GENERALIST SOCIAL WORK PRACTICE

Advisory Editor

Thomas M. Meenaghan, *New York University*

Related books of interest

An Experiential Approach to Group Work, Second Edition
Rich Furman, Kimberly Bender, and Diana Rowan

Interviewing for the Helping Professions: A Relational Approach
Fred McKenzie

Practicing Rural Social Work
Paul Force-Emery Mackie, Kimberly Zammitt, and Michelle Alvarez

The Helping Professional's Guide to Ethics: A New Perspective
Valerie Bryan, Scott Sanders, and Laura Kaplan

Essential Skills of Social Work Practice: Assessment, Intervention, and Evaluation, Second Edition
Thomas O'Hare

The Practice of Social Work in North America: Culture, Context, and Competency Development
Kip Coggins

Breaking Out of the Box: Adventure-Based Field Instruction, Third Edition
Kelly Ward and Robin Sakina Mama

Clinical Assessment for Social Workers: Quantitative and Qualitative Methods, Fourth Edition
Catheleen Jordan and Cynthia Franklin

Modern Social Work Theory, Fourth Edition
Malcolm Payne

Social Welfare Policy: Responding to a Changing World
John G. McNutt and Richard Hoefer

GENERALIST SOCIAL WORK PRACTICE
A Worktext

Charles H. Zastrow
University of Wisconsin–Whitewater

LYCEUM
BOOKS, INC.

5758 South Blackstone Avenue
Chicago, Illinois 60637

© 2016 by Lyceum Books, Inc.

Published by

LYCEUM BOOKS, INC.
5758 S. Blackstone Avenue
Chicago, Illinois 60637
773-643-1903 fax
773-643-1902 phone
lyceum@lyceumbooks.com
www.lyceumbooks.com

ISBN 978-0-19-065708-6

Printed in the United States of America.

Library of Congress Cataloging-in-Publication Data

[to come]

Contents

Preface

Carlos is a sophomore in a social work program at a university. He recently decided to try out social work as a major, after doing well in his Introduction to Social Work course, and in his two Human Behavior and Social Environment courses. He still has a number of questions as to whether he really wants a career in social work. He recognizes that friends and a number of relatives view him as a "good listener," as they seek him out to share their personal challenges. He has had some traumatic experiences in the past, one of which was his parents divorcing eight years ago; he still does not quite understand why they decided to separate. Carlos as yet is somewhat unaware of what social workers actually do. He is interested in being a protective services worker, but is keeping an open mind about other areas of social work that might be a "good fit" for him. He has a number of questions as to whether he truly has the skills to be of help to other people.

Yolanda is a graduate student in an MSW program. She attained a Bachelor's degree in social work four years ago. For the past four years she has worked as a probation and parole agent. She enjoyed being a probation and parole agent but now is interested in attaining her MSW degree—which she hopes will facilitate her securing a supervisor position, or in her becoming a clinical social worker. She recognizes that she has skills in working with individuals, treatment groups, and families, and recognizes that her employing agency valued her, considered her a team player, and encouraged her to pursue an MSW degree so that "more doors would be opened" to her. She is focused on acquiring in her MSW program the necessary knowledge, skills, and values to work more effectively with individuals, groups, families, organizations, and communities.

The focus of this text is to facilitate Carlos and Yolanda (and other BSW and MSW students) in comprehending what social workers do, and to acquire the knowledge, skills, and values needed for generalist social work practice.

Prior editions of *Generalist Social Work Practice: A Worktext* (11th ed.) were titled *The Practice of Social Work: A Comprehensive Worktext*. The title was changed in this edition because of: a) the increasing emphasis of the Council on Social Work Education (CSWE) on "generalist practice" and b) the added material on generalist practice in this edition.

The Council on Social Work Education (CSWE) is the national organization in the United States that accredits baccalaureate and master's degree programs in social work education. In 2015, CSWE published *Educational Policy and Accreditation Standards (EPAS)* for baccalaureate and master's degree programs. A major thrust of *Generalist Social Work Practice: A Worktext* is to present material that is consistent with the following mandated content on social work practice in EPAS:

This text provides the theoretical and practical knowledge needed for entry levels of practice in social work. Material is presented covering generalist practice, social work values, confidentiality, principles of interviewing, contemporary theories of counseling, social work with individuals, social work with groups, social work with families, social work with organizations, social work community practice, assessment, evaluation, evidence-based practice, general systems theory, cross-cultural social work, working within a bureaucratic system, burnout, and the frustrations and satisfactions of being a social worker. Numerous case examples are included to illustrate the theory that is presented.

Generalist Social Work Practice: A Worktext is designed for use in practice courses in social work at both undergraduate and graduate levels. Social work practitioners also will find the text valuable because it describes a variety of approaches to social work practice, including relaxation approaches, mediation, milieu therapy, task-centered practice, family counseling concepts, feminist intervention, reality therapy, rational therapy, and behavior therapy. An eclectic approach is used in presenting these diverse types of therapies. After each therapy approach is described, a critical review of the theory is presented to help the reader assess its merits and shortcomings.

The skill-building exercises in this text may be used in a variety of ways. The instructor may request that students complete certain exercises as a homework assignment before the next class period; the exercises are then reviewed when the class next meets. The instructor may have students complete one or more exercises during class. The instructor may assign certain exercises as written homework to be submitted for evaluation. The instructor may have each student complete several exercises and then place them in a portfolio, which the instructor may periodically review for evaluation purposes.

This book is unique in that it combines the key components of existing practice texts, both traditional and contemporary, into one volume. As much as possible, jargon-free language is used so the reader can more readily grasp the theory. Exercises for students are presented in each chapter to illustrate key concepts and to help students learn how to apply the theoretical material to social work practice. These exercises are largely skill-building exercises that are designed to facilitate students' developing social work practice skills. Exercises also are presented at the end of each chapter to facilitate students' learning how to apply the theoretical material to social work practice.

PLAN OF THE BOOK

The chapters in this text (1 through 14) describe various components of Generalist Social Work Practice. The following is a brief summary of each chapter.

Chapter 1, "Overview of Social Work Practice," conceptualizes generalist practice in social work. It describes what social workers do, explains how social work is distinct from other professions, and summarizes the knowledge, values, and skills needed for beginning-level social work practice. This chapter also describes the goals of social work practice, gives a brief history of social work, indicates that social work is a multiskilled profession, and summarizes professional activities performed by social workers, including casework, case management, group work, group counseling, family counseling, and community organization. Various role models of social work practice are defined, including that of a counselor, broker, advocate, and activist.

Chapter 2, "Social Work Values," summarizes social work values. Values described include: self-determination, individualization, confidentiality, belief in the institutional approach for the delivery of social services, focus on family, advocacy for those being discriminated against, and accountability.

Chapter 3, "Assessment" describes the components of assessments in social work, including attending to Bio-Psycho-Social and Cultural components. Material is presented on assessing individuals, families, groups, organizations, and communities.

Chapter 4, "Social Work with Individuals: Interviewing," describes three types of social work interviews: informational or social history, assessment, and intervention. Guidelines are provided on how to begin and end interviews, how to phrase interview questions, and how to take notes while interviewing.

Chapter 5, "Social Work with Individuals: Counseling," presents material on counseling from the worker's perspective, and from the client's perspective. Eight stages of a problem-solving approach to counseling clients are presented.

Chapter 6, "Social Work with Groups: Types of Groups and Guidelines for Leading Them," describes a number of groups that social workers are involved in, including: recreation, recreation-skill, task, problem-solving and decision-making, focus, self-help, socialization, counseling, and encounter. Guidelines are presented on how to start, lead, terminate, and evaluate groups.

Chapter 7, "Social Work with Groups: Concepts and Skills" summarizes three group development models, describes five leadership approaches, and presents material on group dynamics. Conflict resolution strategies are summarized. Guidelines are presented on starting, leading and ending counseling groups.

Chapter 8, "Social Work with Families," describes family problems and the nature of social work with families. Eco-maps and genograms are described. Family counseling is conceptualized.

Chapter 9, "Social Work with Organizations" indicates that most social workers are employed by an agency (i.e., organization). Several models of organizational behavior are described. The following two perspectives on the provision of social services are described: liberalism and conservatism. Guidelines are presented on how social workers can thrive and survive in a bureaucracy.

Chapter 10, "Social Work Community Practice," describes three models of community practice: locality-development, social planning, and social action. Knowledge and skills needed for community practice are summarized. The Community Assets Model to community practice is presented.

Chapter 11, "Practice Evaluation and Program Evaluation," describes the importance of both practice evaluation and program evaluation. Process evaluation, outcome evaluation, evidence-based practice, and the ethics of evaluation are described. Approaches to outcome evaluation include: single-subject design, goal achievement scaling, task achievement scaling, and satisfaction questionnaire.

Chapter 12, "Social Work Practice with Diverse Groups" outlines key terms involving diversity. It helps readers identify their stereotypes. It describes: empowerment, the strengths perspective, and cultural competence. It has information on cultures of diverse groups, and material on effective intervention approaches with diverse groups. Macro strategies to promote social and economic justice are summarized.

Chapter 12, "Social Work with Diverse Groups," describes challenges faced, and desired intervention strategies, with African American clients, First Nations People clients, Latino clients, women, persons with disabilities, and LGBT clients. Culturally competent practice is described. Macro strategies are presented on promoting social and economic justice for populations-at-risk.

Chapter 13, "Spirituality and Religion" presents a rationale for the use of spirituality and religion in social work practice. Material is presented on assessing spiritual and religious beliefs of clients, and on spiritual and religious interventions with clients. Social work and religious organizations are in a limited partnership in providing social services to people. Four different religions are summarized.

Chapter 14, "Surviving and Enjoying Social Work" focuses on the importance of social workers taking care of themselves. To be of help to others, social workers must first take care of themselves. Suggestions are presented for resolving common concerns of students receiving professional training in social work. Techniques to manage stress and prevent burnout are described. Mindfulness is summarized. Safety guidelines for social workers are described. This part concludes with a discussion of the importance for social workers (as well as other people) of developing a positive identity and provides guidelines on how to develop a positive sense of self.

The final section of the book is a Counseling Theories Resource Manual (CTRM). To highlight the uniqueness of the CTRM, material is presented in modules, rather than chapters. This CTRM presents and critiques the prominent theories of counseling that are widely used by social workers, including reality therapy, rational therapy, and behavior therapy. Specific intervention techniques are also described, including assertiveness training, token economies, aversive techniques, crisis intervention, parent effectiveness training, mediation, solution-focused therapy, and narrative therapy.

The instructor does not have to cover all the theories of intervention presented in this text. Rather, he or she (with the consultation of other faculty in the program) should decide which of the intervention theories described in the CTRM are most important for students to learn to best serve clients in the school's geographic area.

NEW TO THIS EDITION

Content has been added on:

- The new Educational Policy and Accreditation Standards (EPAS, 2015) statement of the Council on Social Work Education
- Material and exercises on assessing the extent to which students are attaining the competencies and behaviors of 2015 EPAS
- Student learning objectives for each chapter and module
- Motivational interviewing
- Major mental disorders according to DSM-5
- The servant leadership approach
- New material on improving one's self-concept
- Expanded description of Total Quality Management
- Instructions for three relaxation exercises
- Force field analysis
- Culturagrams
- Mindfulness
- Cultural humility
- New technology and social work

COUNSELING AS A COMPONENT OF GENERALIST PRACTICE

A small minority of social work educators assert that counseling is not a component of generalist social work practice. I, however, strongly assert that counseling is a key component of generalist practice. A generalist practitioner uses the problem-solving approach to bring about positive changes when working with individuals, families, groups, organizations, and communities. Much of social work practice with individuals, treatment groups, and families requires the social worker to use counseling principles and theories extensively. Competence in counseling is as essential for generalist-practice social workers to have as are competencies in other areas (such as brokering, policy making, lobbying, and planning). Most baccalaureate and master's degree social workers are engaged primarily in providing direct services to individuals, treatment groups, and families—and the provision of counseling services is a major component of the direct services provided. Conversely, when a social worker identifies himself or herself as a clinical social worker or a psychotherapist, it does not mean that the person is uninvolved in other areas of generalist practice. Every clinical social worker (at times) works with changing organizations and communities to benefit clients. And because I believe that counseling is a key component of generalist social work practice, the Counseling Theories Resource Manual (CTRM) is provided near the end of the text, which presents contemporary theories of counseling that are useful in working with individuals, treatment groups, and families.

From one point of view, the 14 chapters of the text focus on generalist practice, whereas the CTRM focuses exclusively on counseling. However, the reader will note that in describing social work practice with individuals, families, and groups, it is essential to discuss aspects of counseling. Not surprisingly, most of the 14 "generalist" chapters describe some aspects of counseling, as the following list indicates:

Chapter 1, "Overview of Social Work Practice," links the social work goal "Enhance people's problem-solving, coping, and developmental capacities" with counseling. It also describes how counseling is an integral component of "social casework," "group therapy," and "family therapy."

Chapter 2, "Social Work Values," describes a number of values that relate to counseling—such as confidentiality, privileged communication, whether to inform partners of clients in counseling that a client is HIV-positive, and establishing professional boundaries with clients.

Chapter 3, "Assessment," discusses strategies and approaches to assessing the issues of clients in counseling and features counseling case examples.

Chapter 4, "Social Work with Individuals: Interviewing," focuses on interviewing, which is directly related to counseling.

Chapter 5, "Social Work with Individuals: Counseling," focuses exclusively on counseling.

Chapter 6, "Social Work with Groups: Types of Groups and Guidelines for Leading Them," presents considerable content on counseling groups.

Chapter 7, "Social Work with Groups: Concepts and Skills," presents a section on starting, leading, and ending counseling groups.

Chapter 8, "Social Work with Families," describes family counseling.

Chapter 11, "Practice Evaluation and Program Evaluation" describes evaluation approaches to assess the effectiveness of counseling and other direct practice services.

Chapter 12, "Social Work Practice with Diverse Groups," provides considerable content on cultural competence for social workers who provide culturally sensitive services to clients who receive counseling and other services.

Chapter 13, "Spirituality and Religion in Social Work Practice," describes the importance of assessing the religious and spiritual aspects of clients, including clients receiving counseling. Also described are religious and spiritual interventions with clients receiving counseling.

Chapter 14, "Surviving and Enjoying Social Work," features content on common concerns of social work students who are preparing to provide services to clients, including clients receiving counseling. (In covering this material, some instructors may choose to assign this chapter after chapter 2 or 3 because it covers material that is essential to thriving as a social work practitioner.)

ACKNOWLEDGMENTS

I wish to express my sincere appreciation to Vicki Vogel, who assisted in conceptualizing various chapters and helped in a number of ways with the writing of this text. My thanks also to the reviewers of this edition.

Charles H. Zastrow

OVERVIEW OF SOCIAL WORK PRACTICE

LEARNING OBJECTIVES

Generalist Practice of Social Work, Eleventh Edition, is intended for use in social work practice courses. The focus of this book is on the theoretical and practical knowledge students need to perform the tasks of workers in entry-level positions that require either a bachelors (BSW) or master's (MSW) degree in social work. This book is designed to be read by students preparing for, or already in, field placement. This chapter will help prepare students to:

Understannd a brief history of social work
Define social work
Describe the relationship between social work and social welfare
Define generalist social work practice
Understand the roles of social workers in practice
Comprehend that counseling is a component of generalist practice
Understand the relationship between counseling and therapy
Understand that social workers use a systems perspective
Understand the medical model, and the ecological model, of human behavior
Decsribe the goals of social work practice
Understand the knowledge, skills, and values needed for social work pracrice

THE HISTORY OF SOCIAL WORK

Social work as a profession is of relatively recent origin. The first social welfare agencies appeared in urban areas in the early 1800s. These agencies, or services, were private and were developed primarily at the initiation of the clergy and religious groups. Until the early 1900s, these services were provided exclusively by the clergy and affluent "do-gooders" who had no formal training and little understanding of human behavior or of how to help people. The focus of these private services was on meeting such basic physical needs as food and shelter and on attempting to cure emotional and personal difficulties with religious admonitions.

An example of an early social welfare organization is the Society for the Prevention of Pauperism, founded by John Griscom in 1820 (Bemner, 1962, p. 13). This society investigated the habits and circumstances of the poor, suggested plans by which the poor could help themselves, and encouraged the poor to save and economize. One of the remedies used was house-to-house visitation (a very elementary type of social work).

By the latter half of the 1800s, a fairly large number of private relief agencies had been established in large cities to help the unemployed, the poor, the ill, persons with physical or mental disabilities, and orphans. Their programs were uncoordinated and sometimes overlapping, and so an English invention—the Charity Organization Society (COS)—soon caught the interest of a number of American cities (Cohen, 1958). Starting in Buffalo, New York, in 1877, COS was rapidly adopted in many cities. In charity organization societies, private agencies joined together (1) to provide direct services to individuals and families—in this respect, they were the forerunners of social casework and of family counseling approaches—and (2) to plan and coordinate the efforts of private agencies to meet pressing urban social problems—in this respect, they were the precursors of community organization and social-planning approaches. Charity organizations conducted a detailed investigation of each applicant for services and financial help, maintained a central client registration system to avoid duplication, and used volunteer *friendly visitors* extensively to work with those in difficulty. The friendly visitors were primarily "doers of good works," as they generally gave sympathy rather than money and encouraged the poor to save and to seek employment. Poverty was viewed as a personal shortcoming. Most of the friendly visitors were women.

Concurrent with the COS movement was the establishment of settlement houses in the late 1800s. Toynbee Hall was the first settlement house, established in 1884 in London; many others were soon formed in larger U.S. cities. Many of the early settlement house workers were the daughters of ministers. The workers, who were from the middle and upper classes, lived in poor neighborhoods to experience the harsh realities of poverty. Simultaneously, in cooperation with neighborhood residents, they sought to develop ways to improve living conditions. In contrast to friendly visitors, they lived in impoverished neighborhoods and used the missionary approach of teaching residents how to live moral lives and improve their circumstances. They sought to improve housing, health, and living conditions; find jobs; teach English, hygiene, and occupational skills; and change environmental surroundings through cooperative efforts. The change techniques that settlement houses used are now called social group work, social action, and community organization.

Settlement houses emphasized "environmental reform" while "they continued to struggle to teach the poor the prevailing middle-class values of work, thrift, and abstinence as the keys to success" (Becker, 1968, p. 85). In addition to dealing with local problems by local action, settlement houses played important roles in drafting legislation and in organizing to influence social policy and legislation. The most noted leader in the settlement house movement was Jane Addams of Hull House in Chicago, who summarized settlement houses as follows: "The Settlement, then, is an experimental effort to aid in the solution of the social and industrial problems which are engendered by the modern conditions of life in a great city" (Addams, 1959, pp. 125–126). Settlement house leaders believed that by changing neighborhoods they would improve communities, and through altering communities they would develop a better society.

The first paid social workers were executive secretaries of charity organization societies (Dolgoff & Feldstein, 1980, pp. 233–234). In the late 1800s charity organization societies received some contracts from the cities in which they were located to administer relief funds. To administer these programs, COS hired people as executive secretaries to organize and train the friendly visitors and to establish accounting procedures to show accountability for the funds received. To improve the services of friendly visitors, the executive secretaries established standards and training courses. In 1898, a training course was first offered by the New York Charity Organization Society. By 1904, the New York School of Philanthropy offered a one-year program. Soon after, colleges and universities began offering training programs in social work. Initially, social work education focused on environmental reform approaches to meet social problems. (Such approaches focus on changing the system to better meet people's needs. The enactment in 1935 of the Social Security Act to meet the needs of the poor and the unemployed is an example of an environmental reform approach.)

Richard Cabot introduced medical social work into Massachusetts General Hospital in 1905 (Dolgoff & Feldstein, 1980, pp. 233–234). Gradually, social workers were employed in schools, courts, child guidance clinics, and other settings.

In 1917 Mary Richmond published *Social Diagnosis,* a text that presented for the first time a theory and methodology for social work. The book focused on how the worker should intervene with individuals. The process is still used today and involves study (collecting information), diagnosis (stating what is wrong), prognosis, and treatment planning (stating what should be done to help clients improve). This book was important because it formulated a common body of knowledge for casework.

In the 1920s, Freud's theories of personality development and therapy became popular. The concepts and explanations of psychiatrists appeared particularly appropriate for social workers, who also worked in one-to-one relationships with clients. The psychiatric approach emphasized intrapsychic processes and focused on enabling clients to adapt and adjust to their social situations. For the next three decades, social workers switched their emphasis from reform to therapy. In the 1960s, however, social workers expressed renewed interest in sociological approaches, or reform. Several reasons account for this change. Questions arose about the relevance and appropriateness of talking approaches with low-income clients who have urgent social and economic pressures. Furthermore, the effectiveness of many psychotherapeutic approaches was questioned

(Eysenck, 1961). Other reasons for the renewed interest included the increase in status of sociology and the mood of the 1960s, which raised questions about the relevance of social institutions in meeting the needs of the population. Social work at the present time embraces both reform and therapy approaches.[1]

Not until the end of World War I did social work begin to be recognized as a distinct profession. The Depression of the 1930s and enactment of the Social Security Act in 1935 brought about an extensive expansion of public social services and job opportunities for social workers. Since 1900, there has been a growing awareness by social agency boards and the public that professionally trained social workers are needed to provide social services competently. In 1955, the National Association of Social Workers was formed to represent the social work profession in this country. Its purpose is to improve social conditions and to promote high-quality and effective social work practice.

In recent years, considerable energy has been expended to develop a system of registration or licensing of social workers. Such a system helps assure the public that qualified personnel are providing social work services and also advances the recognition of social work as a profession. All states have passed legislation to license or certify the practice of social work.

Social work is one of the most important professions in our society in terms of the number of people affected, the human misery treated, and the amount of money spent.

A DEFINITION OF SOCIAL WORK

The National Association of Social Workers (NASW) defines *social work* as follows:

> Social work is the professional activity of helping individuals, groups, or communities to enhance or restore their capacity for social functioning and to create societal conditions favorable to their goals.
>
> Social work practice consists of the professional application of social work values, principles, and techniques to one or more of the following ends: helping people obtain tangible services; providing counseling and psychotherapy for individuals, families, and groups; helping communities or groups provide or improve social and health services; and participating in relevant legislative processes.
>
> The practice of social work requires knowledge of human development and behavior; of social, economic, and cultural institutions; and of the interaction of all these factors. (Barker, 2003, p. 408)

The term *social worker* is generally applied to graduates of educational programs (either with bachelor's or master's degrees) in social work who are employed in the field of social welfare. A social worker is a *change agent,* a helper who is specifically employed for the purpose of creating planned change (Pincus & Minahan, 1973, p. 54). As a change agent, a social worker is expected to be skilled at working with individuals, groups, families, and organizations and at bringing about community changes.

THE RELATIONSHIP BETWEEN SOCIAL WORK AND SOCIAL WELFARE

The goal of social welfare is to fulfill the social, financial, health, and recreational requirements of all individuals in a society. Social welfare seeks to enhance the social functioning of all age groups, both rich and poor. When other institutions in our society (such as the market economy and the family) fail at times to meet the basic needs of individuals or groups of people, social services are needed and demanded. Barker (2003) defined *social welfare* as follows:

> A nation's system of programs, benefits, and services that help people meet those social, economic, educational, and health needs that are fundamental to the maintenance of society. (p. 408)

Examples of social welfare programs and services are foster care, adoption, day care, Head Start, probation and parole, public assistance programs, public health nursing, sex therapy, suicide counseling, recreational services (Boy Scouts and YWCA programs), services to minority groups and veterans, school social services, medical and legal services to the poor, family planning services, Meals on Wheels, nursing home

---

[1] I believe there is little difference between therapy and counseling (for emotional and behavioral problems); therefore, these terms are used interchangeably in this text. In addition, because counseling (or therapy) is an intervention with a client, sometimes the term *intervention* is used to refer to *counseling.*

services, shelters for battered spouses, services to persons with acquired immune deficiency syndrome (AIDS), protective services for victims of child abuse and neglect, assertiveness training, public housing projects, family counseling, Alcoholics Anonymous, runaway services, services to people with developmental disabilities, and rehabilitation services.

Almost all social workers are employed in the social welfare field. There are, however, many other professional and occupational groups working in the field, as illustrated in Figure 1.1.

WHAT IS THE PROFESSION OF SOCIAL WORK?

The National Association of Social Workers (NASW) (1982, p. 5)) describes the social work profession as follows:

> The social work profession exists to provide humane and effective social services to individuals, families, groups, communities, and society so that social functioning may be enhanced and the quality of life improved. . . .
>
> The profession of social work, by both traditional and practical definition, is the profession that provides the formal knowledge base, theoretical concepts, specific functional skills, and essential social values which are used to implement society's mandate to provide safe, effective, and constructive social services.[2]

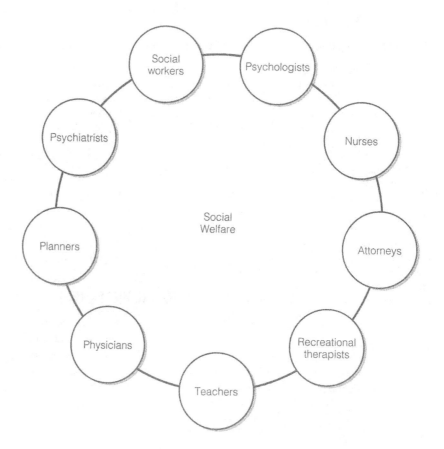

Figure 1.1

Examples of professional groups within the field of social welfare include attorneys providing legal services to the poor; urban planners in social planning agencies; physicians in public health agencies; teachers in residential treatment facilities for those with emotional and behavioral disorders; psychologists, nurses, and recreational therapists in mental hospitals; and psychiatrists in mental health clinics.

---

[2]Published 1982, National Association of Social Workers, Inc. Reprinted with permission, from *Standards for the Classification of Social Work Practice,* Policy Statement 4, p. 5. Copyright material reprinted with permission from the National Association of Social Workers, Inc.

Social work is thus distinct from other professions (such as psychology and psychiatry) because it has the responsibility and mandate to provide social services.

A social worker needs training and expertise in a wide range of areas to effectively handle problems faced by individuals, groups, families, organizations, and the larger community. Although most professions are increasingly becoming more specialized (for example, most medical doctors now specialize in one or two areas), social work continues to emphasize a generic (broad-based) approach. The practice of social work is analogous to the old general practice of medicine. A general (or family) practitioner has professional education to handle a wide range of common medical problems; a social worker has professional education to handle a wide range of common social and personal problems. The Case Example "Domestic Abuse" highlights some of the skills that social workers need.

Exercise 1.1: Your Areas of Interest in Social Work

Goal: This exercise is designed to help you identify the social work areas that you desire to work in.

Step 1:   Rank the following five client systems that you prefer to work with (with one being your first choice).

_____ Individuals

_____ Families

_____ Groups

_____ Organizations

_____ The larger community

Step 2:   Describe the reasons for your ranking.

Step 3:   Describe the areas of social work (such as services to battered spouses) that you prefer to work in. Also specify your reasons for your selected areas.

CASE EXAMPLE   DOMESTIC ABUSE

Sherry Gulag lived in an 8-unit two-bedroom apartment building in a medium size city. She frequently heard screaming in the next door unit where Richard and Julie Landel lived with their six-year-old son, Alan. The screaming between the spouses frequently went on for over an hour at a time, with Alan crying much of this time. Sherry Gulag hated to interfere in her neighbors' business, but she was fearful someone was being physically abused. Sherry could not stand it anymore, so she picked up the phone and reported what she knew to protective services at the public Social Services Department. She asked that the Landels not be told who had reported the situation. She was assured that the report would remain confidential. (State law protects persons who report suspected child abuse or neglect by ensuring their anonymity if they desire.)

Guillermo Gomez was the protective services worker assigned to the case. He visited the Landels' home the next day. All three members of the Landel family were at home. He explained to them that he had come to investigate potential child abuse. Mrs. Landel became very angry, grabbed her coat, and left the house. While leaving, she stated it was outrageous someone was suspecting her of child abuse. Mr. Gomez examined Alan's arms, legs, neck, and face—and did not see any bruises. He also asked Alan if he had ever been hit by either parent. Alan stated that his dad had slapped him on "his butt" a few months ago when he did something wrong, but otherwise said his parents never hit him.

Mr. Gomez then asked Mr. Landel what is happening in the family between him and his wife. Mr. Landel gradually revealed that he had been married to Julie for the past 9 years. He indicated that their marriage was one that had a long history of marital discord. Mr. Landel stated Julie has been diagnosed as bipolar, with a number of cycles of manic behavior and depression. Mr. Landel indicated he also has been diagnosed as bipolar and has been on lithium (antidepressant medication) for the past 10 years. With both spouses having frequent mood swings, Mr. Landel stated their marriage was full of severe tension, some episodes of hitting one another, and rarely times of happiness. Mr. Landel indicated both he and his wife loved Alan, and had never struck Alan. (Mr. Gomez was aware that child abuse was more likely to occur in families where there was marital turmoil, but it appeared Alan was not being physically abused. Mr. Gomez was aware that Alan was probably suffering emotional abuse from marital discord, but he knew that the court system is unlikely to remove a child from a home for marital turmoil.)

Mr. Landel stated he had tried numerous strategies to persuade his wife to enter marital counseling with him. For example, a year ago he had voluntarily committed himself to a psychiatric hospital for depression—as he was informed that part of his treatment would involve mandated couple's counseling at the hospital. However, his wife refused counseling, and Mr. Landel was then released after staying for a few days.

CASE EXAMPLE   (continued)

Mr. Landel added that occasionally there were physical confrontations with his wife. She had a pattern of screaming at him and shoving him when she was upset with him. A few times he stated he shoved back at her. She then would respond by calling 911. When police came, they usually calmed the situation, but twice the police took him to jail for a night because of domestic abuse.

Mr. Gomez asked Mr. Landel if he would be willing to see Rachel Torrez, a counselor at the Social Services Department to work on his marital challenges. Mr. Gomez added that hopefully Mrs. Landel would agree to join in the counseling. Mr. Landel thought that was a good idea. Mr. Landel said he would leave the protective services case "open" for awhile, while Mr. and Mrs. Landel received counseling.

Mr. Landel did receive counseling for several months from Ms. Torrez. Mrs. Landel refused to attend. Mr. Landel did learn some strategies to better handle the conflict with his wife, when he sensed a potentially violent situation may occur—one strategy was for him to leave by either taking a walk, or going for a drive. After several months of little improvement in their relationship, Ms. Torrez asked Mr. Landel to complete a homework assignment of writing down a "pro-con" list as to whether it would be desirable to continue the marriage. The next week, Mr. Landel

came in with his list. Practically all of his items were on the side of ending the marriage. After considerable discussion, including the possible impact of the divorce on Alan, Mr. Landel decided to retain a divorce attorney and file for divorce.

The divorce took eleven months to obtain. Mr. and Mrs. Landel had major confrontations on custody issues, visitation schedules, and dividing the finances. Mr. Landel occasionally met with Ms. Torrez during this time period to vent his emotions and to problem-solve present and future issues. Ms. Torrez also referred Mr. Landel to a "Rebuilding" support group (a self-help group), which Mr. Landel found to be quite helpful, as it was a group of men and women who were also going through a divorce and working on rebuilding their lives.

During this time period Mr. Gomez occasionally kept in contact with Ms. Torrez on the progress that Mr. and Mrs. Landel were making. Mr. Gomez noted there were no additional child abuse complaints occurring. After the Landels obtained a divorce (and joint custody was arranged), Mr. Gomez closed the protective service case involving Alan. A few months after the divorce was granted, Mr. Landel stopped seeing Ms. Torrez. He indicated he and Alan were now "doing better," and thanked her and Mr. Gomez for their help. On a negative note, he indicated Julie had increasingly become "bitter" about him.

GENERALIST SOCIAL WORK PRACTICE

There used to be an erroneous belief that a social worker was a caseworker, a group worker, or a community organizer. Practicing social workers know that such a belief is faulty because every social worker is a change agent working with individuals, groups, families, organizations, and the larger community. The amount of time spent at these levels varies from worker to worker, but every worker will, at times, work at each of these levels and therefore needs training in all of them.

The Council on Social Work Education (CSWE, the national accrediting entity for baccalaureate and master's programs in social work) requires that all bachelor's and master's programs train students in generalist social work practice. (MSW programs, in addition, usually require students to select and study in an area of concentration. They generally offer several choices, such as family therapy, administration, corrections, or clinical social work.)

A generalist social worker is trained to use problem solving to assess and intervene in the problems confronting individuals, families, groups, organizations, and communities.

The Baccalaureate Program Directors Organization (BPD, 2006, p. 2) defined *generalist practice* as follows:

> Generalist social work practitioners work with individuals, families, groups, communities and organizations in a variety of social work and host settings. Generalist practitioners view clients and client systems from a strengths perspective in order to recognize, support, and build upon the innate capabilities of all human beings. They use a professional problem solving process to engage, assess, broker services, advocate, counsel, educate, and organize with and on behalf of client and client systems. In addition, generalist practitioners engage in community and organizational development. Finally, generalist practitioners evaluate service outcomes in order to continually improve the provision and quality of services most appropriate to client needs.
>
> Generalist social work practice is guided by the NASW Code of Ethics and is committed to improving the well-being of individuals, families, groups, communities and organizations and furthering the goals of social justice.

The Council on Social Work Education (2015), in *Educational Policy and Accreditation Standards*, also defined *generalist practice*:

Generalist practice is grounded in the liberal arts and the person-in-environment framework. To promote human and social well-being, generalist practitioners use a range of prevention and intervention methods in their practice with diverse individuals, families, groups, organizations, and communities based on scientific inquiry and best practices. The generalist practitioner identifies with the social work profession and applies ethical principles and critical thinking in practice at the micro, mezzo, and macro levels. Generalist practitioners engage diversity in their practice and advocate for human rights and social and economic justice. They recognize, support, and build on the strengths and resiliency of all human beings. They engage in research-informed practice and are proactive in responding to the impact of context on professional practice.

This text teaches the generalist-practice approach in social work by describing a variety of assessment and intervention strategies. Once you have learned these strategies, you can select the approaches that hold the most promise in facilitating positive changes in your clients.

In working with individuals, families, groups, organizations, and communities, social workers use a problem-solving approach. The process can be described in a variety of ways but includes these steps:

1. Identify as precisely as possible the problem or problems.
2. Generate possible alternative solutions.
3. Evaluate the alternative solutions.
4. Select a solution or solutions to be used and set goals.
5. Implement the solution.
6. Follow up to evaluate how the solution worked.

Exercise 1.2: Applying the Problem-Solving Approach

Goal: This exercise is designed to help you understand the problem-solving approach.

Step 1: Identify a situation in your past where you faced a challenge or an issue in which you used the problem-solving approach. What was the situation?

Step 2: Specify as precisely as possible the problem or problems.

Step 3: Specify the resolution strategies that were generated by you (and perhaps by someone else).

Step 4: Specify how these resolution strategies were evaluated.

Step 5: Specify the resolution strategy that was selected to be used to seek to resolve the issue.

Step 6: Specify how the resolution strategy was implemented.

Step 7: Specify how the resolution strategy (after it was implemented) was evaluated.

Step 8: Was the outcome judged to be "successful/satisfactory"? If not, what was the next resolution strategy that was tried?

Step 9: What do you see as the strengths and shortcomings of the problem-solving approach?

A Variety of Roles

In working with individuals, groups, families, organizations, and communities, a social worker is expected to be knowledgeable and skillful in filling a variety of roles. Particular roles should (ideally) be determined by what will be most effective, given the circumstances. The following list identifies some, but certainly not all, of the roles assumed by social workers.

Enabler/Counselor. In this role, a worker *helps* individuals or groups articulate their needs, clarify and identify their problems, explore resolution strategies, select and apply a strategy, and develop their capacities to deal with their own problems more effectively. The enabler is perhaps the most frequently used role in counseling individuals, groups, and families. The model is also used in community practice, primarily when the objective is to help people organize to help themselves.

(This definition of *enabler* is very different from the definition used in the context of chemical dependency. There the term refers to a family member or friend who facilitates the substance abuser in continuing to use and abuse the drug of his or her choice.)

Broker. A broker links individuals and groups who need help (and do not know where to obtain it) with community services. For example, a wife who is frequently physically abused by her husband might be referred to a shelter for battered women. Nowadays even moderate-size communities have 200 or 300 social service agencies/organizations providing community services. Even human services professionals are often only partially aware of the total service network in their community.

Advocate. This role is borrowed from the law profession. It is an active directive role—that is, the social worker advocates for a client or for a citizens' group. When a client or a citizens' group is in need of help and existing institutions are uninterested (and sometimes openly negative and hostile) in providing services, the advocate's role may be appropriate. The advocate provides leadership for collecting information, arguing the correctness of the client's need and request, and challenging the institution's decision not to provide services. The object is not to ridicule or censure a particular institution but to modify or change one or more of its service policies. In this role, the social worker is a partisan who serves the interests of a client or of a citizens' group exclusively.

Empowerer. A key goal of social work practice is *empowerment*, the process of helping individuals, families, groups, organizations, and communities increase their personal, interpersonal, socioeconomic, and political strength and influence by improving their circumstances. Social workers who engage in empowerment-focused practice seek to develop the capacity of clients to understand their environment, make choices, take responsibility for their choices, and influence their life situations through organization and advocacy. Empowerment-focused social workers also seek to gain a more equitable distribution of resources and power among different groups in society. This focus on equity and social justice is a hallmark of the social work profession, as evidenced through the early settlement workers such as Jane Addams.

Activist. An activist seeks basic institutional change; often the objective involves a shift in power and resources to a disadvantaged group. An activist is concerned about social injustice, inequity, and deprivation. Tactics involve conflict, confrontation, and negotiation. Social action is concerned with changing the social environment to better meet the recognized needs of individuals. The methods used are assertive and action oriented (for example, organizing welfare recipients to work toward improvements in services and increases in money payments). Activities of social action include fact finding, analysis of community needs, research, dissemination and interpretation of information, organization of activities with people, and other efforts to mobilize public understanding and support on behalf of some existing or proposed social program. Social action can be geared toward a problem that is local, statewide, or national in scope.

Mediator. Mediators intervene in disputes between parties to help them find compromises, reconcile differences, or reach mutually satisfactory agreements. Social workers use their value orientations and unique skills in many forms of mediation between opposing parties (for example, divorcing spouses, neighbors in conflict, landlord-tenant disputes, labor-management disputes, and child custody disputes). A mediator remains neutral, not siding with either party in the dispute. Mediators make sure they understand the positions of both parties. They clarify positions, recognize miscommunication, and help the parties present their cases clearly.

Negotiator. A negotiator brings together those who are in conflict over one or more issues, then helps them bargain and compromise to arrive at mutually acceptable agreements. Somewhat like mediation, negotiation involves finding a middle ground that all sides can live with. However, unlike a mediator (which is a neutral role), a negotiator usually is allied with one of the sides involved.

Educator. Educators give information to clients and teach them adaptive skills. To be an effective educator, the worker must first be knowledgeable. In addition, the worker must be a good communicator so that information is conveyed clearly and is readily understood by the receiver. Examples include teaching parenting skills to young parents, instructing teenagers in job-hunting strategies, and teaching anger-control techniques to individuals with difficulties in this area.

Initiator. An initiator calls attention to a problem or to a potential problem. A problem does not have to exist before attention can be called to it. For example, a proposal to renovate a low-income neighborhood by building middle-income housing units may raise the problem of dispossessing current residents who cannot afford the cost of the new units. Because calling attention to problems usually does not resolve them, the initiator role must often be followed by other kinds of work.

Coordinator. In this role, the worker brings components together in an organized manner. For example, in the case of a multiproblem family, several agencies often work together to meet the complicated financial, emotional, legal, health, social, educational, recreational, and interactional needs of the family members. Frequently, one social worker assumes the role of case manager and coordinates services from the different agencies to avoid duplication of services and conflicting objectives.

Researcher. At times, every worker is a researcher. Research in social work practice includes researching the literature on topics of interest, evaluating the outcomes of one's practice, assessing the merits and shortcomings of programs, and studying community needs.

Group Facilitator. A group facilitator is a leader for some group experience. The group may be a counseling group, an educational group, a self-help group, a sensitivity group, a family counseling group, or a group with some other focus.

Public Speaker. Social workers occasionally talk to a variety of groups (for example, high school classes, public service organizations such as Kiwanis, police officers, staff at other agencies) to inform them of available services or to advocate developing new services for clients whose needs are not being met. In recent years, various new services have been identified as being needed (for example, family preservation programs and services for persons with AIDS). Social workers who have public speaking skills are better able to explain services to groups of potential clients and also are likely to be rewarded (including financially) by their employers for their public speaking services.

Exercise 1.3: Your Interest in Various Social Work Roles

Goal: This exercise is designed to help you identify the social work roles that you want to become involved in.

Step 1: With a check, indicate your interest in each of the indicated roles.

	I want to become involved in	Uncertain	I do not want to become involved in
Enabler/Counselor			
Broker			
Advocate			
Empowerer			
Activist			
Mediator			
Negotiator			
Educator			
Initiator			
Coordinator			
Researcher			
Group Facilitator			
Public Speaker			

Step 2: Describe your reasons for wanting to become involved in some roles.

Step 3: Describe your reasons for not wanting to become involved in other roles.

COUNSELING AS A COMPONENT OF GENERALIST PRACTICE

A small minority of social work educators assert that counseling and clinical social work are not components of generalist social work practice. For instance, in *Understanding Generalist Practice*, Kirst-Ashman and Hull (2008) do not use the terms *counseling* and *clinical social work*, nor do they describe contemporary theories of counseling (such as rational therapy, reality therapy, and behavior therapy). In *Social Work Practice: A Generalist Approach*, Johnson (1986) does not use the terms *counseling* and *clinical social work* either, although she does give a half-page introduction to each of the contemporary theories of counseling.

I believe that counseling and clinical social work are key components in generalist practice. A generalist practitioner uses the problem-solving approach to bring about positive changes when working with individuals, families, groups, organizations, and communities. Much of social work practice with individuals, intervention groups, and families involves counseling and what has been called clinical social work. Clinical social workers diagnose and treat a wide variety of clients, using different treatment techniques and strategies to address different emotional and behavioral problems. Licensure for independent clinical social workers has been achieved in all 50 states, with the specific requirements varying from state to state (Groshong, 2009).

Every social worker who provides services to individuals, intervention groups, and families uses counseling principles and theories extensively. Competence in counseling is as essential for generalist-practice social workers to have as are competencies in other areas (such as brokering, policy making, lobbying, and planning). The vast majority of baccalaureate degree and master's degree social workers is engaged primarily in providing direct services to individuals, intervention groups, and families—with counseling services a major component of the direct services provided (Hopps & Collins, 1995). More social workers are psychotherapists in the United States than psychologists or psychiatrists are psychotherapists (Hepworth, Rooney, Rooney, Stromm-Gottfried, & Larsen, 2010). For many social workers, the term *clinical social worker* is synonymous with *social work psychotherapist.*

When a social worker identifies himself or herself as a clinical social worker or a psychotherapist, it does not mean that the person is uninvolved in other areas of generalist practice. In fact, in providing quality services to individuals, intervention groups, and families, every clinical social worker at times seeks to make positive changes in organizations and communities to benefit clients. One example would be advocating that social service agencies in the community change their eligibility guidelines for services so that clients (and individuals with similar needs in the community) can receive services to meet their health, welfare, and recreational needs.

Because counseling is a key component of generalist social work practice, in this text I emphasize principles and guidelines for counseling and present contemporary theories of counseling that are useful in working with individuals, intervention groups, and families.

Modules 1–5 in the Counseling Theories Resource Manual present and critique the prominent theories of counseling that are widely used by social workers, including reality therapy, rational therapy, and behavior therapy. Numerous specific intervention techniques are also described, including assertiveness training, token economies, aversive techniques, crisis intervention, parent effectiveness training, meditation, and solution-focused therapy.

COUNSELING VERSUS THERAPY/PSYCHOTHERAPY

One of the reviewers of a draft of this text commented that I needed to make it clear that graduates of accredited baccalaureate social work programs can counsel clients but cannot provide therapy/psychotherapy to clients. As far as the profession of social work is concerned, it is accurate to say that only licensed clinical social workers can be reimbursed by third-party payers (usually health insurance companies) for providing psychotherapy. (Other helping professionals, such as clinical psychologists and psychiatrists, also are reimbursed for providing psychotherapy.)

The question that arises is, What differentiates "counseling" from "therapy" or from "psychotherapy"? I believe this question is very important because graduates of accredited baccalaureate programs are supposed to limit the services they provide to "counseling." So I researched a variety of sources, seeking a definition that would differentiate "counseling" from "therapy" and "psychotherapy," including three state licensing/certification boards in social work and the Association of Social Work Boards. I also asked baccalaureate social work educators who are on the Baccalaureate Program Directors (BPD) listserv to respond to this question.

I received a variety of definitions of these three terms. One example of the definitions of each of these terms is the following:

Counseling—Professional guidance of individuals, families or groups to assist them in coping with life challenges through such techniques as problem solving, identifying alternatives, articulating goals, and providing needed information.

Therapy—Therapeutic treatment, especially of bodily, emotional or behavioral disorders. (Social workers frequently use this term as a synonym for psychotherapy.)

Psychotherapy—Treatment of emotional or behavioral disorders, or of related bodily ills, by professional therapists—such as clinical social workers, psychologists, and psychiatrists. Psychotherapists are licensed in all 50 states in the United States.

From the BPD listserv, I received a variety of responses regarding what differentiates "counseling" from "therapy" or "psychotherapy." The following are illustrative:

- The licensed professions should limit the use of the term *psychotherapy* to only the licensed mental health professions for the protection of the public.
- In this state, there is no control of therapy/psychotherapy We may think that these terms convey work that is done by only the most skilled professionals; however, in reality anybody off the street can perform the duties of a therapist/psychotherapist.
- No difference among them.
- Although psychotherapy and counseling overlap considerably, there are also some differences. The work with clients may be of considerable depth in both modalities; however, the focus of counseling is more likely to be on specific problems or changes in life adjustment. Psychotherapy is more concerned with the restructuring of the personality or self.
- Although both psychotherapists and counselors work with a wide variety of clients, psychotherapists are more likely to work very intensively with more deeply disturbed individuals who are seen more frequently over a longer period of time.
- Counseling is an educative modality, and therapy is an emotional, understanding restorative modality.
- Counseling is problem solving, and therapy/psychotherapy deals with deeper psychological or mental health issues.
- Psychotherapy is concerned with some type of personality change whereas counseling is concerned with helping individuals utilize full coping potential.
- Counseling is best for routine maintenance, and psychotherapy is best for a major overhaul of the client's personality.
- The distinction between counseling and psychotherapy is murky at best, even at the master's and doctoral level.
- Licensed clinical social workers can diagnose clients, using the classifications in *Diagnostic and Statistical Manual of Mental Disorders-5* (American Psychiatric Association, 2013), but BSW persons cannot. (It should be noted that some states require that licensed clinical social workers need to be supervised by a psychiatrist or by a clinical psychologist.)

Given this list, what can be concluded is that there is considerable overlap between "counseling" and "therapy/psychotherapy." At the present time, there appear to be no major clear-cut distinctions between these terms. It is true that licensed clinical social workers can diagnose clients using *DSM-5*, but BSW persons cannot.

Some key unanswered questions are the following: First, are some intervention techniques (such as hypnosis) beyond the limit of authority for a BSW graduate to use? If so, what are they? Also, how do we determine if a BSW graduate has exceeded the limit of his or her authority?

I put this last question to a social worker in my state who is a member of the state social work certification/licensing board. This person responded, "To date, the board has only concluded that a BSW person is acting outside the scope of his or her certification when that person states in a resume or in an ad that s/he provides psychotherapy."

A SYSTEMS PERSPECTIVE

Social workers are trained to have a systems perspective in their dealings with individuals, groups, families, organizations, and communities. A systems perspective emphasizes looking beyond presenting the problems of the client to assess the complexities and interrelationships of problems. Wholeness, relationship, and homeostasis are key concepts in systems theory.

The concept of *wholeness* means that the objects or elements within a system produce an entity that is greater than the sum of the parts. Systems theory is antireductionistic; it asserts that no system can be adequately understood or totally explained once it has been broken down into its component parts. (For example, the central nervous system carries out thought processes that would not occur if only parts were used.)

The concept of *relationship* asserts that the patterning and structuring among the elements in a system are as important as the elements themselves. For example, Masters and Johnson (1970) found that sexual dysfunctions occur primarily because of the nature of the husband–wife relationship rather than the psychological makeup of each partner.

Systems theory opposes simple cause-and-effect explanations. For instance, whether a child will be abused in a family is determined by a variety of variables and the patterning of these variables: the parents' capacity to control their anger, relationships between the child and the parents, relationships between the parents, degree of psychological stress, characteristics of the child, and opportunities for socially acceptable ways for parents to ventilate anger.

The concept of *homeostasis* suggests that most living systems endeavor to maintain and preserve the current system. Jackson (1965), for example, noted that families tend to establish a behavior balance or stability and to resist any change from that predetermined level of stability. Thus, a state of imbalance typically is driven back toward the previous state of balance *or* is driven forward to a new balance. If one child is abused in a family, that abuse often serves a function in the family as indicated by the fact that if that child is removed a second child is often selected to be abused. Or, if one family member improves through counseling, the improvement often upsets the balance within the family; other family members will have to change (which may be adaptive or maladaptive) to adjust to the new behavior of the improved family member.

Ecological theory is a subcategory of systems theory. Ecological theory has emerged as a prominent force in social work practice, as discussed in the next section.

THE MEDICAL MODEL VERSUS THE ECOLOGICAL MODEL OF HUMAN BEHAVIOR

The Medical Model

From the 1920s to the 1960s, most social workers used a medical model for assessing and changing human behavior. This model, initiated primarily by Sigmund Freud, views clients as *patients*. The service provider first diagnoses the causes of a patient's problems and then provides treatment. The patient's problems are viewed as being inside the patient.

The medical model has a lengthy classification of mental disorders defined by the American Psychiatric Association. The major categories of mental disorders are listed in Exhibit 1.1.

Exercise 1.4: Understanding the Major Mental Disorders

Goal: This exercise is designed to assist you in understanding the major mental disorders.

Briefly describe people you know who have the mental disorders identified in Exhibit 1.1. For confidentiality reasons, do not use their real names. Here is an example of a desired brief description: Jenny, age 22 and a college student, has been bulimic for at least the past three years. She has been binging and purging four or more times a week. Recently, she stated some of her vomit sometimes contains blood (which may suggest a serious medical issue).

The medical model conceptualizes emotional and behavioral problems as *mental illnesses*. People with emotional or behavioral problems are then given medical labels such as schizophrenia, paranoia, psychosis, and insanity. Adherents of the medical approach believe the disturbed person's mind is affected by some generally unknown internal condition that is thought to result from a variety of possible causative factors: genetic endowment, metabolic disorders, infectious diseases, internal conflicts, unconscious uses of defense mechanisms, and traumatic early experiences that cause emotional fixations and prevent future psychological growth.

Several specific mental disorders are described briefly here.

Schizophrenia.   This malady encompasses a large group of disorders, usually of psychotic proportion, manifested by characteristic disturbances of language and communication, thought, perception, affect, and behavior and lasting longer than 6 months.

Delusional Disorder.   The essential feature is the presence of one or more delusions that persist for at least 1 month. A delusion is something that is falsely believed or propagated. An example is the persecutory type, in which an individual erroneously believes that he or she is being conspired against, cheated, spied on, followed, poisoned or drugged, maliciously maligned, harassed, or obstructed in the pursuit of long-term goals.

Exhibit 1.1 Major Mental Disorders According to the American Psychiatric Association

NEURODEVELOPMENTAL DISORDERS include, but are not limited to intellectual disabilities (sometimes called cognitive disabilities), communication disorders (such as language disorder), autism spectrum disorder, attention-deficit/hyperactivity disorder, specific learning disorder (such as impairment in reading), and motor disorders (such as developmental co-ordination disorder, stereotypic movement disorder, and Tourette's disorder).

SCHIZOPHRENIA SPECTRUM AND OTHER PSYCHOTIC DISORDERS include, but are not limited to schizotypal (personality) disorder, delusional disorder, schizophrenia, schizoaffective disorder, and catatonic disorder.

BIPOLAR AND RELATED DISORDERS include, but are not limited to bipolar I disorder, bipolar II disorder, and cyclothymic disorder.

DEPRESSIVE DISORDERS include, but are not limited to disruptive mood dysregulation disorder (such as major depressive disorder), persistent depressive disorder, and premenstrual dysphoric disorder.

ANXIETY DISORDERS include separation anxiety disorder, specific phobia (such as fear of injections and transfusions), social anxiety disorder, panic disorder, and agoraphobia.

OBSESSIVE-COMPULSIVE AND RELATED DISORDERS include obsessive-compulsive disorder, trichotillomania (hair-pulling disorder), and excoriation (skin-picking) disorder.

TRAUMA- AND STRESSOR-RELATED DISORDERS include reactive attachment disorder, posttraumatic stress disorder, and acute stress disorder.

DISSOCIATIVE DISORDERS include dissociative disorder and dissociative amnesia.

SOMATIC SYMPTOM AND RELATED DISORDERS include somatic symptom disorder, illness anxiety disorder, and factitious disorder (includes factitious disorder imposed on self, and factitious disorder imposed on another).

FEEDING AND EATING DISORDERS include pica, rumination disorder, avoidant/restrictive food intake disorder, anorexia nervosa, bulimia nervosa, and binge-eating disorder.

ELIMINATION DISORDERS include enuresis and encopresis.

SLEEP-WAKE DISORDERS include insomnia disorder, hypersomnolence disorder, narcolepsy, breathing-related sleep disorder (such as central sleep apnea), and parasomnias (such as sleepwalking type, sleep terror type, nightmare disorder, rapid eye movement sleep behavior disorder, restless leg syndrome, and substance/medication-related sleep disorder).

SEXUAL DYSFUNCTIONS include delayed ejaculation, erectile disorder, female orgasmic disorder, female sexual interest/arousal disorder, genitor-pelvic pain/penetration disorder, male hypoactive sexual desire disorder, and premature (early) ejaculation.

GENDER DYSPHORIA includes gender dysphoria.

DISRUPTIVE, IMPULSE-CONTROL, AND CONDUCT DISORDERS include oppositional defiant disorder, intermittent explosive disorder, conduct disorder, antisocial personality disorder, pyromania, and kleptomania.

SUBSTANCE-RELATED AND ADDICTIVE DISORDERS include alcohol-related disorders (such as alcohol use disorder and alcohol intoxication); caffeine-related disorders (such as caffeine intoxication); cannabis-related disorder (such as cannabis use disorder and cannabis intoxication); hallucinogen-related disorders; inhalant-related disorders; opioid-related disorders; sedative-, hypnotic-, or anxiolytic-related disorders; stimulant-related disorders (such as cocaine abuse); tobacco-related disorders; and non-substance-related disorders (such as gambling disorders).

NEUROCOGNITIVE DISORDERS include delirium, major and mild neurocognitive disorders (such as Alzheimer's disease, vascular disease, traumatic brain injury, substance/medication use, HIV infection, Parkinson's disease, and Huntington's disease).

PERSONALITY DISORDERS include paranoid personality disorder, schizoid personality disorder, schizotypal personality disorder, antisocial personality disorder, borderline personality disorder, histrionic personality disorder, narcissistic personality disorder, avoidant personality disorder, dependent personality disorder, and obsessive-compulsive personality disorder.

PARAPHILIC DISORDERS include voyeuristic disorder, exhibitionistic disorder, frotteuristic disorder (such as recurrent sexual arousal from touching or rubbing against a nonconsenting person), sexual masochism disorder, sexual sadism disorder, fetishistic disorder, and transvestic disorder.

OTHER MENTAL DISORDERS include mental disorders due to another medical condition.

MEDICATION-INDUCED MOVEMENT DISORDERS AND OTHER ADVERSE EFFECTS OF MEDICATION include neuroleptic-induced Parkinsonism and medication-induced acute dystonia.

OTHER CONDITIONS THAT MAY BE A FOCUS OF CLINICAL ATTENTION include relational problems (such as parent-child relational problems), abuse and neglect (such as child abuse and neglect, child sexual abuse, child psychological abuse, spouse or partner violence or neglect, and adult abuse by non-spouse), educational and occupational problems, housing and economic problems (such as homelessness), problems related to crime or interaction with the legal system, religious or spiritual problems, victim of terrorism or torture, personal history of military deployment, and overweight or obesity.

Source: Diagnostic and Statistical Manual of Mental Disorders-5, Fifth Edition by the American Psychiatric Association, 2013. Washington, DC: American Psychiatric Association.

Hypochondriasis. This is a chronic maladaptive style of relating to the environment through preoccupation with shifting somatic concerns and symptoms, a fear or conviction that one has a serious physical illness, the search for medical treatment, inability to accept reassurance, and either hostile or dependent relationships with caregivers and family

Bipolar Disorder. This is a major affective disorder characterized by episodes of both mania and depression; it was formerly called manic-depressive psychosis. Bipolar disorder may be subdivided into manic, depressed, or mixed types on the basis of currently presenting symptoms.

Phobia. A phobia is characterized by an obsessive, persistent, unrealistic, intense fear of an object or situation. Common phobias include *acrophobia* (fear of heights), *algophobia* (fear of pain), *claustrophobia* (fear of closed spaces), and *erythrophobia* (fear of blushing).

Personality Disorders. Some of the most common personality disorders and their characteristics are as follows:

- *Paranoid.* A pattern of distrust and suspicion such that others' motives are interpreted as malevolent
- *Schizoid.* A pattern of detachment from social relationships and a restricted range of emotional expression
- *Schizotypal.* A pattern of acute discomfort in close relationships, cognitive or perceptual distortions, and eccentricities of behavior
- *Antisocial.* A pattern of disregard for, and violation of, the rights of others
- *Borderline.* A pattern of instability in interpersonal relationships, self-image, and affect; also characterized by marked impulsivity
- *Histrionic.* A pattern of excessive emotionality and attention seeking
- *Narcissistic.* A pattern of grandiosity, need for admiration, and lack of empathy
- *Avoidant.* A pattern of social inhibition, feelings of inadequacy, and hypersensitivity to negative evaluation
- *Dependent.* A pattern of submissive and clinging behavior related to an excessive need to be taken care of
- *Obsessive-compulsive.* A pattern of preoccupation with orderliness, perfectionism, and control

The medical model arose in reaction to the historical notion that the emotionally disturbed were possessed by demons, were mad, and were to be blamed for their disturbances. These people were "treated" by being beaten, locked up, or killed. The medical model viewed the disturbed as in need of help, stimulated research into the nature of emotional problems, and promoted the development of therapeutic approaches.

The major evidence for the validity of the medical model comes from studies that suggest that some mental disorders, such as schizophrenia, may be influenced by genetics (heredity). The bulk of the evidence on the case for heredity comes from studies of twins. For example, in some studies identical twins have been found to have a concordance rate (that is, if one twin has it, both have it) for schizophrenia of about 50% (Comer, 2005, pp. 251–260). Keep in mind that the rate of schizophrenia in the general population is about 1% (p. 251). When one identical twin is schizophrenic, the other is 50 times more likely than the average to be schizophrenic. This suggests a causal influence of genes, but not genetic determination, for concordance for identical twins is only 50%, not 100%.

The Ecological Model

In the 1960s, some social work scholars began to question the usefulness of the medical model. Environmental factors were shown to be at least as important as internal factors in causing a client's problems. Research also was demonstrating that psychoanalysis was probably ineffective in treating clients' problems (Stuart, 1970).

In the 1960s, social work shifted at least some of its emphasis to a *reform approach*, which seeks to change systems to benefit clients. Enactment of antipoverty programs (such as Head Start) is an example of an effort to change systems to benefit clients.

In the past several years, social work has increasingly focused on an *ecological model*. This model integrates both treatment and reform by conceptualizing and emphasizing the dysfunctional transactions between people and their physical and social environments. Human beings are viewed as developing and adapting through transactions with all elements of their environments. An ecological model gives attention to both internal and external factors. It does not view people as passive reactors to their environments but, rather, as being involved in dynamic and reciprocal interactions with them.

This model tries to improve the coping patterns of people and their environments so that a better match can be attained between an individual's needs and the characteristics of his or her environment. One emphasis of the model is on the person-in-environment. The person-in-environment conceptualization is depicted in Figure 1.2.

As is evident in the figure, people interact with many systems. With this conceptualization, social work can focus on three separate areas. First, it can focus on the person and seek to develop his or her problem-solving, coping, and developmental capacities. Second, it can focus on the relationship between a person and the systems he or she interacts with and link the person with needed resources, services, and opportunities. Third, it can focus on the systems and seek to reform them to meet the needs of the individual more effectively.

The ecological model views individuals, families, and small groups as having transitional problems and needs as they move from one life stage to another. Individuals face many transitional changes as they grow older, such as learning to walk, entering first grade, adjusting to puberty, graduating from school, finding a job, getting married, having children, having children leave home, and retiring.

Families also have a life cycle. Here are only a few of the events that require adjustment: engagement, marriage, birth of children, parenting, children going to school, children leaving home, and loss of a parent (perhaps through death or divorce).

Small groups have transitional phases of development as well. Members of small groups spend time getting acquainted, gradually learn to trust one another, begin to self-disclose more, learn to work together on tasks, develop approaches to handle interpersonal conflict, and face adjustments to the group eventually terminating or some members leaving.

The model's central concern is to articulate the transitional problems and needs of individuals, families, and small groups. Once these problems and needs are identified, intervention approaches are then selected and applied to help individuals, families, and small groups resolve the transitional problems and meet their needs.

An ecological model can also focus on maladaptive interpersonal problems and needs in families and groups, including communication processes and dysfunctional relationship patterns. These difficulties cover an array of areas, including interpersonal conflicts, power struggles, double binds, distortions in communicating, scapegoating, and discrimination. The consequences of such difficulties are usually maladaptive for some members. An ecological model seeks to identify such interpersonal obstacles and then apply appropriate intervention strategies. For example, parents may set the price for honesty too high for their children. In such families, children gradually learn to hide certain behaviors and thoughts, and even learn to lie. If the parents discover such dishonesty, an uproar usually occurs. An appropriate intervention is to open up

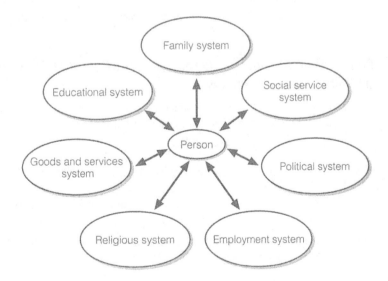

Figure 1.2

Person-in-environment conceptualization.

communication patterns and help the parents understand that, if they really want honesty from their children, they need to learn to be more accepting of their children's thoughts and actions.

Two centuries ago, people interacted primarily within the family system. Families were nearly self-sufficient. In those days, the person-in-family was a way of conceptualizing the main system that individuals interacted with. Our society has become much more complex. Today, a person's life and quality of life are interwoven with and inter-dependent on many systems, as shown in Figure 1.2.

The ecological model "opens up many more doors" of intervening with clients in contrast to the medical model. With the medical model the problems faced by clients are viewed as being inside the clients, which limits the interventions to be focused on the clients making changes to improve themselves. With the ecological model interventions can focus not only on clients making changes to improve their well being, but also on: a) linking clients to systems and resources which will improve their lives, b) changing ineffective systems and resources to better serve clients, and c) changing broader social policies to better serve clients; e.g., establishing a universal health care system to meet the medical needs of all residents in a country.

Exercise 1.5: Understanding the Medical Model and the Ecological Model

Goal: This exercise is designed to help you understand the medical model and the ecological model. In understanding why people become involved in dysfunctional behavior (such as being anorexic, committing a crime, or becoming a batterer), which model (the medical model or the ecological model) do you believe is more useful? State the reasons for your choice.

GOALS OF SOCIAL WORK PRACTICE

The National Association of Social Workers (1982) has conceptualized social work practice as having five major goals.

Goal 1: Enhance People's Problem-Solving, Coping, and Developmental Capacities

Using the person-in-environment concept, social work practice at this level focuses on the "person." With this focus, a social worker serves primarily as an *enabler*. In this role, the worker may take on the activities of a counselor, teacher, caregiver (providing supportive services to those who cannot fully solve their problems and meet their own needs), and behavior changer (that is, changing specific parts of a client's behavior).

Goal 2: Link People with Systems That Provide Them with Resources, Services, and Opportunities

Using the person-in-environment concept, social work practice at this level focuses on the relationships between individuals and the systems they interact with. In this situation, a social worker serves primarily as a *broker*.

Goal 3: Promote the Effective and Humane Operation of Systems That Provide People with Resources and Services

Using the person-in-environment concept, the focus of social work practice at this level is on the systems people interact with. One role a worker may fill at this level is an *advocate*. Additional roles include

Program developer: The worker seeks to promote or design programs or technologies to meet social needs.

Supervisor: The worker seeks to increase the effectiveness and efficiency of the delivery of services through supervising other staff.

Coordinator: The worker seeks to improve a delivery system by increasing communications and coordination between human service resources.

Consultant: The worker seeks to provide guidance to agencies and organizations by suggesting ways to increase the effectiveness and efficiency of services.

Goal 4: Develop and Improve Social Policy

Similar to goal 3, social work practice at this level focuses on the systems people interact with. The distinction between goal 3 and goal 4 is that the focus of goal 3 is on the available resources for serving people. Goal 4 works on the statutes and broader social policies that underlie such resources. The major roles at this level are *planner* and *policy developer*. In these roles, workers develop and seek adoption of new statutes or policies and propose elimination of ineffective or inappropriate ones. In these planning and policy development processes, social workers may take on an advocate role and, in some instances, an activist role.

The Council on Social Work Education (CSWE) is the national accreditating body for social work education in the United States. It describes the purpose of social work as follows (CSWE, 2015):

> The purpose of the social work profession is to promote human and community well-being. Guided by a person-in-environment framework, a global perspective, respect for human diversity, and knowledge based on scientific inquiry, the purpose of social work is actualized through its quest for social and economic justice, the prevention of conditions that limit human rights, the elimination of poverty, and the enhancement of the quality of life for all persons, locally and globally.

This description of the purpose of social work is consistent with the four goals of social work mentioned earlier. However, it adds one additional goal, as follows.

Goal 5: Promote Human and Community Well-Being

The social work profession is committed to enhancing the well-being of all human beings and to promoting community well-being. It is particularly committed to alleviating poverty, oppression, and other forms of social injustice. About 15% of the U.S. population has an income below the poverty line. Social work has always advocated for developing programs to alleviate poverty, and many practitioners focus on providing services to the poor.

Poverty is global; every society has members who are poor. In some societies, as much as 95% of the population lives in poverty. Social workers are committed to alleviating poverty not only in the United States but also worldwide. Alleviating poverty is obviously complex and difficult. Social work professionals work with a variety of systems to make progress in alleviating poverty, including educational systems, healthcare systems, political systems, business and employment systems, religious systems, and human services systems.

Oppression is the unjust or cruel exercise of authority or power. In our society, numerous groups have been oppressed—including African Americans, Latinos, Chinese Americans, Native Americans, women, persons with disabilities, gays and lesbians, various religious groups, and people living in poverty (The listing of these groups is only illustrative and certainly not exhaustive.) Social injustice occurs when some members of a society have less protection, fewer basic rights and opportunities, or fewer social benefits than other members of that society. Social work is a profession that is committed not only to alleviating poverty but also to combating oppression and other forms of social injustice.

Social justice is an ideal condition in which all members of a society have the same basic rights, protection, opportunities, obligations, and social benefits. Economic justice is also an ideal condition in which all members of a society have the same opportunities to attain material goods, income, and wealth. Social workers have an obligation to help groups at risk increase their personal, interpersonal, socioeconomic, and political strength and influence through improving their circumstances. Empowerment-focused social workers seek a more equitable distribution of resources and power a mong the various groups in society. Diverse groups that may be at risk include those distinguished by "age, class, color, culture, disability and ability, ethnicity, gender, gender identity and expression, immigration status, marital status, political ideology, race, religion/spirituality, sex, sexual orientation, and tribal sovereign status" (Council on Social Work Education, 2015).

Exercise 1.6: Your Interest in Achieving the Goals of Social Work

Goal: This exercise is designed to assist you in identifying your interest in becoming involved in activities that are consistent with the five goals of social work.

Step 1:   Check which of the following identifies your interest level in each of the five goals of social work.

	Highly Interested	Somewhat Interested	Uncertain	Somewhat Disinterested	Not Interested
Goal 1					
Goal 2					
Goal 3					
Goal 4					
Goal 5					

Step 2:   For the goals that you checked "Highly Interested," state the reasons for these selections.

Step 3:   For the goals that you checked "Somewhat Disinterested" or "Not Interested," state your reasons for these markings.

MICRO, MEZZO, AND MACRO LEVELS OF PRACTICE

Social workers practice at three levels: (1) *micro*—working on a one-to-one basis with an individual; (2) *mezzo*—working with families and other small groups; and (3) *macro*—working with organizations and communities or seeking changes in statutes and social policies.

The specific activities performed by workers include, but are not limited to, the following categories.

Social Casework

Aimed at helping individuals on a one-to-one basis to meet personal and social problems, casework may be geared to helping the client adjust to his or her environment or to changing certain social and economic pressures that adversely affect an individual. Social casework services are provided by nearly every social welfare agency that provides direct services to people. *Social casework* encompasses a wide variety of activities, such as counseling runaway youths; helping unemployed people secure training or employment; counseling someone who is suicidal; placing a homeless child in an adoptive or foster home; providing protective services to abused children and their families; finding nursing homes for stroke victims who no longer need to be hospitalized; counseling individuals with sexual dysfunctions; helping alcoholics acknowledge they have a drinking problem; counseling those with a terminal illness; being a probation and parole officer; providing services to single parents; and working in medical and mental hospitals as a member of a rehabilitation team.

Case Management

Many social service agencies have labeled their social workers *case managers*. The tasks performed by case managers are similar to those of caseworkers. The job descriptions of case managers vary from service area to service area. For example, case managers in a juvenile probation setting supervise clients, provide some counseling, monitor clients to make certain they are following the rules of probation, link clients and their families with needed services, prepare court reports, and testify in court. Case managers at a sheltered workshop are likely to provide job training and counseling, arrange transportation, discipline clients for unacceptable behavior, act as an advocate, and act as liaison with the people who supervise clients during their nonwork hours (which may be at a group home, foster home, residential treatment facility, or their parents' home). Hepworth and Larsen (1986) described the role of a case manager this way:

> Case managers link clients to needed resources that exist in complex service delivery networks and orchestrate the delivery of services in a timely fashion. Case managers function as brokers, facilitators, linkers, mediators, and advocates. A case manager must have extensive knowledge of community resources, rights of clients, and policies and procedures of various agencies and must be skillful in mediation and advocacy. (p. 563)

Group Work

The intellectual, emotional, and social development of individuals may be furthered through group activities. In contrast to casework or group counseling, *group work* is not primarily therapeutic, except in a broad sense. Different groups have different objectives, such as socialization, information exchange, curbing delinquency, recreation, changing socially unacceptable values, and helping achieve better relations between cultural and racial groups. For example, through group activities a group worker at a neighborhood center may seek to curb delinquency patterns and change socially unacceptable values, or a worker at an adoption agency may meet with a group of applicants to explain adoption procedures and help applicants prepare for becoming adoptive parents. Activities and focuses of groups vary: arts and crafts, dancing, games, dramatics, music, photography, sports, nature study, woodwork, first aid, home management, information exchange, and discussion of such topics as politics, sex, marriage, religion, and selecting a career.

Group Counseling

Group counseling is aimed at facilitating the social, behavioral, and emotional adjustment of individuals through the group process. Participants in group counseling usually have emotional, interactional, or behavioral difficulties. Group counseling has several advantages over one-to-one counseling, such as the operation of the helper therapy principle, which maintains it is therapeutic for the helper (who can be any member of a group) to feel he or she has been helpful to others. In contrast to one-to-one counseling, group pressure is often more effective in changing individuals' maladaptive behavior, and group counseling is a time saver because it enables the group facilitator to treat several people simultaneously. For example, group counseling might be used for individuals who are severely depressed, have drinking problems, are rape victims, are psychologically addicted to drugs, have a relative who is terminally ill, are single and pregnant, are recently divorced, or have an eating disorder.

Family Counseling

A type of group counseling aimed at helping families with interactional, behavioral, and emotional problems, *family counseling* can be used with parent–child interaction problems, marital conflicts, and conflicts with grandparents. A wide variety of problems are dealt with in family treatment or family counseling, such as communication problems and disagreements between parents and youths on choice of friends, drinking and other drug use, domestic tasks, curfew hours, sexual values and behavior, study habits and grades received, and choice of dates.

Community Organization

The aim of *community organization* is stimulating and assisting the local community to evaluate, plan, and coordinate efforts to provide for the community's health, welfare, and recreation needs. Although it is not possible to define precisely the activities of a community organizer, they often include encouraging and fostering citizen participation, coordinating efforts between agencies or groups, public relations and public education, research, planning, and being a resource person. A community organizer acts as a catalyst in stimulating and encouraging community action. Such specialists are apt to be employed in community welfare councils, social planning agencies, health planning councils, and community action agencies. The term *community organization* is now being replaced in some settings by *planning, social planning, program development, policy development*, and *macro practice.*

Barker (2003) defined *community organization* as:

> An intervention process used by social workers and other professionals to help individuals, groups, and collectives of people with common interests or from the same geographic areas to deal with social problems and to enhance social well-being through planned collective action. Methods include identifying problem areas, analyzing causes, formulating plans, developing strategies, mobilizing necessary resources, identifying and recruiting community leaders, and encouraging interrelationships between them to facilitate their efforts. (p. 84)

Policy Analysis

Policy analysis involves systematic evaluation of a policy and the process by which it was formulated. Those who conduct such an analysis consider whether the process and result were clear, equitable, legal, rational, compatible with social values, superior to other alternatives, cost-effective, and explicit. Such an analysis frequently identifies shortcomings in the policy. Those conducting the policy analysis then usually recommend modifications in the policy that are designed to alleviate these shortcomings.

Administration

Administration involves directing the overall program of a social service agency. Administrative functions include setting agency program objectives; analyzing social conditions in the community; making decisions about what services will be provided; employing and supervising staff members; setting up an organizational structure; administering financial affairs; and securing funds for the agency's operations. Administration also involves setting organizational goals; coordinating activities to achieve the selected goals; and monitoring and making necessary changes in processes and structure to improve the effectiveness and efficiency of processes that contribute to transforming social policy into social services. In social work, the term *administration* is often used synonymously with *management*. In a small agency, administrative functions may be carried out by one person, whereas several people may be involved in administrative affairs in a larger agency.

Exercise 1.7: Identifying Your Interest in Various Social Work Activities

Goal: This exercise is designed to help you reflect on the kinds of activities you want to engage in as a social worker.

Step 1:   Check which of the following indicates your interest in engaging in a variety of social work activities.

	Highly Interested	Somewhat Interested	Uncertain	Somewhat Disinterested	Not Interested
1. Social Casework					
2. Case Management					
3. Group Work					
4. Group Counseling					
5. Family Counseling					
6. Community Organization					
7. Policy Analysis					
8. Administration					

Step 2:   For the activities that you checked "Highly Interested," state the reasons for these selections.

Step 3:   For the activities that you checked "Somewhat Disinterested" or "Not Interested," state your reasons for these markings.

Other areas of professional activity in social work include research, consulting, supervising, planning, program development, policy development, and teaching (primarily at the college level). Social casework, case management, group work, group counseling, family counseling, and community organization constitute the primary professional activities that beginning-level social workers are likely to provide. All of these activities require social workers to have counseling skills. (Counseling involves helping individuals or groups resolve social and personal problems through the process of developing a relationship, exploring the problems in depth, and exploring alternative solutions. This process is described in Chapter 5.) Caseworkers, case managers, group workers, group counselors, and family counselors need high levels of counseling skills to work with individuals and groups. Community organizers need to be perceptive, and they need skills in relating to other people in assessing problems and developing resolution strategies—skills that parallel or are analogous to counseling skills. Therefore, a major emphasis of this text is on counseling.

Counseling skills, however, are not the only skills social workers need. For example, caseworkers also need to be able to construct social histories and to link clients with other human services. Some agencies require skills in public speaking, preparing and presenting reports to courts and to other agencies, and teaching parents better parenting techniques. Research capacities to evaluate one's own practice and other programs are also important. The essential skills needed for social work practice are further described in the next section. As you will see, generalist social workers are expected to have an extensive knowledge base and numerous skills and to adhere to a well-defined set of professional social work values.

KNOWLEDGE, SKILLS, AND VALUES NEEDED FOR SOCIAL WORK PRACTICE

In *Educational Policy and Accreditation Standards (EPAS)*, the Council on Social Work Education (2015) identified knowledge, skills, values and cognitive and affective processes that accredited baccalaureate and master's degree programs are mandated to convey to social work students. *EPAS* is based on a competency approach. The following material is reprinted with permission from *Educational Policy and Accreditation Standards* (Council on Social Work Education, 2015); the mandated content that BSW and MSW programs are required to provide to students are summarized in the following 9 competencies:

Social Work Competencies

The nine Social Work Competencies are listed below. Programs may add competencies that are consistent with their mission and goals and respond to their context. Each competency describes the knowledge, values, skills, and cognitive and affective processes that comprise the competency at the generalist level of practice, followed by a set of behaviors that integrate these components. These behaviors represent observable components of the competencies, while the preceding statements represent the underlying content and processes that inform the behaviors.

Competency 1—Demonstrate Ethical and Professional Behavior

Social workers understand the value base of the profession and its ethical standards, as well as relevant laws and regulations that may impact practice at the micro, mezzo, and macro levels. Social workers understand frameworks of ethical decision-making and how to apply principles of critical thinking to those frameworks in practice, research, and policy arenas. Social workers recognize personal values and the distinction between personal and professional values. They also understand how their personal experiences and affective reactions influence their professional judgment and behavior. Social workers understand the profession's history, its mission, and the roles and responsibilities of the profession. Social workers also understand the role of other professions when engaged in interprofessional teams. Social workers recognize the importance of life-long learning and are committed to continually updating their skills to ensure they are relevant and effective. Social workers also understand emerging forms of technology and the ethical use of technology in social work practice. Social workers:

- make ethical decisions by applying the standards of the NASW Code of Ethics, relevant laws and regulations, models for ethical decision-making, ethical conduct of research, and additional codes of ethics as appropriate to context;
- use reflection and self-regulation to manage personal values and maintain professionalism in practice situations;
- demonstrate professional demeanor in behavior, appearance, and oral, written, and electronic communication;
- use technology ethically and appropriately to facilitate practice outcomes; and
- use supervision and consultation to guide professional judgment and behavior.

Competency 2—Engage Diversity and Difference in Practice

Social workers understand how diversity and difference characterize and shape the human experience and are critical to the formation of identity. The dimensions of diversity are understood as the intersectionality of multiple factors including but not limited to age, class, color, culture, disability and ability, ethnicity, gender, gender identity and expression, immigration status, marital status, political ideology, race, religion/spirituality, sex, sexual orientation, and tribal sovereign status. Social workers understand that, as a consequence of difference, a person's life experiences may include oppression, poverty, marginalization, and alienation as well as privilege, power, and acclaim. Social workers also understand the forms and mechanisms of oppression and discrimination and recognize the extent to which a culture's structures and values, including social, economic, political, and cultural exclusions, may oppress, marginalize, alienate, or create privilege and power. Social workers:

■ apply and communicate understanding of the importance of diversity and difference in shaping life experiences in practice at the micro, mezzo, and macro levels;
■ present themselves as learners and engage clients and constituencies as experts of their own experiences; and
■ apply self-awareness and self-regulation to manage the influence of personal biases and values in working with diverse clients and constituencies.

Competency 3—Advance Human Rights and Social, Economic, and Environmental Justice

Social workers understand that every person regardless of position in society has fundamental human rights such as freedom, safety, privacy, an adequate standard of living, health care, and education. Social workers understand the global interconnections of oppression and human rights violations, and are knowledgeable about theories of human need and social justice and strategies to promote social and economic justice and human rights. Social workers understand strategies designed to eliminate oppressive structural barriers to ensure that social goods, rights, and responsibilities are distributed equitably and that civil, political, environmental, economic, social, and cultural human rights are protected. Social workers:

■ apply their understanding of social, economic, and environmental justice to advocate for human rights at the individual and system levels; and
■ engage in practices that advance social, economic, and environmental justice.

Competency 4—Engage in Practice-Informed Research and Research-Informed Practice

Social workers understand quantitative and qualitative research methods and their respective roles in advancing a science of social work and in evaluating their practice. Social workers know the principles of logic, scientific inquiry, and culturally informed and ethical approaches to building knowledge. Social workers understand that evidence that informs practice derives from multi-disciplinary sources and multiple ways of knowing. They also understand the processes for translating research findings into effective practice. Social workers:

■ use practice experience and theory to inform scientific inquiry and research;
■ apply critical thinking to engage in analysis of quantitative and qualitative research methods and research findings; and
■ use and translate research evidence to inform and improve practice, policy, and service delivery.

Competency 5—Engage in Policy Practice

Social workers understand that human rights and social justice, as well as social welfare and services, are mediated by policy and its implementation at the federal, state, and local levels. Social workers understand the history and current structures of social policies and services, the role of policy in service delivery, the role of policy in service delivery, and the role of practice in policy development. Social workers understand their role in policy development and implementation within their practice settings at the micro, mezzo, and macro levels and they actively engage in policy practice to effect change within those settings. Social workers recognize and understand the historical, social, cultural, economic, organizational, environmental, and global influences that affect social policy. They are also knowledgeable about policy formulation, analysis, implementation, and evaluation. Social workers:

■ identify social policy at the local, state, and federal level that impacts well-being, service delivery, and access to social services;
■ assess how social welfare and economic policies impact the delivery of and access to social services;
■ apply critical thinking to analyze, formulate, and advocate for policies that advance human rights and social, economic, and environmental justice.

Competency 6—Engage with Individuals, Families, Groups, Organizations, and Communities

Social workers understand that engagement is an ongoing component of the dynamic and interactive process of social work practice with, and on behalf of, diverse individuals, families, groups, organizations, and communities. Social workers value the importance of human relationships. Social workers understand theories of human behavior and the social environment, and critically evaluate and apply this knowledge to facilitate engagement with clients and constituencies, including individuals, families, groups, organizations, and communities. Social workers understand strategies to engage diverse clients and constituencies to advance practice effectiveness. Social workers understand how their personal experiences and affective reactions may impact their ability to effectively engage with diverse clients and constituencies. Social workers value principles of relationship-building and interprofessional collaboration to facilitate engagement with clients, constituencies, and other professionals as appropriate. Social workers:

- apply knowledge of human behavior and the social environment, person-in-environment, and other multidisciplinary theoretical frameworks to engage with clients and constituencies; and
- use empathy, reflection, and interpersonal skills to effectively engage diverse clients and constituencies.

Competency 7—Assess Individuals, Families, Groups, Organizations, and Communities

Social workers understand that assessment is an ongoing component of the dynamic and interactive process of social work practice with, and on behalf of, diverse individuals, families, groups, organizations, and communities. Social workers understand theories of human behavior and the social environment, and critically evaluate and apply this knowledge in the assessment of diverse clients and constituencies, including individuals, families, groups, organizations, and communities. Social workers understand methods of assessment with diverse clients and constituencies to advance practice effectiveness. Social workers recognize the implications of the larger practice context in the assessment process and value the importance of interprofessional collaboration in this process. Social workers understand how their personal experiences and affective reactions may affect their assessment and decision-making. Social workers:

- collect and organize data, and apply critical thinking to interpret information from clients and constituencies;
- apply knowledge of human behavior and the social environment, person-in-environment, and other multidisciplinary theoretical frameworks in the analysis of assessment data from clients and constituencies;
- develop mutually agreed-on intervention goals and objectives based on the critical assessment of strengths, needs, and challenges within clients and constituencies; and
- select appropriate intervention strategies based on the assessment, research knowledge, and values and preferences of clients and constituencies.

Competency 8—Intervene with Individuals, Families, Groups, Organizations, and Communities

Social workers understand that intervention is an ongoing component of the dynamic and interactive process of social work practice with, and on behalf of, diverse individuals, families, groups, organizations, and communities. Social workers are knowledgeable about evidence-informed interventions to achieve the goals of clients and constituencies, including individuals, families, groups, organizations, and communities. Social workers understand theories of human behavior and the social environment, and critically evaluate and apply this knowledge to effectively intervene with clients and constituencies. Social workers understand methods of identifying, analyzing and implementing evidence-informed interventions to achieve client and constituency goals. Social workers value the importance of interprofessional teamwork and communication in interventions, recognizing that beneficial outcomes may require interdisciplinary, interprofessional, and interorganizational collaboration. Social workers:

- critically choose and implement interventions to achieve practice goals and enhance capacities of client and constituencies;
- apply knowledge of human behavior and the social environment, person-in-environment, and other multidisciplinary theoretical frameworks in interventions with clients and constituencies;

- use inter-professional collaboration as appropriate to achieve beneficial practice outcomes;
- negotiate, mediate, and advocate with and on behalf of diverse clients and constituencies; and
- facilitate effective transitions and endings that advance mutually agreed-on goals.

Competency 9—Evaluate Practice with Individuals, Families, Groups, Organizations, and Communities

Social workers understand that evaluation is an ongoing component of the dynamic and interactive process of social work practice with, and on behalf of, diverse individuals, families, groups, organizations, and communities. Social workers recognize the importance of evaluating processes and outcomes to advance practice, policy, and service delivery effectiveness. Social workers understand theories of human behavior and the social environment, and critically evaluate and apply this knowledge in evaluating outcomes. Social workers understand qualitative and quantitative methods for evaluating outcomes and practice effectiveness. Social workers:

- select and use appropriate methods for evaluation of outcomes;
- apply knowledge of human behavior and the social environment, person-in-environment, and other multi-disciplinary theoretical frameworks in the evaluation of outcomes;
- critically analyze, monitor, and evaluate intervention and program processes and outcomes; and
- apply evaluation findings to improve practice effectiveness at the micro, mezzo, and macro levels.

TEXT OBJECTIVES

This text uses an integrative approach to present prominent methods in social work practice. Thus, the key objectives of this text are as follows:

- Provide content on social work practice, social work values and ethics, diversity, human rights, and promotion of social and economic justice that is consistent with *EPAS*.
- Prepare students for generalist social work practice by informing them of contemporary assessment and intervention strategies.
- Develop students' interviewing and counseling skills and capacities so they can intervene effectively with individuals, families, and groups.
- Develop students' macro practice skills and capacities in intervening with organizations and communities.
- Help students develop a philosophical value orientation that is consistent with social work practice.
- Develop students' capacities to function effectively in a variety of social work roles, including enabler, empowerer, broker, advocate, activist, mediator, negotiator, educator, initiator, coordinator, researcher, and group facilitator.
- Foster in students an awareness, understanding, and appreciation of how to intervene effectively with people of diverse racial, ethnic, cultural, social, and class backgrounds.
- Expand students' capacities to evaluate and modify human service programs and systems to make human services more equitable, humane, and responsive to consumers.
- Foster philosophical conceptual skills so that graduates can critically evaluate and further develop their own practice capacities throughout life.
- Help students develop a positive sense of self and an awareness and appreciation of the importance of continuing to evaluate their professional skills and professional growth.
- Inform students of the prominent theories of counseling that are used by social workers.

WHICH INTERVENTION STRATEGIES SHOULD SOCIAL WORKERS LEARN?

Literally hundreds of intervention approaches have been developed at the micro, mezzo, and macro levels of practice. A partial list of available techniques that can be used at the micro and mezzo levels of practice appears in Exhibit 1.2.

Exhibit 1.2   Partial List of Intervention Therapies at the Micro and Mezzo Levels

Task-centered therapy	Mindfulness
Psychoanalysis	Solution-focused therapy
Client-centered therapy	Gestalt therapy
Transactional analysis	Assertiveness training
Feminist intervention	Token economies
Rational-emotive therapy	Contingency contracting
Reality therapy	Systematic desensitization
Crisis intervention	In vivo desensitization
Behavior modification	Implosive therapy
Provocative therapy	Covert sensitization
Radical therapy	Aversive techniques
Adlerian therapy	Thought-stopping
Analytical therapy	Sex therapy
Existential therapy	Milieu therapy
Encounter therapies	Play therapy
Ego psychology approaches	Parent effectiveness training
Cognitive approaches	Muscle relaxation
General systems approaches	Deep breathing relaxation
Role theory approaches	Imagery relaxation
Time management	Meditation
Biofeedback	Hypnosis
Marathon groups	Self-hypnosis
Alcoholics Anonymous	Encounter groups
Weight Watchers	Sensitivity groups
Psychodrama	Parents Anonymous
	Neuro-linguistic programming

It is impossible for social workers to have an effective working knowledge of all of these intervention approaches. What social workers can do, however, is continue to learn additional approaches throughout their careers and also learn to apply the approaches they already use more effectively. Social work agencies encourage this continual learning by offering in-service training and workshops, sending workers to conferences, and encouraging workers to take additional college courses in the helping professions.

Workers should continue to learn a wide variety of intervention approaches so they can select from their "bag of tricks" the approach that is likely to be most effective (given each client's unique set of problems and circumstances). Workers soon become aware that their own personalities also partially determine which intervention approaches they are most comfortable with and effective in applying.

Because there are so many intervention techniques (as suggested in Exhibit 1.2), students may be bewildered about which intervention approaches to learn. It is therefore crucial that faculty guide students by (1) making carefully thought-out decisions, as a group, regarding the intervention theories that are most useful for students in their geographic area to learn; (2) giving an overview so that students are familiar with a wide number of theories; and (3) conveying material on each theory's merits and shortcomings. Later chapters in this text summarize many of the intervention approaches listed in Exhibit 1.2. The instructor of this course, along with the other social work faculty members, should decide which intervention approaches to cover in this class.

Once you graduate and obtain employment, your work setting will be a deciding factor in which intervention approaches you should use. If you are working with shy or aggressive people, assertiveness training may be appropriate. Alcoholics Anonymous may be appropriate for people with drinking problems, rational therapy for people who are depressed, in vivo desensitization for people who have phobias, and so on.

A competent social worker generally has a working knowledge of a variety of intervention approaches. In working with clients, the worker should focus on selecting effective intervention approaches that help clients solve their problems rather than trying to redefine the problems in terms of the worker's favorite intervention approach (see the material on evidence-based practice in Chapter 11).

SUMMARY

The following summarizes the chapter's content in terms of the learning objectives presented at the beginning of the chapter.

1. Understand a brief history of social work.
   Social work as a profession is of relatively recent origin. The first paid social workers were executive secretaries of charity organization societies in the late 1800s. Colleges and universities began to offer training programs in social work in the early 1900s.
2. Define social work.
   Social work is the professional activity of helping individuals, families, groups, organizations, and communities enhance or restore their capacity for social functioning and create societal conditions favorable to their goals. The term *social worker* is generally applied to graduates of bachelor's- or master's-level social work programs who are employed in the field of social welfare. A social worker is a change agent who is skilled at working with individuals, groups, families, organizations, and communities. Almost all social workers are employed in the field of social welfare.
3. Describe the relationship between social work and social welfare.
   The goal of social welfare is to fulfill the social, financial, health, and recreational requirements of all individuals in a society. Social welfare is a broader term than social work. Social workers are one of several professionals employed in social welfare; other professionals include psychiatrists, psychologists, and guidance counselors.

   The profession of social work is distinct from other helping professions because it has the responsibility and mandate to provide social services and it uses the person-in-environment concept.
4. Define generalist social work practice.
   Educational Policy and Accreditation Standards (Council on Social Work Education, 2015) defines generalist practice as:

   Generalist practice is grounded in the liberal arts and the person-in-environment framework. To promote human and social well-being, generalist practitioners use a range of prevention and intervention methods in their practice with diverse individuals, families, groups, organizations, and communities based on scientific inquiry and best practices. The generalist practitioner identifies with the social work profession and applies ethical principles and critical thinking in practice at the micro, mezzo, and macro levels. Generalist practitioners engage diversity in their practice and advocate for human rights and social and economic justice. They recognize, support, and build on the strengths and resiliency of all human beings. They engage in research-informed practice and are proactive in responding to the impact of context on professional practice.

5. Understand the roles of social workers in practice.
   The following list identifies some, but certainly not all, of the roles assumed by social workers: counselor, broker, advocate, empowerer, activist, mediator, negotiator, educator, initiator, coordinator, researcher, group facilitator, and public speaker.
6. Comprehend that counseling is a component of generalist practice.
   A small minority of social work educators assert that counseling and clinical social work are not components of generalist social work practice. This text asserts that counseling and clinical social work are key components in generalist practice.
7. Understand the relationship between counseling and therapy.
   At the present time, there appear to be no major clear-cut distinctions between "counseling" and "therapy/psychotherapy."
8. Understand that social workers use a systems perspective.
   Social workers are trained to have a systems perspective in their dealings with individuals, groups, families, organizations, and communities. A systems perspective emphasizes looking beyond present-

ing the problems of the client to assess the complexities and interrelationships of problems. Ecological theory is a subcategory of systems theory. Ecological theory has emerged as a prominent force in social work practice.

9. Understand the medical model, and the ecological model, of human behavior.

The medical model generally views clients as "patients." The patient's problems are generally viewed as being inside the patient.

The ecological model has a person-in-environment conceptualization. This model integrates both the treatment approach and the reform approach by conceptualizing and emphasizing the dysfunctional transactions between people and their physical and social environments.

10. Describe the goals of social work practice.

Social work has a number of goals, including to (1) enhance the problem-solving, coping, and developmental capacities of people; (2) link people with systems that provide them with resources, services, and opportunities; (3) promote the effectiveness and humane operation of systems that provide people with resources and services; (4) develop and improve social policy; and (5) promote human and community well-being.

A social worker needs training and expertise in a wide range of areas to effectively handle problems faced by individuals, groups, families, organizations, and the larger community. Most professions are becoming increasingly specialized, but social work continues to emphasize a generalist (broad-based) approach.

Social work uses a problem-solving approach. Social workers practice at three levels: micro, mezzo, and macro. Specific activities include social casework, case management, group work, group counseling, family counseling, community organization, policy analysis, planning, program development, policy development, research, consulting, supervision, and administration.

11. Understand the knowledge, skills, and values needed for social work practice.

In *Educational Policy and Accreditation Standards (EPAS)*, the Council on Social Work Education (2015) identified knowledge, skills, and values that accredited baccalaureate and master's degree programs are mandated to convey to social work students. This material is reprinted in this chapter.

Literally hundreds of intervention approaches have been developed for social work practice. It is impossible for any social worker to have an effective working knowledge of all of these theories. Educational programs have an obligation to provide social work students with an overview of the commonly used theories and to convey information on the merits and shortcomings of these approaches. Social workers have an obligation to continue throughout their careers to learn a variety of intervention approaches. In working with clients, a worker should focus on selecting the most effective intervention approaches for solving clients' problems rather than redefining clients' problems to fit the worker's favorite intervention approach.

EXERCISES

1. Breaking the Ice

Goal: To get acquainted and to reduce anxiety.

Step 1:   Starting a new class can be exciting and anxiety-producing for both students and instructors Brainstorm about what you would like to know about other members of the class. Examples might include marital status, hometown, work or volunteer experience in social work, and most unforgettable experience. List these questions on the blackboard.

Step 2:   Answer the questions developed in step 1.

Step 3:   Ask your instructor questions you may have about her or his educational background and professional experiences.

Step 4:   (Optional) In groups of two, share an experience that has had a profound effect on your life. Listeners should be encouraged to ask questions to seek clarification. After each person has had a chance to speak, class re-forms to report on what students have learned about their partners.

Step 5:   (Additional option) Ask each student to share "what is something surprising that we do not know about you?"

2. Searching for Descriptors

Goal: To facilitate student interaction and to establish a positive class atmosphere.

Step 1:   A list of descriptors is distributed to the class. (A descriptor is a word or phrase that identifies an item.) Some possibilities are listed below.

Step 2:   Each student finds one student (or two or three students in large classes) who says "yes" to having specific descriptors. (Each student can be listed only once on the sheet by each "searcher.")

Step 3:   After several minutes the instructor indicates time is up. The instructor then reads each descriptor and asks for the names of those who were listed by at least one "searcher."

Step 4:   The instructor ends the exercise by finding out who has the largest list and then giving a small prize (such as a nutritious candy bar) to the winner.

SAMPLE DESCRIPTORS

Plays golf	Has meditated
Likes classical music	Has water-skied
Is a fan of the Dallas Cowboys	Likes the psychoanalytic approach to therapy
Has had a paid or volunteer job in social work	Has been hypnotized
Was born west of the Mississippi River	Has been to a gay pride festival
Has traveled in Mexico	Has traveled in Canada
Has traveled in Europe	Enjoys fishing
Is married	Attends church regularly
Likes to jog	Has received a speeding ticket
Has never flown in an airplane	Has visited, or lived on, a reservation

SOCIAL WORK VALUES

LEARNING OBJECTIVES

Most people tend to believe that decisions rest primarily on objective facts and figures. But in fact, values form the bases of most decisions. For example, in the political arena in the United States, political decisions largely reflect which party controls the most votes—Republicans or Democrats. This chapter will help prepare students to:

Describe value dilemmas in social work
Understand the distinction between knowledge and values
Distinguish value dilemmas of clients from the value dilemmas of social workers
Describe respect for the dignity and uniqueness of individuals
Describe the client's right to self-determination
Understand confidentiality and privileged communication
Understand the residual view and the institutional view of social welfare
Understand the importance of establishing professional boundaries with clients
Understand the worker's obligation to promote social and economic justice and to safeguard human rights
Describe value dilemmas in social work

VALUE DILEMMAS IN SOCIAL WORK

Let's assume that you are a social worker and are assigned the following case. What would you do to help this family?

Mrs. Kehl is 2 months pregnant. She works part-time in a shoe factory and is paid the minimum wage. Her husband is a janitor in a business office and earns only slightly more. They already have seven children and are living in substandard poverty conditions. They do not wish to have additional children; this pregnancy resulted from a failure of the birth control method they were using. The family is Catholic and attends church regularly. On the one hand, they want to have an abortion; they feel their family is already being hurt because of a lack of money. On the other hand, they believe having an abortion is immoral.

This case raises a number of questions about values. As a social worker, how would you help this family weigh their views about abortion against their desire to limit their family size to improve their living conditions?

This case is not unique. Most situations that clients face involve, at least partially, value dilemmas. Here are a few more examples.

Mr. Ritter is 82 years old and has terminal cancer. He has lived a full life but now is in severe pain. He is rather depressed and is seriously considering taking his own life. Should he be allowed to?

Mr. and Mrs. Sinclair have a 2-year-old child who has a profound cognitive disability and who also needs extensive medical care. They have three older children. The family's emotional and physical resources are being severely drained, and family relationships are increasingly tense. Yet the family feels the child will develop at a faster pace in their home than in an institution or in a group home. What should they do?

Mr. and Mrs. Fedders have been married for 6 years and have two children. Their love for each other has been practically nonexistent for the past 3 years. Mr. Fedders recently discovered his wife has been having an affair. They both hold religious beliefs against divorce, but they are seriously considering terminating their marriage. How should a social worker help them?

Mr. Franzene is on probation for 2 years for theft. For the past 18 months he has stayed out of trouble. He inadvertently reveals to his probation officer that he took two pens from a discount store. Should his probation officer make a report on this?

LaVonne Hall recently left a mental hospital and was helped by her aftercare worker to obtain a filing job. While intoxicated and angry, Ms. Hall calls her worker and says that she has been fired. She then says that she is going to shoot her former employer and hangs up. What should the worker do?

Mr. Townsend's neighbors occasionally hear cries of anguish from Mr. Townsend's two children. The neighbors report this to protective services because they suspect abuse. A protective service worker investigates, and Mr. Townsend and the children state the cries are the result of spankings. How does the worker decide when harsh spanking should be considered abuse?

Mr. and Mrs. Stonek's only child was taken away 2 years ago and placed in a foster home because of neglect. The father drank excessively, and the mother was very depressed. Over the past 2 years, the Stoneks have occasionally made efforts to improve their lives but have always "slid back" For the past 2 months, Mr. Stonek has been involved in Alcoholics Anonymous and has only occasionally gotten drunk. Mrs. Stonek presently seems less depressed and feels having her son back would make her life more meaningful. The Stoneks ask to have their child returned. Should the child be returned? How would you as the worker arrive at a decision?

Mrs. Barta seeks counseling at a comprehensive mental health center. She states her husband is having intercourse with their 11-year-old daughter. The counselor arranges a joint meeting with the Bartas. Mr. Barta first denies the accusation but then admits it after being confronted with what his wife has seen and heard. How should the worker attempt to help this family?

Mrs. Johnson is a caseworker at a public welfare agency in a rural county. She observes and collects evidence that the director makes a range of decisions that deny migrant workers in the area (most of whom are Mexican Americans) public assistance benefits for which they are eligible. If she confronts the director with this evidence, Mrs. Johnson believes she will be fired or at least denied merit increases and promotions at work. What should she do?

Mrs. Gordon seeks counseling from a sex therapist. She indicates she is fairly content with her marriage and has an enjoyable sex life with her husband. Yet she feels substantial guilt about her desire and following through on her desire to masturbate. How can the therapist help her?

A community worker in an inner city is working with residents to organize a rent strike against a landlord who neglects making essential repairs. The building does not have adequate heat and is infested with rats and roaches. The organizer wonders whether she should fully inform the residents of the risks involved in a rent strike (such as being evicted). She fears that if she fully informs the tenants of the risks, they probably will decide not to strike, and essential improvements in living conditions will not be made. What should she do?

These examples highlight the fact that much of social work practice involves value dilemmas. Social work is both an art and a science. Because social work is partly an art, a worker must frequently make decisions based on values rather than on knowledge. It also means that the change techniques workers use are often based on theory and value assumptions rather than on proven intervention techniques.

One value assumption that is frequently useful in helping clients resolve value dilemmas is the principle of *self-determination*. According to this principle, clients have the right to hold and express their own opinions and to act on them, as long as in so doing they do not infringe on the rights of others. When clients face a dilemma, a worker can often proceed effectively by helping the clients first define their problems precisely and then examine fully the merits and shortcomings of the various alternatives to resolving the problem. After this is done, clients are then given the responsibility to decide which course of action they desire to pursue. This problem-solving format might be useful for many of the situations we listed. For example, the Kehls might list all their reasons for and against having an abortion and then make a decision. This same approach might also be useful in helping the Sinclairs decide whether to place their child with the profound cognitive disability in an institution or a group home and in helping the Fedders decide whether to terminate their marriage.

Although this self-determination principle can be useful, *there are no absolutes* in *social work practice.* Guidelines are simply guidelines. What works in one situation may not resolve problems in others. Suppose, for example, that Mr. Ritter makes a list of the reasons for and against taking his life and decides that there is no rational reason for him to endure further pain. Such a decision raises a value dilemma for the social worker regarding whether the worker should attempt to stop Mr. Ritter from taking his life. Or suppose the Bartas decide they do not want further counseling on the incestuous relationship between Mr. Barta and his daughter because they both conclude that delving into it further will break up their marriage and their family What should the worker do then?

Much of social work practice depends on the worker's professional judgment. Directors of social welfare agencies frequently tell me that their best workers are those who have common sense and who are able to "trust their guts" (that is, trust their feelings, intuition, and perceptions). This chapter spells out value assumptions and principles of social work practice. These guidelines (and all other guidelines presented in this text) are to be applied not as absolutes but simply as concepts that may be useful in working with people. An effective worker understands and uses these guidelines to make a professional judgment on whether a guideline is, or is not, appropriate when working with particular people.

KNOWLEDGE AND VALUES

It is important for workers to be able to distinguish between values and knowledge and to be aware of the role each plays in social work practice. Pincus and Minahan (1973) concisely defined the difference between values and knowledge:

> Values are beliefs, preferences, or assumptions about what is desirable or good for man [humans]. An example is the belief that society has an obligation to help each individual realize his fullest potential. They are not assertions about how the world is and what we know about it, but how it *should* be. As such, value statements cannot be subjected to scientific investigation; they must be accepted on faith. Thus we can speak of a value as being right or wrong only in relation to the particular belief system or ethical code being used as a standard.
>
> What we will refer to as knowledge statements, on the other hand, are observations about the world and man [humans] which have been verified or are capable of verification. An example is that black people have a shorter life expectancy than white people in the United States. When we speak of a knowledge statement as being right or wrong, we are referring to the extent to which the assertion has been confirmed through objective empirical investigation. (p. 38)

The distinction between values and knowledge can be illustrated in some of the cases described earlier. First, let's look at the abortion question. Suppose a woman questions the abortion procedure because she feels it is immoral. She believes it means killing an unborn baby. Implicit in this value statement is the belief that life begins at or shortly after conception—a belief that is not verifiable.

Now suppose that a woman has qualms about abortion because she fears the risks of the medical procedure or fears there is a high probability of feeling remorseful after the abortion. Informational questions are raised, and knowledge, or empirical evidence, can be presented showing that the health risks of abortion are less than those of carrying the child to full term, and evidence can be presented showing that only a small percentage of women who have an abortion experience severe remorse (Hyde & DeLamater, 2011).

Mrs. Gordon's guilt over masturbating is also a useful illustration. If she feels guilty because she believes masturbating is immoral and sinful, then she obviously has a belief system that asserts it is wrong to masturbate. To resolve this value dilemma, she must decide either to change her belief system or to stop masturbating. However, if she feels guilty because she fears she is hurting herself physiologically or hindering her sex life with her husband, she could be shown that both of these beliefs are erroneous by pointing out that most married men and women masturbate, masturbation is highly recommended by sex therapists, and masturbation usually fosters rather than hinders a sexual relationship (Hyde & DeLamater, 2011).

As these case examples suggest, it is much easier to change a client's belief if it conflicts with current knowledge. Changing a belief that is based on a value is much more difficult because the "rightness" or "wrongness" of the belief cannot be determined with empirical evidence.

Exercise 2.1: Clarifying My Values

Goal: This exercise is designed to help you identify and clarify your values on a number of prominent issues related to social work.

Step 1:   It should be noted that for most of these questions there are no right or wrong answers. Each student should answer the following questions.

Values Questionnaire

	Yes	Uncertain	No
1. Assume you are single. Would you marry someone of a different race?			
2. If you were going to adopt a child, would you adopt a child of a different race?			
3. Are you in favor of a woman becoming president of the United States?			
4. Do you believe busing should be used to attempt to achieve racial integration in schools?			
5. Do you support affirmative action programs that assert that certain minority groups and women should be given preference in hiring over white males?			
6. Do you believe a father who commits incest with his 10-year-old daughter should be placed in jail?			
7. Do you believe prostitution should be legalized?			
8. Do you or your partner were pregnant and in a situation where it would be very difficult to raise a child, would you seriously consider abortion?			
9. Do you support a constitutional amendment to make abortion illegal?			
10. Would you be willing to be a surrogate mother? If you are male, would you be willing to have your wife or future wife become a surrogate mother?			
11. Do you believe that the death penalty should be used for certain crimes?			
12. Do you believe that the United States should support an extensive program to develop the capacity to clone human beings?			
13. Do you support artificial insemination for humans?			
14. Do you believe people should remain virgins until they marry?			
15. Would you vote for an African American candidate for president of the United States?			
16. If you were married, would you seriously consider having an extramarital affair?			
17. Do you believe that persons who have a profound cognitive disability (so severe that they are functioning at less than a 6-month intellectual level) should be kept alive indefinitely at taxpayers' expense?			
18. Do you believe that marijuana should be legalized?			
19. Would you be upset if a son or daughter of yours were gay/lesbian?			
20. Do you believe you could objectively counsel someone who had brutally raped four women?			
21. Do you think people should limit the size of their families to two children?			
22. Do you favor a law to limit families to two children?			
23. Do you think a person who is gay/lesbian should be allowed to teach in elementary and secondary schools?			
24. Do you approve of a young couple trying out marriage by living together before actually getting married?			

25. Would you be in favor of a group home for drug addicts being located in your neighborhood?			
26. Do you think the government should help support day-care centers for working mothers?			
27. Do you think women in the military service should take part in active combat?			
28. Do you think the United States should build more nuclear power plants to generate electricity?			
29. Would you encourage your son to have premarital sex?			
30. Would you encourage your daughter to have premarital sex?			
31. When you become an older person and unable to care for your needs, would you be willing to be placed in a nursing home?			
32. Do you support physician-assisted suicide when the victim is terminally ill and in intense pain?			
33. Would you consider marrying someone who is divorced and has two children? (Assume you are single in answering this question.)			
34. Do you believe you would enjoy being a social worker at a group home for persons with severe cognitive disability?			
35. Do you believe the legal drinking age should be less than 21 years?			
36. Would you marry someone who is of a different religion than you?			
37. Do you believe there are circumstances that justify a person taking his or her own life?			
38. Would you divorce your spouse if you found out he or she had had an extramarital affair?			
39. Would you allow a child of yours to play frequently with a child who has AIDS?			
40. Do you believe that most welfare recipients are able-bodied loafers?			
41. Do you believe you would be comfortable in hugging a person who has AIDS?			
42. Do you believe you would be comfortable rooming with a person who has AIDS?			
43. Do you think social workers should inform a client's current sexual partners that the client is HIV positive if the client refuses to do so?			
44. Are you supportive of same-sex marriages?			

Step 2: This an optional step. The instructor collects the questionnaires so that anonymity is assured and lists the question numbers on the blackboard. After tallying the results (with the help of volunteers), the instructor seeks to open a discussion. For example, if most students indicate that they would not marry someone of a different race, the instructor asks, "Does this suggest that most of you have some racial prejudices?"

VALUE DILEMMAS OF CLIENTS AND SOCIAL WORKERS

It is important for social workers to recognize exactly who is confronting a value dilemma. (This will be discussed in more detail later.) An important guideline in social work practice is not to become overly emotionally involved in a client's case. (If you find yourself frequently taking clients' problems home with you so that your dwelling on their problems interferes with your life, then you are overly involved.) If a client faces a dilemma about whether to obtain a divorce, or have an abortion, or place a member of the family in an institution, it is important for you to be aware that the dilemma is the *client's,* not yours. This awareness will help you to remain objective and thereby be most helpful to your client. If, however, you feel strongly that a client is doing something immoral (for example, if you believe abortion is murder), then *you* face a value dilemma. In such a situation it will be very difficult for you to remain objective.

When you face a dilemma about a client's actions or plans, the following guidelines are sometimes helpful:

1. The first step in resolving such a question is to recognize its existence. Such self-awareness is often difficult to attain. Ethical questions are often ambiguous and make us feel uncomfortable. Therefore, we like to avoid them.

2. Self-awareness is not enough unless it is put to use with clients. Kelman (1965) recommended that workers should "label" their values for the client and allow the client to "talk back" in a sort of mutual influence situation. Such an approach *may* be useful in working with clients who are involved with drugs, or are having extramarital affairs, or have been arrested for stealing, and so forth. However, there is a danger to this approach. The worker's values may not be in the client's best interest. When the workers share their values, they are influencing (and perhaps also manipulating) the client. For example, if a worker is morally opposed to abortion, sharing those values with a young unmarried and pregnant woman probably will influence her not to have an abortion, which may or may not be in this woman's best interest. In deciding whether to share values, that worker has to make a professional judgment about what will be most constructive and helpful for the client.

3. When a worker's personal values conflict with the values of the social work profession (for example, in the area of sexual orientation), it is generally advisable for the worker to adhere to the values of the profession when providing services to clients. The Code of Ethics of the National Association of Social Workers is a useful guide to the values of the social work profession. (A copy of this code appears at www.naswdc.org.)

4. Clients should be encouraged to explore their own values and to relate alternative actions to their own value systems. Clients need protection against manipulation that would encroach on their freedom of choice. For example, if a worker is morally opposed to abortion, clients might well be encouraged to see (and referral arrangements be made to see) someone who views abortion as a viable alternative.

5. A useful moral code advanced by Glasser (1965) allows clients to fulfill their needs and to do what they want to do, as long as by doing so they do not deprive others of the ability to fulfill their needs. I have found this code very useful in counseling people considering abortion and in a wide variety of other situations—counseling gays and lesbians, people involved in premarital relationships, and so forth. The code is also useful in working with adults involved in child abuse, incest, and extramarital affairs because those involved need to examine the effects of their actions on others. There is no one right moral code—what works for one person may not work for another because of differences in lifestyles, life goals, and personal values.

6. Loewenberg and Dolgoff (2004) have developed a rank order of ethical priorities. They suggest that social work practitioners can use these prioritized values when making ethical decisions. In the event that two values are competing, the social worker should abide by the one higher in the order. For instance, if the worker is debating between value 1 (protection of life) and value 2 (right to equality), the worker should act in accordance with value 1. Likewise, value 2 should take precedence over values 3–7, and so on.

Dolgoff, Loewenberg, and Harrington's (2009) prioritized values are as follows:

1. *Protection of life.* This might include provision of adequate food, shelter, clothing, or health care. It might concern acting in response to a person's suicide threat or threat of physically harming another.

2. *Right to equality.* This means that people should be treated fairly and equally A social worker should seek to facilitate fairness and equality—except when there is a value conflict involving protection of life.

3. *Right to autonomy.* Persons should be allowed to make their own choices about their lives.

4. *Right to experience least harm.* People have the right to be protected from injury. If injury is unavoidable, they have the right to experience the least injury possible, the least lasting harm, or the most easily reversible harm.

5. *Right to a decent quality of life.* People have the right to seek and attain a "better quality of life" than they currently have.

6. *Right to privacy and confidentiality.* People have the right not to have their private information made public.

7. *Right to truth and all relevant information.* People have the right to know the truth and the right to receive accurate information.

Exercise 2.2: Applying Dolgoff, Loewenberg, and Harrington's Rank Order of Ethical Priorities

Goal: This exercise is designed to assist you in understanding Dolgoff et al.'s rank order of ethical priorities.

Step 1:   You are a social worker for a county human services department. In a city neighborhood you encounter a group of African Americans in a heated conflict over a race-related issue with members of the Ku Klux Klan. There is imminent danger of physical violence erupting. Using Dolgoff et al.'s rank order of ethical priorities, which of the following values is the one that you need to first attend to? (circle this value)

    a. Protect life.
    b. Maintain autonomy, independence, and freedom.
    c. Promote a better quality of life.
    d. Strengthen every person's right to privacy/confidentiality.
    e. Speak the truth and fully disclose all relevant information.
    f. Practice in accord with rules and regulations voluntarily accepted.

Step 2:   What action(s) would you take to seek to support the value you selected?

Elaine Congress (2000) has developed the following five-step ETHIC process model of decision makings:

E   Examine relevant personal, societal, agency, client, and professional values.
T   Think about what ethical standard of the NASW Code of Ethics applies, as well as relevant laws and case decisions.
H   Hypothesize about possible consequences of different decisions.
I   Identify who will benefit and who will be harmed in view of social work's commitment to the most vulnerable.
C   Consult with supervisor and colleagues about the most ethical choice.

Exercise 2.3: Applying Congress's ETHIC Process Model of Decision Making

Goal: This exercise is designed to assist you in applying the ETHIC process model.

Step 1:   You are a social worker who works for a hospice organization in California. You have a client who has an advanced case of amyotrophic lateral sclerosis (also referred to as Lou Gehrig's disease, and also known as ALS). ALS is a progressive, fatal disease caused by the degeneration of the nerve cells in the central nervous system that control voluntary muscle movement. Affected individuals eventually lose the ability to initiate and control all voluntary movement.

    Your client, John Hawkins, has lost control of most of his muscles. He has a prognosis of 4 months left to live. He and his wife ask you to find a state in which Mr. Hawkins could legally end his life through physician-assisted suicide. Physician-assisted suicide, at the time of this writing, is not legal in California, but is legal in Oregon, Washington, and Montana. Using the following ETHIC model, speculate how you would proceed in arriving at a decision of how to respond to the Hawkinses' request.

Step 2:   What do you see as the relevant personal, societal, client, and professional values in regard to the Hawkinses' request?

Step 3:   Are there ethical standards of the NASW Code of Ethics that apply, as well as relevant laws and case decisions?

Step 4:   Hypothesize about possible consequences of different decisions.

Step 5:   Identify who will benefit and who will be harmed in view of different decisions.

Step 6:   Speculate what your supervisor and colleagues at hospice are apt to advise about the most ethical choice.

Step 7:   What do you see as the strengths and shortcomings of using the ETHIC model?

RESPECT FOR THE DIGNITY AND UNIQUENESS OF INDIVIDUALS

Every human being is unique in a variety of ways—value system, personality, life goals, financial resources, emotional and physical strengths, personal concerns, past experiences, peer pressures, emotional reactions, self-identity, family relationships, and deviant behavioral patterns. In working with a client, a social worker needs to perceive and respect the uniqueness of the client's situation. *Individualization* is the ethical value in social work and other helping professions of viewing, and relating to, the client as a person or group rather than as one whose characteristics are simply typical of a class.

Individualization is relatively easy for a social worker to achieve when the worker is assisting clients who have values, goals, behavioral patterns, and personal characteristics similar to the worker's. Individualization is harder to achieve when a worker is assigned clients who have values or behavioral patterns that the worker views as disgusting. For example, a worker may have difficulty viewing a client with respect when that client has raped a young girl, or is involved in an incestuous relationship, or has killed a member of his family, or has severely abused a child. A general guideline in such situations is that the worker should accept and respect the client but not accept the deviant behavior that needs to be changed. If a worker is unable to convey acceptance of the client, a helping relationship will not be established. If such a relationship is not established, the worker will have practically no opportunity to help the client change deviant behaviors. A second guideline is that if a worker views a client as being disgusting and is unable to establish a working relationship, then the worker should transfer the case to another worker. There should be no disgrace or embarrassment in having to transfer a case for such reasons; it is irrational for a worker to expect to like every client or for every client to like the worker (Ellis & Harper, 1977).

Exercise 2.4: Clients I Would Be Uncomfortable Working With

Goal: This exercise is designed to assist you in identifying types of clients that you may be uncomfortable (and thereby not fully objective) in working with.

Step 1:   Check from the following list those clients you believe you would experience discomfort in working with:

____ A serial rapist

____ A child molestor

____ Someone with intense body odor

____ Someone who has a profound cognitive disability

____ A hit man for the mafia

____ A pathological liar

____ A father who is sexually involved with his 11-year-old daughter

____ A member of the Ku Klux Klan

____ A bigamist

____ A terrorist who has killed several people

____ A young person who is suicidal

____ A 17-year-old who wants an abortion

____ A person who is gay or lesbian

____ A child-care provider who shook a baby to death

____ A person whose religious beliefs are sharply different from yours

____ A person who is severely addicted to alcohol or cocaine

____ Someone who is labeled schizophrenic

____ A husband who battered his wife on several occasions

____ A wife who has a history of extramarital affairs

Step 2:   For the items that you checked, specify as precisely as you can why you believe you would be uncomfortable in working with such a client.

Step 3:   Review the list of the clients you checked. Specify the types of clients with whom you believe you would have considerable difficulty in establishing a working relationship and therefore should transfer to another worker.

> Social workers occasionally encounter "raw" situations. For a while I worked in a mental hospital for the criminally insane and had a variety of clients who had committed a wide range of asocial and bizarre acts, including incest, rape, decapitation of a girlfriend, sodomy, sexual exhibitionism, and removing corpses from graves. I've worked in a variety of other settings and encountered other raw situations. Achieving an attitude of respect for people who commit bizarre actions is difficult at times, but rehabilitation will not occur unless it is achieved.

Social psychologists have firmly established the theoretical principle that people's images of themselves develop largely out of their interactions and communications with others. A long time ago Charles Cooley (1902) called this process the *looking glass self-concept*. The looking glass says that people develop their self-concept in terms of how other people relate to them, as if others were a looking glass or mirror. For example, a person who receives respect from others and is praised for positive qualities is likely to feel good about himself or herself, will gradually develop a positive sense of worth, will be happier, and will seek responsible and socially acceptable ways to maintain the respect of others.

Exercise 2.5: Components of My Self-Concept That Contain Remnants from the Past

Goal: This exercise is designed to help you recognize that some "tapes in your head" about who you are have remnants from your past.

Step 1: Reflect back to when you were younger (perhaps in the age range from 4 to 12 years of age). Write down what people significant in your life (parents, teachers, siblings, peers, etc.) said about your:

____ Intelligence

____ Health

____ Looks

____ Worth as a person

____ Morals

____ Sexuality

____ Abilities

____ Friends

____ Future

Step 2: Reflect on your current self-concept. Specify all these views that remain as part of your current self-concept.

Step 3: Specify whether you believe your current self-concept was partly formed in terms of the "looking glass self-concept."

Conversely, if a person commits a deviant act and *then* is shunned by others, viewed as different, and treated with disrespect, that person will develop a *failure identity*. According to Glasser (1972), people with failure identities withdraw from society, become emotionally disturbed, or express their discontent in delinquent and deviant actions.

For example, if a neighborhood identifies a youth as being a troublemaker (a delinquent), the neighbors are likely to relate to the youth as if she were not to be trusted, may erroneously accuse her of delinquent acts, and will label her semidelinquent and aggressive behavior as being delinquent. In the absence of objective ways to gauge whether she is, in fact, a delinquent, she will rely on the subjective evaluations of others. Thus, gradually, as she is related to as being a delinquent, she is likely to perceive herself in that way and will begin to enact the delinquent role.

Compton and Galaway (1975) expanded on the importance of social workers' attending carefully to their communications with clients:

Social workers and other professionals intervening in the lives of people are well advised to be constantly sensitive to the message they are extending to others about their worth. Do we, in the little things we do, communicate to the other person that he is a unique individual to be highly prized? What, for example, is the message communicated when we safeguard time and provide a client with a specific time to be seen as opposed to a catch-me-on-a-catch-as-catch-can basis for visits? Do appointments in advance communicate to the client a higher sense of respect than unannounced visits or hurriedly arranged telephone appointments? And, speaking of telephoning, how about the all too frequently overlooked return call? What message does the client get from the worker in terms of the client's worth when the worker does not have the courtesy or good sense to return telephone calls promptly? How about the ability to listen to clients, to secure from them their own account of their situation, and to avoid prejudgments? And does not privacy, both in terms of how the social worker conducts the interviews and how he treats the material gained from interviews, communicate something to clients about the esteem in which they are held? A worker attempting to operationalize the premise of individual uniqueness and dignity may find it useful to repeatedly inquire of himself, "What does this action on my part communicate to the client about my perception of his personhood?" (pp. 106–107)

The principle of individualization also plays a key role in social work treatment. Various problems, needs, goals, and values of clients involve different patterns of relationships with clients and different methods of helping. For example, consider the needs of a teenage male who is placed in a group home for being beyond parental control. At times he may need an understanding but firm counselor who sets and enforces strict limits. At times he may need encouragement and guidance in how to perform better at school. If conflicts develop between the youth and other boys at the group home, the counselor may need to play a mediating role. If the youth is shy, counseling on how to be more assertive may be needed. If his parents are fairly ineffective in their parenting role, the counselor may seek to have the parents enroll in a parent effectiveness training program (Gordon, 1970). If the youth is being treated unfairly at school or by the juvenile court, the counselor may play an advocate role and attempt to change the system. If the youth has behavior problems, the reasons need to be explored and an intervention program developed.

A thorny problem facing social workers involves striking an effective balance between classification and individualization. There is a need in all human service areas to generalize beyond individuals and to organize data on the basis of common characteristics. Classification is essential to make sense out of a mass of data and is an essential part of developing theories. The danger of putting people into a particular category is that such a classification may lead social workers to respond to people as objects rather than as individuals. Compton and Galaway (1975) commented about the labeling process:

> The pitfalls of this process are being documented in a growing body of literature from sociologists studying deviance from a labeling perspective. Not only does labeling or classification lead to a distortion of individual differences, but, as labeling theorists and their supporting research are noting, a person labeled deviant, those doing the labeling, and the surrounding audience frequently respond to the deviant on the basis of the label rather than on the basis of individual characteristics. This creates conditions for the development of a self-fulfilling prophecy in which the person becomes what he has been labeled. (p. 107)

This labeling process, most simply stated, occurs because of Cooley's *looking glass self* in which people define who and what they are by how others relate to them. A person labeled as mentally ill or as being hyperactive, or a delinquent, or an ex-con, or a welfare mother is then likely to define himself or herself by these labels and unfortunately begin playing these roles. Social workers have to continue to be alert to the dangers of labeling and should interact with each client (or judge, attorney, professor, and so forth) as a person rather than as a label.

Exercise 2.6: Labeling Becoming a Self-Fulfilling Prophecy

Goal: This exercise is designed to show you the powerful effects of labeling.

Step 1:   Specify a situation in your life where someone conveyed something positive to you, and it was a factor in leading you to excel in that area. (Perhaps it was someone saying you were good at _____, and it led you to excel in that area.)

Step 2:   Specify a situation in your life where someone conveyed something negative to you, and it was a factor in leading you to do something dysfunctional/deviant or to put forth minimal effort and you then failed. (Perhaps it was someone saying you were "stupid," or terrible at _____, and it led to your failing or doing something you know you should not have done.)

Step 3:   Comment on the following: "If, as social workers, we want clients to make positive changes, we first need to treat clients with respect and convey that we strongly believe they have the potential for making the kind of choices that will result in a better life for them."

THE CLIENT'S RIGHT TO SELF-DETERMINATION

Social workers believe that clients have the right to express their own opinions and to act on them, as long as by so doing clients do not infringe on the rights of others. This principle is in sharp contrast to the layperson's views that a social worker seeks to "remold" clients into a pattern chosen by the worker. Instead, the workers' efforts are geared to enhancing clients' abilities to help themselves. Client self-determination derives logically from belief in the inherent dignity of each person. If people have dignity, then it follows that they should be permitted to determine their own lifestyles as far as possible.

Social workers believe that making all decisions and doing everything for a client is self-defeating, because it leads to increased dependence rather than greater self-reliance and self-sufficiency. For people to grow, to mature, to become responsible, they need to make their own decisions and take responsibility for the consequences. Mistakes and emotional pain will occur. But that is part of life. We learn by our mistakes and by trial and error. Respect for the clients' ability to make their own decisions is associated with the principle that social work is a cooperative endeavor between clients and workers (client participation). Social work is done *with,* not *to,* a client. Plans imposed on people without their active involvement have a way of not turning out well.

Four points should be made in operationalizing the principle of *client self-determination.* First, self-determination implies that clients should be made aware that there are alternatives for resolving the personal or social problems they face. Self-determination involves having clients make decisions—that is, making a choice selected from several courses of action. If there were only one course of action, there would be no choice, and therefore clients would not have the right of self-determination. As will be discussed further in later chapters, the role of a social worker in helping clients involves (1) building a helping relationship, (2) exploring problems in depth with clients, and (3) exploring alternative solutions with clients, then choosing a course of action. This third step is the implementation of the principle of self-determination.

Second, self-determination means that the client, rather than the worker, is the chief problem solver. Workers need to recognize that the client *owns* the problem and therefore has the chief responsibility to resolve the problem. This is an area in which social work differs markedly from other professions. Most professionals, such as physicians and attorneys, advise clients about what they believe clients ought to do. Doctors, lawyers, and dentists are experts in advising clients. The client's decision making after receiving the expert's advice in such situations is generally limited to the choice of whether to accept the professional's advice.

In sharp contrast, social workers should seek to establish not an expert-inferior relationship but a relationship between equals. The worker's expertise does *not* lie in knowing or recommending what is best for the client. Rather, the expertise lies in assisting clients to define their problems, develop and examine the alternatives for resolving the problems, maximize their capacities and opportunities to make decisions for themselves, and implement the decisions they make. In conjunction with this principle, Dumont (1968) noted,

> The most destructive thing in psychotherapy is a "rescue fantasy" in the therapist—a feeling that the therapist is the divinely sent agent to pull a tormented soul from the pit of suffering and adversity and put him back on the road to happiness and glory. A major reason this fantasy is so destructive is that it carries the conviction that the patient will be saved only through and by the therapist. When such a conviction is communicated to the patient, verbally or otherwise, he has no choice other than to rebel and leave or become more helpless, dependent, and sick. (p. 60)

Third, self-determination does not prohibit or restrict social workers from offering an opinion or making a suggestion. In fact, social workers have an obligation to share their viewpoints with their clients. Compton and Galaway (1975) noted,

> Workers have the obligations of sharing with clients their own thinking, perhaps their own experiences, not as a way of directing the clients' lives but rather as an additional source of information and input for the clients to consider in their own decision making. It is imperative, however, that the social workers' input be recognized as information to be considered and not an edict to be followed. (p. 111)

The key to implementing this principle is for the social worker to phrase the alternative as a suggestion rather than as advice. For example, if a client is worried about how her older mother, who is living alone and whose physical and mental capacities are deteriorating, will be able to have her physical, emotional, and social needs met, the social worker should not advise: 'The best thing for you to do is to place her in a nursing home." Instead the worker should offer a suggestion for the client to consider: "Have you thought about placing your mother in a nursing home?"

Fourth, client self-determination is possible and should be encouraged even in areas in which the social worker has the additional function to protect society. Three areas in social work for which the worker has this additional function are in protective services, in prisons, and in probation and parole. Compton and Galaway (1975) noted,

> A probation agency, for example, may enforce the legal requirement that the probationer must report to the probation officer; this is not a matter for client self-determination. But the sensitive officer can allow for considerable client self-determination in the frequency of reporting, the length of the interviews, the time of reporting, and the content to be discussed during the interviews. (p. 112)

Actually, probationers can also be informed that they even have a choice in reporting to the probation officer. In working with involuntary clients who are angry with the legal authority held by the social worker, it is often helpful for the worker to inform the clients that they do have a choice regarding whether they are willing to meet the minimum legal requirements. The consequences of not cooperating (such as being sent to prison or having their children taken away in the case of abusive parents) are also made clear to them. This approach appears to be useful because it reduces the clients' inclination to view the social worker as a parent or a cop. Instead of playing the game of how much they can get away with, this approach puts the responsibility for their future squarely on the clients. They are faced with the decision of reporting or suffering the consequences of not reporting; of deciding whether to stop abusing their children or of suffering the consequences of making no effort to refrain from abusing their children. In this connection O'Connor (1972) noted,

> The recognition of man's [a person's] right to free choice guarantees that he may choose to run his life as he sees fit. This choice may run counter to society's welfare and even his own, yet essentially it is his choice and his prerogative. Society may censure, but it cannot take from him his right; nor would society strip him of his dignity by a censure. The criminal then has a right to say "crime is my choice and I am willing to pay the price. If you send me to prison, I am paying my debt to society and refuse to submit to your attempts to reform me." The principle of self-determination makes it incumbent upon society to honor such a plea. (pp. 485-486)

In working with involuntary clients whose actions have adversely affected other people in the past (for example, abusive parents), the worker's obligation is to outline the minimum legal requirements (for example, no further incidents of abuse) and specify the consequences if these clients decide not to meet these requirements. Even in such situations, clients have a choice in deciding whether they will meet the requirements. If they are not met by a client, the worker must follow through and implement the consequences to maintain credibility with the client. Often the consequences have therapeutic shock value as clients learn they can no longer manipulate the system and are responsible for the consequences they suffer.

CONFIDENTIALITY

Confidentiality is an implicit or explicit agreement between a professional and a client that the professional will maintain the private nature of information about the client. An *absolute* implementation of confidentiality means that the professional will not share client disclosures with anyone, unless authorized by the client in writing or required by law. Because of the principle of confidentiality, professionals can be sued if they disclose information that the client is able to document has a damaging effect on him or her.

Confidentiality is important because clients may decide not to share their secrets, personal concerns, and asocial thoughts and actions with a professional if they believe the information will be revealed to others. A basic principle of counseling is that clients must feel comfortable in fully revealing themselves to the professional without fear that their secret revelations will be used against them.

Confidentiality is "absolute" when information revealed to a professional is *never* passed on to anyone in any form. Such information would never be shared with other agency staff, fed into a computer, or written in a case record. A student or beginning practitioner tends to think in absolutes and may naively promise clients absolute confidentiality Absolute confidentiality, however, is seldom achieved.

Social workers today generally function as part of a larger agency. Much of the client's communication is written into case records and shared orally with staff in the system as part of the service-delivery process. Social workers share details with supervisors, and many work in teams and are expected to share information. Therefore, instead of absolute confidentiality, it is more precise to indicate that a system of *relative* confidentiality is being used in social work practice (Wilson, 1978, p. 3).

Confidentiality is a legal matter, and there is a fair amount of uncertainty about what is an unlawful violation. In addition, there have been few test cases in court to determine this issue. Let me provide a brief summary of how agencies handle issues related to confidentiality.

Practically all agencies allow (and in fact encourage) their workers to discuss a client's circumstances with other professionals employed at the same agency. At many agencies (such as a mental hospital) the input of many professionals (psychiatrist, psychologist, social workers, nurses, physical therapist, and so forth) is used in assessing a client and developing a treatment plan.

Many agencies feel it is inappropriate to share or discuss a client's case with a secretary. (Yet the secretary does the typing and usually knows as much about each client as the professional staff does.)

Most agencies believe it is inappropriate to discuss a client's case with professionals at another agency unless the client first signs a release-of-information form (see Figure 2.1). (Yet, informally, professionals employed by different agencies do at times share information about a client without the client's authorization.)

Nearly all agencies share case information with social work interns. (Whether it is legally permissible to share information with student interns has not been determined.)

It is certainly permissible to discuss a case with others for educational purposes if no identifying information about the client is given. But this too is a gray area because the person talking about the case will not be able to determine precisely when identifying information is being given. Let me give you an example.

Some years ago I was employed at a maximum-security hospital for the criminally insane and had on my caseload a young male who had decapitated his 17-year-old girlfriend. Such a criminal offense is indeed shocking and rare. People in the client's local area will never forget the offense. If I were to discuss this case in a class at a university (which I occasionally do), I would never be fully assured that no one would be able to identify the offender. There is always the chance that one of the students may have lived in the client's home community and would recognize the offender.

A question that is sometimes raised in relation to confidentiality is whether clients have a right to see the agency's records on them. According to the 1974 Federal Privacy Act, any agency receiving federal funds must allow clients to see their records. Furthermore, if a client requests a copy of the record, the agency must

---

Lakeview Counseling Center
Consent to Release Confidential Information to Another (third) Party

_____ at Lakeview Counseling Center requests permission from _____
(Name of social worker)

_____ to release confidential information about _____. This information will be released to:
(Name of client)   (Name of client)

Name: _____   Address: _____

Position: _____   _____

Agency: _____

Material to be released: _____

_____

_____

The information will be used/disclosed for the following purposes: _____

_____

_____

My signature verifies that I know what information is being disclosed. I am aware that this consent can be revoked (in writing) at any time. My questions about this form have been answered.

This consent form expires on _____ unless revoked by me in writing prior to that date.
(Date)

_____   _____   _____
(Client's signature or "X")   (Date signed)   (Witness)

_____   _____   _____
(Client's guardian—If applicable)   (Date signed)   (Witness)

_____   _____
(Lakeview Counseling Center representative)   (Date signed)

Figure 2.1

Release-of-information form (sample copy of a suggested format).

provide one. If the client is a minor, both the child and the child's parents have the right of access to the client's records. (For individuals who are 18 years old or older or who attend postsecondary institutions, the access to educational records and the consent required before access by others resides with them rather than their parents.)

It is probably a good idea not to put anything into a client's record that you do not want the client to see. Numerous private agencies that receive no federal funds also now have policies to allow clients access to their records.

Another problematic area is the thorny question of when a professional should violate confidence and inform others. Again, many gray areas surround this question (Wilson, 1978). Most state statutes permit or require the professional to inform the appropriate people when a client admits to a past or intended *serious* criminal act. Yet the question of how serious a crime must be before there is an obligation to report it has not been resolved. On the extreme end of the severity continuum, it has been established that a professional *must* inform the appropriate people.

A precedent-setting case occurred in *Tarasoff v. Regents of the University of California,* 1974 (*University of Pittsburgh Law Review,* 1975). In this case a university student informed his psychiatrist that he was going to shoot his girlfriend. The psychiatrist informed the campus police of this threat but did not inform the intended victim or her parents. Campus security picked up and questioned the student and soon released him, concluding that he "appeared rational." Shortly afterward he murdered his girlfriend. Her parents sued the psychiatrist, and the U.S. Supreme Court ruled,

> When a doctor or a psychiatrist, in the exercise of his professional skills and knowledge, determines, or shall determine that a warning is essential to avert danger arising from a medical or psychological condition of his patient, he incurs a legal obligation to give that warning. (*University of Pittsburgh Law Review,* 1975, p. 159)

The Court also concluded,

> The public policy favoring protection of the confidential character of patient-psychotherapist communication must yield in instances in which disclosure is essential to avert danger to others. The protective privilege ends where the public peril begins. (p. 161)

Thus, the Court set a precedent holding that a professional is liable for failure to warn the intended victim. This precedent has continued to be upheld in court decisions involving a helping professional's obligation to inform the intended victim (Schwartz, 1989, pp. 225–226).

For what intended crimes must a helping professional inform the police and the intended victim? Do such crimes include embezzlement, pornography, and larceny? Apparently not. Schoener (2000) has reviewed court decisions in this area and concludes helping professionals are obligated to inform the intended victim (along with the police) only when a client threatens serious physical violence to a specific person. Student interns or beginning practitioners are advised to ask their supervisors when questions in this area arise.

Several years ago I was the faculty supervisor for a student in a field placement at a public assistance agency. The student intern had an unmarried mother on his caseload. A trusting, working relationship between the intern and the mother was developed. The mother then informed the student she was dating a person who was sometimes abusive to her when he was drunk. The mother further indicated there was a warrant for the boyfriend's arrest in another state for an armed robbery charge. The student intern contacted me inquiring whether it was his obligation to inform the police, thereby violating confidentiality. My response was that he should discuss this with his agency supervisor to find out the agency's policy in regard to this question.

Wilson (1978) further concluded,

> In summary, a professional whose client confesses an intended or past crime can find himself in a very delicate position, both legally and ethically. There are enough conflicting beliefs on how this should be handled, so that clear guidelines are lacking. Social workers who receive a communication about a serious criminal act by a client would be wise to consult an attorney for a detailed research of appropriate state statutes and a review of recent court rulings that might help determine the desired course of action. (p. 121)

In a number of other areas a professional is permitted, expected, or required to violate confidentiality.[1] These areas include the following:

---

[1] An extended discussion of these areas is contained in Suanna J. Wilson, *Confidentiality in Social Work: Issues and Principles* (New York: Free Press, 1978), and in Donald T. Dickson, *Confidentiality and Privacy in Social Work* (New York: Free Press, 1998).

When a client formally (usually in writing) authorizes the professional to release information.

When a professional is called to testify in a criminal case (state statutes vary regarding guidelines on what information may be kept confidential in such criminal proceedings, and therefore practitioners must research their own particular state statutes in this area).

When a client files a lawsuit against a professional (for example, for malpractice).

When a client threatens suicide and a professional may be forced to violate confidentiality to save the client's life. (The treating professional is encouraged to violate confidentiality in such circumstances, but there is not necessarily a legal requirement to do so.)

When a client threatens to harm his or her therapist.

When a professional becomes aware that a minor has committed a crime, when a minor is used by adults as an accessory in a crime, or when a minor is a victim of criminal actions. In such situations most states require that counselors inform the legal authorities. Again, the question arises of how serious the crime must be before it is reported.

When there is evidence of child abuse or neglect. Most states require professionals to report the evidence to the designated child-protection agency.

When a client's emotional or physical condition makes his or her employment a clear danger to self or others (for example, when a counselor discovers that a client who is an airplane pilot has a serious drinking problem).

In all these areas, professional judgment must be used in deciding when the circumstances justify violating confidentiality.

Exercise 2.7: Do You Violate Confidentiality to Blow the Whistle on Embezzling?

Goal: This exercise is designed to help you understand the complexities surrounding a potential whistle-blowing situation. You are a social worker for the United Way. Tim Mehan, hired 4 years ago as director of United

Way, is a charismatic, creative fund-raiser who in 4 years has doubled the amount of United Way money being raised in your community. United Way agencies are now being allocated significantly more funds, and more clients are being served. However, there is a major issue. Helen Jarvis, bookkeeper for United Way, shows you evidence that Mr. Mehan is systematically embezzling money—he apparently has a severe gambling addiction at a casino in the area. Ms. Jarvis asks you whether the two of you should "blow the whistle" on this embezzling. The United Way's books will be audited in the next 5 weeks by an accounting firm, and there is a high probability the missing funds will be noted. If this embezzlement becomes public knowledge, the resulting scandal will undoubtedly lead to a sharp reduction in contributions to United Way. Revealing this situation may also jeopardize your employment and that of Ms. Jarvis. What do you recommend that you and Ms. Jarvis should do?

Privacy and Confidentiality in the Computer Era

Protecting the confidentiality of files and records in human service organizations is becoming much more difficult as the technology of compiling, storing, and receiving information on clients expands exponentially. Vast amounts of data can be gathered, recorded, stored, and processed quickly, easily, and inexpensively. More than a decade ago, Dickson (1998) noted,

> At one time, a patient's or client's record might have consisted of some basic information on a single file card, or a number of pages of personal data, process notes, and observations. Today, such a record might consist of hundreds of pages of text along with still or moving visual images and recorded sound, all stored on tape, disk, hard drive, or CD-ROM as electronic/magnetic impulses. The record might be copied into a central database of case records and could be linked with or contain cross-references to other databases containing other records for the same individual, family, or condition. The records could be accessed, sorted, merged, compiled, and transmitted. They could be downloaded and printed, instantly copied, and transmitted by fax or computer modem to numerous other locations, anywhere in the country or internationally. And with the appropriate linkages, the record could be accessed by other computers or other data systems near and far. Along with all this, the expansion of federal and state government and private third-party insurers in monitoring and reimbursing service delivery has greatly increased the potential for broad access to and dispersion of recorded information. (pp. 124–125)

It is possible (although some legislative acts prevent certain linkages) to link or combine a client's health, mental health, social service, juvenile court, adult court, education, and law-enforcement records. At times, individuals learn that inaccuracies in their records have found their way into computerized databases, with severe, adverse consequences.

The preservation of privacy and confidentiality is a major challenge. Faxed and computer-transmitted records and e-mails can be intercepted by third parties. Confidential information can be posted on the Internet, where it is seen and can be copied by millions of people anywhere around the world. Even the destruction of records is complicated. Records can be shredded and erased from computer files, but a record that was assumed to have been destroyed or has been deleted may exist in another location or under another name or identification number. Therefore, it is important for human service agencies to keep a log of what client information has been transmitted, when, to whom, and in what form.

Because of the potential for violations of privacy and confidentiality, social workers need in-depth understanding of the privacy rights and confidentiality rights of individuals and families. What information to gather, store, replicate, transmit, and who has access and for what purposes, are crucial issues.

Confidentiality and HIPAA Regulations

Congress recognized the need for national public record privacy standards in 1996 when it enacted the Health Insurance Portability and Accountability Act (HIPAA). The law included provisions designed to save money for health-care businesses by encouraging electronic transfers, but it also required new safeguards to protect the security and confidentiality of that information.

A major concern was the security and privacy of electronic health records and their transmission between health-care entities. The security standards HIPAA mandated are designed to establish industry "best practice." Health-care providers must have security policies that are documented and implemented. Health-care providers generally utilize a number of security mechanisms to permit only the sender, recipient, and authorized personnel to have access to data passing through electronic systems.

Most health-care providers require all employees to read and sign a confidentiality agreement, in which the employees agree not to directly or indirectly disclose confidential information in an inappropriate manner. Confidential or protected health-care information is information pertaining to the physical or mental health or condition of an individual, how health care is delivered to an individual, and the source of payment for an individual's health care.

Under HIPAA, patients

- Must be told (in writing) how their health-care information may be used
- Have a right to see their medical records
- Have a right to amend (change) incorrect or incomplete information in their records
- Must give authorization before information is released (with a few exceptions)
- Have a right to complain formally if they believe their privacy was not protected

HIPAA also requires health-care providers to observe all existing state and federal laws and regulations relating to the transmission and storage of, and access to, records and other health care data and to maintain the security and confidentiality of patient-specific information.

Privileged Communication

Privileged communication is closely related to confidentiality but is narrower in scope. *Privileged communication* is a legal term pertaining to the admission of evidence in a court; *confidentiality* refers to laws or rules of professional ethics that regulate the disclosure of information by a client to a professional. Bernstein (1975) defined *privileged communication* as follows:

> In states where certain professional groups are granted privileged communication, the client or his attorney has the privilege of preventing the professional from answering questions about their communication when called as a witness in court. (p. 521)

Privileged communication protects the client, and the right to exercise this privilege belongs to the client, not to the professional.

Four fundamental conditions are necessary to establish privilege against disclosure:

1. Communications must originate in the confidence that they will not be disclosed.
2. The element of confidentiality must be essential to the maintenance of the relationship between the parties.

3. The relationship is one which in the opinion of the community ought to be fostered.

4. The injury that would inure to the relationship as a result of disclosure must be greater than the benefit gained in regard to the correct disposal of litigation. (Wigmore, 1961, p. 52)

These conditions lay the foundation for the determination of privileged communication by the judiciary. Every case that raises the issue of privileged communication is evaluated by whether it meets these conditions.

Many state statutes contain exceptions to privileged communication whereby the professional must testify in court. A list of these exceptions is contained in Wilson (1978). Examples of such exceptions include the following:

- The client waives privilege.
- The client introduces privileged material into litigation.
- A communication does not meet Wigmore's four criteria.
- The social worker is called to testify in a criminal case.
- A client sues his or her counselor.
- A client commits or threatens a criminal act.
- A patient threatens suicide.
- A client threatens to harm his or her therapist.
- Physicians must report certain medical conditions and treatments.
- A minor is involved in criminal activity
- Child abuse or neglect is suspected.
- A client is using certain types of drugs.
- A client's condition makes his or her employment hazardous to others.
- The court orders a professional examination.
- Involuntary hospitalization is needed for someone's protection.
- The client dies.
- A treating professional needs to collect fees for services rendered.
- Information is learned outside the professional treatment relationship.
- Information is shared in the presence of a third person.
- The federal government needs certain information.
- The right of privileged communication is not transferable from one state to another.
- Emergency action is needed to save a client's life.
- Legal action is needed for protection of a minor.
- A client engages in treasonous activities.
- A presentence investigation report is prepared.

In the past few decades, social workers have been successful in most states in attaining passage of state legislation that recognizes social worker–client privileged communication to avoid forced disclosures of confidential information in court. In states in which social workers are not granted privileged communication, they can be subpoenaed by any party to a court action and thereby forced to testify in court fully and under oath about all that transpired between the client and the social worker. If they fail to testify, they can be found in contempt of court by the judge and fined, sent to jail, or both. Such court appearances can be detrimental to the client-worker relationship and to future work with the client.

Social workers in recent years have been successful in all states in securing passage of legislation that licenses (or certifies) social workers. A section of such legislation usually contains a provision that recognizes social worker–client privileged communication. In various states a number of other professionals have been licensed and have secured recognition of privileged communication with clients. These professionals include attorneys, accountants, physicians, the clergy, guidance counselors, marriage counselors, nurses, psychiatrists, and psychologists.

Explaining Confidentiality to Clients

How should a worker respond to clients' questions about confidentiality? Clients often wonder when they seek services how the information they reveal will be used. Clients need to be assured that the information they divulge will be kept confidential; otherwise they are unlikely to share their secret concerns. Compare the following two responses to a question asked by a husband who is seeking marriage counseling for himself and his wife:

First response:

Husband: Will what we say here be told to others?

Worker: Our agency operates on a system of relative confidentiality. This means I may discuss certain aspects of your case with other staff members at this agency, but I will not discuss your case with anyone else outside the agency. There is one exception to this: if I am subpoenaed (which might happen if you decide to get a divorce and the divorce is contested), then I would have to reveal what we talked about. I guess there might be one additional exception. Should the need arise for me to talk with professionals at other agencies (for example, your doctor), then, I would first ask you to sign a release-of-information form allowing me to discuss your case.

Second response:

Husband: Will what we say here be told to others?

Worker: No, what you say here will be kept within this agency. I know when clients first come to an agency they often wonder how the in formation they reveal will be used. I assure you that what we talk about will be kept confidential.

The second response is probably the most desirable at agencies where the chances of subpoenas are unlikely. The first response, though more thorough, is likely to suggest to clients that there is a moderate chance that information they reveal will be used against them at some future time, which will inhibit them from sharing their "secret" concerns.

However, if a worker is providing services in an area with a moderate or high chance of court action, then clients should be more fully informed about the limits of confidentiality. For example, a probation and parole officer should inform clients (early in the supervision period) about his or her obligations to the court if a client reveals a violation of the conditions of probation (for example, by committing another offense), as illustrated in this excerpt from an interview:

Probation Officer: I'm here to help you in any way I can. If you have personal concerns and want to talk to someone, I'd be happy to talk with you. If you choose to talk with someone else, that's certainly okay with me. The important thing is that when you have personal concerns, you get them worked out. We all have personal concerns at times. If you choose to talk to me, it will be kept confidential. The only information that will not be kept confidential is a violation by you of the conditions of probation, which we have discussed and which you have a copy of. If you violate the conditions of probation, and I find out, either by your telling me, or in some other way, I am required to make a report to the court of the violation. Do you have questions about this?

Probationee: No.

Probation Officer: All right, if you have some concerns now, or in the future, I'll be happy to talk with you.

Probationee: There is one concern I have. My girlfriend's parents as yet don't know I've been arrested and placed on probation. He's a minister, and his wife is a schoolteacher. I don't know what they will say when they find out I'm in trouble. How do you think I should handle this? [The interview continues— and a trusting, helping relationship begins to develop.]

Confidentiality and AIDS

The major social concerns and controversies encompassing AIDS are far too numerous to be addressed here, so the focus will be on confidentiality and AIDS. Once a person has been positively diagnosed as having antibodies to HIV and therefore is capable of transmitting the virus to others, who else should have access to this information? Do social workers have an obligation to help protect the public health that outweighs their clients' interests? Is it ethically permissible for social workers to notify identifiable partners who are in danger of contracting the AIDS virus, if their clients refuse to change high-risk behaviors or to warn their partners? Where does a social worker's obligation to preserve client confidentiality end and duty to protect or warn another person begin?

Clients who are HIV-positive may be reluctant to inform their sexual partners for a variety of reasons. They may be concerned about the possibility of being abandoned. They may be angry because they suspect their partners infected them. They may fear that their partners might tell others that they are HIV-positive.

The NASW's policy statement (Landers, 1993) on HIV/AIDS concerning whether there is a duty to inform is as follows:

> Practitioners and agencies may perceive a responsibility to warn third parties of their potential for infection if their spouses, other sexual partners, or partners in intravenous drug use are HIV-infected and the partners refuse to warn them. (p. 3)

In this HIV/AIDS policy statement, NASW refers to the "duty to warn" principle, which was established by the 1974 case *Tarasoff v. Regents of the University of California* (*University of Pittsburgh Law Review*, 1975). In this precedent-setting case, the California Supreme Court ruled that psychotherapists have a duty to warn a potential victim when the professional believes there is a clear danger, even if this means breaching confidentiality. The court concluded, "The protective privilege ends where the public peril begins." Whether *Tarasoff* applies to AIDS cases has not been tested. All *Tarasoff* cases tested in court have involved threats with weapons or arson, not sexually transmitted diseases.

In regard to the thorny issue of partner notification, Dickson (1998) states,

> For social workers—and other professionals—disclosure of a patient's or client's HIV/AIDS status to others presents significant ethical and perhaps legal problems. Ethically, a strong argument can be made that if the patient or client refuses to tell a spouse, sexual partner, or other who is in danger of exposure, the social worker should take steps to protect that individual. . . . However, there is often a conflicting state confidentiality statute, with penalties for unauthorized disclosure of HIV or AIDS. Until the case and statutory law are better harmonized, the best course for the social worker is to work with the patient or client to get him or her to notify those at risk or, failing that, to gain an informed consent for notification. If this is unsuccessful, a court-ordered release of the confidential information is possible. As always, consultation and careful documentation are called for. (p. 212)

Exercise 2.8: Do You Have a Duty to Inform a Person at Risk of Acquiring HIV?

Goal: This exercise is designed to better inform you of the complicated issues surrounding whether to violate confidentiality.

You are a social worker, and one of your clients informs you that he recently tested positive for HIV You begin to assist him with his feelings and concerns and also give him the name of a physician who has expertise in medically treating HIV-positive individuals. The client further informs you that he has a female sexual partner who is unaware of his HIV status. You urge him to inform her so that precautions can be taken to prevent the transfer of the HIV virus to her—and to suggest it may be in her best interest to be tested to determine her HIV status. He refuses to inform her, saying she'll leave him if she finds out. Do you seek to get a court-ordered release of confidential information, which may (or may not) be attained over a period of weeks? Do you contact the girlfriend and violate confidentiality by revealing his HIV status—which in the long run may lengthen her life and her quality of life? What other options do you have? Please specify what you believe you would do.

OTHER VALUES

Additional values and principles of social work practice are briefly summarized in this section. You should also study the Code of Ethics of the National Association of Social Workers and the Canadian Association of Social Workers' Code of Ethics, which summarize important practice ethics for social workers. The NASW is the largest professional association representing the social work profession in the United States, and the Canadian Association of Social Workers is the largest professional association representing the social work profession in Canada. (The NASW Code of Ethics appears at www.naswdc.org. The Canadian Association of Social Workers' Code of Ethics and Guidelines for Ethical Practice appears at www.casw-acts.ca.)

Another important statement of ethics relevant to social work is the "Ethics in Social Work, Statement of Principles," developed jointly by the International Federation of Social Workers and the International Association of Schools of social work (2004). It can be accessed at http://www.ifsw.org.

Residual and Institutional Orientations toward Social Welfare

There are two conflicting views of the role of social welfare in our society (Wilensky & Lebeaux, 1965). The *residual* view promotes a gap-filling or first-aid role. This view holds that social welfare services should be provided only when an individual's needs are not properly met through other societal institutions, primarily the family and the market economy. Social services and financial aid should not be provided until all measures or efforts have failed (other efforts include the exhaustion of the individual's or the family's resources). In addition, the residual view asserts that funds and services should be provided on a short-term basis (primarily during emergencies) and withdrawn when the individual or the family again becomes self-sufficient.

The residual view has characterized social welfare as "charity for unfortunates" (Wilensky & Lebeaux, 1965, p. 14). Funds and services are seen not as a right (something to which one is entitled) but as a gift, with the receiver having certain obligations (for example, to receive financial aid the recipient may be required to perform certain low-grade work assignments). An associated belief holds that the causes of recipients' difficulties are rooted in their own malfunctioning (that is, recipients are brought to their predicament through their own fault because of some personal inadequacy, or ill-advised activity, or sin). Under the residual view, a stigma is usually attached to receiving services or funds.

Exercise 2.9: The Residual View Stigma

Goal: This exercise is designed to help you recognize the stigma about receiving social welfare funds or services that is associated with the residual view.

Reflect on a time when you were aware that you had intense unwanted emotions (such as depression, anger, or confusion) related to a personal situation or dilemma that you faced (please do not specify the dilemma or situation). Did you experience reluctance to seek counseling because you were wary of what others might think of you? If "yes," please specify your concerns related to this residual stigma. Also specify whether you did, or did not, seek counseling for this dilemma or situation.

The opposing point of view has been called the *institutional* view. According to this view, social welfare programs are to be "accepted as a proper, legitimate function of modern industrial society in helping individuals achieve self-fulfillment" (Wilensky & Lebeaux, 1965, p. 14). Under this view, there is no stigma attached to receiving funds or services; recipients are entitled to such help. Associated with this view is the belief that individuals' difficulties result from causes largely beyond their control (for example, a person is unemployed because of a lack of employment opportunities).

The residual approach characterized social welfare programs from our early history to the Depression of the 1930s. Since the Great Depression, both approaches have been applied to social welfare programs, with some programs being largely residual in nature while others are more institutional in design and implementation. Social workers generally believe in the institutional approach and strive to develop and provide programs with this orientation.

At the present time a so-called devolution revolution is occurring with regard to the provision of human services in our society. Decisions about the provision of key social welfare programs are being transferred from the federal government down to the state level. A major program affected by the devolution revolution was Aid to Families with Dependent Children (AFDC).

From 1935 to the middle 1990s, the federal government required all states to provide the AFDC program to eligible families. (The program was created by the 1935 Social Security Act.) This public assistance program provided monthly checks primarily to low-income mothers with children under age 18. The precise parameters of eligibility for AFDC varied from state to state. Payments were made for both the parent (or parents) and the children in eligible families. Financing and administration of the AFDC program was shared by federal and state governments. In many states, counties also participated in financing and administration. In 1996, federal legislation was enacted that dismantled the AFDC program. The entire concept that poor families are entitled to basic human and health services has now been questioned. As Chapter 13 indicates, many policy makers now believe that private charities can respond, at a lower cost, to local social problems than public services can. The 1996 Welfare Reform Act (the Personal Responsibility and Work Opportunity Reconciliation Act) called for the following: (1) Each state sets its own eligibility rules and amounts for financial assistance. The federal government provides block grants to states to assist in financing the programs that are developed. (2) Recipients of financial benefits receive no more than 2 years of assistance without working, and there is a 5-year lifetime limit of benefits for adults.

In 1935, when the AFDC program was enacted, it was thought best for single mothers to stay at home to raise their children. The 1996 welfare reform legislation asserts that single mothers (and fathers) have an obligation to work for a living. The safety net for poor families with young children now has some major holes. Clearly, the legislation marks a shift by our society to the residual approach. The profession of social work is being challenged to confront the devolution revolution and to respond to the needs of those who are falling through the holes in the safety net.

Establishing Professional Boundaries with Clients

Is it appropriate for a social worker to have lunch or dinner with a client? Is it appropriate to attend a party (where alcoholic drinks are being served) where clients may be present? Is it appropriate to hug a client who is experiencing emotional distress? These are examples of *boundary questions* that arise in interactions with clients.

As the years have passed, I have seen a variety of boundary problems. A well-meaning male psychotherapist was charged by a female client for unethical conduct because he occasionally gave her hugs and because he overstepped (according to her) the boundaries of a professional relationship by giving her his room air-conditioner after he had central air installed in his home. In another case, a man charged a female psychotherapist with alienation of affection after the psychotherapist and the man's wife, who was a client of the female therapist, had dinner a few times and the wife became attracted to the therapist. Some social work faculty members have dated social work students, and now universities across the country are questioning the propriety of such relationships. (A power differential exists between students and faculty, and many campuses now view such dating relationships as evidence that the involved students could use to prove sexual harassment.) A female social work intern at a group home for adolescent males was confronted by her agency supervisor because she sought to become friends with the residents. She frequently played pool with them and occasionally shared some of her "partying" stories, and one of the residents became infatuated with her. A male intern at a shelter for runaway youths occasionally related jokes that had some sexual connotations; one of the female residents charged that such behavior was evidence that the intern was making romantic advances toward her. A female intern was terminated at her field placement at a halfway house for chemically addicted correctional residents after she began dating one of the residents. A male intern at a shelter for battered women was confronted by his agency supervisor about the "provocative and revealing" clothes he tended to wear, which was a factor in some of the residents becoming infatuated with him.

Social workers have an obligation to establish appropriate boundaries in professional relationships with clients. The Canadian Association of Social Workers' Code of Ethics and Guidelines for Ethical Practice (2005) contains the following statements on these boundary issues:

> Dual or multiple relationships occur when social workers relate to clients in more than one relationship, whether professional, social or business. Dual or multiple relationships can occur simultaneously or consecutively. While having contact with clients in different life situations is not inherently harmful, it is the responsibility of the social worker to evaluate the nature of the various contacts to determine whether the social worker is in a position of power and/or authority that may unduly and/or negatively affect the decisions and actions of their client.

> Social workers avoid engaging in physical contact with clients when there is a possibility of harm to the client as a result of the contact. Social workers who engage in appropriate physical contact with clients are responsible for setting clear, appropriate and culturally sensitive boundaries to govern such physical contact.

> Social workers do not engage in romantic relationships, sexual activities or sexual contact with clients, even if such contact is sought by clients.

> Social workers who have provided psychotherapy or in-depth counselling do not engage in romantic relationships, sexual activities or sexual contact with former clients. It is the responsibility of the social worker to evaluate the nature of the professional relationship they had with a client and to determine whether the social worker is in a position of power and/or authority that may unduly and/or negatively affect the decisions and actions of their former client.

> Social workers do not engage in a romantic relationship, sexual activities or sexual contact with social work students whom they are supervising or teaching.

The NASW Code of Ethics (2008) contains these statements on boundary issues:

> Social workers should not take unfair advantage of any professional relationship or exploit others to further their personal, religious, political, or business interests.

> Social workers should not engage in dual or multiple relationships with clients or former clients in which there is a risk of exploitation or potential harm to the client. In instances when dual or multiple relationships are unavoidable, social workers should take steps to protect clients and are responsible for setting clear, appropriate, and culturally sensitive boundaries. (Dual or multiple relationships occur when social workers relate to clients in more than one relationship, whether professional, social, or business. Dual or multiple relationships can occur simultaneously or consecutively.)

Social workers should under no circumstances engage in sexual activities or sexual contact with current clients, whether such contact is consensual or forced.

Social workers should not engage in activities or sexual contact with clients' relatives or other individuals with whom clients maintain a close, personal relationship where there is a risk of exploitation or potential harm to the client. Sexual activity or sexual contact with clients' relatives or other individuals with whom clients maintain a personal relationship has the potential to be harmful to the client and may make it difficult for the social worker and client to maintain appropriate professional boundaries. Social workers—not their clients, their clients' relatives, or other individuals with whom the client maintains a professional relationship—assume the full burden for setting clear, appropriate, and culturally sensitive boundaries.

Social workers should not engage in sexual activities or sexual contact with former clients because of the potential for harm to the client.

Social workers should not provide clinical services to individuals with whom they have had a prior sexual relationship.

Social workers should not engage in physical contact with clients where there is a possibility of psychological harm to the client as a result of the contact (such as cradling or caressing clients). Social workers who engage in appropriate physical contact with clients are responsible for setting clear, appropriate, and culturally sensitive boundaries that govern such physical contact.

(The NASW Code of Ethics appears at www.naswdc.org.)

Exercise 2.10: Dual Relationships in Small Rural Communities

Goal: This exercise is designed to help you understand the complexities of avoiding dual relationships in small rural communities.

Step 1:   In small rural communities, nearly everyone knows everyone else, and there is considerable social interaction. A dual relationship arises for a social worker when he or she provides professional services to a client and then enters into a social or business relationship with that client. Assume that you are a social worker in a rural community, that you are serving on a church committee, and that one of your clients joins this committee. What do you do?

Step 2:   You are on a volleyball team in your community. The team has a ritual of having a few beers after playing volleyball. A client of yours joins the team. What do you do?

Step 3:   One of your clients is the only cement contractor in your community. You own a house, and you need a new driveway. Are you going to contact this cement contractor to pour a new driveway for you? Give your rationale for what you will do.

Exercise 2.11:   Hugging a Client and Going to Lunch with a Client

Goal: This exercise is designed to help you clarify when hugging and having lunch with a client may be appropriate.

Step 1:   We all need positive physical contact with others. It may be constructive and desirable to ask a 7-year-old child whether she or he would like a hug when the child is experiencing emotional distress. But a hug may send the wrong message to a client. State your guidelines about when, and when not, to hu a client.

Step 2:   Having lunch with a shy 8-year-old at a fast-food restaurant may have therapeutic value. But dining with a client, at times, may send the wrong message. State your guidelines on when, and when not, to have lunch with a client.

It is impossible to develop guidelines that answer every question that might arise when social workers set boundaries with clients, but the following guidelines may be useful in resolving some boundary dilemmas:

- In your professional *and* your personal life, try to be a role model for the values and principles of the social work profession.
- In relationships with clients, try to gain their respect and to exemplify the values and principles of the social work profession, rather than establish a friend-to-friend relationship.
- Never try to meet your personal needs or wants in relationships with clients.
- Try to increase your awareness of your own needs, feelings, values, and limitations so you become increasingly aware of how such factors may affect client relationships.

■ When questions arise about the appropriateness of certain interactions with a client (such as whether to go to lunch), try to arrive at an answer by gauging whether the interaction will have a constructive impact on the client and your relationship. If a concrete, beneficial impact cannot be objectively specified, do not engage in the interaction.

■ Constructive professional relationships with clients require a certain amount of distance. If you have questions about whether contemplated social interactions will interfere with the boundaries of a professional relationship, consult your supervisor or a respected colleague.

■ In your professional social work role with clients, be aware of any inappropriate behavior, verbal communications, and dress on your part. For example, sharing details of your "wild" parties with clients is unprofessional.

Promoting Social and Economic Justice and Safeguarding Human Rights

Social workers have an obligation to promote social and economic justice for those who are oppressed or victimized by discrimination. According to the Council on Social Work Education, social work educational programs need to provide a learning environment "through which students learn about differences, to value and respect diversity, and develop a commitment to cultural humility" (Council on Social Work Education [CSWE], 2015). In EPAS (CSWE, 2015) social work educational programs are mandated to have a commitment to diversity, "including but not limited to age, class, color, culture, disability and ability, ethnicity, gender, gender identity and expression, immigration status, marital status, political ideology, race, religion/spirituality, sex, sexual orientation, and tribal sovereign status."

According to the NASW Code of Ethics (1996, p. 27), "Social workers should act to prevent and eliminate domination of, exploitation of, and discrimination against any person, group, or class on the basis of race, ethnicity, national origin, color, sex, sexual orientation, age, marital status, political belief, religion, or mental or physical disability."

The social work profession holds that society has a responsibility to all of its members to provide security, acceptance, and satisfaction of basic cultural, social, and biological needs. Only when basic needs are met is it possible for individuals to develop their maximum potentials. Therefore, social workers have a special responsibility to protect and secure civil rights based on democratic principles and a moral responsibility to work toward eradicating discrimination for any reason. Clients' civil rights need to be protected to preserve human dignity and self-respect.

In promoting social and economic justice for oppressed populations, social workers are expected to have an understanding of (1) the consequences and dynamics of social and economic injustice, including the forms of human oppression and discrimination, and (2) the impact of economic deprivation, discrimination, and oppression on populations-at-risk. Social workers have an ethical obligation to understand and appreciate human diversity. They are expected to have and use skills to promote social change that furthers the achievement of individual and collective social and economic justice.

In recent years the Council on Social Work Education has placed increased emphasis on human rights. For example, in 2015 EPAS (Council on Social Work Education, 2015) there is the following statement on values: "Service, social justice, the dignity and worth of the person, the importance of human relationships, integrity, competence, human rights, and scientific inquiry are among the core values of social work." The 2015 EPAS adds,

> Social workers understand that every person regardless of position in society has fundamental human rights such as freedom, safety, privacy, an adequate standard of living, health care, and education. Social workers understand the global interconnections of oppression and human rights violations, and are knowledgeable about theories of human need and social justice and strategies to promote social and economic justice and human rights.

Reichert (2007), however, has noted that "human rights" has received very limited attention in social work curricula and in social work course materials and lectures. Often, a human rights focus is "invisible" in social work curricula. Social work literature continually prefers the term *social justice* in analyzing core values relevant to the social work profession.

Social justice is an ideal condition in which all members of a society have the same basic rights, protection, opportunities, obligations, and social benefits. Economic justice is also an ideal condition in which all members of a society have the same opportunities to attain material goods, income, and wealth.

Human rights are commonly understood as inalienable fundamental rights to which a person is inherently entitled simple because he or she is a human being. Human rights are universal (applicable everywhere) and egalitarian (the same for everyone).

Reichert (2007, p. 4) compares the concept of "human rights" to the concept of "social justice":

> Human rights provide the social work profession with a global and contemporary set of guidelines, whereas social justice tends to be defined in vague terminology such as fairness versus unfairness or equality versus inequality. . . . This distinction gives human rights an authority that social justice lacks. Human tights can elicit discussion of common issues by people from all walks of life and every corner of the world.

What are basic "human rights"? A clear specification of basic human rights has not been agreed upon. A key starting point in articulating such rights is the UN's *Universal Declaration of Human Rights* (United Nations, 1948). The following rights are identified in this document:

> All humans are born free and equal in dignity and rights.
> Everyone is entitled to all of the rights in the UNDR regardless of any distinction.
> The right to life, liberty, and the security of the person.
> Prohibition of slavery.
> Prohibition of torture.
> Right to recognition as a person before the law.
> All must be treated equally under the law.
> Right to a remedy of any violation of these rights.
> Prohibition of arbitrary arrest, detention, or exile.
> Right to a fair trial.
> People shall be presumed innocent until proven guilty.
> Right to freedom from arbitrary interference with private life.
> Right to freedom of movement.
> Right to seek asylum.
> Right to a nationality.
> Right to marry; marriage must be consented to by both parties; the family is entitled to protection from the state.
> Right to property.
> Right to freedom of thought, conscience, and religion.
> Right to freedom of opinion and expression.
> Right to freedom of assembly and association.
> Right to participate in the government of one's country.
> Right to economic, social, and cultural rights necessary for dignity and free development of personality.
> Right to work and equitable compensation.
> Right to rest and leisure from work.
> Right to an adequate standard of living, including food, clothing, housing, and medical care.
> Right to education.
> Right to participate in cultural activities and to share in scientific achievements.
> Right to a world order in which these rights can be realized.
> Each has duties to their community; rights shall be limited only in regards to respecting the rights of others.
> None of the rights may be interpreted as allowing any action to destroy these rights.

Every member nation of the UN has approved the *Universal Declaration*, but it is not legally binding on any nation. Because it articulates human rights in somewhat vague terms, determining when (or if) a country/government is violating basic human rights is sometimes difficult. Most countries recognize that the safeguarding of human rights has evolved into a major worldwide goal. Yet identifying violations is currently an imprecise science. It is common for a government to accuse other governments of violating human rights while at the same time "overlooking" its own violations. Reichert (2007, p. 8) states:

> The United States; compared to many other countries, fails to fulfill its obligation to promote human rights for all. . . . For instance, our failure to provide adequate health care for children and all expectant mothers violates the same Universal Declaration of Human Rights that U.S. political leaders continually call upon to denigrate China, Cuba, and Iraq, among other countries. The infant mortality rate is higher in the United States than in any other industrialized nation . . . and, within the U.S. itself, infant mortality rates are disparate among racial groups, with African-American infants suffering a mortality rate more than twice that of non-Hispanic whites.

It is hoped that greater attention to articulating basic human rights will lead countries to initiate programs that safeguard such rights for all citizens. Increased attention to articulating and protecting basic human rights has promise of being a key countervailing force to facilitate curbing discrimination against people of color, women, persons with a disability, gays and lesbians, and other groups who are currently victimized by discrimination.

Focus on Family

The focus of social work services is often on the family. A family is seen as an interacting independent system. The problems faced by any person are usually influenced by the dynamics within a family, as illustrated in the following example.

A schoolteacher became concerned when one of her pupils was consistently failing, and she referred the child for psychological testing. Testing revealed a normal IQ, but failure was found to be caused by a low self-concept (the girl was reluctant to do her academic work because she saw herself as being incapable of doing it). A school social worker met with the family and observed that the low self-concept was primarily a result of the parents' ridiculing and criticizing the child and seldom giving emotional support, encouragement, or compliments.

A family is an interacting system, and change in one member affects other members. For example, in some abusive families, the abused child is a scapegoat on which the parents vent their anger and hostility. If the abused child is removed from the home, another child within the family is at times selected to be the scapegoat (Leavitt, 1974).

Another reason for the focus on the family rather than on the individual is that the other family members are often needed in the treatment process. For example, other family members can put pressure on an alcoholic to have him or her acknowledge that a problem exists. The family members may also need counseling to help them cope with the person when he or she is drinking, and these family members may play important roles in providing emotional support for the alcoholic's efforts to stop drinking.

Exercise 2.12: When Rights of Family Members Clash

Goal: This exercise is designed to show you that a client's right to privacy sometimes clashes with the rights of others to be informed.

A client of yours, Kelly North, is married and wants to have children. She informs you that she is a carrier of Huntington's disease. As yet there is no cure for this disease, but there may be in 10 to 20 years. Ms. North is 26 years old. Huntington's disease is an inherited condition. It is transmitted by a dominant gene and affects half of the offspring of those who carry the gene. The symptoms include hallucinations, profound mood swings, dementia, and spasmodic movements of limbs and facial muscles. Symptoms generally begin to occur around age 30. Ms. North refuses to tell her husband about her condition, and she requests that you do not tell him—because she fears her husband would be unwilling to have children if he found out. When the well-being of other people is at risk, does their right to such information take precedence over your client's right to privacy? What are you going to do?

Accountability

Increasingly, federal and state governmental units and private funding sources are requiring that the effectiveness of service programs be measured. Gradually, programs found to be ineffective are being phased out. Although some social workers view accountability with trepidation and claim the paperwork involved interferes with serving clients, members of the social work profession have an obligation to funding sources to provide the highest-quality services. Two hundred years ago, bloodletting was thought to be an effective treatment technique. Only a few decades ago, lobotomies were erroneously thought to be effective. Now the value of electroshock therapy, psychoanalysis, and some other therapy techniques is being questioned. Program outcome studies have also demonstrated that orphanages are not the best place to raise homeless children; long-term hospitalization is not the best way to help those who are emotionally disturbed; probation generally has higher rehabilitative value than long-term confinement in prison; the Job Corps program of the 1960s was too expensive for the outcomes achieved; children with a cognitive disability can be better served in their home communities through local programs than by confinement in an institution; and so on.

Social workers need to become skilled at evaluating the extent to which they are being effective in providing services. Widely ranging evaluation techniques are now available to assess the effectiveness of current services and to identify unmet needs and service gaps. One of the most useful approaches is management by objectives (MBO). This technique involves specifying the objectives of a program, stating in measurable terms how and when these objectives are to be met, and then periodically measuring the extent to which the objectives are being met.

MBO is also one of the most useful approaches that social workers can use to assess their own effectiveness in providing services. Many agencies now require their workers, with the involvement of their clients, to (1) identify and specify what the goals will be for each client—generally this is done together with clients during the initial interviews; (2) write down in detail what the client and the worker will do to accomplish the goals—deadlines for accomplishing these tasks are also set; and (3) assess, when treat ment is terminated (and perhaps periodically during the treatment process), the extent to which the goals have been achieved. (See the section on evidence-based practice in Chapter 11.)

If goals are generally not being achieved, the worker needs to identify and examine the underlying reasons. Perhaps unrealistic goals are being set. Perhaps the program or the treatment techniques are ineffective. Perhaps certain components of the treatment program are having an adverse effect. Perhaps other reasons account for the low success rate. Appropriate changes then need to be made.

Conversely, if the goals are generally being met, workers can use this information to document to funding sources and to supervisors that high-quality services are being provided.

NEW TECHNOLOGY AND SOCIAL WORK

For many individuals, their main form of communication is done through technology—such as social media, emails, chatrooms, online classrooms, and text messaging. This relatively new technology allows individuals from different regions or time zones to communicate with one another. It also allows those who lack adequate transportation or who are homebound to communicate with others. A number of social workers have entered this technology world through providing online individual/group counseling, telephone counseling, cyber therapy, social network sites, self-guided web-based interventions, and text messaging.

Due to the increasing nature of the use of technology in social work, NASW has developed guidelines for workers engaging in these technologies (Reamer, 2013). Social workers need to be aware of how technology can impact communication and take necessary steps to prevent any miscommunication or disruption that may occur. For example, displaying one's excessive alcohol use or illegal drug use on Facebook has caused a number of social workers to lose their job.

SUMMARY

The following summarizes the chapter's content in terms of the learning objectives presented at the beginning of the chapter.

1. Describe value dilemmas in social work.

   Much of social work practice involves value dilemmas. A number of such dilemmas are described in this chapter. Social work is both an art and a science. Because social work is partly an art, a worker frequently must make decisions based on values rather than on knowledge. Change techniques used by workers are often based on theory and value assumptions rather than on proven therapy techniques.

2. Understand the distinction between knowledge and values.

   Values are beliefs, preferences, or assumptions about what is desirable or good for people. Knowledge statements are observations about the world and people that have been verified or are capable of verification. It is much easier to change a client's belief that conflicts with current knowledge than it is to change a belief based on values. Guidelines were presented for how a worker should handle a value conflict between the worker and the client.

3. Distinguish value dilemmas of clients from the value dilemmas of social workers.

   It is important for social workers to recognize who is confronting a value dilemma. A social worker at times may make the mistake of thinking he or she must resolve a dilemma faced by a client (such as whether or not to have an abortion). Such erroneous thinking by the social worker may lead the worker to become overly emotionally involved in the client's case. It is important for the worker to recognize when the dilemma is the client's—so that the worker will be able to remain objective and thereby be most helpful to the client.

4. Describe respect for the dignity and uniqueness of individuals.

   An important value of social work is respect for the dignity and uniqueness of the individual. The importance of individualizing each client was discussed, and guidelines were presented on how to relate to clients whose behavior is viewed as disgusting by the worker. Involved in individualization is the ability to accept clients but not the deviant behavior to be changed, careful attendance to clients' communications, and the discreet use of labeling.

5. Describe the client's right to self-determination.

Self-determination is the clients' right to express their own opinions and to act on them, as long as clients do not infringe on the rights of others. Clients should be made aware that there are alternatives for resolving the personal and social problems they face. Self-determination means that the client, not the worker, is the chief problem solver, although the worker has an obligation to suggest resolution approaches that the client may not be aware of.

6. Understand confidentiality and privileged communication.

Confidentiality is the implicit or explicit agreement between a professional and a client to maintain the private nature of information about the client. In professional practice, a system of relative confidentiality currently exists, rather than a system of absolute confidentiality Numerous unresolved questions surrounding confidentiality were raised, and some guidelines on how beginning practitioners should handle these questions were presented. At times, circumstances arise in which a professional is permitted, expected, or required to violate confidentiality, and many of these circumstances were listed—for example, when a client admits to a past or intended serious criminal act. Protecting the confidentiality of clients' files and records in human service organizations is becoming much more difficult as information technology expands exponentially.

Privileged communication is a legal term pertaining to the admission of evidence in a court. In states where certain professional groups (such as social workers) are granted privileged communication, the client or his/her attorney has the privilege in court of preventing the professional from answering questions about what the client has communicated to the professional.

7. Understand the residual view, and the institutional view, of social welfare.

The residual view promotes a gap-filling or first-aid role. This view holds that social welfare services should be provided only when an individual's needs are not properly met through other societal institutions, primarily the family and the market economy.

The institutional view asserts that social welfare programs are to be accepted as a proper function of society. Contrary to the residual view, there is no stigma attached to receiving funds or services. Recipients are viewed as being entitled to such help.

8. Understand the importance of establishing professional boundaries with clients.

Social workers have an obligation to establish appropriate boundaries in professional relationships with clients. For example, social workers should not engage in dual or multiple relationships with clients (or with former clients) in which there is a risk of potential harm to the clients. Also, social workers should not engage in sexual activities, or sexual contact, with current or former clients.

9. Understand the worker's obligation to promote social and economic justice and to safeguard human rights.

Social workers have an obligation to promote social and economic justice for those who are oppressed or victimized by discrimination. Social workers also have an obligation to advocate for human rights for all individuals.

EXERCISES

1. Confidentiality

Goal: To get a feel for when to uphold, and when to violate, confidentiality.

Step 1: Divide into groups of about five students. Each group answers the questions raised in the following vignettes.

a. You are a social worker at a public school, and you have been working with a family that has multiple problems. Two of the children are in special education programs for the emotionally disturbed. The mother has occasionally been hospitalized for emotional problems. The father has been investigated by protective services for child abuse in the past. Mother and father are having marital problems and are presently separated. The father comes to your office and demands to see the school's records on his children and his family. As a social worker, would you show him these records?

b. You are a social worker at a mental health center, and you are working with a client who appears to be emotionally upset. He states he has heard that his girl friend is seeing someone else. While saying this, he becomes enraged and says he intends to shoot her. He asks you not to tell anyone what he has said. As you endeavor to discuss his threat, he becomes more upset and walks out, stating, "I'll make sure she doesn't cheat on me." Should you violate confidentiality and inform someone? If so, whom would you inform?

c. You are a social worker at a drug abuse treatment center, and you have been working with a 23-year-old female. You establish a good working relationship with her. She says something has been bothering her for a long time, but she states she won't discuss it unless you agree not to tell anyone. You assure her that what she reveals will be kept confidential. She then reveals that she had an incestuous relationship with her stepfather that started when she was 14 and lasted nearly 3 years. She believes her unresolved feeling about this experience is one of the reasons she sometimes drinks too much. In a staff meeting on this client, would you reveal to the other staff what she has said?

Step 2: Groups share their answers with the class. The instructor then summarizes the text's answers to the questions, which involve (a) the 1974 Federal Privacy Act, (b) the 1974 *Tarasoff v. Regents of the University of California* decision, and (c) guidelines about sharing information with other staff.

Step 3: Class discussion about how social work practice uses a system of relative, rather than absolute, confidentiality. Class review of chapter guidelines on when to uphold and when to violate confidentiality.

2. Clarifying Values

Goal: To clarify values on a number of prominent issues in social work.

Step 1: Class discussion of why social workers need to be aware of their personal values and aware of professional values, when workers should take a nonjudgmental position with clients, and when they should seek to sell to clients (or enforce to clients) a particular set of values.

In groups of three, develop answers, and reasons for your answers, to the following 10 questions.

a. You are a protective service worker and you have evidence that a father is committing incest with his 10-year-old daughter. Would you seek to end the incest by (1) providing counseling services to all family members to keep the family intact, (2) bringing legal charges against the father, or (3) seeking to do both at the same time?

b. Do you support a constitutional amendment to make abortion illegal?

c. Does a social worker have an obligation to preserve confidentiality if an HIV-infected client refuses to inform his or her sexual partner of the infection (while persisting in behavior that places the partner at risk), or does the social worker have an obligation to warn the partner about the peril?

d. Do you support affirmative action programs that assert that certain minority groups and women should be given preference in hiring over white males?

e. If an older person who is terminally ill and in intense pain wants to end his or her life, should physicians be allowed to provide assistance in helping this person die?

f. Do you believe the United States should support an extensive program to develop the capacity to clone human beings?

g. Do you believe in capital punishment for certain crimes?

h. Do you think a gay or lesbian teacher should be allowed to teach in elementary and secondary schools?

i. Do you think women in military service should fight in combat?

j. Should condoms and other contraceptives be provided to requesting students through health-care clinics located in middle schools and high schools?

Step 2: Groups present and discuss their answers. Each question is taken one at a time. (*Note:* The purpose of this exercise is to help you clarify your values and not to sell any particular value system.)

Step 3: Discuss how you felt when others in class expressed views that you strongly disagree with.

3. New Frontier to Rings of Fire

Goal: To help you clarify your values about humanity.

Step 1:   Form groups of about five. Your instructor reads the following vignette to the students:

The United States has recently completed building a remarkable spaceship, named *New Frontier*, that is capable of carrying seven people to planets in other galaxies. *New Frontier* uses nuclear power and is guided by a new computer system that does not require a pilot to fly the spaceship.

Our government has recently discovered a new planet in a faraway galaxy that has an atmosphere very similar to Earth's atmosphere and appears capable of supporting life. This planet has been named Rings of Fire as it has a red hue and several rings around it, similar to those of Saturn.

Your group has been chosen by the president of the United States to select the seven people who will take the first flight. *New Frontier* is presently located on a remote Samoan island.

Suddenly a nuclear war breaks out in the Middle East, and the superpowers quickly enter the conflict. The bombs and the radioactive fallout will destroy civilization as we know it. The chief scientist frantically calls your group. She indicates your group has 15 minutes to select the seven people to go on *New Frontier* to Rings of Fire. A country we are fighting in this war has sent a nuclear missile to this Samoan island to destroy *New Frontier*. There are 13 people close enough to board *New Frontier*. The chief scientist wants your group to select the 7 people so that these 13 people do not begin fighting among themselves. If your group does not select seven people in 15 minutes; there is a danger the human race will cease to exist. The seven people selected may well be the only hope for continuing the human race. Your group has only the following information about the 13 people.

1. Chief scientist, 57 years old, has a husband and three children who live in Beaumont, Texas.

2. Male Korean medical student, 24 years old.

3. White male rabbi, 28 years old.

4. Female Samoan prostitute who has herpes, 35 years old.

5. White male professional baseball player, 26 years old and gay.

6. Protestant male child, 8 years old.

7. White female who has a cognitive disability from not having enough oxygen at birth, 10 years old.

8. White Catholic male who is unemployed and has cerebral palsy, 27 years old.

9. White male truck driver who has a history of not getting along with people and of getting into numerous fights, 34 years old.

10. Samoan farmer who has had a vasectomy, 22 years old.

11. Female Japanese stockbroker, 27 years old.

12. White female who is depressed and has a long history of being hospitalized for emotional problems, 35 years old.

13. White female who is a millionaire via inheritance and detests working, 26 years old.

Step 2:   Distribute copies of this list to each group. Each group has 15 minutes to complete the task; your instructor will announce when 10, 5, 3, and 1 minute remain.

Step 3:   Group presentation of its choices and the reasons for its selections. Class discussion of (a) the values underlying the selections and (b) the merits and shortcomings of this exercise.

ASSESSMENT

Here is a simplified paradigm of the problem-solving process in social work:

Assessment → Intervention → Termination and Evaluation

In this chapter, we discuss the first element: assessment. This chapter will help prepare students to:

Identify the components of an assessment
Describe the strengths perspective
Identify sources of information for an assessment
Specify the knowledge used in making an assessment
Describe the environmental systems emphasis in conducting an assessment
Describe bio-psycho-social and cultural components in assessment
Identify guides for assessing problem systems

COMPONENTS OF AN ASSESSMENT

Assessment is a critical process in social work practice. The selection of goals and interventions depends largely on what is being assessed. An inaccurate or incomplete assessment can lead to inappropriate goals and inappropriate interventions. When an inaccurate or incomplete assessment is made, positive changes are unlikely to occur.

Hepworth and Larsen (1986) defined *assessment* as follows:

Assessment is the process of gathering, analyzing, and synthesizing salient data into a formulation that encompasses the following vital dimensions: (1) the nature of clients' problems, including special attention to the roles that clients and significant others play in the difficulties; (2) the functioning (strengths, limitations, personality assets, and deficiencies) of clients and significant others; (3) motivation of clients to work on the problems; (4) relevant environmental factors that contribute to the problems; and (5) resources that are available or are needed to ameliorate the clients' difficulties. (p. 165)

Assessment has sometimes been referred to as *psychosocial diagnosis* (Hollis, 1972). But the term *diagnosis* focuses on what is wrong with the client, family, or group being diagnosed—such as having a disease, dysfunction, or mental problem. Because diagnosis has a negative connotation, many other social work educators, myself included, prefer *assessment*. Assessment includes not only what is wrong with the client[1] but also the resources, strengths, motivations, functional components, and other positive factors that can be used to resolve difficulties, to enhance functioning, and to promote growth. Actually, assessment in its broadest sense is the base for the development of an intervention plan.

The *nature* of the assessment task varies significantly with the setting in which the social worker practices, but the *process* is similar in all settings. A social worker in a nursing home who is assessing an applicant for potential placement will look at variables that are radically different from those examined by a social worker in a protective service setting who is assessing an allegation of child abuse.

---

[1]In this chapter the term *client* is often used in a generic sense to refer to an individual, family, group, organization, or community that a practitioner is working with.

In some settings (as in many protective services programs), the social worker makes an independent assessment. With independent assessments, the social worker may consult with colleagues or professionals in other disciplines on complicated cases. In other settings (for example, mental health clinics, schools, and medical hospitals), the social worker is likely to be a member of a clinical team that makes an assessment. Other team members may include a psychologist, psychiatrist, nurse, and perhaps professionals from other disciplines. Team members have specific roles in the assessment process—roles based on their special professional expertise. The psychologist, for example, focuses primarily on psychological functioning and would probably administer a variety of psychological tests (including personality and intelligence tests). The social worker compiles a social history to assess family background, marital dynamics, environmental factors, and employment and educational background. In settings in which the social worker is the primary assessor, the assessment is generally completed in one to three sessions. With a clinical team approach, the case is usually more complicated, and assessment by the various professionals may take a few weeks.

Assessment is sometimes a product and sometimes an ongoing process. As a product, an assessment is a formulation at a point in time regarding the nature of a client's difficulties and resources. An example is a mental status assessment at a psychiatric hospital. Such an assessment is first focused on determining whether the client is sane or psychotic. If the client is assessed as psychotic, a psychiatric label is assigned and a recommended treatment approach is then stated. A product assessment usually has to be updated and revised months or sometimes years later. Such an assessment is, in essence, a working hypothesis of a client's difficulties and resources based on current data. As time passes, the client may change and so will environmental factors. Such changes require the assessment to be updated and revised periodically.

Assessment can also be an ongoing process, from the initial interview to the termination of the case. The length of time a client receives services may be weeks, months, or even years. During this period, the professionals working with the case are continually receiving and analyzing new information. In the early stages of client contact, the focus is primarily on gathering information to assess the client's problems and resources. Once these are tentatively specified, problem solving is emphasized. Resolution strategies are suggested and analyzed, and then one or more strategies are selected and implemented. But even in the problem-solving phase, new information related to the client's difficulties and resources is likely to emerge, necessitating a revision of the assessment. In fact, as contact between the professional and client continues, the client may disclose additional problems that need to be assessed and then resolved. It is common in initial contact for a client to withhold vital information for fear of condemnation. For example, a parent who is abusing a child may initially deny that the abuse is occurring. As time passes, if the parent comes to trust the worker, the parent may disclose that she at times loses control and then hits the child. As new information is provided, the initial assessment needs to be revised.

Hepworth and Larsen (1986) noted that assessment continues to occur even during the termination phase:

> The process of assessment continues even during the terminal phase of service. During the final interviews, the practitioner carefully evaluates the client's readiness to terminate, assesses the presence of residual difficulties that may cause future difficulties, and identifies possible emotional reactions to termination. The practitioner also considers possible strategies to assist the client to maintain improved functioning or to achieve additional progress after formal social work service is concluded. (p. 166)

THE STRENGTHS PERSPECTIVE

For most of the past several decades, social work and the other helping professions focused primarily on diagnosing the pathology, shortcomings, and dysfunctions of clients. One reason may be that Freudian psychology was the primary theory used in analyzing human behavior. Freudian psychology is based on a medical model, and its concepts are therefore geared to identify illness or pathology. It has very few concepts for identifying strengths. As described in Chapter 1, social work is now shifting to a systems model in assessing human behavior. This model focuses on identifying both strengths and weaknesses.

It is essential that social workers include clients' strengths in the assessment process. Today, social workers routinely focus on the strengths and resources of clients to help them resolve their difficulties. To use a client's strengths effectively, social workers must first identify those strengths, but, unfortunately, Maluccio (1979) found that many social workers focus too much on clients' perceived weaknesses and underestimate or are blind to their strengths. Maluccio concluded, "There is a need to shift the focus on social work education and practice from problems or pathology to strengths, resources, and potentialities in human beings and their environments" (p. 401).

A primary focus on weaknesses can impair a worker's capacity to identify a client's growth potential. Social workers strongly believe that clients have the right (and should be encouraged) to develop their potential fully. Focusing on pathology undermines this commitment.

Another reason for attending to clients' strengths is that many clients need help in enhancing their self-esteem. Many have feelings of worthlessness, feelings of inadequacy, a sense of being a failure, and a lack of self-confidence and self-respect. Glasser (1972) noted that low self-esteem often leads to emotional difficulties, withdrawal, or criminal activity. To help clients view themselves more positively, social workers must first view their clients as having considerable strengths and competencies. Berwick (1980) underscored this point in working with neglectful parents of children who fail to thrive:

> Self-esteem is already at a low ebb in many of the parents of these children, and the success of the hospital in nourishing a child when the mother has failed only serves to accentuate the pain of failure. . . . Even in the few cases that require foster care, the health care team's task is to seek strengths and to develop a sense of competence in both the parents and the child that will permit a synchronous nurturant relationship to emerge. (p. 270)

Dennis Saleeby (2012) is recognized as the founder of the strengths perspective.

According to Graeme Stuart (2012), seven principles underlie the guiding assumptions of the strengths perspective:

1. *People have many strengths and have the capacity to continue to learn, grow and change.* People have an inherent power to learn, grow, and change. When clients come to the social worker for assistance with some problem, they are much more than that problem. They also have a number of strengths and abilities which have allowed them to survive, and thrive, in the face of past and present challenges. Social workers need to understand that all clients have hopes, skills, aspirations, and other people that have helped them to survive; and that positive changes are most apt to occur when social workers understand and collaborate with clients' aspirations and strengths. Positive changes are likely to occur only when the worker conveys a strong belief to clients that they will improve.

    Clients who have been victimized in the past are seen as active and developing individuals who, through their traumas, learn skills and develop personal attributes that help them cope with future struggles. There is dignity to be found in having prevailed over obstacles. We often grow more from crises in which we find ways to handle situations effectively than from periods in our lives when we are content and comfortable.

2. *The focus of intervention is on the strengths and aspirations of clients.* Too often service providers have focused on the deficits, problems and pathologies of clients. Such a focus empowers the problem and disempowers the person. It leads the client to feel powerless and creates a victim stance (where the client feels victimized). A focus on strengths does not mean that clients' concerns and problems are ignored, but they are not the main focus of the intervention. Intervention works best when there is a focus on the skills, interests, hopes, desires and resources of clients to improve their lives. Clients are much more motivated to use their capacities to change when the focus is on their strengths.

3. *The community or social environment is seen as being full of resources.* If the social environment (i.e., the community) is viewed as being dangerous, hostile, pathological, or even toxic, then potential resources are often overlooked. For every individual in need, there are a wide range of groups and organizations in every community that can provide help, including family, work, friends, sporting groups, churches, schools, police, hospitals, libraries, social service agencies, medical clinics, and local businesses.

    It is true that many American (and foreign) cities have pockets of deeply troubled communities. These pockets have high rates of: crime, violence, unemployment, welfare dependency, gangs, drug involvement, homelessness, and vacant and abandoned land and buildings.

    There are two paths for seeking to find solutions for deteriorated communities: the deficiency-oriented model, and the asset-based approach. Both of these approaches will be briefly described.

    The deficiency model focuses attention on what is "wrong" with a community. A key instrument used in the deficiency model is a "needs" survey, which focuses on the deficits in a community. The deficiency model often leads to the creation of "client neighborhoods." The creation of a client neighborhood is often accelerated by the mass media with its focus on emphasizing the spectacularly problematic components of a client neighborhood. It is apt to lead residents in these neighborhoods to view themselves as deficient victims who are incapable of taking charge of their lives and of their community's future. Targeting resources based on a "needs map" directs funding to service providers rather than directly to the residents. The service providers, with the deficiency approach, then relate to the residents as "clients." This approach furthers the perception that only outside experts can provide "real help." Such an approach hinders the development of the leadership capacities of the residents. Furthermore, service providers are under funding pressure to provide annual evidence that problems continue to intensify—in order for funding to be renewed. All of these factors tend to lead to the deepening of the cycle of dependence.

The asset-based model focuses on the development of policies and activities based on the assets, skills, and capacities of lower-income people and their neighborhoods (Kretzmann & McKnight, 1993). The asset-based approach believes that significant community development occurs only when local community people are committed to investing themselves and their resources in improving the community. This approach believes sustainable development of a community must start from within the community—rather than waiting for significant help to arrive from outside the community. Instead of viewing the residents of a deteriorated neighborhood as being "clients," this model views residents as being "citizens"—who have untapped resources, assets, capabilities, and potential. The focus is on the community's assets, capacities, and abilities. In addition, every community has a number of citizens' associations—where the citizens assemble to share common interests and activities, and to solve problems. (Every community has associations with religious, athletic, cultural, and recreational purposes.) These associations are key instruments in having the potential for community development.

The key to asset-based community development is mobilizing the assets of individuals, associations, businesses, and public institutions to build a community from inside out (see Chapter 10).

4. *The service provider collaborates with clients.* Clients are usually experts on their own situations. Service providers in the role of "expert" or "professional" are often not at the best vantage point to understand and appreciate the strengths of clients. Clients are most motivated to improve their situations when they feel they have an egalitarian relationship with the service providers. Clients are the primary problem solvers of their problems—not the worker. For all these reasons, the strengths perspective asserts that social workers need to focus on developing collaborative, egalitarian relationships with clients.

5. *Interventions are based on client self determination.* Clients are the primary problem solvers of their problems. As indicated in Chapter 2, a basic ethical principle of social work practice is the client's right to self determination. The power of decision making in regard to what course of action a client will take needs to be placed with the person living that life.

6. *There is commitment to empowerment.* Empowerment is the process of helping individuals, families, groups, organizations, and communities to increase their interpersonal, personal, political, and socioeconomic strengths so that they can improve their circumstances.

The strengths perspective seeks to identify, use, build, and reinforce the strengths and abilities people already have. This is in contrast to the pathological perspective, which focuses on deficiencies and inabilities. The strengths perspective is useful across the life cycle and throughout all stages of the helping process—assessment, intervention, and evaluation. It emphasizes people's abilities, values, "interests, beliefs, resources, accomplishments, and aspirations" (Weick, Rapp, Sullivan, & Kisthardt, 1989).

7. *Problems are seen as the result of interactions between individuals, organizations or structures rather than deficits within individuals, organizations or structures.* In the model of social work that uses a deficit approach to the problem is viewed as being with the client (the "client" may be an individual, family, group, organization, or community). With the deficit approach, the client is the problem. The client is viewed as being responsible for having the problem, which often results in the client being blamed for the problem. The strengths approach uses a person-in-environment model, which is described in Chapter 2. With a person-in-environment model, and the strengths approach, the focus is not on assigning blame, but on identifying strengths of individuals, families, groups, organizations, and communities that can be utilized for improving the lives of the people.

Exercise 3.1: Assessing an Individual

Goal: This exercise is designed to assist you in learning how to write an assessment of an individual. (Please code the name of the individual for confidentiality reasons.)

Step 1: Briefly describe the individual—including coded name, age, gender, height, weight, occupation or school grade level, family information, overall health, financial resources, religion, race or ethnic background, personality characteristics, school performance, health status, arrests and convictions, marital or dating status, hobbies, special interests, outside systems impacting this individual, and so on.

Step 2: Describe the current problems and challenges this person has.

Step 3: Specify the strengths or resources this person has for meeting his or her problems and challenges.

Step 4: Specify the recommended courses of action you believe this person should take to better handle his or her problems and challenges.

SOURCES OF INFORMATION

Information used in making an assessment comes from a variety of sources. The following are the principal sources.

The Client's Verbal Report

A client's verbal report is often the primary source and in some cases the only source of information. (For example, social workers in private practice sometimes obtain information only from the client.) A variety of information can be obtained in this way: description of the problems; feelings about the problems; views of the client's personal resources to combat the problems; motivations to make efforts to resolve the problems; the history of the problems; views of the causes; a description of what has already been done in attempting to resolve the problems.

Although clients are often fairly accurate in describing their difficulties and resources, workers should be aware that verbal reports are sometimes distorted by embarrassment, bias, distorted perceptions, and strong emotions. For example, a married woman whose husband left her for someone else may be so immersed in her emotional reactions that she cannot be objective about the role she played in the breakup of her marriage. In some settings, clients deliberately try to conceal, or even distort, information. Abusive parents, for example, may deny they have abused their children. Alcoholics, because of the nature of the addictive process, are likely to deny they have a drinking problem. Correctional clients may try to conceal some of their illegal activities.

A client's verbal report should be respected as valid until additional information indicates otherwise. In some settings, as in protective services, it is often necessary to verify a client's denial that a problem exists by checking with other sources, such as neighbors, relatives, and school personnel.

Assessment Forms

Many agencies, before or after the first interview, ask clients to supply such information as name, address, telephone number, employer, years of school completed, marital status, description of problem, and names of family members. Such information is most efficiently collected by having the client fill out a form.

Self-report forms can also be used in the assessment process. Some clients, particularly adolescents, may be more relaxed and more truthful if they can answer questions on a form, while being assured that only helping professionals at the agency will see the answers. Sources such as Fischer and Corcoran (2006), Thyer and Wodarski (2004), and Bloom, Fischer, and Orme (2006) can acquaint social workers with available assessment forms and their proper use.

A worker who chooses to use a self-report instrument should be knowledgeable about the instrument and guidelines for its use. Research on its reliability and validity should be carefully studied to evaluate its usefulness. Also, the worker needs to use common sense in interpreting the results. Like so many other parts of the assessment process, a test result is a starting point, rather than an end product.

Computer-Assisted Assessment Forms

Nurius and Hudson (1993) developed a computer-based evaluation tool that includes the Walmyr Assessment Scales. These scales were developed by Hudson (1992) and include scales that measure self-esteem, depression, anxiety, clinical stress, peer relations, homophobia, sexual attitudes, alcohol involvement, marital satisfaction, sexual satisfaction, physical abuse of partner, nonphysical abuse of partner, parental attitude toward children, children's attitudes toward father and mother, family relations, sibling relations, children's behavior, and a general screening inventory. Clients can complete the scales manually or on a personal computer.

Computer programs accommodate different types of scales, including self-anchored, single-item, multiple-item, checklists, and multidimensional rating scales. Hepworth, Rooney, and Larsen (1997) note,

> Computer-aided assessment deserves the attention of practitioners. Clients reportedly respond well to this technology. The greatest potential for use of this tool derives from the computer's ability to process, integrate, and synthesize data from expanded sources of information. The computer's objectivity also reduces evaluative errors caused by subjective interpretations of data by practitioners. (p. 202)

Collateral Sources

Information is sometimes collected from collateral sources: friends, relatives, neighbors, physicians, other social agencies, teachers, and others who may be able to provide relevant information. In some cases, clients have received social services from a number of other agencies. Summary information about such clients is often obtained from these agencies.

Some workers overlook collateral sources; as a result, potentially valuable information is not collected. Less frequently, workers spend too much time gathering collateral information. In social work practice, a practitioner needs to exercise prudence in deciding what information is needed. In many circumstances, it is essential to get the client's verbal consent and have the client sign release-of-information forms before contacting collateral sources. (See Chapter 2 for a description of confidentiality and release-of-information forms.)

Psychological Tests

There are a variety of personality and intelligence tests. Most psychological tests are designed to be administered by psychologists. The tests that Hudson (1992) developed for clinical social workers, however, are an exception.

Caution should be used with psychological tests, because most are not designed to be administered or interpreted by social workers. Such administration and interpretation is the responsibility of psychologists. In addition, most personality tests have low validity and reliability and should be used with extreme caution, if at all.

Nonverbal Behavior

Clients' nonverbal behavior provides a valuable source of information. As practitioners become more experienced, they give greater attention to, and become more competent at, identifying and interpreting nonverbal cues. These cues are invaluable in identifying what clients are actually thinking and feeling. Nonverbal cues include gestures, posture, breathing patterns, tension in facial and neck muscles, facial color, eye movements, choice of clothes, physical appearance, eye contact, and tone of voice. Such cues give information about stress levels, kinds of feelings being experienced, and whether the client is telling the truth. For example, a client who folds his arms over his chest and frowns every time a worker brings up a particular topic is conveying valuable information about his feelings related to that topic.

Interactions with Significant Others and Home Visits

Observing a client interacting with people who are important in her life reveals a lot of information. These significant others include family members, other close relatives, peers, friends, and neighbors. The way a client presents herself in an office may differ dramatically from the way she interacts at home. In an office setting, a client may present an image that is atypical for her. A home visit provides information not only about how a client interacts with significant others but also about environmental factors. For example, a home visit investigating a charge that a single mother is neglecting her children will reveal information about home cleanliness, available food and diet, presence of animals (including pets and rats), presence of cockroaches and insects, available clothing, possible drug abuse by the parent, home interactions between mother and children, interactions between the mother and neighbors, type of neighborhood, and financial circumstances.

Social work emphasizes the importance of assessing the person-in-environment, and home visits by the social worker are an integral part of assessing the environmental factors that affect a client. Remember that an office setting is an unnatural arena for family interaction. In an unnatural setting, families are less likely to interact as they do at home. Most people are more relaxed in their own homes, and a home visit can help clients feel more accepted and less anxious.

Nevertheless, like conclusions drawn from any source of information, conclusions drawn from observed interaction, even at the client's home, can be erroneous. The way family members interact while being observed may be atypical of how they interact when they know they are not being observed. In addition, many clients feel some discomfort if the worker is better educated than they and has a higher societal status.

Worker's Conclusions from Direct Interactions

Clients often manifest similar interactional patterns in their social relationships. The way clients interact with a worker therefore provides clues to their difficulties or successes in interactions with others. Some of the many ways in which a worker may experience clients include their being nonassertive, passive, submissive, aggressive, withdrawn, passive-aggressive, personable, caring, manipulative, highly motivated, insecure, or dependent. Such observations can provide valuable information about a client's problematic behavior.

I once counseled a 22-year-old college student who complained that her roommates used her as a "doormat." They frequently borrowed her car, failed to pay for gas, wore her clothes without asking, and ate the food she bought without asking. In the interview she came across as nonassertive (in her verbal and nonverbal communication) and as making extraordinary efforts to please me. I pointed out these specific behaviors to her and asked whether she might be inadvertently communicating through these behaviors that she would not object to her roommates "using her things." She thought about it for awhile and acknowledged that my assessment was probably accurate. She was then instructed in how to express her concerns assertively to her roommates. With role-playing, she gradually acquired the confidence to confront her roommates about these concerns.

There are cautions and limitations to using your personal conclusions to assess a client's interactions with others. A client may interact atypically with a social worker because she or he wants to convey an atypical image. Just as some people change their patterns when interacting with a police officer, some clients seek to convey an atypical image when interacting with a worker. Also, the workers personality may lead clients to interact atypically. For example, if a worker comes across as aggressive and highly confrontative, the client is likely to become either passive and submissive or aggressive. Therefore, to use observations effectively in assessing clients' behaviors, the worker must have substantial awareness of self and of how he or she tends to affect others during interactions. The worker also must convey a nonjudgmental attitude. For lasting change to occur, most clients need to feel competent. To feel competent, most clients need to value and believe in themselves.

Exercise 3.2: Assessing a Family

Goal: This exercise is designed to assist you in learning how to write an assessment of a family. (Please code the names of the family members for confidentiality reasons.)

Step 1:   Briefly describe a family-including coded names of the members, ages, gender of each member, race or ethnic background, occupations of members, educational levels achieved by each, religion, relationships among family members, health issues, arrests and convictions, important personality characteristics of members, special interests of members, political orientations, family values, family activities, other systems affecting this family, and so forth.

Step 2:   Describe the current problems and challenges this family has.

Step 3:   Specify the strengths or resources this family has for meeting its problems and challenges.

Step 4:   Specify the recommended courses of action you believe this family should take to better handle its problems and challenges.

KNOWLEDGE USED IN MAKING AN ASSESSMENT

Extensive knowledge of human behavior and the social environment is needed for a high degree of accuracy when assessing the problems of a client system. As Hepworth and Larsen (1986) noted,

> To assess the problems of a client system (individual, couple, or family) . . . requires extensive knowledge about that system as well as careful consideration of the multifarious systems (e.g., economic, legal, educational, medical, religious, social, interpersonal) that impinge upon the client system. Moreover, to assess the functioning of an individual entails evaluating various aspects of that person's functioning. For example, one must consider dynamic interactions among the biophysical, cognitive, emotional, cultural, behavioral, and motivational subsystems and the relationships of those interactions to problematic situations. (p. 172)

At first glance, learning about all the factors that Hepworth and Larsen mention seems overwhelming, but such knowledge is obtained in college from a variety of social work courses. A key course or courses in most social work programs is human behavior and the social environment. Practice and policy courses also cover some of these areas. Other disciplines that provide background information are sociology, psychology, anthropology, biology, political science, women's studies, ethnic studies, history, communication, philosophy, religious studies, and economics.

In addition, the overall purpose of an assessment gives considerable focus to what knowledge is needed. For example, a social worker assessing an older adult applicant for placement in a nursing home would first need to know the nursing home's criteria for accepting applicants. Such criteria may include financial resources, medical conditions, physical strengths and impairments, emotional and behavioral patterns, special needs, level of cognitive functioning, and degree of willingness to enter a nursing home. Based on the nursing home's criteria, the social worker would then obtain information from the client, family members, physicians, and other relevant sources to determine the extent to which the client meets the criteria.

A careful assessment sharpens the focus on what factors should be examined. For example, for a fourth-grade child who is performing considerably below his grade level in schoolwork, the following variables might be examined: Does he have a learning disability? What is his IQ? Is he having emotional difficulties? Does he have low self-esteem? Is low self-esteem contributing to his low level of performance? Does he have a visual or hearing impairment or other medical problems? Are factors in his home and family life influencing his school performance? What specific educational subjects and tasks *is* he doing fairly well at, and which is he having the most trouble with? How does he interact with peers and with teachers? Has he experienced significant traumas in the past that may still be affecting him? Is he involved in using and perhaps abusing drugs? Is he motivated to do his best in school? How does he feel about his school performance?[2]

The theory or theories a practitioner uses have a major influence on what is examined during an assessment. For example, Freudian psychology focuses on pathology, or unconscious processes, on fixations during a child's development, on sexuality, and on traumatic experiences during childhood. In contrast, rational therapy asserts that thinking patterns determine emotions and actions, and therefore the focus is on identifying client self-talk that leads to unwanted emotions and dysfunctional behaviors. (Module 1 summarizes rational therapy.) What workers look for in their analysis has a big effect on the outcome. For example, practically everyone has traumatic early childhood experiences—so it is not surprising that an adherent of Freudian psychology doing an assessment would identify some traumatic early childhood experiences and then hypothesize them as causes of the client's current problems. Similarly, all individuals talk to themselves in negative ways at times, so it is not surprising that a rational therapist would find evidence to support his or her theory in an assessment.

The worker's favorite theories of assessment and intervention can have enormous consequences for the client. For example, adherents of Freudian psychology are much more inclined to assess a person as psychotic (because they believe mental illness exists) than are adherents of reality therapy, who believe that mental illness is a myth. (Module 3 describes reality therapy.)

---

[2]Additional material elsewhere in this text may be valuable in conducting an assessment: Chapter 4, how to write a social history; Chapters 4 and 5, interviewing and counseling (helpful when gathering information from clients and from collateral resources); Chapters 6 and 7, group dynamics; Chapter 8, family functioning and family systems (useful in assessing families); Chapter 9, how to analyze social welfare organizations; Chapter 10, how to assess community needs and how to conduct a community needs assessment; Chapter 12, diversity and populations-at-risk; Chapter 13, spirituality.

Most theories of human behavior have not been proven. Many practitioners make the mistake of assuming that their favorite theory or theories are factual. When an assessment is based on a theory of human behavior, the practitioner should be aware that the results of the assessment rest on the accuracy of the theory. Practitioners need to realize that their assessment of someone is not "gospel" but only a hypothesis. (See the section on evidence-based practice in Chapter 11.)

Exercise 3.3: Assessing a Group

Goal: This exercise is designed to assist you in learning how to assess a group. (In writing this assessment, it may be valuable to read Chapters 6 and 7.)

Step 1:   Briefly describe a group you have participated in—such as a student social work club, a church group, or a group in high school. In your description, cover the following:

- Goals of the group
- Characteristics of members
- When the group was formed
- How decisions are made
- Who has the most power in making decisions
- Group norms
- Group activities and projects
- Hidden agendas of some group members
- Level of cohesiveness of group
- Disruptive behavior displayed by some members
- Roles of officers in the group
- Outside systems affecting this group

Step 2:   Describe the current problems and challenges this group has.

Step 3:   Specify the strengths or resources this group has for meeting its problems and challenges.

Step 4:   Specify the recommended courses of action that you believe this group should take to better handle its problems and challenges.

ENVIRONMENTAL SYSTEMS EMPHASIS

As described in Chapter 1, social work is increasingly using an ecological perspective in assessing human behavior. The ecological perspective involves considering the adaptive fit of human beings and their environments—that is, the ecology of people in their "life space," which includes all the components of the social and physical environments that affect them. The ecological perspective stresses the importance of assessing the person in the environment. Such an assessment therefore focuses not only on the person but also on environmental systems.

When assessing environment, the worker should limit his or her attention to those elements that are affecting (positively or negatively) the problem situation. In some cases the elements may be obvious (for example, substandard housing and serious financial problems). In other cases the elements may be subtle (for instance, having aloof parents who give little encouragement).

Although the assessment of environmental factors should be limited to those that affect the client's problematic situations, certain basic environmental needs are universal. A partial list of these includes the following:

- Adequate housing
- Safety from hazards and safety from air, noise, and water pollution
- Opportunities for a quality education
- Adequate social support systems (for example, family and relatives, neighbors, friends, and organized groups)
- Access to quality health care
- Access to recreational facilities
- Adequate police and fire protection

- Adequate financial resources to purchase essential items for an acceptable standard of living
- Sufficient food and opportunities for a nutritional diet
- Adequate clothing
- Emotional support from significant others
- Support from significant others to be drug free

Some students majoring in social work have the misconception that social workers sit in offices and counsel clients. True, counseling is a function, but workers have many more responsibilities. They work with families, of course, but they also work with organizations and a variety of other groups to assess community needs and to meet unmet needs. For most social workers, in-office counseling is only a small fraction of the total services provided. A major part of their work involves assessing environmental systems and then endeavoring to change those systems that have a negative impact on clients. To change the environment, a worker may use a variety of skills, such as brokering, advocacy, program development, mediation, research, enabling, and case management. Here are a few examples:

- A protective services worker removes a child from a family in which she is being sexually abused and places her in a foster home.
- A worker arranges for visiting nurses and Meals on Wheels (home-delivered hot meals for homebound persons) to serve an elderly couple so they can continue to live independently.
- A worker arranges for homemaker services for a single mother with three young children; such services involve shopping, cleaning, budgeting, preparing balanced meals, doing the laundry, and teaching these skills to the mother.
- A worker works with a women's group to develop a shelter for battered women and their children in the community.
- A worker helps a community develop local chapters of needed self-help groups, such as Alcoholics Anonymous, Narcotics Anonymous, and Parents Anonymous.
- A worker refers a family with a terminally ill member to a hospice program.
- A practitioner works with parents of children with special needs to establish closer collaboration with schoolteachers to enhance the children's functioning in school.
- A worker joins with other health professionals in seeking to raise the state's licensing standards for residential treatment centers, nursing homes, or day-care centers.

Exercise 3.4: Assessing an Organization

Goal: This exercise is designed to assist you in learning how to assess an organization. (In writing this assessment, it may be valuable to read Chapter 9.)

Step 1: Briefly describe an organization. This may be an organization you have participated in, such as the department in which your social work program is located. It may be a sorority or a fraternity, a church you attend, and so on. In your description, cover the following:

- The mission and goals
- Services provided
- Organizational structure
- Funding sources
- Eligibility criteria for clients and customers
- Characteristics of clients and customers
- Number of members and employees
- Characteristics of members and employees
- Morale of members and employees
- Public image of organization
- Your overall impression of the organization

Step 2: Describe the current problems and challenges this organization has.

Step 3: Specify the strengths or resources this organization has for meeting its problems and challenges.

Step 4: Specify the recommended courses of action that you believe this organization should take to better handle its problems and challenges.

ATTENDING TO BIO-PSYCHO-SOCIAL AND CULTURAL COMPONENTS IN ASSESSMENT

As indicated earlier in this chapter, social work is increasingly using an ecological perspective in assessing human behavior; with such an emphasis, social workers need to attend to biological, psychological, sociological and cultural variables in doing an assessment. In using this conceptualization it is important to recognize that there is sometimes overlap between some of these variables. For example, the favorite leisure patterns of a family (such as practicing tai chi) can be considered to be both a sociological and a cultural factor. For another example, a person's IQ score can be considered to be both a biological and a psychological variable. To illustrate assessing a family in terms of bio-psycho-social and cultural variables, we will examine the Gomez family.

Maria Gomez came into the office of Concetta Martinez, a county protective services worker. Ms. Gomez had two black-and-blue, swollen eyes, and a cast on her wrist and lower forearm. She stated her husband had beaten her while intoxicated the previous day. She added he had also hit her two older children yesterday.

Ms. Gomez gave the following additional information. Her husband, Carlos, is generally a good husband, except when he is intoxicated—which occurs once or twice a week. Carlos and Maria have been married for the past 4 years. They have a 3-year-old daughter, Carla, Ms. Gomez has a son, Santos, 9 years old, who has a mild cognitive disability from lack of oxygen at birth. She has a daughter, 7 years old, Karina, who has been diagnosed with autism. Carlos Gomez is not the biological father of either Santos or Karina.

Ms. Gomez indicated the first few months of her marriage to Carlos were wonderful. However, after the birth of Carla, Ms. Gomez saw a side of Carlos that she had never witnessed before. Instead of coming directly home from work as a roofer, he would occasionally stop at a tavern, with some of his fellow workers, and sometimes become intoxicated. Carlos also began neglecting Maria's two older children and would become irate with Maria when she was attentive to them. Carlos also began to abuse both Maria and her two older children. Carlos would sometimes tell Maria that he was the "boss" of the family, and would not allow Maria to work outside the home—even though the family's income was below the poverty line.

The protective services agency became involved with the family after the social worker at Santos's school questioned him about his bruises. The school social worker then reported the case to the county protective services agency.

Ms. Gomez indicated her Catholic upbringing has led her to believe it would be a sin to divorce her husband.

POSSIBLE BIOLOGICAL VARIABLES IN THIS CASE

- A genetic component to Carlos Gomez's drinking behavior
- A genetic component to Karina Gomez having autism
- Santos Gomez having a cognitive disability

POSSIBLE PSYCHOLOGICAL VARIABLES IN THIS CASE

- Carlos Gomez having anger-management issues
- Carlos Gomez's drinking behavior (perhaps he is drinking due to certain unidentified psychological needs)
- The lower IQ of Santos Gomez as a result of his cognitive disability
- The learning challenges faced by Karina Gomez due to having autism

POSSIBLE SOCIOLOGICAL VARIABLES IN THIS CASE

- The family being a blended family
- Carlos Gomez's drinking behavior may partially involve the socialization patterns and expectations of his fellow workers
- The perspective of Ms. Gomez that he has to be the "boss" of his family, that he has a right to physically hit his wife and children, and that his wife should not work outside the home
- The belief of Mrs. Gomez that getting a divorce is a sin
- The family living below the poverty line
- The family facing a domestic abuse crisis, which may result in a divorce

POSSIBLE CULTURAL VARIABLES

- The perspective of Mr. Gomez that he has to be the boss of his family, and that his wife should not work outside the home
- The belief of Mrs. Gomez that her church believes it is a sin for her to divorce her husband

GUIDES FOR ASSESSING PROBLEM SYSTEMS

Assessments focus on evaluating clients' needs and problems, and the concept of "problem system" is helpful. Hepworth and Larsen (1986) defined *problem system:*

> The configuration of the client(s), other people, and elements of the environment that interact to produce the problematic situation are designated as the problem system. The problem system revolves around the client's concerns and is limited to those persons and factors directly involved in the client's ecological context. (p. 174)

The following 16 questions are useful guides for assessing problem systems.

1. What specifically are the problems? Many problems have several dimensions. It is crucial in an assessment to articulate the subproblems and dimensions of the problem as specifically and accurately as possible. For example, a 27-year-old wife with two children whose husband is killed in a traffic accident caused by a drunk driver may have a variety of needs and problems. She will probably undergo several emotional reactions to the death (including denial of the tragedy, depression, anger at the drunk driver, possible guilt over unresolved conflicts she had with her husband, anger that the husband left her with two children to raise alone) and nightmares. Because intensive grieving is highly stressful, she may come down with one or more stress-related illnesses (such as skin rashes, ulcers, or hypertension). She may seek to escape her problems by using drugs. She is likely to have financial difficulties caused by loss of her husband's income. She will need companionship and emotional support. Her children may have a variety of emotional reactions to the death, which they will need help in handling. She may need help in learning to take on the child-care responsibilities previously performed by her husband. She may face a sharp reduction in her standard of living with the loss of her husband's income. She may be forced to seek a job (if she is not working) or to seek a higher-paying job. She may be forced to apply for public assistance benefits and have to cope with the embarrassment she may feel about being on welfare. She may need legal help to receive any death benefits she is entitled to. At some point in the future, she may have to decide whether to begin dating again. To do an accurate assessment, the social worker must identify, prioritize, and specify these problems and subproblems. Subproblems not identified in an assessment will not be combated in the problem-solving phase.

2. How does the client view the problems? The meanings that clients assign to negative events in their lives are often as important as, or more important than, the events themselves. For example, a woman may end a relationship with a man she has been engaged to for over a year. The man's view of the breakup will largely determine the problems he faces.

Let's assume he tells himself the following: "Life is not worth living. My life is ruined forever. I might just as well end it right now." Such a person is very depressed and perhaps suicidal. These are the problems he then needs help with. In contrast, let's assume he tells himself the following: "I'll miss her somewhat, but it's probably best we end it now. The last 3 or 4 months we apparently grew in different directions. I'm somewhat relieved she broke up with me, as I was thinking about ending the relationship myself. It's easier with both of us wanting out of the relationship. I'll soon find someone else to date." In this case, the man will probably be somewhat sad but also relieved that the relationship is over. With such views, he may have little need for social services.

3. Who is involved in the problem system? The problem system includes all the people who are involved in producing the problematic situation. In the example in which the husband was killed in a traffic accident, the problem system would definitely include the surviving wife and her two children. The problem system also may include others who are highly involved with this family, such as in-laws, other relatives, neighbors, friends, or employers. Such people may need help for the grief they are experiencing, and some may be part of the intervention process by becoming a social support system for the wife and her children. Another problem system that may or may not be identified is the drunk driver and his close family members. The drunk driver and his family may need help for the guilt and remorse they are experiencing, and the driver is probably also in need of help for his drinking problem.

4. *How are the participants involved?* In this aspect of the assessment process, the focus is on identifying the roles that each person plays in the problem system. Some systems become very complex. For example, a multiproblem family will require considerable analysis to determine the roles played by each member. In a multiproblem family, several problems need to be identified. For each problem, each family member may be playing one or more roles. Detailed information is needed about how each person affects and is affected by others.

5. *What are the causes of the problems?* Frequently, identifying the causes of problems will suggest ways to intervene. If a husband abuses his wife when he is angry, then helping him learn alternative ways to vent his anger (such as jogging or expressing his feelings in an assertive rather than an aggressive manner) may be constructive. If he abuses his wife when under stress, then instructing him in stress management techniques (such as relaxation techniques) may be useful. If he abuses his wife only when intoxicated, he may benefit from an alcohol treatment program.

When making an assessment, remember that all human behavior is purposeful. A powerful way of analyzing human behavior is as follows:

$$\text{Antecedents} \rightarrow \text{Thought Processes} \rightarrow \text{Behavior} \rightarrow \text{Consequences}$$

The following is an example:

Antecedent: Jim Schroeder, age 20, is raised in a family and peer culture that glorifies sexual conquests. He is on his second date with a woman and is alone with her late in the evening in her apartment.

Thought Processes: "She is really sexy. Since I've wined and dined her twice, it's time for her to show her appreciation. She wants it as much as I do. I'll show her what a great lover I am. She may protest a little, but I can overcome that. Once we get involved sexually, she'll be emotionally committed to me."

Behavior: Date rape.

Consequences: The woman is traumatized. She calls the police after Mr. Schroeder leaves. He is arrested and charged with first-degree sexual assault. The police also immediately refer the victim to a rape crisis center, and she receives medical services and extensive counseling.

Why did Mr. Schroeder commit date rape? Analyzing behavior through this model identifies the antecedents and the thought processes that led to the date rape. Once these antecedents and thought processes have been identified, interventions can be made to prevent and deter such victimization in the future. For example, Mr. Schroeder might have benefited from educational programs in middle school and high school that emphasize (a) communication about sexual interest between people who are dating rather than aggressive behavior, (b) the rights of women in our society, and (c) the consequences of date rape and the long-term effects on victims. Current interventions for Mr. Schroeder may include (a) individual counseling, (b) correctional time for having committed a serious offense, (c) probation, (d) community service, and (e) group therapy for sexual offenders—perhaps with a component that has victims of sexual assaults describe the long-term adverse effects that they experience. The only way to prevent Mr. Schroeder from committing sexual assaults in the future is to change his thought processes.

6. *Where does the problematic behavior occur?* Problematic behavior tends to occur in certain locations and not in others. A child may throw temper tantrums at home but not at school or when visiting relatives. Perhaps the child has learned that having a tantrum at home manipulates his parents into giving him what he wants; perhaps he has also learned that throwing a tantrum elsewhere results in ridicule instead of getting what he wants. Identifying where problematic behavior does *not* occur is as important as identifying where it does occur. Both may provide clues to factors that trigger the behavior and factors that prevent it from occurring. For example, a married couple may get into heated arguments when they visit the wife's parents but not when they visit the husband's parents. Perhaps certain factors lead to increased tension when the couple visits the wife's parents—such as the husband's feeling he is being put down and not accepted by the wife's parents. An excellent way to determine why arguments occur at the wife's parents' home is to ask each spouse what the arguments were about and why they occurred.

7. *When does the problematic behavior occur?* Closely related to *where* the problematic behavior occurs is the question of *when* it occurs. The process of identifying when problematic behavior occurs and when it does not occur frequently reveals valuable clues to factors that trigger the behavior. A client who frequently becomes depressed at a certain time of the year may be grieving about a serious loss that occurred at that time some years ago—such as the death of a loved one or a divorce—or the client may be suffering from seasonal affective disorder (SAD). Identifying when serious arguments occur for a married couple may suggest factors that trigger the conflict: one or both drinking at a party, one having contact with someone she or he dated in the past, one spouse participating in activities that the other is excluded from, or a misbehaving child (the parents may disagree about discipline). A child may feign a headache or throw a temper tantrum when she has to go someplace she does not want to go or when she is told to do something (such as studying her spelling words) that she views as unpleasant. A male in a romantic relationship may start talking about taking his life whenever his woman friend suggests they stop dating. A person with a drinking problem may drink to excess whenever she has intense unwanted emotions, such as anger, frustration, depression, and feelings of insecurity. Once the antecedents that trigger the problematic behavior are identified, the intervention phase can then focus on making the kinds of changes that will reduce the frequency of the behavior.

8. What are the frequency, intensity, and duration of the problematic behavior? Someone who becomes intoxicated once or twice a year may not have a drinking problem, whereas someone who becomes intoxicated once or twice a week probably does. Someone who becomes depressed for a day or two every 3 months probably does not have a serious problem with depression, but someone who is depressed daily certainly does.

Closely related to the frequency of the problematic behavior is its intensity. Someone who is mildly depressed is much more functional than someone who is so severely depressed that he sleeps 15 hours a day, cries frequently during his waking hours, and cannot think rationally. Many other problematic behaviors have varying degrees of intensity, such as extent of intoxication, extent of violent behavior when angry, intensity of family arguments, and extent of overeating.

The duration of the behavior is also an important assessment variable. For example, when someone is intoxicated, how long does she continue to drink to maintain the intoxication? Or, if he is angry or depressed or under high stress, what is the typical duration of the problem behavior? A marital disagreement that lasts 3 weeks is obviously much more serious than one that lasts 20 minutes.

An assessment of the frequency, intensity, and duration of the behavior helps specify its severity and clarify its impact on the client and members of the family

9. What is the history of the problematic behavior? Examining the history of a problem often identifies the events that triggered the dysfunctional behavior. For example, if an eighth-grade child develops a school phobia, looking into the history of the problem would first seek to identify when the phobia began to occur. Then what was happening in the child's life at this time could be identified. What made her fear going to school? Perhaps she was not getting the grades she desired. Perhaps her classmates were making her life miserable. Perhaps her parents were having severe marital conflict, and she erroneously believed that by staying home she could help ease the marital conflict. Perhaps it is part of a larger anxiety-related problem that has been developing for years. Identifying the antecedents or triggers will help in designing an intervention plan to reduce the frequency and severity of the behavior.

However, identifying the antecedents that initially caused the dysfunctional behavior may not fully isolate the current factors that are maintaining the behavior. For example, a child may have developed a school phobia because two of his classmates were bullying him; but they moved to another city, so other factors are probably causing the child to want to stay home, such as being able to watch television or play all day and not having any schoolwork to do.

For voluntary clients, it is also often revealing to seek out the *precipitating events* that led them to seek help. Often, their problems have existed for months, even years, and identifying the precipitating events yields valuable information. For example, a person who has been bulimic for 2½ years seeks help after she notices blood in her vomit. She believes she might have internal bleeding; she is referred to a physician who finds that her esophagus is severely damaged. A married couple who have been arguing periodically for 3 years seek counseling after they have their first serious physical fight; both are fearful their feuding has entered a new phase that could potentially be life threatening to both. Precipitating events can usually be identified by the practitioner's asking (and probing) clients to identify the reasons for seeking help at this time.

Involuntary clients usually have a crisis or a series of crises that result in their being seen by a practitioner. A practitioner needs to obtain as much information about these crises as possible (often from collateral sources) to determine why an involuntary client is being referred and what his or her problems are. Such information is also useful in confronting the involuntary client. (Many involuntary clients deny they have a problem.)

10. What does the client want? A key social work value is to start where the client is at. In an initial interview with a client, whether voluntary or involuntary, it is crucial to address any problems that the client identifies. Failure to do so may leave the client feeling helpless or annoyed, either of which interferes with the eventual intervention effort. In addition, too often assessment is made from the practitioner's perspective rather than from the client's. An adult services worker for a public welfare department was assigned the following case. A 78-year-old man was living alone in a house on a farm where he had been born and raised. The house was in a shambles; it was filthy and had no running water or toilet facilities. Dishes were washed (when they were washed) in rainwater. A small wood-burning stove in the kitchen was used to heat the house. The elderly man was mentally alert but suffered from a variety of minor medical problems: He was overweight and had gout and hypertension. He drank to excess and also rolled and smoked his own cigarettes, which was a potential fire hazard especially when he was intoxicated. The worker decided it would be best for the man to be placed in a nursing home where adequate care could be given. To the worker's surprise, the man refused and bluntly stated, "I was born and raised here, and I'm going to die here. If you would get a court order to place me in a nursing home, which I don't believe you will be able to get, I'll give up the will to live, and die quickly there." The worker was shocked. She discussed the case with her supervisor, and her supervisor pointed out that she may have been viewing the situation from what she wanted rather than what the client wanted. The worker agreed.

This example points out that what a worker views as being a problem may not be viewed as a problem by a client. If the client chooses to live in a substandard living situation, that is *his* choice—and he has a right to do so, *as long as he is not hurting anyone else in the process* If, however, young children were living with this elderly man, then child neglect would need to be considered. Should that be the case, changes in living conditions would need to be made, or the children might need to be removed from the home.

In any assessment, it is crucial to accurately obtain the client's view of the problem and what the client wants. If the client's desires are realistic and obtainable, satisfying them should generally be a major goal of the helping process. If what the client wants is not realistic, the reasons that his or her desires cannot be fulfilled need to be tactfully explained.

11. How has the client attempted to handle the problem? The ways in which clients have attempted to cope with their problems provide valuable information during an assessment. Clients may have tried ways of resolving their problems that did not work. Those strategies can be then eliminated from consideration in the problem-solving phase.

Suppose a client has tried strategies that were partially successful. Perhaps with increased effort or some modifications, they will work. For example, a client suffering from a high level of stress learned to relax using imagery relaxation. However, she did not think to use the technique when she was highly anxious or frustrated. She was then instructed to set aside 15 minutes every morning before going to work and 15 minutes in the evening to practice the technique. Structuring imagery relaxation into daily activities proved to be a useful way of helping her combat the stress.

Examining the strategies that clients have used to try to resolve their problems can reveal valuable information about their coping and problem-solving skills. If clients have marked deficits in problem solving, it may be helpful to instruct them in the problem-solving approach (see Chapter 7 for a description).

Some clients respond to interpersonal difficulties by becoming passive or nonassertive. Others become aggressive. If either is the case, it may be desirable to instruct clients in using assertiveness to handle interpersonal conflict (see Module 2 for a description of assertiveness training).

Often, clients have good problem-solving and interpersonal skills in some situations but not in others. For example, a schoolteacher was able to handle disruptive students in his classroom but was ineffective in dealing with his own children. A closer examination revealed that he was divorced and was fearful that if he disciplined his children they would want to live with his ex-wife. Through counseling, he came to realize that his children would respect him more if he more clearly specified and enforced behavioral limits. Once this was accomplished, he was able to use the same child management skills he used in the classroom with his own children.

12. What skills does the client need to combat the problem? An assessment of a problematic situation should also identify the skills that clients need to resolve their difficulties. If a parent is having difficulties with a child, needed skills may include listening, negotiating, setting limits, following through on consequences, and nurturing. If a couple is having marital conflicts, they may need problem-solving, communication, listening, and conflict management skills. (Sometimes helping a couple learn these skills is more productive in the long run than helping them resolve their present conflicts.) If a client frequently loses considerable sums of money while gambling, he may need to learn how to say no assertively when his friends ask him to play poker or go to the racetrack. If a client is depressed, she may need to learn what she can do to counter the depression (see Module 1 for some strategies).

13. What are the bio-psycho-social and cultural components of the problem? See a discussion and illustration in the prior section in this chapter.

14. What external resources are needed to combat the problem? An assessment should identify not only the skills that clients need to combat their problems but also the external resources they need. A single mother on public assistance may need day-care services, transportation, and job training to help her become employable. Someone addicted to gambling may need a self-help group, such as Gamblers Anonymous, to give him the emotional support and guidance he needs to combat his addiction. A bulimic may need medical attention to assess and treat physical damage from binging and purging, one-to-one counseling to stop the binge-purge cycle, support from a self-help eating disorders group, and instruction in what is a nutritious and well-balanced diet. Once an assessment is made, a social worker often acts as a broker or case manager in connecting clients with needed services and resources. Frequently, some or all of the needed services are not provided by the practitioner's agency, and arrangements need to be made for the services to be provided by other agencies, organizations, self-help groups, and natural support systems (such as neighbors, family members, fellow workers, church groups, and social groups).

15. What are the client's resources, skills, and strengths? A quality assessment also identifies the resources, strengths, and skills that clients already possess to combat their problems. The importance of identifying such strengths has been described. Sometimes problems are resolved by empowering clients to use resources and skills they already have to mitigate their problematic behavior. Through counseling, clients who have frequent stress-related illnesses may learn that applying the following techniques will help them relax and reduce their high stress levels: positive thinking, problem solving rather than "awfulizing" about their problems, using social support systems, and being more assertive with significant others in expressing their feelings and concerns. A couple with marital problems may find their relationship improving when they treat each other with the same kind of respect that they give to strangers and acquaintances; many spouses use tact in communicating with acquaintances but not in communicating with each other. A person who is grieving about the death of a loved one may find that discussing her grief with friends and relatives not only helps ventilate her grief but also helps her develop a social support system for putting her life back together.

16. What are the recommended courses of action? The recommended courses of action are also called the *treatment plan* and the *intervention plan.* Once a client's difficulties and strengths have been assessed, the next step is to set goals and arrive at a course of action to accomplish the goals. Some authorities conceptualize goal setting and specifying recommended courses of action as a process that follows an assessment. However, in social work practice, most assessments contain a recommended course of action; therefore, this process is discussed briefly here.

Goals should be jointly agreed to by the client and the worker and should be realistic and obtainable. Goals should be geared to resolving the identified problems and should be stated in such a way that they are operational and measurable. An *operational goal* is a goal that can be directly translated into a course of action so it can be accomplished. For example, an operational goal for a nonassertive client might be to learn to be assertive with significant others, and assertiveness training might be the course of action to accomplish this goal. A *measurable goal* is a goal that is stated in such a way that the extent of progress toward attaining the goal can be measured. For example, one way to measure whether a client is making progress in becoming more assertive is for the client to record for 2 weeks the number of times he is assertive and nonassertive in interactions with significant others. The client is then given training in being assertive. Afterward, he keeps records for another 2 weeks. If the number of assertive behaviors after treatment is higher, measurable progress has occurred.

The stated courses of action should be realistic and obtainable. Generally they also should be agreed to by the client. A client who disagrees with these courses of action is unlikely to carry them out. (With some involuntary clients, there are exceptions to this guideline that the recommended courses of actions should be agreed to by the client. For example, a battering husband may not agree with his probation officer's presentence recommendation to the court that he have no contact with his abused wife, who has filed for a divorce.)

The stated courses of action should usually be selected through the following process. After a goal is set, the client and the worker generate a list of feasible courses of action to accomplish the goal. The strengths and shortcomings of each alternative are considered. Then the client and the worker together select the course of action.

In some settings, the worker or the clinical team selects the recommended courses of action, with minimal input from the client. For example, when an assessment is done for an elderly person's admission application for a nursing home, the recommendation is usually based on the extent to which the elderly person's characteristics meet the nursing homes criteria for admission.

Exercise 3.5: Assessing a Community

Goal: This exercise is designed to assist you in learning how to assess a community. (In writing this assessment, it may be valuable to read Chapter 10.)

Step 1:   Briefly describe a community. (This may be a community you've lived in or a community you visited. It may be a community that you viewed in a movie, such as *The Help* (a film about how African American maids are treated by their white employers in the early 1960s in the South). It may be your college community.) In your description, cover the following:

- Population size
- Racial and ethnic characteristics of the population
- Major industries
- Financial circumstances of population
- Unemployment rate
- Housing patterns (homes, condos, apartments, deteriorating units, etc.)
- Major religions of the population
- Governing structure
- Who the main decision makers are
- Human services that are provided
- Transportation systems
- Climate and geography
- Self-help groups
- Community values
- Significant community activities

Step 2:   Describe the current problems and challenges this community has.

Step 3:   Specify the strengths or resources this community has for meeting its problems and challenges.

Step 4:   Specify the recommended courses of action that you believe this community should take to better handle its problems and challenges.

Step 5:   (Optional) The instructor may have each student present his or her assessment to the class, with a discussion after each presentation.

SUMMARY

The following summarizes the chapter's content in terms of the learning objectives presented at the beginning of the chapter.

1. Identify the components of an assessment.
   Assessment is a critical process in social work practice. The selection of goals and interventions largely depends on the assessment. An assessment should include not only what is wrong with a client but also the client's resources, skills, and strengths that can be used in resolving difficulties and promoting growth. Too often in the past, assessments focused only on clients' shortcomings and pathology.

   The nature of the assessment process varies significantly with the type of setting in which the social worker practices. In some settings the social worker makes an independent assessment, and in other settings the social worker is a member of a clinical team that makes an assessment. An assessment is, in essence, a working hypothesis of a client's difficulties and resources based on current data. As time passes, assessments have to be revised and updated as changes occur in the client and in his or her environment.

2. Describe the strengths perspective.

This perspective emphasizes the client's capabilities, resources, motivations, and support systems to overcome adversities and to meet challenges. This approach does not ignore the existence of social problems and dysfunctions; it instead emphasizes the client's assets in handling adversities and challenges.

3. Identify sources of information for an assessment.

Data used in making an assessment are derived from various sources: the client's verbal report, assessment forms, computer-assisted assessment forms, collateral sources, psychological tests, the client's nonverbal behavior, home visits, observation of the client interacting with significant others, and the worker's intuition after interacting with the client.

4. Specify the knowledge used in making an assessment.

To do a quality assessment, a worker needs extensive knowledge of human behavior and the social environment. An assessment may require knowledge about multifarious systems, biophysical factors, behavioral factors, motivational factors, family systems, and environmental factors. Such knowledge is obtained from a variety of courses that social work majors typically take in college. The purpose of an assessment is to give focus to the kinds of factors that are examined.

5. Describe the environmental systems emphasis in conducting an assessment.

The theory or theories of human behavior that a practitioner subscribes to will have a major influence on what is examined during the assessment. What a worker examines when conducting an assessment has a large effect on the outcome. Most theories of human behavior have not been proven; therefore, practitioners need to be aware that their assessment of someone is only a hypothesis.

Social work is increasingly using an ecological perspective to assess human behavior. An ecological perspective asserts that it is important to assess the person-in-environment.

6. Describe bio-psycho-social and cultural components in assessment.

Social workers need to attend to biological, psychological, sociological and cultural variables in doing an assessment.

7. Identify guides for assessing problem systems.

This chapter presented 16 questions that serve as guides for what to examine in conducting an assessment.

EXERCISES

1. Writing an Assessment

Goal: To give you experience in writing an assessment.

Step 1: Your instructor explains the purpose of the exercise and then summarizes the 16 key questions for writing assessments. (Alternatively, you can read these questions in the text.)

Step 2: A volunteer constructs a *contrived* problem prior to the next class period. At the next class period, your instructor interviews the volunteer about the contrived problem. The other students in the class then independently write up an assessment that covers the following topics:

a. Specific problems
b. Client's views of problems
c. People involved in the problem system
d. Roles of participants in problem system
e. Causes of problems
f. Where the problematic behavior occurs
g. When the behavior occurs
h. Frequency, intensity, and duration of the behavior
i. History of the behavior
j. Client's goals regarding this behavior
k. Strategies client has used to handle the problem

l.   Skills client needs to resolve the problem

m. External resources needed to combat the problem

n.   Client's resources, skills, and strengths

o.   Recommended courses of action

During the interview your instructor will ask questions that provide you with the data for topics a–n. A significant percentage (40%) of your grade will be based on the quality of your response to "Recommend courses of action."

Step 3:   Write up your assessment and turn it in on the designated date. Before returning the graded papers, your instructor will read one or two high-quality recommended courses of action.

Step 4:   Student discussion of the merits and shortcomings of this assignment.

2. Assessing Bio-Psycho-Social and Cultural Components

Goal: To learn to have a bio-psycho-social and cultural perspective in assessing clients.

Step 1:   Review the material in this chapter on bio-psycho-social and cultural assessment.

Step 2:   Answer the following questions about this case.

William Weatherford is a social worker, employed as a parole officer. He is assigned the case of Jim Mills, a man who has recently been paroled. The following is background information.

When Jim Mills was 2 years old his mother remarried. His stepfather beat him with 2×4's when he did not eat his food fast enough or when he did not finish what was put on his plate. He was tied with ropes and locked in closets. When Jim turned 5 he was not allowed in the house during the day. If he wet his pants he was made to wear those clothes unwashed the next day. Covered with bruises, dried urine, and feces, Jim was put outside and told to behave himself. School was another torment. He was placed in the "slow" class and labeled as antisocial when he did not play with the other children. By this time Jim recoiled if anyone came too close to him or tried to touch him.

Eventually, relatives, who believed he would soon be killed, talked his mother into allowing them to adopt him. The short, skinny child was moved from a deteriorated inner-city neighborhood to a middle-class suburb. He was given tutors to help him catch up with his schoolwork. He joined cub scouts and had his own body-building equipment. It sounds like a happy ending—it wasn't.

One snowy winter evening his family went out to dinner with the next-door neighbors. Jim, now a teenager, walked over to talk to that neighbor's daughter, a friend who attended the same high school. They drank some Coke and watched television. They snacked on some pizza. The girl told Jim to leave because their parents would soon be getting home. Jim did something entirely different. He picked up a knife and stabbed her over 50 times. Knife in hand, he walked home, leaving a trail of blood in the sparkling snow. He climbed into bed without changing his bloody clothes and went to sleep. Police found him there within the hour.

The girl's family was well known in the community. The press had a heyday. Jim answered any question he was asked, except for questions about the night of the murder. The court showed some leniency. Jim was sentenced to 25 years of prison. His survivor instinct intact, he learned many things in prison, some good and some bad. He became the prison Brewmeister when he found out that drinking would take away some of the pain. He discovered drugs. He found out they would take away some of the pain. He found out he was not "slow," but had an exceptionally high IQ. He found the prison library, where he devoured books on philosophy, religion, history, and metaphysics. He was initiated into the Native American Sweat Lodge. The Sweat Lodge is a ceremonial sauna and is an important event in many Native American cultures. It represents acceptance and respect from fellow Native Americans.

When Jim had done a little over 15 years of his time, he was paroled. The family that adopted him had stayed in touch but did not want him to return to their neighborhood. So he returned to the first neighborhood in the inner city to live with his aunt.

a.   What are the possible biological variables in this case?

b.   What are the possible psychological variables in this case?

c.   What are the possible sociological variables in this case?

d.   What are possible cultural variables in this case?

Step 3:   The leader asks for volunteers to share with the class what they wrote. The class then discusses the usefulness of identifying these variables when conducting an assessment.

SOCIAL WORK WITH INDIVIDUALS: INTERVIEWING

LEARNING OBJECTIVES

Social work practice with individuals is aimed at helping them on a one-to-one basis to resolve personal and social problems. Perhaps the two most essential skills social workers need in working with individuals are interviewing and counseling skills. This chapter presents material on how to interview; the next chapter focuses on how to counsel. This chapter will help prepare students to:

Describe three types of social work interviews
Comprehend how to begin and close interviews
Describe how to phrase effective questions
Understand guidelines on note taking during interviews
Comprehend guidelines for tape recording and videotaping of interviews

THREE TYPES OF SOCIAL WORK INTERVIEWS

Most social work interviews can be classified as informational (to obtain data for a social study or for a social history), assessment (to arrive at an appraisal), or intervention (to help clients change). Often, the three types overlap. For example, a protective services worker in the initial interview with a couple suspected of child abuse will often obtain background information about the family members and seek to arrive at an appraisal of whether child abuse has occurred. If abuse is occurring, the worker may also begin helping the family make changes to end further abuse. Despite overlap, the three types of interviews differ in the way they are structured and conducted.

Informational or Social History Interviews

Informational interviews are designed to obtain background or life history material related to the client's personal or social problem. The purpose is not to learn all there is to know about the person's background but to seek information that will enable the worker (or agency) to better understand the client so that decisions can be made regarding the kinds of services that should be provided. Such information includes both objective facts and subjective feelings and attitudes. In addition to the client, others interviewed or contacted may include parents, friends, other relatives, employers, and other agencies having contact with the client (such as social service agencies, police departments, and schools).

The specific information desired in a social history varies somewhat from agency to agency. An adoption agency, for example, is interested in information about the child-rearing philosophies of potential adoptive parents, whereas a sheltered workshop is interested in the specific work capacities of potential clients. As the social history example in Exhibit 4.1 shows, a social history usually has fact sheet information (name, age, occupation, and so on), plus information about the presenting question or problem, early childhood experiences and development, family background, school performance, dating and marital history, employment history, contact with other agencies, and general impressions. The desired objectives and formats of social histories vary greatly from agency to agency

Here are a few examples of informational interviews: A social worker at a mental hospital seeks background information to better understand the problems and social functioning of an inpatient. A probation officer conducts a social investigation to guide the court in dealing with someone charged with a felony. A

Exhibit 4.1   Example of a Social History

WISCONSIN STATE HOSPITAL
SOCIAL HISTORY
Donald Cooper*

Birth date: June 30, 1986

Occupation: Accountant

Race: White

Religion: Unaffiliated

Marital status: Divorced, and currently engaged

Height: 5'10"

Weight: 180

Home Address: 2030 Lincoln Drive
Milwaukee, Wisconsin

Phone: (414) 726-4567

PRESENTING PROBLEMS: Mr. Cooper was committed to this hospital by Judge Chewenka of Washington County for a 60-day observation period. Mr. Cooper was arrested on August 1 on the charge of sexually molesting a minor earlier in the day. The reported victim was an 8-year-old girl whom Mr. Cooper reportedly enticed into his car at the girl's school, and then fondled her genitals after driving to a secluded area.

Mr. Cooper has been arrested on three previous occasions for fondling young girls; each time the charges were dropped after Mr. Cooper consented to receiving psychiatric care. Besides minor traffic violations, he has no other arrest record.

FAMILY BACKGROUND AND EARLY HISTORY: Mr. Cooper's father, Dave Cooper, has been a dairy farmer near Stevens Point all his life. His income has been marginal through the years. Dave Cooper gives the impression of being a meek, submissive person who reportedly has a drinking problem. Dave Cooper indicated he has no idea why his son would become involved in his current difficulties.

Dave Cooper's wife died when Donald was 8 years old, after being ill with cancer for a relatively short time. Dave Cooper mentioned this was a substantial blow to the children and to himself. He added that he has not as yet fully adjusted to his wife's death.

Donald has one sibling, Mary, who is 1 year older. She is currently married to a serviceman, and they are now stationed in San Diego.

Dave Cooper reported his son's developmental milestones were normal, except he sometimes was enuretic until age 5. Dave Cooper reported Donald had a very close relationship with his mother but seemed to adjust satisfactorily to her death. Dave Cooper continued to provide and care for the two children after his wife died.

SCHOOL PERFORMANCE: Mr. Cooper received slightly above-average grades in elementary and high school and received a 2-year associate degree in accounting from Portage County Vocational School. Mr. Cooper reported he neither disliked nor liked school and that he was somewhat of a loner during his school years.

GENERAL HEALTH: Mr. Cooper reports his health has been good. He had a hernia operation at age 20 with no lingering complications.

MARITAL HISTORY: Mr. Cooper was married at age 19 to Nancy Riehle, whom he met in high school. It was a forced marriage and ended after 1 year because of "incompatibility." His ex-wife was interviewed and had no explanation for his involvement in his current difficulties. She is currently receiving $400 per month in child support, and is currently a typist and caring for their 10-year-old daughter. The daughter has not been informed of her father's current confinement; she seldom has contact with her father. The ex-wife appeared to be very dominating and overly critical of Donald, whom she views as "morally immature."

Mr. Cooper is currently engaged to Mary Gautier, and the marriage was planned for December 2 of this year. Miss Gautier indicated she is now reconsidering the upcoming marriage. She is a charming, attractive, petite person currently employed at Jones High School as a secretary. She mentioned she was shocked on being informed of her fiance's arrest, and had not previously known about his prior arrests. She mentioned she still loves Donald, but feels that unless his reported involvement with young girls is discontinued, it would be better for them to break their engagement. She mentioned she has had sexual relations with Mr. Cooper about twice a week for the past 6 months, which she described as "satisfying" for her, and she also thought for her fiance.

EMPLOYMENT HISTORY: Mr. Cooper has been employed as an accountant at Paul Realty Company for the past 5 years. His supervisor, John Namman, reported his work is reliable, that he associates well with other employees, but is sometimes "moody." Mr. Cooper reported he likes his current job and hopes he can return after his confinement.

Prior to this position, Mr. Cooper worked as an accountant for two other firms where his work was also reported as acceptable. While in high school and in vocational school, he helped his father on the farm.

PRIOR CONTACT WITH SOCIAL AGENCIES: Since Mr. Cooper's first arrest for fondling young girls 6 years ago, he has been seeing Dr. Timmer at Midwest Psychiatric Center occasionally.

---

*Names and other identifying information have been changed in this social history.

Exhibit 4.1 *(continued)*

Dr. Timmer reported Mr. Cooper's difficulty is due to the following past history. (Mr. Cooper also related these events in an interview.)

Mr. Cooper mentioned his family life was fairly normal until his mother died when he was 8 years old. His father then began drinking. When sober, his father was considerate, quiet, and an adequate family provider. However, when intoxicated, he was verbally, and sometimes physically, abusive to the children. The children became terrified when they knew their father was drinking. Therefore, when they heard him coming home, they learned to hide by crawling under a blanket. While under the blanket, in fear, they began fondling each other, which seemed to make them feel better. Now, Mr. Cooper mentioned that when he feels "moody" or depressed, he seeks young girls to fondle, hoping to feel better again.

In treating Mr. Cooper, Dr. Timmer has been using a modified psychoanalytic approach, but he admits the therapy has apparently not yet curbed Mr. Coopers involvement with young girls.

GENERAL IMPRESSIONS: In the interviews, Mr. Cooper appeared to be very concerned about his fondling behaviors with young girls and displayed motivation to curb the deviant behavior. He appears to have traditional middle-class values. He is fairly attractive, and has a pleasant personality.

Mr. Cooper, however, has had repeated incidents of involvement with young girls, even while under psychiatric care. The latest incident occurred at a time when Mr. Cooper is engaged, and as his fiancee reported, when he is having satisfying relations with her. His deviant behavior is apparently deeply entrenched. Sexual activities such as Mr. Cooper's are difficult to change. Perhaps rational therapy (see Module 1) might be used to teach him other ways of handling his emotions of depression and moodiness, instead of through seeking to fondle young girls. Also, an arrangement might be made with the local mental health center to have Mr. Cooper call and receive immediate counseling (perhaps staying overnight at the center) whenever he has a strong urge to fondle young girls.

---

worker for a community welfare council interviews people in a multiproblem neighborhood to identify what they view as their most urgent unmet needs. A worker at a nursing home does a social history on a new resident to obtain information about current social and personal problems and about special interests, which will help determine the kinds of services and activities that are needed to meet the resident's needs and interests.

Assessment Interviews

Assessment or decision-making interviews are more focused in purpose than informational interviews. The questions asked in assessment interviews are aimed at making *specific* decisions involving human services. For example, a protective services worker investigates a child abuse complaint to determine whether abuse is occurring. A public assistance worker interviews an unmarried woman who is pregnant to determine eligibility for financial assistance. A vocational rehabilitation counselor interviews a client with a developmental disability to determine eligibility for a range of services, including financial assistance, vocational training, and sheltered workshop participation. A social worker at a residential facility for persons with developmental disabilities interviews the parents of a child with a severe cognitive disability to obtain information that will be used by the admissions committee to determine whether the child should be admitted. A director of a group home for adolescent boys interviews a youth on juvenile probation who is having severe conflict with his parents to determine whether he would benefit from the group home or whether a correctional school would be more appropriate.

Intervention Interviews

The purpose of intervention interviews is to help clients make changes, or to change the social environment to help clients function better, or both. A shy parent is counseled on how to be more assertive. A depressed, lonely, or suicidal client is counseled on how to handle such problems better. A client on probation is counseled on how to apply for and find a job. A couple having marital problems are counseled on how to communicate and handle their problems better. A newly married couple distressed by the husband's premature ejaculation are counseled on how to resolve such a dysfunction (Hyde & DeLamater, 2006). A couple with problems disciplining their children might be given instructional sessions in parent effectiveness training techniques (Gordon, 1970). These are all examples of helping clients make changes.

Other intervention interviews are geared to changing the social environment to facilitate a client's social functioning. For example, the spouse of a client with a drinking problem is counseled on how to help the spouse stop drinking and develop a meaningful life separate from alcohol. Interviews may have an intervention goal without the person for whom the change is sought being present. Two examples are the following. A social worker for a family with an aging grandfather who has alzheimer's disease may meet with the admission person at a nursing home to gather information for the family for possible placement of the gentleman. A social worker working with a family with a ten-year-old autistic child (with the child failing to thrive at a public school) may meet with the principal at a private school to gather information for the family on educational and social services at this school.

Intervention interviews are the most common in social work, and therefore this text focuses mainly on this type.

THE PLACE OF THE INTERVIEW

Social work interviews can take place anywhere—in the office, in the client's home, on street corners, in restaurants, in institutions. Office interviews permit control of the physical setting, usually make the interviewee comfortable, and usually can be arranged to ensure privacy. Office interviews also reduce the worker's travel time between interviews.

Home visits have an advantage in helping the interviewer better understand the living conditions of the interviewee. Family interactions can also be observed. Some clients, such as those with severe disabilities, find it difficult or impossible to travel to an office; therefore, home visits are common in social work. Other clients find an office "foreign" to them and are more comfortable in their home or in other settings.

The home visit also offers opportunities for the worker to enter the life of the interviewee as a participant—opening a stuck door, moving furniture, holding a crying baby. However, there is also the chance that the interviewer may have to respond to conflict between family members if it occurs, and some clients may feel that a home visit suggests that the worker is spying on them. Distractions are also more likely to occur—for example, phone calls, TV programs that other family members want to watch, friends dropping by to visit.

In practice I have found that although the physical setting may have an effect on the start of an interview, the effect can almost always be handled by a skillful interviewer. For example, on a home visit where a number of other people are present, the worker can suggest to the client that they go to a restaurant where they can have a soda and talk without interruptions from other family members. The interviewer's skills are almost always more important than the setting in determining the productivity of an interview.

OPENING THE FIRST INTERVIEW

When Interviewee-Initiated

If someone has asked to see a social worker and has come to the appointment, it is best to let that person state exactly what he or she is concerned about. The counselor should, of course, greet the client with something like "Hi, I'm Jane Bernes, and I'm a counselor at this agency." After the client has been seated, the client often begins indicating his or her concerns. If this does not happen, the worker should say something brief and neutral (not to sidetrack the client) to help the client get started, such as: "You came in here to see me about something today."

Openings that are *not* as desirable include the following: (1) "I'm glad you came in this afternoon." The client may know that you are being superficial and may not in fact be glad to hear what he or she has to say. (2) "In what way can I help you?" The worker should not erroneously convey that he or she is the chief problem solver. The client owns the problem and is the primary problem solver. (3) "You have a problem?" The word *problem* in a counseling situation may suggest to the client that the worker is viewing the client as a psychiatric case.

The following are useful suggestions for starting an interview. The worker should state his or her name, and the position she holds at the agency. The worker should then ask the client his or her name. (We will now use "her" for the worker, and "his" for the client.) She invites him in, and follows the familiar social amenities—taking his coat, if he has one, offering a chair, and engaging in a little small talk (such as "it's good to see the sun today after several cloudy days"). Such small talk is designed to allow him time to check out the room, to begin to check out the worker, to start to become comfortable, and to catch his breath.

Exercise 4.1: Introducing Yourself When the Interview Is Interviewee-Initiated

Goal: This exercise is designed to give you the opportunity to practice the skill of introducing yourself.

You are a social worker at a nursing home. A family member (whom you have not previously met) of a resident wants to discuss something with you. Write the words you would say to introduce yourself—using some small talk and also inviting the family member to have a seat in your office.

When Interviewer-Initiated

Whether talking to a client, to a client's relative, or to professionals at other agencies, the worker should indicate his or her role or position at the agency and then state the purpose of the interview. Thus, a school counselor may say to a student who is receiving failing grades, "Hi, John. I'm Mr. Roberts, a social worker at this school. I asked that you see me today because I was looking at your grade report. It looks as if you are having difficulty in some of your courses. Perhaps we can talk about the reasons." A protective services worker might say, "Hi, I'm Mary Seely, a protective services worker with Rock County Social Services. Information that raises questions about the care your child is receiving has come to our attention. I realize there are always two sides to any such report, and therefore I would like to talk with you about this."

Exercise 4.2: Introducing Yourself When the Interview Is Interviewer-Initiated

Goal: This exercise is designed to give you the opportunity to practice the skill of introducing yourself while stating the purpose of the interview.

You are a juvenile probation officer for Wood County Human Services Department. Amy Harper, age 15, has recently been arrested by the police for shoplifting, Ms. Harper has not yet appeared in juvenile court. This is your first meeting with Ms. Harper. The purpose of your meeting is to begin to get information from Ms. Harper regarding her views of what happened and background information about her and her family. This information is needed so you can begin to compile your recommendation to the juvenile court about whether Ms. Harper should be placed on juvenile probation or should be offered an opportunity to attend a juvenile diversion program (which consists of 1-hour group meetings each week for 10 weeks with other first-time juvenile offenders). Write the words you would say to introduce yourself, to invite Ms. Harper to have a seat in your office, and to state the purpose of this first meeting.

CLOSING AN INTERVIEW

Closing is not always easy. Ideally, both the interviewer and the interviewee would accept the fact that the interview is ending, and the subjects being discussed would not be left hanging. Saying something like "Well, you really have serious problems, but I've got to catch my ride. When can we talk further?" would be abrupt and unprofessional. Such abrupt endings are likely to be perceived by the interviewee as being discourteous and uncaring.

It is often useful for the worker to indicate at the beginning of an interview the amount of time s/he has available for the interview. When the allotted time is nearly up, the interviewer may inform the interviewee by saying something like this: "Well, our time is just about up. Is there anything you'd like to add before we look at where we have arrived and where we now go from here?" At the end of the interview, it is often helpful to summarize what was discussed. If the interview focused only on exploring the client's problems, another interview should be set up for fuller exploration and to begin looking at alternatives.

I find it helpful to give clients "homework" assignments between interviews. A couple who are having trouble communicating with each other, for example, might be encouraged to set aside a certain amount of time each evening to discuss their personal thoughts with each other. At the next interview, this "homework" assignment is reviewed.

Reid and Shyne (1969) found that if an agency establishes a set, limited period for contact with the client (including both the number of interviews and the length of each interview), both worker and client make more productive use of the time as they mobilize their efforts to accomplish the tasks within the designated time.

Ideally, the interviewee would be emotionally at ease when the interview ends. Therefore, the interviewer should not introduce emotionally charged content at the end but should seek a reduction in intensity of emotion.

If an interviewee displays reluctance to end the interview, it is sometimes helpful to confront this directly by saying, "It appears to me that you wish we had more time." The reasons for the interviewee's reluctance can then be discussed, and perhaps another appointment can be made.

Just as it is sometimes advisable to begin an interview with small talk, a short social conversation at the end can be useful because it provides a transition out of the interview. There are many styles of closing. The style used will depend on the interviewer, the interviewee, and what was said during the interview.

At times, an interview can be closed with a restatement of the way the interviewer and interviewee agreed to proceed. Here is an example: "I'm glad you have decided to have the pregnancy test. If it's positive, give me a call so we can arrange another time to further discuss the options we briefly talked about here."

At times, the interviewer may make a more explicit summation of what was discussed, what decisions were arrived at, what questions remain to be resolved, and what actions will be taken. A somewhat different approach is to ask the interviewee to summarize the decisions he arrived at during the interview and what actions he now intends to take.

Sometimes as an interview is closing, concerns that were alluded to but not fully discussed might be mentioned as topics to be discussed at the next interview. I find that some clients first reveal their most serious concerns at the end of the interview, perhaps because they needed time to become comfortable and to gain confidence that the interviewer is a competent person who may have some useful suggestions. In such instances, the interviewer has to decide whether to extend the interview beyond the allotted time or to set up another appointment to discuss these concerns.

Benjamin (1974) observed:

> Closing is especially important because what occurs during this last stage is likely to determine the interviewee's impression of the interview as a whole. We must make certain that we have given him full opportunity to express himself, or, alternatively, we must set a mutually convenient time for this purpose. We should leave enough time for closing so that we are not rushed, since this might create the impression that we are evicting the interviewee. (p. 32)

Exercise 4.3: Closing an Interview

Goal: This exercise is designed to give you the opportunity to practice the skill of closing an interview.

You are a social worker for a hospice program. Dr. Richard Miller has referred Karen Meersman, age 83, to your hospice services. Ms. Meersman is in an advanced stage of ovarian cancer. She has received both chemotherapy and radiation therapy, and the cancer has not gone into remission. Ms. Meersman refuses to have additional chemotherapy, as research indicates the side effects would be more adverse than the potential benefits. It is estimated by Dr. Miller that Ms. Meersman has less than 6 months left to live.

You have your first meeting with Ms. Meersman and her 57-year-old daughter, Helen Kraft, at an assisted living facility. You are compassionate and empathetic. You listen to the mother and daughter briefly trace the struggles they have had with Ms. Meersman having ovarian cancer. You seek to lighten the tone of the interview, at times, by asking Ms. Meersman questions such as "Tell me about some of your most memorable occasions in your life" and 'Tell me about your son and two daughters." You then explain that Ms. Meersman meets the eligibility criteria for hospice services. You also summarize the services that hospice is able to provide, including medication for pain relief, emotional support for Ms. Meersman and close family members, nursing care assistance at this assisted living facility, assistance with helping Ms. Meersman get her financial circumstances in order, being available during crises, assisting with funeral arrangements, and providing bereavement services for close family members. You indicate tomorrow at a certain time you will return with a hospice nurse, whom you will introduce.

There are several acceptable ways to close the interview. Write the words you would say to close it. Then summarize your rationale for choosing this approach.

QUESTIONING

Questions are asked for a variety of purposes: to obtain information, to help clients tell their stories, to build a relationship, to help clients look at alternative strategies, and to help clients select solutions. The tone in which the question is asked is often as important as the question itself. For a client who is depressed, an appropriate tone should indicate caring and understanding. For someone who is angry, the tone should imply recognition of the anger and willingness to examine the anger. For someone who is anxious, the tone should convey reassurance.

In exploring clients' problems and alternative solutions, a series of questions with an increasingly specific focus is usually advisable. Kadushin (1972) expanded on this point:

> The successive questions should act as a funnel, moving from general to more specific aspects of the content being discussed. As discussion of one area is completed at the more specific end of the funnel, the new content area introduced for discussion should start with another general, open-ended question. (p. 149)

"How do you feel about that?" is a common question that I find useful for a variety of situations—for example, when a client is pregnant or is involved in a failing romance. Another common question that I ask when a client has a problem that involves someone else is "Could you describe what kind of a person (*name*) is?" Such questions facilitate getting a rapid impression of the client's thoughts and feelings about the other person.

Skilled interviewers use probing questions to help clients elaborate on the specific details of their concerns and to help clients look in greater detail at the merits, shortcomings, and consequences of possible resolution strategies. Probing questions with a client who feels her husband drinks too much might include the following: "How much does he drink?" "How often does he drink?" "How does he act when intoxicated?" "What concerns you most about his drinking'" The concerns she mentions also need to be explored in depth, using probing questions such as the following: "Given his drinking, how do you now feel about him?" "Does he recognize that he has a drinking problem?" "Do you think he would be willing to come in to talk about these concerns?" Probes should be used not in a cross-examining fashion but in a manner that gradually permits the interviewer and the interviewee to see the situations more clearly.

Various errors should generally be avoided in phrasing questions. Some of these are shown in Exhibit 4.2. The questions classified there as "errors" should not be used unless a worker has a *specific, constructive* purpose for phrasing the question in that way.

Exercise 4.4: Phrasing Questions

Goal: This exercise is designed to assist you in learning to phrase questions professionally and constructively.

Step 1.   You are a social worker at a high school, and you have had several meetings with Kara Whitford about dating issues she has and about her future (which she is confused about) when she graduates in 3½ months. You are informed by one of her teachers that her parents have recently decided to get a divorce and that this has been very upsetting to Kara. You meet with Kara. Write the words you would say to her to express your compassion and to encourage her to share her concerns related to the divorce of her parents. Summarize your rationale for your phrasing of this question.

Step 2.   You are a child protective services worker for Lincoln County Human Services. A school system reports that 7-year-old John Komarek has several bruises on his arms, legs, back, and face. You meet with John at school, and he informs you that his dad hit him several times last night. You call the Komareks to make an appointment to discuss this. Mr. Komarek answers the phone. Write the words you would say to him to arrange a time for you to go on a home visit (taking another worker along) to discuss this incident. Summarize your rationale for phrasing your approach this way.

Step 3.   You are a social worker at a Temporary Assistance for Needy Families (TANF) agency. You have assisted Ms. Marcella Gomez (a single mother with two young children) in receiving job training for a secretarial position and in making child-care arrangements. Although Ms. Gomez is one of your most competent clients, she was not hired for any of the six positions she applied for. You note that Ms. Gomez is untidy in her personal appearance and usually has an unpleasant body odor. Write the words you would say to her that will tactfully assist her in examining whether her personal appearance and lack of showering may be a factor in her not being successful in attaining a position. Summarize your rationale for phrasing your question this way.

Step 4.   You are a social worker at an adoption agency. A couple (both in their early 30s), Harold and Emily Nolan, have applied to adopt a child. This is your third meeting for the adoption study. You visit the Nolans at their home. It is 10 a.m. When you arrive for the appointment, you are surprised when you detect the odor of alcohol on Mrs. Nolan's breath. Write the words you would say to her that will tactfully assist in exploring why it appears she may have had one (or more) alcoholic beverages this early in the morning. Summarize your rationale for your phrasing of this question.

Step 5.   You are a social worker at a Planned Parenthood clinic. Ms. Roberta Greene has been a client for the past several months. She is 16 years old, has been on a birth control pill, but has a history of skipping 3 or 4 days in taking the pill. She fears she may be pregnant. The clinic performs a pregnancy test, and the result is "positive." You meet with her to give her the result. Write the words you would say in informing her of the result—and write the words you would say to her to encourage her to share her feelings, concerns, and questions about being pregnant. Summarize your rationale for phrasing what you say this way.

Exhibit 4.2   Phrasing Questions

Errors in Phrasing Questions	A Desirable Neutral Formulation
THE LOADED QUESTION: This question assumes an unknown action is occurring.	
"When did you last hit your wife?" "What are you going to do when John breaks up with you?"	"Have you ever hit your wife?" "Do you think John is considering breaking up with you?"
THE SUGGESTIVE, OR LEADING, QUESTION: The interviewer suggests a "desired" answer.	
"Don't you think it's high time you stop drinking and shape up?" "You're really making good progress—aren't you?"	"Do you think you have a drinking problem?" "What progress do you think you're making?"
YES-NO QUESTION: Such questions do not encourage elaboration.	
"Do you ever do anything together with your husband?" "You really don't like Mary—do you?"	"What kinds of things do you and your husband do together?" "How do you feel toward Mary?"
EITHER-OR QUESTION: The interviewee might prefer both or neither or a third.	
"Would you like to talk about your marriage or your job this morning?" "Have you and Tim decided to get married or to have an abortion?"	"What would you like to talk about this morning?" "What alternatives have you and Tim talked about?"
BOMBARDING: The interviewer asks two or more questions at the same time.	
"How are you feeling today, and did you and your husband get a chance to further discuss what we talked about last week?" "What were your parents' reactions when you told them you were pregnant? Did they suggest getting an abortion? How do you feel about having an abortion?" "Since graduating from high school have you found a job, a place to live, and are you still dating the same person?"	Such questions should be asked separately.
GARBLED QUESTION: Such questions usually occur when the interviewer is unclear about what he or she wants to ask.	
"You've been considering, uh, what was it, oh yeah, something about what we talked about last time—now how do you feel about that?" "Have you thought about—no, that wouldn't work, another possible thing you could do is—I don't know. What were we talking about?"	Interviewers need to be clear about what they want to ask before speaking. Pauses are better than asking garbled questions.

NOTE TAKING

Note taking is an integral part of counseling. Workers need notes to refresh their memory of past interviews, to record the contracts made with clients, to record information for social histories, to share important facts with colleagues, and to record what has been done or left undone. Benjamin (1974) observed,

In our culture, when note taking is discriminately handled, it is not resented. On the contrary, its absence may be looked upon as negligence or lack of respect. Usually no explanation of our recording practice is required. However, should an explanation be requisite because of the needs of either or both partners in the interview, it can be easily provided. (p. 58)

Note taking should be subordinate to interviewing. Don't let note taking interfere with the flow of the interview. For example, avoid saying or conveying, "I wish you would talk slower, I can't write that fast." Don't turn note taking into cross-examination—for example, "Let's see if I got it right, you state you sometimes think about getting a divorce because you find marriage confining." Convey that you are relaxed and comfortable with note taking. Don't be secretive about taking notes; otherwise, the client may become suspicious or anxious. At times, it is important for a worker to record certain kinds of information to demonstrate an interest in the client. Such expected information includes certain addresses, names, telephone numbers, contract goals, and tasks.

Note taking presents a possible distraction to interview interaction. When a worker breaks eye contact to make notes, the focus may shift from what *is being* said to what *has been* said. Ideally, workers should acquire the capacity to take notes unobtrusively without seeming to shift their attention from the client to what is being written. Kadushin (1972) advised,

> The effect of note taking needs to be assessed periodically during the interview. If at any point the interviewee appears to be upset or made hesitant by note taking, this should be raised for explicit discussion. If, despite the interviewee's stated assent, note taking appears to be a disruptive tactic, one might best forget it. (p. 206)

Note taking generally decreases in quantity as a worker gains experience. When recording, don't emphasize the importance of note taking by, for example, sitting with a pen and paper between you and the client or by recording most of what a client says. Most experienced interviewers find they often don't need to make notes during the interview. Frequently, writing down a few key phrases and points afterward enables the worker to recall important points.

Exercise 4.5: Explaining Note Taking to a Client

Goal: This exercise is designed to give you the opportunity to practice the skill of explaining why you are taking notes during an interview.

You are an adult probation and parole officer. Mr. Rodney Wyler has been convicted of embezzling more than $200,000 from his employer. You meet with Mr. Wyler, introduce yourself, and indicate that one of your first responsibilities is to write a presentencing report, which the judge will review before determining the sentence that she will impose. (A presentencing report is similar to the social history in Exhibit 4.1). You ask Mr. Wyler if he has any questions at this time. He indicates he does not have any. You start asking Mr. Wyler questions to obtain background information about him. How do you briefly explain to him the necessity for you to take notes? Write the words you would use. Also summarize your rationale for phrasing what you say this way.

TAPE RECORDING AND VIDEOTAPING

Audio and video recording of interviews are increasingly being used. Both have advantages over note taking because they provide a full record of what was said. However, a worker cannot refer to tapes as readily as to written notes. Tapes can be transcribed, but this is expensive.

When an interview is tape recorded or videotaped, the client's permission to record the interview should be obtained, and the purpose and use of the recording should be explained.

Tape recordings and note taking are generally used for different purposes. Tape recordings are used as a mirror to reflect to interviewer or to interviewee exactly what was said and how. As such they have a *self-confrontation* or *sensitivity* value, because they reflect how a person interacts with others. Playing back tapes can show clients where they have interactional problems (for example, shyness). For interviewers, the tapes can improve counseling and interviewing skills.

An initial concern of interviewers in deciding whether to use tape recordings is how the interviewee will react to being taped. I have used both audiotaping and videotaping extensively and find that clients soon forget the interview is being taped.

Some counselors routinely videotape interviews. When clients review the tape, they can more fully grasp what was said and gain valuable feedback about how they interact. Videotaping allows both interviewer and interviewee to study their verbal and nonverbal communication simultaneously.

VIDEOTAPING FOR TRAINING PURPOSES

Most educational programs in social work and counseling use videotaping of simulated counseling situations to help students develop and assess their interviewing and counseling skills. Growing numbers of programs use videotaping as one approach to assess students' aptitude for social work. An essential capacity of social work is the ability to counsel and relate to people. This capacity is necessary in social work practice with individuals, groups, families, organizations, and communities, and for performing competently in micro, mezzo, and macro practice.

In many undergraduate and graduate programs in social work, students must now demonstrate, usually in a practice course, that they have a sufficient level of counseling and interviewing skills that will give field placement agencies substantial assurance that they will be able to counsel clients. One way of helping students to develop their interviewing and counseling skills is by videotaped role-playing. Each student in the class is videotaped (usually in a video lab) in the role of a counselor while counseling someone else about a contrived problem. This videotape is later reviewed jointly by student and instructor. Students are usually graded on a pass/fail basis on this videotaped role-play. They are permitted to videotape a role-playing situation as many times as they want. If they fail to make an acceptable tape, they are not allowed to pass the course and are encouraged to transfer to another major. This course, therefore, serves as a first step in screening out students from the program. The emphasis of this requirement, however, is not on culling students from the program but on helping them develop their interviewing and counseling techniques. If a student feels the instructor's review of the tape is unfair, an appeal process is available in which the student can take the tape to other social work faculty members for their review.

When Zastrow and Navarre (1979) studied the effectiveness of videotapes as a training tool, they found that students are initially apprehensive about the videotaped role-playing. This apprehensiveness is partially reduced by lecture material and class discussions on "how to counsel" and by role-playing counseling situations in class (generally two students counseling two other students about a contrived problem). Following the videotaped role-playing, most students express considerably increased confidence in their capacities to counsel and a substantial reduction in their apprehensiveness about being videotaped in the future. These student responses of how videotaping is helpful are typical (Zastrow & Navarre, 1979):

> It helped make me comfortable in a counseling situation. I was able to test out different ways in helping a client and when reviewing the tape I saw what things I did well, and what I need to work on to become a better counselor.

> I became aware of my own voice, posture, and gestures and the importance they play in counseling.

> I was able to see an actual picture of myself, not what I thought I looked like, and was able to see where I made my mistakes and could have done something different.

> I feel that the best way to learn something is to actually do it, instead of just talking about it. I also thought it was useful to watch the tape and look for your mistakes. This is the best way to correct them.

> I became aware of exactly how I came across to the client and I noticed that I was suggesting things to him—which I didn't even realize before reviewing the tape.

> Made me more aware of my self-presence (mannerisms). Gave me the opportunity early in my academic career to have a slight taste of what counseling is about and what I might be in store for!

> I was not confident in my counseling skills at first. But after seeing the videotape I saw that I could do it. Videotaping is a good confidence builder. (pp. 201–202)

The benefits of using videotaped role-playing to assess and develop counseling skills include the following:

1. Students report it is a valuable tool in learning how to counsel.
2. Difficulties that a student has in counseling and relating to people can be identified and shown to the student; then efforts can be made to make improvements.
3. Students whose capacities lie elsewhere can be identified early in their college career and counseled into some other major.
4. Videotaping links theory with practice and thereby makes the course more meaningful and relevant.
5. Students report that videotaping provides considerable feedback about themselves and about how they relate to others.
6. Students report that videotaping builds their confidence for counseling "real" clients in the future and gives them an opportunity to test their skills and interpersonal behaviors in a safe setting.
7. This laboratory approach helps students make the transition from theory to real practice.
8. The approach provides assurance to field placement agencies that student interns will have an acceptable level of counseling expertise.

Zastrow and Navarre (1979) also found that almost all students are able (sometimes after three or four attempts) to develop their interviewing and counseling skills to an acceptable level. It is interesting that most of the few students identified with this approach as not having an aptitude for social work voluntarily decided to switch to another major. They also concluded after viewing their videotapes that they didn't have the capabilities to be a social worker.

SUMMARY

The following summarizes the chapter's content in terms of the learning objectives presented at the beginning of the chapter.

1. Describe three types of social work interviews.
   Most social work interviews are for information (to obtain data for a social study or for writing a social history), assessment (to arrive at an appraisal), or intervention (to help clients change). Often, the three types overlap. Intervention interviews are the most common in social work. Their purpose is to help clients make changes or to change the social environment to help clients function better, or both.
2. Comprehend how to begin and close interviews.
   Social work interviews can take place anywhere. Most commonly, they occur in the interviewer's office or in the client's home. Although location does affect an interview, the interviewer's skills are almost always more important in obtaining a productive interview.

   Material about how to begin and how to end interviews is presented. In interviewee-initiated interviews, the initial focus is on helping clients become comfortable and start relating their concerns. In interviewer-initiated interviews, the initial focus, after the introductions, is for the interviewer to state the purpose concisely and then begin the dialogue. There are a variety of ways to close interviews. The style used depends on the interviewer, the interviewee, and what was said during the interview. Ideally, both interviewer and interviewee should accept the fact that the interview is ending. Topics being discussed should not be left hanging. Most interviews end with either the interviewer or the interviewee summarizing what was said or summarizing what courses of action are now planned.
3. Describe how to phrase effective questions.
   Questions in interviews are used for a variety of purposes—to gather information, to help clients tell their stories, to help them look at alternative solutions, and to help them select a strategy. The tone in which a question is asked is often as important as the question itself. Probing questions are common in social work practice. Several types of questions should usually be avoided: loaded questions, suggestive questions, yes-no questions, either-or questions, clustered questions (bombarding), and garbled questions.

4. Understand guidelines on note taking during interviews.

   Note taking is an integral part of counseling and should be unobtrusive so it does not interfere with the flow of the interview.

5. Comprehend guidelines for tape recording and videotaping of interviews.

   Audiotape and videotape recordings are increasingly used to provide a full record of what was said. They are generally used for different purposes than note taking. Reviewing tapes helps clients grasp more fully what was said and gives them valuable feedback on how they interact. Reviewing tapes is particularly valuable for counselors, helping them assess and hone their interviewing skills.

   When an interview is tape recorded or videotaped, the client's permission to record the interview should be obtained, and the purpose and use of the recording should be explained.

EXERCISE

Writing a Social History

Goal: The purpose of this exercise is to give students practice in writing a social history.

Step 1:   At an earlier class session, the instructor informs the class there will be an exercise in a future session designed to teach them how to write a social history. Students read the material in this chapter on how to write a social history. The instructor informs the students they may use the format and subheadings in the example of a social history presented in this chapter (see Exhibit 4.1) or an adaptation of it. The instructor asks for a volunteer to develop (1) a contrived story about some unusual incident that has led him or her to become a client of an agency and (2) background information covering the following material:

Birth date	Education*
Religion	Kindergarten
Occupation	Grade school
Marital status	Junior high
Height	High school
Weight	College
Address	Employment history
Home phone	Where worked
Why referred	How long
By whom	Health
Early developmental history	Family life
Toilet trained (what age)	Dating
First walked (what age)	Courtship
First talked (what age)	Prior contact with other
Relationship to parents, brothers, sisters	social agencies

*Places, grades, relationships to other students, and attitudes about these schools

The instructor informs the class that at a future session she or he will interview the "client" and that each student will have to write a social history based on this interview. (The volunteer may be excused from having to write the social history.) The instructor informs the students that a significant part of their grade for this project will depend on their *realistic* recommendations on how to intervene effectively to help this "client." The instructor indicates that bringing tape recorders to the interview for the write-ups is acceptable.

Step 2:   The instructor interviews the "client" during a future class session, covering the information contained in step 1. In this interview the instructor explores problems but ends the interview before the client chooses specific courses of action to resolve the situation. A major focus of this exercise is to give students practice in arriving at recommendations for how to intervene. The instructor sets a deadline for when students are to hand in their social histories. After grading them, the instructor reads to the class one or two (without naming the writers) that were particularly well done.

SOCIAL WORK WITH INDIVIDUALS: COUNSELING[1]

LEARNING OBJECTIVES

Counseling someone with personal problems requires neither magic nor mysticism. Training and experience in counseling are beneficial, but everyone has the potential to help others by listening and talking through their difficulties. Counseling with a beneficial outcome can be done by a friend, neighbor, or relative; the local barber, hairdresser, banker, and bartender; as well as by social workers, psychiatrists, psychologists, guidance counselors, and the clergy. This is not to say that everyone is effective at counseling. Professional people, because of their training and experience, have a higher probability of being effective, but competence and rapport, rather than degrees or certificates, are the keys to desirable outcomes. All of us at one time or another counsel others; the closer that counseling (including friend-to-friend counseling) approaches professional counseling, the higher is the probability of a successful outcome. This chapter will help prepare students to:

Describe counseling from the worker's perspective
Summarize guidelines on counseling clients
Describe counseling from the client's perspective
Describe clients' reactions to having a personal problem

COUNSELING FROM THE WORKER'S PERSPECTIVE

Simply stated, counseling consists of three phases: (1) building a relationship, (2) exploring problems in depth, and (3) exploring alternatives solutions with the client and selecting a course of action. (These phases are components of the problem-solving approach, described in Chapter 1.) Successful counseling gradually proceeds from one phase to the next, with some overlap. While problems are explored, the relationship between counselor and client continues to develop in many cases, and problems are generally being examined in greater depth even as alternative solutions/strategies are explored. At the end of a series of counseling interviews, there is often the fourth phase of termination and evaluation. (Guidelines on the counselor's role in each of these phases are presented in the next section.)

Before the initial interview, a counselor is often unaware of the concerns (or problems) new clients have. What should be the counselor's objective in the first interview? Simply put, to build a helping relationship and to begin exploring the client's problems. The third phase—examining alternative solutions—may or may not be arrived at in the initial interview. Every interview has a goal or an objective, and the counselor should use this goal to give focus to the interview.

On many occasions the first problem that clients present may not be the one that they are most concerned about. Clients sometimes initially present problems that they believe are more socially acceptable to test how objective, accepting, and helpful the counselor will be. I once had a client who mentioned six "presenting" problems before sharing the one she was most concerned about, which was the guilt she experienced over masturbating.

---

[1]This chapter is adapted from a chapter written by this author, "Self-Talk in Counseling," in *Talk to Yourself: Using the Power of Self-Talk,* © 1979, pp. 266–279.

Exhibit 5.1 Summary of Key Guidelines in Counseling Clients

1. Establish a working relationship
   a. Introduce yourself and begin with a little small talk.
   b. Have client talk about his or her concerns by saying something like "Do you have some concerns you'd like to talk about today?"
   c. After the client discusses his or her concerns for 3 or 4 minutes, "connect" with the feelings by saying something like, "How are you feeling about this?" "This must really be difficult for you." "I sense you're feeling (such and such) about this." Such "connections" with a client generally facilitate the client comprehending that the counselor understands and cares about his or her feelings and concerns. Such "connections" validate the client's feelings and concerns.

2. Explore the client's concerns in depth.
3. Explore alternative solutions to the concerns with the client.
   a. In doing this, please *first* ask the client what he or she has tried, and what he or she is thinking about trying.
   b. Don't give advice, but instead phrase your resolution options as suggestions, such as "Have you thought about trying _____?"

COUNSELING FROM THE CLIENT'S PERSPECTIVE

The counseling process also can be conceptualized from the client's point of view. For counseling to be successful, clients must arrive at a progressive series of "self-talk" statements (that is, clients must arrive at having certain thoughts and beliefs). These self-talk stages are the following:

Stage 1 *Problem awareness:* "I have a problem."

Stage 2 *Relationship to counselor:* "I think this counselor has what it takes to help me."

Stage 3 *Motivation:* "I want to improve my situation and am willing to put forth the effort to do so."

Stage 4 *Conceptualizing the problem:* "My problem is not overwhelming but has specific components that can be changed."

Stage 5 *Exploration of resolution strategies:* "I see there are several courses of action that I might try in order to do something about my situation."

Stage 6 *Selection of a strategy:* "I think this approach might help, and I am willing to try it."

Stage 7 *Implementation:* "This approach is helping me."

Stage 8 *Termination and evaluation:* "Although this approach takes a lot of my time and effort, it's worth it."

This conceptualization of the counseling process presents a framework for assessing and improving the effectiveness of counseling. When counseling is not producing positive changes in clients, this framework helps identify reasons for the lack of progress. Once reasons are identified, changes can be made.

Stage 1: Problem Awareness

At this initial stage, clients must say to themselves, "I have a problem—I need to do something about my situation." If clients refuse to acknowledge that they have problems, they will not be motivated to change. In some areas of counseling (for example, working with problem drinkers), people have difficulty acknowledging that they have a problem. Involuntary clients (those forced to seek counseling) frequently deny that a problem exists. Social workers encounter involuntary clients in a variety of settings: protective services, corrections, certain public school settings, group homes, mental health facilities, nursing homes, and hospitals.

For people in denial, constructive changes are not likely to occur unless counselors find a way to convince them that there is a problem. Counselors focus on the denial by exploring why clients believe the problem doesn't exist and by gathering evidence to document the existence of the problem. Clients then need to be confronted (in a tactful manner) with this evidence. If after such a confrontation they are still in denial, counselors must accept that the client *owns* the problem, and there is little more that counselors can do constructively at this time, except perhaps to indicate they will be available in the future if the client wants to talk. (For additional strategies on how to work with hostile, involuntary clients, see Exhibit 5.2.)

Exhibit 5.2 Strategies for Working with Hostile, Involuntary Clients

Significant numbers of involuntary clients are openly hostile in initial (and sometimes later) contacts with their assigned workers. What strategies can workers use to develop rapport with such clients and to motivate them to make positive changes? Six strategies are summarized here.

1. Treat such clients with respect. Workers need to understand that such clients probably do not want to discuss their situation with a social worker. Modeling respect can help calm clients and may then lead clients to show respect for the worker.

2. Allow clients to vent their unhappiness over being forced to see a worker. In many cases, it is useful to indicate, "It is understandable that you are upset about having to be here. If the tables were turned and I was in your situation, I wouldn't want to be here either. It may help us to begin by you summarizing your concerns about being forced to be here." Venting concerns can have a calming effect.

3. Allowing clients to vent concerns may also generate goals that the worker can help clients work toward. For example, if a client is seeing a child welfare worker because he physically abused his son while disciplining him, the worker can say, "I know you disciplined your child because you want the best for him—however, hurting a child is not acceptable. I wonder if we could explore some alternatives, like timeouts for Timmy and anger management techniques?" *A key ingredient in working with involuntary clients is establishing goals that are personally meaningful to them.* Workers should seek to limit involuntary goals to legal mandates and then seek to add real-

istic goals that clients desire. The strategy here is to search for common ground between the legal mandates and clients' personal goals. Often, redefining the problem in a way that adequately addresses the concerns of both client and referral source reduces the client's resistance and makes a workable agreement possible.

4. Use the "disarming" technique (described in greater detail in Chapter 7), which involves finding some truth in what involuntary clients are saying even when workers believe they are largely wrong, irrational, unfair, or unreasonable. There is always a grain of truth to be found. When workers disarm clients with this technique, clients may recognize that workers are offering respect; this may make them more cooperative. This technique also facilitates open (rather than defensive) communication.

5. Do not subject yourself to extensive verbal abuse. If hostile clients become overly verbally abusive, postpone the contact with something like "Sir, I'm treating you with respect, and in exchange I also have a right to be treated with respect. I see we presently are not getting anywhere. I will contact you tomorrow—by that time we will hopefully be better able to more calmly discuss this."

6. If clients continue to be verbally abusive in subsequent meetings, workers should meet with their immediate supervisor to discuss available options—such as referring the involuntary client back to the original referral source or transferring the case to another worker.

At times someone who acknowledges a problem may prefer to try to resolve it without help from others. The person "owns" the problem and therefore has a right to decide how to handle it. If the person decides to work on it alone, the counselor should respect this decision but also indicate that he or she will be available in the future by saying something like "If you do decide later that you'd like to talk about it, my door is always open."

Exercise 5.1: Stating Goals for Involuntary Clients in Terms of Legal Mandates

Goal: This exercise gives you an opportunity to practice phrasing goals for involuntary clients in terms of legal mandates.

You are the facilitator for a group dynamics group. Group members are individuals who were arrested and convicted for driving while intoxicated. (The group has 2-hour meetings each week, for a period of 8 weeks.) Before the start of the first meeting, Mr. Ron Lewis comes to you and says he does not want to be here, that he will not participate in saying anything at the meetings, and that he does not have a drinking problem. He indicates his arrest occurred the first time he ever drove after having too much to drink.

You are aware that when the group sessions end you need to make a report (to the court) on each member who was ordered to attend. The minimal legal mandates for "passing" this group are as follows: (1) attendance at each meeting—unless a medical excuse is provided in writing, (2) staying awake during sessions, and (3) not interfering with the educational experiences of the other members. If any member fails to meet these minimal requirements, the court has the right to review the case of that person and impose a harsher sentence.

Write the exact words you would use to tell Mr. Lewis what he needs to do to "pass" this course. In your statement to him, you may want to add that he has the option not to attend but that if he exercises that option you will inform the court, and the court is likely to impose an even harsher sentence.

Stage 2: Relationship to Counselor

The client–counselor relationship operates in every stage of the counseling process. For counseling to be effective, clients must arrive at the point where their self-talk is, "I think this counselor has what it takes to help me." If clients think, "This counselor can't help me. I don't need a head shrinker. I don't trust this counselor," counseling will fail unless a more positive relationship is established. Throughout counseling, and especially in the initial meetings, counselors must be aware of and give attention to the kind of relationship that is developing with each client. Eriksen (1979) emphasized the importance of a helping relationship being formed with clients:

> The relationship that develops between worker and client is the very cornerstone of helping. Through the helping relationship, the client and worker come together to unblock communication that is preventing problem solving. . . .
>
> Through the vehicle of the helping relationship, the client can communicate to the worker what she thinks, knows and feels about her problem. This kind of in-depth communication, when reinforced by effective responses by her worker, will strengthen the helping relationship itself and will soon open the door to problem solving. (p. 54)

Exercise 5.2: Identifying a Client's Concerns about a Counselor

Goal: This exercise is designed to have you identify the concerns of a client about seeing a counselor and to then have you speculate about what the counselor needs to do to alleviate these concerns.

Step 1:   Imagine that you are a client going to a counselor. What concerns would you have about the counselor? Consider such factors as level of expertise, empathy, arrogance, confidentiality, personal appearance, verbal communication, non-verbal communication, problem-solving skills, being nonjudgmental, and capacity to relate to you.

Step 2:   Specify the qualities and characteristics that you would like your counselor to have.

Step 3:   Specify what you would want your counselor to do to alleviate the concerns that you identified in step 1.

The following guidelines can help build a constructive relationship.

1. Try to establish a nonthreatening, comfortable atmosphere where clients feel safe to communicate fully their troubles while feeling accepted as individuals.
2. In initial contacts with clients, you need to "sell" yourself, not arrogantly but as a knowledgeable, understanding person who may be able to help and who wants to try.
3. Be calm. Do not laugh or express shock when clients begin to open up about their problems. Even subtle responses can lead clients to believe that you are not going to understand their difficulties, and they usually will stop discussing them. Remaining calm is not always easy. I remember one interview with a client who had brutally murdered his estranged partner by decapitating her. It took 45 minutes for the client to explain his reasons for killing her and to recount how he had planned and carried out this murder. The details were shocking, but I had to continue to take a professional approach, to remain calm, and to continue to maintain a nonthreatening atmosphere so that he would feel free to relate what occurred.
4. Be nonjudgmental, not moralistic. Show respect for clients' values and do not try to sell your own. Values that work for you may not be best for someone else in a different situation. For example, if a single client is pregnant, do not attempt to force your values on adoption or abortion on her. Let her decide on the course of action after a full examination of the problem and an exploration of alternative solutions.
5. View clients as equals. Rookie counselors sometimes make the mistake of thinking that because clients are sharing intimate secrets the counselor must be very important, and they end up constructing a superior-inferior relationship. If clients feel they are being treated as inferiors, they will be less motivated to reveal and discuss personal difficulties.
6. Use a shared vocabulary. This does not mean using the same slang words and the same accent as clients. If clients see counselors as artificial in their use of slang or accent, they may be seriously offended. Use words that clients understand and that are not offensive.

7. Your tone of voice should convey that you empathetically understand and care about the client's feelings.

8. Keep what clients say confidential. People unfortunately have nearly irresistible urges to share juicy secrets. If clients discover that their confidentiality has been violated, a working relationship can be quickly destroyed. (See the material on confidentiality in Chapter 2.)

9. If you counsel a relative or a friend, you are probably emotionally involved, and you may get upset or begin to argue. If that happens, it is almost always best to drop the subject immediately, as tactfully as possible. Perhaps after tempers cool, the subject can be brought up again, or perhaps you should refer the individual to someone else. When you find yourself becoming upset, further discussion will not be productive. Many professional counselors refuse to counsel friends or relatives because of the emotional involvement. A calm, detached perspective is needed to help clients objectively explore problems and alternative solutions.

Stage 3: Motivation

For counseling to be effective, clients must (sooner or later) conclude, "I want to improve my situation and am willing to put forth the effort to do so." Unless clients become motivated to change, constructive changes are not likely to occur. In counseling, the key variable in determining whether clients will improve their circumstances is their motivation to want to improve and put forth the necessary effort (Losoncy, 1977).

Exercise 5.3: Understanding Lack of Motivation

Goal: This exercise is designed to help you understand some of the reasons why certain people are not motivated to improve their life circumstances.

Step 1: Briefly summarize (using a coded name) three or four people you know who are making little effort to improve their life circumstances. An example is the following. Barth is 26 years old and very healthy, yet he has not worked for the last 18 months in a community that has a very low unemployment rate.

Step 2: Speculate about the reasons why these people are displaying little motivation to improve their life circumstances.

Step 3: If you were the counselor for these people, what would you do to seek to motivate these people to put forth effort to improve their life circumstances?

Counselors can best motivate discouraged or apathetic people by being encouraging. According to Losoncy (1977), encouraging people have the following characteristics:

1. Complete acceptance of the discouraged person, but not of the dysfunctional behavior that has to be changed. Convey "I accept you exactly as you are, with no conditions attached."

2. A nonblaming attitude, so the discouraged person no longer feels a need to lie, pretend, or wear a mask.

3. Empathy. Be aware of and to some extent feel what the discouraged person is feeling. Empathy occurs when a counselor imaginatively enters into the inner life of the other person.

4. Genuine interest in the client's progress; convey that the client is an important, worthwhile person.

5. Confidence in the capacity of the discouraged person to improve.

6. Sincere enthusiasm about the discouraged person's interests, ideas, and risk-taking actions. Discouraged people need to believe in themselves, and they also need an encouraging person who conveys that they are important, worthwhile persons.

7. Nonjudgmental listening, so the discouraged person's real thoughts and feelings can be expressed freely, without fear of censure.

8. The ability to notice (reward) every small instance of progress (particularly during the beginning of the relationship) and to notice (reward) positives about the client. Even small compliments about something unrelated to the counseling goals go a long way toward motivating clients.

9. The ability to motivate. Motivating a discouraged person takes a long, long time. Discouraged people often have a long history of failures. Reversing this trend requires time. Listen to and understand this person as fully as possible.

10. A sincere belief in the discouraged person's ability to find a purpose in life (see Exhibit 5.3: Motivational Interviewing).

11. The ability to allow the person to take risks without passing judgment.

Exhibit 5.3 Motivational Interviewing

One of the biggest reality shocks of a "new" social worker is that many, perhaps most, clients are simply not motivated to make the necessary changes to improve their emotional and physical well-being. Examples are infinite. An alcoholic with accompanying serious health problems will often choose to continue to drink. A person who is depressed because his/her spouse recently attained a divorce will wallow in misery and not seek to make life changes that will bring happiness. A compulsive gambler who has lost a lot of money will continue gambling. A person with a stressful job will not seek to learn and practice stress management techniques. A person who is imprisoned for selling drugs may return to selling drugs upon being released from incarceration.

A number of years ago it was thought that the best way to motivate a client who does not want to make constructive changes to improve his or her well-being was to hold an "intervention" with that person. For example, if one has a serious drinking problem it was thought that his or her counselor should gather as much evidence as possible, and enlist friends and relatives to have a meeting with the alcoholic to confront the person with all the evidence and incidents of the negative effects of drinking, which might include health challenges, relationship issues, loss of jobs, physical and verbal altercations, and arrests for driving under the influence. Sometimes such an intervention did prove beneficial, but often it did not. For alcoholics, drinking has become their "best friend," which they will not give up. So—how does a social worker seek to motivate a client to make changes, when that client denies that a problem exists, and refuses to make changes?

Social workers need to recognize that people go through a process when they make positive changes in their lives. This process has been conceptualized by Prochaska & DiClemente (1982) as involving the following five stages:

Stage 1. PRECONTEMPLATION	A person is not seeing a need for a lifestyle change.
Stage 2. CONTEMPLATION	A person is considering making a change but has not decided yet.
Stage 3. PREPARATION	A person has decided to make changes and is considering how to make them.
Stage 4. ACTION	A person is actively doing something to change.
Stage 5. MAINTENANCE	A person is working to maintain the change or new lifestyle. There may be some temptations to return to the former behavior or even small relapses.

The aim of motivational interviewing is to help clients who are in stages 1, 2, or 3 to move toward stages 4 and 5. It should be noted that clients are apt to move back and forth between these stages. Someone at stage 1, for example, may recognize that he does in fact have a problem, and move, for awhile, to stage 4 where he is actively making some constructive changes; then he may regress and return to stage 1 or 2; then move at a later date to stage 3 or 4; and so on.

Motivational interviewing is not a specific technique, but rather is a style of interacting with clients, with the objective of calmly encouraging clients to move towards stages 4 and 5. William R. Miller and Stephen Rollnick (1981) are generally recognized as the founders of motivational interviewing. They developed this approach in their work with substance abusers who had high relapse rates while being in treatment. Motivational interviewers seek to convey understanding of the challenges that clients face in recognizing they have an issue, and being supportive of the efforts that clients need to make in order to make constructive changes. Motivational interviewing is now used with a wide variety of clients, including: substance abusers, those with an eating disorder, depressed persons, those with a gambling addiction, persons with anger management issues, and those with a dysfunctional sexual addiction.

Key principles of motivational interviewing are the following:

- Express Empathy: The social worker needs to place him/herself into, as much as possible, the "shoes" of the client. The social worker needs to focus on what a client (who is resisting making positive changes) is thinking and feeling, and then convey to the client his or her understanding of what the client is thinking and feeling. When clients feel they are being understood, they are much more apt to further open up and share their innermost thoughts—which may well lead them to start to move from stages 1, 2, or 3 to stage 4. When they feel support and understanding from the social worker, clients become more comfortable with examining their ambivalence about putting forth the efforts to make constructive changes. An example of a social worker's empathetic response to a client who has a drinking problem but is reluctant to taking action to reduce his drinking is the following, "In a sense, alcohol has become your best friend, as it helps to ease the pain of unwanted emotions that you feel; but are you aware that there are other ways (besides drinking) that we might explore to help you make it through each day?"
- Develop Discrepancy: Clients tend to be more motivated to make constructive changes when they perceive a discrepancy between where they are, and where they want to be. A social worker can assist a client in recognizing the discrepancies between where their current behavior is at and what their short- and long-term goals are by gently asking questions. For example, with a client who has a drinking issue, the social worker can ask questions like the following:

"Could you tell me some good things that drinking does for you?" After the client responds, the social worker asks, "Could you now tell me some less good things about your drinking?"

"Do you remember what your life was like before you started having problems with drinking?"

"Do you believe your life might improve if you stopped drinking?"

"Have you thought about what your life might be like 10 years from now if you continue to drink as much as you do?"

Exhibit 5.3 (*continued*)

■ Roll with Resistance: The social worker expects resistance with motivational interviewing. The social worker does not fight the resistance, but seeks "to roll with it." Statements made by a client that indicate resistance are not challenged. Instead, the worker uses the client's momentum to further explore the client's views. A useful technique when a client is resisting change is using a reflection. A reflection enables the worker to respond to resistance with a nonresistant response by reflecting the client's statement in a neutral form. The following is an example with a client who drinks too much: "Let's talk about the incident when you spent the night in jail after receiving a citation for driving under the influence." The client responds, "What's to talk about? The police and you have already concluded that it was all my fault." The worker responds with the reflection, "So you feel like your opinion does not matter?" instead of confronting the client with the facts contained in the police report.

Rolling with resistance avoids confrontations with clients on issues they have.

■ Support Self-Efficacy: Self-efficacy is one's belief in one's ability to succeed in specific situations. One's self-efficacy plays a major role in how one approaches tasks, goals, and challenges. In motivational interviewing, the social worker focuses on helping clients stay motivated to put forth the efforts to move toward stages 4 and 5. A competent social worker knows, and conveys to the client, that there is no one right way to change. The worker wants the client to develop the argument for change, and to also develop the courses of action to be taken for making changes. The more a client develops his or her own strategies for attaining change, the more the client will be committed to implementing those strategies.

One technique for assisting the client to assess his or her readiness for change is the following "Readiness to Change Ruler": The worker shows the client the following scale and asks him or her to state the number that best reflects how ready, at the present time, he or she is to change his or her dysfunctional behavior:

Not Ready to Change	Thinking of Changing	Undecided/ Uncertain	Some- what Ready	Very Ready to Change
1	2	3	4	5

It is important for the worker to identify the client's readiness to change, as the worker needs to focus his or her attention on the same level of readiness to change that the client is at, in order to minimize resistance and gain cooperation. For example, if the client states he is "Thinking of changing his drinking behavior" the worker may make progress by gently asking, "What do you see as the benefits to reducing the number of drinks that you have?" And, after the client responds, the worker may then ask, "Could you tell me your thoughts as to why you still want to continue drinking as much as you do?" Such communication may lead the client to further explore why he continues to drink to excess, and may increase his chances to making a commitment to moving towards stage 4—taking some actions to reduce the amount of alcohol that he consumes.

■ Encourages Supportive Relationships: The worker encourages the client to develop supportive relationships with friends and relatives who believe in the person's potential to improve. Also, self-help groups (such as AA for alcoholics) are also a critical source of support. Members of self-help groups have experienced similar difficulties as the client, and are on a similar journey of recovery; they can help the client develop coping strategies for the challenges that arise.

■ Finding Meaning in Life: The worker assists the client in developing a sense of meaning to living, which is important in sustaining the recovery process.

■ Developing Coping Strategies: The worker assists the client in developing coping and problem-solving skills to resolve other personal and family challenges that the client is facing.

■ Being an Encouraging Person: The worker conveys to the client that the client has the resources (internal strengths and social support networks) to conquer his or her issues and challenges. The worker has a nonjudgmental attitude so that the client no longer feels a need to lie, pretend, or wear a mask. The worker conveys to the client that she or he is genuinely interested in the client's progress and conveys that the client is an important, worthwhile person. The worker conveys sincere enthusiasm in the constructive interests, ideas, and risk-taking actions of the client. The worker takes the time to spend listening and understanding the client as fully as possible. Motivating a discouraged person take a long, long, time; discouraged clients generally have a long history of failures. The worker reinforces efforts made by the client, even when the actions taken do not bring immediate success; the important thing is that the client tries to improve his or her life. The worker is a nonjudgmental listener so that the client's real thoughts and feelings can be expressed freely, without fear or censure.

12. The ability to reinforce the person's *efforts*. The important thing is that people try, not that they necessarily succeed. As long as they are making efforts to improve, there is hope.

13. The ability to help the discouraged person see the falseness and negative consequences of self-defeating statements (such as "I'm a failure"). Every person has skills and deficiencies, and every person should be encouraged to build strengths and lessen weaknesses.

14. The capacity to recognize that all that you can do is give your best effort in trying to motivate the person. Success is not guaranteed. A counselor with no hope of motivating is no longer effective.

15. The skill to look for the client's uniquenesses and strengths. These should be communicated so that clients begin to realize they are special and worthwhile. This process leads to a sense of improved self-worth and gives them courage to take risks and change.

16. Awareness of the negative consequences of overdependency. As clients begin to take risks and make constructive changes, counselors should start to help them develop self-encouragement, in which they are encouraged to make and trust their own decisions and to take more risks.

(*Note:* These guidelines on motivating clients are also useful in building counseling relationships with them.)

Stage 4: Conceptualizing the Problem

For counseling to be effective, clients need to say to themselves, "My problem is not overwhelming but has specific components that can be changed." Many clients view their situation as so complex that they become highly anxious and emotional and cannot see that their problem is solvable.

Exercise 5.4: Understanding the Tendency to Awfulize

Goal: This exercise is designed to show you that most of us have a tendency to awfulize when bad events happen to us.

Step 1:   Specify your awfulizing thoughts when a bad event happened to you, such as getting a traffic ticket, someone breaking up with you, a pet dying, or failing a test. For example, when someone ends a romantic relationship, we may awfulize by telling ourselves such things as the following: 'That jerk—he/she just used me!" "My life is ruined—I'll never find anyone else as special to love me again." 'That jerk—s/he probably found someone else to love—I'll find out who it is, and make both their lives miserable." "This is absolutely the worst thing that could happen to me—life is no longer worth living."

Step 2:   Awfulizing thoughts lead us to feel bad, hurt, or angry. When we have severe negative emotions, we focus on our emotions, preventing ourselves from focusing on realistically problem-solving our issues or challenges. Specify how your awfulizing thoughts in step 1 interfered with your capacities to problem-solve your issues or challenges.

Several years ago I counseled a teenager who had missed her menstrual period for 3 months and was so overwhelmingly afraid of being pregnant that she was unable to figure out on her own that the first step was to have a pregnancy test. (When she finally took the test, the results showed she was not pregnant.) To help clients conceptualize their problems, counselors need to explore the problems together in depth with clients. The following guidelines focus on how to explore problems in depth:

1. Many rookie counselors suggest solutions as soon as a problem is identified, without exploring the problem area in depth. For example, an advocate of abortion may advise this solution as soon as a single female reveals that she is pregnant, without taking the time to discover whether she is strongly opposed to abortion, really wants a baby; or intends to marry soon.

2. In exploring problems in depth, counselor and client need to examine the severity of the problem, how long the problem has existed, its causes, how the client feels about the problem, and the client's physical and mental coping capacities and strengths before exploring alternative solutions. For example, the counselor and a single pregnant client need to explore the following: How does she feel about being pregnant? Has she seen a doctor? About how long has she been pregnant? Do her parents know? What are their feelings and concerns if they know? Has she informed her sexual partner? What are his feelings and concerns if he knows? What does she feel is the most urgent situation to deal with first? Answers to such questions will determine the future direction of counseling.

3. Once a problem area is identified, usually a number of subproblems can be identified. Explore all of them—for example, deciding how to tell the father, obtaining medical care, obtaining funds for medical expenses, deciding where to live, deciding whether to leave school or stop working during the pregnancy, deciding whether to terminate the pregnancy, and making plans for after the child is delivered or the pregnancy is terminated.

4. In a multiproblem situation, the best way to decide which problem to handle first is to ask clients which problem they perceive as most pressing. If that problem can be solved, explore it in depth and together develop a solution strategy. Problem-solving success will increase clients' confidence in the counselor and thereby further solidify the relationship.

5. Convey empathy, not sympathy. Empathy is the capacity to show that you are aware of and can to some extent feel what the client is saying. Sympathy is also a sharing of feelings, but it offers pity. The difference is subtle. Empathy facilitates problem solving; sympathy is often problem prolonging. Giving sympathy usually causes clients to dwell on their emotions without taking action to improve the situation.

   The difference between sympathy and empathy is apparent in responses to the following statement by a client whose male friend recently ended their 3-year relationship: "How could he do this to me, after all I've done for him? He's hurt me so much."

   Sympathetic response: "He's such a schnook! I don't see how you can ever face the world. You're probably going to be miserable for a long, long time."

   Empathic response: "I know ending this relationship hurts deeply. Part of your emotional pain appears to be related to your confusion as to why he wants to end the relationship. Have you discussed this with him?"

   Keith-Lucas (1972) gave a cogent example separating sympathy, pity, and empathy:

   > Consider three reactions to someone who has told us that he strongly dislikes his wife. The sympathetic person would say, "Oh, I know exactly how you feel. I can't bear mine, either." The two of them would comfort each other but nothing would come of it. The pitying person would commiserate but add that he himself was most happily married. Why doesn't the other come to dinner sometime and see what married life could be like? This, in most cases, would only increase the frustration of the unhappy husband and help him to put his problem further outside himself, on to his wife or his lack of good fortune. The empathetic person might say something like, "That must be terribly difficult for you. What do you think might possibly help?" and only the empathetic person, of the three, would have said anything that would lead to some change in the situation. (pp. 80–81)

6. "Trust your guts." The most important tool counselors have is their feelings and perceptions. Counselors should continually strive to place themselves in their client's situation (with the client's values and pressures). To use the earlier example, if the client is 17 years old, single, and pregnant, and has parents who are very critical of the situation and who want her to have an abortion, a competent counselor will continually strive to feel what the client is feeling and to perceive the world from her perspective, with her goals, difficulties, pressures, and values. We are never 100% accurate in placing ourselves in our client's situation, but 70 to 80% is usually sufficient to gain an awareness of the client's pressures, problems, and perspectives. This information is very useful in determining what additional areas need to be explored, what she should say to her parents, and what might be possible solutions. Stated somewhat differently, counselors should wonder, "What is this person trying to tell me, and how can I make it clear that I understand not only intellectually but empathically?"

7. When you believe that the client has touched on an important area of concern, further communication can be encouraged in the following ways:

   ■ Show interest nonverbally.
   ■ Pause. Rookie counselors usually become anxious when there is a pause and hasten to say something, anything, to have conversation continue. This is usually a mistake, especially when it leads to a change in an important topic. Pauses give clients time to think about the important area of concern, so they can explore it thoughtfully.
   ■ Probe neutrally. "Could you tell me more about it?" "How do you feel about that?" "I'm not sure I understand what you have in mind."
   ■ Summarize what the client is saying. "During this past hour you made a number of critical comments about your spouse; it sounds as if some things about your marriage are making you unhappy."
   ■ Reflect feelings. "You seem angry," or "You appear to be depressed about that."

Exercise 5.5: Reflecting Feelings and Meanings

Goal: This exercise is designed to give you the opportunity to practice the skill of reflecting feelings and meanings.

Step 1.   You are a social worker at a social service agency. Ann Marie Caleb states, "My life is ruined. John broke up with me 2 days ago. I'll never find anyone else as good for me as him. I am so confused as to why he broke up. I guess I'm not a lovable person. I thought we would get married in a couple of years. Life is no longer worth living." Write the words you would say in reflecting the feelings and meanings in what Ms. Caleb has said.

Step 2.   You are a counselor at a campus counseling center. A 20-year-old female student, Ellen Megan states, "I'm flunking biology. It is a required course that I must pass. I'm so stupid. I study and study for that course, but just can't get a passing grade. I should drop out of college right now—at least that way I'd save my parents a lot of money. Nothing is going well for me. No one wants to date me. I have no money, and now I'm flunking out of college." Write the words you would say in reflecting the feelings and meanings in what Ms. Megan has said.

Step 3.   You are a social worker at a Planned Parenthood clinic. You have just informed a client, Peggy Putnam, that she has a positive test for being pregnant. Ms. Putnam begins to cry, and says, "My life plans just went 'poof.' I don't want an abortion as it is immoral. I'm no longer dating the guy who is the father of this child—he's now dating my former best friend. The worst of it is I'll never be able to go to college. How could I be so stupid to get pregnant! I don't know how to take care of a baby. No one will ever want to date a single mother with a young child." Write the words you would say in reflecting the feelings and meanings in what Ms. Putnam has said.

Step 4.   You are a social worker for a social service agency. A 52-year-old client, Tom Cherwenka, states, "I have really screwed up. Last week I got arrested for drunk driving. When my wife found out, she said it was the 'last straw' and she has now contacted an attorney to draw up divorce papers. My two adult sons have told me they are really embarrassed about what I did. Life without my wife will really be empty and lonely. I'm so confused about what I can now do to put my life back together. I'm a real 'loser'!" Write the words you would say in reflecting the feeling and meaning in what Mr. Cherwenka has said.

Step 5.   You are a social worker at a hospice program. A 22-year-old male, Gregorio Maldonado, is reflecting on his loss: "My mother was my best friend. I so wanted to make her proud of me. When she was killed in that car accident, part of me also died. My upcoming graduation from college now seems insignificant. I'm without a job, have little money, and have no one to share my thoughts and feelings with. You will never know how much her death has affected me. I can hardly sleep at night." Write the words you would say in reflecting the feelings and meanings in what Mr. Maldonado has said.

8.   Approach socially unacceptable topics tactfully. Tact is an essential quality of competent counselors. Try not to ask a question in such a way that the answer puts the respondent in an embarrassing position. Suppose you have a good relationship with a teenage client and you have reason to suspect that this person has concerns about masturbating. How would you tactfully bring up the subject? One possible approach is "When I was your age, I had a number of concerns about masturbating. That was unfortunate. Most teenagers masturbate, and many have strong feelings of guilt or shame about it. Although masturbation has been stigmatized, it is a natural outlet for sexual feelings and is not harmful. In fact, most sex therapists recommend masturbating as a way to release sexual tensions.

I'm wondering if you have some questions or concerns about masturbation that would be helpful for us to discuss." Informing the youth that you also had concerns about this subject personalizes it and informs the teenager that you successfully dealt with concerns similar to those he or she is currently facing. This self-disclosing process fosters communication and relationship building.

Exercise 5.6: Exploring a Socially Unacceptable Topic with Tact

Goal: This exercise is designed to give you an opportunity to phrase tactfully a question that is designed to have a client give you information about a socially unacceptable topic.

Step 1.   You are a social worker at a social service agency A client has told you that he has been unemployed for the past 6 months, that his girlfriend recently broke up with him (the loss of whom he deeply regrets), and that he is so depressed that he sometimes sleeps 12 to 13 hours a night. He also says that he drinks too much and that his future looks really bleak. Write the words you would use in inquiring whether he sometimes thinks about ending his life.

Step 2.   You are a social worker at a social service agency. You have a client who rather frequently expels intestinal gas. You and the other staff at the agency find such behavior to be obnoxious. The person has been unemployed for the past 3 months, and in the past 14 years (the client is age 34), he has frequently been fired from janitorial jobs. You wonder if his frequent expulsion of intestinal gas may be a factor in causing his spotty work history. Write the words you would use in having him look at whether his obnoxious habit is a reason for his being discharged from jobs and a reason he has difficulty in now being hired.

A question occasionally arises about when counselors should self-disclose by sharing past experiences. An advantage of self-disclosure is that the client will then think you have expertise on the issue (because you have dealt with an issue similar to what the client is dealing with). The client is also likely to feel that you will be understanding of his or her feelings and concerns about the issue—because you too have "lived" the issue. A disadvantage of self-disclosing is that the client may come to view the counselor as needing counseling. (The client is particularly likely to reach this conclusion if counselors reveal, by nonverbal and verbal communication, that they still have unresolved issues surrounding these experiences.) Also, when working in certain settings (for example, drug treatment centers), a statement that the counselor continues to engage in behaviors that the client needs to change (such as getting drunk or smoking pot) may be used as an excuse for the client to continue problematic behaviors. A good rule to follow in deciding whether to self-disclose is to first ask yourself, "If I share these personal experiences, are they likely to have a constructive effect?" If you are unable to objectively specify a possibly beneficial effect, you should not self-disclose the experience.

9.   When pointing out clients' limitations, mention and compliment them on their assets. Mentioning a limitation causes clients to feel that something is being laid bare or taken away A compliment in another area gives something back.

10.   Watch for nonverbal cues. Competent counselors generally use such cues to identify when a sensitive subject is being touched on because clients display their anxiety by changes in tone of voice, fidgeting, tightening facial or neck muscles, yawning, assuming a stiff posture, or flushing. Some counselors even claim they can tell when clients become anxious by observing when their pupils dilate.

11.   Be honest. An untruth always runs the risk of being discovered. If that happens, your client's confidence in you will be seriously damaged, and your relationship may be seriously jeopardized. If a client asks an important question that you cannot answer, it is usually best to say, "Unfortunately I don't know the answer, but let me check into it and I'll let you know by _____ (a specified time)." Being honest goes beyond not telling lies. Counselors should always tactfully inform clients of shortcomings that they really need to attend to. For example, if an individual is being fired from jobs because of poor grooming habits, this fact needs to be brought to his or her attention. Or if a trainee's relationship skills and intervention capacities are not suited for the helping profession, that person needs to be "counseled out" in the interest of clients and in the trainee's own best interests.

12.   Listen attentively. View clients' words from their perspective, not from yours. Unfortunately, some counselors, caught up in their own interests and concerns, don't always tune out these personal thoughts while clients are speaking. This guideline seems simple, but it is not always easy to follow. Kadushin (1972) expanded on why listening attentively is difficult:

The nature of spoken communication presents a special hazard, seducing the interviewer into an easy nonlistening. The hazard lies in the great discrepancy between the number of words that are normally spoken in one minute and the number of words that can be absorbed in that time. Thought is much more rapid than speech. The average rate of spoken speech is about 125 words per minute. We can read and understand an average of 300–500 words per minute. There is, then, a considerable amount of dead time in spoken communication, during which the listener's mind can easily become distracted. (p. 188)

Kadushin (1972) gave the following suggestions on how to listen effectively:

Rather than becoming preoccupied as a consequence of the availability of the spare time between the slow spoken words, the good interviewer exploits this time in the service of more effective listening. The listener keeps focused on the interviewee but uses the time made available to the mind by slowness of speech to move rapidly back and forth along the path of the interview, testing, connecting, questioning: How does what I am hearing now relate to what I heard before? How does it modify what I heard before? How does it conflict with it, support it, make it more understandable? What can I anticipate hearing next? What do I miss hearing that needs asking about? What is he trying to tell me? What other meanings can the message have? What are his motives in telling me this? (p. 190)

Stage 5: Exploration of Resolution Strategies

After (or sometimes while) a problem is explored in depth, the next step is to consider alternative solutions. In exploring solutions, it is almost always best for counselors to begin by asking something like "Have you thought about ways to resolve this?" Clients generally have been aware for some time that they have a problem. In most cases, they have already tried to resolve the problem. Therefore, this question often elicits alternatives that the client has tried but that have not worked. They can then be discarded. In addition, this question can elicit from the client high-quality alternatives that the counselor has not thought of and that may well work for the client. Merits, shortcomings, and consequences of the client's alternatives should be tactfully and thoroughly examined. Counselors should then mention other potential solutions, and their merits and shortcomings should also be examined.

Each client is unique, and so are his or her problems. What works for one client may not work for another. Abortion, for example, may be compatible with one client's values and circumstances but undesirable for another client. If counseling is going to be effective, the client needs to say, "I see there are several courses of action that I might take to try to do something about my situation." Unless clients realize that resolution strategies exist, counseling is likely to fail.

Exercise 5.7: Generating Options and Resolution Strategies

Goal: This exercise is designed to give you practice in generating options and resolution strategies.

(The more options we can generate and the more creative we can be in generating options, the higher is the probability of high-quality options being available for the client to consider.) You are a social worker at a social service agency. A 28-year-old woman has arrangements made to be married in 5 weeks. She now has "cold feet at the altar," as she indicates she is confused about whether (1) she really loves the person she is engaged to, (2) she should call off the wedding, and (3) she ever wants to be married. Write down all the options that would be worthwhile for this woman to consider regarding this dilemma.

Stage 6: Selection of a Strategy

After counselor and client discuss the probable effects and consequences of possible resolution strategies, it is essential that the client conclude, "I think this approach might help me, and I am willing to try it." If a client is indecisive or refuses to commit to a course of action, constructive change will not occur. For example, if a client says, "I know I have a drinking problem, but I am unwilling to take any action to cut down on my drinking," counseling probably will not be successful.

Clients usually have the right to self-determination—that is, to choose the course of action they want to take. The counselor's role is to help clients clarify and understand the likely consequences of each alternative. It is generally not the counselor's role to give advice or choose the alternative. If the counselor selects the alternative, there are two possible outcomes: (1) The alternative may prove to be undesirable, in which case the client will blame the counselor for the advice and the future relationship will be seriously hampered. (2) The alternative may prove to be beneficial. This immediate outcome is desirable, but clients will not "own" the result—*they* didn't make the outcome happen, the counselor did. The client will then become overly dependent on the counselor, seeking his or her advice far too often and becoming reluctant to make decisions on his or her own. In practice, most courses of action have both desirable and undesirable consequences. An unmarried mother who keeps her child may receive considerable gratification from being with and raising the child, but she may also blame the counselor for her long-term financial hardship and isolated social life.

Not giving advice does not mean that counselors should not suggest alternatives. On the contrary, it is the counselor's responsibility to suggest and explore all viable alternatives with clients. A good rule to follow is that when you believe a client should take a certain course of action, phrase it as a suggestion, "Have you thought about . . .?" rather than as advice, "I think you should . . ."

Clients' rights to self-determination should be taken away only if the selected course of action will seriously hurt others or themselves. For example, if it is highly probable that a parent will continue to abuse a child or if the client attempts to take her own life, counselor intervention is suggested. For most situations, however, clients have the right to select their resolutions, even when counselors believe that another alternative would be a better course of action. Frequently, clients are in a better position to know what is best for their situation, and if it doesn't work out, they should not be deprived of the opportunity to learn from the mistake.

Stage 7: Implementation

Counseling will be successful only if clients follow through on their commitment to try a resolution approach and then conclude, "This approach is beginning to help me." If clients follow through on the commitment but instead conclude, "I don't believe this approach is helping me," counseling is again failing. If this occurs, counselor and client need to examine the reasons for no gain and perhaps try another strategy. Here are some guidelines for implementing a resolution approach:

1. Attempt to form an explicit, realistic "contract" with clients. When clients do select an alternative, they should clearly understand the goals, what tasks need to be carried out, how to do the tasks, and who will carry out each task. Frequently, it is desirable to write a "contract" for future reference, with a time limit set for accomplishing each task. For example, if an unmarried mother decides to keep her child and now needs to make long-range financial plans, this goal should be understood and specific courses of action decided on—seeking public assistance, seeking support from the alleged father, securing an apartment within her budget, and so on. Furthermore, who will do what task within a set time limit should be specified.

   Negotiating a contract (and perhaps renegotiating it in future interviews) brings a focus to the interview. Client and counselor are less likely to get sidetracked by extraneous issues, and the interview's productivity can be sustained.

   If the client and the counselor differ in their expectations of desired goals or in their expectations of who will do what tasks, the contract negotiation process forces client and counselor to discuss and, one hopes, resolve their differences. For additional material on contracts, see Exhibit 5.4.

2. Counseling is done *with* clients, not *to* or *for* them. Clients should have the responsibility of doing many of the tasks necessary to improve the situation. Here is a good rule to follow: Clients should take responsibility for those tasks that they can carry out, and counselors should attempt to do only those that are beyond the clients' capacities. Doing things *for* clients, such as giving advice, risks creating a dependency relationship. Furthermore, succeeding at tasks leads to personal growth and prepares clients for future responsibilities.

3. Role-play certain tasks that clients lack confidence or experience in carrying out. For example, if a pregnant single woman wants help in telling her male friend about the pregnancy, role-playing will assist her in selecting words and the strategy for informing him. The counselor can first play the woman's role and model an approach, with the woman playing the male role. Then the roles are reversed so the woman can practice telling her male friend.

Exercise 5.8: Contracting

Goal: This exercise is designed to assist you in learning how to write behavioral contracts.

Step 1. Specify a behavior of yours that you know you should change, such as drinking to excess, procrastinating in writing papers, or lack of exercising.

Step 2. Prepare a contract, answering the following:

a. What behavior do you want to change? Be as specific as possible.
b. What is your goal?
c. What will you do to achieve this goal?
d. How will you reward yourself for achieving the goal and adhering to your contract?
e. If you fail to adhere to the contract, what adverse consequences will you give yourself (such as donating $10 to a charity each time you "screw up")?

Stage 8: Termination and Evaluation

If constructive change is to be long lasting or permanent, clients must conclude, "Although this approach takes a lot of my time and effort, it's worth it." If they conclude, "This approach has helped a little, but it's really not worth what I'm sacrificing for it," then an alternative course of action needs to be developed and implemented.

When clients meet commitments, reward them orally or in other ways. Rewarding clients increases their self-esteem and self-respect and motivates them to continue working to improve their circumstances.

Exhibit 5.4   Guidelines for Formulating a Contract

Contracts in social work practice specify goals and the tasks to be performed to accomplish them. In addition, contracts set deadlines for completing tasks and identify rewards for successful task completion. Contracts also specify consequences for unsuccessful completion of tasks. A contract is, therefore, an agreement between a social worker and one or more clients in their joint efforts to achieve specified outcomes. Formulating an explicit contract is directly related to a positive outcome for clients (Hepworth & Larsen, 1993, p. 365).

A contract, in outline format, should contain the following components:

1. Goals to be accomplished (ranked in order of priority)
2. Tasks to be accomplished by the client and by the worker (These tasks must be directly related to accomplishing the goals, so that accomplishing the tasks results in successfully meeting the goals.)
3. Time frame for completing the tasks
4. Means of monitoring progress in task completion and goal accomplishment
5. Rewards for the client if the terms of the contract are met
6. Adverse consequences to the client upon nonfulfillment of the terms of the contract

Some workers prefer written contracts, and others prefer oral contracts. A written contract has the advantage of emphasizing the commitment to the contract by both worker and client, and it also minimizes the risks of misunderstandings. An oral contract avoids the sterility of a written contract. Research comparing the effectiveness of written versus oral contracts shows that oral contracts are generally as effective as written contracts with regard to meeting goals (Hepworth & Larsen, 1993, p. 381). If workers use an oral contract, they should still record the essential elements of the contract in their notes for future reference.

The most difficult element in an effective contract is formulating goals. Goals specify what the client wishes to accomplish and should directly relate to the needs, wants, or problems being encountered by the client. Goals serve the following important functions:

1. Goals ensure that workers and clients are in agreement about the objectives to be accomplished.
2. Goals provide direction to the helping process and thereby reduce needless wandering.
3. Goals guide selection of appropriate tasks (and interventions) to achieve the objectives.
4. Goals serve as outcome criteria in evaluating the extent to which the tasks (and interventions) are succeeding.

Useful guidelines when setting goals include the following:

1. *Goals must relate to the desired end results sought by the client.* Clients must believe that accomplishing the selected goals will enhance their well-being. Therefore, workers need to integrally involve clients in selecting and specifying the goals.
2. *Goals should be stated in specific and measurable terms.* Nebulous goals (such as "Client gaining increased control over his emotions") are not sufficient and often lead the client to "drift" or wander in the helping process. A specific goal (such as 'The client will express his angry feelings with his mother in an assertive rather than an aggressive manner when they are having conflicts") is more effective. In addition, it is also measurable, whereas a nebulous goal is not. The client's mother (and others) can monitor the number of times, over a specified period, that the client expresses his angry feelings assertively rather than aggressively. Clients tend to define goals nebulously, so it is important for workers to help clients state goals that are both specific and measurable.
3. *Goals should be feasible.* Unachievable goals set clients up for failure, which then leads to disappointment, disillusionment, and a sense of defeat. It is vital that the goals chosen can be accomplished. For clients with grandiose tendencies, it is important for workers to assist them (tactfully) in lowering their expectations to what can reasonably be attained.

When arriving at feasible goal statements with clients, workers should agree only to assist them in working toward goals for which the workers have the requisite skills and knowledge. If the goal is beyond the worker's competence (for example, assisting the client in overcoming a complex sexual dysfunction), the worker should refer the client to a more appropriate resource.

Once clients settle on their goals, the final step in negotiating goal statements is to assign priorities to the goals. This ensures that the initial change efforts are directed to the goal that is most important to the client.

The following scenario provides an example. First, background information: Ray and Klareen Norwood have been married for 3 years. They seek counseling because Klareen is increasingly afraid of Ray's angry outbursts. Ray is physically and verbally abusive to her when he is angry. He has not hit Klareen yet, but she is afraid that Ray's escalating aggressiveness will lead to her being battered. Klareen is seriously considering separating from Ray. She has already contacted an attorney to discuss divorce proceedings. Both partners, however, state that they want to maintain the marriage. At the end of the second meeting with the Norwoods, this contract is prepared:

Goals: (a) Ray will cease being physically abusive to Klareen and will reduce by at least two-thirds his verbal abuse incidents over the next 30 days. (This goal is rated number one.) (b) The Norwoods will begin discussing, at some future date, raising a family. (This goal is rated number two.) The Norwoods both agree to put off further discussion at this time because Klareen says she first needs to decide whether she wants to remain in the marriage.

Tasks of the participants: Worker: The social worker will instruct Ray in the following anger control techniques: (1) Expressing his angry feelings to Klareen in an assertive rather than aggressive manner (see Module 2). (2) Reducing the intensity and frequency of his outbursts by countering his negative and irrational self-talk with rational and positive self-talk (Module 1). (3) Countering his feelings of anger with deep-breathing relaxation (Chapter 14). And (4) learning to blow off steam nondestructively through such physical activities as jogging or hitting a pillow (Chapter 14).

Exhibit 5.4   (*continued*)

Mr. Norwood: Ray will attend weekly counseling sessions to learn and practice anger control techniques. His main task is to use these techniques to cease his physical abuse of Klareen and to substantially reduce his verbal abuse of Klareen. After 30 days, if Ray succeeds, a renegotiation of the terms of the contract will occur.

Mrs. Norwood: Klareen will attend weekly counseling sessions with Ray. In addition, she will seek to calmly discuss issues she has with Ray (in and outside the counseling sessions) to avoid provoking Ray's anger. Klareen also has the responsibility to record any incidents in which Ray is physically or verbally abusive to her in the next 30 days.

Duration of contract: 30 days

Means of monitoring progress: Klareen will record incidents where Ray expresses his anger toward her in assertive or nondestructive ways. (This measures the positive ways in which Ray is learning to express his anger.) Klareen will also record any incidents in which Ray is verbally or physically abusive to her.

Rewards for Ray and Klareen if contract is met: They will continue their marriage, which is what both partners want.

Consequences for Ray and Klareen if contract is not met: If Ray hits Klareen one time in the next 30 days, she will separate. If Ray does not reduce by two-thirds the number of times he is verbally abusive in the next month, she will separate. (To get baseline information, Klareen is asked to identify in the past week—taking each day at a time—the number of times Ray was verbally abusive. Nine incidents are identified. As a result, Ray agrees he will, at most, be verbally aggressive to Klareen no more than 12 times in the next 28 days. If he exceeds this limit, it is agreed that Klareen will move in with her parents.)

One of the biggest reality shocks of new trainees entering the helping professions is that many clients, even after making commitments to improve their situations, do not carry out the steps outlined. If clients fail to meet the terms of the contract, effective workers generally do not punish. Punishment usually increases hostility without producing positive lasting changes. Also, don't accept excuses when commitments are not met. Excuses let people off the hook; they provide temporary relief, but they eventually lead to more failure and to a failure identity. Simply ask, "Do you still wish to try to fulfill your commitment?" If clients answer affirmatively, another time deadline acceptable to the client should be set.

Whether or not clients reach all their goals, careful attention should be given to terminating the relationship. If clients still have unresolved problems, a referral should be made to an appropriate agency or professional. Care should be taken in terminating the contact so that clients do not erroneously conclude that the counselor is rejecting them. Also, clients should be asked whether there are additional concerns that they would like help with.

The nature and intensity of the feelings clients experience as they end a relationship with a counselor vary according to a number of factors, including their personal characteristics, the progress they made, the nature of the relationship with the counselor, and the issues worked on. Because ending is an important event in the lives of most clients, the counselor should give them an opportunity to express feelings related to the ending of the counseling.

Clients may experience a variety of emotions about the ending, such as gratitude, ambivalence, anger, sadness, guilt, and fear. If they conclude the relationship without sharing their feelings, they may experience a sense of incompleteness. Therefore, the counselor should encourage clients to express their feelings about ending. The counselor may say something like the following to encourage the expression of feelings about ending: "In the weeks we met we discussed the following issues: _____. You have stated you have made progress on _____. We as yet have not shared our feelings about ending the relationship with one another. Since this is our final meeting with one another, what emotions are you now feeling?" After the client expresses his or her feelings, it is appropriate for the counselor to express those feelings that would add to a pleasant and appropriate ending. (It perhaps is best for the counselor to choose which feelings are most constructive to express. For example, it probably would be counterproductive to express feelings of annoyance that the counselor has about the client.)

Often, when the counselor shares his or her feelings about the ending, clients may respond by sharing additional emotions of their own. The counselor may reflect their feelings and perhaps share more of his or her own. It then is time for the counselor and the client to complete the ending process by saying good bye.

Exercise 5.9: Terminating and Encouraging Clients to Share Their Ending Feelings

Goal: This exercise is designed to give you an opportunity to practice the skills of terminating and encouraging clients to share their feelings about ending.

Step 1.   You are a social worker at a social service agency. You have worked with Andy Morrissey for the past 2½ months. Andy is a 28-year-old computer programmer. You have helped him with several issues, including the recent death of his mother to whom he was very close, his girlfriend of 7 years breaking up with him (he is now beginning to date again), his struggling to keep his job as he mourned the loss of his mother and his girlfriend, and his drinking to excess (he now limits himself to two drinks when he goes out). You believe he no longer has acute issues that need to be worked on. Write the words that you would say to Mr. Morrissey to suggest that it now may be time to terminate his coming to see you.

Step 2.   Assume you and Mr. Morrissey agree to terminate. Write the words that you would use in encouraging Mr. Morrissey to express his feelings about ending.

At the final interview or a few weeks after termination, it is usually beneficial to ask clients (orally or with a brief questionnaire) the following questions:

■ Did the counseling help you? If "yes," how? If "no," why did it not help?
■ What did the counselor do well?
■ What were the shortcomings of the counseling that was received?
■ What suggestions do you have for improving counseling services at this agency?
■ Do you have some concerns for which you desire additional counseling?

This information is very useful in improving the counseling process and in determining whether the client needs additional help.

These guidelines on counseling should not be followed dogmatically because they will probably work only 70 to 80% of the time. The most important tools counselors have are their feelings, perceptions, relationship capacities, and interviewing skills.

One final important guideline: Counselors should refer a client to someone else, or at least discuss the case with another professional counselor, in any of the following situations: (1) if counselors are unable to empathize with the client, (2) if they feel the client is choosing unethical alternatives (such as seeking an abortion) that conflict with the counselor's basic value system, (3) if they feel the problem is of such a nature that they will not be able to help, or (4) if a working relationship is not established. Competent and secure counselors know that it is possible to work with and help some people but not all and that it is in the client's and the counselor's best interests to refer clients they cannot help to others who may be able to provide the counseling needed.

Counseling Skills at Work in Generalist Practice.   As you read the Case Example "Counseling Mrs. H: Principles in Action," (pp. 106–107), notice that the social work intern uses the following roles, which, as described in Chapter 1, are components of generalist social work practice: brokering Mrs. H to enroll in a work-training program; facilitating Mrs. H to receive employment; educating Mrs. H to understand she needed to seek employment; brokering Mrs. H to receive dental care; helping Mrs. H to problem-solve; and being an encouraging role model.

CLIENTS' REACTIONS TO HAVING A PERSONAL PROBLEM

In counseling clients, a crucial area that counselors need to be aware of and learn to handle effectively is clients' emotional reactions to having a personal problem. Lee Askew's example underscores the importance of this area. Mr. Askew has been an alcoholic for many years, and for most of these years he has been in denial. Why? First seen in counseling nearly 3 years ago, Mr. Askew has experienced a variety of problems related to his drinking. The following is a summary of Mr. Askew's social history:

Lee Askew is 43 years old and has been drinking heavily since he was 16 years of age. For the past several years, he has drunk an average of a quart of vodka each day. His second marriage is in trouble because his wife, Callie, claims their money is spent on alcohol rather than on paying bills. Also, his wife has informed him she can no longer tolerate his drunken behavior—nearly every evening he is in a drunken stupor and rambles on, repeating himself until he finally falls asleep, often by passing out. Mr. Askew's first wife divorced him because of his drinking. When he is sober, he is friendly and enjoyable to be with. But as the day moves along, he increasingly becomes intoxicated, and his behavior becomes intolerable. Five years ago he had a serious automobile accident while intoxicated and was nearly killed. Three and one-half years ago he was again arrested for drunken driving. In the past 10 years he has held a variety of sales jobs and has been fired from three of these jobs for being intoxicated. Last night Mr. Askew physically abused his wife for the first time. This morning Mrs. Askew informed Lee that he must either seek help for his drinking or she will leave. Mr. Askew apologized for hitting his wife, claiming he had had a bad day at work. Lee, however, refuses to acknowledge he has a drinking problem.

Mr. Askew's denial of his drinking problem is not unique. Clients display a variety of emotional reactions when confronted with evidence of a personal problem. The effectiveness of counseling frequently depends on counselors understanding such emotional reactions so they can help clients recognize that they do have a personal problem and need certain services.

An important contribution in this area has been made by Elisabeth Kübler-Ross. In *On Death and Dying*, Kübler-Ross (1969) describes five stages of dying that terminally ill people typically experience. These stages are not absolute, and not everyone goes through each one. But helping professionals who counsel the terminally ill have found this paradigm, when used in a flexible, insight-producing way, to be valuable in explaining why patients behave the way they do. The five stages also typify individuals' reactions when confronted with serious personal problems.

Kübler-Ross's Five Stages of Dying

Mauksch (1975, p. 10) provided a concise summary of Kübler-Ross's five stages of dying:

1. *Denial:* "No, not me." This is a typical reaction when patients learn that they are terminally ill. Denial, says Dr. Ross, is important and necessary. It helps cushion the impact of the patient's awareness that death is inevitable.
2. *Rage and anger:* "Why me?" Patients resent the fact that others will remain healthy and alive while they die. God is a special target for anger, since He is regarded as imposing, arbitrarily, the death sentence.
3. *Bargaining:* "Yes, me, but . . ." Patients accept the fact of death but strike bargains for more time. Mostly they bargain with God—"even among people who never talked with God before." They promise to be good or to do something in exchange for another week or month or year of life. Notes Dr. Ross, "What they promise is totally irrelevant, because they don't keep their promises anyway."
4. *Depression:* "Yes, me." First, people mourn past losses, things not done, wrongs committed. But then they enter a state of "preparatory grief," getting ready for the arrival of death. Patients grow quiet and don't want visitors. "A dying patient who doesn't want to see you anymore," says Dr. Ross, "is signaling he has finished his unfinished business with you, and it is a blessing. He can now let go peacefully."
5. *Acceptance:* "My time is very close now and it's all right." Dr. Ross describes this final stage as "not a happy stage, but neither is it unhappy. It's devoid of feelings but it's not resignation, it's really a victory."

In presenting these five stages, Kübler-Ross (1969) warns it is a mistake to expect that all terminally ill patients methodically pass through all five. Some never reach the fifth stage of acceptance. Others display reactions from two stages at the same time—for example, anger and denial. Still others waver between stages—reaching the depressed stage, then returning to an earlier stage of denial or anger.

Kübler-Ross's Five Stages as Emotional Reactions

Kübler-Ross's five stages also typify clients' emotional reactions when they are confronted with evidence of their personal problem. Denial, rage and anger, bargaining, depression, and acceptance are, in my experience, common reactions in numerous situations: A husband is informed his wife is having an affair; a single teenager is informed she is pregnant; an employee is fired for incompetence; a woman is informed she has a malignant tumor in her breast; a woman informs her fiance she is ending their engagement. This list could be expanded infinitely, because we are all likely to have these emotional reactions. When clients recognize they have a personal problem, they experience a sense of loss, and Kübler-Ross's five stages are emotional reactions to loss. Lee Askew's case illustrates each stage.

CASE EXAMPLE   COUNSELING MRS. H: PRINCIPLES IN ACTION

Our social work program (similar to social work programs at other universities) places students in social service agencies for internships. As social work interns, students observe, and soon begin to do, the kind of work that social workers do. A frequent "reality shock" reported by interns is that many clients are apathetic, discouraged, and simply not motivated to improve. Often, the result is that clients do not follow through on commitments made during counseling sessions to improve their circumstances.

Last year at a county social services agency, I was supervising an intern who was surprised and frustrated when clients failed to follow through on commitments. The intern was working with a small caseload of Temporary Assistance to Needy Families (TANF) mothers. The intern commented, "The case examples discussed in textbooks are always successes, and I have not yet seen improvement in my cases." I reassured her that she was not at fault and that lack of improvement is more often the rule than the exception. I added that textbooks are very selective in that they usually present success cases, rather than typical cases, to illustrate theory. I cautioned that if she became discouraged and gave up being an "encouraging person," she had *no* hope of being effective. After further discussion, she developed an approach in which she used the counseling principles presented in this chapter. At the end of her internship, not all of the TANF mothers she was working with showed substantial improvement. Yet she had formed a respectful working relationship with each client, and some were making significant efforts to improve their circumstances. At the end of the semester, she wrote the following summary about her contacts with one client:

I was assigned the case of Mrs. H. She was 33 years of age and had three children, ages 15, 11, and 7. She had been receiving TANF assistance for the past 6 years, ever since her husband deserted her. During the past 4 years, the agency had made several efforts to get her a job, without success. The records showed Mrs. H did not want a full-time job, because she felt she was too busy taking care of her children. She applied for several part-time jobs but was not hired. Mrs. H felt she did not have any marketable skills, as she had never worked outside of her home.

I was assigned Mrs. H's case when she requested a social worker's help with a problem she was having with her 15-year-old son. Mrs. H had found some pot in her son's clothes drawer and didn't know how to handle the situation. I met with Mrs. H. Her home had a general unclean appearance. Mrs. H's physical appearance gave the impression she had been through a war. Her clothes were wrinkled and had what appeared to be food stains on several places. Her hair was greasy, she was quite obese, and she had few teeth left in her mouth. Dark circles were under her eyes, suggesting a great deal of fatigue and stress.

We met for about an hour and a half, and Mrs. H related much of her life history. She had never held a full-time job and had a "forced marriage" (due to becoming pregnant) shortly after she graduated from high school. Her husband had been a road construction worker and had a drinking problem. She had not heard from him in the previous year. She felt if he did come back, she would not even want to see him. She had heard also that when he left he moved to a distant state with another woman.

My aim in the first interview was to build a working relationship, obtain Mrs. H's trust, and help her explore what she saw as her problems. Her immediate problem appeared to be what to do about her discovery of pot. We discussed to some extent the legalities of smoking marijuana and the effects and consequences of the drug. I also said I could bring over some brief reading material on the drug the next day, and she responded by saying she would very much appreciate receiving such material.

We then role-played how she might bring up the subject of smoking marijuana with her son. First I played her role to model a possible approach, and she played her son. Then we reversed roles to give her practice in trying out an approach. Before discussing the subject with her son, she mentioned she wanted to look at the reading material I had promised her. I dropped off this material the next day. We also set another meeting for the following week.

At our next appointment, Mrs. H indicated she had discussed smoking marijuana with her son. Her son responded first with some surprise and some displeasure that Mrs. H had gone through his clothes drawer. The son, Jerry, indicated he had tried smoking marijuana only twice and was not that interested in smoking in the future. Mrs. H added that another related concern she had about Jerry was his interest in occasionally drinking beer with some of his friends. She indicated that she and Jerry had had some moderate disagreements in this area, and they were working on it.

I asked if she felt she needed help from our agency for this issue. She responded, "No, not at this time." I then asked if she needed any other additional help from our agency. She thanked me for the help I had given and said she was not aware of other areas where she needed help. I could have left, but I thought that as I had a good relationship established with her and had been of some prior help this might be an opportunity to have her take a look at her future.

I began by asking her what she would like to see herself doing 10 years from now. She responded by saying, "I haven't given that much thought. I probably will be doing what I'm doing now." I asked if she was satisfied with her current life. She rather firmly said no and went on at length about how difficult it is to live on an inadequate TANF budget and to raise three children by herself. She was also critical of her husband, who placed her in this situation by deserting her.

I conveyed an understanding of her concerns and mentioned that it was certainly true that past events had led to her current circumstances. But I added that what she wanted for the present and the future was largely up to her. She asked what I meant.

I said, 'Take your financial situation, for example. You have a choice between staying home or seeking a job. Now, I know at the present time that working would not improve your finances very much. But if you don't begin learning an employable skill now and gradually working your way up in a job, what's going to happen when, in a year, your TANF benefits expire?" I explained to her that under the TANF program current (and future) single parents can only receive financial assistance for a maximum of 2 years. During that 2-year period, they need to prepare themselves for holding a job and then find a job. I added, "There are also other areas that we could work on, for example, dental care. But the choice is totally up to you. If you want to work on some of these areas, I'm very interested in working with you. If you aren't interested at the present time, there's little I can do."

Mrs. H responded by indicating she was aware that her teeth needed attention but added she didn't have the money to pay a

CASE EXAMPLE   (*continued*)

dentist. I indicated the expenses were covered under her medical card (Medicaid program). She expressed surprise and indicated she would make an appointment with a dentist. She thanked me for the information, and I noted her face showed a spark of interest.

I then asked if she had thought about obtaining a job. She mentioned that would be nice but then started citing a number of reasons she thought that it would not be possible. Many of these appeared to me to be "self-defeating self-talk." The material below contains a summary of her negative self-talk, along with a more positive view for each reason that I suggested to her.

At this point I asked her to think over what we had talked about and indicated that I would ask Mrs. S to contact her.

A week later I stopped by to see Mrs. H. She mentioned that she had had an "inspirational" talk with Mrs. S. At that point she asked to be enrolled in our work-training program. I praised her decision. Within 3 months, she had obtained a receptionist job for a new car dealer. Equally important, she appeared to have a renewed interest in living and had improved her personal appearance with increased grooming attention, some new clothes, and a set of dentures. For me, as a student social work intern, this turned out to be a deeply rewarding, gratifying person to work with.

Mrs. H's Reasons for Not Seeking a Job	A More Positive View
1. "I've tried finding a job several times in the past and was not able to obtain one."	1. "Having tried in the past and failed does not mean you can't obtain a job at this time. We could provide you with work training in an area that you are interested in and also help you obtain a job after the training. You need to start thinking about your future, because in a year you will no longer be eligible for TANF assistance. Having a job now will help you prepare for the future. Also, there are other benefits in working, such as the opportunity to get to know other people."
2. "I'm really not skilled at any job. Frankly, it is very embarrassing to be turned down when I apply."	2. "Nothing ventured, nothing gained. As far as not having a skill, we can enroll you in a work-training program. We can also help you find a job. You are not alone in being turned down for a job. I have a friend who applied to 67 teaching positions before being hired. This person was becoming quite discouraged but kept on trying. She finally found one and really liked it. The key is to keep on trying and hoping."
3. "I won't be able to work and also take care of my home and family."	3. "A working mother does have a lot to do and limited time to get it all done. However, many mothers are able to do both." (At this point I asked if she would be interested in discussing this area with a friend of mine, Mrs. S has four children and used to receive financial assistance but now works full-time as a secretary. Mrs. S is an "encouraging" person. She got her job by first having work training, then volunteering at an agency to do clerical work. By volunteering, she developed her typing skills, and after a year the agency hired her. Mrs. H indicated she would be interested in talking with Mrs. S.)
4. "Frankly, my personal appearance is such that I don't think that anyone would hire me."	4. "You're selling yourself short. Our agency can help you with dental care and in getting some new clothes. When you meet with Mrs. S, you will see she probably will not win a beauty contest but has an inner beauty (personality) that helped her get a job. I think with a more positive attitude, people would note an inner beauty on your part."
5. "I wouldn't, if I worked, be able to watch some of my favorite game shows and soap operas during the day. My present daily routine would be greatly altered."	5. "This is true. But you would be able to meet more people if you worked and perhaps grow more as a person. Also, wouldn't your children be prouder of you if you worked? Are you really satisfied and contented with your present circumstances and current daily routine?"
6. "I don't own a car, and therefore don't have a way to get to a job even if I did get one."	6. "We can help you here by paying the cost of transportation and by helping you arrange for transportation. For example, we have volunteer drivers who would be able to provide transportation when you go for job interviews."

Stage 1: Denial ("Not me.") Admitting the existence of a problem is difficult because clients often then (erroneously) perceive themselves as weak, sinful, or irresponsible. Also, recognition brings with it an acknowledgment that change is inevitable. Clients often mourn the loss of that which must be changed. Alcoholics thus mourn the loss of their drinking because their social activities are centered around it. Unless clients already have an openness or reaching-out pattern with others, it can be very difficult for them to share a new problem openly. Denial helps cushion the impact of the client's awareness that change is inevitable.

Constructive changes are not likely to occur for people in denial unless counselors find a way to convince them that the problem exists. Counselors therefore need to focus on the denial and explore why the person believes there is no problem. They should gather evidence to document the existence of the problem. Clients can then be confronted with this evidence in a tactful manner.

For more than 20 years, Mr. Askew has denied that he has a drinking problem. He believes that he needs alcohol to get through each day. He feels such a strong need for alcohol that he allowed his drinking to end his first marriage, and he will not face the fact that drinking is ruining his second marriage. He will not acknowledge that he nearly lost his life while driving when intoxicated, nor will he acknowledge that he has lost several jobs because of his drinking.

Mrs. Askew gave her husband an ultimatum: Either he sees a counselor or she is leaving now. Mr. Askew reluctantly decided to see a counselor. In counseling, Mr. Askew denied he had a drinking problem. He had excuses for everything: His car accident resulted from slippery roads. He was fired because his employers didn't like his suggestions for increasing sales. He ended his first marriage because rus wife was a "nag." He denied having more than a couple of drinks a day.

Stage 2: Rage and Anger ("Why me?") Clients resent the fact that they have to change while others do not. Old friends, relatives, or society at large are doing the things that the clients must change. Anyone can be the target for their anger. Sometimes the anger is used to avoid discussing the issue at hand. At other times the anger is directed at the counselor for confronting the client with reality.

The underlying reasons for this anger need to be remembered here. Certain therapeutic techniques are especially helpful during this stage. Allowing clients to vent their anger reduces its intensity; once this happens, they are better able to examine their difficulties realistically. Conveying empathy and emotional support creates an atmosphere in which clients feel more comfortable examining their difficulties. Clients often feel overwhelmed by their problems, which is a factor in their intensely felt "Why me?" They need to see that their problems are not overwhelming but can be broken down into subproblems that are resolvable in a step-by-step fashion. During this stage, it is helpful for counselors to realize that clients angrily attacking them should not be taken personally. Reacting personally or angrily to clients' anger will only prolong their hostile behavior.

Lee Askew at times displayed anger while in counseling with Paul Decker. As indicated earlier, Mr. Askew at first denied he had a drinking problem. He had excuses for all the problems that were being caused by drinking. Mr. Decker knew counseling would not be productive unless this denial was broken through. Mr. Decker suggested that at the next session the Askews meet jointly to get both their perceptions of their marital problems. Mr. Askew reacted angrily to this suggestion, castigating his wife for making up stories about him, particularly his drinking. The counselor allowed Mr. Askew to vent his anger and then asked, "Are you fearful of what your wife might say?" Mr. Askew stated "no" and agreed to a joint meeting.

Several joint meetings were held with the Askews. Mr. Askew continued to deny his drinking problem. These denials were countered by Mr. Decker asking him questions that served to confront Mr. Askew with his problem, including how much he drank each day, how he acted while drunk, how Mrs. Askew felt about seeing her husband intoxicated, and whether his drinking has gotten him in trouble at work and with the police. Mr. Askew used anger to avoid confronting his alcoholism. Mr. Decker let Mr. Askew "spit fire" and vent. On a few occasions after Mr. Askew calmed down, Mr. Decker asked, "I wonder why you are reacting angrily to what is being said?" or "It appears we are touching a sensitive chord with you." Such questions were designed to help Mr. Askew understand why he was reacting angrily.

At other times, Mr. Askew would go into a tirade about how many of his friends drank and had a good time. He fumed about his wife pressuring him to stop drinking. He was clearly going through the "Why me?" stage. After allowing Mr. Askew to vent, Mr. Decker pointed out that unlike the drinking of social drinkers, his drinking controlled him; he was not in control of his drinking. Specific incidents were tactfully mentioned.

On one occasion Mr. Askew, with his wife present, castigated Mr. Decker for meddling in his family affairs. The counselor calmly listened and then replied, "Are you feeling angry at me because I'm forcing you to see that you face a choice between giving up drinking or losing your wife?" Mr. Askew at first reacted angrily to this but later acknowledged the statement was true.

Stage 3: Bargaining ("Yes, me, but . . .") During this stage, clients are beginning to accept the problem but will bargain for "just one more time." They promise to be good or to do something in exchange for another week or month before they embrace change. During this stage, counselors should confront clients with the reality of their circumstances and their bargaining efforts. During the bargaining stage, clients usually try to change a few circumstances in their lives, and they generally believe that just a few changes will allow them to continue in their old ways. They tell themselves that "if such and such changes, I can still continue to . . ." Bargaining is a common reaction. People who are urged to lose weight bargain for "strawberry shortcake"; smokers who are urged to quit bargain to smoke when tense; some spouses seek to preserve a marriage that is in trouble by means of a pregnancy.

Mr. Askew tried several bargains. He asked if he continued in counseling whether he could continue to drink socially. Both the counselor and Mrs. Askew doubted that he could quit after a few drinks and expressed their misgivings. Social drinking was tried for a week, and Mr. Askew became intoxicated on three occasions. At the next session Mrs. Askew again stated her ultimatum: "Stop drinking, or I'm leaving." Efforts were then made to get Mr. Askew involved in Alcoholics Anonymous (AA) meetings. Initial results in AA were good. Then a wedding came up, and Mr. Askew bargained with his wife (outside of counseling) that he would continue in AA if he could socially drink at special occasions such as the wedding. His wife struck the bargain on the condition that he quit after a few drinks. Mr. Askew became intoxicated at the wedding, and his actions (including wetting his pants) were intensely embarrassing to Mrs. Askew. At the next counseling session, Mrs. Askew again stated her ultimatum: "Stop drinking completely, or else I'm leaving." After other similar bargaining efforts, Mr. Askew was confronted by Mr. Decker with the statement that it appeared he was not committed to giving up drinking but was striking bargains to continue his drinking. Mr. Askew at first reacted angrily (back to the anger stage) but gradually acknowledged he was bargaining.

Stage 4: Depression ("Yes, me.") Clients in the depression stage become very quiet. They have, by now, stopped denying their problem. Their anger has subsided, and they no longer try to bargain. They have gained insight into their particular problem and realize they must change. Alternatives, however, are not yet perceived as viable solutions. They blame themselves in a "self-downing" manner for their problems and frequently mourn what they will have to give up. During this stage, counselors need to convey empathy and help clients see that their problems are not overwhelming. Clients need hope; frequently this can be accomplished by helping them develop resolution strategies.

Mr. Askew and his wife had been coming to weekly counseling for 3½ months. During this time Mr. Askew made some efforts to give up drinking. At times he would go for a week or two without drinking, but he always returned to the bottle. In counseling sessions, he vacillated between making excuses for his drinking (denial) and displaying anger or bargaining when confronted with the need to stop drinking. At the counseling session following a drinking episode, he would usually be depressed, acknowledging he was ruining his life. He would deprecate himself and beg his wife to give him one more chance. When she did, a week or two later he would find an excuse to start drinking again.

Mr. Askew came into counseling one day a little hung over and very depressed. He indicated he had gotten drunk the day before, and he and his wife had argued. He wasn't certain, but he thought he may have slapped her a few times. He added that afterward she packed a bag, indicated she was going to file for divorce, and left. Mr. Askew stated that life was not worth living without his wife. He fully acknowledged he had a drinking problem and had to abstain completely. The counselor and Mr. Askew discussed various alternatives. Mr. Askew stated with emotion that he would never take another drink and that he would demonstrate this to his wife. He further decided to wait for 2 weeks before contacting her so that she could sort out her feelings and thoughts. Mr. Askew left the interview depressed, realizing that his drinking may have ruined his marriage forever.

Stage 5: Acceptance ("I have a problem, but it's all right." "I can.") Clients make a concentrated effort at this stage to work out alternatives, not only those suggested earlier in treatment but also some of their own. Their attitude is now one of "I can do it." There is hope. A plan for rehabilitation can be presented if one was lacking or dismissed in the earlier stages. Fear is still present but very much reduced.

After 2 weeks Mr. Askew called his wife. They talked, and she agreed to attend the next counseling session. At this session, Mrs. Askew indicated she was ambivalent about ending her marriage, but she had totally had it with her husband's drunken behavior. They agreed to live apart for the next 4 months. If Lee participated in AA meetings and did not drink at all, then they would live together again, on the condition that he would never drink again.

That was over 2 years ago. Lee Askew has not had a drink, and he is active in AA helping other problem drinkers. He is also active in a speakers bureau in which he talks to high school students and businesses and organizations about the dangers of alcohol and about treatment programs. After 3 months of separation, his wife returned, and both report their marriage and their careers are going well.

Exercise 5.10: Understanding Clients' Emotional Reactions to Having a Problem

Goal: This exercise is designed to help you better understand the Kübler-Ross model of emotional reactions to a loss.

Step 1.   Reflect on a significant loss that you had—such as the ending of a relationship, getting a speeding ticket, or a pet dying. Specify the loss.

Step 2.   Specify the extent to which you experienced emotional reactions consistent with Kübler-Ross's five reactions.

     a. Denial:

     b. Rage and anger:

     c. Bargaining:

     d. Depression:

     e. Acceptance:

SUMMARY

The following summarizes the chapter's content in terms of the learning objectives presented at the beginning of the chapter.

1. Describe counseling from the worker's perspective.
   Counseling can be divided into three phases:
   a. Building a relationship
   b. Exploring problems in depth
   c. Exploring alternative solutions with the client and selecting a course of action
2. Summarize guidelines on counseling clients.
   a. Establish a working relationship:
      i. Introduce yourself and begin with a little small talk.
      ii. Have client talk about his or her concerns by saying something like "Do you have some concerns you'd like to talk about today?"
      iii. After the client discusses his or her concerns for 3 or 4 minutes, "connect" with the feelings by saying something like the following: "How are you feeling about this?" "This must really be difficult for you." "I sense you're feeling (such and such) about this."
   b. Explore the client's concerns in depth.
   c. Explore alternative solutions to the concerns with the client:
      i. In doing this, *first* ask the client what he or she has tried and what he or she is thinking about trying.
      ii. Don't give advice. Instead, phrase your resolution options as suggestions, such as "Have you thought about trying _____?"
3. Describe counseling from the client's perspective.
   The counseling process can be conceptualized from the client's point of view. For counseling to be successful, clients must arrive at a progressive series of "self-talk" statements (that is, clients must arrive at having certain thoughts and beliefs). These self-talk stages are the following:

   Stage 1   *Problem awareness:* "I have a problem."

   Stage 2   *Relationship to counselor:* "I think this counselor has what it takes to help me."

   Stage 3   *Motivation:* "I want to improve my situation and am willing to put forth the effort to do so."

   Stage 4   *Conceptualizing the problem:* "My problem is not overwhelming but has specific components that can be changed."

   Stage 5   *Exploration of resolution strategies:* "I see there are several courses of action that I might take to try to do something about my situation."

Stage 6   *Selection of a strategy:* "I think this approach might help and I am willing to try it."

Stage 7   *Implementation:* "This approach is helping me."

Stage 8   *Termination and evaluation:* "Although this approach takes a lot of my time and effort, it's worth it."

4. Describe client's reactions to having a personal problem.

Counselors need to be aware of and learn to handle clients' emotional reactions to having a personal problem. Kübler-Ross's five stages of emotional reactions to loss are not unique to the terminally ill but are also typical reactions that clients display when confronted with evidence of a personal problem. Any time clients first recognize that they have a personal problem, a sense of loss occurs. Kübler-Ross's five stages are denial, rage and anger, bargaining, depression, and acceptance. Only when clients reach the fifth stage of acceptance are they ready to work effectively on alternatives for resolving their problems. With a better understanding of these emotional reactions, counselors will be more effective in selecting appropriate intervention strategies.

EXERCISES

1. Understanding Clients' Reactions to Having a Personal Problem

Goal: This exercise is designed to help students understand clients' reactions to having a personal problem.

Step 1. The instructor explains the purpose of the exercise. The instructor indicates that when a person acknowledges he or she has a personal problem, almost always that person experiences a loss of some kind. The loss may involve giving up something one has had (such as an alcoholic giving up drinking). Or the loss may involve recognition that a desired goal is not obtainable (for example, parents who have a child with a cognitive disability may feel the loss of not having a child of normal intelligence). When a loss is experienced, the person almost always has the emotional reactions described by Kübler-Ross. The instructor describes the following reactions to students: denial, anger and rage, bargaining, depression, and acceptance.

Step 2. The instructor asks students to volunteer to describe a loss they have had and has them comment on whether they experienced the five reactions described by Kübler-Ross.

Step 3. The instructor explains that clients frequently are not ready emotionally to work on resolving a personal problem or a loss until they reach the fifth stage of acceptance. The instructor asks the students who describe a loss if, in fact, they had to reach the stage of accepting their loss before they were able to make a concentrated effort to work on alternatives for resolving the problems.

2. Learning How to Counsel through Role-Playing

Goal: The purpose of this exercise is to help students develop their counseling skills through role-playing counseling situations.

Step 1. The instructor describes the goal of the exercise. The instructor indicates that the counseling process from the counselor's view can be divided into five phases: (1) starting the interview; (2) building a relationship; (3) exploring problems in depth; (4) exploring alternative solutions with the client, then choosing one or more of the alternatives; and (5) ending the interview. (Material on these five phases is summarized in Chapters 4 and 5.) The instructor briefly summarizes guidelines on how a counselor should handle each of these phases.

Step 2. Two students volunteer to role-play being clients. The "clients" come up with their own contrived problems. Here are some examples of possible problems:

   a. Two college students are roommates. One believes the other has a drinking problem, but the other refuses to acknowledge a problem exists.

   b. Two siblings are concerned about their mother living alone. Her health is failing, and her husband recently died. The siblings also believe they are unable to care for their mother because each is married and has a family and the mother is not easy to live with.

   c. A husband and wife both want children, but the husband is infertile. The wife wants to become pregnant through artificial insemination. The husband objects to his wife getting pregnant using this means.

Step 3:   The instructor counsels the two students who have contrived problems to demonstrate the five phases of counseling. After the counseling is completed, the class discusses the strengths and shortcomings of the counseling that was given.

Step 4.   The instructor asks four more students to volunteer—two as clients having contrived problems and two as counselors for the two "clients." (It is useful to have two people, at this early stage, volunteer to be counselors to offset the potential of one counselor becoming "stuck" by not knowing what to say.) Role-play the interview.

Step 5.   As an additional step, the instructor requires each student in the class to role-play as counselor and also as client (for some other student who role-plays being a counselor). Ideally each student should be videotaped in the role of the counselor, and this videotape should then be played back so students can assess the interview. (As described in Chapter 4, the videotaping may be used not only to help students develop their counseling skills but also as a screening device to counsel out students from the social work major if they are unable, after several tries, to make an acceptable videotape.)

Step 6.   The instructor shows each videotape to the class. A brief class discussion is held after each tape is shown. This discussion should review the strengths and shortcomings of the counseling and also look at what else might be done. If each tape is shown to the class, it is helpful for each student to fill out the "Interviewer Skills Rating Sheet" on the following page, which is then given to the "counselor" for feedback purposes. (One advantage of showing each tape to the class is that students learn what should, and should not, be done in counseling.)

Note: Role-playing contrived counseling situations (and also videotaping such situations) can be structured in a variety of ways. This exercise presents some ideas, but the instructor of course has the autonomy to structure the role-playing in ways that he or she believes will be most beneficial.

Interviewer Skills Rating Sheet

Student _____   **Date** _____

Skills	Needs Improvement	Satisfactory	Excellent
1. Opening remarks			
2. Explanation of counselor role			
3. Voice quality and volume			
4. Body posture			
5. Eye contact			
6. Behavioral congruence/facial expression (therapist's words match his/her outward appearance)			
7. Frequency of open-ended questions (not yes-no or multiple-choice questions)			
8. Amount of therapist's verbal activity			
9. Verbal following behavior (sequencing questions with client's answers, preparing client for shift in subject matter)			
10. Clarity of questions			
11. Ability to confront client with inconsistencies			
12. Use of humor			
13. Warmth/ability to put client at ease			
14. Use of silence			
15. Ability to help client define problems			

Interviewer Skills Rating Sheet (*continued*)

Skills	Needs Improvement	Satisfactory	Excellent
16. Ability to have client specify goals			
17. Paraphrasing			
18. Reflection of client's feelings			
19. Summarization of client information			
20. Ability to answer client's questions/provide useful information			
21. Extent to which interviewer presented him-herself as a professional			
22. Extent to which necessary data about the problem was obtained			
23. Ending the interview/length of interview			
24. Completeness of interview			
25. Extent to which a helpful relationship was developed			
26. Extent to which alternative solutions to the problem were begun to be explored			

Positive Comments about Strengths Demonstrated during the interview:

_____

_____

_____

Areas Needing Attention:

_____

_____

_____

3. Responding Effectively to Critical Statements from Clients

Goal: This exercise is designed to help students learn how to respond more effectively to highly emotional and complex statements made by clients.

Step 1.   The instructor explains the purpose of the exercise. The instructor then reads to the class the first of the client statements listed below and asks the class for suggestions on the most effective way for a counselor to respond. There are various effective responses. (One way of responding to each of these statements is presented in the Appendix.) A class discussion of the merits and shortcomings of some of the students' suggested responses is likely to be a productive learning experience.

Step 2.   After the class responds to and discusses the first statement, the instructor reads the second statement and again seeks responses and discussion from the students. This process continues with the remaining statements.

CLIENT STATEMENTS

1. *Male client* (fifth interview): "There's something that's been bothering me for the past few weeks (pause). I'm beginning to feel that you're not really interested in me as a person. I have the feeling that the only reason you're meeting with me is because you're getting paid to see me."

2. *Engaged female*, age 20: "I'm engaged to marry Kent. My uncle thinks he's terrific, but my parents are telling me I'm making the biggest mistake of my life to marry him. They dislike him and also think I'm too young to marry. I'm so confused about what I should do. Kent is putting a lot of pressure on me to elope."

3. *Juvenile probationee,* age 16—who is recognized as being a con artist—in required weekly visit with probation agent: "Your office is really cool. You've really got it made. I admire your taste in furnishing this office. You deserve what you've got in life. I admire you. Those are great photographs on the wall. Did you take them?" The probation officer is aware that students received their midterm grade reports this past week.

4. *Male client,* age 27 (fourth interview): "I'm feeling real tense today. I've got a lot on my mind (pause). I don't think we've made much progress in the last three meetings, although I am gradually coming to trust you (pause). I haven't been fully honest with you. You know the marital problems I've been having? Well, the main reason our marriage hasn't gone well, and Karen doesn't even know this, is because for the past few years I've been involved with someone else—who happens to be a male. Karen no longer turns me on because I guess I'm more attracted to males."

5. *African American client* from an inner city who has a white therapist: "You honkies don't know what life is really like for us who live in a ghetto. You say you want to help me, but I don't buy that jive. How can you possibly help me when you have no idea what it is like to be black and living in a ghetto?"

6. *Teenage male delinquent* caught with marijuana in his possession at a correctional institution: "Please don't report this. You know I've been doing really well here at school and have a clean record. If you report this, my stay will be extended. I was only holding the drugs for a friend here. I'm not using any of it myself. Give me a break—everyone needs one in life." The youth was involved with drugs when he committed the offenses for which he was sent to this correctional facility.

SOCIAL WORK WITH GROUPS: TYPES OF GROUPS AND GUIDELINES FOR LEADING THEM

LEARNING OBJECTIVES

The practice of social work in groups is not a new phenomenon. The ideological roots of social work with groups can be traced most directly to the settlement houses, informal self-help recreational organizations (YMCA, YWCA), Jewish centers, and scouting, all of which developed during the first three decades of the twentieth century. During this period, many social workers found group-based methods of intervention effective and efficient for confronting a variety of personal and social problems. The last 75 years have witnessed progressive interest in, and expansion of, group services in our society. The involvement of the social work profession in groups has broadened accordingly. Today it is not uncommon to find social workers as both group leaders and participants in a myriad of settings, helping solve or ameliorate human or social problems and planning for and creating change. There are many reasons behind the attractiveness of groups for members and for practitioners.

Johnson and Johnson (2000) define a group as "two or more individuals in face-to-face interaction, each aware of his or her membership in the group, each aware of the others who belong to the group, and each aware of their positive interdependence as they strive to achieve mutual goals" (p. 20). From this description, we can see that the members of a group relate to one another within a context of sensing they form a distinct entity, that they share a common goal or purpose, and that they have confidence that together they can accomplish as much as or more than would be possible were they to work separately. This commonality is characteristic of a wide variety of groups dealing with a multitude of societal problems.

The beginning social worker is likely to be surprised at the diversity of groups in existence and excited by the challenge of practicing social work in groups. The period from 1960 to the present has witnessed an explosion in the number of groups and group-based techniques used by the social work profession. This chapter will help prepare students to:

Describe types of groups in which social workers become involved
Understand guidelines on how to start, lead, evaluate, and terminate groups

TYPES OF GROUPS

This section describes a significant sample of the types of groups in which social workers may become involved. The following types of groups are briefly described: recreation groups, recreation-skill groups, educational groups, task groups, problem-solving and decision-making groups, focus groups, self-help groups, socialization groups, counseling groups, and encounter groups. This list is not exhaustive; only the creativity of the helping professional and the client group served will provide such limits. However, the groups discussed here are frequently encountered by social workers.

Recreation Groups

The objective of recreation groups is to provide activities for enjoyment and exercise. Often such activities are spontaneous, and the groups are practically leaderless. The group service agency (such as YMCA, YWCA, or neighborhood center) may offer little more than physical space and the use of some equipment.

Spontaneous playground activities, informal athletic games, and an open game room are examples. Some group agencies providing such physical space claim that recreation and interaction with others help build character and prevent delinquency among youth by providing an alternative to the street.

Recreation-Skill Groups

The objective of a recreation-skill group is to improve a set of skills while providing enjoyment. In contrast to recreational groups, this group has an adviser, coach, or instructor; also, there is more of a task orientation. Examples of activities include golf, basketball, needlework, arts and crafts, and swimming. Competitive team sports and leagues may emerge. Frequently such groups are led by professionals with recreational training rather than social work training. Social service agencies providing such services include YMCA, YWCA, Boy Scouts, Girl Scouts, neighborhood centers, and school recreation departments.

Educational Groups

The focus of educational groups is to help members acquire knowledge and learn complex skills. The leader generally is a professional person with considerable training and expertise in the subject area. Examples of topics include child-rearing practices, assertiveness training, techniques for becoming a more effective parent, preparing to be an adoptive parent, and training volunteers to perform a specialized task for a social service agency. Educational group leaders often function in a didactic manner and frequently are social workers. These groups may resemble a class, with considerable group interaction and discussion being encouraged. The Case Example "Assertiveness Training—An Educational Group" below shows how assertiveness training can be taught in an educational group.

Exercise 6.1: My Most Rewarding and Least Rewarding Educational Group

Goal: This exercise is designed to assist you in identifying the factors that lead to rewarding and unrewarding educational group experiences.

Step 1.   Briefly describe an educational group in which you participated that you found to be highly rewarding. Indicate why this group was highly rewarding to you. (The group may be a class.)

CASE EXAMPLE   ASSERTIVENESS TRAINING—AN EDUCATIONAL GROUP

There are several advantages of group assertiveness training. A group provides a "laboratory" for testing or experimenting with new assertive behaviors. A group has a broader base for social modeling because each member sees the other members trying out various assertive approaches. A wider variety of feedback is also offered. Furthermore, a group is generally understanding and supportive. Finally, group pressure and expectations motivate members to conscientiously develop and practice new assertive responses.

A typical format for an assertiveness training group is as follows: The size of such groups generally ranges from 5 to 20 members. The first session is devoted to a lecture presentation on differences between assertive, nonassertive, and aggressive behavior. The specific steps in assertive training are then summarized. (These steps are presented in Module 2.) Several examples of typical situations are given to illustrate that assertive responses are generally more effective than aggressive or nonassertive responses.

In later sessions, specific situations calling for assertive responses are examined. It may be desirable to begin with situations not brought forth by members of the group (group members may at first be reluctant to reveal personal situations they face).

Alberti and Emmons (1975, pp. 183–184) suggested the following situations be practiced:

1. Starting a conversation with a small group of strangers who are already engaged in conversation at a party
2. Saying "no" assertively when a roommate or friend asks to borrow something that you do not want to lend
3. Returning faulty or defective items to a store
4. Asking someone next to you to extinguish a cigarette
5. Asking someone to turn down a television that is too loud or not talk so loudly in the library or theater
6. Asking for a date or refusing a date on the phone and face-to-face
7. Expressing positive feelings; "soft assertions"
8. Responding assertively to a date or spouse who is giving you put-down comments
9. Assertively refusing to take an alcoholic beverage from a friend when you prefer not to drink

For each situation the following steps are used: (1) Each member is asked to visualize (form a mental image of) his or her response. (2) One member is selected to role-play an assertive response. (3) The group briefly discusses the strategy after it is

CASE EXAMPLE   (continued)

role-played. (4) If a more effective response is desired, a new assertive response is role-played by a member. (5) The group discusses the strategy.

After this exercise, group members are encouraged to bring to the group real-life situations that are troubling them. These are often complex situations involving close, intimate relationships. Such situations may not have pat, simple resolutions.

The following steps are recommended for group leaders trying to help members become more assertive:

1. Help each group member identify the situations and interactions in which it would be to his or her benefit to be more assertive. Usually group members will bring up these situations themselves. Some members, however, may be reluctant to reveal problem interactions, or they may be unaware they could handle certain situations better by being more assertive. Considerable tact and skill by the leader is necessary in initiating problem areas of the latter type. (One approach that usually works is to have the members anonymously write the situations they want role-played on a note card.)
2. When a problem interaction is identified, each member of the group is asked to visualize a response silently. For complicated situations with no simple solutions, considerable discussion may arise about possible ways of resolving the matter.
3. A member (often someone other than the person with the problem situation) is asked to role-play an assertive response. The member with the problem may be asked to play the role of the person with whom he or she is having difficulty. The situation is then role-played.

4. The group briefly discusses the merits of the assertive strategy that was modeled in step 3.

If the strategy is effective and the person with the problem is comfortable with it, that person is then asked to role-play the approach. If the group believes there may be a more effective approach, steps 3 and 4 are repeated. If the person with the problem is uncomfortable about using a strategy that is effective, the reasons for the discomfort are then explored. For example, for very shy people, certain attitudes, such as "don't make waves" or the "meek shall inherit the earth" may need to be dealt with.

5. The person with the problem is asked to rehearse an assertive strategy silently, thinking of what he or she will say and what the consequences may be.
6. The person with the problem is asked to role-play an assertive strategy.
7. The group gives feedback about the merits of the strategy. Generally the person is praised for the effective aspects and coached on how to improve other aspects. This approach is practiced via role-playing until it is perfected and the person has developed sufficient comfort and self-confidence for the "real event." For feedback purposes, if possible, the approach is recorded on audiotape or videotape.
8. The person tries out the new response pattern in an actual situation.
9. The person describes at the next group meeting how the real-life test went. The person is complimented on the degree of success attained, and assistance is given on aspects that could be improved.

Step 2.   Briefly describe an educational group in which you participated that you found to be very unrewarding. Indicate why this group was not very rewarding for you.

Task Groups

Task groups are formed to achieve a specific set of tasks or objectives. Social workers are likely to interact with or become involved in a variety of task groups. A *board of directors* is an administrative group charged with responsibility for setting the policy governing agency programs. A *task force* is a group established for a special purpose and is usually disbanded after the task is completed. A *committee* of an agency or organization is a group formed to deal with specific tasks or matters. An *ad hoc committee,* like a task force, is set up for one purpose and usually ceases functioning after completion of its task.

Problem-Solving and Decision-Making Groups

Both providers and consumers of social services may become involved in groups concerned with problem solving and decision making. There is considerable overlap between task groups and these groups; thus, problem-solving and decision-making groups can be considered a subcategory of task groups.

Providers of services use group meetings for such objectives as developing a treatment plan for a client or a group of clients, deciding how to best allocate scarce resources, deciding how to improve the delivery of services to clients, arriving at policy decisions for the agency, deciding how to improve coordination efforts with other agencies, and so on. Potential *consumers* of services may form a group to study an unmet need in the community and to advocate for the development of new programs to meet the need. Data on the need may be gathered, and the group may be used as a vehicle either to develop a program or to influence existing agencies to provide services. Social workers may function as stimulators and organizers of such group efforts as well as participants (see Chapter 10 on social work community practice).

One type of problem-solving group is the *nominal group,* which can be helpful in identifying problems. The case example "Nominal-Group Approach—A Problem Identification Technique for Problem-Solving Groups" below describes one such group.

In problem-solving and decision-making groups, each participant normally has some interest or stake in the process and may gain or lose, depending on the outcome. Usually, there is a formal leader of some sort, although other leaders sometimes emerge during the process. Three issues are of importance to problem-solving and decision-making groups: group versus individual decision making, groupthink, and decision by consensus versus decision by majority vote.

Group versus Individual Decision Making. Is group decision making superior to individual decision making? Evidence indicates that group decision making usually is superior to individual decision making (Johnson & Johnson, 2000), even when an individual decision is made by an expert.

There appear to be several reasons why group decision making is generally superior. First, through group interaction, the knowledge, abilities, and resources of each member are pooled. An individual acting alone often lacks some of the information, skills, or resources needed to arrive at the highest-quality decision. Second, working in the presence of others motivates a person to put forth more effort, to be more careful, and to increase the quality of the work. Third, having more people working on a problem increases the probability that someone in the group will suggest the highest-quality solution. Fourth, through group interaction the members can build on one another's ideas and develop a high-quality decision based on this building-block approach. Fifth, through group discussion there is a greater chance of identifying the positive and negative consequences of each alternative. Therefore, the negative consequences of an inferior decision are more likely to be identified. Sixth, it is easier to identify other people's mistakes than it is to identify your own. Through group interaction you are more likely to identify the problem areas in the favorite alternatives of others, and others are more likely to identify the problem areas in your favorite alternative.

CASE EXAMPLE   NOMINAL-GROUP APPROACH—A PROBLEM IDENTIFICATION TECHNIQUE FOR PROBLEM-SOLVING GROUPS

The nominal-group approach was developed by Delbecq and Van de Ven (1971) as a problem identification technique in social program development efforts. The approach involves meeting with potential users of a service. A *nominal group* is defined as "a group in which individuals work in the presence of others but do not verbally interact" (Van de Ven & Delbecq, 1971, p. 205). This need-identification approach emphasizes the importance of understanding clearly the view of the population that the group is trying to serve and asserts that potential consumers of new services should articulate their needs, problems, and goals. The main orientation is to respond to consumers' needs rather than independently develop programs for them. To accomplish this objective, the nominal-group approach is designed to receive input from all group members rather than just the more vocal or aggressive ones, as often happens in conventional group discussions. This technique has successfully been used in such applications as determining the housing difficulties of college students, reasons that have led delinquent youth into difficulty with police (Zastrow, 1973), and specific course topics wanted by students enrolling in social work courses (Zastrow & Navarre, 1977).

Research indicates that the nominal-group approach is superior to brainstorming and other types of interaction in groups in generating information relevant to a problem situation. Both quantity and quality of suggestions are enhanced with this technique (Van de Ven & Delbecq, 1971). Several features appear to be involved in leading to this superiority. The approach has a game mystique that stimulates the interest of participants. Creative tension is stimulated by the presence of others, which fosters individual commitment to the task. Evaluation of items is avoided, which substantially reduces the pressure against expressing minority opinions or conventional ideas. Conflicting, incompatible ideas are tolerated. Furthermore, the approach appears to be "a time-saving process since it can be activated and concluded with greater rapidity than interacting group processes" (Van de Ven & Delbecq, 1971, p. 210).

The mechanics of conducting a nominal group are as follows:

1. Gather together a group of participants, any size, ranging up to about 100, and explain the nature of the study Emphasize the importance of their ideas related to this topic. Care should be taken to obtain a representative cross-section of the populations of interest.
2. Randomly divide the participants into small groups ranging in size from five to eight. Seat each group around a separate table or in desks arranged in a circle.
3. Distribute to each participant a sheet of paper containing a question that must be answered. For example, the wording for

CASE EXAMPLE *(continued)*

determining what social work students in a class see as short-comings in the social work program that should be addressed might be: "What do you see as shortcomings in our social work program?"

Please—No Talking

4. For 15 to 20 minutes, the participants privately list items they feel are in response to the question being asked; no talking is permitted during this period.

5. A round-robin listing technique is then used in which each individual in turn is given the opportunity to disclose one item at a time to the group. This listing is done separately for each group with one of the members acting as a recorder. Ideas may be recorded on flip-chart paper or on a chalkboard. This round-robin listing continues until all members indicate they have no further ideas to share. Until this point is reached, there is no discussion or evaluation of ideas presented.

6. Following the listing of all ideas, the flip-chart sheets are posted on the wall with masking tape. There is a brief, informal discussion of the items, which is focused on clarifying what the ideas mean. There are two different approaches to reviewing the items. Either (1) all items are made known to all participants, or (2) members of each group briefly review only the items recorded for their group. Both approaches appear to work. With smaller groups, the first is usually used. With larger groups, in which the total number of listed items becomes very large, the second approach is generally used.

7. Once the participants are familiar with the items listed, each is asked to write privately on index cards the five items he or she feels are the most important.

8. These selections are then tabulated and posted. The highest-ranked problems or topics represent those considered most important by the group members.

In general, the effectiveness of group decision making is enhanced when there is high involvement by all group members. High involvement increases the willingness of members to share their information and abilities in making a decision, increases their allegiance to the group, increases their commitment to implementing the decision, and increases their commitment to working for the group in the future. Most groups can become more effective by seeking to increase the involvement of all group members in making decisions.

There are only a few situations in which decisions might best be made by one or a few individuals: (1) when a decision has to be made so quickly it is not possible to have a meeting; (2) when the decision is relatively unimportant and the person making the decision follows precedents previously set by the group; and (3) when the decision is relatively unimportant, does not require committed action by most members of a group, and there is no reason to believe the group will object to the decision.

But there are also problems with group decision making. At times a subgroup will seek to "railroad" a decision that benefits them but is counterproductive for the whole group or for certain people outside the group. (Hitler, for example, used many tactics to sway groups he worked with to begin World War II and to exterminate 6 million Jews.) Railroading tactics include pressuring a group to make a quick decision without giving members time to analyze all the consequences, withholding information that is adverse to the desired decision, buying votes with promises, and suggesting there may be negative consequences for members who do not vote for the desired decision.

Another problem in group decision making is that friendships and paybacks for past favors sometimes lead members to vote for "the person" rather than for a decision based on thorough analysis of the consequences of the alternatives. Republicans and Democrats in Congress, for example, largely vote along party lines.

Sometimes groups reach incorrect or ineffective decisions because of a phenomenon known as *groupthink*

Groupthink. Irving Janis (1971) identified groupthink as an unusual condition that prevents effective problem solving. Janis studied groups that advised presidents of the United States and found that powerful social pressures were often exerted whenever a dissident began to voice objections to what otherwise appeared to be a group consensus. *Groupthink* is a problem-solving process in which proposals are accepted without a critical, careful review of the pros and cons of the alternatives and in which considerable social pressure is brought to bear against expressing opposing points of view. Groupthink occurs partially because the norms of the group hold that it is more important to bolster group morale than to evaluate all alternatives critically. Another group norm that increases groupthink is that members should remain loyal to the group by sticking with the policies to which the group has already committed itself, even if those policies are not having the intended effects or are having disturbing unintended consequences.

Janis (1971) listed a number of factors that promote groupthink, including the following:

- Members have an illusion of being invulnerable, which leads them to become overly optimistic about their selected courses of action, to take extraordinary risks, and to fail to respond to clear warnings of danger.
- Members have an unquestioning belief in the group's moral rightness, which leads them to ignore the ethical consequences of their decisions.
- The group applies social pressures of disapproval on any member who momentarily questions the basic policies or who raises questions about a policy alternative favored by the majority.
- The group constructs rationalizations to discount warnings and other forms of negative feedback that would, if taken seriously, lead the members to rethink basic assumptions about policies that are not working out well.
- Group members hold stereotyped views of the leaders of opposing groups. Either these leaders are viewed as being so evil that it would be a mistake to try genuinely to negotiate differences, or they are viewed as so stupid or so weak that they will not be able to prevent the group from attaining its objectives.
- Members sometimes assume "mind guard" roles in which they attempt to protect their leader and the group from negative information that might lead them to question the morality and effectiveness of past decisions.
- Members keep quiet about their misgivings and even minimize to themselves the importance of these misgivings. Through self-censorship members avoid deviating from what appears to be group consensus.
- Members believe practically everyone in the group fully agrees with the policies and programs of the group.

Numerous poor decision-making practices result from groupthink. The group limits its discussion to only those courses of action that are consistent with past decisions and policies. As a result, divergent strategies (some of them viable) are not considered. The group fails to reexamine a selected course of action, even when it discovers risks, drawbacks, and unintended consequences not previously considered. The group makes little effort to get cost-benefit information on possible strategies from experts who might be able to supply more accurate information. Members seek primarily to obtain facts and listen to opinions that support their preferred policy and tend to ignore facts and opinions that do not. The group fails to work out contingency plans to cope with foreseeable setbacks, and it spends little time considering how the chosen strategy might be sabotaged by political opponents or hampered by bureaucratic red tape.

Groupthink apparently affected decision making prior to the 2003 invasion of Iraq. Yahoo News (2004) reported the following:

> The key U.S. assertions leading to the 2003 invasion of Iraq—that Saddam Hussein had chemical and biological weapons and was working to make nuclear weapons—were wrong and based on false or overstated CIA analyses, a scathing Senate Intelligence Committee report asserted Friday. Intelligence analysts fell victim to "groupthink" assumptions that Iraq had weapons that it did not, concluded a bipartisan report.

Exercise 6.2: My Groupthink Experience

Goal: This exercise is designed to assist you in understanding and applying the theoretical material on groupthink.

Step 1: Describe an experience in which you believed your group was going in the wrong direction yet you failed to express your thoughts or opinions.

Step 2: Specify why you failed to express your thoughts or opinions.

Step 3: Do you believe your reasons for not expressing your thoughts or opinions are consistent or inconsistent with groupthink? Explain your views.

Consensus versus Majority Voting. Decision making by consensus is usually the most effective approach for getting all members to support and work for a decision. Consensus means that everyone is willing to go along with the decision, at least temporarily. This approach is also the most time-consuming because the concerns of each member need to be dealt with. For many decisions, consensus is difficult to achieve because members are likely to have diverse opinions about what should be done.

To use consensus effectively, group members need to have a certain mind-set, and the group has to have a trusting, cooperative atmosphere. For consensus to be arrived at, members need to feel free to present their views as clearly and logically as possible but to avoid blindly arguing their own individual views. They need to listen to and respect the views of other members. Members should *avoid* going along with the group if they believe the majority opinion is a mistake. It is a mistake to yield to the majority if the only reason is to avoid conflict and appear united. Members, however, might yield to the majority opinion if that position appears to have merit and is a position they believe has a fair chance of having positive outcomes.

To make consensus work effectively, differences of opinion are sought out and respectfully dealt with. Disagreements and divergent views are advantageous because they increase the chances that all crucial aspects will be reviewed, that members will build on the views of others, and that viable decisions will be made.

With consensus, the participation of all members is encouraged. The emphasis is on finding the best solution that everyone can agree on and support. If a group becomes stalemated between two possible alternatives, a vote is not taken to allow one subgroup to win while the other loses. Instead, a third alternative is sought to incorporate the major desires of both subgroups.

There are a number of benefits to consensus. Consensus resolves controversies and conflicts, so it increases the group's ability to make future high-quality decisions. If group members feel they have participated in the decision and support it, they are more likely to contribute their resources to implement the decision. Consensus is useful in making important, serious, and complex decisions in which the success of the decision depends on the commitment of all members.

There are some disadvantages to consensus. It takes a great deal of time and psychological energy. The pressure for group consensus can lead to groupthink In this situation members go along with what they believe is the majority opinion, even when they have evidence or information (which they fail to share for fear of making waves) that the probable decision will be unproductive or even destructive. In addition, consensus will not work in many groups for a variety of reasons. A high level of trust may not exist in the group, thereby not allowing candor, honesty, and directness. Some members may try to dominate or manipulate the group rather than listen to and support one another as individuals. Some members may see the slow process required to arrive at consensus as painful, aggravating, and a waste of time.

Most groups make decisions by simple majority vote. With this approach, issues are discussed until they are clarified and a simple majority of the members has arrived at an alternative. A vote is then taken. There are several advantages to this type of decision making. Decisions are arrived at much faster than with the consensus approach. Most decisions in a group are not so important that full support of all members is necessary to achieve the objectives of the decision. Also, majority vote does not require, to as great an extent, the characteristics that are essential for consensus (such as trust, open communication, and willingness to give up one's favorite position).

There are also shortcomings of the simple majority approach. Minority opinions are not always safeguarded. Racial groups, women, certain ethnic groups, gay men and lesbians, and people with disabilities are minority groups that in the past have suffered from adverse decisions made by simple majority voting. Majority voting frequently splits a group into winners and losers, with the losers often becoming angry, frustrated, and apathetic. Sometimes the group of losers is nearly as large as the winners (such as having 49% of the vote), but they end up feeling their concerns are ignored. A large-size minority that feels it was outvoted may not lend its resources to implement the decision and may even work to subvert or overturn it. If the final vote alienates a minority, the group's future effectiveness is diminished. The majority rule approach may be interpreted by the minority as being an unfair means of control and manipulation by the majority. Therefore, to maintain effective group functioning, groups that use majority voting should seek to create a climate in which members feel they have "had their day in court" and have an obligation to go along with the group decision.

A compromise between consensus and simple majority is a high-percentage majority vote (such as two-thirds or three-fourths). This approach requires more time to arrive at a decision than a simple majority because more votes are needed. But it takes less time than consensus because not everyone has to be convinced or persuaded. A strong minority (such as 45%) can block a decision it dislikes, but a small majority cannot force its views on a strong minority. However, a small minority may still feel it is being controlled and manipulated by a high-percentage majority vote. A high-percentage majority vote will generally draw stronger support from group members than the simple majority approach, but it will not generate as much support as the consensus approach.

Focus Groups

Closely related to task groups and problem-solving and decision-making groups are focus groups. Focus groups are formed for a variety of purposes: to identify needs or issues, to generate proposals to resolve an identified issue, to test reactions to alternative approaches to an issue, and so forth. A focus group is a specially assembled collection of people who respond through a semistructured or structured discussion to the concerns and interests of the person, group, or organization that invited the participants. Members of the group are invited and encouraged to bring up their own ideas and views.

A *representative group* is a version of the focus group. Its strength is that its members have been selected specifically to represent different perspectives and points of view in a community. At its best, a representative group is a focus group that reflects the diversity in the community and seeks to bring these diverse views to the table; at its worst, it is a front group manipulated by schemers to make the community think that it has been involved.

Self-Help Groups

Self-help groups are increasingly popular and often successful in helping individuals with certain social or personal problems. Katz and Bender (1976) provided a comprehensive definition of *self-help groups:*

> Self-help groups are voluntary, small group structures for mutual aid and the accomplishment of a special purpose. They are usually formed by peers who have come together for mutual assistance in satisfying a common need, overcoming a common handicap or life-disrupting problem, and bringing about desired social, and/or personal change.

CASE EXAMPLE   PARENTS ANONYMOUS—A SELF-HELP GROUP

Parents Anonymous (PA) is a national self-help organization for parents who have abused or neglected their children. PA was originally established in 1970 by Jolly K. in California, who was desperate to find help to meet her needs. For 4 years prior to this time, she struggled with an uncontrollable urge to severely punish her daughter. One afternoon she attempted to strangle her daughter. Desperate, she sought help from the local child-guidance clinic. She was placed in therapy. When asked by her therapist what she could do about this situation, she developed an idea; as she explained (Zauner, 1974, p. 247), "if alcoholics could stop drinking by getting together, and gamblers could stop gambling, maybe the same principle would work for abusers, too." With her therapist's encouragement, she formed "Mothers Anonymous" in 1970, and started a few local chapters in California. Nearly every major city in the United States and Canada now has a chapter, and the name has been changed to Parents Anonymous (because fathers who abuse their children are also eligible to join).

PA uses some of the basic therapeutic concepts of Alcoholics Anonymous. PA is a crisis intervention program that offers two main forms of help: (1) a weekly group meeting in which members share experiences and feelings and learn better control of their emotions and (2) personal and telephone contact among members during periods of crisis, particularly when a member feels a nearly uncontrollable desire to take his or her anger or frustration out on a child. Parents may be referred to PA by a social agency (including protective services) or may be self-referrals of parents who are aware they need help.

Starkweather and Turner (1975) described why some parents who abuse their children would rather participate in a self-help group than receive professional counseling:

> It has been our experience that most (abusive) parents judge themselves more harshly than other more objective people tend to judge them. The fear of losing their children frequently diminishes with reassurance from other members that they are not the monsters they think they are.
>
> Generally speaking, PA members are so afraid they are going to be judged by others as harshly as they judge themselves that they are afraid to go our and seek help. Frequently our members express fears of dealing with a professional person, seeing differences in education, sex, or social status as basic differences that would prevent easy communication or mutual understanding.
>
> Members express feelings of gratification at finding that other parents are "in the same boat." They contrast this with their feelings about professionals who, they often assume, have not taken out the time from their training and current job responsibilities to raise families of their own. (p. 151)

PA emphasizes honesty and directness. In the outside world, parents who are prone to abuse their children learn to hide this problem because society finds it difficult to stomach. In contrast, the goal of PA is to help parents admit and accept the fact that they are abusive. The term *abuse* is used liberally at meetings. PA has found that this insistence on frankness has a healthy effect. Parents are relieved because they've finally found a group of people who are able to accept abusive parents for what they really are. Furthermore, only when they are able to admit they are abusive can they begin to find ways to cope with this problem.

During PA meetings parents are expected actually to say they are beating their child or engaging in other forms of abuse, and the members challenge each other to find ways to curb such activities. Members also share constructive approaches that each has found useful, and efforts are made to help one another develop specific plans for dealing with situations that have in the past resulted in abusive episodes. Members learn to recognize danger signs and to then take necessary action to curb the potential abuse.

Leadership in the group is provided by a group member selected by the parents themselves. The leader, called a "chairperson," is normally assisted by a professional sponsor who serves as resource and backup person to the chair and the group members. The social worker who becomes the sponsor must be prepared to perform a variety of roles, including teacher-trainer, broker of community services needed by parents, advocate, consultant, and, in some instances, behavior changer (Check the parents Anonymous website at http://parentsanonymous.org).

The initiators and members of such groups perceive that their needs are not, or cannot be, met by or through existing social institutions. Self-help groups emphasize face-to-face social interactions and the assumption of personal responsibility by members. They often provide material assistance as well as emotional support; they are frequently cause-oriented, and promulgate an ideology or values through which members may attain an enhanced sense of personal identity. (p. 9)

To convey the varieties and focuses of self-help groups that now exist (see Exhibit 6.1), two different classifications of these groups are summarized in the following paragraphs. Katz and Bender (1976) classified self-help groups into the following five categories:

1. Groups that focus on self-fulfillment or personal growth. Examples include Alcoholics Anonymous, Recovery Inc. (for former mental patients), Gamblers Anonymous, and Weight Watchers.
2. Groups that focus on social advocacy. Examples include Welfare Rights Organizations, MADD (Mothers Against Drunken Drivers), and the Committee for the Rights of the Disabled. Katz and Bender (1976) noted that the advocacy "can be both on behalf of broad issues, such as legislation, the creation of new services, change in the policies of existing institutions and so on, or it can be on behalf of individuals, families, or other small groups" (p. 38).

Exhibit 6.1   Examples of Self-Help Groups

Organization	Service Focus
Abused Parents of America	For parents who are abused by their adult children
Adoptees' Liberty Movement Association	For adoptees searching for their natural parents
Alcoholics Anonymous	For adult alcoholics
American Diabetes Association	Clubs for diabetics, their families, and friends
American Sleep Apnea Association	For persons with sleep apnea and their families
Burns United Support Group	For burn victims
Candlelighters Childhood Cancer Foundation	For parents of young children with cancer
Conjoined Twins International	For families of conjoined twins
CROHNS	For persons with Crohns disease and their families
CUB (Concerned United Birthparents)	For adoption-affected people in coping with adoption, including assistance for locating family members
Depressed Anonymous	For depressed persons
Divorce Care	For divorced persons
Emotions Anonymous	For persons with emotional problems
Encephalitis Support Group	For those with encephalitis and their families
Families Anonymous	For relatives and friends of drug abusers
Fortune Society	For ex-offenders and their families
Gam-Anon	For families of gamblers
Gray Panthers	An intergenerational group
Herpes Anonymous	For persons with herpes and their families and friends
High Risk Moms, Inc.	For women experiencing a high-risk or problem pregnancy
Impotents World Association	For impotent men and their partners
Make Today Count	For persons with cancer and their families
Molesters Anonymous	For men who molest children
National Organization for Women	For women's rights
Overeaters Anonymous	For overweight persons
Parents Anonymous	For parents of abused children
Sexaholics Anonymous	For those with sexually self-destructive behavior
WINGS Foundation, Inc.	For men and women traumatized by incest

3. Groups that focus on creating alternative patterns for living. Examples include Gay Liberation and certain religious cults such as the Moonies.

4. *Outcast haven* or *rock-bottom* groups. Katz and Bender (1976) defined this type as follows:

> These groups provide a refuge for the desperate, who are attempting to secure personal protection from the pressures of life and society, or to save themselves from mental or physical decline. This type of group usually involves a total commitment, a living-in arrangement or sheltered environment, with close supervision by peers or persons who have successfully grappled with similar problems of their own. (p. 38)

Examples include ex-drug addict organizations.

5. Groups of mixed types that have characteristics of two or more categories. One such group is Parents Without Partners, which promotes personal growth, advocacy, and social events for its members.

Powell (1987) classified self-help groups into these five categories:

1. *Habit-disturbance organizations:* These organizations focus on a problem that is specific and concrete. Examples include Alcoholics Anonymous, Smokestoppers, Overeaters Anonymous, Gamblers Anonymous, Take Off Pounds Sensibly (TOPS), Women for Sobriety, Narcotics Anonymous, and Weight Watchers.

2. *General-purpose organizations:* These organizations address a wide range of problems and predicaments. Examples are Parents Anonymous (for parents of abused (children), Emotions Anonymous (for persons with emotional problems), Compassionate Friends (for persons who have experienced a loss through death), and GROW, an organization that works to prevent hospitalization of mental patients through a comprehensive program of mutual aid. In contrast to habit-disturbance organizations, general-purpose organizations address a wider range of problems and predicaments.

3. *Lifestyle organizations:* These organizations seek to provide support for, and advocate for, the lifestyles of people whose members are viewed by society as being different (the dominant groups in society are generally indifferent or hostile to that difference). Examples of this category include Widow-to-Widow programs, Parents Without Partners, ALMA society (Adoptees' Liberty Movement Association), PFLAG (Parents, Families, and Friends of Lesbians and Gays), National Gay and Lesbian Task Force, and Gray Panthers, an intergenerational group that advocates for the elderly.

4. *Physical handicap organizations:* These organizations focus on major chronic diseases and conditions. Some are for people with conditions that are relatively stable, some for conditions that are likely to get worse, and some for terminal illnesses. Examples of this category include Make Today Count (for the terminally ill and their families), Emphysema Anonymous, Lost Chord clubs (for those who have had laryngectomies), stroke clubs, Mended Hearts, the Spina Bifida Association, and Self-Help for Hard of Hearing People.

5. *Significant-other organizations:* The members of these organizations are parents, spouses, and close relatives of troubled and troubling persons. Very often, members of significant-other groups are last-resort caregivers. Significant others contend with dysfunctional behavior. Through sharing their feelings, they obtain a measure of relief. In the course of sharing, they may also learn about new resources or new approaches. Examples of such organizations include Al-Anon, Gam-Anon, Tough love, and the National Alliance for the Mentally Ill.

Why are self-help groups successful? Many self-help groups stress (1) members admitting to the group that they have a problem, (2) members recounting to the group their past experiences with their problem and their plans for handling the problem in the future, and (3) support from members (for example, a member who feels an intense urge to drink or to abuse a child is encouraged to call another member of the group to come over to stay with the person until the urge subsides).

Members of self-help groups have visceral understanding of one another's problems, which helps them help others. Having experienced the misery and consequences of the problem, they are highly motivated and dedicated to finding ways to help themselves and their fellow sufferers. The participants also benefit from the *helper therapy principle:* A helper gains psychological rewards by helping others (Riessman, 1965). Helping others makes a person feel good and worthwhile; it also enables the helpers to put their own problems into perspective as they see that others' problems may be as serious as, or even more serious than, their own.

When people help each other in self-help groups, they tend to feel empowered because they are able to control important aspects of their lives. When help is given from the outside (from an expert or a professional), there is a danger that dependency may develop, which is the opposite effect of empowerment. Empowerment increases motivation, energy, personal growth, and an ability to help that goes beyond helping oneself or receiving help.

Some self-help groups advocate for the rights and lifestyles of people whose members are viewed by society as being different. One such group is the National Gay and Lesbian Task Force. Some self-help groups (such as the National Association for Retarded Citizens) raise funds and operate community programs. Many people with a personal problem use self-help groups in the same way others use social agencies. An additional advantage is that self-help groups generally are able to operate with a minimal budget. Hundreds of these groups are in existence. Social workers often act as brokers in linking clients to appropriate self-help groups.

Riessman (1987, pp. ix–x) summarizes the distinctive characteristics of self-help groups as follows:

- A noncompetitive, cooperative orientation
- An anti-elite, antibureaucratic focus
- An emphasis on the indigenous—people who have the problem and know a lot about it from the inside, from experiencing it
- An attitude of do what you can, one day at a time (you can't solve everything at once)
- A shared, often revolving leadership
- An attitude of being helped through helping (the helper-therapy principle) . . .
- An understanding that helping is not a commodity to be bought and sold
- A strong optimism regarding the ability to change
- An understanding that although small may not necessarily be beautiful, it is a place to begin and the unit to build on
- A critical stance toward professionalism, which is often seen as pretentious, purist, distant, and mystifying. Self-helpers like simplicity and informality
- An emphasis on the consumer. . . . The consumer is a producer of help and services
- An understanding that helping is at the center—knowing how to receive help, give help, and help yourself . . .
- An emphasis on empowerment

Exercise 6.3: Merits and Shortcomings of a Self-Help Group

Goal: This exercise is designed to assist you in having a better understanding of the merits and shortcomings of self-help groups.

Step 1: Interview someone who has participated in a self-help group. (If you have participated yourself, you may answer the questions in this exercise by sharing your personal experiences.) Most colleges have several self-help groups on campus—such as an eating disorder group, a gay and lesbian group, and groups combating substance abuse. The student counseling center is usually a good resource for identifying contact persons for the available self-help groups. Describe the goals of the self-help group that you gather information on.

Step 2: Describe the activities of this self-help group.

Step 3: Ask the person you interview to summarize the merits and shortcomings of this self-help group, and then record this information here.

The American Self-Help Group Clearinghouse is a web-based database of over 1,100 national and international self-help support groups for health, mental health, addictions, abuse, disabilities, parenting, caregiver concerns, and other stressful life situations. It is compiled and edited by Barbara Jo White and Edward J. Madara, with the web version updated by Nicole Klem. To access any self-help group contained in the database, type in a keyword on the website. The website can be easily accessed by typing "American Self-Help Group Clearinghouse," into your web browser.

Exercise 6.4: Checking Out Online Self-Help Groups

Goal: This exercise is designed to familiarize you with online self-help groups.

Using the Internet, check out the web pages of three online self-help groups. Some suggested websites are the following:

Alcoholics Anonymous: www.alcoholicsanonymous.org

Adult Children of Alcoholics: www.adultchildren.org

American Foundation for Suicide Prevention: www..afsp.org

Gamblers Anonymous: www.gamblersanonymous.org

Overeaters Anonymous: www.overeatersanonymous.org

Sexaholics Anonymous: www.sa.org

(You can locate over 1,100 additional self-help groups by typing "American Self-Help Group Clearinghouse" into your web browser. When this website is accessed, type in a keyword of the support group that you want.)

Summarize the information you find about the three online self-help groups.

Socialization Groups

The objective of socialization groups generally is to develop or change the attitudes and behaviors of group members to make members more socially acceptable. Developing social skills, increasing self-confidence, and planning for the future are other goals. Illustrations include working with the following: a group of pre-delinquent youth in group activities to curb delinquency trends, a youth group of diverse racial backgrounds to reduce racial tensions, a group of elderly residents at a nursing home to remotivate them and get them involved in various activities, and a group of boys at a correctional school to help them make plans for returning to their home community. Leadership of such groups requires considerable skill and knowledge in using the group to foster individual growth and change. These leadership roles are frequently filled by social workers. (See the Case Example "Socialization—A Group at an Assisted Living Facility.")

Counseling Groups

This category of groups has also been called "treatment groups." Counseling groups are generally composed of members with rather severe emotional or personal problems. Leadership of such groups requires considerable skill, perceptiveness, knowledge of human behavior and group dynamics, group counseling capaci-

---

CASE EXAMPLE   SOCIALIZATION—GROUP AT AN ASSISTED LIVING FACILITY

Winterhaven is an assisted living facility that has 32 beds for mostly elderly residents. All the residents have either beginning-stage dementia issues or mobility issues—such as difficulty in walking because of medical conditions such as severe arthritis or stroke. The facility is staffed with nurses, nursing assistants, food preparation personnel, and one social worker, Jean Schible.

Every weekday evening at 7 p.m. a group meeting is held. All the residents are invited, but usually only about half of them attend. Some are too ill, some have visitors, and a few may be away on an outing.

This group meeting has three main objectives. One is to serve as a vehicle for residents to express their satisfactions and dissatisfactions with the facility and its programs. Sometimes the group meeting appears to be primarily a gripe session, but the social worker (who leads the meetings) makes sure the staff make conscientious efforts at improvement when the residents' con-

cerns are legitimate. A frequent request is for greater variation in the meals that are served.

Another objective is to provide interesting lectures and activities. Speakers from the surrounding community are invited to talk about topics of interest to the residents. Often the speakers encourage residents to engage in discussions. Winterhaven is near a university, so faculty members are sometimes invited to talk. If there are no speakers, the social worker may lead the group in playing a game—such as a card game. At other times, musicians are invited to play for an hour or an hour and a half. Speakers and these activities have the benefit of giving residents something to look forward to. Many of them spend hours and hours in their own rooms—which can lead to melancholy and a sense of isolation. The group meeting helps to combat loneliness and melancholy.

The third objective of the group meeting is to convey information about planned daily activities and changes in the overall program at Winterhaven.

ties, and ability to use the group to bring about behavioral changes. Among other skills, the group leader needs to be highly perceptive regarding how each member is being affected by what is being communicated. Considerable competence is needed to develop and maintain a constructive atmosphere within the group. Like the goal of one-to-one counseling, the goal of counseling groups is generally to have members explore their problems in depth and then to develop one or more strategies for resolving them. The group facilitator generally uses one or more therapy approaches as a guide for changing attitudes and behaviors. These approaches include reality therapy, learning theory, rational therapy, and psychodrama.

Group counseling is being used increasingly in social work. It has several advantages over one-to-one counseling. The *helper therapy principle* (in which members interchange roles and sometimes become the helper for someone else's problems) is generally operative. In such roles, members receive psychological rewards for helping others. Groups also help members put their problems into perspective as they realize others have equally serious problems. Groups also help members who are having interaction problems test out new interaction approaches. Research has shown that it is generally easier to change the attitudes of an individual in a group than in one-on-one counseling (Johnson & Johnson, 2009). Research on conformity has found that group pressure can have a substantial effect on changing attitudes and beliefs (Johnson & Johnson, 2009). Furthermore, group counseling permits the social worker to help more than one person at a time, with potential savings in the use of professional effort.

CASE EXAMPLE   COUNSELING GROUP FOR SPOUSES OF ADULTS WITH CANCER

Eight years ago Linda Sonsthagen's husband was diagnosed with cancer. Linda was a social worker, and her husband was a successful life insurance agent. They had two sons in grade school. Mr. Sonsthagen died 4½ years ago, after having gone through a variety of treatment programs and experiencing considerable pain. He lost weight and his hair fell out. These years were extremely difficult for the Sonsthagens. Linda had to take a larger role in raising the children and was the primary caregiver to both her husband and the children. During these years, the Sonsthagens found that relatives and friends shied away from them. It took several months before they became aware that the reason was that friends and relatives saw cancer as something they didn't understand and wanted to avoid. Even more difficult was dealing emotionally with not knowing the course of the disorder, going through cycles of hope and then disappointment as different treatment approaches were tried. As her husband became more incapacitated, Linda found she had to assume more of his tasks—for example, home repairs, maintaining their two cars, disciplining the children, and other daily household tasks.

After her husband's death, Linda and the two children went through several months of mourning and grief. Linda discovered it was somewhat awkward to go to social functions alone. Fortunately, she had two single female friends with whom she increasingly socialized. These were very difficult years for Linda. She needed more than 2 years after her husband's death to rebuild her life in such a way that she was again comfortable. During these years, she received some financial help from the local chapter of the American Cancer Society. Through this organization, she met another woman whose husband was dying of cancer. They gave each other emotional support and shared useful ideas for handling problems.

Eighteen months ago Linda told the local chapter of the American Cancer Society that she was willing to volunteer her time to start a group for spouses of people with cancer and for spouses adjusting to a recent cancer death. The Cancer Society gave its approval and endorsement.

Linda started with nine members. The objectives were to give emotional support, to help members handle the new responsibilities they had to take on, and to help them deal with their emotional reactions. Linda used primarily a combination of rational therapy and reality therapy (see Modules 1 and 3). Reality therapy helped group members better understand and make decisions and plans for the problems they faced. For example, for members whose spouses had cancer, one focus was how to inform and handle their friends' and relatives' reactions to the illness. Survivors focused on rebuilding their lives. Rational therapy countered unwanted emotions. Common emotions included depression, guilt, anxiety, the feeling of being overwhelmed, and anger (particularly resulting from "Why does this have to happen to me?"). Members were instructed on how to do a rational self-analysis (see Module 1) of their unwanted emotions, and members often shared and discussed their analyses at group meetings.

On several occasions group members stated that the group was very helpful. They mentioned that knowing others faced similar plights was beneficial in and of itself. Seeing how others handled difficult decisions inspired them and gave them useful ideas on how to handle crises they faced. When a member suffered a serious crisis (for example, a spouse hospitalized for a serious operation), other members were available for phone contact and to lend physical assistance.

After 8 months, the local chapter of the American Cancer Society was so encouraged by the results that it offered Linda a full-time position to run additional groups and to be available for individual counseling for people with cancer and for their relatives. Linda gave up her part-time job as a counselor at the YWCA and took this position. Her first effort was to divide her group, which was growing, into two groups. The definition of eligible membership was expanded: One group was for adults who have a family member with cancer, the other for survivors. At this time, Linda is leading one group of the first type and two groups of the second type.

In essence a group facilitator uses the principles of one-to-one counseling (discussed in Chapter 5) and of group dynamics (see Chapter 7) to work with clients to change dysfunctional attitudes and behavior. Generally the group facilitator also uses the principles of certain treatment techniques (such as reality therapy, rational therapy, parent effectiveness training, and assertiveness training) to help clients resolve personal and emotional problems. The selection of the techniques to use should be based on the nature of the problems presented.

Encounter Groups

Encounter groups and sensitivity training groups (these terms are used somewhat synonymously) are groups in which members relate to each other in a close interpersonal manner and self-disclosure is required. The goal is to improve interpersonal awareness. An *encounter group* is a typically unstructured group in which participants seek to increase their sensitivity, responsiveness, and emotional expressiveness, as by freely verbalizing and responding to emotions. It is designed to promote the personal growth of the participants.

A *sensitivity group* is a nonclinical group (not intended for persons with severe emotional problems), which focuses on interpersonal interactions and on self-awareness and self-understanding in an effort to help them become more aware of their own feelings and behaviors, and of the feelings and behaviors of others.

Sensitivity groups usually generate an outpouring of emotion rarely found in other groups.

An encounter group may meet for a few hours or for a few days. Once increased interpersonal awareness is achieved, it is anticipated that attitudes and behaviors will change. For these changes to occur, a three-phase process generally takes place: unfreezing, change, and refreezing.

Unfreezing occurs through a deliberate process of interacting in nontraditional ways. Our attitudes and behavior patterns have been developed through years of social experiences, experimentation, and refinement. Such patterns have now become nearly automatic. Our interpersonal style generally has considerable utility in our everyday interactions. Deep down, however, we may recognize a need for improvement but are reluctant to make the effort, partly because our present style is somewhat functional and partly because we are afraid to reveal things about ourselves. Unfreezing occurs when we decide certain patterns of our present behavior need to be changed and we are psychologically ready to explore ways to make changes.

Tubbs and Baird (1976) described the unfreezing process in sensitivity groups:

> Unfreezing occurs when our expectations are violated. We become less sure of ourselves when traditional ways of doing things are not followed. In the encounter group, the leader usually does not act like a leader. He or she frequently starts with a brief statement encouraging the group members to participate, to be open and honest, and to expect things to be different. Group members may begin by taking off their shoes, sitting in a circle on the floor, and holding hands with their eyes closed. The leader then encourages them to feel intensely the sensations they are experiencing, the size and texture of the hands they are holding and so forth.
>
> Other structured exercises or experiences may be planned to help the group focus on the "here-and-now" experience. Pairs may go for "trust walks" in which each person alternatively is led around with his eyes closed. Sitting face-to-face and conducting a hand dialogue, or a silent facial mirroring often helps to break the initial barriers to change. Other techniques may involve the "pass around" in which a person in the center of a tight circle relaxes and is physically passed around the circle. Those who have trouble feeling a part of the group are encouraged to break into or out of the circle of people whose hands are tightly held. With these experiences, most participants begin to feel more open to conversation about what they have experienced. This sharing of experiences or self-disclosure about the here and now provides more data for the group to discuss. (p. 48)

The second phase of the process is *change*. In sensitivity groups, change is facilitated by spontaneous reactions or feedback to how a person "comes across" to others. In everyday interaction we almost never get spontaneous feedback, and we tend to repeat ineffective interaction patterns because we lack knowledge of our effect on others. But in sensitivity groups, such feedback is strongly encouraged. The following set of interactions illustrates such feedback:

Carl: All right (in a sharp tone), let's get this trust walk over with, and stop dilly-dallying around. I'll lead the first person around—who wants to be blindfolded first?

Judy: Your statement makes me feel uncomfortable. I feel you're saying this group is a waste of your time. Also, it's the third time tonight you've ordered us around.

Jim: I feel the same way, like you're trying to tell us peons what to do. Even the tone of your voice sounds autocratic, and I get the message you're really down on this group.

Carl: I'm sorry, I didn't mean it to sound like that. I wonder if I do that outside the group too?

Such feedback provides new insights on how we affect others. Once problem interactions are identified, members are encouraged to try out new response patterns in the relative safety of the group.

The third and final phase is *refreezing*. Unfortunately, this term is not the most descriptive because it implies rigidity with a new set of response patterns. The goal in this phase is to experiment with new sets of behaviors so that members become growing, continually changing people who increasingly become more effective in their interactions with others. In terminating a sensitivity group, the leader may alert the participants to be on guard because former dysfunctional behavior patterns tend to creep back in.

The goal of sensitivity groups provides an interesting contrast to that of most counseling groups (see Exhibit 6.2). In counseling groups, the goal is for all members to explore their personal or emotional problems and develop a strategy to resolve the problems. In comparison, sensitivity groups foster increased personal and interpersonal awareness and then develop more effective interaction patterns. Sensitivity groups generally do not attempt to identify and change specific emotional or personal problems (drinking problems, feelings of depression, sexual dysfunctions, and so on). The philosophy behind sensitivity groups is that with increased personal and interpersonal awareness, people will be better able to avoid, cope with, and handle specific personal problems that arise.

Sensitivity groups are used for a wide variety of purposes: to train professional counselors to be more perceptive and effective in interpersonal interactions with clients and with other professionals, to train managers to be more effective in their business interactions, to help clients with overt relationship problems become more aware of how they affect others and to help them develop more effective interaction patterns, and to train interested citizens in becoming more aware and effective in their interactions.

Despite their popularity, sensitivity groups remain controversial. In some cases, inadequately trained and incompetent individuals have become self-proclaimed leaders and have enticed people to join through sensational advertising. If handled poorly, the short duration of some groups can intensify personal problems—for example, when a person's defense mechanisms are stripped away without developing adaptive coping patterns. Many authorities on sensitivity training disclaim the use of encounter groups as a form of psychotherapy and discourage those with serious personal problems from joining such groups.

In some cases, the popularity of sensitivity groups has led individuals to enter harmful groups with incompetent leaders where normal ethical standards have been abused. Shostrom (1969, pp. 38–39) has identified means by which those interested in encounter groups can prevent exploitation: (1) Never participate in a group of fewer than a half-dozen members. The necessary and valuable candor generated by an effective group cannot be dissipated, shared, or examined by too small a group, and scapegoating or purely vicious ganging up can develop. (2) Never join an encounter group on impulse—as a fling, binge, or surrender to the unplanned. (3) Never stay with a group that has a behavioral ax to grind. (4) Never participate in a group that lacks formal connection with a professional on whom you can check.

After reviewing the research on the outcome of sensitivity groups, Lieberman, Yalom, and Miles (1973) provided an appropriate perspective for those interested in the intensive group experience:

> Encounter groups present a clear and evident danger if they are used for radical surgery to produce a new man [person]. The danger is even greater when the leader and the participants share this misconception. If we no longer expect groups to produce magical, lasting change and if we stop seeing them as panaceas, we can regard them as useful, socially sanctioned opportunities for human beings to explore and to express themselves. Then we can begin to work on ways to improve them so that they may make a meaningful contribution toward solving human problems. (p. 73)

Exhibit 6.2   Contrasting Goals of Counseling Groups and Sensitivity Groups

Counseling Groups		Sensitivity Groups	
Step 1	**Step 2**	**Step 1**	**Step 2**
Examine problems in depth.	Develop and select from various resolution approaches a strategy to resolve the problem.	Help each person become more aware of self and how she or he affects others in inter-personal interactions.	Help person develop more effective interaction patterns.

HOW TO START, LEAD, TERMINATE, AND EVALUATE GROUPS

In the remainder of this chapter we focus on guidelines for starting, running, and terminating groups. This section covers homework, session planning, relaxing before a meeting, cues on entering the meeting room, seating arrangements, introductions, role clarification, agendas, additional guidelines for leading a group, terminating a group, and evaluating a group. Many students fear taking a leadership role in groups. They are uncertain about what leaders do, and they fear they do not have the qualities or traits to be a leader. Amazingly, the truth is that even the most fearful and anxious students have already taken leadership roles in many groups. Every student has in the past been a member of several groups and has performed some essential tasks for these groups. As we shall see in Chapter 7, performing an essential task is simultaneously an effective leadership action.

Homework

Extensive preparation is the key to a successful experience for group members (including yourself. Even experienced leaders prepare carefully for each group and for each meeting.

When planning a new group, be sure to answer the following questions: What are the group's overall purpose and goals? What possible ways can these general goals be accomplished? What are the characteristics of the members? Do some members have unique, individual goals or needs? What resources do members need to accomplish the general goals? What should the agenda be for the first meeting? Group members should have considerable input in suggesting and deciding on the specific goals of the group. How can this best be accomplished? When the group first meets, should an icebreaker exercise be used—if so, what? Should refreshments be provided? How should the chairs be arranged? What type of group atmosphere will best help the group accomplish its tasks? What is the best available meeting place? Why have you been selected to lead the group? What do the members expect you to do?

As you plan for the first meeting, it is helpful to view the group as a new member would view it. Here are some questions and concerns that a new member might have: What are the goals of this group? Why am I joining? Will my personal goals be met in this group? Will I feel comfortable in this group? Will I be accepted by other members? Will the other members be radically different from me in backgrounds and interests? If I do not like this group, can I get out of attending meetings? Will other members respect what I have to say, or will they laugh and make fun of me? By considering such concerns, the leader can plan the first meeting in a way that helps members feel comfortable and will clarify their questions about the group's goals and activities.

Exercise 6.5: My Concerns about Joining a Group

Goal: This exercise is designed to help you identify (a) the concerns that you would have about joining a group and (b) what you want the leader to do to make you feel comfortable.

Step 1:   Assume the dean of your college has invited you to be a member of the newly formed Dean's Student Advisory Council. Specify your concerns and reservations about joining this group. (The dean will be leading the group.)

Step 2:   What would you like to see the dean say and do to meet your concerns and reservations and to help you feel comfortable?

Step 3:   Do you believe your concerns and reservations are unique or similar to those that other members would have? Explain your reasons.

Step 4:   If you stated in step 3 that your concerns and reservations are similar to those of other new members, does this exercise help you identify what you would need to say and do to help members feel comfortable if you were leading a group? Please explain.

It is *absolutely essential* for a group leader to identify needs and expectations before the first meeting. The quickest way to fail as a leader is to try to lead a group in a direction different from what the members want. For example, I once attended a workshop with other counselors titled "Grief, Death, and Dying." The counselors expected material on how to counsel clients who were grieving about the death of a loved one. The presenter instead gave a historical review of how present-day funeral rituals evolved since the Middle Ages. The audience was very disappointed.

There are various ways to identify what members want. Before the first meeting, try to ask at least some members about their expectations. If you are asked by someone to lead the group, it is essential to ask that person about the expectations for the group. At the first meeting, ask members to give their views about what they desire from the group. Another way (which needs to be done for preparatory reasons anyway) is to "scout" the following about the members:

1. How many members are expected?
2. What are their characteristics—ages, socioeconomic status, racial and ethnic backgrounds, gender mix, educational and professional backgrounds, and so on?
3. How knowledgeable and informed are members about the topics that will be dealt with?
4. What are likely personal goals and agendas of the various members?
5. How motivated are members to accomplish the group purposes? This can partly be determined by examining how voluntary the membership is. Groups composed of involuntary members (for example, a person who is court ordered to attend because of conviction for driving while intoxicated) may have little motivation and may even be hostile because they are being forced to attend.
6. What are the underlying value systems of members? A group of teenagers on juvenile probation will differ significantly from a group of retired priests. (That said, take care to view the members as unique persons rather than by stereotypes.)

When planning for the first meeting (and additional meetings), visualize in great detail how you, as leader, want the meeting to go. Here is an example:

> The members will arrive at various times. I will be there early to greet them, introduce myself, help them feel comfortable, and engage in small talk. Small talk likely to be of interest to these new members: ___, ___, and ___.
>
> I will begin the meeting by introducing myself and stating the overall purpose of the group. As an icebreaker exercise, I will ask the group to give me a list of four or five facts they would like to know about other members and then have members introduce themselves and give these facts about themselves. I will also briefly summarize my professional experience and encourage members to ask questions about me and the group.
>
> After the icebreaker exercise, I will again briefly state the group's overall purpose and ask if members have questions about this. Possible questions that may arise are ___. If such questions arise, my answers will be ___.
>
> We will then proceed to items on the agenda (which I previously mailed to the members). During the discussion of these items, the questions that may arise are ___. My answers to such questions, should they arise, are ___.
>
> The kind of group atmosphere I will seek to create is democratic. Such an atmosphere is best suited for encouraging all members to participate in formulating the group goals and then to contribute their time and resources toward accomplishing them. I will seek to do this by arranging the chairs in a circle, by drawing out through questions those who are silent, by using humor, and by making sure that I don"t dominate the conversation.
>
> I will end the meeting by summarizing what has been covered and the decisions that have been made. We will set a time for the next meeting. Finally, I will ask if anyone has additional comments or questions. Throughout the meeting I will encourage a positive atmosphere, partly by complimenting the members on the contributions they make.

After a group has met for one or more times, the leader should review these questions: Have our overall goals been sufficiently clarified? If not, what needs to be done in this clarification process? Are we making adequate progress in accomplishing its goals? If not, what obstacles that we need to confront are slowing us down? Have we selected adequate courses of action to reach our goals, or are there more effective courses of action that we could consider? What items should be on the agenda for our next meeting? What activities should we plan? Will successful completion of these activities move us toward accomplishing our overall goals? If not, perhaps other activities need to be selected. Does each member seem sufficiently interested and motivated to help us accomplish its goals, or do some members appear to be disinterested? If so, why do they appear to be disinterested, and what could we try to stimulate their interests?

Session Planning

In planning a session, it is essential to be fully aware of the group's overall goals. It is also essential to identify specific goals for each session. Know *exactly* what you want to accomplish in each session and make sure that all the items on the agenda relate to these goals. Here are some suggestions.

1. *Select content that is relevant.* The material should be relevant not only to the specific goals for the session but also to the backgrounds and interests of participants. For example, in a time management presentation, the time-saver tips you give to college students probably will be quite different from those for business executives. An excellent way to evaluate the relevance of your material is to define precisely how it will be valuable to members. Ask yourself, "If a group member asks why should I know this, can I give a valid reason?" If you are unable to come up with more than a vague answer, consider discarding that material and selecting more relevant material.

2. *Use a number of examples.* Examples illustrate key concepts. They also stimulate interest. People remember examples much more than statistics. Thus, in a presentation on spouse abuse, vivid real-life stories of the drastic effects of battering will stay with members much longer than statistics on spouse abuse.

3. *Present materials in a logical order.* It is generally a good idea to begin by summarizing the agenda for the session. Ideally, one topic will blend into the next. If group exercises are used, place them next to the related theoretical material.

4. *Plan the time.* Once you have the content of the session fairly well organized, estimate how long each segment will take. Accurate estimations will help you determine if you have too much or too little material planned for the allotted time. Plan what you will do if the content is covered faster or slower than what you are estimating. Always be prepared to cover extra material should the anticipated content be covered more quickly than you estimated. If you are showing a videotape or have a guest speaker, have appropriate substitute material in case something goes awry.

5. *Be flexible with your agenda.* A variety of events can make it desirable to change the agenda during a session. The material may be covered much faster than anticipated, or interpersonal conflict may erupt that may take considerable time to process. Some members may bring up subjects related to the group's overall purpose that are valuable for the group to focus on at the moment.

6. *Change pace occasionally.* People pay attention for longer periods if there is an occasional change of pace. Long, long lectures or discussions are boring. Change pace in a variety of ways: Use a group exercise, show a film, invite a guest speaker, take a break, have a debate, make a PowerPoint presentation, change topics, and so on. In group counseling sessions, change pace by switching from one member's problems to another's concerns. If you are presenting a lecture, you can increase attention in several ways:

   - Speak extemporaneously rather than read the material.
   - Occasionally walk around the room rather than stand or sit in one place.
   - Draw out the participants by asking questions.

   (An excellent way to learn how to give more stimulating presentations is to observe the nonverbal and verbal communication patterns of dynamic speakers.) Remember to use appropriate transitions so the topics blend into one another rather than becoming choppy and confusing. As you select methods, be aware that people remember information better if they receive it actively (such as through an exercise) than if they receive it passively (through listening).

Relaxing before a Meeting

Before a meeting, you may be nervous about how it will go. Some anxiety is helpful; you will be mentally alert, and you will attend more carefully to what is being communicated. Some leaders, however, have an excessively high level of anxiety that reduces their effectiveness. If your anxiety is too high, you can reduce it by engaging in relaxing activities. Relaxation techniques are highly recommended and are described in Chapter 14. Other suggestions include taking a walk, jogging, listening to relaxing music, and finding a place where you can be alone to clear your mind. Effective group leaders learn they can reduce their level of anxiety by using one or more of these techniques. Practice in leading groups will also build your confidence.

Cues on Entering the Meeting Room

It is important for you, as leader, to be on time, and perhaps a little early. Being early allows you to see that everything is arranged as you planned. You'll be able to do what needs to be done—seeing that the refreshments are available, erasing the chalkboard, arranging the chairs, and so on. It also allows you to observe the moods of the members. If you have not previously met the group, arriving early gives you an opportunity to gain information about the participants' interests by observing their age, gender, clothes and personal appearance, small talk, and the way they interact with one another. Effective leaders notice such cues and generally find ways to "join" the participants.

I was once asked to give a workshop on suicide prevention to a high school class. On arriving, I was informed by the teacher that a classmate had recently taken his life. Instead of beginning with my planned presentation, I acknowledged that I had just been informed about their former classmate, and I asked each of them anonymously to jot down one or two concerns or questions. We then proceeded to have a lively discussion related to these. This discussion was no doubt more valuable than the formal presentation I planned to give because it zeroed in on their immediate concerns.

Seating Arrangements

Seating arrangements are important. They affect who talks to whom and influence who plays leadership roles. As a result, they can affect group cohesion and morale.

It is important in most groups for members to have eye contact with one another. It is even more important for the group leader to be able to make eye contact with everyone to obtain nonverbal feedback about what members are thinking and feeling.

A circle is ideal for generating discussion, for encouraging a sense of equal status, and for promoting openness and cohesion. The traditional classroom arrangement (with the leader in front and everyone facing that person while sitting in rows) has the effect of placing the leader in a position of authority It also tends to inhibit communication because members can make eye contact only with those closest to them.

Tables have advantages and disadvantages. They provide a place to write and to put work materials. Some members feel more comfortable at a table because it gives them something to lean on. However, tables also restrict movement and can serve as a barrier. Carefully consider whether tables are desirable or undesirable for your group. If members are to sift through papers or are expected to take notes, tables are useful. In counseling groups, tables are seldom used because they act as a barrier. In many settings, tables can be arranged to best meet the goals of the meeting. For example, arranging small tables in a circle facilitates communication.

Tables influence how group members interact with each other. If the table is rectangular, it is customary for the leader to sit at one end, at the "head" of the table. This positioning creates an "authority" dynamic wherein the "head" does more talking and has a greater influence on the discussion. If an egalitarian atmosphere is desired, use a round or square table. The "head of the table" effect can also be reduced by placing two rectangular tables together to make a square.

Tables also influence interactions by where people sit. People are most likely to talk to those sitting at right angles to them and then to those next to them. People sitting directly across receive less communication, and those sitting anywhere else are even less likely to be addressed.

When a group meets for the first time (and often later), members are most likely to sit next to friends. If it is important for everyone in the group to interact, it may be desirable to ask people to sit next to people they don't know to counteract potential cliquishness and to encourage members to get to know each other.

Introductions

During the introduction, summarize your credentials in such a way that members gain a sense of confidence that you as the leader can fulfill their expectations. If you are being introduced by someone else, a brief and concise summary of your credentials *for the expected role* is desirable. If you are introducing yourself, summarize your important credentials in a nonarrogant fashion. Deliver your summary in a way that creates the desired atmosphere—whether it is informal or formal, fun or serious, and so on. An excellent way to handle the introduction is to use an icebreaker exercise (described in Chapter 1).

In meeting with a group, it is highly desirable to learn members' names as quickly as possible. This requires extra attention by you. Name tags facilitate this process for everyone. Members appreciate being called by name—it conveys that they have importance.

If the group is small, it is generally advantageous for members to introduce themselves—perhaps by using an icebreaker. This is also a good time for members to state their expectations for the group. This helps uncover hidden agendas. If a stated expectation is beyond the scope of the group, you should tactfully state this and discuss it to prevent unrealistic expectations from becoming a source of frustration or dissatisfaction.

Role Clarification

As the leader of the group, you should be clear about your roles and responsibilities. If you are unclear, discuss with the group their expectations about the appropriate roles for the leader and members. One way of doing this is for the group to select goals and then decide which tasks and responsibilities each member will have in achieving those goals. In most situations, it is clearly a mistake for the leader to do most of the work. Groups are most productive if all members make substantial contributions. The more members contribute to the group, the more they will feel a part of the group psychologically.

Even if you are fairly clear about what you would like your role to be, other members may be confused about your role or may have different expectations of you. If there is a realistic chance that the other members are unclear about your role, explain carefully what you perceive your role to be. If members indicate they have different expectations, take time here to decide who will do what. In explaining what you perceive your role to be, be humble about your skills and resources. You want to come across as a knowledgeable "human" rather than as an authority figure who has all the answers.

Always be prepared to explain the reasoning behind the things you do. If you are leading an exercise, inform the group about its goals or objectives. If questions arise about whether its goals are consistent with the group's overall goals, be prepared to provide an explanation.

The role that leaders assume in groups varies from situation to situation. For example, there are marked differences in responsibilities of the leader of a therapy group and those of a committee assessing the social service needs of a community.

Agendas

Most meetings have agendas. Ideally, all group members should have an opportunity to suggest items for the agenda. If possible, send the agenda to members several days before the meeting to give them an opportunity to prepare.

Agenda items should be briefly reviewed at the start of the meeting, before consideration of the first item. This review gives members a chance to suggest additions, deletions, or other changes. In some meetings it may be appropriate for the group to discuss, and perhaps vote on, the suggested changes in the agenda.

Additional Guidelines for Leading a Group

1. Remember that leadership is a shared responsibility. Every member at times will take on leadership roles. Designated leaders should not dominate a group, nor should they believe they are responsible for directing the group in all of its task functions and group maintenance functions (these functions are described in Chapter 7). Actually, productivity and group cohesion are substantially increased when everyone contributes.
2. Use decision-making procedures that are best suited for the issues facing the group. (The merits and shortcomings of decision making by consensus and by majority voting were discussed earlier in this chapter.)
3. Create a cooperative group atmosphere rather than a competitive one (see Chapter 7).
4. View controversy and conflict as natural and desirable for resolving issues and furthering discussion. In resolving conflicts and in handling the issues and problems facing the group, use a problem-solving approach rather than a win-lose approach (see Chapter 7).
5. Try to create an atmosphere of open and honest communication.
6. Give attention to how you end a session. A few minutes before the session is scheduled to end or when it appears the group has exhausted a subject, conclude with a brief summary of the key points made in the meeting. This helps members remember major points, and it leaves them with a sense of achievement. Closing also helps members transition to the outside world.

Terminating a Group

Termination is about separating from the group and from group members. Separation typically generates mixed feelings that vary in intensity according to a number of factors. The greater the members' emotional closeness and investment in a group, the greater is their feeling of loss. The greater the feeling of success in accomplishing group goals, the greater is the feeling of "sweetness and sorrow"—sweetness from feeling that they have grown and had success and sorrow from separating from the group that has come to be an important and meaningful part of their lives. The more emotionally dependent members become on a group, the more likely they are to feel anger, rejection, and depression over termination. The more they have experienced difficulties in separating in the past from significant others, the more likely they are to experience group separation as difficult.

There are several types of termination: (1) termination of a successful group, (2) termination of an unsuccessful group, (3) a member dropping out, (4) transfer of a member, and (5) departure of the leader.

Termination of a Successful Group. In a successful group, members have generally accomplished their goals. Termination of such a group can generate the "sweetness and sorrow" reaction. They are delighted with their accomplishments, which are increasing their self-confidence and self-esteem. But they may also experience varying levels of loss because they are emotionally invested in the group. Such groups may decide to have dinner together or have some other ceremony to commemorate and recognize the group's accomplishments.

In terminating a successful group, it is essential that formal termination begin one or more meetings before the final meeting. Ideally, the date of the last meeting should be discussed and agreed on well in advance. (The final meeting of some groups is scheduled even before the group begins to meet.) Sufficient time has to be allowed in terminating successful groups so that (1) group progress can be evaluated; (2) plans can be made for continued work; (3) work can be done on unresolved, last-minute issues; (4) emotional reactions to terminating can be handled; and (5) members can discuss whether they want to plan a special social event for the group's ending.

Good-byes are often sad, but negative feelings can be offset by emphasizing what members have given and received, the ways they have grown, the skills they have learned, and the accomplishments of the group. In some cases, an extra session is held to complete unfinished business items. The members may decide to have periodic "class reunions" or social get-togethers.

Termination of an Unsuccessful Group. In an unsuccessful group, most or all of the group's goals are largely unmet. Members' reactions to the lack of progress will vary considerably: anger, frustration, disappointment, despair, guilt (for unproductive efforts or lack of effort), scapegoating, blaming, and apathy. In rare cases, it is possible for an unsuccessful group to be fairly pleased and accepting of its efforts. For example, a group formed to write a grant (when there was limited hope of funding from the federal government) may be pleased with its efforts and with the new relationships formed and only mildly disappointed by the failure of the group's objective.

Terminating an unsuccessful group is as important as terminating a successful one. As with all groups, plans for termination should be made well in advance. The date of the last meeting should be discussed and agreed on by the members long before the final meeting. Sufficient time should be allowed so that (1) the reasons for the lack of progress of the group can be assessed and analyzed; (2) alternatives for achieving the goals can be discussed (these may involve changing the format of the present group, referral of members to other groups, and alternatives involving individual actions rather than group efforts); (3) emotional reactions to terminating and to the lack of progress can be handled; (4) members can work on unresolved, last-minute issues; and (5) members can discuss whether they want to plan for the group's ending.

At times, ending an unsuccessful group is chaotic and abrupt. A group appointed to write a grant may be nearly finished when they are informed the funding organization has a financial shortfall and is therefore withdrawing its request for funding proposals. This group may end abruptly in despair. Or, in a group of involuntary members (such as at a prison or at an adolescent residential treatment facility), the leader may decide that continuing the group is counterproductive because members are continually goofing off and are not putting effort into achieving the group goals. In any case, the reasons for the group's ending should be fully explained and time given to handle members' reactions to the closing. If there is insufficient time at the last meeting to deal with these tasks, it is sometimes advisable either to have another session or for the leader to meet individually with members to discuss their reactions to the group's failure, alternatives for reaching goals, reactions to the group's ending, and unresolved concerns. When an unsuccessful group ends abruptly, some group members may be highly critical of the leader, of other members, or of group experiences. If the leader contacts members to learn their thoughts about the group, he or she should be prepared to respond to highly critical feedback. To prepare, the leader can "visualize" possible criticisms and then formulate positive and realistic responses.

Exercise 6.6: Successful and Unsuccessful Group Experiences

Goal: This exercise is designed to have you reflect about how you felt when you participated in a successful group and when you participated in an unsuccessful group.

Step 1:   Describe a successful group in which you participated. Indicate why you defined this group to be successful. Perhaps the goals were accomplished, or perhaps you enjoyed the camaraderie.

Step 2:   What feelings did you experience about participating in this group?

Step 3:   Describe an unsuccessful group in which you participated. Indicate why you defined this group to be unsuccessful. Perhaps the goals were not accomplished, or you disliked certain members, or you were asked to leave.

Step 4:   What feelings did you experience about participating in this group?

Dropping Out. When a member drops out, that member terminates even though the group continues on. A member drops out for a variety of reasons. She becomes disenchanted with the group and feels that neither she nor the group will accomplish the goals. He disagrees with or dislikes another group member. She is a parent who must now provide child care at the time the group meets or has begun a new job with work hours that conflict with meeting times. There are numerous reasons.

When a member drops out without informing the group of his or her reasons, you as leader should contact the individual to learn why he or she decided to terminate. In some instances, it is desirable for you to explain that leaving is a major decision that should not be made abruptly and that you would like an opportunity to explore the reasons that led to the decision. If the reason is conflict with another member, perhaps the conflict can be resolved. Perhaps other actions can be taken that will enable the member to return.

If the member decides not to return after being contacted and encouraged to return, the reasons for leaving should be attended to. The member may be raising legitimate concerns that need to be dealt with so that other members do not become discouraged and leave. If a person drops out of a counseling group, a sensitivity group, or an educational group and still has unresolved personal concerns, referral to another group or to one-to-one professional help may be advisable.

Whenever members drop out, you need to inform them of their positive contributions to the group. Dropping out is often viewed as a personal failure, and therefore you need to thank the person for any positive contributions to help dispel any sense of personal failure.

Don't neglect remaining members; they too experience a variety of emotions. Some will feel they failed this person. Some will feel guilt for what they said or did—or for failing to do or say what they believe would have led the member to stay. Some will feel relief or joy; perhaps they view the member as unworthy of the group or as an obstacle in the group's efforts to accomplish its goals. Others will feel sadness and be concerned that something tragic has happened to that member. Some will be angry, feeling the person is abandoning the group. Still others will feel personally rejected. Often rumors begin to circulate about the person's reasons for leaving. Therefore it is essential that the group be informed of the reasons. A member's leaving can be devastating to group morale. And if other members have also recently left, the group's survival can be jeopardized.

Ideally, members leaving should inform the group of their reasons, either in person or in writing. If they do not, you or another member should contact them to ascertain their reasons for leaving and inform the group.

Transfer of a Member. Transfer of a group member to another group or to some other type of professional services generally involves a planned arrangement between the group leader and the member. The transfer can occur for a variety of reasons. In a problem-solving group, the employing agency may decide that the member's talents and skills could be better used in another capacity. In a counseling group, the leader and person leaving may jointly decide that the transferee will be served better by receiving more specialized services with a somewhat different intervention. A member may be transferred because of a conflict that cannot be resolved, especially when the conflict is severely interfering with group goals. For example, a serious and insurmountable gap in mutual understanding and communication caused by differences in religious beliefs, values, or language may exist.

When a transfer occurs, you as leader should do everything possible to prevent it from being unexpected or abrupt. The member being transferred should clearly understand the reasons for the transfer and ideally should be accepting of it. Be sure to explain to the group why the person is transferring. Ideally, the member should explain his or her reasons to the group; this gives other members an opportunity to wish the person well and to gain a sense of closure.

Departure of the Leader. Sometimes you must terminate your work with a group. This termination is often difficult for both you and the members. Emotional reactions can be intense, and adequate time for working through them may not be available. You may experience intense emotions, including guilt, for not being able to follow through on your commitment to lead the group until its goals are accomplished. Members who feel vulnerable and depend on you may be devastated. Some may erroneously personalize your leaving as resulting from something they said or did. Some may feel anger and betrayal; they made a commitment to the group, confided and trusted in you, and now feel rejected.

When you leave, you should encourage members to express their feelings. You may want to initiate this expression by explaining fully why you are leaving, giving members positive comments about the group, and stating your feelings of sadness and guilt over leaving. Before leaving, you or the group should select a new leader. If the new leader is not a member of the group, you should inform the new leader (privately) about the goals, member characteristics, current tasks and difficulties in the group, and progress toward group goals. The new leader should be introduced to the group by you; your goal is a smooth transition shifting your responsibilities to the new leader.

Evaluating a Group

In the past few decades, accountability has become a major emphasis in social welfare. Funding sources demand research evidence that allocated funds are having a beneficial effect. An essential component of accountability is evaluation.

In broad terms, evaluation is designed to assess whether the services provided were effective and efficient. When the services provided by a group are evaluated, there are two dimensions of evaluation: process evaluation and outcome evaluation.

Process Evaluation. *Process evaluation* is an assessment, generally by group members, of the aspects of the process that were useful or detrimental. Feedback about techniques and incidents that blocked or enhanced process is of immense value to you as group leader. With this information, you can hone certain skills, eliminate materials, and give direction for approaches and materials to add. Positive feedback generally helps build your confidence. Feedback that is highly critical can be humbling and even devastating. It is far better to make changes suggested by the evaluation than to reject and "deny" the feedback and repeat the same mistakes in future groups. You need to welcome criticism and be prepared to respond to it constructively. After all, this is the way social workers expect clients to respond to constructive criticism.

Process evaluation can be conducted orally by asking group members to discuss the aspects, techniques, materials, and incidents that were constructive and those that were counterproductive. An advantage of oral evaluation is that most members enjoy a spoken discussion. A disadvantage is that some members may not give constructive negative feedback verbally because the social norm in such situations is to focus on the positives.

Process evaluation also can be accomplished by means of a brief questionnaire in which members address three key areas:

1. The group's strengths. (Cite specific materials and incidents. Also cite skills and techniques used by the leader.)
2. The group's shortcomings. (Cite specific materials and incidents. Also cite skills and techniques used by the leader.)
3. Specific suggestions for changes.

In process evaluations, group members typically cite positive factors more than negative ones (Hepworth & Larsen, 1986, p. 590). Such positive feedback not only has a "stroking value" but also enables leaders to be more aware of their strengths, so they can increase the use of these strengths in the future. Nevertheless, negative feedback is as valuable as, and often more valuable than, positive feedback. It informs you of aspects that need improvement, which you can then attend to.

Another way of evaluating process is by *peer review.* Peer review is conducted by having one or more "peers" (usually other group leaders) periodically sit in on your group. (Some agencies have one-way mirrors so the group can be unobtrusively observed.) Before a peer review, the agency or organization should agree on a set of principles or criteria that reflect quality group leadership. A peer review is a review of a small portion of the total functioning of the group. That small portion may be typical, or atypical, of the total functioning of the group. (Many colleges and universities use a peer review process in which tenured faculty in a department sit in on classes of recently hired faculty.)

In a variation of the peer-review process, meetings may be taped (either audio or video). The tape is played back and reviewed by you and a peer (or by your supervisor). Before taping a meeting, you should explain to the members the reasons for taping, indicate who will view the tape, and then ask members for their permission to tape the session.

Outcome Evaluation. *Outcome evaluation* assesses the extent to which the goals formulated when the group began have been accomplished. Specific approaches to measure goal attainment are single-subject design, task achievement scaling, and satisfaction questionnaire.

Single-Subject Design. Single-subject design has become increasingly popular in the helping professions in the past several decades. There are more than a dozen variations of single-subject design, some of them complex and rigorous. Fortunately, the simpler designs can be used by entry-level social workers in many situations. Single-subject design is described in considerable detail in Chapter 11.

Task Achievement Scaling. The objective of this approach is to gauge the degree to which group members and the leader have completed agreed-on tasks. Work toward member and group goals is broken into many separate actions or tasks. Tasks are selected by mutual agreement, and members are assigned or select specific tasks to reach their personal goal and the group's overall goal. Usually, a deadline is set for completing each task. *Task achievement scaling* rates the degree to which each agreed-on task has, in fact, been achieved.

Reid and Epstein (1972) used a 4-point scale to record progress on each task: 4 = completely achieved; 3 = substantially achieved, action is still necessary; 2 = partially achieved, considerable work remains to be done; and 1 = minimally achieved or not achieved. Where appropriate, they have a fifth rating, "no," for "no opportunity to work on task" With this approach, only results are rated—not effort, motivation, or good intentions. The appealing features of task achievement scaling are its simplicity and the fact that it can be used when more rigorous procedures are not feasible because of insufficient time or data, or difficulties in finding a suitable way to measure changes in the target behavior.

Task achievement scaling has some limitations. For example, if the tasks were incorrectly conceptualized as being constructive in meeting the goals of the group, then completing the tasks will have little effect on accomplishing group goals.

Satisfaction Questionnaire. Another way to assess a group outcome is to have members fill out a questionnaire that measures satisfaction. An example is the "Group Member Satisfaction Questionnaire" shown in Exhibit 6.3. Such questionnaires are a relatively simple and inexpensive way to measure members' satis-

---

Exhibit 6.3   Group Member Satisfaction Questionnaire

Thank you for taking a few minutes to evaluate your experiences in our group. Your answers to this brief questionnaire will help us improve future groups. Feel free to offer your comments. To ensure anonymity, please do not sign your name.

1. Did you accomplish what you expected when you joined the group?
   ___ Yes, completely
   ___ Mostly
   ___ No real progress
   ___ Worse off now than before
   Comments _____

2. Do you feel the group accomplished its goals?
   ___ Yes, completely
   ___ Mostly
   ___ No real progress
   ___ The group was an utter failure
   Comments _____

3. How do you feel about the group leader?
   ___ Very satisfied
   ___ Satisfied
   ___ No feelings one way or another
   ___ Dissatisfied
   ___ Very dissatisfied
   Comments _____

4. How do you feel about the other members in the group7
   ___ Satisfied with everyone
   ___ Satisfied with some and dissatisfied with others
   ___ No feelings one way or another
   ___ Dissatisfied with most of the other members
   ___ Dissatisfied with all of the other members
   ___ Very dissatisfied with all of the other members
   Comments _____

faction with the group. The questionnaire can be filled out at the last meeting or mailed to members some time later. Questions that evaluate process (described in this chapter) can also be included.

Satisfaction questionnaires have some limitations. Responses are affected by the respondent's mood. In addition, dissatisfied members are less likely to fill out the questionnaire, particularly if it is administered by mail (Sheafor, Horejsi, & Horejsi, 1988, p. 390).

A few concluding comments are in order about the personal benefits you will receive in leading groups. Through learning how to lead effectively, you will grow as a person, become more self-confident, feel good about yourself, develop highly marketable skills, improve interpersonal relationships, and help yourself and other members accomplish important tasks. Leaders are not born. They are trained. We all have the potential to become effective group leaders. You can do it!

SUMMARY

The following summarizes the chapter's content in terms of the learning objectives presented at the beginning of the chapter.

1. Describe types of groups in which social workers become involved.
    The historical roots of social group work lie in informal recreational organizations such as the YWCA and YMCA, scouting, Jewish centers, settlement houses, and 4-H Clubs. Today almost every social service agency provides some group services. Most undergraduate and graduate social work programs provide practice courses to train students to lead groups, particularly socialization, educational, and therapeutic groups. Groups frequently encountered in social work practice include recreation, recreation-skill, educational, task, problem-solving and decision-making, focus, self-help, socialization, counseling, and encounter groups.

    Group decision making in problem-solving and decision-making groups is usually superior to individual decision making. Problem-solving groups sometimes fall victim to groupthink, which can lead a group to make ineffective and even destructive decisions. Decisions made by consensus have the best chance of gaining members' support. Decisions made by simple majority voting are arrived at much faster than those made by consensus. The decision-making technique a group uses will depend on many factors.

    Socialization groups generally endeavor to develop or change attitudes and behaviors of group members in some socially accepted direction. Social skill development, increasing self-confidence, and planning for the future are other objectives.

    Counseling groups generally strive to help members explore personal or emotional problems and then develop strategies to resolve the problems. Group facilitators use principles of one-to-one intervention and group dynamics to assist members in achieving positive changes in attitudes and behaviors. In contrast, sensitivity groups foster increased personal and interpersonal awareness and develop more effective interaction patterns.
2. Understand guidelines on how to start, lead, evaluate, and terminate groups.
    The chapter concluded with guidelines for starting, leading, terminating, and evaluating groups. Topics included homework, planning a session, relaxing before starting a meeting, cues on entering the meeting room, seating arrangements, introductions, clarifying roles, agenda, terminating a group, and evaluating a group.

EXERCISES

1. Assertiveness Training

Goal: Demonstrate to the class how to run an educational group by illustrating how to run an assertiveness training group.

Step 1: The instructor indicates the purpose of this exercise. The instructor describes nonassertive, aggressive, and assertive behaviors (see Module 2 for descriptions).

Step 2: The instructor distributes a handout that describes the 12 steps of assertiveness training (contained in Module 2). The instructor summarizes these steps.

Step 3: The instructor asks for volunteers (two for each situation) to role-play assertively the situations that the instructor gives them, such as

    a. Asking someone who is smoking next to you to put out a cigarette
    b. Asking for a date and refusing a date
    c. Indicating to your objecting father that you want to live with the person you are dating

    After a situation is role-played, the class discusses the assertiveness strategy.

Step 4: Students write anonymously on a note card one or two situations involving assertiveness that they are struggling with and that they would like others in the class to role-play.

Step 5: The instructor collects these note cards and selects some situations for volunteers to role-play. After a situation is role-played, the class discusses the merits and shortcomings of the assertiveness strategy that was used.

2. The Nominal Group

Goal: This exercise is designed to have the class learn how a nominal group is conducted.

    The instructor asks a question for the nominal group to consider, such as "What do you see as the shortcomings of our social work program?" (Do not mention the names of faculty members.) The class follows the steps for conducting a nominal group as described in this chapter.

3. Trust Walk

Goal: This exercise is designed to demonstrate an approach—the trust walk—that is frequently used in sensitivity groups. A trust walk helps students get in touch with aspects of themselves that they are unaware of.

Step 1: The instructor informs the class of the purpose of the exercise. The students form groups of two. (If a member is without a partner, the instructor can be a partner.) A member of each subgroup closes his or her eyes and keeps them closed during the first part of this exercise. The "seeing" partner is instructed to lead the "blind" partner down corridors, around the room, and perhaps outside. The "seeing" partner can lead the "blind" partner with spoken directions and by taking a hand. The "seeing" person has the responsibility to watch that the "blind" partner does not run into objects, fall, stumble, or get hurt in any way. (The instructor tells students to be very careful going up and down stairs.)

Step 2: After 8 to 10 minutes, the partners reverse roles and continue the exercise for another 8 to 10 minutes.

Step 3: The students then discuss their feelings about the trust walk The instructor asks questions such as the following: Did you occasionally open your eyes when you were the "nonseeing" partner? Did you have trust in your partner? Did you feel you would run into objects and hurt yourself? Were you afraid? If yes, how did you handle these fears? Did you become aware of feelings or thoughts about yourself that you previously were unaware of? If yes, what thoughts and feelings?

SOCIAL WORK WITH GROUPS: CONCEPTS AND SKILLS

LEARNING OBJECTIVES

Effective groups are exhilarating and exciting for both the group leader and the members. This chapter will help prepare students to:

Understand key group dynamic concepts
Describe conflict resolution strategies
Comprehend guidelines for leading counseling groups

MEMBERSHIP GROUPS AND REFERENCE GROUPS

A *membership group* is any group we belong to. Membership in a group is clearly defined—either we belong or we don't. Membership is thus a boundary condition.

Some people are marginal members of a group. For example, Tim Kelly attends classes, works evenings, and doesn't live on campus. He likes his coworkers but knows very few students. He comes to campus only for classes and leaves immediately afterward. Tim is a marginal member of the student body:

Full psychological membership in a group occurs only when a person is positively attracted to being a member and is positively accepted as a member. Tim Kelly has limited psychological membership with the student body because he has only a slight identification with the campus. The more a person is attracted to a group, the greater is that persons commitment to accomplishing the goals of the group.

Aspiring members include those who are seeking admission to a group but have not yet been admitted. They are not members but act as if they are. For example, students who want to join a fraternity or sorority will act like members to increase their chances of being admitted. Aspiring members identify psychologically with the group even though they are not as yet formally admitted.

There is also a difference between voluntary membership and involuntary membership. Individuals who deliberately choose to belong to a group, such as a fraternity or athletic team, are voluntary members. In many situations, people have little or no choice about becoming a group member. Social workers routinely work with groups whose membership is involuntary—for example, in prison settings, mental hospitals, and residential treatment facilities. Involuntary group members may initially be uninterested in participating and are sometimes hostile and disruptive.

Reference groups are groups whose influence we are willing to accept. We closely identify with these groups. Tim Kelly's work group is his reference group; the student body, for all practical purposes, is not.

Reference groups have two distinct functions. First, members' behavior, attitudes, and other characteristics become standards we use to judge and evaluate ourselves and others. Second, reference groups have a normative function in that we seek to conform to their standards.

In a given group, only some members are referents for us. Referents are people who influence us and whom we, in turn, seek to influence. In a large group, we normally have only a small subgroup of referents. These referents may be selected because they have ideas, values, or beliefs similar to ours, because we can easily identify with them, or just because we enjoy associating with them. Referents may or may not be in positions of power. For example, some adolescents reject the norms of their parents and other adults and become members of Goth groups that dress and act differently from the norm. Others join gangs that offer acceptance and friendship despite their location on the margins of society. Still others are drawn toward athletes and other student leaders because they are perceived as being influential or powerful members of the student body. We tend to tune out and interact with others who do not belong to our reference group.

Exercise 7.1: Understanding Membership Groups and Reference Groups

Goal: This exercise is designed to help you understand the concepts of reference groups and membership groups.

Step 1:   Identify a group that you are a member of that is not a reference group for you. Explain why it is not a reference group for you.

Step 2:   Identify a group that you are a member of that is a reference group for you. Explain why you identify with this reference group.

GROUP DEVELOPMENT

Groups change over time. Numerous models or frameworks describe group change. In this section we examine two sequential-stage models and one recurring-phase model.

The Garland, Jones, and Kolodny Model

Garland, Jones, and Kolodny (1965) identified five sequential stages of development in social work groups. Their model describes problems that commonly arise as groups form and develop. Understanding these problems, it is theorized, enables leaders to anticipate and respond to member reactions more effectively. The conceptualization of Garland and his colleagues is particularly applicable to socialization groups and counseling groups. To a lesser extent, the model also applies to self-help groups, problem-solving and decision-making groups, educational groups, recreation-skill groups, and some task groups.

Closeness (how emotionally close members will allow themselves to become) is the central focus of this model. Degrees of closeness are reflected in *struggles* that occur at the five stages of group growth identified by Garland, Jones, and Kolodny: preaffiliation, power and control, intimacy, differentiation, and separation.

In the first stage, *preaffiliation*, members are ambivalent about joining the group. Interaction is guarded. Members test, often through approach and avoidance behavior, whether they really want to belong to the group. New situations are frightening, and members try to protect themselves from being hurt or taken advantage of. They attempt to maintain a certain amount of distance and to get what they can from the group without risking much. Individuals are aware that group involvement will make demands that may be frustrating or even painful. However, they are attracted to the group because they have had satisfying experiences in other groups and membership in this group offers similar rewards.

In the first stage, the leader seeks to increase members' attraction to the group. The leader accomplishes this by explaining the purpose of the group, inviting members' input, explaining the importance of confidentiality, and helping members feel that they are important to the group. Group activities may be used to enhance member participation. The first stage gradually ends as members come to feel fairly safe and comfortable and view the rewards as worth a tentative emotional commitment.

The second stage, *power and control*, emerges as group characteristics begin to develop. Patterns of communication emerge, alliances and subgroups begin to appear, members take on certain roles and responsibilities, norms and methods for handling tasks develop, and membership questions arise. Such processes are necessary for the group to conduct its business. However, these processes lead to struggle as the members establish their places in the group. Each member seeks power, partly for self-protection and partly to gain greater control over the gratifications and rewards to be received from the group. In this struggle, the group leader is a major source of gratification. The leader is perceived as having the greatest power to influence the group's direction and to give or to withhold emotional and material rewards. At this point, members realize that the group is becoming important to them.

The second stage is a transitional stage wherein certain basic issues need to be resolved. Who has primary control over the group's affairs—the group or its leader? Limits of power for the leader and group are questioned. This uncertainty results in anxiety among, and considerable testing by, members as they gauge the limits and seek to establish norms for power and authority. Rebellion is not uncommon, and dropout rates are often highest at this stage. During this struggle, leaders should (1) help members understand the nature of the power struggle, (2) give emotional support to weather the discomfort of uncertainty, and (3) help the group establish norms to resolve the uncertainty. It is very important that group members develop trust in the leader so that the leader can maintain a safe balance of shared power and control. When trust is achieved, members make a major commitment to become involved in the group.

In the third stage, *intimacy*, likes and dislikes are expressed. The group becomes a "family," with "sibling rivalry" arising between members and the leader sometimes even referred to as a parent. Feelings about the group at this stage are more openly expressed and discussed. The group is now viewed as a place where growth and change take place. Individuals examine and make efforts to change personal attitudes, concerns, and problems. Group tasks are worked on, and there is a feeling of "oneness" or cohesiveness. Struggle or turmoil during this stage leads members to explore and make changes in their personal lives and to examine what the group is all about.

During the fourth stage, *differentiation*, members increasingly experiment with new and alternative behavior patterns. There is a recognition of individual rights and needs and a high level of communication among members. The group is able to organize itself more efficiently. Leadership is shared, and roles are more functional. Power problems are now minimal, and decisions are made and carried out with less emotion and on a more objective basis.

During the differentiation stage, the group is analogous to a high-functioning family in which the children have reached adulthood and are pursuing their own lives successfully. Relationships are between equals, members are mutually supportive, and members relate to each other in ways that are rational and objective. Members value each other and the group as a whole. The leader encourages the group to run itself and helps members begin to evaluate what they have accomplished with respect to their individual and group goals.

The final stage is *separation*. The purposes of the group have been achieved, and members have learned new behavioral patterns that enable them to move on to other social experiences. Termination is not always easy. Members are sometimes reluctant to move on and may even display regressive behavior in an effort to prolong the safety of the group. They also may express anger over ending the group or even psychologically deny the end is near. The leader's (or worker's) role in termination is to help members separate from the group by emphasizing activities that increase their connection with others outside the group and reduce those connections that have helped pull members together. The focus is on evaluation of accomplishments, acknowledgment of feelings about ending, and providing support as the group ends.

Exercise 7.2: The Garland, Jones, and Kolodny Model

Goal: This exercise is designed to help you use the Garland, Jones, and Kolodny model to analyze groups.

Write a description of a group that you have participated in that has at least some of the group development stages identified by the Garland, Jones, and Kolodny model. Identify the stages of your group that are consistent with the model. Describe any developmental stages of your group that are inconsistent with this model.

The Tuckman Model

Tuckman (1965) reviewed more than 50 studies of counseling and sensitivity groups with limited duration and concluded that groups go through the following predictable stages:

1. *Forming:* Members become oriented toward each other, work on being accepted, and learn more about the group. A period of uncertainty ensues in which members try to determine their place in the group and the rules and procedures of the group.
2. *Storming:* Conflicts begin to arise as members resist the influence of the group and rebel against accomplishing the tasks. Members often confront their various differences, and management of conflict becomes the focus of attention.
3. *Norming:* The group establishes cohesiveness and commitment, and in the process group members discover new ways to work together. Norms are set for appropriate behavior.
4. *Performing:* The group works as a unit to achieve the group's goals. The group gains proficiency in achieving its goals and becomes more flexible in its patterns of working together.
5. *Adjourning:* The group disbands. The feelings that members experience are similar to those in the "separation stage" of the Garland, Jones, and Kolodny model.

Exercise 7.3: The Tuckman Model

Goal: This exercise is designed to help you use the Tuckman model to analyze groups.

Write a description of a group that you have participated in that has at least some of the group development stages identified by the Tuckman model. Identify the stages of your group that are consistent with the model. Describe any developmental stages of your group that are inconsistent with this model.

The Bales Model

The Garland, Jones, and Kolodny model and the Tuckman model are sequential-stage models—that is, they specify sequential stages of group development. In contrast, Bales (1965) developed a recurring-phase model. He hypothesized that groups continuously strive to achieve equilibrium between task-oriented work and emotional expressions, in order to build better relationships among group members. (Task roles and social/emotional roles are described in the next section.) According to Bales, groups tend to oscillate between these two concerns—sometimes focusing on identifying and performing work tasks that must be conducted to achieve goals and at other times focusing on building morale and improving the social and emotional atmosphere.

Note that the sequential-stage and recurring-phase perspectives are not necessarily contradictory. Both are useful for understanding group development. The sequential-stage perspective assumes that groups move through various stages while dealing with basic themes that surface as they become relevant to the group's work. The recurring-phase perspective assumes that the issues underlying the basic themes are never completely resolved and tend to recur.

It is common for leaders just beginning their work with groups to expect a smooth transition between stages, and they are often disappointed if this transition doesn't occur. In addition, many new practitioners, lacking experience and trust in the group process, tend to prematurely force the group out of certain stages—that is, they rush the process of group development. Experience will demonstrate the futility of such efforts. Barring unforeseen circumstances, groups move at their own pace and eventually arrive at the same destination. Groups that skip stages or groups whose development is otherwise thwarted often return to a stage with "unfinished business." Good leaders recognize this and allow natural group processes to evolve. Although groups sometimes do get mired in one stage, this happens less often than neophyte leaders fear it will.

TASK ROLES AND MAINTENANCE ROLES

All groups (whether organized for therapeutic reasons, for problem solving, or for other objectives) rely on members performing a variety of roles. Group needs require that both task roles and group-building roles be performed satisfactorily. *Task roles* are roles needed to accomplish specific group goals; *maintenance roles* are roles that strengthen the social and emotional aspects of group life (Pfeiffer & Jones, 1976).

Johnson and Johnson (1975, p. 26) summarized *task roles* as follows:

Information and opinion giver: Offers facts, opinions, ideas, suggestions, and relevant information to help group discussion.

Information and opinion seeker: Asks for facts, information, opinions, ideas, and feelings from other members to help group discussion.

Starter: Proposes goals and tasks to initiate action within the group.

Direction giver: Develops plans on how to proceed, and focuses attention on the task to be done.

Summarizer: Pulls together related ideas or suggestions, and restates and summarizes major points discussed.

Coordinator: Shows relationships among various ideas by pulling them together, and harmonizes activities of various subgroups and members.

Diagnoser: Figures out sources of difficulties the group has in working effectively and obstacles to progress in accomplishing the group's goals.

Energizer: Stimulates a higher quality of work from the group.

Reality tester: Examines the practicality and workability of ideas, evaluates alternative solutions, and applies them to real situations to see how they will work.

Evaluator: Compares group decisions and accomplishments with group standards and goals.

The Johnsons (1975, p. 27) also identified *group maintenance roles,* which strengthen social and emotional bonds within the group:

Encourager of participation: Warmly encourages everyone to participate, gives recognition for contributions, demonstrates acceptance and openness to ideas of others, and is friendly and responsive to group members.

Harmonizer and compromiser: Persuades members to analyze constructively their differences in opinions, searches for common elements in conflicts, and tries to reconcile disagreements.

Tension reliever: Eases tensions and increases the enjoyment of group members by joking, suggesting breaks, and proposing fun approaches to group work.

Communication helper: Shows good communication skills, and makes sure that each group member understands what other members are saying.

Evaluator of emotional climate: Asks members how they feel about the way in which the group is working and about each other, and shares own feelings about both.

Process observer: Watches the process by which the group is working, and uses the observations to help examine group effectiveness.

Standard setter: Expresses group standards and goals to make members aware of the direction of the work and the progress being made toward the goal and to get open acceptance of group norms and procedures.

Active listener: Listens and serves as an interested audience for other members, is receptive to others' ideas, goes along with the group when not in disagreement.

Trust builder: Accepts and supports openness of other group memberts, reinforcing risk taking and encouraging individuality.

Interpersonal problem solver: Promotes open discussion of conflicts between group members to resolve conflicts and increase group togetherness.

Hersey and Blanchard (1977) developed a situational theory of leadership that serves as a guideline for when leaders should focus on task behaviors, on maintenance behaviors, or on both. In essence, the theory asserts that when members have low maturity for accomplishing a specific task, leaders should engage in high-task and low-maintenance behaviors. Hersey and Blanchard refer to this situation as *telling,* because leader behaviors are most effective when leaders define members' roles and tell them how, when, and where to do needed tasks. The task maturity of members increases as their experience and understanding of the task increases. For moderately mature members, leaders should engage in high-task and high-maintenance behaviors. This combination of behaviors is referred to as *selling,* because leaders should not only provide clear direction for role and task responsibilities but should also use maintenance behaviors to get members to "buy into" decisions.

Also, according to Hersey and Blanchard, when group members' commitment to the task increases, so does their maturity. When members are committed to accomplishing the task and have the ability and knowledge to complete the task, leaders should engage in low-task and high-maintenance behaviors, referred to as *participating.* Finally, for groups in which members are both willing and able to take responsibility for directing their own task behavior, leaders should engage in low-task and low-maintenance behaviors, referred to as *delegating.* Delegating allows members considerable autonomy.

Exercise 7.4: Your Task and Maintenance Contributions to a Group

Goal: This exercise is designed to assist you in understanding your task and maintenance contributions to a group.

Step 1:   Identify a group you are currently participating in or participated in, in the past. Briefly describe this group, including its goals.

Step 2:   Review the list of task roles, and then describe your task contributions to this group.

Step 3:   Review the list of maintenance roles, and then describe your maintenance contributions to this group.

LEADERSHIP THEORY

Five approaches to leadership theory are discussed in this section: trait, position, style, distributed functions, and servant leadership.

The Trait Approach

Aristotle observed, "From the hour of their birth some are marked for subjugation, and others for command" Johnson & Johnson, 2000, p. 186). As implied by this comment, the trait approach to leadership has existed for millennia. This approach assumes that leaders have personal characteristics or traits that make them different from followers. It also implies that leaders are born, not made, and that leaders emerge naturally rather than being trained. The trait approach has been called the *great person* theory of leadership.

Krech, Crutchfield, and Ballachey (1962) reviewed research studies on leadership traits. Their results suggested leaders need to be perceived as (1) being a member of the group they are attempting to lead, (2) embodying to a special degree the norms and values that are central to the group, (3) being the most qualified group member for the task at hand, and (4) fitting members' expectations about how the leader should behave and what functions he or she should serve.

Research on personality traits indicates that leaders, compared with followers, tend to be better adjusted, more dominant, more extroverted, and more assertive; they often have greater interpersonal sensitivity. Other traits, such as intelligence, enthusiasm, self-confidence, and equalitarianism, also frequently characterize leaders (Hare, 1962).

Although potential leaders tend to have more of all positive attributes than other members have, they cannot be so extreme that they become deviates. In a classic study, for example, Davie and Hare (1956) found that B students were the campus leaders and A students were sometimes treated as outcasts for being "curve wreckers." Also, people who do most of the talking often win most of the decisions and become leaders, unless they talk *too* much and antagonize the other members (March, 1956).

Two leadership traits that have received considerable attention are charisma and Machiavellianism.

Charisma. Johnson and Johnson (2000, p. 189) defined *charisma* as "an extraordinary power, as of working miracles." Johnson and Johnson (1987) gave the following definition of a *charismatic leader:*

> A charismatic leader has (1) an extraordinary power or vision and is able to communicate it to others or (2) unusual powers of practical leadership that will enable him or her to achieve the goals that will alleviate followers' distress. The charismatic leader has a sense of mission, a belief in the social-change movement he or she leads, and confidence in himself or herself as the chosen instrument to lead the movement to its destination. The leader appears extremely self-confident in order to inspire others with the faith that the movement he or she leads will prevail and ultimately reduce their distress. (p. 190)

Some charismatic leaders inspire their followers to adore and be extraordinarily committed to them. Others offer members hope and promise of deliverance from distress.

Charisma has proven difficult to define precisely. Qualities and characteristics of charismatic leaders differ dramatically. Consider, for example, the characteristics of these charismatic leaders: Martin Luther King, Jr., General George Patton, Gandhi, and Hitler.

One difficulty with quantifying charismatic leadership is that charismatics express this quality in numerous ways. A second difficulty is that many leaders do very well without being charismatic.

Exercise 7.5: The Charismatic Leader

Goal:　This exercise is designed to assist you in identifying charismatic people and to understand the various characteristics that lead to charisma.

Step 1:　Write the names of three people you identify as being charismatic—presidents, political leaders, religious leaders, teachers, acquaintances of yours, and so on. For each person you identify, list the characteristics that make this person (in your view) charismatic.

Step 2:　For the three persons you wrote about, identify the charismatic characteristics that all three appear to have.

Step 3:　Do any of these persons have unique charismatic characteristics (that is, characteristics that are not held by the other two)? If "yes," identify the person, and state his or her unique characteristics.

Machiavellianism. Niccolò Machiavelli (1469–1527) was an Italian statesman who advocated that rulers use cunning, craft, deceit, and duplicity to increase their power and control. (Machiavelli was not the originator of this approach; earlier theorists also conceptualized leadership as manipulation for self-enhancement. However, the term *Machiavellianism* is now synonymous with the notion that politics is amoral and that unscrupulous means can therefore justifiably be used to achieve political power.) Machiavellian leadership is based on the concepts that followers (1) are basically fallible, gullible, untrustworthy, and weak; (2) are impersonal objects; and (3) should be manipulated for leaders to achieve their goals.

Christie and Geis (1970) concluded that Machiavellian leaders have four characteristics: (1) They have little emotional involvement in interpersonal relationships because it is easier emotionally to manipulate others if they are seen as "impersonal objects." (2) They are not concerned with conventional morality and take a utilitarian view (what they can get out of it) rather than a moral view of their interactions. (3) They have a fairly accurate perception of the needs of their followers, which facilitates their capacity to manipulate them. (4) They have a low degree of ideological commitment; they manipulate others for personal benefit rather than for achieving ideological goals.

Although some leaders have Machiavellian characteristics, most do not. Groups simply do not function effectively or efficiently with Machiavellian leaders.

In recent years, the trait theory of leadership has declined in popularity, partly because research results raise questions about its validity. For example, different leadership positions often require different leadership traits. The characteristics of a good military leader differ markedly from those of a good group therapy leader. Moreover, traits found in leaders are also found in followers. Qualities such as intelligence and a well-adjusted personality have some correlation with strong leadership, but many intelligent, well-adjusted people never get top leadership positions. The best rule for selecting leaders involves choosing people with the necessary skills, qualities, and motivation to help a group accomplish its goals.

Exercise 7.6: Machiavellian Leaders

Goal:　This exercise is designed to assist you in understanding the characteristics of Machiavellian leaders.

Some authorities view Joseph Stalin, Adolf Hitler, and Saddam Hussein as being Machiavellian leaders. Identify three persons you view as being Machiavellian leaders. (These persons may include one or more of the leaders just mentioned.) For each person you list, write the characteristics he or she had (or has) that are Machiavellian.

The Position Approach

Large organizations have several levels of leadership. The position approach defines leadership in terms of the authority associated with a particular position and focuses on the behavior of people in high-level positions. Training and personal background of leaders have also been examined.

Studies using the position approach, however, reveal little consistency in how people assume leadership positions. Individuals with little training become leaders; others spend years developing their skills. Also, individuals in different leadership positions display a variety of appropriate behaviors. A drill sergeant is not expected to be empathetic, but a therapy group leader is. It is difficult to compile a list of leadership traits using this approach. Not surprisingly, the position approach has shown that what constitutes leadership behavior depends on the particular requirements of the position.

It is also difficult to define which behaviors are leadership behavior and which are not. Certainly not all the behavior of designated authority figures is leadership behavior. Also, leadership behavior among group members who are not designated leaders is often difficult to clarify. An experienced supervisor who joins a new firm, for example, may categorize her staff members according to guidelines set by her former employer. If the positions she uses are not interchangeable with those already in use at her new place of employment, communication problems may develop, and her leadership abilities or the ability of her staff will be questioned.

The Style Approach

Because research on the trait approach was turning out contradictory results, Lewin, Lippitt, and White (1939) focused on leadership *styles.* These researchers described three leadership styles: authoritarian, democratic, and laissez-faire.

Authoritarian leaders have more absolute power than democratic leaders. They alone set goals and policies, dictate the activities of members, and set major plans. They alone reward and punish, and they alone know the succession of future steps in the group's activities. In contrast, democratic leaders seek maximum involvement and participation of members in all decisions affecting the group. They spread responsibility rather than concentrate it.

Authoritarian leadership can be efficient and decisive. One hazard, however, is that group members often do what they are told out of necessity and not because of their commitment to group goals. The authoritarian leader who anticipates approval from subordinates for accomplishments achieved may be surprised to find backbiting and bickering common in the group. Unsuccessful authoritarian leadership generates factionalism and behind-the-scenes jockeying and maneuvering for position among members, and it leads to a decline in morale.

Democratic leadership, in contrast, is slow in decision making and sometimes confusing but is frequently more effective because strong cooperation emerges when members participate in decision making. With democratic leadership, interpersonal hostilities between members, dissatisfactions with the leader, and concern for personal advancement are discussed and acted on. The danger is that the private, behind-the-scenes complaining that can happen in the authoritarian approach becomes public conflict in a democratic approach. However, once the public conflict is resolved, strong personal commitments develop that motivate members to implement group decisions rather than to subvert them. The potential for sabotage in authoritarian groups is high, and therein lies the advantage of the democratic style.

Democratic leaders know that mistakes are inevitable and that the group will suffer from them. Yet such mistakes require that leaders stand by without interfering because to do otherwise harms the democratic process and impedes group progress.

In certain situations, authoritarian leadership is most effective, whereas in others democratic leadership is most effective (Hare, 1962). As in any situation, groups are more effective when members' expectations about behavior are met. When group members anticipate a democratic style, as they do in educational settings, classrooms, and discussion groups, the democratic style produces the most effective groups. When members anticipate forceful leadership, as in industry or military service, authoritarian leadership results in more effective groups.

In the *laissez-faire* style, there is very little participation by the leader. Group members function (or flounder) with little input by the designated leader. There are a few conditions in which group members function best under laissez-faire leadership (when the members are committed to a course of action, have the resources to implement it, and need a minimum of designated leader influence to work effectively).

Because different leadership styles are required in different situations (even within the same group), research interest in recent years has switched to the distributed-functions approach.

Exercise 7.7: Authoritarian, Democratic, and Laissez-Faire Leaders

Goal: This exercise is designed to help you understand these three types of leadership styles.

Step 1:   Identify someone who used an authoritarian style in leading a group. State what the leader did that led you to conclude his or her style was authoritarian. Also state what the reactions of the other group members were to this authoritarian style.

Step 2:   Identify someone who used a democratic style in leading a group. State what the leader did that led you to conclude his or her style was democratic. Also state what the reactions of the other group members were to this democratic style.

Step 3:   Identify someone who used a laissez-faire style in leading a group. State what the leader did that led you to conclude his or her style was laissez-faire. Also state what the reactions of the other group members were to this laissez-faire style.

The Distributed-Functions Approach

This approach defines *leadership* as the performance of acts that help the group reach its goals and maintain itself in good working order (Johnson & Johnson, 1975). Leadership functions include setting group goals, selecting and implementing tasks to achieve goals, and providing resources to accomplish goals. Leadership functions also include the group maintenance tasks of improving group cohesion and seeking to ensure that individual members are satisfied. This approach seeks to discover what tasks are essential to achieve group goals under various circumstances and how different group members take part in these actions.

The distributed-functions approach stands in direct contrast to the great person theory of leadership. It asserts that at times any group member may be a leader by taking actions that serve group functions. Leadership is viewed as specific to a particular group in a particular situation. Telling a joke, for example, may relieve tension in some situations and thus may be leadership behavior. According to the functional approach, leadership occurs whenever any member influences other members to help the group reach its goals. Because at times all group members influence other members, each member leads.

The functional approach asserts that leadership is a learned set of skills that anyone with certain minimal requirements can acquire. Responsible membership is the same thing as responsible leadership; both involve doing what needs to be done to help the group maintain itself and accomplish its goals. This approach asserts that people can be taught the skills and behaviors that help the group accomplish its tasks and maintain good working relationships. The implication for a social work practice course is that practically everyone can learn to be an effective leader. However, being a *designated leader* and engaging in leadership behavior are different. A designated leader has responsibilities that continue for the duration of the group, whereas members who engage in leadership behaviors do so temporarily—this leadership role shifts from member to member.

Like any member of the group, the designated leader may need to adopt one or more of the task roles or maintenance roles discussed earlier in this chapter. Indeed, designated leaders have a special obligation to be alert for such occasions and to assume or assist others to assume whichever roles are timely and appropriate. The designated leader's contribution to the group is not limited, however, by assuming specified roles. He or she is responsible for functions that range from performing intake to planning for termination. The needs and developmental stage of a group will require a leader who can at different times assume the previously described roles and also the following ones:

- Executive (the top coordinator of group activities)
- Policymaker (establishing group goals and policies)
- Planner (deciding the means by which the group will achieve its goals)
- Expert (source of readily available information and skills)

- External group representative (the official spokesperson for the group)
- Controller of internal relations (managing the structure as a way to control in-group relations)
- Purveyor of rewards and punishments (promotions, demotions, and pleasant and unpleasant tasks)
- Arbitrator and mediator (both judge and conciliator with the power to reduce or to increase factionalism within the group)
- Exemplar (shows what members should be and do)
- Ideologist (the source of the group's beliefs and values)
- Scapegoat (the target for members' frustrations and disappoint ments)

Exercise 7.8: Applying the Distributed-Functions Approach

Goal: This exercise is designed to show you that you already have taken on leadership functions in a group.

The distributed-functions approach asserts that every member of a group will be a leader at times by taking actions that serve group functions. Identify a group that you are currently in or that you were a member of in the past. Describe actions that you took that were useful to the group. (When you made positive contributions to this group, you were taking on leadership responsibilities.)

The Servant Leadership Approach

Servant leadership is an approach to leadership that was initially developed by Robert K. Greenleaf (Greenleaf, Spears, and Covey, 2002). A servant leader is someone who looks to the needs of the group. The servant leader asks herself how he or she can help the members to solve problems and promote their personal development. The servant leader places the main focus on the members, as he or she believes that content and motivated members are best able to reach their goals. In contrast to an autocratic style of leadership, in which the autocratic leader makes most of the decisions, decision-making responsibilities are shared with the members in the servant leadership style. The highest priority of a servant leader is to support, encourage, and enable members to unfold their full potential and abilities. (A highly competent teacher probably uses many of the concepts of a servant leader.)

Larry C. Spears (Greenleaf, Spears, and Covey, 2002) has identified the following 10 concepts that characterize a servant leader:

- Listening: A servant leader is motivated to listen to members, is supportive of their opinions, and validates their concerns. The servant leader attends not only to verbalized concerns, but also to what is "unspoken."
- Empathy: A servant leader seeks to understand and empathize with the members. The members are viewed as people who need respect and appreciation in order to facilitate personal development; and the more that members develop, the more successful and productive they are apt to become.
- Healing: A servant leader seeks to help members solve their issues and conflicts in relationships, as he or she wants to encourage and support the personal development of each member. Such "healing" is postulated to lead to a working environment in the group that is dynamic, fun, and free of the fear of failure.
- Awareness: A servant leader seeks to have a high level of self-awareness, and to be perceptive of what the members are thinking and feeling. He or she also seeks to be aware of the interpersonal relationships in the group.
- Persuasion: A servant leader does not try to coerce members into compliance with what he or she wants, but instead seeks to convince members to share decision-making responsibilities.
- Conceptualization: A servant leader thinks beyond day-to-day realities by conceptualizing long-term goals and strategies for teaching those goals. He or she has a personal vision that incorporates what is in the best interests of all members of the group.
- Foresight: A servant leader has the capacity to foresee the likely outcome of possible implementation strategies. (This characteristic is closely related to conceptualization.)
- Stewardship: A servant leader not only seeks to facilitate the personal development and productivity of the group, but also realizes that he or she has an obligation to do what is best for the greater society. Openness and persuasion are more important than control.
- Commitment to the growth of people: A servant leader focuses on nurturing the professional, personal, and spiritual growth of members. He or she seeks to validate the ideas of all the members, and involves them in decision making.

■ Building community: A servant leader not only seeks to develop a productive and contented group, but also seeks to build a strong community. It is postulated that members will have considerable growth with this style of leadership, which will lead these members to add to the development of the communities in which they live.

Servant leadership is a lifelong journey that includes self-discovery, a desire to serve others, and a commitment to developing the group members that one works with. Servant leaders are humble, caring, visionary, empowering, relational, competent, good stewards, and community builders. They put others first, are skilled communicators, are compassionate collaborators, are systems thinkers, and are ethical. Instead of a top-down hierarchical style, servant leaders emphasize trust, collaboration, empathy, and ethical use of power. Servant leaders do not seek to increase their own power, but seek to lead by better serving others.

Servant leadership not only facilitates the personal development of group members, but has the potential to influence the broader society in a positive way. Group members tend to be attracted to this style of leadership, and tend to be happier and more productive. (Servant leadership is not only an effective approach to leading a group, but is also an effective management style for a supervisor to use in supervising employees. Managers who empower and respect their staff tend to get better performance in return.)

Will servant leadership work well in all groups? Undoubtedly not! Certain settings probably require a more forceful form of leadership—such as in the military or in a prison setting.

Exercise 7.9: Applying the Servant Leadership Approach

Goal: This exercise is designed to help you understand the servant leadership approach. Identify someone who used the servant leadership approach in leading a group. Perhaps the person was a teacher or a member of the clergy.

State what the leader did that led you to conclude his or her style was servant leadership. Also state what the reactions of the other group members were to this style.

SOCIAL POWER BASES IN GROUPS

French and Raven (1968) developed a framework for understanding the extent to which group members have influence or power over each other. They identified five types of power: reward, coercive, legitimate, referent, and expert. This framework allows group leaders to analyze the source of their power and also suggests when, and when not, to use their power.

Power is often viewed negatively. But *every* interaction involves power. In groups, it is natural and generally desirable that every member seeks to influence other members—this is how personal goals and group goals are accomplished.

Reward power is based on the perception of B (one member) that A (another member or the entire group) has the capacity to dispense rewards or remove negative consequences in response to B's behavior. A's power will be greater the more group members value the reward and the more they believe they cannot get the reward from anyone else. Rewards include such things as promotions, pay increases, days off, and praise. Group members often work hard for someone who has high reward power, will usually like the person, and will communicate effectively with him or her. But reward power can backfire if members feel they are being conned or bribed into going along, which can lead to dislike of the high-reward person. If A uses reward power in a conflict situation with B, B may feel he is being bribed and controlled.

Coercive power is based on B's perception that A can dispense adverse consequences or remove positive consequences. Coercive power stems from B's expectation that she will be punished by A if she fails to conform to A's wishes. The ability to fire workers if they fall below a given level of production is a common example of coercive power. The distinction between reward and coercive power is important. French and Raven noted that reward power tends to increase the attraction of B toward A, whereas coercive power decreases this attraction. If A uses coercive power to settle a conflict, it increases B's hostility, resentment, and anger. Threats often lead to aggression and counterthreats. Thus, coercive power can exacerbate the conflict by leading both A and B to distrust each other and to retaliate. Therefore, whenever possible, coercive power should not be used in a conflict situation. (Unfortunately, it often is, with the result that conflict is exacerbated. For example, military threats often increase conflict between rival countries.)

Legitimate power is based on B's perception that A has a legitimate right to prescribe behavior for him and that B has an obligation to accept this influence. Legitimate power is the most complex of the five power bases and is based on some internalized value or norm. Cultural values constitute one common basis for legitimate power and include such things as intelligence, age, caste, and physical characteristics. For example, in some cultures the elderly are highly respected and granted the right to prescribe behavior for others. Acceptance of a social structure is another basis; legitimate power in a formal organization is largely a relationship between positions rather than between people (such as the perceived right of supervisors to assign work). A third basis is a legitimizing agent; the process of electing a group leader is a common way to legitimize a person's right to a position that has legitimate power associated with it.

The areas in which legitimate power may be used are generally specified (for example, in a job description). The attempted use of power outside the prescribed range decreases the legitimate power and attractiveness of the authority figure.

Referent power is based on B's identification with A. Identification in this context means either a feeling of oneness with A or a desire for such an identity. The stronger B's identification with A, the greater is B's attraction to A and the greater A's referent power: "I am like A, and therefore I will believe or behave as A does," or "I want to be like A, and I will be more like A if I believe or behave as A does." In ambiguous situations, B will evaluate his thoughts, beliefs, and values in terms of what A thinks, believes, and values. In ambiguous situations, B is likely to adopt the thoughts, beliefs, and values of the individual or group with which he identifies. French and Raven noted that B is often not consciously aware of the referent power that A exerts.

Expert power is based on the perception that A has some special knowledge or expertise. Accepting a physician's advice in medical matters is a common example. Another is accepting directions from a service station owner when in a strange city. For expert influence to occur, it is necessary for B to think that A has the right answer and for B to trust that A is telling the truth. A client accepting a counselor's suggestion exemplifies the effect of expert power. Expert power is more limited than referent power because the expert is seen as having superior knowledge or ability only in specific areas. French and Raven (1968) noted that the attempted exertion of expert power outside the perceived range of that power will reduce it—that is, an undermining of confidence will take place.

French and Raven (1968) theorized that for all five types, the stronger the basis of power, the greater will be the power. Referent power is thought to have the broadest range of power. Attempts to use power outside the prescribed range may reduce the power.

Exercise 7.10: The Power Bases in This Class

Goal: This exercise is designed to assist you in understanding and applying the power bases identified by French and Raven.

This class can be viewed as being a group. For each of the following types of power, please write the following: Who in this class has this type of power? Has the person (or persons) engaged in actions that demonstrated this type of power? If "yes," describe these actions.

Reward power:

Coercive power:

Legitimate power:

Referent power:

Expert power:

PERSONAL GOALS AND GROUP GOALS

A *goal* is an end toward which an individual or a group of people are working. It is an ideal or a desired end point that people value. A personal goal is a goal held by a member. A group goal is a goal held by enough members that the group can be said to be working toward its achievement. All groups have goals, and every person who joins a group has personal goals. Groups have both short- and long-range goals. The short-range goals are stepping-stones to reaching the long-range goals.

It is very important to set group goals. The effectiveness and efficiency of the group can be measured by the extent to which its goals are achieved. Goals give direction to groups and to their members. They direct the group's programs and efforts. Conflicts of opinion between members are often resolved by deciding which opinion is most helpful in achieving group goals. Group goals are a motivating force. Once members commit to achieving a certain goal, they feel an obligation to put forth their abilities, efforts, and resources to attain this end.

Members' motivation to work to accomplish group goals is increased by involving members in setting the goals. Through involvement, members (1) have a greater chance of having their personal goals for joining the group become a component of the group goals, (2) have an increased awareness of the importance of choosing these goals, and (3) feel a greater commitment to providing their resources to achieve the goals.

The more congruence there is between members' personal goals and the group's goals, the more attracted to the group the members will be and the more willing to provide their resources and energies to the group. Members' personal goals can be heterogeneous (different) or homogeneous (alike). The more homogeneous personal goals are, the more likely are members to agree on group goals and work together to achieve them. They also tend to be happier with the group when personal goals are homogeneous.

When members have heterogeneous personal goals, hidden agendas can develop. A *hidden agenda* is a personal goal held by a member that is unknown to the other group members and that interferes with group goals. Hidden agendas can be very destructive. I have participated in groups where an individual observed the comments and actions of others to obtain evidence to bring legal harassment charges. Usually, however, hidden agendas are less destructive. For example, a lonely person who enjoys talking may slow a group down by monopolizing meetings with irrelevant small talk.

Because hidden agendas can severely hamper group processes, it is important that groups set goals that incorporate members' personal goals. With such a focus, hidden agendas are likely to be minimized.

Note, however, that *all* groups operate on two levels: the surface task and the hidden needs and motivations. Although hidden agendas siphon energy, they also reflect individual needs and may or may not be known to the person who holds them. All members join groups with the intention of meeting their personal needs. Sometimes after initial needs are met, other, less obvious ones surface. Such needs are normal and expected. The real issue is the effect these needs have on the group. The important question is whether meeting A's needs will prevent B (or the group) from satisfying needs. The goal is to find a means to legitimize individual needs in ways that allow for effective problem solving.

Managing hidden agendas requires that members and leaders be on the lookout for them and support members who try to bring hidden agendas to the surface. One such approach might involve saying, "I wonder if we've said all that we feel about this idea. Perhaps we should go around the room once more and see whether anyone has anything to add." At the same time, leaders and members should be aware that some hidden agendas are best left hidden. Criticizing a member for a hidden agenda can create defensiveness and inhibit problem solving.

Exercise 7.11: Group Goals, Personal Goals, and Hidden Agendas in This Class

Goal: This exercise is designed to assist you in understanding the dynamics between group goals, personal goals, and hidden agendas.

Step 1: Specify the group goals that the instructor wants for this class. (Usually the "course objectives" section of the syllabus will specify the group goals desired by the instructor.) In his or her lectures, the instructor may have identified additional desired group goals.

Step 2: Have all the students in the class "accepted" the desired group goals of the class? If "no," describe why you believe some students have not accepted the instructor's group goals.

Step 3: Did the instructor ask the students for additional group goals that they desired for the class? If "yes," did the students suggest additional group goals? If "yes" to the latter question, what were the additional group goals that were suggested—and then were they adopted for this class?

Step 4: Specify the personal goals that you have for this class. Are they consistent with the group goals?

Step 5: Do you believe some members of the class have "personal goals" or "hidden agendas" that are inconsistent with the group goals? (These personal goals or hidden agendas may include "not wanting to study very much" or "wanting help in resolving a personal dilemma.") If "yes," specify these inconsistent personal goals or hidden agendas.

GROUP NORMS

Group norms are rules that specify proper group behavior. To be a norm, a rule must be accepted by a majority of the group. If a person recognizes a norm and believes the benefits of conforming outweigh the consequences of deviating, the norm can influence that person's behavior. At first, members may conform because of pressures from the group. As time passes, though, members generally internalize norms and conform automatically. Norms provide one of the most important mechanisms of social control over members of groups and over society as a whole.

Every group has norms. If you frequently socialize with a certain group of students, for example, your group will gradually set norms as to what is acceptable and unacceptable behavior at gatherings. Your classes will have certain norms covering smoking, arriving late, absences, meeting deadlines, raising a hand before speaking, and cheating on exams.

Some norms are set formally—bylaws and constitutions of organizations, for instance, specify responsibilities for the officers. Other norms are set informally. During a department meeting, the department chair may frown at a faculty member who is reading his mail. If that faculty member responds to the nonverbal communication and puts aside his mail, other faculty members may observe the nonverbal interaction and decide never to read their mail during meetings. Through this process, a norm against reading mail has informally been established.

Norms have an "ought to" or "must" quality, and they vary in importance. There are strong pressures to obey and, in some cases, severe penalties for violating *important* norms—confidentiality in counseling groups, for example. If a member violates confidentiality by revealing personal information about another member to others outside the group, he may be penalized by expulsion from the group. Failure to obey less important norms, such as not belching at meetings, generates only mild disapproval and little or no penalty.

Members are often only subconsciously aware of many of the norms that are guiding their behavior. If one were to ask a group member to define her group's norms, she would probably be able to list only a few because many norms are taken for granted. Norms relating to dress, promptness, or foul language are often given little thought by group members.

When a person enters a new group, he generally feels strange and uncomfortable because he is unaware of the norms. So he searches for clues to norms, asking himself such questions as these: What is appropriate to disclose, and what is not? Who is in the in-group, and who is left out? Is smoking permissible? Can I tell a joke? Do members raise their hands before speaking? What role does each member play? Is the group competitive or cooperative? Are there hidden agendas? Are there coalitions? Which members are more powerful?

Some group norms are fairly universal, so new members who have worked in groups before will be aware of many norms that are likely to be operating. For example, an individual who joins a counseling group will expect other members to be honest, open, and self-disclosing. Many groups have norms such as reciprocity (if someone does something kind or helpful for you, you should do something kind or helpful in return); fair play (don't lie or cheat to get what you want); social responsibility (you should help those who need help); and shared air time (everyone should have a chance to talk, and no one should monopolize the conversation).

New members may learn norms by talking privately with a group member they trust. They may ask questions such as the following: Who has the power? Is it acceptable to say or do such and such? Are there coalitions in the group? Do some members have hidden agendas? Are there personal matters that some members are sensitive about? Someone who is overweight, for example, may express discomfort with comments on dieting, and other members may individually decide not to mention dieting when the overweight person is present.

Although norms are learned in a variety of ways, the most common way is through positive and negative reinforcement. Through a process of trial and error, members identify which of their behaviors are accepted and rewarded by the group and which are judged inappropriate or destructive. Another way members identify norms is through "modeling," which involves learning through observing another member's behavior.

Some norms are in the bylaws, constitution, minutes, or other documents of a group or organization. For example, there may be guidelines for placing an item on the agenda, the duties and responsibilities of the officers, and the decision-making procedures for resolving crucial issues. Furthermore, norms can take the form of role expectations that can be official or unofficial. Officially, the chair of a group is expected to call and run meetings; the secretary keeps minutes. Unofficially, a wealthy member is expected to make donations when the group needs funds. Likewise, a member who is skilled at reducing tension is expected to ease the tension level when it gets too high.

Some norms develop less formally through nonverbal communications. For example, the leader of a counseling group may shake his head in disapproval of one member mimicking another. The other members note the gesture and then individually (without discussion) decide not to mimic anyone in the group in the future.

New norms may develop from suggestions on group policy or procedures made by group members. For example, a member may suggest, "For an item to be placed on the agenda, the members must be informed of it at least forty-eight hours before the meeting to give them an opportunity to think about it." If the group approves of the suggestion, it becomes a policy and a norm.

Exercise 7.12: Group Norms in This Class

Goal: This exercise is designed to assist you in identifying group norms and to understand the processes that led to their development.

Step 1:   Specify the group norms that exist for proper behavior in this class.

Step 2:   Identify the processes that occurred that led to these group norms. (For example, the department may have standards for acceptable behavior in a class. The NASW Code of Ethics has statements on confidentiality, honesty, and opposition to making racist and sexist remarks. The CSWE's *Educational Policy and Accreditation Standards* has statements on diversity, populations at risk, and promoting social and economic justice. The instructor may have made statements about proper behavior in this class. Some students may have made statements about what they view as offensive remarks and behaviors.)

CONFORMITY

Some classic studies have examined conforming behavior. Sherif (1936) examined the "autokinetic effect." In this experiment, subjects were placed in a darkened room and asked to judge how far a dot of light moves. Although the light appeared to move (the autokinetic effect), it actually did not. Each subject saw the dot of light and made a series of individual judgments about how far the light moved. The subjects were then brought together in groups of three to judge again how far the light moved. In this situation, their judgments tended to converge to a group standard. Later, when they again viewed the light alone, they often retained the group standard and gave that answer. The key finding from this study and many after it is that when a situation is ambiguous and there is no objective way to determine the "right" answer, members rely on the group to define "reality." This means membership in a group determines for individuals many of the things they will see, learn, think about, and do.

Asch (1955) also examined conforming behavior. Asch investigated what happens when an individual's judgment conflicts with the judgments of other group members. The experiments were designed as follows. There were two sets of cards, as shown in Figure 7.1. Subjects were arranged in groups of seven to nine, seated at a table, and asked to state in turn which line was closest in length to the standard. In the control groups, practically all subjects chose line 2. Now, here is where things get interesting: In the experimental groups, all members, except for one subject, were accomplices of the experimenter. The subject was seated

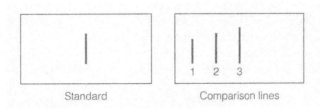

Standard   Comparison lines

Figure 7.1

Cards used in Asch's conformity studies.

at or near the end of the line for giving his or her judgment. Accomplices all chose the same *incorrect* line. When it came to the subject's turn, he or she was then faced with relying on individual judgment or conforming to the group judgment. In a variety of similar studies, Asch found that more than one-third of the subjects conformed to the group judgment. Such a large percentage is amazing because there was no overt group pressure to conform, the situation was not ambiguous, and the subjects did not know each other. In addition, there were neither promises of future favor or advancement, nor threats of ostracism or punishment.

Conformity is the yielding to group pressure. For there to be conformity, there must be conflict—conflict between the influences exerted by the group and those forces in individuals that tend to lead them to value, believe, and act in some other way. For members experiencing such conflict, there are two available options: Announce an independent decision, or conform with the group's position. Conforming takes two forms: (1) The expedient conformer outwardly agrees but inwardly disagrees. (2) The true conformer both outwardly and inwardly comes to agree with the group.

A number of conclusions have arisen from conformity research (Krech et al., 1962, pp. 509–512):

1. Considerable amounts of yielding are produced by group pressure, even when the bogus group consensus is obviously wrong. In one study, 50 military officers were asked to indicate which of two figures, a star and a circle presented side by side, was larger in an area. The circle was clearly about one-third larger, but under group pressure 46 percent of the men agreed with the bogus group consensus.

2. Many people can be pressured into yielding on attitude and opinion items, even those with significant personal implications. For example, 50 military officers were asked privately and under bogus group consensus to state their opinion on the following: "I doubt whether I would make a good leader." In private, none of the officers expressed agreement, but under unanimous group pressure, 37 percent expressed agreement.

3. Yielding is far greater on difficult, subjective items than on easy, objective ones.

4. Individual differences in yielding are extremely large. A few people yield on almost all items; a few yield on none; most people yield on some and not on others.

5. When people are retested individually and privately on the same items some time later, the yielding effect mostly disappears as they tend to revert to their own unchanged private judgment. But a small part of the yielding effect remains, indicating group pressure has a lasting effect on changing attitudes.

6. As a group increases in size, the pressure for yielding increases, and more yielding occurs. When a person is opposed by a single other person, there is very little yielding.

7. Yielding is markedly reduced when a person has the support of one other person (a partner) in the group. Apparently, a dissident opinion has a tremendous effect in strengthening the independence of like-minded people.

In a dramatic series of studies, Milgram (1963) demonstrated that subjects in an experimental situation would administer electric shocks of dangerous strength to another person when instructed to do so by the experimenter. (Unknown to the subject, the person did not actually receive the electrical shocks.) Most subjects complied with the experimenter's commands, even when instructed to give increasingly stronger shocks to the victim, and despite the victim's protests and cries of anguish. These studies demonstrated that people will yield to "authoritative" commands even when the behavior is incompatible with their own moral, normal standards of conduct. Milgram suggested his studies help us understand why the German people complied with the unethical commands of Hitler. Group pressures, especially when viewed as authoritative, have a tremendous effect on our actions, attitudes, and beliefs.

Schachter (1959) developed a theory of social comparison. Schachter assumed that we all have a need to evaluate the "rightness" of our feelings, opinions, values, and attitudes. He also assumed that we all have a need to evaluate the extent of our abilities. Schachter then theorized and conducted studies to demonstrate that in the absence of objective, nonsocial means of evaluation, a person will rely on other people as comparison points of reference. To a large extent, the groups we belong to define social reality for us. For most of our opinions, values, beliefs, and abilities, there is no objective, nonsocial way to evaluate ourselves, so we rely on others.

Exercise 7.13: Your Yielding to Group Pressure

Goal: This exercise is designed to help you understand that all of us have yielded (at one time or another) to group pressure. The exercise also helps you understand your feelings about yielding.

Step 1:   Describe a group that you participated in, in which you yielded to group pressure. Specify the issue or action that you yielded to. (If you have difficulty in identifying a time when you yielded, feel free to identify an issue in which you yielded to pressure from your parents.)

Step 2:   Specify your thoughts and feelings during the time when you yielded. Also specify your thoughts and feelings after you yielded.

Step 3:   If you had to do it over, would you still yield? Why, or why not?

IDIOSYNCRATIC CREDITS

Every member of a group gains credits (and status) by showing competence and by conforming to expectations at that time. Eventually these credits allow a person to break the group's norms and rules without being chastised. To some extent, after credits accumulate, nonconformity to general procedures or expectations serves as a confirming feature of one's status. Yet there is a limit on the number of earned idiosyncratic credits. Nonconformity beyond this limit can result in a dramatic decrease in status and even rejection by other group members.

COMPETITIVE GROUPS AND COOPERATIVE GROUPS

Groups basically have either a cooperative or a competitive group atmosphere. In a cooperative group, open and honest communication, trust, pooling of resources, and cohesion prevail. Research has found a number of positive consequences for a cooperative group atmosphere in problem-solving groups. Cooperation among members increases creativity, coordination of effort, division of labor, emotional involvement in group accomplishment, helping and sharing, interpersonal skills, cooperative attitudes and values, positive self-attitudes, liking among group members, positive attitudes toward the group and tasks, divergent thinking, acceptance of individual and cultural differences, and problem-solving skills.

Cooperative group atmospheres result when members' personal goals are perceived as compatible, identical, or complementary. An example of a highly cooperative group is a successful basketball team in which the main goal of each member is to win and the main goal of the team is to win. In a cooperative group, members seek to coordinate their efforts with those of other members to achieve the goals of the group. To establish a cooperative atmosphere, rewards to members must be based on the quantity and quality of group performance rather than on individual performance.

In contrast, competitive atmospheres can be detrimental and destructive. Competitive atmospheres exist when members perceive their personal goals as incompatible, different, conflicting, or mutually exclusive. In highly competitive groups, a member achieves his or her goal only if other members fail to obtain their goals. An example is a job group interview held for several job applicants. The consequences of competition in problem-solving groups are numerous. Competition decreases creativity, coordination of effort, division of labor, helping and sharing, and cohesion. Competition promotes ineffective communication, suspicion and mistrust, high anxiety, competitive values and attitudes, negative self-attitudes, dislike among group members, and negative attitudes toward the group and its tasks. Competition encourages rejection of differences of opinion, divergent thinking, and cultural and individual differences. A competitive atmosphere often leads to low effectiveness in solving complex problems.

Kelly and Stahelski (1970) examined the question of what happens when a competitive person joins a group that has a cooperative atmosphere. Because cooperative groups are much more effective in problem solving than competitive groups are, the question is significant. Three consequences were found to occur: (1) The competitive behavior of the new member leads other members to behave competitively. (2) The competitive person views the former cooperative members as having always been competitive. (3) The former cooperative members are generally aware that their competitive behavior is largely a consequence of the new member's competitiveness. Thus, it appears that one competitive person can change a cooperative group into a competitive group. Why does a competitive person have such a strong, destructive effect? Apparently, the cooperative members realize the competitive person, if given a chance, will take advantage of their cooperativeness and use it to his or her own advantage. In many situations, their only recourse to prevent exploitation is to also become competitive. If a cooperative group is to survive, it is important that new members have an orientation compatible with that of the other members.

CONFLICT AND CREATIVITY

Conflict is an antagonistic state of action involving divergent ideas or interests and is inevitable in groups. Johnson and Johnson (1975) summarize the potential merits and dangers of a conflict in a group:

> A conflict among group members is a moment of truth in group effectiveness, a test of the group's health, a crisis that can weaken or strengthen the group, a critical event that may bring creative insight and closer relationships among members—or lasting resentment, smoldering hostility, and psychological scars. Conflicts can push members away from one another or pull them into closer and more cooperative relationships. Conflicts may contain the seeds of group destruction or the seeds of a more unified and cooperative unit. . . . They have the potential for producing both highly constructive and highly destructive consequences for group functioning. (p. 139)

Many people in our society erroneously believe that conflicts produce only negative results and should be avoided. Conflict is seen as a cause of divorce, low work morale, deterioration of friendships, psychological trauma, violence, and social disorder. In reality, the cause of these destructive events is the ineffective and harmful management of conflicts. People have divergent interests, beliefs, values, and goals, so it is inevitable that conflicts will occur in interpersonal relationships.

Conflicts are a natural part of any relationship within a group, and they are desirable because, when handled effectively, they have a number of payoffs. Without conflict, members may become bored; disagreements often spark the interest and curiosity of group members and produce lively discussions. Conflicts motivate members to define issues more sharply, search harder for resolution strategies, and work harder in implementing solutions. Conflicts also can lead to greater commitment, cohesion, communication, and cooperation and can revitalize stagnant groups. By expressing and working out their dissatisfactions, group members can assess their beliefs, values, and opinions. Therefore, verbal conflicts can lead to personal growth and encourage innovation and creativity.

Exercise 7.14: My Tolerance for Conflicts

Goal: This exercise is designed to assist you in assessing whether you need to become more assertive in confronting interpersonal conflicts.

Step 1:   Do you shy away (by usually giving in) from interpersonal conflicts? If "yes," explain your reasons.

Step 2:   If you shy away from interpersonal conflicts, do you feel when you give in that the other person is "treading" on your personal rights?

Step 3:   Do you believe that you need to more assertively confront your interpersonal conflicts? If "yes," what do you intend to do to become more assertive in confronting conflicts?

STRATEGIES FOR RESOLVING CONFLICTS

There are a variety of strategies for resolving conflicts. Among them are the win-lose approach, no-lose problem solving, role reversal, empathy, inquiry, I-messages, disarming, stroking, mediation, letting go or forgiving, and the law of requisite variety.

Win-Lose Approach

In ineffective groups, resolutions of conflict between opposing positions become win-lose situations. In many competitive fields, such as sports, business, and politics, individuals or teams are pitted against each other. In groups, conflicts are often cast in the same competitive mold. Because each side denies the legitimacy of the other's interests and concerns, members attempt to sell their position without really listening to the other side. Power blocks are formed to support one position against another. The original goals and objectives of the group may fade into the background as only a "win" on issues becomes the objective of the warring sides.

In win-lose situations, the group as a whole loses because it fails to achieve its long-range goals and objectives. The losing side is not motivated to carry out the winning decision. The losers resent the winners and may attempt to reverse the decision or impede its implementation. In such an atmosphere, distrust increases between opposing sides, communication becomes more limited and inaccurate, and group cohesion decreases. Members' unresolved feelings often result in biased judgments and actions; members will frequently refuse to vote for a good idea simply because they dislike the person who suggested it.

Communication is severely hampered in groups that handle conflict in a win-lose fashion. Conflict in win-lose situations leads to the denial or distortion of unpleasant facts and information, as each side is likely to deny, hide, or distort information inconsistent with its position in an effort to win. Members misinterpret the ideas and actions of those perceived as opponents, causing "blind spots" in communication. A win-lose approach leads to deceitful expression of ideas and feelings because winning sometimes receives higher priority than honesty. Disagreement tends to be interpreted as personal rejection by opposing group members, and the group's future decisions are generally poor.

No-Lose Problem Solving

The no-lose problem-solving approach asserts that it is almost always possible for both sides to have their needs met in a conflict situation. This approach, a variation of the problem-solving approach described earlier in this chapter, was developed by Thomas Gordon (1970) and is based on two basic premises: (1) All persons have the right to have their needs met. (2) What is in conflict between the two sides is almost never their *needs* but their *solutions* to those needs.

The distinction between needs and solutions is all-important. Assume that a student social work club is arguing over whether to fund a graduation party for seniors or a campus day-care center that is in danger of being closed. An analysis of needs and solutions in this discussion would reveal that the club is arguing over solutions rather than needs. There is a need to honor the graduating seniors and a need for the day-care center to receive operating funds. However, there are a variety of ways of meeting both needs. The club may spend its current funds on a graduation party and then hold a fund-raiser for the day-care center; or fund the center and hold a graduation party by having members donate food, refreshments, and a few dollars at the party. Half of the club's funds could go to the center, the remainder to a reduced-cost graduation party. In addition, many other solutions could be generated to meet these needs.

The six steps to the *no-lose problem-solving approach*, as described by Gordon (1970), are the following:

1. Identify and define the needs of each opposing side.
2. Generate possible alternative solutions.
3. Evaluate the alternative solutions.
4. Decide on the best acceptable solution.
5. Work out ways of implementing the solution.
6. Evaluate how the solution worked.

The first step is by far the most difficult because group members often view conflicts in terms of win-lose and attempt to identify and meet primarily their own needs. When each side's needs in a conflict are identified, however, what usually is in conflict are not the *needs* of each side but their *solutions*. No-lose problem solving will generally lead to creative solutions, after all six steps are followed. (Readers will note the "no-lose problem-solving process" is identical to the "problem-solving process" described in Chapter 1.)

The advantages of this no-lose approach are that both sides fulfill their needs and group harmony and cohesion are increased. Also, the resentment, hostility, and subversive actions *of* a win-lose situation are eliminated. Actually, it is in each group member's best interest to resolve conflicts in a way that will help all members achieve their short-term goals and needs and increase the long-term effectiveness *of* the group, so that the long-term goals and needs of all members have a better chance of being achieved. Frequently, when groups function through win-lose, the winning side may win some battles, but the effectiveness of the group may diminish. All members may thus fail to accomplish their long-term goals and satisfy their needs.

With a problem-solving approach, members tend to listen to one another, recognize the legitimacy of one another's interests, and influence one another with rational arguments. Instead of a competitive environment, problem solving encourages an atmosphere of cooperation.

The differences between a win-lose strategy and a problem-solving strategy are summarized in Exhibit 7.1.

Exhibit 7.1   Differences between Strategies

Win-Lose Strategy	Problem-Solving Strategy
The conflict is defined as a win-lose situation.	The conflict is viewed as a problem.
Each side seeks solutions to meet only its needs.	Each person seeks to find solutions to meet the needs of all members.
Each side attempts to force the other side into submission.	Each person cooperates with others to find mutually acceptable compromises.
Each side increases its power by emphasizing its independence from the other and the other's dependence on itself.	Each person equalizes power by emphasizing interdependence.
Each side inaccurately, deceitfully, and misleadingly communicates its goals, needs, and ideas; information inconsistent or harmful to one's position is not shared.	Each person honestly and openly communicates goals, needs, and ideas.
No expression of empathy or understanding is made of the views, values, and opinions of the other side.	Efforts are made to convey empathy and understanding of the views, values, and opinions of others.
Threats are used to attempt to force the other side into submission.	Threats are avoided to reduce the defensiveness of others.
Rigid adherence to one's position is expressed.	A willingness to be flexible is expressed.
Changes in position are made very slowly, in an effort to force concessions from the other side.	Positions are changed readily to help in problem solving.
No suggestions are sought from third parties because the focus is on forcing the other side to give in.	Third parties are sought to help in problem solving

Role Reversal

A useful strategy for resolving both intragroup and intergroup conflict is role reversal. Here is the basic rule for role reversal: *Each person expresses his or her opinions or views only after restating the ideas and feelings of the opposing person.* These ideas and feelings should be restated in your own words rather than parroted or mimicked in the exact words of the other person. It is advisable to begin your restatement with "Your position is . . . ," "You seem to be saying . . . ," or "You apparently feel. . . ." Approval or disapproval, blaming, giving advice, interpreting, or persuading should be avoided.

In addition, nonverbal messages should be consistent with the verbal paraphrasing and convey interest, openness, and attentiveness to the opposition's ideas and feelings. Above all, role reversal should be the expression of a sincere interest in understanding the other person's feelings, ideas, and position.

Role reversal can result in a reevaluation and a change of attitude concerning the issue by both parties, for the group members involved are likely to be perceived as people who are understanding, willing to compromise, cooperative, and trustworthy. The approach has also been found to increase cooperative behavior between role reversers, to clarify misunderstandings, to change win-lose situations into problem-solving situations, and, most important, to allow the issue to be perceived from the opponent's frame of reference.

Empathy

A technique closely related to role reversal is the expression of empathy. Empathy is imaginatively putting yourself in the inner life of the person you are in conflict with and expressing your understanding of what the person is thinking and saying. Here are some phrases that help you get started:

"What you seem to be saying is . . ."

"I take it that you think . . ."

"I sense you feel ___ about this issue."

When you express empathy, it is essential to mirror what was said in a nonjudgmental way and to grasp the essence of what the other person is thinking or feeling. Similar to role reversal, the use of empathy facilitates open communication, assists in clarifying misunderstandings, increases cooperative behavior, and facilitates the process of no-lose problem solving.

Inquiry

If you are in conflict with someone and are confused about his or her thoughts and feelings, the inquiry technique is often useful. This technique involves using gentle, probing questions to learn more about what the other person is thinking and feeling. Tone of voice is crucial in this technique; asking a question sarcastically or defensively is likely to result in defensive responses.

I-Messages

Most of us are raised to respond to conflict with "you-messages." There are two types of you-messages: a *solution* message and a *put-down* message. A solution message orders, directs, commands, warns, threatens, preaches, moralizes, or advises. A put-down message blames, judges, criticizes, ridicules, or name-calls. Examples of you-messages include "You stop that," "Don't do that," "I hate you," and "You should know better." You-messages tend to inhibit open communication. You-messages are generally counterproductive because people do not like to be ordered or criticized. You-messages frequently result in an ongoing struggle between the two people involved.

In contrast, I-messages foster open communication. They are nonblaming messages that communicate how the sender of the message believes the receiver is affecting the sender. I-messages do not provide solutions, and they do not criticize. It is possible to send an I-message without using the word *I*.

I-messages communicate much more honestly the effect of behavior, and they help the other person to assume responsibility for his or her behavior. An I-message conveys to the person you are in conflict with that you trust him or her to respect your needs and to handle the conflict constructively. I-messages are much less likely to provoke an argument. They facilitate honesty, openness, and more cordial relationships. (I-messages and you-messages are described in Module 4.)

Disarming

When you are in conflict with someone, the disarming technique is an effective way to move toward resolution. This technique involves finding some truth in what the other person (or side) is saying and then expressing this "agreement"—even if you feel that what the other person is saying is largely wrong, unreasonable, irrational, or unfair. When using the disarming technique, it is important for you to be genuine in what you say and express your agreement in a sincere way.

There is always a grain of truth in what someone else is saying, even if it sounds obnoxious and insulting. When you disarm the other side with this technique, those disagreeing with you will recognize that you respect them. As a result, they won't feel so dogmatic and will have less of an urge to insist that they are right and you are wrong. They are then likely to be more willing to examine the merits of your point of view. If you want respect, you have to give respect first. If you want to be listened to, this technique helps you listen to the other person first and avoids defensive communication. Friendly responses facilitate open communication; hostile responses usually result in defensive communication.

Stroking

Stroking is closely related to disarming. When using this technique, you say something genuinely positive to the person (or side) you are in conflict with, even in the heat of (verbal) battle. Stroking is a sign of respect. During an argument or conflict, we have a tendency to reject the other person before we get rejected (so we can save face). Often we overreact, and differences of opinion blow out of proportion. To prevent this, let those with whom you disagree know that although you are at odds with them you still think highly of them. This strategy makes it easier for them to open up and to listen.

Mediation

Mediation is increasingly used to resolve conflicts. Mediation involves intervention by an acceptable, impartial, and neutral third party, who has no decision-making power, to assist contending parties in voluntarily reaching their own mutually acceptable settlement of issues in dispute. Mediation leaves decision making in the hands of the people in conflict. It is a voluntary process: The participants must be willing to accept the assistance of the mediator. Mediation is usually initiated when the parties no longer believe they can resolve the conflict on their own and when the only means of resolution appears to be impartial third-party assistance. (Mediation is described more fully in Module 4.)

Letting Go or Forgiving

If we hold long-term grudges against others, the primary people we are hurting, (both emotionally and health-wise) are ourselves. Emotionally we hurt ourselves by being in a state of periodic anger (which occurs when we think about the perceived "wrong"). By holding a grudge, we also raise our level of stress, which (as described in Chapter 14) often leads to a variety of stress-related illnesses. Mentally nursing a grudge puts your body through the same strains as a major stressful event: muscles tense, blood pressure rises, and sweating increases.

Two strategies to get rid of holding a long-term grudge are "letting go" and forgiving. With the letting-go strategy, we reframe our thinking so that we no longer dwell on the perceived wrong. One way of reframing our thinking is to do a rational self-analysis (described in Module 1). If there is no way to change a perceived "wrong," the best thing we can do for our mental and physical well-being is to "let go" of it.

Forgiveness is actually another strategy for letting go. When you forgive someone who has hurt you, you make yourself—rather than the person who hurt you—responsible for your happiness.

The Law of Requisite Variety

If used appropriately, the strategies described so far will help resolve interpersonal conflicts in most cases. If these strategies fail, you can probably correctly conclude that the person you are in conflict with does not want to resolve the conflict. Perhaps, for reasons beyond your control, the person is very hostile and wants to generate conflicts to meet personal needs. Or perhaps he or she wants to make your life uncomfortable!

What can you do when you realize that another person really wants to sustain a conflict? The law of requisite variety provides one option. According to this law, if you continue to come up with creative new ways of responding to the daggers being thrown at you, eventually the other person will tire of the turmoil and decide to "bury the hatchet." Here is an example:

Janice and Pete Palmer were married about a year ago. Unknown to Janice, Pete was having lunch about once a month with a former partner (Paula) whom he dated over a 3-year period. Seven months ago Janice walked into a restaurant at noon and saw her husband with Paula. In a fit of rage, Janice stomped out. That evening she and Pete had a major blowup. Pete claimed that Paula was just a friend and that nothing romantic was occurring. Janice yelled and screamed. Pete indicated he would stop having lunch with Paula. But he didn't keep his promise. About once a month he continued to see her, and when Janice found out, they again had a major argument. Janice suggested a number of resolution options, including marriage counseling. Pete refused to go to counseling and also indicated (the win-lose approach) that he was going to continue having lunch with Paula. Then one day Janice ran into one of her former partners—Dave. Dave invited Janice for lunch or dinner. A light bulb went on for Janice—she accepted the invitation. Later she gleefully told Pete (Pete knew Dave had dated Janice in the past). Pete became jealous and tried to talk Janice out of the dinner. Janice of course said "No way. What's good for the rooster is good for the hen." This threw Pete into fits of anguish. When Janice came home, Pete politely said he had called Paula that evening to inform her he was canceling their next scheduled lunch, and that he felt it was best that they no longer meet for lunch. Pete then asked Janice if she also would no longer get together with Dave. She indicated "Yes." Through this experience, Pete and Janice learned to respect and appreciate each other to a greater extent.

Exercise 7.15: Resolving Your Conflicts Effectively

Goal: This exercise is designed to inform you about how to resolve interpersonal conflicts more effectively.

Step 1: Describe a serious interpersonal conflict that you had with someone who was important to you.

Step 2: What conflict resolution strategies did you use to attempt to resolve the conflict?

Step 3: What conflict resolution strategies did the other person seek to use?

Step 4: Was the conflict successfully resolved? If "yes," describe what led to the resolution. If "no," specify why it was not resolved.

Step 5: Review the conflict resolution techniques described in this chapter. Specify those that you believe might have been effective in more rapidly resolving the conflict. Provide an explanation for your views.

Step 6: Which of the conflict resolution techniques do you intend to use in the future?

HANDLING DISRUPTIVE BEHAVIOR

There may be hostile or disruptive members in any group, even in groups whose members come voluntarily. However, they are more likely to be found in involuntary groups. Involuntary members often (at least at the initial meetings of the group) wish they were a thousand other places rather than in the group. They are often angry because they are forced to come, and they may believe that the group will be a "complete waste of time."

Social workers encounter involuntary clients in various settings: corrections, protective services, mental health facilities, certain public school settings, group homes, residential treatment facilities, nursing homes, and hospitals. In such settings, groups are often established that unwilling clients are required to attend and social workers are expected to lead. Disruptive behavior includes being aggressive, competing, fooling around, sympathy seeking, and failing to finish tasks on time. To more vividly describe these disruptive behaviors, I will ascribe "personalities" to the behaviors.

Bears openly express anger, rage, frustration, resentment, and hostility, They are unhappy as members of the group or with what is happening in the group. They express discontent in a variety of ways: verbally, by attacking other members; nonverbally, by facial expressions; or physically, by aggressively pushing and shoving other members.

Bears who directly express unhappiness in an active fashion can also express unhappiness in passive-aggressive ways through indirect aggression. Bach and Wyden (1981) have called indirect aggression "crazy-making." Indirect aggressors maintain a front of kindness but find subtle, indirect ways to express their anger, rage, or frustrations. Bach and Wyden label direct aggression "clean fighting" because feelings are expressed openly and can be identified and resolved. "Dirty fighters" use indirect tricks and never clearly express their feelings, which often causes a great deal of pain and can destroy effective communication. Most disruptive behaviors involve an element of indirect aggression.

If you have a relationship with a "dirty fighter," he or she will identify what will "press your buttons." Dirty fighters casually and subtly press these buttons to get you going.

Eager beavers volunteer to do crucial tasks but have little intention of completing them; they seduce other members into believing they are willing contributors. They may partially perform some tasks to show good faith but then employ a variety of excuses to explain why the tasks can't be completed on time.

Clowns are disrupters who are rarely serious. They are always joking and clowning around, even when other members want to be serious. A clown inhibits other members from expressing their thoughts and feelings because they fear they will be ridiculed.

Psychoanalyzers continually analyze what other members do and say. They often use psychological terms and delight in analyzing what others really mean and what's wrong with them. The psychoanalyzer often slows a group by getting members to engage in mind reading rather than task completion. Other members are inhibited from expressing their thoughts and feelings; they don't want to be analyzed.

Withholders have important information or resources that would help the group accomplish its task, but they intentionally withhold assistance. They are more interested in watching the group struggle and spin its wheels.

Beltliners are dirty fighters. Everyone has a psychological "beltline" under which lie subjects that we are extremely sensitive about. Beltline items include physical characteristics, intelligence, past behavior, past unhappy events, or personality characteristics. An overweight person, for example, may be highly sensitive about comments related to obesity. Beltliners make subtle negative comments about sensitive areas to threaten group cohesion and morale.

Guiltmakers attempt to control others by making them feel guilty. They trap the group into helping them with personal needs and goals, rather than working toward group goals. Guiltmakers use common expressions such as "You never do anything for me" and "All I've done for you and this is the thanks I get" to trigger the guilt response.

Catastrophe criers, by exaggerating the seriousness of a problem, would have group members believe that consequences will be not minor but disastrous. "Catastrophiers" focus only on examining the severity of the problem and not on developing and implementing problem-solving approaches, so they exacerbate problems.

Subject changers do not want the group to deal with crucial issues or with controversy and conflict. When difficult situations arise, they change the subject. They prevent the group from dealing with crucial topics. There are a variety of reasons for seeking to change a subject; for example, changers may detest heated debates or may fear the debate will reveal something they wish to keep hidden.

Whiners continually complain about one thing or another without taking action to resolve the problem. Because they seek attention and sympathy, they slow group progress.

If a group is competing with another group, a betrayer, or **Benedict Arnold**, supplies confidential information to the other group. The betrayer encourages people outside the group to ridicule or disregard it or slyly arranges to have the group's funding cut back. Within a group, Benedict Arnolds attempt to prevent the group from accomplishing its goals.

Instead of honestly sharing concerns, frustrations, and discontent, **trivial tyrannizers** annoy the group with constant interruptions and digressions. They arrive late and leave early, fail to show up for crucial meetings, or bring up concerns the group has already acted on. Besides raising unnecessary questions about the wording of the minutes, for instance, trivial tyrannizers may yawn or read something when other members are speaking.

Shirkers are disruptive simply by failing to do anything for the group. When assigned certain tasks, shirkers will evade these responsibilities by using a variety of excuses.

Power grabbers attempt to become the group leader or the power behind the leader by convincing other members that they have more expertise than anyone else in the group or by buying the support of others with money, favors, or promises. Power grabbers create conflicts that make the leader look bad, and sabotage the efforts of the leader, even though they may not assume leadership power.

Because **paranoiacs** are excessively or irrationally suspicious and distrustful of others in the group, they always feel picked on. Much of their time is spent defending themselves and finding fault with other members. Paranoiac individuals often feel that other members must be discredited before they can amass enough evidence to discredit the paranoiacs.

Note that disrupters are often intentionally aware of the effects of their behavior. Most of these examples are of this type. However, some disrupters act out of unconscious personal needs and may not be aware that their behavior is disruptive. The following suggestions for handling disruptive behavior apply whether disrupters are aware or unaware of the effects of their behavior.

There are three main ways leaders can handle hostile and disruptive behavior. The approach you choose should be based on your judgment about which will be most helpful to the group:

1. *Allow the member to continue to express the disruptive behavior.* Such expression has a vent effect, so the member may become less disruptive as time goes on. It is often helpful to tactfully ask disruptive members to express their concerns.

    Tactfully asking the member probing questions about his concerns and modeling good listening skills while reflecting his feelings often helps defuse a disruptive situation. In certain instances there may be benefit in using a role reversal: Ask the disrupter to argue the alternate point of view while you take the disrupter's position. Whenever possible, disruption should be dealt with as a group issue, and the group may, in fact, decide to deal with at least some of the disrupter's concerns, especially those that are legitimate. Through resolution of some of these concerns, the disruptive member may become less unhappy and begin to see that the group has some payoffs.

Most of the time, my first strategy in responding to a disgruntled group member when he or she voices a concern is to "kill that person with kindness." I seek to convey that the disgruntled person has a legitimate concern (or at least a partially legitimate concern), which often leads that person to feel validated. Usually, once the disgruntled person feels validated, she or he will "buy into" what the group is trying to accomplish, and then make positive contributions.

2. *Assertively confront the member about how her behavior is disrupting the group.* This confrontation can take place with other group members present, or leaders can meet privately with the person. (When confronting a disruptive member, it is helpful to use one or more of the conflict resolution strategies described in the previous section.) Whether you confront privately or publicly should be based on your judgment of which will be most beneficial. If other members are present, they may be able to help by elaborating on the ways in which the behavior is disruptive. Also, having others present emphasizes the seriousness of the problem. A disadvantage of confrontation when others are present is that hostile members may feel ganged up on and may be more inhibited in fully expressing what they are unhappy about. In some instances, simply indicating to the members in private that you are concerned about their behavior and are considering opening it up as a matter of discussion for the entire group will help them reconsider whether the disruptions are accomplishing the desired purpose.

3. *Have other members do the confronting.* Certain situations are best handled by someone other than the leader. Another member may have better rapport with the person, and the disruptive member may be more responsive if the confrontation comes from the neutral member.

Any of these approaches may prove fruitful. It is important to realize that conflict and differences in opinion are not uncommon or unnatural in groups and in fact may be healthy.

Exercise 7.16: Handling the Disruptive Behavior of a Group Member

Goal: This exercise is designed to help you handle the disruptive behavior of a group member.

Step 1: Describe the disruptive behavior of someone who was also a member of a group that you were involved in.

Step 2: How did the disruptive behavior affect the group7

Step 3: What actions (if any) did the other group members take to attempt to minimize the effects of the disruptive behavior? Were these actions effective?

Step 4: If the actions were not very effective, review the material on handling disruptive behavior in this chapter. What actions might have been taken by you (or by other group members) to more effectively handle the disruptive behavior?

GROUP SIZE

The size of a group affects members' satisfactions, interactions, and output. Smaller groups often rate more favorably in these aspects (Toseland & Rivas, 2007). Larger groups tend to create more stress, have more communication difficulties, and, though successful in some tasks because of the greater number of skills available, be generally less efficient or productive. In larger groups, each person has less opportunity to talk, and some people feel inhibited and reluctant to talk. In discussion groups, it has been shown that as the size of the group increases, the most frequent contributor assumes an increasingly prominent role in the discussion. The bigger the group, the greater is the gap in participation between the most frequent contributor and other members of a group.

In one classic study, Slater (1958) found that groups of five persons were considered most satisfactory by members. Observations of the interactions of groups smaller than five indicated the members were inhibited from expressing their ideas through fear of alienating one another and thereby destroying the group. With more than five, members felt restrictions on participating.

Groups of two tend to avoid expressing disagreement and antagonism. This size also has high tension levels because each member is "on the spot," as each is forced to react to what the other says. In disputes, deadlock often arises because there is no majority and the group then breaks up.

Groups of even size tend to have higher rates of disagreement and antagonism than odd-size groups. The "group of two" dynamic is apparently at work here.

Groups of three have majority-over-minority problems. A two-to-one split leaves the minority feeling isolated.

To sum up, for any given task there is an optimal group size. The more complex the task, the larger is the optimal size to ensure the greatest number of needed abilities and skills.

STARTING, LEADING, AND ENDING COUNSELING GROUPS

Extensive preparation is needed for leading counseling groups. Leaders should have considerable training in (1) assessing human behavior and human problems; (2) comprehensive intervention approaches—such as reality therapy, behavior therapy, and rational therapy (see Modules 1–3); (3) specialized intervention techniques—such as assertiveness training (Module 2) and relaxation techniques (Chapter 14); (4) interviewing and counseling; and (5) principles of group dynamics—such as cohesion, task roles, social and emotional roles, and effects of authoritarian versus democratic styles of leadership. Baccalaureate and master's programs in social work generally provide considerable material on these areas. For any counseling group, leaders also need to study the literature on the causes of the problems that members are experiencing, the most effective intervention strategies, the prognosis for positive changes, and expectations about the length of time intervention strategies need to be applied to induce positive changes.

In this section I summarize a number of guidelines for starting, leading, and ending counseling groups. Chapter 6 covered substantial material on preparation and homework, relaxing before starting a session, cues on entering the meeting room, seating arrangements, introductions, and clarifying roles. This material is directly applicable to counseling groups and will not be repeated here. (Students studying how to lead counseling groups should review this material.) In this section we focus on building rapport, exploring problems in depth, exploring alternative solutions, ending a session, and ending a group.

Building Rapport

In group counseling, as in individual counseling, there are two types of members: voluntary and involuntary. In *voluntary* groups, group facilitators can take a more casual, less directive approach to begin with. In such groups facilitators may begin by involving members in small talk. This preliminary chitchat may be about the weather, parking problems, baseball, something currently in the news, and so on. Such casual conversation lets group members get acquainted with the facilitator and other members. In *involuntary* groups, facilitators often begin by introducing themselves and making a formal statement about the purpose of the group. Then members may be asked to introduce themselves. Generally, in involuntary groups, less is left up to the members themselves because they have less motivation for being there and less commitment to the group itself.

Sometimes, with both voluntary and involuntary clients, it is helpful (after introductions) to begin a session by providing some factual information. You as group leader can do this in a brief presentation or by showing a short film or videotape. For example, if your group comprises involuntary clients who have been convicted of driving while intoxicated, you might show a film that vividly demonstrates that as alcohol consumption increases, reaction times slow and the chances of serious accidents occurring dramatically increase. Factual information provides educational material and triggers discussion. Sometimes after factual information is presented, it is useful to involve members in an exercise related to the material.

When members are forced to attend a group they do not want to attend, as is the case with involuntary clients, you may begin by saying something like "I know most of you really don't want to be here, and I wouldn't either if I were forced to come. I wonder if we might begin by talking about your anger and unhappiness about being here." Then you can convey the purposes of the group, what is going to happen, and how the members can satisfy the minimal requirements of "passing." Mention that each member can (1) choose to participate actively and get as much out of the group as possible, (2) remain silent and listen to what others have to say, (3) vent anger and unhappiness in disruptive ways (which will probably anger and alienate others in the group), or (4) refuse to come, which will have certain consequences. You can then indicate that you can in no way control their behavior, so the choice is up to them. Such an approach almost always leads involuntary clients to choose either the first or second alternative, perhaps because they conclude that you understand their anger. They then focus on fulfilling the requirements of their forced attendance in the least painful way.

If the group has met previously, you may choose to begin by bringing up for discussion a topic that was not fully discussed at the last meeting. Or, if homework assignments were given out, you may begin with "Jim, at the last meeting you indicated you were going to do (such and such). How did that work out?"

Try to establish a nonthreatening group atmosphere in which members feel accepted and safe enough to communicate their troubles fully. During the initial contacts, you need to "sell" yourself (but not arrogantly) as a knowledgeable, understanding person who may be able to help and who wants to try. Your tone of voice should convey the message that you understand and care about group members' feelings. Be calm and never laugh or express shock when members begin to open up about problems. Emotional outbursts, even if subtle, will lead group members to believe that you are not going to understand or accept their difficulties, and so they will usually stop discussing them.

View group members as equals. Inexperienced facilitators sometimes make the mistake of thinking that because someone is sharing intimate secrets with them, they must be very important, and they end up assuming a superior position relative to their clients. If members feel that they are being treated as inferiors, they will be less motivated to reveal and discuss personal issues.

Use a "shared vocabulary" with members. This does not mean that you should use the same slang and the same accent as group members. If clients perceive you are mimicking their speech patterns, they may be seriously offended. To communicate effectively, use words that members understand and do not find offensive.

You (and other members) need to keep what members say confidential. Unfortunately, many people have nearly irresistible urges to share secrets with someone else. If a group member discovers that confidentiality has been violated, that member's trust in the group will be quickly destroyed. It is essential that you underscore the importance of "what is said in the group, remains in the group."

Exploring Problems in Depth

In exploring a member's problems in depth, you and group members need to examine such areas as the extent of the problem, how long the problem has existed, its causes, how the member feels about the problem, and what physical and mental capacities and strengths the individual has to cope with the difficulty, before exploring alternative solutions.

A problem area is often multidimensional—that is, numerous problems are usually involved. Explore all of these. A good way to decide which problem to handle first is to ask members which problems they feel are most pressing. If a problem can be solved, start by exploring that problem in depth and develop a solution together. Success in solving one problem will increase members' confidence in you and thereby further solidify rapport.

Convey empathy, not sympathy, and encourage group members to do so, too. Empathy is the capacity to understand and to share in another person's feelings. Sympathy also involves sharing feelings, but it results in offering pity. The difference is subtle, but empathy encourages problem solving, whereas sympathy encourages members to dwell on their problems without taking action to improve the situation. For example, if you offer sympathy to a person who is frustrated and angry about someone ending a romantic relationship with him, that person will keep telling his sad story over and over, each time having an emotional outpouring reinforced by your sympathy, without taking any action to improve the situation. Telling the story over and over only reopens old wounds and prolongs the anger and frustration.

"Trust your guts." Your most important resources are your own feelings and perceptions. Continually strive to place yourself in members' shoes, understanding that their values and pressures may be different from your own. You will probably never be 100% on target in your appraisal of a client's pressures, problems, and perspectives, but 70% to 80% is usually sufficient to be helpful. Empathizing is very useful in helping you determine what additional areas need to be explored, what you should say, and what the possible solutions are.

When you believe that a client has touched on an important area of concern, further communication can be encouraged in a number of ways. Show interest nonverbally (by making and continuing eye contact, leaning forward, and raising eyebrows slightly); this encourages further sharing. Allow for pauses. Inexperienced facilitators usually become anxious during pauses and hasten to say something—anything—to have conversation continue. This is usually a mistake, especially when it leads to a change in the topic. Although a pause may make members anxious, it gives them time to think about what areas of concern are most important and then usually motivates them to continue conversation in that area.

Neutral probes that do not control the direction of conversation but encourage further communication are helpful. For example, "Could you tell me more about it?" "Why do you feel that way?" and "I'm not sure I understand what you have in mind" all ask for further information, but just what kind is left up to the member. Reflecting feelings—for example, "You seem angry" or "You appear to be depressed about that"—works the same way. Summarizing what a group member is saying shows that you are listening and that you have received the same message he or she sent. An example is, "During this past hour, you made a number of critical comments about your spouse; it sounds like you're fairly unhappy about certain aspects of your marriage."

Approach socially unacceptable topics tactfully. Tact is an essential quality of a competent facilitator. Try not to ask a question in such a way that the answer will put the respondent in an embarrassing position.

When pointing out a member's limitation, mention and compliment the person on any assets. When a limitation is mentioned, he or she will figuratively feel naked, as if something has been taken away. Therefore, compliment the person in another area to give something back.

Watch for nonverbal cues and use them to identify sensitive subjects. Clients generally display anxiety by a changing tone of voice, fidgeting, yawning, stiff posture, or a flushed face.

Be honest. An untruth always runs the risk of being discovered. If that happens, the group member's confidence in you will be damaged and the relationship seriously jeopardized. But being honest goes beyond not telling lies. Always point out shortcomings that are in the group member's best interest to correct. For example, if a father's negative comments to his son are a factor in the son developing a negative self-concept (which is partly responsible for the son receiving failing grades at school), bring this to the father's attention.

Exploring Alternative Solutions

After a problem is explored in depth, the next step is for you and group members to consider alternative solutions. Your role is generally to begin by asking something like "Have you thought about ways to resolve this?" The merits, shortcomings, and consequences of the alternatives thought of by the member should then be tactfully and thoroughly examined. Next, involve other members by asking them if they are aware of other alternatives that might work for this situation. Those who suggest alternatives temporarily assume a "helper" role. In such a role, the helper therapy principle is operating as a member receives psychological rewards from helping others. If you have additional viable alternatives to suggest, mention them at this time. The merits, shortcomings, and consequences of the alternatives suggested by group members and by you should then be thoroughly explored.

Group members usually have the right to self-determination—that is, to choose a course of action among possible alternatives. Your role is to help each individual clarify and understand the likely consequences of each available alternative but generally not to give advice or choose the alternative. If *you* select the alternative, either of two outcomes is possible: (1) The alternative proves undesirable for the person, in which case he or she probably will blame you for the advice and your future relationship will be seriously hampered. Or (2) the alternative proves desirable for the person, which is advantageous, but the person then becomes overly dependent on you, seeking your advice for nearly every decision and generally being reluctant to make decisions on his or her own.

The warning about giving advice does *not* mean that you should not suggest alternatives that your client hasn't considered. On the contrary, it is your responsibility to suggest and explore all viable alternatives with a client. Here is a good rule to follow: When you believe a client should take a certain course of action, phrase it as a suggestion, "Have you thought about. . . ?" rather than an opinion, "I think you should . . ."

Group counseling is done *with* group members, not *to* or *for* them. Each member should have responsibility for doing many of the tasks necessary to improve a situation. Another good rule to follow is that members should take responsibility for the tasks that they have the capacity to do. Like giving advice, doing things *for* group members brings with it the risk of a dependent relationship. Furthermore, success leads to personal growth and better prepares clients to take on future responsibilities.

A group member's right to self-determination should be taken away only if the selected course of action has a high probability of seriously hurting the client or others. For example, if it is highly probable that a member will attempt to take his life, you must intervene (make arrangements for the member to receive inpatient psychiatric care) even if the intervention is a course of action that he or she objects to. In most situations, however, members should have the right to select an alternative, even when you believe that another course of action would be better. Frequently, clients are in a better position to know what is best for themselves, and if it doesn't turn out—well, they then get to learn from their mistake.

When members select an alternative, they should clearly understand the goals, what tasks need to be carried out, how to accomplish the tasks, and who will do them. Frequently, it is desirable to write a "contract" for future reference, with a time limit set for accomplishment of each task. If group members fail to meet the terms of a contract, do not criticize them or accept excuses. Excuses let people off the hook; they provide temporary relief, but they eventually lead to more failure and to a failure identity. Simply ask, "Do you still wish to try to fulfill your commitment?" If the person answers affirmatively, another time deadline acceptable to the member should be set.

Perhaps the biggest single factor in determining whether a member's situation will improve is his or her motivation to carry out essential tasks. Try to motivate apathetic members. One way to increase motivation is to clarify what will be gained by meeting a goal. When individuals meet commitments, reward them, verbally or in other ways. Never criticize members for failing. Criticism usually increases hostility and rarely leads to positive, lasting change. It serves only as a temporary means of obtaining different behavior; when people no longer believe they are under surveillance, they usually return to their dysfunctional behavior.

If a group member lacks confidence or experience, role-play the task before the member attempts it. For example, if a member wants help in telling his partner that he wants to end the relationship, role-playing the situation in the group will help him select words and an appropriate strategy. You or a group member can play his role and model an approach, letting him play his partner's role. Then reverse the roles so that he can practice telling his partner.

Ending a Session

Ending is not easy. Ideally, you and the group members accept that the session is ending and that subjects being discussed should not be left hanging. Abrupt endings can be perceived as discourteous and rejecting.

There are some useful guidelines on how to terminate a therapy session. Preparation for ending the session should be initiated at the very beginning of the session. Members should be explicitly informed about when the session will end. Unless an unusual situation develops, assertively seek to terminate at the scheduled time.

When the allotted time is nearly up, inform members by saying something like "I see our time is just about up. Is there anything you'd like to add before we look at where we've arrived and where we go from here?" At the end of the session, it is often helpful to summarize what was discussed. If this session focused only on exploring problems, another one should be set up for fuller exploration and to begin looking at alternatives for resolving the problems.

Give members "homework" assignments between sessions. For example, a couple who is having trouble communicating with each other might be encouraged to set aside a certain amount of time each evening to discuss their personal thoughts with each other. At the next session this assignment would be reviewed.

Ideally, group members should be emotionally at ease when the session ends. Therefore, don't introduce emotionally charged content at the end but instead start to reduce the intensity of emotion. Just as it is sometimes advisable to begin a session with small talk, a short social conversation at the end can provide transition. If a member displays reluctance to end a session, it is sometimes helpful to confront this directly by saying, "It appears to me that you wished we had more time." The reasons for the person's reluctance can then be discussed.

At times a session can be ended by restating the way you and the group agreed to proceed. Or you may undertake a more explicit summation of what was discussed, what decisions were arrived at, what questions remain to be resolved, and what actions will be taken.

A somewhat different approach is to ask each member to state one item that was discussed or learned from the session, and what he or she now plans to do. Some counseling groups end by having members state a "bad" feeling they now intend to get rid of and then state a good feeling that will replace the bad one.

Sometimes concerns that were alluded to but not fully discussed are mentioned in closing as topics that will be taken up at the next session. Some members will reveal their most serious concerns for the first time at the end of a session, perhaps because they are ambivalent about whether they are ready to explore these concerns fully with the group. In these instances, you must make a professional judgment about whether to extend the session beyond the allotted time, to set up an appointment to discuss these concerns privately, or to wait until the next group session.

Sometimes it is helpful to end a group session by leading the group in a relaxation exercise. (Relaxation exercises are described in Chapter 14.) A relaxation exercise not only helps members relax but also reduces their level of stress so they can view their problems more objectively and work on resolving them after they leave.

Closing is especially important because what occurs during this last phase is likely to determine members' impressions of the session as a whole. Leave enough time for closing so the members don't feel rushed, which can create the impression that they are being "evicted."

Ending a Group

The ending phase of a group frequently offers the highest potential for powerful, important work. Group members often feel a sense of urgency as they realize there is little time left; this can lead them to reveal their most sensitive and personal concerns. Because the work remaining to be done is usually clearly identified at this point, members can focus on completing it. However, the relationship dynamics are also heightened in this phase as the members prepare to move away from each other. The termination of the group can evoke powerful feelings.

If group members have grown emotionally close, the ending of the group will be viewed as a loss and will produce a variety of emotions. Kübler-Ross's (1969) stages of dying can also be used to describe other important losses, including the ending of a successful and cohesive group. Members may display denial (by ignoring the imminent end of the group), anger and rage, or sadness and depression. They may bargain for an extension of the group in various ways, such as urging that the group deal with additional problems. Ideally, members will vent and work through such feelings and gradually come to accept the ending of the group. (Kübler-Ross's stages are more fully described in Chapter 5.)

Other emotions may also be displayed. Some members may feel guilty because of adverse comments they made or because they believe they failed to take certain actions that would have benefited themselves or other members of the group. If a member left prematurely, some members may feel that the group let that person down. Members may want to share their feelings about the support system they will lose when the group ends. Members who want the group to continue may interpret the ending as a personal rejection. Conversely, members who feel that the group was very successful may want to have a celebration to give recognition to the successes and to say good-bye.

Concluding sessions are in many ways the most difficult. Strong emotions are often generated and should be worked through. It is painful to terminate a group when members have shared their most personal and important concerns and feelings. Our society has done little to train us to handle such separations; many of us adhere to the norm of being "strong" and not expressing feelings.

You can help members accept the ending of the group in a number of ways, and the process of terminating a group should, in fact, begin during the early stages of the group. This guideline is particularly relevant for time-limited groups. Attempt to prevent dependency between members and you. The goal is independence and better functioning; reiterate this whenever appropriate during group sessions.

Summarize the emotional reactions that people have to group endings. An appropriate point for a discussion may occur when some members display denial, anger, guilt, bargaining, or sadness. When discussing these feelings, share your personal feelings and recollections, for the ending of the group has meaning for you as well. You, in effect, provide a model that can help members express their concerns about ending the group. Use a problem-solving approach to alleviate concerns; for example, if a member is apprehensive about future problems, suggest several other counseling resources.

The ending process should provide enough time for you and the members to sort out feelings and use the ending productively. A sudden ending cuts short necessary work and may not allow enough time to work through feelings and complete the remaining tasks. Sometimes, members indirectly express their anger by being late, appearing apathetic, being sarcastic, or battling over minor issues. In these situations, respond directly to the indirect cues by saying something like "I wonder if your recent critical remarks are related to your anger that this group is ending. I know you have invested a lot in this group and may dislike the idea that our meetings are coming to an end." By helping members recognize and articulate their feelings, you can help them express and work through those feelings. Once such feelings are dealt with, members will be more productive during the remaining time.

At or near the end of some groups, members may test new skills and do things independently. They may report having tackled a tough problem or dealt with an issue by themselves. Acknowledge their independence and make positive remarks about the members' ability to "go it alone."

At times, you may be the person leaving the group, perhaps to take a job elsewhere. In these situations, try to create a smooth transition and, if appropriate, involve members in selecting the new leader. At times it is helpful for you and the new leader to be coleaders for a brief period.

The ending of a group is always a transition to something else. The important element during the ending phase is to work with all members to help them develop a game plan so that the transition will enable them to work toward higher goals. The transition should work not to stifle members but to help them progress. Life is full of transitions and passages: from childhood to puberty, from school to the work world, from being single to being married, from working to retirement, and so on. In a transition phase, we have the potential to control our future; the choices we make and the efforts we put forth will determine whether the transition will be constructive or destructive for us. Helping each member make productive, realistic plans for the future is a key goal of the ending phase.

During the process of terminating a group, obtain feedback about how to improve future groups by having members fill out a brief evaluation at the last (or next-to-last) session. This evaluation should be done anonymously. The following questions apply to a variety of therapy groups. For the first seven questions, use the following scale: (1) strongly disagree, (2) disagree, (3) neutral or uncertain, (4) agree, (5) strongly agree.

1. I am very satisfied with what this group accomplished.

    1   2   3   4   5

2. My personal goals in this group have been attained.

    1   2   3   4   5

3. I truly enjoyed being a member of this group.

    1   2   3   4   5

4. The facilitator has done a superb job in leading the group.

    1   2   3   4   5

5. This has been one of the most rewarding groups I have participated in.

    1   2   3   4   5

6. I have grown extensively as a person through participating in this group.

    1   2   3   4   5

7. I have made substantial progress in resolving the personal problems that led me to join this group.

    1   2   3   4   5

The next three questions are open-ended.

8. The strengths of this group are . . .
9. The shortcomings of this group are . . .
10. My suggestions for changes in this group are . . .

At the final session it is also desirable for members to discuss what they got out of the group, the merits of the group, and suggestions for improving it. They should be given a chance to bring up unfinished business. In some cases, an extra session may be held to complete unfinished business items.

COFACILITATING GROUPS

Even though many settings do not have the resources for two leaders facilitating a single group, some programs do allow for this type of group facilitation. Also, many students in internships are given opportunities to cofacilitate groups with either their field instructor or some other professional at their agency. The cofacilitator approach has the following advantages:

- Each facilitator can grow from working with, observing, and learning from the other.
- Group members can benefit from the different life experiences, insights, and perspectives of the two facilitators.
- The two facilitators can complement each other, with the group thereby benefiting.
- The two facilitators can provide valuable feedback to each other by discussing what happened in a session and how to approach a complex issue.
- The two facilitators can serve as models for the members in how they relate to and communicate with each other and with the group.
- If one of the leaders is female and the other is male, barriers that some members have involving gender can be effectively confronted, explored, and resolved.
- While one facilitator is working with a particular member, the other facilitator can scan the group to get a sense of how the other members are reacting.
- Coleading offers a certain safety, especially when practitioners are leading a group for the first time. Beginning group facilitators often experience self-doubt and anxiety. Facing a group for the first time with a cofacilitator whom you respect and trust can make what initially seems a frightening task a delightful learning experience.

The major disadvantages of two facilitators leading a group occur when the facilitators fail to develop and maintain an effective working relationship. To develop a good working relationship, it is essential that they respect each other. Facilitators will have differences in leadership style and will not always agree or share the same perceptions and interpretations; this is normal and healthy. However, when there is mutual respect, they generally will be able to communicate and discuss these differences, trust each other, and work cooperatively instead of competitively. If trust and respect between the facilitators is lacking, the group is bound to sense the disharmony and be negatively affected. Power struggles between incompatible cofacilitators can divide the group. Friction between facilitators can serve as a model for members to focus on negatives within the group and to subtly or overtly verbally hurt one another.

It is important for group facilitators to learn whom they can and cannot cofacilitate with. Even secure, competent, and experienced facilitators who respect one another don't always work effectively together. A facilitator who leads by giving suggestions aimed at providing quick answers for every problem will have trouble working with a facilitator who believes members grow by struggling and arriving at their own answers to their personal issues. If two facilitators discover that they can't work together effectively, it doesn't necessarily mean that one is right and the other wrong or that one or both are incompetent. It simply means that their styles clash and that each would be better off making arrangements to work with someone with a more compatible style.

It is important for cofacilitators to get together regularly (ideally shortly after the end of each session) to discuss where the group is and where it needs to go. Additional areas to discuss include how the facilitators view the group and individual members, how they feel about working with each other, and how to approach complex issues. They also need to make plans for the next session.

LEGAL SAFEGUARDS FOR GROUP FACILITATORS

Unfortunately, filing lawsuits has become a national pastime. The key way group facilitators can avoid malpractice suits (or provide a defense if one arises) is to maintain reasonable, ordinary, and prudent (wise and judicious) practices. The following guidelines translate the terms *reasonable, ordinary,* and *prudent* into concrete actions:

- Screen candidates carefully for a group experience. Many potential problems can be avoided with effective screening practices. Select group members whose needs and goals are compatible with the goals of the group, who will not impede the group process, and whose well-being will not be jeopardized by the group experience.
- Adequately inform members about the group process. Entrance procedures, time parameters of the group experience, expectations of group participation, goals of the group, intervention methods that will be used, rights of members, responsibilities of members and facilitator, methods of payment (where appropriate), and termination procedures should be explained at the outset of the group.
- Obtain written parental consent for all minors who are attending a counseling group.

- Obtain written informed consent contracts at the outset of a group. Barker (2003) defines informed consent as follows:

  The granting of permission by the client to the social worker and agency or other professional person to use specific *intervention,* including diagnosis, treatment, follow-up, and research. This permission must be based on full disclosure of the facts needed to make the decision intelligently. Informed consent must be based on knowledge of the risks and alternatives. (p. 217)

- Have a clear rationale for the techniques and exercises you use in group sessions. Be prepared to concisely explain and defend the theoretical underpinnings of your techniques and exercises.
- Consult with your supervisor or an attorney on issues involving complex legal and ethical matters.
- Avoid becoming entangled in a social relationship with group participants.
- Be aware of those situations in which you legally are required to break confidentiality. (See the section on confidentiality in Chapter 2.)
- Carry malpractice insurance.
- Keep up with theoretical and research developments that apply to group therapy.
- Be knowledgeable about, and abide by, the codes of ethics for social workers. In the United States, refer to the NASW Code of Ethics (2008), which appears at www.naswdc.org. In Canada, refer to the Canadian Association of Social Workers' *Code of Ethics and Guidelines for Ethical Practice* (2005), which appears at www.casw-acts.ca.
- Be aware of when it is appropriate to refer a group member for another form of treatment, and also be aware of when group counseling might be inadvisable.
- Instruct members in how to evaluate their progress toward their individual goals. Also, routinely assess the general progress of the group.
- Write and maintain adequate records on the needs and goals of each member and the progress (or lack thereof) made by each member in the group.
- Do not promise magical cures. Create reasonable expectations about what the group can and cannot achieve.
- Practice within the boundaries of your state and local laws.
- If you work for an agency, have a contract that specifies the agency's legal liability for your professional functioning.
- Abide by the policies of the agency that employs you. If you strongly disagree with agency policies and if they interfere with your ability to do your job, seek first to change these policies. If the policies cannot be changed, consider resigning.
- Define clearly to members what confidentiality means, why it is important, and that what the members disclose should be kept confidential—even though the members should be aware that confidentiality cannot be guaranteed because some members may intentionally or unintentionally breach confidentiality.

SUMMARY

The following summarizes the chapter's content in terms of the learning objectives presented at the beginning of the chapter.

1. A membership group is a group a person belongs to; a reference group is one whose influence a person is willing to accept.

   Three models of group development are presented. The Garland, Jones, and Kolodny model hypothesizes five sequential stages: preaffiliation, power and control, intimacy, differentiation, and separation. The Tuckman model also hypothesizes five sequential stages: forming, storming, norming, performing, and adjourning. Bales developed a recurring-phase model. According to Bales, groups continuously seek equilibrium between task-oriented work and emotional expressions, in order to build better relationships among group members.

   All groups have task roles and maintenance roles to be performed by members. Task roles are needed to accomplish the specific goals set by the group. Maintenance roles strengthen the social and emotional aspects of group life.

   The theory of leadership highlighted in this chapter is the distributed-functions approach. According to this approach, leadership is the performance of acts that help the group reach its goals and maintain itself in good working order, and leadership occurs when any member influences other members to help the group reach its goals. Because all group members at times influence other group members, each member in a group exerts leadership. Four other leadership approaches described in this chapter are trait, position, style and servant leadership.

French and Raven identified five types of power that group members can use to influence each other: reward, coercive, legitimate, referent, and expert. Each type has different effects on those being influenced.

Personal goals and group goals should be identified soon after a group is formed. The more congruent personal goals are with group goals, the more effective the group is likely to be. Conformity studies have found that a group has considerable influence on members' opinions and attitudes.

2. Describe conflict resolution strategies.

Groups often function more effectively in an atmosphere of cooperation than in a competitive atmosphere. If handled constructively, conflict and controversy can have numerous beneficial effects on a group, including increasing creativity. The no-lose problem-solving approach is much more effective in resolving conflict than is the win-lose approach. Additional strategies for resolving conflicts include role reversal, empathy, inquiry, I-messages, disarming, stroking, mediation, letting or forgiving, and the law of requisite variety. Hostile or disruptive members should generally be confronted by the leader or by other group members.

For any given task, there is an optimal group size. The more complex a task is, the larger is the optimal size to ensure a sufficient number of needed abilities and skills.

3. Comprehend guidelines for leading counseling groups.

This chapter concludes with guidelines for leading counseling groups. Aspects discussed include building rapport, exploring problems in depth, exploring alternative solutions, ending a session, and ending a group. Guidelines are also presented on how to cofacilitate counseling groups and on establishing legal safeguards for group facilitators.

EXERCISES

1. Group Therapy in Action

Goal: To give class members an experiential awareness of being in a group therapy session.

Step 1: The instructor indicates that at the next class period a simulated group therapy session will be conducted. Each student is given the "homework" assignment of identifying one or two personal problems that a friend or relative currently has. Students are told that they should not reveal the identity of the person having the problem and that the personal problem should be that of a friend or relative (and not their own).

Step 2: At the next class period, the instructor begins by stating the following ground rules. 'Today we will have a simulated group therapy session to give you an experiential awareness of being in group therapy. Because this is a class, I strongly request that you do not reveal any personal information about any dilemmas or difficulties you are experiencing. Instead, I ask you to describe one or two complicated personal dilemmas that a friend or relative is currently facing. For confidentiality reasons, please do not reveal the identity of the person whose problems you talk about. Remember, for reasons of confidentiality, what is said here stays here. Are there any questions about what we are going to do or about the ground rules?"

Step 3: The instructor asks students to begin sharing the concerns. If the class is reluctant, the instructor may initiate the process by asking a normally vocal student to begin. When a student is sharing, the instructor should encourage other students to probe with questions to explore the problem further and suggest realistic and creative courses of action to resolve the problem. (In group therapy sessions, each member at times takes on the role of a therapist.)

Step 4: After the dilemma revealed by one student is fully discussed and problem-solved, other students share the dilemmas they've brought. Continue until the end of the class period or until no one has anything further to share. At the end of the exercise, the instructor asks students their thoughts about the benefits and shortcomings of the exercise and their suggestions for changes in the format of the exercise when it is again used.

Comment: During the exercise, one or more of the students may begin talking about a personal problem. At this point the instructor needs to make a judgment about whether to let the student continue. The instructor should not allow any students to divulge personal information that they are apt to regret later.

2. Facilitating an Intervention Group

Goal: To develop skills at leading intervention groups.

Step 1:   The instructor states the purpose of the exercise and indicates that a component of most class sessions will be for the students to take turns in facilitating an intervention group. The instructor demonstrates how to do this: The instructor shares a personal issue that she or he is currently dealing with or has dealt with in the past. Possible topics include depression, grief management, ending a relationship, creative financing, stress management, assertiveness, and resolving an interpersonal dispute. The instructor asks if anyone in the group has experienced a similar issue and encourages volunteers to share. The instructor then asks the group for ideas (strategies) on how to seek to resolve dilemmas that have been raised. The merits and shortcomings of these strategies are discussed. The instructor ends the exercise by summarizing important points that were made during the exercise.

Step 2:   The instructor passes out a sign-up sheet, and each student selects a date in class to lead the group as described in step 1. Each student should take 15 to 20 minutes to lead the group. Each student is graded on a pass/fail basis by the instructor. Students who do not "pass" at first are given additional opportunities to lead a group in later class sessions. The instructor should inform those students who have to lead another session about what they need to work on to improve. When students are facilitating such intervention groups, it is advisable for the instructor to sit outside the circle of students, so that the students attend to the facilitator rather than to the instructor. When sitting outside the circle, the instructor should evaluate the facilitator on such areas as facilitation strengths demonstrated, areas needing attention, and suggestions for changes. The instructor also notes to the facilitator whether she or he has "passed" or whether another session has to be led. If someone continues to not receive a "pass" after several tries, the student and the instructor should meet privately to explore options of what to do. (Because of the importance of social work students being able to facilitate intervention groups, the instructor may choose to set the grading requirement that a passing grade on this exercise is needed in order for students to receive a passing grade in the class.)

Note: During these intervention exercises, these two ground rules must be strictly followed:

1. *Confidentiality.* "What is said here stays here" and should not be revealed outside the class.

2. *Emotional safety.* If a student begins to share and then feels that his or her disclosure is becoming too personal, the student should say, "This is becoming too personal," and there should be no group pressure for that person to say more.

3. Resolving Interpersonal Conflicts

Goal: To understand conflict resolution strategies and to become more skillful in resolving future interpersonal conflicts.

Step 1:   Students write down on a sheet of paper a summary of a recent interpersonal conflict that they had—perhaps involving a friend, a relative, another student, or a faculty member. The summary should include who the conflict was with, what was at issue, and how it was resolved. (If the issue has not been resolved, the summary should contain a description of the current status of the conflict.)

Step 2:   The instructor describes the following conflict resolution strategies: the win-lose approach, the problem-solving approach, role reversal, empathy, inquiry, being assertive, I-messages, disarming, stroking, mediation, letting or forgiving, and the law of requisite variety. (These strategies should be written on the chalkboard so students can refer to them later.)

Step 3:   The class for ms groups of three students each. The subgroups share with each other the nature of the interpersonal conflict that they wrote on a sheet of paper. (Students have a right not to reveal what they wrote.) For each conflict that is shared in the subgroup, the students explore whether *needs* or *solutions* of the people involved in the conflict were primarily at issue. The subgroups identify whether any of these strategies were used (or would have been helpful to use) in resolving the conflict: the problem-solving approach, role reversal, empathy, inquiry, being assertive, I-messages, disarming, stroking, mediation, and the law of requisite variety.

Step 4:   When the class re-forms, students have an opportunity to ask questions about conflict resolution. Some students may want to share a complicated unresolved conflict situation they are now experiencing to obtain feedback on how it may be effectively resolved.

SOCIAL WORK WITH FAMILIES

The focus of social work services is often the family, which is an interacting, interdependent system. The problems that people face are usually influenced by dynamics within the family, and dynamics within the family are, in turn, influenced by the wider social and cultural environment. Because a family is an interacting system, change in any member will affect all other members. Tensions between husband and wife, for example, will be felt by their children, who may respond with disturbed behavior. Treating the children's behavior alone would not get to the root of the family problem (Compton & Galaway, 1999).

Another reason for the focus on the family as a whole rather than on certain individuals is that the participation of other family members is often needed in the treatment process. They can help identify family patterns. In addition, the whole family, once members perceive the relationships among their various behaviors, can form a powerful team in reestablishing healthier patterns (Wells, 1998). For example, family members can pressure their alcoholic mother to acknowledge her problem. They may provide important emotional support for her efforts to stop drinking. They may also need counseling themselves (or support from a self-help group) to assist in coping with her when she is drinking.

This chapter will help prepare students to:

Describe the diversity of family forms
Describe the societal functions of families
Understand how to use two family assessment techniques
Comprehend aspects of families for workers to focus on
Describe family problems and the social work services available to families

DIVERSITY OF FAMILY FORMS

The family is a social institution that is found in every culture and has been defined by Coleman and Cressey (1995, p. 124) as "a group of people related by marriage, ancestry, or adoption who live together in a common household." This definition does not cover a number of living arrangements whose members consider themselves a family, such as

- A husband and wife raising two foster children who have been in the household for several years
- Two women, lesbians in a loving relationship, raising children born to one of the partners while in a heterosexual marriage that ended in divorce
- Grandparents raising grandchildren because of illness or addiction of the parents
- Where one spouse lives away from home—perhaps because of military service in a foreign country or because of incarceration
- Where one child who has a severe and profound cognitive disability lives in a residential treatment facility
- A man and a woman who have been living together for years in a loving relationship but never legally married

A broader definition of *family* that encompasses all of the above is: a family is a kinship system of all relatives living together or recognized as a social unit. Such a definition recognizes unmarried same-sex and opposite-sex couples and families, foster families, and any relationship that functions or feels like a family.

A wide diversity of family patterns exists in the world (see the Case Example, "Sex-Role Expectations Are Culturally Determined" on page 178). Families in different cultures take a variety of forms. In some societies, husband and wife live in separate buildings. In others, they live apart for several years after the birth of a child. In some societies, husbands are permitted to have more than one wife. In a few countries, wives are allowed to have more than one husband. Some cultures permit (and a few encourage) premarital and extramarital intercourse.

Some societies have large communes where adults and children live together. There are communes in which the children are raised separately from adults. In some cultures, surrogate parents (rather than the natural parents) raise the children. Some societies encourage certain types of same-sex relationships, and a few recognize same-sex as well as heterosexual marriages.

In many cultures, marriages are still arranged by the parents. In a few societies, an infant may be "married" before birth (if the baby is of the wrong sex, the marriage is dissolved). Some societies do not recognize romantic love. Some cultures expect older men to marry young girls. Others expect older women to marry young boys. Most societies prohibit the marriage of close relatives, but a few subcultures encourage marriage between brothers and sisters or between first cousins. Some expect a man to marry his father's brother's daughter, whereas others insist that he marry his mother's sister's daughter. In some societies, a man, on marrying, makes a substantial gift to the bride's father, whereas in others the bride's father gives a substantial gift to the new husband.

These are indeed substantial variations in family patterns. People in each of these societies feel strongly that their particular pattern is normal and proper, and many feel the pattern is divinely ordained. Suggested changes in their particular form are viewed with suspicion and defensiveness and are often sharply criticized as being unnatural, immoral, and a threat to the survival of the family.

Despite these variations, sociologists note that most family systems can be classified into two basic forms: the extended family and the nuclear family. An *extended family* consists of a number of relatives living together, such as parents, children, grandparents, great-grandparents, aunts, uncles, in-laws, and cousins. The extended family is the predominant pattern in preindustrial societies. The members divide various agricultural, domestic, and other duties among themselves.

A *nuclear family* consists of a married couple and their children living together. The nuclear family type emerged from the extended family. Extended families tend to be more functional in agricultural societies where many "hands" are needed; the nuclear family is more suited to the demands of complex, industrialized societies, because its smaller size and potential geographic mobility enable it to adapt more easily to changing conditions—such as the need to relocate to obtain a better job.

Although the nuclear family is still the predominant family form in the United States, Canada, and many other industrialized countries, it is a serious mistake for social workers and other helping professionals to use the nuclear family as the ideal model that individuals in our society should strive to form. Many other family forms are functioning in our society, such as the following:

- A married couple without children who are the primary caregivers for the wife's mother, who has Alzheimer's disease and resides with the couple
- Two gay men in a committed relationship, each of whom has joint custody of two children with his former wife
- A childless married couple who have decided not to conceive children
- A single parent with three young children
- A blended family in which the husband and wife have children in the current marriage, plus children from earlier marriages, all of whom live in the household
- An unmarried young couple living together in what amounts to a trial marriage

In the past few decades, there has been a trend in the United States for greater diversity in marital arrangements and family forms. There are increasing numbers of transracial marriages, marriages between spouses of diverse ages and cultural backgrounds, transracial adoptions, single-parent families, and blended families. Although some social workers may personally judge a few of these types to be "wrong," it is essential that they not allow their personal beliefs to reduce the quality or quantity of professional services that are provided to these family units. It is also essential that social workers who work with families of diverse cultural backgrounds learn about those backgrounds and understand the customary norms for family functioning.

Some family forms have been discriminated against, such as a single-parent household and a gay or lesbian couple with children. Recognizing this discrimination, the Council on Social Work in Education's *Educational Policy and Accreditation Standards* (2008) identified "marital status" as a population at risk and thereby a group that social workers are obligated to work with to end discrimination.

CASE EXAMPLE   SEX-ROLE EXPECTATIONS ARE CULTURALLY DETERMINED

In the classic study *Sex and Temperament in Three Primitive Societies*, Margaret Mead (1935) demonstrated that sex-role expectations are culturally rather than biologically determined. The study further showed that family socialization patterns are immensely influenced by the larger culture. The study was conducted with three tribes in New Guinea in the early 1930s. Mead found that many characteristics that Americans classify as typically feminine or masculine are classified differently in these tribes.

Both sexes among the Arapesh would seem feminine to us. Both men and women are gentle, nurturant, and compliant. The personalities of males and females in this society are not sharply differentiated by sex. Both girls and boys learn to be unaggressive, cooperative, and responsive to the needs and wants of others. Relations between husband and wife parallel the traditional mother-child relations in our society, with the Arapesh husband often seeing his role as providing training to his much younger wife.

In contrast, among the Mundugamors, both sexes would seem masculine to us. Both are headhunters and cannibals, are nonnurturant and aggressive, and actively initiate sexual involvement.

The most interesting society that Mead studied was the Tchambuli. This society virtually reverses our traditional sex-role expectations and stereotypes. The men spend much more time than the women in grooming and decorating themselves. Also, the men spend much of their time painting, carving, and practicing dance steps. In contrast, the women are efficient, impersonal, unadorned, managerial, and brisk. The women are the traders and have most of the economic power.

Exercise 8.1: Description of My Family

Goal: This exercise is designed to assist you in better understanding your family dynamics.

Write a description of your family. Provide information on who is a member (may include aunts, uncles, grandparents, foster children, etc.), ages and gender of members, occupation or professions of members, religious orientations, political orientations, family values, educational levels attained by members, significant qualities or characteristics of members, hobbies or interests of members, significant family activities, current stresses or challenges faced by members or by the family, significant resources and strengths of the family, and past family crises.

SOCIETAL FUNCTIONS OF FAMILIES

Families in modern industrial societies perform the following essential functions that help maintain the continuity and stability of society:

1. *Replacement of the population.* Every society has some system for replacing its members. Practically all societies consider the family as the unit in which children are to be produced. Societies define the rights and responsibilities of the reproductive partners within the family unit. These rights and responsibilities help maintain the stability of society, although they are defined differently from one society to another.

2. *Care of the young.* Children require care and protection until at least the age of puberty. The family is a primary institution for the rearing of children. Modern societies have generally developed supportive institutions to help in caring for the young—for example, medical services, day-care centers, parent training programs, and residential treatment centers.

3. *Socialization of new members.* To become productive members of society, children have to be socialized into the culture. Children are expected to acquire a language, learn social values and mores, and dress and behave within the norms of society. The family plays a major role in this socialization process. In modern societies, as numerous other groups and resources are also involved in this socialization process. Schools, the mass media, peer groups, the police, movies, and books and other written material are important influences. (Sometimes these different influences clash by advocating opposing values and attitudes.)

4. *Regulation of sexual behavior.* Failure to regulate sexual behavior results in clashes between individuals because of jealousy and exploitation. Every society has rules that regulate sexual behavior within family units. Most societies, for example, have incest taboos, and most disapprove of extramarital sex.

5. *Source of affection.* Humans need affection, emotional support, and positive recognition from others (including approval, smiles, encouragement, and reinforcement for accomplishments). Without such affection and recognition, our emotional, intellectual, physical, and social growth would be stunted. The family is an important source for obtaining affection and recognition, because family members generally regard each other as among the most important people in their lives and gain emotional and social satisfaction from family relationships.

FAMILY ASSESSMENT

There are a variety of ways to assess families. Conducting a social history of a family and its members is a widely used approach (see Chapter 4). With regard to family assessment, however, two techniques have received considerable discussion in recent years: eco-maps and genograms.

Eco-Maps

The eco-map is a paper-and-pencil assessment tool used to assess specific troubles and plan interventions for clients. The eco-map, a drawing of the client family in its social environment, is usually drawn jointly by the social worker and the client. It helps both parties achieve a holistic or ecological view of the client's family life and the nature of the family's relationships with groups, associations, organizations, and other families and individuals. The eco-map has been used in a variety of situations, including marriage and family counseling and adoption and foster-care home studies. It has also been used to supplement traditional social histories and case records. The eco-map is a shorthand method for recording basic social information. The technique helps clients and workers gain insight into the clients' problems by providing a "snapshot view" of important interactions at a particular point in time. Ann Hartman (1978) is the primary developer of this tool.

A typical eco-map consists of a family diagram surrounded by a set of circles and lines used to describe the family within an environmental context. Eco-map users can create their own abbreviations and symbols, but the most commonly used symbols are shown in Figure 8.1.

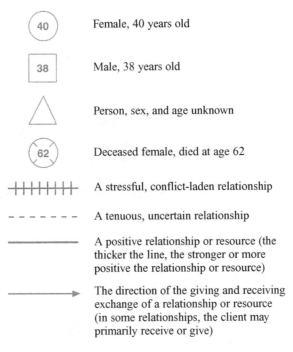

Figure 8.1

Symbols commonly used in an eco-map.

First, a circle (representing the client's family) is drawn in the center of a large blank sheet of paper (see Figure 8.2 below). The composition of the family is indicated in the circle. Other circles are then drawn around the family circle. These circles represent other systems—that is, the groups, other families, individuals, and organizations—with which the family ordinarily interacts. Lines are drawn to describe the relationships that members of the client family have with these systems. Arrows show the flow of energy (giving or receiving resources and communication between family members and significant systems). Figure 8.3 on page 181 shows the eco-map for the family described in the Case Example "Using an Eco-Map: The Wilbur Family."

An eco-map helps both worker and client view the client's family from a systems and ecological perspective. Sometimes, as happened in the Wilbur case example, clients and workers gain greater insight into the social dynamics of a problematic situation. For the worker, a completed eco-map graphically displays important interactions of a client family with other systems (that is, the groups, other families, individuals, and organizations) that the family ordinarily interacts with at a particular point in time. Such a diagram allows the worker to better understand the environmental factors affecting the family. It thus helps the worker generate hypotheses of problematic dynamics in the family-environmental system, which the worker can then further explore by questioning the family members. Once problematic dynamics are identified, the worker can focus attention on helping family members generate strategies to resolve the problematic dynamics.

Similarly, an eco-map helps client family members identify and understand problematic dynamics in their family-environmental system. Once these dynamics are identified, family members are in a position to generate strategies (together with their worker) to resolve problems.

Genograms

The genogram is a graphic way of investigating the origins of a client's or client family's presenting problem by diagramming the family over at least three generations. The client and worker usually jointly construct the family genogram, which is essentially a family tree. Murray Bowen is the primary developer of this technique (Kerr & Bowen, 1988). The genogram helps the worker and family members examine problematic emotional and behavioral patterns in an intergenerational context. Patterns tend to repeat them-

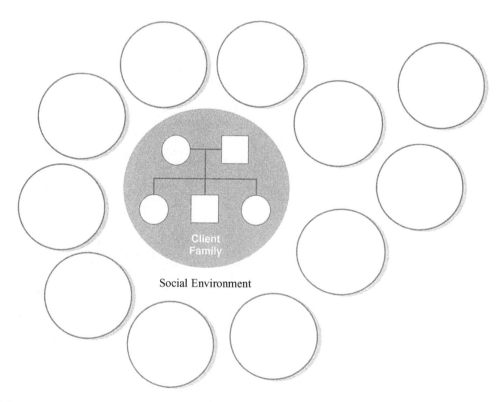

Figure 8.2

Setting up an eco-map.

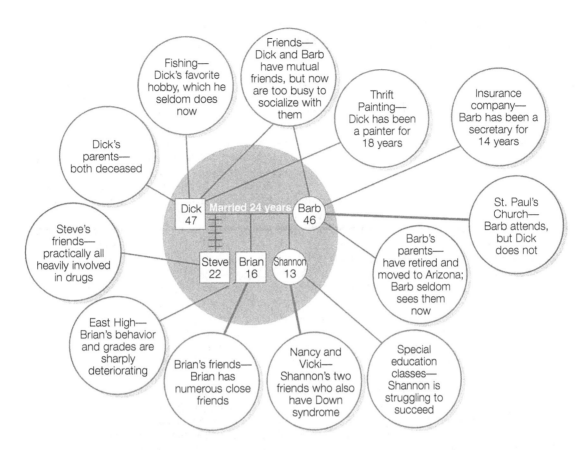

Figure 8.3

Sample eco-map: The Wilbur family.

selves; what happens in one generation often occurs in the next. Genograms help family members identify and understand family relationship patterns.

Commonly used genogram symbols are shown in Figure 8.4. Together, the symbols provide a visual picture of a family tree, for at least three generations, including the following: who the members are; their names, ages, and gender; marital status; and sibling positions. When relevant, additional items of information are included, such as emotional difficulties, behavioral problems, religious affiliation, ethnic origins, geographic locations, occupations, socioeconomic status, and significant life events. The use of the genogram is illustrated in the Kull family case example on page 184.

In summary, genograms are useful to both worker and clients. For the worker, a completed genogram graphically points out intergenerational family dynamics. Such a diagram allows the worker to better understand the intergenerational patterns affecting a client family. It then helps the worker generate hypotheses of problematic patterns from prior generations, which the worker can further explore by questioning family members. Once problematic dynamics are identified, the worker can then focus attention on helping family members generate strategies to resolve the patterns. A strengths perspective should also be used by workers—that is, they should also focus on helping family members identify intergenerational patterns that are *resources* that will help the family confront challenges. (Such resources include longevity, high educational achievement levels, valuing and practicing good health patterns, low rates of divorce, and high levels of constructive community participation.)

Similarly, for the client family, a genogram helps family members identify and understand problematic intergenerational patterns and resources. Once such patterns are identified, family members can begin to generate strategies (together with their worker) to break these patterns.

The genogram and the eco-map have a number of similarities. With both techniques, users gain insight into family dynamics. Some of the symbols used in the two approaches are identical. There are differences, however. The eco-map focuses attention on the family's interactions with groups, resources, organizations, associations, other families, and other individuals. The genogram focuses attention on intergenerational patterns, particularly those that are problematic or dysfunctional.

CASE EXAMPLE   USING AN ECO-MAP: THE WILBUR FAMILY

Barb and Dick Wilbur are contacted by Mary Timm, school social worker at East High School. The Wilburs' second-oldest son, Brian (age 16), had a knife in his jacket at school and liquor on his breath. The Wilburs are shocked. They agree to meet with Ms. Timm the next day to discuss these incidents. Brian will also be present.

At the meeting, Ms. Timm asks Brian why he brought a knife to school. At first, he refuses to respond. Ms. Timm also notes that records show he used to receive mainly B's, but now his grades are primarily D's and F's. Mr. and Mrs. Wilbur also sternly ask Brian what is happening. They add that the school system has informed them that he apparently has been drinking during school hours. Gradually tears come to Brian's eyes. He says no one cares about him. He asserts his parents are too busy at work and too busy looking after his older brother, Steve, and his younger sister, Shannon.

At first, Mr. and Mrs. Wilbur are surprised. They indicate they love Brian very much. Gradually they disclose they have been so involved with the demands of their other two children that they may have been "shortchanging" Brian in recent months. Shannon, age 13, has Down syndrome and requires considerable individual attention, especially with her coursework. (Shannon is enrolled in special education courses.)

Brian is asked where he obtained the knife. He hesitantly indicates his older brother, Steve, gave it to him for "protection." Brian adds that he sees nothing wrong with carrying a knife; Steve frequently carries a pistol. In addition, Brian says Steve urged him to take the knife to school because some people who are unhappy with Steve have said they may come after Brian. Ms. Timm asks Mr. and Mrs. Wilbur if they know anything about this. Barb and Dick suggest it may be best if Brian is excused at this point. Ms. Timm sets up a later meeting with Brian, and he leaves.

Both Barb and Dick then become teary-eyed. They indicate they are nearing their wit's end. Both work full-time, and in recent years Steve and Shannon have required so much of their attention that they now no longer are able to spend any time with their former friends. In addition, they have been arguing more and more. They feel that their family is disintegrating and that they are "failing" as parents. They also disclose that Steve is addicted to both alcohol and cocaine and has been for several

years. He has been in for inpatient treatment three times but always goes back to using soon after leaving treatment. They don't know where Steve is getting the money for his cocaine habit. They fear he may be dealing. He hasn't been able to hold a full-time job. He is usually terminated because he shows up for work while under the influence. Currently, he is working part-time as a bartender.

Mr. and Mrs. Wilbur fear that unless something is done soon, Brian may follow in Steve's footsteps. They add they have contemplated asking Steve to leave but are reluctant to do so, because they feel it is their parental obligation to provide a house for their children as long as the children want to stay.

At this point, Ms. Timm suggests it may be helpful to diagram their present dilemma. Together the Wilburs and Ms. Timm draw the eco-map shown in Figure 8.3.

While drawing the map, Ms. Timm asks whether providing housing for Steve is helping him or whether it may be a factor in enabling him to continue his drug use and his irresponsible behavior. The eco-map helps the Wilburs see that as a result of working full-time and spending the remainder of their waking hours caring for Shannon, Steve, and Brian, they are gradually becoming too emotionally and physically exhausted to cope. During the past few years, they have stopped socializing.

The Wilburs ask Ms. Timm to explain what she means by "enabling" Steve to continue his drug use and his irresponsible behavior. Ms. Timm explains enabling and indicates that a "tough love" approach may be an option. (In this case, a tough love approach would involve the Wilburs' demanding that Steve live elsewhere if he continues to abuse alcohol and cocaine.) Ms. Timm also gives them pamphlets that describe enabling and tough love. They make an appointment for the next week.

For the next several weeks, Ms. Timm continues to meet weekly with the Wilburs and individually with Brian. The Wilburs eventually decide to use a tough love approach with Steve. Steve leaves but continues to use alcohol and cocaine. However, living on his own docs appear to be somewhat beneficial as he now works full-time at a maintenance job to pay his bills. With Steve out of the house, Barb and Dick Wilbur are able to spend more time with Brian and Shannon, and they begin to socialize again with some of their former friends.

ASPECTS OF FAMILIES FOR WORKERS TO FOCUS ON

In assessing families, and providing services to families, there are certain aspects of families that provide significant information about their challenges, and about their strengths. Frequently, the strengths (assets and resources) can be utilized to resolve their challenges, and to enhance their overall functioning. Aspects that social workers should attend to are: verbal communication patterns; nonverbal communication patterns; family roles of members; personal goals and family goals; norms and cultural values; and culturagrams.

Verbal Communication Patterns

All cooperative family interaction, whether verbal or nonverbal, depends upon effective communication. Through communication, members argue, trade insults, debate issues, arrive at goals, assume tasks and responsibilities, laugh, and work out differences. Effective communication occurs between two or more peo-

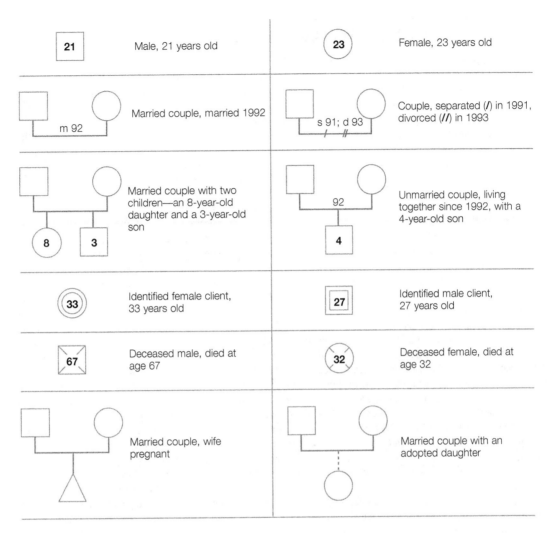

Figure 8.4

Symbols commonly used in a genogram.

ple when the receiver interprets the sender's message in the way the sender intended. *The meaning of a communication is the response it elicits in the receiver, regardless of the intent of the sender.*

We will begin this section by describing a model of communication. Although most people think they understand what communication is all about, they are not fully aware of the process that goes on whenever people share ideas. This section will briefly summarize the process. We will begin by assuming that you, a sender, want to express a thought or a feeling.

The first thing you do is translate your thoughts and feelings into symbols (usually spoken words, but also nonverbal signals) that others can understand. This process is called *encoding*. Finding the precise symbols to express what you think or feel can be difficult. The next step is to *send the message*. There are a number of ways of sending a message: by letter, e-mail, telephone, note, spoken word, touch, posture, gestures, and facial expressions. When your message reaches a receiver, the receiver *decodes* the message by interpreting it in terms of thoughts or feelings that mean something to the receiver. The completed process is shown in Figure 8.6.

This process is one-way communication, in which a sender directs a message to a receiver. Most communication is a two-way process, however, as the initial sender directs a message to a receiver and the receiver responds. Two-way communication is diagrammed in Figure 8.7.

With effective communication, what the receiver decodes is what the sender sends. However, frequently something goes wrong. A friendly joke is taken as an insult. A subtle request is missed. A constructive suggestion is taken as a put-down.

CASE EXAMPLE   USING A GENOGRAM: THE KULL FAMILY

Jim Kull is referred by Rock County District Attorney's Office to the Rock County Domestic Violence Program. He was arrested two nights ago for an incident in which his wife, Diane, received several severe bruises on her body and her face. Kris Koerner, a social worker, has an intake interview with Mr. Kull. Mr. Kull is an involuntary client and is reluctant to discuss the incident. Ms. Koerner informs Mr. Kull he has a right not to discuss it, but if he chooses not to, she is obligated to inform the district attorney that he refused services. She adds that in such cases the district attorney usually files a battery charge with the court, which may lead to jail time.

Mr. Kull reluctantly states he and his wife had a disagreement, which ended with her slapping him and him defending himself by throwing a few punches. He adds that yesterday, when he was in jail, he was informed she left home with the children and is now staying at a women's shelter. He is worried she may contact an attorney and seek a divorce.

Ms. Koerner inquires about the specifics of the "disagreement." Mr. Kull indicates he came home after having a few beers, his dinner was cold, and he "got on" Mrs. Kull for not cleaning the house. He adds that Mrs. Kull then started "mouthing off," which eventually escalated into them pushing and hitting each other. Ms. Koerner then inquires whether such incidents had occurred in the past. Mr. Kull indicates "a few times" and then adds that getting physical with his wife is the only way for him to "make her shape up." He indicates he works all day long as a carpenter while his wife sits home watching soap operas. He feels she is not doing her "fair share"; he states the house usually looks like a "pigpen."

Ms. Koerner asks Mr. Kull if he feels getting physical with his wife is justifiable. He responds with "sure" and adds that his dad frequently told him "spare the rod, and spoil both the wife and the kids." Ms. Koerner asks if his father was at times abusive to him when he was a child. He indicates that he was and adds that to this day he detests his dad for being abusive to him and to his mother.

Ms. Koerner then suggests that together they draw a "family tree," focusing on three areas: episodes of heavy drinking, episodes of physical abuse, and traditional versus modern gender stereotypes. Ms. Koerner explains that a traditional gender stereotype includes the husband as the primary decision maker and the wife as submissive to him and primarily responsible for domestic tasks. The modern gender stereotype involves an equalitarian relationship between husband and wife. After an initial reluctance (related to his expressing confusion as to how such a "tree" would help get his wife back), Mr. Kull agrees to cooperate in drawing such a "tree." The resulting genogram is presented in Figure 8.5.

The genogram helps Mr. Kull see that he and his wife are products of family systems that have strikingly different values and customs. In his family the males drink heavily, have a traditional view of marriage, and use physical force in interactions with their spouses. (Mr. Kull further adds his father also physically abused his brother and sister when they were younger.) On questioning, Mr. Kull mentions he frequently spanks his children and has struck them "once or twice." Ms. Koerner asks Mr. Kull how he feels about repeating the same patterns of abuse with his wife and children that he despises his father for using. Tears come to his eyes, and he says "not good."

Ms. Koerner and Mr. Kull then discuss courses of action that he might take to change his family interactions and how he might best approach his wife in requesting that she and the children return. Mr. Kull agrees to attend Alcoholics Anonymous (AA) meetings as well as a therapy group for barterers. After a month of attending these weekly meetings, he contacts his wife and asks her to return. Mrs. Kull agrees to return *if* he stops drinking (since most of the abuse occurred when he was intoxicated), *if* he agrees to continue to attend group intervention and AA meetings, and *if* he agrees to go to counseling with her. Mr. Kull readily agrees. (Mrs. Kull's parents, who have never liked her husband, express their disapproval)

For the first few months, Mr. Kull is on his best behavior, and there is considerable harmony in the family. Then one clay, on his birthday, he decides to stop for a few beers after work. He drinks until he is intoxicated. When he finally arrives home, he starts to verbally and physically abuse Mrs. Kull and the children. For Mrs. Kull, this is the last straw. She takes the children to her parents' house, where they stay for several days, until they are able to find and move into an apartment. She also files for divorce and follows through in obtaining one.

At first glance, this case is not a "success." In reality, many social work cases are not successful. However, Mr. Kull now realizes that he has acquired, and acts out, certain dysfunctional family patterns. Unfortunately, he is not ready to make lasting changes. Perhaps in the future he will be more committed. At the present time he has returned to drinking heavily. Mrs. Kull and the children are safer and can now stan to break the cycle of abuse.

Our model identifies the areas in which misinterpretations may occur. First, the sender may have difficulty putting into symbolic form the thoughts and feelings he or she wishes to express. Second, the message may not be sent effectively. There may be too much noise for the sender to be fully heard, or the sender may not speak loudly enough. Although nonverbal cues tend to be ambiguous, words also have a variety of meanings and may connote something different from what the sender intends. Third, during the decoding process, the receiver may misunderstand the sender's message as a result of several factors, including: individual attitudes, values, beliefs, defense mechanisms, and stereotypes; and perceptual factors, such as not listening. Later in this chapter, we will take a closer look at how these factors influence communication.

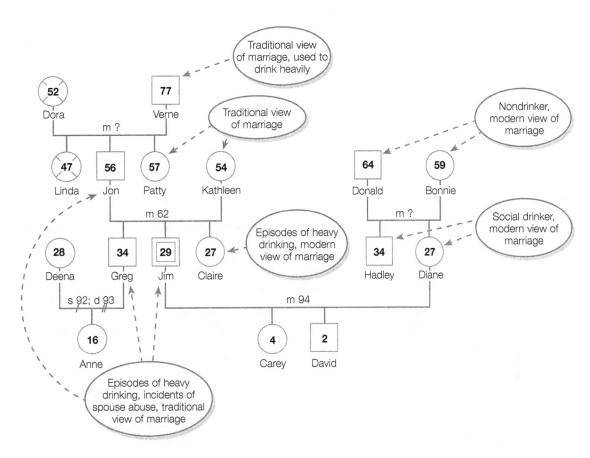

Figure 8.5

Sample genogram: The Jim and Diane Kull family.

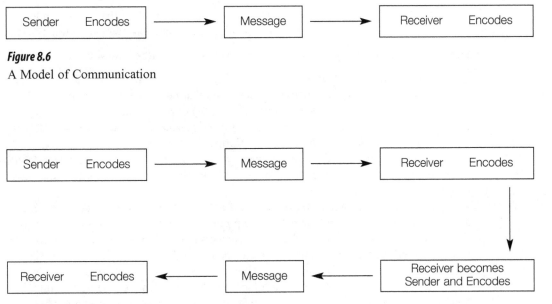

Figure 8.6

A Model of Communication

Figure 8.7

A Model of Two-Way Communication

In most families the members communicate with a pattern of two-way communication. One-way communication, however, is apt to occur with an autocratic head (which is apt to be the father or mother) of the family. With an autocratic head, the other family members are apt to feel constrained in expressing their thoughts and feelings. Some serious drawbacks exist with one-way communication. Those who feel constrained to express themselves may feel they are being related to as being "second-class citizens." In addition, they may have valuable information that could improve the family's functioning, but because it is not communicated, it is never considered. The adage, "children should be seen, but not heard", fosters one-way communication.

Exercise 8.2: The Emotional Effects of One-Way Communication

Goal: This exercise is designed to assist you in understanding the emotional impact of one-way communication.

Step 1:   Describe a situation where someone in your family used one-way communication with you.

Step 2:   How did you feel when you were not allowed to voice your opinion, were not allowed to share your thoughts, and were not allowed to ask a question?

Step 3:   Were you motivated to do what the person who used one-way communication wanted you to do?

There are numerous benefits to be gained through two-way communication. It improves family morale, trust, and openness. Conflicts and controversies are more readily resolved, as the resources and ideas of all the family members are pooled.

With communication, sociopsychological factors (including defense mechanisms, beliefs, attitudes, values, and stereotypes) influence what we perceive.

A defense mechanism is a psychological attempt to avoid or escape from painful conditions such as anxiety, frustration, hurt, and guilt. An individual's defense mechanisms are usually activated when he or she faces information that conflicts with his or her self-image. Defense mechanisms preserve self-concept and self-esteem, and soften the blows of failure, deprivation, or guilt. Common defense mechanisms are briefly summarized in Figure 8.8.

Although everyone uses defense mechanisms to cope with unpleasant situations, defense mechanisms can become destructive when a person's perception of reality becomes seriously distorted.

Exercise 8.3: Using Defense Mechanisms

Goal: This exercise is designed to assist you in better understanding defense mechanisms.

Step 1:   Reread the list of defense mechanisms discussed in this section. List the ones that you remember someone else using. Indicate for each who the user was (first name only) and describe how this person used the defense mechanism.

Step 2:   List the defense mechanisms that you remember using yourself. Describe how you used each of these mechanisms.

Communication That Fosters Defensiveness. Gibb (1961) has found that we are more likely to respond defensively to certain types of communication and that defensiveness is *reciprocal*. If the sender begins to respond defensively, the receiver will react by putting up defenses, which will then increase the sender's defensiveness. Gibb has identified six types of messages that increase a receiver's defensiveness: evaluative, controlling, manipulative, indifference, superiority, and certainty.

Any message perceived as *evaluative* or *judgmental* increases the receiver's defensiveness. When an individual is being evaluated or rated, he or she is more on guard. In contrast, nonblaming communication reduces defensiveness.

Communication meant to *control* behavior or thoughts also increases defensiveness. For example, when a salesperson aggressively attempts to sell a product, many customers react defensively. Gibb indicates that defensiveness is decreased when the sender projects a willingness to share in the solution of a problem, for example, "Let's find a solution that works for both of us."

Defensiveness also increases when people discover that someone is trying to *manipulate* them. Because people would rather be asked to do something directly than be tricked into doing it, manipulative communication leads to distrust and defensiveness. An honest request may not always produce an immediate positive response, but it will lead to more open and honest communication and support in crucial situations.

Rationalization: One of the most common defense mechanisms is rationalization, the development of a logical but false explanation that protects a person's self-concept. Family members who use this mechanism actually believe the excuses they have dreamed up. For example, a student who fails an exam may blame it on poor teaching or having to work outside of classes rather than acknowledging the real reasons, such as not studying.

Projection: By using this defense mechanism, family members can unconsciously attribute their unacceptable ideas and impulses to others. An example would be a person who wanted to make himself look good by making others look bad. Psychologically, this person does not want to admit to himself that he has such selfish motives. So, he projects the selfishness onto others by believing they are trying to make him look bad, which then justifies his own negative behavior.

Denial: An individual can escape psychic pain by rejecting or denying reality. When people are confronted with a serious loss, they are likely to initially deny it. For example, a person can deny that a loved one has died. Many alcoholics deny they have a drinking problem.

Reaction Formation: Family members can avoid facing an unpleasant truth by acting opposite to the way they feel. Individuals who are angry and cannot admit it to others or themselves often act as if there is nothing wrong. By using the reaction-formation defense mechanism, sad and lonely individuals can act as if they are the life of the party, laughing and telling jokes. Also, people at funerals who are grieving deeply may behave as if everything is fine. The defense mechanism of denial is generally involved in reaction formation, as the individual seeks to deny painful facts, events, or feelings.

Compensation: This mechanism involves offsetting a real or fancied defect or inferiority by creating a real or fancied achievement or superiority. A recently divorced father may attempt to soften his children's pain by buying them expensive toys. Also, just as unhappily married college students can avoid dealing with their marriage by putting all their energies into their studies, people who have "failed" in their careers and personal life can compensate for their failure by getting "high" on alcohol or drugs.

Identification: When you were seven or eight you had heroes or heroines that you idealized and imitated. Some adults hide their real feelings in certain situations and instead of being themselves imitate someone they admire. The problem with this mechanism is that people "hooked" on identification cannot respond to a situation genuinely. They deny their real feelings and instead act as their hero would.

Fantasy: This mechanism involves using fantasy to dull the pain of reality. It is not uncommon, for example, for an unhappy adopted child to fantasize that her natural parents are exalted, loving people who will one day rescue her. Everyone daydreams, but most people soon return to reality. Some fantasies, however, endure and have destructive effects. For example, a former client of mine thought he could bring his deceased mother back to life by bringing female corpses to his home. After digging up several graves, he was arrested.

Regression: Some adults regress to an infantile or childlike state when ill or in trouble, with the subconscious goal of receiving more care and attention. When certain family members are confronted about their failings, they shed tears in an attempt to be excused for not fulfilling crucial commitments.

Isolation: The separation of an object (idea, experience, or memory) from the emotions associated with it results in the person showing no emotion to the object. This mechanism makes it possible for an individual to avoid the pain of anxiety, shame, or guilt. For example, a person uses this mechanism when discussing a violent act he or she has committed and shows no emotion.

Displacement: This mechanism occurs when hostile or aggressive feelings are vented against safer objects or people rather than against those who caused the feelings. A husband who has had a frustrating day at work, for example, may verbally or physically abuse his wife, children, or family pets.

Undoing: When a person feels guilty about some act or wish, she can undo her guilt by acting in a manner that reflects the reverse of this act or wish. The classic example is an unfaithful spouse who lavishes attention on his or her mate.

Figure 8.8

Common Defense Mechanisms

Indifference to another person's feelings and thoughts increases defensiveness by conveying a lack of concern and implying that the person involved is not important. Defense mechanisms then allow the receiver to maintain a sense of value to offset the indifference. Gibb has found that empathy reduces defensiveness and is much more beneficial to relationships than indifference.

When someone relates to us in a *superior* way, we often become angry, tune that person out, or use defense mechanisms to maintain our self-respect. Some individuals go to great lengths to cut the superior person "down to size." Relating on an *equal basis* is much more conducive to openness, sharing, and reducing defensiveness.

The final type of communication that, as Gibb notes, increases defensiveness is *certainty*. This type involves messages from people who steadfastly assert that their way of doing things is the *only* way or who act as if they have all the answers. Gibb notes that people who work hard at demonstrating certainty usually feel insecure and inferior; their certainty is a reaction formation. In this case, defensiveness can be reduced when openness to new information and ideas is communicated.

Defensiveness is probably the greatest barrier to effective communication and should be avoided. Messages should be sent in ways that do not make either senders or receivers defensive.

Exercise 8.4: Defensive Communication

Goal: This exercise is designed to assist you in understanding the types of communication that foster defensiveness.

For each of the following types of communication, describe a time when someone used this type of communication with you, and also describe your emotional reactions in each situation.

Step 1:   Evaluative or judgmental communication:

Step 2:   Communication to control you:

Step 3:   Communication to manipulate you:

Step 4:   Indifferent communication:

Step 5:   Superior communication, which suggested you were inferior:

Step 6:   Certainty communication:

> Beliefs, Values, and Attitudes. Individuals use their beliefs, values, and attitudes to select, interpret, and organize information. If a member in a family is liked, her comments receive more attention and support. Dislike sparks disagreement or strenuous opposition.
>
> The importance of beliefs and values in communication can be illustrated with a few examples. If parents are conservative and strongly opposed to interracial marriages, they will probably be opposed to interracial dating. A Roman Catholic who strongly opposes abortions will feel close to a speaker who supports that belief and be repelled by someone who favors choice. Deeply religious individuals often become threatened when someone professes that some other religion than theirs is the one, true religion. Finally, people with different sexual values will usually avoid discussing sexuality with each other.
>
> Beliefs have a major impact on perception and sometimes lead to inaccurate interpretations of a message. For example, some people incorrectly believe that others are generally attempting to control them or put them down. Under this system of belief, they are apt to misinterpret general statements, jump to conclusions, and become defensive. Open and honest communication is unlikely to occur. This type of misinterpretation of messages has also been called the tendency to *personalize* messages.
>
> *Stereotypes.* Stereotypes are fixed mental images of a group that are applied to all of its members. Stereotypes may be partially accurate or completely erroneous. You can discover some of the stereotypes you hold by considering the mental images you get in response to the following phrases: "a macho male," "a Republican," "a welfare mother," "a policeman," "a person who is gay," "a handicapped person," "an ex-con." For most of these phrases, you probably were able to get a mental picture of such people, and you probably have beliefs about their lifestyles, values, interests, and attitudes. During your first interaction with someone who fits into one of these categories, you are apt to respond in terms of your preconceived expectations. For example, if you distrust and fear police officers, you will probably be guarded in what you say and do if you meet an officer, and you will be apt to end the interaction as rapidly as possible.
>
> *Double-Bind Communication.* In a double bind communication, the sender of a message places the receiver in a situation where, no matter how he or she responds, the sender will criticize. This situation can occur when Father says, on the one hand, that all good children pick up their toys, yet on the other hand tells his son that all "real" boys are messy. The boy who receives these two messages will be unable to please his father whether he keeps his toys neat or messy. He may solve the problem by refusing to listen at all. At the extreme, he may pull away from reality to such a degree that he develops a severe emotional disturbance.

Exercise 8.5: Analyzing Verbal Communication Patterns in Families

Goal: This exercise is designed to assist you in analyzing constructive and problematic verbal communication patterns in families.

Step 1: Specify the constructive verbal communication patterns in your family.

Step 2: Specify the problematic verbal communication patterns in your family.

Step 3: Summarize your thoughts on how the problematic verbal communication patterns in your family could be improved.

Nonverbal Communication Patterns

It is impossible not to communicate. No matter what we do, we transmit information about ourselves. Even an expressionless face at a funeral communicates something. As you are reading this, stop for a minute and analyze what nonverbal messages you would be sending if someone were observing you. Are your eyes wide open or are they half closed? Is your posture relaxed or tense? What are your facial expressions communicating? Are you occasionally gesturing? What would an observer deduce you are feeling from these nonverbal cues?

Nonverbal cues often reveal feelings a person is intentionally trying to hide. Bodily reactions such as sweating, stammering, blushing, and frowning often reveal the presence of emotions—fear, embarrassment, or discomfort—that people would rather hide from others.

Nonverbal communication may take many forms. We communicate by the way we move, the expressions we make, the clothes we wear, even by the way we arrange our homes. We communicate by our posture, gestures, the way we touch others, choice of clothing, facial expressions, rings, tattoos, eye contact with others, and our personal appearance.

Nonverbal communication interacts with verbal communication and can repeat, substitute for, accent, regulate, or contradict what is spoken. When receivers perceive a contradiction between nonverbal and verbal messages, they usually believe the nonverbal (Adler and Towne, 1981).

Exercise 8.6: Analyzing Nonverbal Communication Patterns in Families

Goal: This exercise is designed to assist you in analyzing constructive and problematic nonverbal communication patterns in families.

Step 1: Specify the constructive nonverbal communication patterns in your family.

Step 2: Specify the problematic nonverbal communication patterns in your family.

Step 3: Summarize your thoughts on how the problematic nonverbal communication patterns in your family could be improved.

Family Roles of Members

A family role is a culturally determined pattern of behavior that is prescribed for a person who occupies a specific status or rank in relation to other family members. There are an infinite number of roles that different family members may play. Some roles are quite common for family members. Parents have the roles of guiding, directing, and raising the children. Parents also generally have the role of earning financial support for the family. Children are generally assigned the role of "student" and "helper" with household tasks. The "helper" role may be further divided among the children, with one being the "dish washer," another being the one who "takes out the garbage," and so on. There are many other possible roles for both the children and the parents. Examples for children include "princess," "trouble maker," "star athlete," "pianist," "bully," and "clown." Mom or dad may have the roles of "family protector," "primary decision maker," "cook," "grocery shopper," "coach for a sport," and "alcoholic."

Sharon Wegscheider (1981) indicates that members of alcoholic families tend to assume roles that both protect the chemically dependent person from taking responsibility for his or her behavior and actually serve to maintain the drinking problem. She identifies several roles that are typically played by family members in addition to the chemically dependent person: the chief enabler, the family hero, the scapegoat, the lost child, and the mascot.

The chief enabler's main purpose is to assume the primary responsibility for the family functioning. The abuser typically continues to lose control and relinquishes responsibility. The chief enabler, on the other hand, takes on more and more responsibility and begins making more and more family decisions. A chief enabler is often the parent or spouse of the chemically dependent person.

Conditions in families of chemically dependent people often continue to deteriorate as the dependent person loses control. A positive influence is needed to offset the negative. The family hero fulfills this role. The family hero often is the "perfect" person who does well at everything he or she tries. The hero works very hard at making the family appear to be functioning better than it is. In this way, the family hero provides the family with self-worth.

Another typical role played by someone in the chemically dependent family is the scapegoat. Although the alcohol abuse is the real problem, a family rule may mandate that this fact be denied and the blame be placed elsewhere. Frequently, another family member is targeted with the blame. The scapegoat often behaves in negative ways (for example, gets caught for stealing, runs away, becomes extremely withdrawn), which draws the spotlight to him or her. The scapegoat's role is to distract attention away from the dependent person and onto something else. This role helps the family avoid addressing the problem of chemical dependency.

Often there is also a lost child in the family. This is the person who seems rather uninvolved with the rest of the members yet never causes any trouble. The lost child's purpose is to provide relief to the family from some of the pain it is suffering. At least there is someone in the home who neither requires much attention nor causes any stress. The lost child is simply there.

Finally, chemically dependent families often have someone playing the role of mascot. The mascot is the person who probably has a good sense of humor and appears not to take anything seriously. Despite how much the mascot might be suffering inside, he or she provides a little fun for the family.

In working with a family, it is important for a social worker to identify the specific roles that each family member is filling, and to determine which roles are functional for a family, and which are dysfunctional. For the dysfunctional roles, the worker needs to make a decision whether seeking to change some of these roles would be beneficial.

Exercise 8.7: Functional Roles and Problematic Roles in Families

Goal: This exercise is designed to assist you in identifying functional and problematic roles in families.

Step 1:   Specify the functional roles that members of your family play.

Step 2:   Specify the problematic roles that some members of your family may play.

Step 3:   Speculate how these problematic roles can realistically be changed in a constructive direction.

Personal Goals and Family Goals

Chapter 7 described "Personal Goals and Group Goals." As a reader, it may be useful for you to review this material. Since a family is a group, it is important for a worker to recognize that each family member has personal goals, and the family has family goals. The personal goals of family members may be supportive of the family goals. For example, a family may have a goal of having each family member living a happy and productive life. If each of the children have a personal goal of doing well academically in school, such a goal is supportive of the family goal. On the other hand, if one of the family members has a goal of seeking to be "high," daily, on a chemical substance, such a goal is in conflict with the family goal of each member living a productive life.

Sometimes a family member may have a hidden agenda. A hidden agenda is a personal goal held by a member that is unknown to the other family members and that interferes with the family goals. Assume, again, that a family has a goal of each family member living a happy and productive life. If a family member thinks he or she can get rich quickly by gambling in casinos, and seeks to do so weekly without the other members being aware of the activity, such an activity is probably a "hidden agenda."

Often, in working with a family, it is important for a worker to identify the personal goals of each family member, determine the family goals, identify any hidden agendas, and work towards the personal goals becoming more consistent with constructive family goals.

Exercise 8.8: Personal Goals, Family Goals, and Hidden Agendas

Goal: This exercise is designed to assist you in identifying personal goals, family goals, and hidden agendas in families.

Step 1:   Specify the personal goals of each member of your family.

Step 2:   Specify the family's goals.

Step 3:   Specify any hidden agendas that you have, which your family is unaware of.

Norms and Cultural Values

Norms are rules that specify proper behavior in a group. Family norms are rules that specify proper behavior in a family. Family norms ideally should allow the entire family and each individual member to function effectively and productively. There is considerable variation between families in their set of norms or rules for the family. It should be noted that not all family norms are considered to be constructive; for example, most Americans view the practice of female circumcision in some Middle Eastern countries to be highly dysfunctional and destructive.

A cultural value is a culture's idea about what is good, fair, right, and just. A family tends to take on the values of its culture, and make those values part of its family norms. But there are exceptions. For example, many Roman Catholics do not adhere to the church's prohibitions against premarital intimacy, and prohibitions against using most forms of contraceptives.

In families with problematic family norms, the family rules do not allow the family or individual members to function effectively and productively. In many families, the parents may set rules that the children do not agree with (and which the children may actively violate). Common areas of disagreement are: when to go to bed, study habits, keeping one's bedroom neat and tidy, smoking, choice of friends, use of alcohol, selection of friends, what to spend money on, etc.

A social worker needs to attend to family norms, and seek to do what is reasonable to make the rules more beneficial for constructive family functioning. Social workers also need to comprehend the cultural values of the clients they are working with. Clients are apt (but there are a number of exceptions) to adopt their cultural norms as family norms. As a start in learning cultural values of clients of ethnic groups that they are unfamiliar with, workers can discover information by Googling the cultural values of the ethnic group of the client. For example, by googling the following ethnic groups, I received the following cultural values:

Hmong in America: Family is very important. They often have large networks of cousins and other relatives working together. Extended families are a basic part of Hmong life. There is a tendency for Hmong girls in their teen years to marry older men.

Mexican-Americans: Place high value on family over individualism. Have numerous extended family get-togethers. They tend to value traditions, including celebrations. Many adhere to the Catholic religion.

Chinese-Americans: High value placed on group cooperation and individual modesty. Tend to have a small number of close lifelong friends who feel obligated to give each other whatever help might seem required. Tend to avoid direct confrontation.

Swedish Americans: Culture in Sweden values "socialism" (for example, Swedes have 5 weeks of paid vacation each year, free schooling for children from preschool through college, and a year of paid maternity leave for each child). Swedish Americans are apt to place a higher value on socialism than most other Americans.

Japanese Americans: Place a high value on education. A substantial percentage of Japanese Americans attain college degrees.

Arab Americans: Family is very important. Believe that men and women are different and complementary. The husband is often the primary decision maker. Older persons are valued for their wisdom. Tend to believe that dignity, honor, and reputation are more valuable than material success. Tend to believe that much of one's fate in life is dependent on God's will.

Exercise 8.9: Norms and Cultural Values in Families

Goal: This exercise is designed to assist you in understanding the significance of norms and cultural values in families.

Step 1:   Specify the functional norms in your family.

Step 2:   Specify the problematic norms in your family, and briefly indicate why they are problematic.

Step 3:   Specify norms in your family that are also cultural values of your ethnic group.

Culturagrams

A culturagram is a family assessment instrument developed by Congress (2004) to help social workers better understand culturally diverse clients and their families. It identifies ten areas of culturally diverse families that social workers are urged to attend to. These ten areas will be specified, and briefly discussed.

- Reasons for Relocation: The reasons for relocating vary among families. Some come to the United States because of economic opportunities. Some relocate because of religious or political discrimination in their country of origin. Some revisit their country of origin on a regular schedule. Some never go home again. Some have found memories of their country of origin, and some never want to return due to an array of adverse circumstances. Social workers need an awareness of this area in order to better understand the stresses and attractions impacting families. (In asking questions to gather information in this area, as well as in the nine other areas, the social worker needs to tactfully phrase his or her questions so as to not offend the family members. For example, the family may have lived a long time in the community, and may be offended if they believe the worker is stereotyping them as being "recent arrivals.")
- Legal Status: If a family is undocumented and fears deportation, the members are apt to become more secretive and socially isolated. They may fear the social worker may report their undocumented status to officials who may arrest them. Undocumented family members may not be eligible for certain services. For undocumented clients it is particularly important for the social worker to establish trust and assure the family members about the confidentiality of contact.
- Length of Time in the Community: Family members who have arrived a fairly long time ago are apt to be more acculturated than recent arrivals. The ages of family members when they arrived is also of significance. Children, because of attending school and thereby developing peer relationships, often become more rapidly assimilated than their parents.
- Language: Often families who have a native language other than English use their native language at home, and then begin to speak English with the outside community. Children are apt, because of school, to more rapidly learn English than their parents. Conflicts sometimes arise in families in which the parents speak little English and therefore use their native language, while the children may see the value of speaking English.
- Health Beliefs: Families from different cultures may have a wide range of health beliefs. Some may only believe in "spiritual healing," or see the preferred treatment when they are ill as coming from a person in their culture who has very little professional medical training. Some may believe the only treatment that should be used is "prayer," or some other spiritual ritual that is unique to their culture. Some immigrants may choose to use a combination of western medicine and traditional folk beliefs.
- Crisis Events: Every family, and every family member has crises. A social worker needs to be aware of the crises that families have experienced, as well as the "interpretations" that are assigned to the crises. For example, in a culture in which the father is expected to be the primary financial provider and then develops a disability that prevents him from working, what "meaning" is assigned to the disability by each of the family members? Also, if a family highly values virginity prior to marriage, what meaning is attached to the rape of a teenage daughter?
- Holidays and Special Events: Every culture has holidays (some of which are unique) and special events. Some events celebrate transitions from one developmental stage to another—such as a bar mitzah, wedding, christening, or funeral. It is important for a social worker to learn the significance of important holidays and events, and to show respect for these holidays and events.
- Contact with Cultural and Religious Institutions: There are hundreds of religions in the world, with varying beliefs. Some religions believe in reincarnation. Some believe in sacrificing animals. Some believe in such practices as female circumcision. Some terrorist groups value a "holy war." It is essential for a social worker to have knowledge of the cultural and religious practices of their clients.

- Values About Education and Work: Some families believe it is more important for young adults to remain at home than seek a college education away from home. Some families have beliefs that members of their family can only obtain jobs that pay minimum (or slightly above) wages. Some families believe the mother's place is at home, rather than having a job outside the home.
- Values About Family—Structure, Power, Myths, and Rules: Some families desire an extended family structure, and others place a higher value on a nuclear family structure. Some families value a patriarchal structure, some a matriarchal structure, and some an egalitarian structure. In a few families, one (or more) child may control what happens in a family. Who does what domestic tasks in a family varies substantially among families. Child-rearing practices vary substantially—with the mother, or father, or older child, or grandparent being the primary person in charge of young children.

FAMILY PROBLEMS AND SOCIAL WORK SERVICES

Family Problems

An infinite number of problems occurs in families. Exhibit 8.1 lists a few of them.

Exhibit 8.1   A Sampling of Family Problems

Divorce	Unemployment of wage earners
Alcohol or drug abuse	Money management difficulties
Unwanted pregnancy	Injury from serious automobile accident involving one or more members
Bankruptcy	A child with a severe cognitive disability
Poverty	Incarceration or institutionalization of one or more members
Terminal illness	Compulsive gambling by one or more members
Chronic illness	Victim of a crime
Death	Forced retirement of a wage earner
Desertion	Caregiver for an elderly relative
"Empty-shell" marriage	Involvement of a child in delinquent and criminal activities
Emotional problems of one or more members	Illness of a member who acquires AIDS
Behavioral problems of one or more members	A runaway teenager
Child abuse	Sexual dysfunctions of one or more members
Child neglect	Infidelity
Sexual abuse	Infertility
Spouse abuse	
Elder abuse	

Thorman (1982) indicates problems within families tend to be clustered in the following four categories:

1. Marital problems: These include communication difficulties, disagreements over children, conflicts over finances, sexual difficulties, infidelity, and conflicts over recreational time. Marital counseling is one of the social services that may be useful in resolving some of the issues.
2. Parent/child relationship difficulties: Parents and children may have many disagreements over a wide range of areas, including choice of friends, assigned tasks and responsibilities, study habits, grades in school, when to start dating, use of alcohol and other drugs, smoking, choice of clothes, how to spend leisure time, and choice of career. Social services available include: family counseling, parent effectiveness training (see Module 4), and use of behavior therapy (see Module 2).
3. Personal problems of individual family members: An immense array of personal challenges may develop, including health issues, being depressed or anxious, a learning disability, shyness, low self-esteem, an addiction (such as alcohol or gambling), and being a single parent. The social services that are available are numerous, and most of them are problem specific. For example, rational therapy (see Module 1) might be used for someone who is depressed, assertiveness training (see Module 2) may be used for someone who is shy or who has anger management issues, medical care should probably be sought for someone who has health issues, etc.

4. Stresses imposed on the family by the external environment: Such stresses may include loss of a job, inadequate income, being homeless, inadequate access to transportation, inadequate schools, living in a dangerous neighborhood, car accident, and house damaged by a tornado. Social services that are available again are problem specific. Red Cross services may assist for a weather disaster, job training may be useful for someone who is unemployed, homeless shelters are sometimes available for the homeless, etc.

Exercise 8.10: Challenges Faced by My Family

Goal: This exercise is designed to assist you in identifying challenges your family is currently facing and to begin problem solving these challenges.

Step 1: Specify the challenges/difficulties that one or more members of your family are currently facing. (You have the right to not reveal challenges you do not wish to reveal.)

Step 2: For each of these challenges, what actions are being taken to confront these challenges?

Step 3: If one or more challenges are currently not being effectively confronted, specify other options for each that might be tried. (Feel free to consult with others about identifying other options.)

Social Work Services

When problems arise in a family, social services are often needed. The types and forms of services that social workers provide to troubled families are extremely varied. We can group them into two major categories: in-home services and out-of-home services.

In-home services are preventive. Although not all are offered literally within the home itself, they are specifically designed to help families stay together. They include financial aid, protective services (services to safeguard children or frail older adults from abuse and neglect), family preservation services (intensive crisis intervention within the home setting where children are so seriously at risk that removal to foster care would otherwise be required), family therapy (intensive counseling to improve family relationships), day care (caretaking services for children or older adults to provide respite for caregivers who might otherwise be overwhelmed or to permit them to work outside the home), homemaker services (for the same purpose), and family-life education (classes, often offered at traditional family service agencies, that cover such topics as child development, parenting skills, and communication issues). Not all of these services can be provided by social workers, but workers must know where to find them and how to help the family obtain them when needed (Suppes & Wells, 2003).

Out-of-home services are services that must be operationalized when the family can no longer remain intact. They are a manifestation that something has gone seriously wrong, because the breakup of any family amounts to a tragedy that will have ramifications beyond family boundaries. Although family members usually receive the blame, the larger system (social environment and the level of support it provides to troubled families) may be called into question. Out-of-home services include foster care, adoption, group homes, institutional care (for example, residential treatment centers), and the judicial system (which provides a different kind of institutional care, prison, or jail, for family members who have run into difficulty with the law).

To perform these services, social workers engage in a variety of roles (for example, broker, educator, advocate, supporter, mediator). The following examples illustrate many common services and important roles.

■ Mark Schwanke, age 32, has AIDS. Ms. Seely, a social worker with the AIDS Support Network in the community, serves as a case manager in providing a variety of services to Mark, his wife (who is HIV-positive), and their two children. These services include medical information and care, housing, counseling, emotional support services, and financial assistance. Because of frequent discrimination against persons with AIDS and persons with the AIDS virus, Ms. Seely often must advocate on the family's behalf to ensure that they receive the services they need.

■ Beth Roessler, age 15, has been convicted of committing six burglaries. Steve Padek, a juvenile probation officer and social worker, is her juvenile probation officer. Mr. Padek provides the following services to

Beth and her mother, who is divorced: He holds weekly supervision meetings with Beth to monitor her school performance and leisure activities, links Beth's mother with a Parents Without Partners group, and conducts several counseling sessions with Beth and her mother to mediate conflicts in their relationship.

- The aunt of Amy Sund, a 3-year-old child, has contacted Protective Services about Amy's mother (Pat) and her lover's physical abuse of Amy. Investigators confirm the abuse; Amy has bruises and rope burns on her body. Instead of referring the case to court, Protective Services refers the case to Family Preservation for services. Maria Gomez, social worker at Family Preservation, meets with Pat Sund and Amy a total of 37 times over the next 90 days. Pat Sund terminates her relationship with her abusive lover, is accepted into a financial assistance program through the Social Services Department for a 2-year period, and enrolls in a job training program. Ms. Gomez arranges for child care for Amy when Ms. Sund is attending the job training program. Ms. Gomez also arranges for a temporary housekeeper who provides training in cleaning the apartment and in making meals. Ms. Gomez encourages Ms. Sund to join the local chapter of Parents Anonymous, which she does. (Parents Anonymous is described in Chapter 6.) Had family preservation services been unavailable or unsuccessful, Amy would have had to be placed in a foster home.

- Cindy Rogerson, age 27, has three young children. She is badly battered by her husband and contacts the House of Hope, a shelter for battered women and their children. Sue Frank, a social worker at the shelter, makes arrangements for shelter for Mrs. Rogerson and her children. The oldest child is attending school, so Ms. Frank arranges for him to continue attending school. Ms. Frank provides one-to-one counseling to Mrs. Rogerson at the shelter to help her explore her options and to inform her of potential resources that she may not be aware of. Ms. Frank also leads groups at the shelter for residents and nonresidents, which Mrs. Rogerson is required to attend while at the shelter. After 2½ weeks, Mrs. Rogerson decides she wants to return to her husband. Ms. Frank convinces Mrs. Rogerson to give her husband an ultimatum prior to returning—he must receive family counseling together with her from the Family Service agency in the community and must attend a group for batterers in the community. Mrs. Rogerson reluctantly agrees. Mrs. Rogerson, at the urging of Ms. Frank, only then returns to live with her husband, with the understanding that she will leave immediately if he hits her again or if he drops out of either family counseling or the group for batterers.

- Katy Hynek, age 76, has Alzheimer's disease. She has been living alone in her house since her husband died 3 years ago. Her physician contacts Adult Services of the Department of Social Services and requests that an assessment of living arrangements be conducted. Linda Sutton, social worker, does an assessment and determines that Katy Hynek can no longer live alone. Katy's son Mark and his wife Annette agree to have Katy move in with them. During the next 19 months, Ms. Sutton has periodic contact with the Hyneks. As is common with this disease, Katy Hynek's physical and mental condition continues to deteriorate. Ms. Sutton listens to Mark and Annette's concerns and seeks to answer their questions about the disease. She also provides suggestions to help them cope with the changes in Katy's condition. As Katy's condition deteriorates, Ms. Sutton makes arrangements for Katy to attend an adult day-care center during the daytime, partly for respite care for Mark and Annette. At the end of 19 months, Mark and Annette request a meeting with Ms. Sutton to discuss the possibility of placing Katy in a nursing home as her condition has so deteriorated that she now needs 24-hour care. (For example, she gets up in the middle of the night and gets lost in closets; she is also now incontinent.) The pros and cons of placing Katy in a nursing home are identified and discussed. Making the decision is exceedingly emotional and agonizing for Mark and Annette. With a careful discussion of the entire situation with Ms. Sutton, Mark and Annette decide they have no choice but to seek a nursing home placement. Ms. Sutton gives them the names of three nursing homes, which they visit, and then they select one.

- Mr. and Mrs. Logan have been married for seven years, and have been trying to have one or more children for the past five years. They eventually go to a fertility clinic and discover that Mrs. Logan has endometriosis, which prevents her from conceiving. The Logans are distraught. Three months later, they decide to adopt. Being Catholic, they contact Catholic Social Services. Rhonda Lopez, a social worker, is assigned to work with them. The Logans undergo a three-month home study to determine their eligibility to adopt. They meet the eligibility requirements. They anxiously wait 8 months, and two older children (Jessica, age 7, and her brother Mark, age 5) become available. A trial placement is arranged. The Logans and the two children experience some adjustments, which Ms. Gomez assists them with. After 7 months, the adoption is finalized.

SUMMARY

The following summarizes the chapter's content in terms of the learning objectives presented at the beginning of the chapter.

1. Describe the diversity of family norms.

    A wide diversity of family patterns exists in the world. Although the nuclear family is still the predominant family form in our society, it is a serious mistake for social workers to use the nuclear family as the ideal model that individuals should strive to form. Many other family forms also function well and deserve respect.

2. Describe the societal functions of families.

    Family patterns and forms are substantially affected by the culture (larger system) in which they are located. Families in our society perform the following functions that help maintain continuity and stability in society: replacement of the population, care of the young, socialization of new members, regulation of sexual behavior, and provision of affection.

3. Understand how to use two family assessment techniques.

    Two assessment techniques are described: eco-maps and genograms. An eco-map provides a snapshot view of important family interactions at a particular point in time. A genogram, essentially a family tree, is a graphic way of investigating the origins of family problems over at least three generations.

4. Comprehend aspects of families for workers to focus on.

    In assessing families, and providing services to families, there are certain aspects of families that provide significant information about their challenges, and about their strengths. Frequently, the strengths (assets and resources) can be utilized to resolve their challenges, and to enhance their overall functioning. Aspects that social workers should attend to are: verbal communication patterns; nonverbal communication patterns; family roles; personal goals and family goals; norms and cultural values; and culturagrams.

5. Describe family problems and the social work services available to families.

    An infinite number of problems can occur in families. Problems with families tend to be clustered in four categories: marital problems; parent/child relationship difficulties; personal problems of individual family members; and stresses imposed on the family by the external environment. When there are problems in a family, social services are often needed. There is extensive variation in the types and forms of services that social workers provide to troubled families.

EXERCISES

1. An Eco-Map of My Family

Goal: To gain insight into the dynamics of families using eco-maps.

Step 1:   Draw an eco-map of your family.

Step 2:   Volunteers share and describe their eco-maps.

Step 3:   Class discussion about problems encountered and the merits and shortcomings of eco-maps.

2. A Genogram of My Family

Goal: To gain insight into the dynamics of families using genograms.

Step 1:   Draw a genogram of your family. This genogram should be prepared outside of class.

Step 2:   Volunteers share and describe their genograms.

Step 3:   Class discussion on the problems encountered and the merits and shortcomings of genograms.

3. Family Counseling

Goal: To demonstrate the dynamics taking place in family counseling.

Step 1: The instructor states the purpose of the exercise. Four students are asked to volunteer to role play the following roles.

Keith is the father and husband in the family. The family bought a house three years ago and struggle financially to make the monthly mortgage payments. Keith is 44 years old and was a salesman for a new car dealership in the community. The community has encountered serious economic challenges, as a General Motors plant closed its doors about 6 months ago; the GM plant was the financial "life line" for the community. Sales of new cars for Keith's dealership have plummeted in recent months, and Keith's job has been terminated. The family is now struggling to pay their bills.

Monica is the mother and wife in the family. She is 39 years old and has been a dental assistant for the past 13 years. Monica has a sister, Cheri, who has recently approached Monica, asking her if she would be willing to be a surrogate mother for her and her husband, Karl. Cheri and Karl have been trying to have a child for the past 6 years and now have been medically found to be "infertile." Cheri and Karl live in a neighboring state and are financially secure; Cheri is a real estate agent and Karl is an attorney. The proposed surrogacy would be a gestational surrogacy, in which a transfer of a previously created embryo (from Cheri and Karl) would be transferred to Monica in a medical setting. Cheri and Karl state they will pay for all the medical expenses and give Keith and Monica $20,000.

Kimberly is the daughter and is 16 years old. Academically she is doing well in high school. She wants to go to college but is worried about how to financially pay for attending college. She has been dating Richard for the past 5 months and is now worried she may be pregnant. She has not told her parents about this concern but is hoping to subtly reveal this concern in family counseling.

Jason is the son and is 15 years old. He is a good athlete, in both basketball and baseball. He was on the junior varsity basketball team but was recently suspended because of his low grades. He has not informed his family, as yet, of his suspension. Academically he was doing "OK" a year ago, but with his father losing his job, he questions whether working hard in school really pays off. Also, he is at an age where he is often embarrassed at being seen with his parents or his sister—he thinks they are "not cool."

Monica states to the family that she would like to be a surrogate for Cheri and Karl; she adds that financially this may be an answer to the family's financial crisis. Keith, Kimberly, and Jason are shocked that Monica wants to be a surrogate mother. Each has a number of questions as to what it would mean to each of them, and to the family. Heated arguments occur, and the family decides to seek family counseling.

Step 2: The instructor asks for two volunteers to be the family counselors. This family counseling situation is then role played.

Step 3: The instructor than asks the class's reactions to the role play. In addition, the instructor asks the class to state what the "family counselors" did well, and what they might have done differently.

4. Analyzing Your Family in Terms of Group Concepts

Goal: To analyze your family in terms of the group concepts described in this text. It is expected students will gain a better understanding of how their family is structured and how it functions from this exercise.

Step 1: The leader explains the purpose of the exercise, indicates it is a visualization exercise, and state the following, pausing briefly after each question.

I want you to get in a comfortable position, and close your eyes . . . take a couple of deep breaths, and relax. . . . Keep your eyes closed during this exercise. . . . I want you to think of your family as I ask you a number of questions. . . . Who is the primary leader in your family? . . . Who makes most of the major decisions in your family? . . . Is the primary leader autocratic, democratic, or laissez faire? . . . Is leadership distributed among different family members in different areas as suggested by the distributed functions theory? . . . Who is generally the task specialist? . . . Who is generally the social-emotional specialist? . . . Who has the most power in your family? . . . For this power person, what is the basis of this power? Is it reward power, coercive power, legitimate power, expert power, or referent power? . . .

What are the rules or norms that exist in your family about: dating, drug and alcohol use, acceptable sexual behaviors, the way you dress, religious expectations, expectations about going to college? . . . Who set these rules or norms, and how were they set? . . . What is your role in your family? . . .

How are disputes usually settled in your family? . . . Is a win-lose approach used or is a problem-solving approach generally used? . . . Are major decisions made by consensus, by simple majority voting, or are they made autocratically? . . . Do members use active listening to further communications? . . . Is the role reversal technique used to foster communication and to settle disputes? . . . Whe your father is angry, how does he communicate his anger nonverbally? . . . When your mother is angry, how does she communicate her anger nonverbally? . . . Do members seek to express their irritations to others or do members seek to hide their irritations in order to attempt to avoid conflict? . . . Does your family have a cooperative atmosphere or a competitive atmosphere? . . . One person can destroy the morale in a family—has this occurred in your family? . . . Think about each family member—who is generally nonassertive, who is usually aggressive, and who is generally assertive?

What are the major sources of stress in your family at the present time? . . . What different stress management techniques are used in your family—such as meditation, positive thinking, exercising, taking vacations, rewarding yourself with personal goodies, taking mental health days, using support groups, talking problems out with others, seeking to change distressing events, seeking to challenge and change negative and irrational thinking? . . .

Probably every person is grieving about something: what are the members of your family grieving about? . . . What are the usual ways of handling grief in your family? . . .

Are some members of your family presently chemically dependent? . . . If so, how are other members of your family reacting to the dependency—for example, are they enablers, are they trying to ignore the problem, are they fighting about it? . . . What can realistically be done to help to reduce problems in this area? . . .

Do the different members of your family have a fairly well thought-out sense of who they are? . . . Do the different members have generally a positive sense of self? . . . For those who have a low self-concept, what might realistically be done to improve their sense of self? . . .

What are the family values about religion, sexual behavior, chemical use, going to college, smoking, whom you associate with, racial integration, politics, majoring in social work?

Do members of your family generally communicate openly with each other? . . . Do some members send vague, indirect messages? . . . Do some members send double bind messages? . . . Are some members afraid to express their needs and desires? . . . How can communication be improved in your family? . . . My questions have ended. Take a minute or two to relax, and then open your eyes.

Step 2: The students discuss whether such concepts are useful in helping them to analyze and better understand their families. Students are invited to share a family situation—such as seeking ideas on how to deal with parents who are autocratic, or how to handle the problems created by someone who is chemically dependent. The students discuss the merits of this exercise.

SOCIAL WORK WITH ORGANIZATIONS

The word *organization* as used here refers to a collectivity of individuals gathered together to serve a particular purpose. The purposes (or goals) that people organize to achieve are infinite in number, ranging from obtaining basic necessities to eliminating the threat of worldwide terrorism or attaining world peace. In each case, an organization exists because people working together can better accomplish tasks and achieve goals than one individual can. Etzioni (1964) described the importance of organizations in our lives:

> We are born in organizations, educated by organizations, and most of us spend much of our lives working for organizations. We spend much of our leisure time paying, playing, and praying in organizations. Most of us will die in an organization, and when the time comes for burial, the largest organization of all—the state—must grant official permission. (p. 1)

Netting, Kettner, and McMurtry (1998) summarized the importance of organizations for social work practice:

> As social workers, our roles within, interactions with, and attempts to manipulate organizations define much of what we do. Clients often come to us seeking help because they are not able to obtain help from organizations that are critical to their survival or quality of life. In turn, the resources we attempt to gain for these clients usually come from still other organizations. . . . Social workers with little or no idea of how organizations operate, how they interact, or how they can be influenced and changed from both outside and inside are likely to be severely limited in their effectiveness. (pp. 193–194)

Although many disciplines (including business, psychology, political science, and sociology) have produced a prodigious amount of theory and research on organizations, the amount of social work literature devoted to organizations is limited, despite the importance of organizations to social work practice. One significant reference in this area is *Social Work Macro Practice*, 5th edition (Netting, Kettner, McMurtry, & Thorman, 2015). Another is *Generalist Practice with Organizations and Communities*, 6th edition (Kirst-Ashman & Hull, 2014).

One subcategory of organizations that is particularly relevant to social work is social agencies. Most social workers are employed by social agencies.

This chapter provides an introduction to social work practice with organizations. This chapter will help prepare students to:

Understand models of organizational behavior
Describe value orientations in organizational decision making
Compare liberalism and conservatism
Understand guidelines for thriving and surviving in a bureaucracy

Exercise 9.1: Appreciating Organizations

Goal: This exercise is designed to increase your interest in participating in organizations and to increase your interest in learning how to thrive in an organization.

Step 1:   Many of my social work students tell me they want to work with individuals, families, and small groups. They also tell me they have little interest in learning about organizations. Please specify your interest (from 1 to 5, with 5 being high) in learning about organizations. Also, give a rationale for your rating.

Step 2:   We have all participated in a number of organizations—schools, clubs at schools, business or social service agencies we have worked for, church organizations, boys and girls organizations (such as Boy Scouts and Girl Scouts). If you are studying to be a social worker, you will have a field placement at an agency and probably will be seeking a job at a social work agency (organization) after you graduate. List three organizations that you have enjoyed participating in, and also briefly describe why you enjoyed participating in each of these.

Step 3:   You will probably be spending most of your career in working for a social work agency: Is it to your benefit to learn about organizations and to learn how to thrive in an organization?

_____ Yes

_____ No

MODELS OF ORGANIZATIONAL BEHAVIOR

The Autocratic Model

The autocratic model has existed for thousands of years. During the Industrial Revolution, it was the prominent model of organizational function. The model depends on *power*. Those who are in power act autocratically. The message to employees is "You do this—or else," meaning that employees who don't follow orders are penalized, often severely.

The autocratic model uses one-way communication—from the top down to workers. Management believes that it knows best. The employees' obligation is to follow orders. The thinking is that employees have to be persuaded, directed, and pushed into performance; this is management's task. Management does the thinking, and the workers obey the directives. Under autocratic conditions, the workers' role is *obedience* to management.

The autocratic model is very effective in some settings. Military organizations throughout the world are formulated on this model. The model was also used during the Industrial Revolution—for example, in building great railroad systems and in operating giant steel mills. Today, it is a legitimate question to wonder whether modern models of organizational behavior might not have worked better in these historic endeavors.

The autocratic model has a number of disadvantages. Workers are often in the best position to identify shortcomings in the structure and technology of the organizational system, but one-way communication prevents feedback to management. The model also fails to generate commitment among workers to accomplish organizational goals. Finally, the model fails to motivate workers to further develop their skills (skills that often would be highly beneficial to the employer).

Exercise 9.2: Working in an Autocratic Organization

Goal: This exercise is designed to assist you in understanding the merits and shortcomings of the autocratic model.

Step 1:   Describe your experiences in working or participating in an organization in which your supervisor, coach, or teacher used the autocratic approach. (Perhaps it was a job where you waited tables; perhaps it was a team sport where you had an autocratic coach; perhaps it was a teacher or a member of the clergy.)

Step 2:   Summarize your thoughts about the benefits and shortcomings of having an autocratic leader.

The Custodial Model

Many decades ago when the autocratic model was the predominant model of organizational behavior, some progressive managers began to study their employees and soon found that the autocratic model had disturbing side effects. Employees felt insecure about their continued employment, were frustrated, and had feelings of aggression toward management. They could not express their discontent directly, so they expressed it indirectly. Among other things, employees sabotaged production. Davis and Newstrom (1989) described sabotage in a wood-processing plant:

> Managers treated workers crudely, sometimes even to the point of physical abuse. Since employees could not strike back directly for fear of losing their jobs, they found another way to do it. They *symbolically* fed their supervisor to a log-shredding machine! They did this by purposely destroying good sheets of veneer, which made the supervisor look bad when monthly efficiency reports were prepared. (p. 31)

In the 1890s and 1900s, progressive employers thought that if these feelings could be alleviated, employees might work harder, which would increase productivity. To satisfy employees' security needs, a number of companies began to provide welfare programs, such as pension programs, child-care centers at the workplace, health insurance, and life insurance. However, researchers found that the custodial approach leads to dependence on the organization. According to Davis and Newstrom (1989, p. 31), "If employees have ten years of seniority under the union contract and a good pension program, they cannot afford to quit even if the grass looks greener somewhere else!"

Employees working under a custodial model tend to focus on economic rewards and benefits. They are happier and more content than under the autocratic model, but they don't have a high commitment to helping the organization accomplish its goals. They give *passive cooperation* to their employer. The model's most evident flaw is that most employees produce substantially below their capacities. They are not motivated to advance to higher capacities. Employees don't feel fulfilled or motivated. The point here is that contented employees are not necessarily the most productive employees.

The Scientific Management Model

One of the earliest and most important schools of thought on the management of workplace functions and tasks was based on the work of Frederick W. Taylor (1947). Taylor was a mechanical engineer, an American industrialist, and an educator. He focused primarily on management techniques that would increase productivity. He asserted that many organizational problems were the result of misunderstandings between managers and workers. Managers erroneously thought that workers were lazy and unemotional, and they mistakenly believed they understood workers' jobs. Workers mistakenly thought that managers only wanted to exploit them.

To solve these problems, Taylor developed the *scientific management model*, which focused on the need for managers to conduct scientific analyses of the workplace. One of the first steps was to conduct a careful study of how each job could best be accomplished. An excellent way to do this, according to Taylor, was to identify the best workers for each job and then carefully study how they effectively and efficiently did the work. The goal of this analysis was to discover the optimal way of doing the job—in Taylor's words, the "one best way." Once this best way was identified, tools could be modified to better complete the work, workers' abilities and interests could be fitted to particular job assignments, and the level of production that the average worker could sustain could be gauged.

Once the level of production for the average worker was determined, the next step was to provide incentives to increase productivity. Taylor's favorite strategy for doing this was the piece-rate wage: Workers were paid for each unit they produced. The goals of management were to produce more units, reduce unit cost, increase organizational productivity and profitability, and provide incentives for workers to produce more.

Taylor's work has been criticized as having a techniques bias because it tends to treat workers as little more than cogs in a wheel. No two workers are exactly alike, so the "one best way" of doing a job is often unique to the person doing it. Actually, forcing the same work approach on different workers may actually decrease both productivity and worker satisfaction. In addition, Taylor's approach has limited application to human services. Each client is unique—with unique needs, unique environmental impacting factors, and unique strengths and capacities—so each human services case has to be individualized, and therefore it is difficult (if not impossible) to specify the "one best way" to proceed.

The Human Relations Model

In 1927, the Hawthorne Works of the Western Electric Company in Chicago began a series of experiments designed to discover ways to increase worker satisfaction and worker productivity (Roethlisberger & Dickson, 1939). Hawthorne Works manufactured telephones on an assembly-line basis. Workers needed no special skills and performed simple, repetitive tasks. The workers were not unionized, and management sought to find ways to increase productivity. If job satisfaction could be increased, employees would work more efficiently, and productivity would then increase.

The company tested the effects on productivity of a number of factors: rest breaks, better lighting, changes in the number of work hours, changes in the wages paid, improved food facilities, and so on. The results were surprising. Productivity increased, as expected, with improved working conditions; but it also increased when working conditions worsened. This latter finding was unexpected and led to additional study.

The investigators discovered that participation in the experiments was extremely attractive to the workers. They felt they had been selected by management for their individual abilities, and so they worked harder even when working conditions became less favorable. In addition, the workers' morale and general attitude toward work improved because they felt they were receiving special attention. By participating in this study, the workers were able to work in smaller groups and became involved in making decisions. Working in smaller groups created a stronger sense of solidarity with their fellow workers. Being involved in decision making decreased their feelings of meaninglessness and powerlessness about their work.

In sociological and psychological research, the results of this study have become known as the *Hawthorne effect*. In essence, when subjects know they are participants in a study, this awareness leads them to behave differently and substantially influences the results.

The results of this study, and of other similar studies, led some researchers to conclude that the key variables affecting productivity are social factors. Etzioni (1964, pp. 34–35) summarized some of the basic tenets of the human relations approach:

- The level of production is set by social norms, not by physiological capacities.
- Noneconomic rewards and sanctions significantly affect the behavior of the workers and largely limit the effect of economic incentive plans.
- Workers do not act or react as individuals but as members of groups.
- The role of leadership is important in understanding social factors in organizations, and this leadership may be either formal or informal.

Numerous studies provide evidence to support these tenets (Netting, Kettner, & McMurtry, 2003).

Workers who are capable of greater productivity often will not excel because they are unwilling to exceed the "average" level set by the norms of the group, even if this means earning less. Studies have also found that attempts by management to influence workers' behaviors are often more successful if targeted at the group as a whole, rather than at individuals. Finally, studies have documented the importance of informal leadership in influencing workers' behavior in ways that can either amplify or negate formal leadership directives. This model asserts that managers who succeed in increasing productivity are most likely responsive to the workers' social needs.

One criticism of the human relations model is (surprisingly) that it tends to manipulate, dehumanize, oppress, and exploit workers. The model leads to the conclusion that management can increase productivity by helping workers become content rather than by increasing economic rewards for higher productivity. It concentrates power and decision making at the top. It is not intended to empower employees in the decision-making process or to assist them in acquiring genuine participation in running the organization. The practice of dealing with people on the basis of their perceived social relationships in the workplace may also be a factor in perpetuating the "good old boys" network; this network has disadvantaged women and people of color over the years. Another criticism of the human relations approach is that a happy workforce is not necessarily a productive workforce, because the norms for worker production may be set well below the workers' levels of capability.

Theory X and Theory Y

Douglas McGregor (1960) developed two theories of management. He theorized that management thinking and behavior are based on two different sets of assumptions, which he labeled Theory X and Theory Y.

Theory X managers view employees as incapable of much growth. Employees are perceived as having an inherent dislike for work and as attempting to evade work whenever possible. Therefore, X-type managers believe they must control, direct, force, or threaten employees to make them work. Employees are also viewed as having relatively little ambition, wishing to avoid responsibilities, and preferring to be directed. Theory X managers therefore spell out job responsibilities carefully, set work goals without employee input, use external rewards (such as money) to force employees to work, and punish those who deviate from established rules. Because Theory X managers reduce responsibilities to a level at which few mistakes can be made, work usually becomes so structured that it is monotonous and distasteful. These assumptions, of course, are inconsistent with what behavioral scientists assert are effective principles for directing, influencing, and motivating people. (Theory X managers are, in essence, adhering to an autocratic model of organizational behavior.)

In contrast, *Theory Y managers* view employees as wanting to grow and develop by exerting physical and mental effort to accomplish work objectives to which they are committed. These managers believe that the promise of internal rewards, such as self-respect and personal improvement, are stronger motivators than external rewards (money) and punishment. They also believe that under proper conditions, employees will not only accept responsibility but seek it. Most employees are assumed to have considerable ingenuity, creativity, and imagination for problem solving. Therefore, they are given considerable responsibility to test the limits of their capabilities. Mistakes and errors are viewed as necessary phases of the learning process, and work is structured so employees have a sense of accomplishment and growth.

Employees who work for Y-type managers are generally more creative and productive, experience greater work satisfaction, and are more highly motivated than employees who work for X-type managers. Under both management styles, expectations often become self-fulfilling prophecies.

Exercise 9.3: Theory X Managers versus Theory Y Managers

Goal: This exercise is designed to assist you in understanding the merits and shortcomings of these two styles of management.

Step 1: Describe someone you have interacted with who relates to others as depicted by Theory X. (This person may have been a manager, coach, teacher, or member of your family). Describe your reactions to interacting with this person.

Step 2: Describe someone you have interacted with who relates to others as depicted by Theory Y. Describe your reactions to interacting with this person.

Step 3: Summarize your views on the merits and shortcomings of relating to others according to Theory X.

Step 4: Summarize your views on the merits and shortcomings of relating to others according to Theory Y.

The Collegial Model

A useful extension of Theory Y, the *collegial model* emphasizes the team concept. It involves employees working closely together and feeling a commitment to achieve a common purpose. Some organizations—such as university departments, research laboratories, and most human services organizations—have a goal of creating a collegial atmosphere to facilitate achieving their purposes. (Sadly, many such organizations are unsuccessful in creating such an atmosphere.)

Creating a collegial atmosphere is highly dependent on management building a feeling of partnership with employees. When such a partnership develops, employees feel needed and useful. Managers are then viewed as joint contributors rather than as bosses. Management is the *coach* who builds a better team. Davis and Newstrom (1989) described some of the approaches to developing a team concept:

> The feeling of partnerships can be built in many ways. Some organizations have abolished the use of reserved parking spaces for executives, so every employee has an equal chance of finding one close to the workplace. Some firms have tried to eliminate the use of terms like "bosses" and "subordinates," feeling that those terms simply create perceptions of psychological distance between managers and nonmanagers. Other employers have removed time clocks, set up "fun committees," sponsored company canoe trips, or required managers to spend a week or two annually working in field or factory locations. All of these approaches are designed to build a spirit of mutuality, in which every person makes contributions and appreciates those of others. (p. 34)

If the sense of partnership is developed, employees produce quality work and seek to cooperate with coworkers, not because management directs them to do so but because they feel an internal obligation to produce high-quality work. The collegial approach thus leads to a sense of *self-discipline*. In this environment, employees are more likely to have a sense of fulfillment, to feel self-actualized, and to produce higher-quality work.

Theory Z

William Ouchi described the Japanese style of management in his 1981 best seller *Theory Z: How American Business Can Meet the Japanese Challenge.* In the late 1970s and early 1980s, the U.S. business world focused on the Japanese approach to management, as markets long dominated by American firms (such as the automobile industry) were taken over by Japanese industries. Japanese industrial organizations had rapidly overcome their earlier reputation for poor-quality work and were selling worldwide standards for quality and durability.

Ouchi asserted that *Theory Z*, the theoretical principles underlying the Japanese style of management, went beyond Theory Y. A business organization in Japan is more than the profitability-oriented entity that it is in the United States. It is a way of life. It provides lifetime employment. It is enmeshed with the nation's political, social, and economic network. Furthermore, its influence spills over into many other organizations, such as nursery schools, elementary and secondary schools, and universities.

The basic philosophy of Theory Z is that involved and committed workers are the key to increased productivity. Ideas and suggestions about how to improve the organization are routinely solicited and implemented, where feasible. One strategy for accomplishing this is the *quality circle*, where employees and management routinely meet to brainstorm about ways to improve productivity and quality.

In contrast to American organizations, Japanese organizations don't have written objectives or organizational charts. Most work is done in teams, and decisions are made by consensus. The teams tend to function without a designated leader. Cooperation within units, and between units, is emphasized. Loyalty to the organization is also emphasized, as is organizational loyalty to the employee.

Experiments designed to transplant Japanese-style management to the United States have met with mixed success. In most cases, American organizations have concluded that Theory Z probably works quite well in a homogeneous culture that has Japan's societal values, but some components do not fit well with the more heterogeneous and individualistic character of the United States. In addition, some firms in volatile industries (such as electronics) have difficulty balancing their desire to provide lifetime employment with the need to adjust their workforces to meet rapidly changing market demands.

Exercise 9.4: Understanding Theory Z

Goal: This exercise is designed to assist you in understanding Theory Z.

Step 1:   Summarize the benefits or merits of a social agency using a Theory Z approach with its employees.

Step 2:   Summarize the shortcomings of a social agency using a Theory Z approach with its employees.

Management by Objectives

Fundamental to the core of an organization is its purpose—that is, the commonly shared understanding of the reason for its existence. Management theorist Peter Drucker (1954) proposed a strategy for making organizational goals and objectives the central construct around which organizational life is designed to function. In other words, instead of focusing on employee needs and wants or on organizational structure as the ways to increase efficiency and productivity, Drucker proposed beginning with the desired outcome and working backward. The strategy is first to identify the organizational objectives or goals and then to adapt the organizational tasks, resources, and structure to meet those objectives. This *management by objectives* (MBO) approach is designed to focus the organization's efforts on meeting these objectives. Success is determined, then, by the degree to which stated objectives are reached.

This approach can be applied to the organization as a whole, as well as to internal divisions or departments. When the MBO approach is applied to internal divisions, the objectives set for each division should be consistent and supportive of the overall organizational objectives.

In many areas, including human services, the MBO approach can also be applied to the cases being serviced by each employee. Goals are set with each client, tasks to meet these goals are then determined, and deadlines are set for completion of these tasks. The degree of success of each case is then determined at a later date (often when a case is closed) by the extent to which stated goals were achieved.

An adaptation of the MBO approach, called *strategic planning and budgeting* (SPB), became popular in the 1990s and early 2000s. The process involves first specifying the overall vision or mission of an organization, then identifying a variety of more specific objectives or plans for achieving that vision, and finally adapting the resources to meet the specific high-priority objectives or plans. Organizations often hire outside consultants to oversee the SPB process.

One major advantage of the MBO approach for an organization (or its divisions) is that it produces clear statements (made available to all employees) about the objectives and the tasks that are expected to be accomplished in specified time periods. This type of activity tends to improve cooperation and collaboration. The MBO approach is also useful because it provides a guide for allocating resources and a focus for monitoring and evaluating organizational efforts.

An additional benefit of the MBO approach is in the area of diversity in the workplace. Before this approach, those responsible for hiring failed to employ women and people of color in significant numbers. As affirmative action programs were developed within organizations, the MBO approach was widely used to set specific hiring goals and objectives. The result was significant changes in recruitment approaches that enabled women and minorities to secure employment.

Exercise 9.5: Understanding Management by Objectives

Goal: This exercise is designed to assist you in understanding the MBO approach.

Step 1: Summarize the benefits or merits of a social agency using the MBO approach.

Step 1: Summarize the shortcomings of a social agency using the MBO approach.

Total Quality Management

The theorist most closely associated with developing the concept of total quality management (TQM) is W. Edwards Deming (1986). Deming formed many of his theories during World War II when he developed statistical methods to speed up military production. Deming taught the Japanese his theories of quality control and continuous improvement after World War II, and he is now recognized, along with J. Juran (1989) and others, for laying the groundwork for Japan's postwar industrial and economic boom.

Omachonu and Ross (1994) defined *total quality management* as follows: "The integration of all functions and processes within an organization in order to achieve continuous improvement of the quality of goods and services. The goal is customer satisfaction" (p. 1). TQM is based on a number of ideas. It means thinking about the quality of every function of the enterprise and is a start-to-finish process that integrates interrelated functions at all levels. It is a systems approach that considers every interaction between the various elements of the organization. TQM asserts that in many businesses and organizations, management makes the mistake of blaming what goes wrong on individual people, not on the system. TQM, instead, affirms the *85/15 rule*: In an organization, 85% of the problems can be corrected only by changing systems (structures, rules, practices, expectations, and traditions that are largely determined by management), and less than 15% can be resolved by correcting individual workers. When problems arise, TQM managers look for causes in the system and work to remove them before casting blame on workers.

TQM asserts that quality depends on continuous improvement of all of the organizations processes that lead to customer satisfaction. Customer satisfaction is the main objective of the organization. The customer is not merely the "point of sale"; the customer is part of the design and production process. Therefore, customers' needs must be monitored continuously.

Numerous organizations have adopted TQM to improve their goods and services. One reason for the emphasis on quality is that more and more consumers are shunning mass-produced, poorly made, disposable products. Companies are realizing that to remain competitive in global markets, high-quality products and services are essential.

There are a variety of approaches to TQM. For a summary of these approaches, see *Principles of Total Quality* (Omachonu & Ross, 1994). In regard to human service agencies, the following are guiding principles of TQM:

■ The first and major principle is to satisfy the customer. The customer is the one paying for the service (which may be the funding source, or if it is paying clients—then it would be these clients). Human service agencies satisfy customers by providing them value for funds they provide. The agencies that provide value for what the customers buy will get more repeat business, referral business, and will have reduced complaints and reduced service expenses. Human service agencies should ask funders what they need, and provide more of what they ask for.

- Human service agencies should instill pride into every employee. Helping every employee to enjoy his or her work will lead to higher motivation of employees to do well, which will result in these agencies becoming more productive. Agencies should provide a forum or seek to create high morale at work so that employees at all levels feel free to voice their opinions when they think they have good ideas. Agencies should review the suggestions and implement the best ones. Employees should be inspired, and empowered, to do their best. The number of layers of authority should be reduced to enhance employee empowerment. A focus of human service agencies should be to instill pride into every employee.
- Complaints from customers or from employees should be viewed as opportunities for improvement. In reviewing a complaint, or a suggestion, the focus should be on quality evaluative information and data, rather than on opinions or egos.
- Supervisors should seek to keep their supervisees happy and productive by providing good task suggestions, the tools they need to do their job, and good working conditions. Supervisors should also reward productive employees with praise and good pay.
- Employees are an excellent source of continuous improvements. They often can provide suggestions on how to improve a system/process and eliminate waste or unnecessary work.

These principles give a "flavor" of TQM.

Summary Comments about Models of Organizational Behavior

The question of which model to apply to obtain the highest productivity depends on the tasks to be completed and on employee needs and expectations. For example, the autocratic model works well in military operations, where quick decisions are needed to respond to rapidly changing crises, but it does not work well in human services organizations in which employees expect Theory Y management style.

In addition, some of these models or approaches can be applied simultaneously. For example, management by objectives can be used at the same time that an organization is using any of the other models described here.

VALUE ORIENTATIONS IN ORGANIZATIONAL DECISION MAKING

In theory, decision making about organizational objectives and goals is a rational process, including identifying problems, specifying resource limitations, weighing advantages and disadvantages of proposed solutions, and selecting the resolution strategy with the fewest risks and the greatest chance of success. In practice, subjective influences (particularly value orientations) can derail the rational process. Most people tend to believe that decisions are made primarily on the basis of objective facts and figures. Decision makers, however, bring not only their objective knowledge and expertise to the decision-making process but also their value orientations, unique attitudes, feelings, biases, and vested interests. Values and assumptions form the bases of most decisions, and facts and figures are used to justify and reinforce these values and assumptions.

Consider the following questions pertinent to providing social services. What do they indicate about how we make our most important decisions?

Should abortion be permitted or prohibited during the first weeks following conception?

Should same-sex behavior be viewed as a natural expression of sexuality?

When does harsh discipline of a child become child abuse?

Should the primary objective of imprisonment be rehabilitation or retribution?

Answers to these questions usually are based not on data uncovered after careful research but on individual beliefs about the value of life, personal freedom, and protective social standards.

Even everyday decisions are based largely on values, and practically every decision also rests on assumptions. Without assumptions, nothing could be proved. Assumptions are made in every research study to test any hypothesis. For example, analysts conducting a market survey assume that the instruments they use (such as a questionnaire) will be valid and reliable. But it cannot even be proved that the sun will rise in the east tomorrow without assuming that history provides the proof.

The term *value orientation* refers to an individual's personal ideas about what is desirable and worthwhile. Most values are acquired through prior learning experiences in interactions with family, friends, educators, organizations such as churches, and anyone else who has made an impression on a person's thinking.

The philosopher Edward Spranger (1928) believed that most people eventually come to rely on one of six value orientations:

1. *Theoretical:* A person with a theoretical orientation strives toward a rational, systematic ordering of knowledge. Personal preference does not count as much as being able to classify, compare, contrast, and interrelate various pieces of information. The theoretical person places value on simply knowing what is—and why.

2. *Economic:* An economic orientation places primary value on the utility of things, and practical uses of knowledge are given foremost attention. Proposed plans of action are assessed in terms of their costs and benefits. If the costs outweigh the benefits, the economic-oriented person is not likely to support the plan.

3. *Aesthetic:* An aesthetic orientation is grounded in an appreciation of artistic values, and personal preferences for form, harmony, and beauty are influential in making decisions. Because the experience of single events is considered an important end in itself, reactions to aesthetic qualities will frequently be expressed.

4. *Social:* A social orientation is an empathetic one that values other people as ends in themselves. Concern for the welfare of people pervades the behavior of the socially oriented decision maker, and primary consideration is given to the quality of human relationships.

5. *Political:* A political orientation involves a concern for identifying where power lies. Conflict and competition are seen as normal elements of group activity. Decisions and their outcomes are assessed in terms of how much power is obtained and by whom because influence over others is a valued goal.

6. *Religious:* A person with a religious orientation is directed by a desire to relate to the universe in some meaningful way. Personal beliefs about an "absolute good" or "higher order" are employed to determine the value of things, and decisions and their outcomes are placed into the context of such beliefs.

Although it is possible for a person to hold values in all six orientations, each person tends to favor one orientation when making decisions.

Exercise 9.6: Understanding Six Value Orientations

Goal: This exercise is designed to assist you in understanding which value orientations you tend to use in your decision making.

Step 1:   Review the description of the theoretical, economic, aesthetic, social, political, and religious value orientations. Specify which orientations have the greatest effect on the major life decisions that you make.

Step 2:   Indicate why you selected the value orientations that you identified in step 1.

LIBERALISM VERSUS CONSERVATISM

Two value orientations that have major impacts on human services organizations are liberalism and conservatism. The decisions that politicians and other decision makers make about human service issues often reflect their adherence to liberal or conservative principles.

Conservatives emphasize tradition and believe that rapid change usually results in more negative than positive consequences. Conservatives feel that government should not interfere with the workings of the marketplace. They encourage the government to support (for example, through tax incentives) rather than regulate business and industry. A free-market economy is thought to be the best way to ensure prosperity and fulfillment of individual needs. Conservatives embrace the adage "Government governs best which governs least." They believe that most government activities pose grave threats to individual liberty and to the smooth functioning of the free market.

Conservatives generally take a residual approach to social welfare programs (see Chapter 2 for a fuller description of the residual and institutional approaches to social welfare programs). They believe that dependency is a result of personal failure and that it is natural for inequality to exist among humans. They assert that the family, the church, and gainful employment should be the primary defenses against dependency. Social welfare should be a temporary function, they assert, that is used sparingly, because prolonged social welfare assistance leads recipients to become permanently dependent. Conservatives believe that charity is a moral virtue and that the "fortunate" are obligated to help the "less fortunate" become productive, contributing citizens in a society. If governmental funds are provided for health and social welfare services, conservatives advocate that such funding go to private organizations, which they believe are more effective and efficient than public agencies in providing services.

In contrast, liberals believe that change is generally good, as it brings progress, and that moderate change is best. They view society as needing regulation to ensure fair competition among various interests. In particular, a free-market economy is viewed as needing regulation to ensure fairness. Government programs, including social welfare programs, are viewed as necessary to help meet basic human needs. Liberals advocate government action to remedy social deficiencies and to improve human welfare. They feel that government regulation and intervention are often necessary to safeguard human rights, to control the excesses of capitalism, and to provide equal opportunities for success. They emphasize egalitarianism and the rights of minorities.

Liberals generally adhere to an institutional view of social welfare. They assert that because modern society has become so fragmented and complex and because traditional institutions (such as the family) have been unable to meet emerging human needs, few individuals can now function without the help of social services (including work training, job location services, child care, health care, and counseling).

Exercise 9.7: Understanding and Applying Liberalism and Conservatism

Goal: This exercise is designed to assist you in understanding your beliefs about liberalism and conservatism.

Step 1:   Specify whether you tend in your political orientation to tilt toward liberalism or conservatism.

Step 2:   Explain your rationale for the political orientation you selected in step l.

THRIVING AND SURVIVING IN A BUREAUCRACY

Basic structural conflicts exist between helping professionals and the bureaucratic systems in which they work. Helping professionals place a high value on creativeness and changing the system to serve clients. Bureaucracies resist change and are most efficient when no one "rocks the boat." Helping professionals seek to personalize services by conveying to each client that "you count as a person." Bureaucracies are highly depersonalized, emotionally detached systems that view every employee and every client as a tiny component of a large system. In a large bureaucracy, employees count *not* as "persons" but only as functional parts of a system. Additional conflicting value orientations between helping professionals and bureaucratic systems are listed in Exhibit 9. l.

Any of these differences in value orientation can become an arena of conflict between helping professionals and the bureaucracies in which they function. Knopf (1979) summarized the potential areas of conflict between bureaucracies and helping professionals:

> The trademarks of a BS (bureaucratic system) are power, hierarchy, and specialization; that is, rules and roles. In essence, the result is depersonalization. The system itself is neither "good" nor "bad"; it is a system. I believe it to be amoral. It is efficient and effective, but in order to be so it must be impersonal in all of its functionings. This then is the location of the stress. The hallmark of the helping professional is a highly individualized, democratic, humanized, relationship-oriented service aimed at self-motivation. The hallmark of a bureaucratic system is a highly impersonalized, valueless (amoral), emotionally detached, hierarchical structure of organization. The dilemma of the HP (helping person) is how to give a personalized service to a client through a delivery system that is not set up in any way to do that. (pp. 21–22)

Numerous helping professionals attribute a "personality" to the bureaucracy. They characterize the bureaucracy as "red tape," "officialism," "uncaring," "cruel," "the enemy." A negative personality is sometimes also attributed to officials, who are derided as "paper shufflers," "rigid," "deadwood," "inefficient," and "unproductive." Knopf (1979) cautioned against this tendency:

> The HP (helping person) . . . may deal with the impersonal nature of the system by projecting values onto it and thereby give the BS (bureaucratic system) a "personality." In this way, we fool ourselves into thinking that we can deal with it in a personal way. Unfortunately, projection is almost always negative and reflects the dark or negative aspects of ourselves. The BS then becomes a screen onto which we vent our anger, sadness, or fright, and while a lot of energy is generated, very little is accomplished. Since the BS is amoral, it is unproductive to place a personality on it. (p. 25)

Exhibit 9.1   Value Conflicts between Helping Professionals and Bureaucracies

Orientations of Helping Professionals	Orientations of Bureaucratic Systems
Desires democratic system for decision making.	Most decisions are made autocratically.
Desires that power be distributed equally among employees (horizontal structure).	Power is distributed vertically.
Desires that clients have considerable power in the system.	Power is held primarily by top executives.
Desires a flexible, changing system.	System is rigid and stable.
Desires that creativity and growth be emphasized.	Emphasis is on structure and the status quo.
Desires a client-oriented focus.	System is organization-centered.
Desires that communication be on a personalized level from person to person.	Communication is from level to level.
Desires shared decision making and shared responsibility structure.	A hierarchical decision-making structure and a hierarchical responsibility structure are characteristic.
Desires that decisions be made by those having the most knowledge.	Decisions are made by the decision-making authority assigned to each position in the hierarchy.
Desires shared leadership.	System uses autocratic leadership.
Believes feelings of clients and employees should be highly valued by the system.	Procedures and processes are highly valued.

In other words, bureaucratic systems are neither good nor bad. They have neither a personality nor a value system. They are simply structures developed to carry out various tasks.

Helping professionals have various emotional responses to these conflicts in orientation with bureaucratic systems.[1] Common reactions are anger at the system, self-blame ("Its all my fault"), sadness and depression ("Poor me"; "Nobody appreciates all I've done"), and fright and paranoia ("They're out to get me"; "If I mess up I'm gone"). Knopf (1979) identified several roles that helping professionals assume in dealing with bureaucracies. **Warriors** lead open campaigns to destroy and malign the system. They discount the value of the system and often enter into a win-lose conflict. Warriors generally lose and are dismissed.

Gossips are covert warriors who complain to others (including clients, politicians, and the news media) about how terrible the system is. Gossips frequently single out a few officials for criticism. Bureaucratic systems often make life very difficult for gossips by assigning them distasteful tasks, refusing to promote them, giving very small salary increases, and perhaps even dismissing them.

Complainers resemble gossips but confine their complaints to other helping persons, to in-house staff, and to family members. Complainers want people to agree so they can find comfort in shared misery. They want to stay with the system and generally do.

Dancers are skillful at ignoring rules and procedures. They are frequently lonely, often reprimanded for incorrectly filling out forms, and have low investment in the system or in helping clients.

Defenders are scared, dislike conflict, and therefore defend the rules, the system, and bureaucratic officials. Defenders are often supervisors and are viewed by others as "bureaucrats."

Machines are "bureaucrats" who take on the orientation of the bureaucracy. Often a machine hasn't been involved in providing direct services for years. They are frequently named to head study committees and policy groups and to chair boards.

---

[1]This description highlights a number of negatives about bureaucratic systems, particularly their impersonalization. In fairness, an advantage of being part of a large bureaucracy is that the potential is there for changing a powerful system to the clients' advantage. In tiny or nonbureaucratic systems, the social worker has lots of freedom but little opportunity or power to influence large systems or mobilize extensive resources on behalf of clients.

Executioners attack persons within an organization with enthusiasm and vigor. They usually have a high energy level and are impulsive. Executioners abuse power by indiscriminately attacking and dismissing not only employees but also services and programs. Executioners have power and are angry (although the anger is disguised and almost always denied). They are not committed to either the value orientation of helping professionals or to the bureaucracy.

Those roles won't get you very far and may destroy your career. There are alternatives, and they do work. Knopf (1979) listed 66 tips on how to survive in a bureaucracy. Some of the most useful suggestions are summarized here:

1. Whenever your needs or the needs of your clients are not met by the bureaucracy, use the following problem-solving approach: (a) Precisely identify your needs (or the needs of clients) that are in conflict with the bureaucracy; this step is defining the problem. (b) Generate a list of possible solutions. Be creative in generating a wide range of solutions. (c) Evaluate the merits and shortcomings of the possible solutions. (d) Select a solution. (e) Implement the solution. (f) Evaluate the solution.

2. Obtain knowledge of how your bureaucracy is structured and how it functions. This knowledge will reduce fear of the unknown, make the system more predictable, and help in identifying rational ways to best meet your needs and those of your clients.

3. Remember that bureaucrats are people who have feelings. Communication gaps are often most effectively reduced if you treat them with as much respect and interest as you treat your clients.

4. If you are at war with the bureaucracy, declare a truce. The system will find a way to dismiss you if you remain at war. With a truce, you can identify and use the strengths of the bureaucracy as an ally, rather than having the strengths being used against you as an enemy.

5. Know your work contract and job expectations. If the expectations are unclear, seek clarity.

6. Continue to develop your knowledge and awareness of specific helping skills. Take advantage of continuing education opportunities (for example, workshops, conferences, courses). Among other advantages, your continued professional development will assist you in being able to contract from a position of competency and skill.

7. Identify your professional strengths and limitations. Knowing your limitations will increase your ability to avoid undertaking responsibilities that are beyond your competencies.

8. Be aware that you can't change everything, so stop trying. In a bureaucracy, focus your change efforts on those aspects that most need change and that you have a fair chance of changing. Stop thinking and complaining about those aspects you cannot change. It is irrational to complain about things that you cannot change or to complain about those things that you do not intend to make an effort to change.

9. Learn how to control your emotions in your interactions with the bureaucracy. Emotions that are counterproductive (such as most angry outbursts) particularly need to be controlled. Doing a rational self-analysis on unwanted emotions (Module 1) is one way of gaining control of your unwanted emotions. Learning how to respond to stress in your personal life will also prepare you to handle stress at work better.

10. Develop and use a sense of humor. Humor takes the edge off adverse conditions and reduces negative feelings.

11. Learn to accept your mistakes and perhaps even to laugh at some of them. No one is perfect.

12. Take time to enjoy and develop a support system with your coworkers.

13. Acknowledge your mistakes and give in sometimes on minor matters. You may not be right, and giving in sometimes allows other people to do the same.

14. Keep yourself physically fit and mentally alert. Learn to use approaches that will reduce stress and prevent burnout (see Chapter 14).

15. Leave your work at the office. If you have urgent unfinished bureaucratic business, do it before leaving work or don't leave.

16. Occasionally take your supervisor and other administrators to lunch. Socializing prevents isolation and facilitates your involvement with and understanding of the system.

17. Do not seek self-actualization or ego satisfaction from the bureaucracy. A depersonalized system is incapable of providing this. Only you can satisfy your ego and become self-actualized.

18. Make speeches to community groups that accentuate the positives about your agency. Do not hesitate to ask after speeches that a thank-you letter be sent to your supervisor or agency director.

19. If you have a problem involving the bureaucracy, discuss it with other employees; focus on problem solving rather than on complaining. Groups are much more powerful and productive than an individual working alone to make changes in a system.
20. No matter how high you rise in a hierarchy, maintain direct service contact. Direct contact keeps you abreast of changing client needs, prevents you from getting stale, and keeps you attuned to the concerns of employees in lower levels of the hierarchy
21. Do not try to change everything in the system at once. Attacking too much will overextend you and lead to burnout. Start small and be selective and specific. Double-check your facts to make certain they accurately prove your position before confronting bureaucratic officials.
22. Identify your career goals and determine whether they can be met in this system. If the answer is no, then (a) change your goals, (b) change the bureaucracy, or (c) seek a position elsewhere in which your goals can be met.

Exercise 9.8: Understanding the Orientations of Bureaucratic Systems

Goal: This exercise is designed to assist you in understanding the value conflicts between helping professionals and top management people in bureaucracies.

Step 1:   Imagine yourself in the shoes of a top management person in a bureaucracy Describe why such a person is likely to choose to adhere to the "orientations of bureaucratic systems."

Step 2:   Imagine yourself in the shoes of a direct service social worker in an agency Describe why this person is likely to adhere to the "orientations of helping professionals."

Step 3:   Summarize the strategies that a direct service social worker should use to survive and thrive in an agency where top management adheres to the "orientations of bureaucratic systems."

SUMMARY

The following summarizes the chapter's content in terms of the learning objectives presented at the beginning of the chapter.

1. Understand models of organizational behavior.
   An organization is a collection of individuals gathered together to serve a particular purpose. This chapter surveys theories that provide a variety of perspectives for viewing and analyzing organizations. The theories covered include the autocratic model, the custodial model, the scientific management model, the human relations model, Theory X, Theory Y, the collegial model, Theory Z, management by objectives, and total quality management. These models are not exhaustive of the numerous models that have been developed. Any of these models can be applied successfully in some situations.
2. Describe value orientations in organizational decision making.
   Values and assumptions (rather than facts and figures) form the bases of most decisions in organizations. Spranger identified six value orientations that frequently have an impact on decision making: theoretical, economic, aesthetic, social, political, and religious.
3. Compare liberalism and conservatism.
   Two diverse value orientations that have major impacts on human service organizations are liberalism and conservatism. Politicians and decision makers often base their decisions on human service issues on whether they adhere to a liberal or conservative philosophy. Conservatives generally advocate a residual approach to social welfare programs, whereas liberals generally take an institutional view of social welfare.
4. Understand guidelines for thriving and surviving in a bureaucracy.
   Knopf (1979) identified numerous potential areas of conflict between bureaucracies and helping professionals. Helping professionals want bureaucratic systems to individualize interactions with clients and employees, to be humanized, to be democratic in decision making, to be relationship oriented, and to quickly change to meet emerging needs. In contrast, bureaucratic systems are generally depersonalized, autocratic, procedures- and process-oriented, emotionally detached, and resistive of change. Such differences in orientations can become arenas of conflict between helping professionals and the systems in which they work. Suggestions are given for surviving and thriving in a bureaucracy.

EXERCISES

1. Hard Choices—Funding Social Programs

Goals: To help students understand that most decisions are based on values and assumptions and to realize that setting budgets for social programs involves hard choices because of scarce resources.

Step 1:   The instructor explains that funding sources (such as the federal, state, and local governments and United Way) have to make difficult choices about how much money to allocate to diverse social programs. Financial resources to fund all social programs are simply unavailable, and some people suffer greatly because they do not receive needed services and funds.

Step 2:   Students form subgroups of five or six members each. The instructor informs each subgroup that it is the funding source for human services in a local community and that it has $10 million to allocate for the following social programs, which requested a total of $15 million. Each subgroup has the task of deciding how much money to allocate to each agency. No subgroup can spend more than $10 million. Read the following material:

The Center for Developmental Disabilities needs $1.5 million to care for adults who have severe or profound cognitive disabilities. These adults have such severe cognitive disabilities that most are unable to walk. It costs $110,000 a year to care for each adult. If the center does not receive its requested funds, some of these clients may not receive necessary medical care and may die.

The Anti-Poverty Agency needs $3.5 million to maintain families at an income level of only 80% of that defined as the poverty line. It costs $20,000 per year to maintain a family of three (generally a single parent with two children). If the agency does not receive its requested funds, many of these families will go hungry, have inadequate shelter, and lack essential clothing for winter.

Protective Services needs $1 million to combat abuse, neglect, and incest. If the agency does not receive all of its needed funds, a number of children will continue to be exposed to abuse, neglect, or incest, which could severely affect them for the rest of their lives.

The Mental Health Center needs $2.5 million to help clients with severe emotional problems, some of whom are so depressed they are suicidal. If the center does not receive all of its needed funds, inadequate services will be provided to clients, and the problems of many clients will intensify. A few may even take their own lives.

The Alcohol and Drug Abuse Treatment Center needs $2 million to help chemically dependent clients and their families. If the center does not receive all of its needed funds, inadequate services will mean that the problems experienced by clients and their families are likely to intensify. Because abuse of alcohol and drugs is a contributing factor to many other problems (such as poverty, mental illness, and family violence), these problems also will intensify.

The Shelter for Battered Women, which is located in a house in a residential area, is requesting $500,000. If funds are cut back, the shelter staff assert they will have to turn away some of the battered wives and their children who request shelter and other services.

Group Homes for Youths runs four group homes: two for young women and two for young men. It needs $500,000. If needed funds are cut back, this agency will have to reduce the number of youths it is serving. Some will be transferred to more expensive residential treatment programs, some will be returned to an unhealthy home environment, and some will simply run away.

The Red Cross needs $1 million for its blood bank and for disaster relief. If funds are cut back, there will be an insufficient supply of blood available for transfusions, and many of the families who are hit by disasters (such as tornadoes and floods) will not be served.

The Rehabilitation Center provides work training and sheltered work to clients with a variety of physical or mental disabilities. It needs $2 million, or it will be forced to turn away clients. If clients are turned away, they will lose hope of becoming productive and perhaps self-supporting. Some of these clients may also end up requesting assistance from the Mental Health Center and from the Anti-Poverty Agency.

Equal Rights is an agency providing a wide range of services to people of color in the area: work training, job placement, and housing location. It also investigates and takes legal action against employers and landlords charged with racial discrimination. The agency needs $500,000. If funds are cut back, discrimination against people of color will increase.

Step 3: Each subgroup shares with the class its decisions for allocating funds (The cuts that are made can be summarized on the chalkboard by having the instructor list the names of the agencies, and then having a representative from each subgroup list the amount of money that was cut—totaling $5 million—from the requested allocations.) Each subgroup states its reasons for making its cuts in funding. The instructor should help the students recognize that most of these reasons are based on values. The instructor asks the students to discuss how they felt making such funding decisions that would (in real life) have significant adverse impacts on potential recipients of services. The instructor asks the class if the exercise helps them understand that making funding decisions for human services involves hard choices caused by scarce resources.

2. Analyzing a Human Services Organization

Goal: To analyze a human services organization.

Visit (perhaps in groups of two or three) a human services agency and write a report covering the following information. (Some agencies may not have information or data on one or more questions. If the information is unavailable, indicate this in your reports.) Include in your report the name and telephone number of the person you met with.

- a. What is the agency's mission statement?
- b. What are its clients' major problems?
- c. What services does the agency provide?
- d. How are client needs determined?
- e. What percentage of clients are people of color, women, gays or lesbians, older persons, or members of other at-risk populations?
- f. What was the total cost of services for the past year?
- g. How much money is spent on each program?
- h. What are the agency's funding sources?
- i. How much and what percentage of funds are received from each source?
- j. What eligibility criteria must prospective clients meet before services will be provided?
- k. What other agencies provide the same services in the community?
- l. What is the organizational structure of the agency? For example, is there a formal chain of command?
- m. Is there an informal organization (that is, people who exert a greater amount of influence on decision making than would be expected for their formal position in the bureaucracy)?
- n. How much decision-making input do the direct service providers have on major policy decisions?
- o. Does the agency have a board that oversees its operations? If yes, what are the backgrounds of the board members?
- p. Do employees at every level feel valued?
- q. What is the morale among employees?
- r. What are the major unmet needs of the agency?
- s. Does the agency have a handbook of personnel policies and procedures?
- t. What is the public image of the agency in the community?
- u. In recent years, what has been the rate of turnover among staff at the agency? What were the major reasons for leaving?
- v. Does the agency have a process for evaluating the outcomes of its services? If yes, what is the process, and what are the outcome results?
- w. What is your overall impression of the agency? For example, if you needed services that this agency provides, would you want to apply at this agency? Why, or why not?

10 SOCIAL WORK COMMUNITY PRACTICE

Most social work students do not consider a career in community practice; they feel that they would rather work directly with people. Many believe that community practice involves skills and techniques that are too complex and too abstract to learn. In addition, they perceive community practice as having too few rewards and as involving a lot of boring, unenjoyable work. All of these beliefs are erroneous. The realities are that (a) the most basic skill needed in community practice is the ability to work effectively with people; (b) community practice primarily involves working with individuals and with groups; (c) every practicing social worker occasionally becomes involved in community practice projects; (d) seeing a community project developed, approved, and implemented is immensely gratifying; and (e) community practice efforts are often fun.

This chapter provides an introduction to social work practice with communities. This chapter will help prepare students to:

Define community and community practice
Understand the history of community practice
Understand three models of community practice
Comprehend knowledge needed for community practice
Describe force field analysis
Identify skills for community practice
Describe the community assets approach

COMMUNITY AND COMMUNITY PRACTICE

Many people think the words "neighborhood" and "community" are synonymous, but a neighborhood is only one type of community. There are many other types. There are communities of associations, such as social work educators or clinical social workers. There are virtual communities, such as members of Facebook. There are political communities, such as members of The Tea Party. Some self-help groups can be viewed as communities, such as members of Alcoholic Anonymous.

Barker (2003) defined a *community* as "a group of individuals or families [who] share certain values, services, institutions, interests, or geographic proximity" (p. 83).

As yet, there is no widely accepted definition of the term *community practice*. The modes of practice performed under this heading have a variety of labels: social planning, community planning, locality development, community action, social action, macro-practice, community organization, and community development.

Community practice will be defined here as the process of stimulating and assisting the local community to evaluate, plan, and coordinate its efforts to provide for the community's health, welfare, and recreational needs. In community practice, a worker's activities include encouraging and stimulating citizen organization around one or more issues, specifying the nature of the problem, coordinating efforts among concerned groups, fact-finding, formulating realizable goals, becoming involved in public relations and public education, conducting research, planning, identifying financial resources, developing strategies to achieve a goal, and being a resource person. Agency settings that employ community practice workers include community welfare councils, the United Way, social planning agencies, health planning councils, neighborhood councils, city planning councils, community action groups, and occasionally some other private or public organization.

Community practice workers become involved in a wide variety of social issues, including civil rights, welfare reform, the needs of poor people, education and health issues, housing, improvement of leisure-time services, race relations, minority-group employment, development of services to counteract alienation of youths, urban redevelopment programs, development of services for teenage runaways and drug users, development of services for the homeless, and development of services for people who are HIV positive or have AIDS.

Other disciplines in addition to social work provide training in community practice. These include community psychology, urban and regional planning, health planning, corrections planning, recreation, and public administration.

In recent years, American citizens have organized around a number of issues. Some that have received national attention include labor-management disputes, women's rights issues, problems of farmers, the abortion question, capital punishment, rights for gays and lesbians, tax cuts, school closings in many cities, the national defense budget, nuclear energy, decriminalization of marijuana, massage parlors, nude dancing, affirmative action guidelines on hiring, and environmental concerns.

A BRIEF HISTORY OF COMMUNITY PRACTICE

For centuries people have organized to change social and political conditions. In the 1700s, for example, Americans organized to revolt against the British and fought what has come to be called the Revolutionary War.

Community practice in social work began in the 1800s with the charity organization movement and the settlement house movement (Kornblum & Julian, 2009).

In the 19th century, private philanthropy bore the major responsibility for the relief of poverty in the United States. During the early 1800s, various private health and welfare agencies were established to provide funds and services (generally combined with religious conversion efforts) to those in need. To avoid duplication of services to the same families, charity organization societies (COSs) were formed to coordinate efforts and to plan for meeting unmet needs.

Reformers associated with the settlement house movement based many of their programs on social action to promote legislation for providing needed services to neighborhoods. These reformers also encouraged neighborhood residents to work together to improve living conditions.

Community welfare councils were first organized in 1908 (Kornblum & Julian, 2009). Continuing the efforts begun by the charity organization movement, these councils served as coordinating organizations for voluntary agencies. The functions of these councils have continued to the present time and include planning, coordinating, avoiding duplication of services, setting standards for services, and improving efficiency and accountability.

Community Chests (now called United Way) were formed around 1920 to serve centralized campaigns for raising funds for voluntary agencies (Kornblum & Julian, 2009). In many communities, United Way has been combined with community welfare councils for fund-raising and for the allocation of funds to voluntary agencies.

All social welfare agencies and organizations become involved at times in community practice efforts.

MODELS OF COMMUNITY PRACTICE

Several approaches have been developed to bring about community change. Rothman and Tropman (1995) categorized these approaches into three models: locality development, social planning, and social action. Real-world approaches to community change tend to have characteristics of all three types. Advocates of social planning, for example, at times use community change techniques such as extensive discussion and participation by a variety of groups, that are characteristic of the other two types. For analytical purposes, however, we'll view the three models as "pure" forms. (Examples of the three models are found in Exhibits 10.1, 10.2, and 10.3.)

Locality-Development Model

The locality-development (or community-development) model rests on the belief that community change can best be brought about through broad-based participation by a wide spectrum of people at the local community level. The model seeks to involve a cross section of individuals (including the disadvantaged and the power structure) in identifying and solving problems. Some themes emphasized in this model are democratic procedures, a consensus approach, voluntary cooperation, development of indigenous leadership, and self-help. For an example, read Exhibit 10.1.

Community practitioners of locality development function as enablers, catalysts, coordinators, and teachers of problem-solving skills and ethical values. It is assumed that conflicts among various groups can be creatively and constructively resolved. People are encouraged to express their differences freely but to put aside self-interests to further the interests of their community. The basic theme of this model is "Together we can figure out what to do and then do it." The locality-development model uses discussion and communication among different factions to reach consensus on which problems to focus on and which strategies and actions to use to resolve these problems.

Examples of such efforts include neighborhood work programs conducted by community-based agencies; Volunteers in Service to America; village-level work in some overseas community-development programs, including the Peace Corps; and activities performed by self-help groups. An analysis of locality-development efforts reveals that there is a greater likelihood of such efforts succeeding under the following conditions:

Exhibit 10.1   The Locality Development Model

The Social Work Student Organization (SWSO) at the University of Wisconsin–Whitewater has been using a locality-development model for the past several years. Its method of proceeding, along with some of its activities, will be briefly described. The SWSO is a social work club; all majors in social work are invited to attend.

The social work program has averaged about 300 student majors for the past 5 years. Current members speak about SWSO in social work classes at the beginning of each semester, inviting nonmembers to join. SWSO also has a listserv of social work students who want to receive the weekly newsletter that SWSO sends out. The newsletter contains information about SWSO "socials," about volunteer opportunities, and about guest speakers at SWSO meetings. Meetings are held every Wednesday afternoon at 5 p.m.

Even though all social work majors are invited to join SWSO, on average about 40 to 60 students become active each semester.

SWSO elects a president, vice president, treasurer, secretary, two representatives to faculty meetings, and one representative to the Deans Advisory Board (composed of one student representative from each department in the College of Letters and Sciences).

Decisions in SWSO meetings are made mostly by consensus. (When there is an issue where SWSO members are divided, a vote is taken.)

The social work program at this campus requires majors to become involved in 70 hours of community service activities before taking the 480-hour internship. (Students are eligible to take the internship after all other required social work courses are completed.) SWSO is highly involved in linking social work students with community service opportunities. Examples of opportunities include mentoring at-risk children at elementary schools in the community, visiting an older person in a nursing home on a weekly basis, tutoring adolescent males at a state correctional school, volunteering at a group home for youths and adults who have a cognitive disability, and volunteering at the campus day-care center.

One of the goals of SWSO is to provide community services to the local community. This goal enriches the community, allows student majors to test out whether they are truly interested in a career in social work, and helps student majors to develop their skills in providing social services. (Two faculty members serve as advisers to SWSO.)

SWSO also engages in several fund-raisers each year. The funds are donated to agencies that serve people in need— such as homeless shelters. One of the fund-raisers is a raffle for items donated by businesses in the community. Another popular fund-raiser is selling hot dogs several evenings a semester at a hot dog stand located in an area where several taverns serve primarily college students.

One of the annual projects of SWSO is "Pass It On." SWSO members notify students living in residence halls that at the end of the school year bins will be placed in the residence halls where students can place their unused canned food and discarded clothes. (All other students are also notified via the campus newspaper of the opportunity to donate their discarded clothes and unused canned goods.) The canned goods and clothes are then donated to food pantries and clothing pantries in the community.

Another activity of SWSO is to hold, once a year, an Employment Seeking Workshop for juniors and seniors majoring in social work. Four or five employers of social workers are invited to discuss the following:

- Where to look for jobs in social work
- What they like and do not like to see in cover letters and resumes
- Dressing and preparing for interviews
- Tips on what to say and what not to say in interviews
- Sending a thank-you letter after an interview, and how to tactfully inquire about the status of an application after an interview

This locality-development model for SWSO is beneficial to the community and develops the social work capacities of the students who actively become involved in SWSO.

1. Leadership and organizational capacity within the community are sufficient.
2. Relatively simple tasks are adequate to accomplish the goal.
3. Small-scale projects will accomplish the goal.
4. The community is sufficiently committed to the project.
5. There is a common interest and people in the community believe that they will benefit from the project.
6. Benefits are tangible and not too far off in the future.
7. Predicted benefits outweigh the costs. (Rothman, 2000)

Community or locality development has expanded in recent years to include community economic development. One example is Chicanos por la Causa in Phoenix, Arizona (Weil & Gamble, 1995, p. 585). This organization received funding from corporations and development groups to improve services and resources to Hispanics in the following areas: job development and training, housing, day care, and educational and training services for adolescent parents and disadvantaged youths. Another example of this type of expansion is community gardening. Efforts to involve residents in urban neighborhoods in community gardens yield more than an increase in healthy foods. The benefits, according to the American Association of Community Gardens (2008), include underrepresented groups becoming more involved in their communities and developing a greater sense of community ownership and the building of community leaders. Also, because community gardeners become more aware of what is going on in their neighborhoods, community gardening has been recognized by the Minneapolis police department and by police elsewhere as an effective crime prevention strategy.

Exercise 10.1: Analyzing the Locality-Development Model

Goal: This exercise is designed to help you recognize the merits and shortcomings of the locality-development model.

Step 1:   Specify the merits of this approach.

Step 2:   Specify the shortcomings of this approach.

Social Planning Model

The social planning model emphasizes problem solving. It assumes that community change in a complex environment requires highly trained and skilled planners who can guide complex change processes. The expert is crucial to identifying and resolving social problems. The expert, or planner, is generally employed by a segment of the power structure, such as an area planning agency, city or county planning department, mental health center, United Way board, or community welfare council. Because social planners are employed by the power structure, they tend to serve the interests of that structure. Marshaling community resources and facilitating radical social change are generally not emphasized in this approach.

In this model, planners gather facts, analyze data, and serve as program designers, implementors and facilitators. Exhibit 10.2 describes this process on a college campus. Community participation in social planning varies from little to substantial, depending on the community's attitudes toward the problems being addressed. For example, an effort to design and fund a community center for the elderly may or may not generate participation by interested community groups, depending on the politics surrounding such a center. Much of the focus of the social planning model is on identifying needs and on arranging and delivering goods and services to people who need them. In effect, the philosophy is "Let's get the facts and take the next rational steps."

Exercise 10.2: Analyzing the Social Planning Model

Goal: This exercise is designed to help you comprehend the merits and shortcomings of the social planning model.

Step 1:   Specify the merits of this approach.

Step 2:   Specify the shortcomings of this approach.

Exhibit 10.2   The Social Planning Model

Emerald College has had an accredited baccalaureate social work program for the past 17 years. The program has an advisory board of 28 members, most of whom are agency practitioners in the community surrounding the college. The social work faculty consists of three people, all of whom have MSW degrees. The chair of the department is Dr. Julie Marzano. Dr. Marzano received her MSW and PhD in social welfare from the University of Wisconsin–Madison.

The advisory board recommends to the social work faculty that they should explore the feasibility of establishing an MSW program at Emerald College because the MSW program closest to Emerald College is 240 miles away.

Dr. Marzano first checks with the campus president and other administrators at the campus about doing a feasibility study for an MSW program. They approve the feasibility study. Dr. Marzano prepares a survey to be filled out by the directors of all the community service agencies in a 125-mile radius of the campus. The survey (among other questions) asks the directors to indicate how many of their social workers who have baccalaureate degrees would be interested in pursuing an MSW degree at Emerald College if the campus decided to offer such a degree. The survey finds overwhelming support for establishing an MSW program at Emerald College and indicates that 247 baccalaureate social workers would (sometime in the future) be interested in applying.

Dr. Marzano also surveys the 73 majors in the social work program to determine their interest in pursuing an MSW degree at this college if such a program were established. Thirty-seven indicate they would be very interested in applying if such a program were offered. Dr. Marzano concludes that the community desires an MSW program be established and that there appears to be a sufficient number of persons who would apply.

Dr. Marzano then checks with the Council on Social Work Education (CSWE) to identify the requirements for an accredited MSW program. An educational specialist at CSWE indicates the program needs to have a minimum of six full-time faculty and that the maximum recommended ratio of faculty to students is 1 to 12.

Dr. Marzano prepares a budget for six additional full-time faculty and for one full-time and one half-time administrative assistant. Dr. Marzano recommends in the budget that funds for the initial start-up costs for the program come from the endowment funds of the college. Dr. Marzano prepares a budget that estimates that an MSW program (charging $25,000 a year in tuition) would be self-sustaining if 70 students were annually enrolled. (The proposed MSW program has an advanced-standing component where as much as 20% of the student body would be given advanced-standing status. The eligibility criteria for advanced standing include the requirement that the student has graduated, in the past 5 years, from a CSWE-accredited baccalaureate program in social work. With advanced-standing status, as many as two semesters of the required four-semester program would be waived.)

Dr. Marzano first presents her MSW proposal (containing the budget) to the Social Work Advisory Board, which gives its approval. Dr. Marzano then presents the proposal to the campus president and other administrators. After raising several questions, these administrators give their approval. The campus president then presents the proposal for this MSW program to the Board of Regents for this campus. The Board, after reviewing it for 2½ months, gives its approval.

Dr. Marzano next prepares the necessary documents, which she submits to CSWE to begin the process of attaining accreditation for this new MSW program.

Social-Action Model

The social-action model assumes that a disadvantaged (often oppressed) segment of the population needs to be organized, perhaps in alliance with others, to pressure the power structure to increase resources or for social justice. Social-action models seek basic changes in major institutions or in basic policies of formal organizations. The objective is the redistribution of power and resources. Whereas locality developers envision a unified community, social-action advocates see the power structure as the opposition—the target of action. Perhaps the best-known social activist was Saul Alinsky (1972, p. 130), who advised, "Pick the target, freeze it, personalize it, and polarize it."

In this model, community practitioners function as advocates, agitators, activists, partisans, brokers, and negotiators. Tactics used in social-action projects include protests, boycotts, confrontation, and negotiation. The change strategy is one of "Let's organize to overpower our oppressor" (Alinsky, 1969, p. 72). The client population is viewed as being "victimized" by the oppressive power structure. Examples of the social-action approach include boycotts during the civil rights movement of the 1960s, strikes by unions, protests by antiabortion groups, and protests by African American and Native American groups. Exhibit 10.3 describes social action at O'Hare airport in Chicago.

A valuable addition to the understanding of "what works?" in social action is Marshall Ganz's *Why David Sometimes Wins: Leadership, Organization, and Strategy in the California Farm Worker Movement* (2009). Ganz explains why Cesar Chavez's United Farm workers organization in California succeeded whereas earlier efforts by radicals and contemporaneous campaigns by the Agricultural Workers Organizing

Exhibit 10.3   The Social-Action Model

Saul Alinsky, one of the nation's most noted organizers, was working in the 1960s in the inner city of Chicago with a citizens' group known as the Woodlawn Ghetto Organization. City authorities had made commitments to this organization to improve several conditions in the neighborhood. However, it became clear that the commitments were not being met by the city. The question arose as how to find a tactic to pressure the city into meeting its commitments. An ingenious strategy was selected to pressure city officials by threatening to embarrass the city by tying up all the lavatories at O'Hare airport—the world's busiest airport. Alinsky (1972, pp. 143–144) describes this effort as follows:

An intelligence study was launched to learn how many sit-down toilets for both men and women, as well as stand-up urinals, there were in the entire O'Hare Airport complex and how many men and women would be necessary for the nation's first "shit-in."

The consequences of this kind of action would be catastrophic in many ways. People would be desperate for a place to relieve themselves. One can see children yelling at their parents, "Mommy, I've got to go," and desperate mothers surrendering, "All right—well, do it. Do it right here." O'Hare would soon become a shambles. The whole scene would become unbelievable and the laughter and ridicule would be nationwide. It would probably get a front page story in the London *Times*. It would be a source of great mortification and embarrassment to the city administration. It might even create the kind of emergency in which planes would have to be held up while passengers got back aboard to use the plane's toilet facilities.

The threat of this tactic was leaked (again there may be a Freudian slip here, and again, so what?) back to the administration, and within 48 hours the Woodlawn Organization found itself in conference with the authorities who said they were certainly going to live up to their commitments and they could never understand where anyone got the idea that a promise made by Chicago's City Hall would not be observed.

Committee (AWOC), sponsored by the AFL-CIO and by the Teamsters, failed. According to Ganz, there was greater motivation, deeper knowledge of the Mexican American culture of the Central Valley, and more open decision making in the United Farm Workers, coupled with an emphasis to learn from those one works with and from successes and mistakes.

Ganz applied his principles to training organizers for Barack Obama's 2008 presidential campaign. Campaign organizers learned to tell their own stories quickly and to form relationships with potential allies and volunteers. These precepts also can be applied to community practice outside of social action.

The social-action model is not widely used by social workers. Involvement in social action can lead employing agencies to penalize those social workers with unpleasant work assignments, low merit increases, and the withholding of promotions. Many agencies will accept minor and moderate changes in their service delivery systems but are threatened by the prospect of the radical changes often advocated by the social-action model.

Exhibit 10.4 on page 220 summarizes the three models.

Exercise 10.3: Analyzing the Social-Action Model

Goal: This exercise is designed to help you comprehend the merits and shortcomings of the social-action model.

Step 1:   Specify the merits of this approach.

Step 2:   Specify the shortcomings of this approach.

KNOW YOUR COMMUNITY

Communities differ in many characteristics from one to another. There are an infinite number of variables that communities may differ from one another. A few of these variables are: religious beliefs, ethnic and racial composition, climate, social economic base, prominent political ideologies, educational levels that are attained, views on same-sex marriages, drug use and abuse patterns, crime patterns, and percent of people over age 65. Because of such diversity, community planning strategies that work in one community (e.g., in Midland, Texas) may not work in another community (e.g., Flint, Michigan).

Therefore it is essential for community practitioners to know, in depth, the community they are working in. The questionnaire in Exhibit 10.5 is a useful tool for obtaining the kind of specific community information that is invaluable in planning for positive community change (or just functioning as a social worker in a community).

Exhibit 10.4   Comparison of the Three Models of Community Practice

Characteristic	Locality Development	Social Planning	Social Action
1. Goals	Self-help; improve community living; emphasis on process goals	Using problem solving to resolve community problems; emphasis on task goals	Shifting of power relationships and resources to an oppressed group; basic institutional change; emphasis on task and process goals
2. Assumptions concerning community	Everyone wants community living to improve and is willing to contribute to the improvement	Social problems in the community can be resolved through the efforts of planning experts	The community has a power structure and one or more oppressed groups; social injustice is a major problem
3. Basic change strategy	Broad cross section of people involved in identifying and solving their problems	Experts using fact gathering and the problem-solving approach	Members of oppressed groups organizing to take action against the power structure, which is the enemy
4. Characteristic change tactics and techniques	Consensus: communication among community groups and interests; group discussion	Consensus or conflict	Conflict or contest: confrontation, direct action, negotiation
5. Practitioner roles	Catalyst, facilitator, coordinator, teacher of problem-solving skills	Expert planner, fact gatherer, analyst, program developer and implementer	Activist, advocate, agitator, broker, negotiator, partisan
6. Views about power structure	Members of power structure as collaborators in a common venture	Power structure as employers and sponsors	Power structure as external target of action, oppressors to be coerced or overturned
7. Views about client population	Citizens	Consumers	Victims
8. Views about client role	Participants in a problem-solving process	Consumers or recipients	Employers, constituents

Exercise 10.4: Know Your Home Community

Goal: This exercise is designed to assist you in better understanding your home community.

Step 1: Specify the name and geographic location of your home community.

Step 2: Using the questions in Exhibit 10.5 as a guide, write a description of your home community. (It is suggested that you do little or no research—simply write what you know about your home community. It is understood there will be a number of questions for which you do not know the answers. That is no problem.) Seek to provide a narrative description of what you know about your home community.

FORCE FIELD ANALYSIS

Force Field Analysis is a method for listing, discussing, and evaluating various forces for a proposed change. It was developed by Lewin (1969). Force Field Analysis helps the planners of a proposed change look at the big picture by analyzing the forces impacting the change and weighing the pros and cons of the proposal. Forces that help in achieving the change are called "driving forces" (pros). Forces that work against the change are called "restraining forces" (cons). Force Field Analysis can be used to develop an action plan to implement a proposed change, as it can help:

1. Determine if a proposed change can get needed support.
2. Identify obstacles to achieving the change.
3. Suggest courses of action to reduce the strength of the obstacles.

Exhibit 10.5   Your Home Community

A Community Characteristics

1. What is the total population? What are the major population characteristics—for example, what percentage is white? African-American? Mexican American? Puerto Rican American? Chinese American? Are there active LGBT organizations? What are the principal religious and ethnic groups? What is the age composition?
2. What are the current issues facing the community? What does the community value—for example, does the majority of the population vote for Democrats, or for Republicans?
3. What is the economic base of the community? Principal types of employment? Major businesses and industries? What percent of the population is living in poverty? What percent is quite wealthy? What is the unemployment rate?
4. Describe the housing characteristics. For example, single-family homes, or apartments, or condos. Is housing affordable for most people? Are there large numbers of deteriorated housing units?
5. Are there one or more colleges/universities in the community? Are the elementary and secondary schools considered to be of high quality? What percent of the adult population achieves a college education?

6. Is alcohol and other drug abuse a major issue? Are delinquent gangs a major issue? Is there a large homeless population?
7. How active are the churches in helping out people who are in need?
8. How many newspapers are there? Television stations? Radio stations?
9. What are the principal communitywide civic and service organizations, such as Rotary? Business organizations? Labor organizations? Cultural groups? Neighborhood groups? What services to the community do these organizations provide?
10. Does the community have a mayor? City council? Police department? Fire department? Are these governmental units effective in the services they provide to the community?
11. Are there self-help groups in the community—such as Alcoholics Anonymous, Narcotics Anonymous, Parents Anonymous, and Gamblers Anonymous?
12. What are the transportation systems—autos, buses, subways, taxis, and airlines?

The stages in conducting a Force Field Analysis are as follows.

1. State a proposed goal.
2. Draw a Force Field Diagram. The goal is written on the top of a page. Divide the page into two columns by drawing a line down the middle of the page. Label the left column the "Driving Forces," and label the right column the "Restraining Forces."
3. Brainstorm a list of driving and restraining forces and record them on the page in the appropriate column.
4. Once the driving and restraining forces are identified, review the driving and restraining forces by asking the following questions:
   • Are the valid?
   • How significant are each of them?
   • What are the strengths of each force?
   • Can the strengths of any of the driving and restraining forces be altered?
   • Is it cost-effective to seek to alter any of these forces?
5. Decide if the goal is feasible. If it is deemed feasible, devise a manageable course of action that seeks to:
   • Strengthen some of the driving forces
   • Weaken some of the restraining forces
   • Create new driving forces

The following is an example of the use of Force Field Analysis that was used by the Community Welfare Council (CWC) in a preliminary analysis of a proposed goal to find affordable housing for all homeless persons in the midwestern city in which this CWC was located.

Goal: Find affordable housing for all the homeless persons in this city: Possible strategies

Driving Forces	Restraining Forces
Strategy 1: Place all the homeless in shelters, with each shelter having social workers as case managers. The homeless could stay up to 90 days. Different shelters would need to be specialized for such populations as: mothers with children, fathers with children, single persons, runaway youths, veterans, persons with mental health issues, and persons with substance abuse issues. These new shelters hold the promise of creating a better life for the homeless in this community.	Strategy 1: The number of homeless persons, and their demographic needs would need to be researched. New shelters would have to be developed to serve the various demographic needs of the diverse categories of the homeless in this city. The estimated costs of developing and maintaining these various types of shelters would need to be determined. Taxpayers are apt to object to the costs of using this strategy to house the homeless.
Strategy 2: Place the homeless in apartments, with the apartments having social workers as case managers. Runaway youths would be placed in foster homes. Landlords and foster parents would be paid the "going rate" for apartments and foster homes. This strategy would provide long-term housing as long as needed for each homeless person.	Strategy 2: This strategy would be substantially more expensive than the first strategy. Taxpayers, therefore, would object even more strenuously to this subsidized housing arrangement. In addition, this form of subsidized housing may attract homeless persons from other communities to relocate to this city.
Strategy 3: Provide job training and job placement services to the adult homeless persons—while they are in a shelter or in an apartment. (This would be an adjunct program to the above two strategies.) The objective would be to help the adult homeless become gainfully employed.	Strategy 3: A certain unknown percentage of the adult homeless would not be able to hold a full time position because of a variety of factors—including some with very young children, transportation issues, mental health issues, and substance abuse issues.

After reviewing the driving forces and restraining forces of each of these strategies, the planners at this Community Welfare Council decided to obtain additional information on:

a) The number of homeless persons, and their demographic needs—such as runaway youths, mothers with young children, father with young children, persons with mental health issues, and persons with substance abuse issues.

b) The costs of developing and maintaining shelters for the diverse homeless populations.

c) The costs of providing long-term apartment housing for the adult homeless and their children; and the costs of foster care for juvenile runaways.

d) The costs of providing job training and job placement service to the adult homeless persons.

COMMUNITY PRACTICE SKILLS

Social workers in community practice need to be skilled at fulfilling the following roles: advocate, empowerer, activist, mediator, negotiator, educator, initiator, coordinator, public speaker, and staff supervisor. These roles are described in Chapter 1 of this text. Additional skills inherent in community practice include the following: evaluating outcomes, fund-raising, budgeting, working with the media, conducting a needs assessment, and influencing decision makers.

Evaluating Outcomes

Agencies and organizations in recent decades have assigned a high priority to evaluating the outcomes of provided services. Funding sources often require outcomes of services to be assessed. The following approaches to outcome evaluation are described in Chapter 11: single-subject design, task achievement scaling, and client satisfaction questionnaires.

Fund-Raising

Social programs cannot exist without financial support. Money is needed to pay staff, rent office space, buy equipment, and for transportation expenses, office supplies, and funds and services provided to clients. Many social programs depend on a combination of public funding and private donations to cover operating expenses.

For many people, asking for money is a distasteful task. Yet agencies cannot survive without fund-raising. Fund-raising involves a variety of approaches, including the following:

Writing a grant proposal to request funds for a specific service or project
Preparing a budget for anticipated service expenditures and submitting it to such funding sources as a town government, a city or county government, a state government, the federal government, or the United Way
Mail solicitations
Person-to-person solicitations
Telephone solicitations
Telethons

Budgeting

Closely related to fund-raising is budgeting. A budget is a statement of probable income from all sources and expenditures during a specified time period. Every agency and organization has a budget regarding how much money it can spend, and on what. When more money is spent than anticipated on one item, less money is available to spend on other items. One of the main tasks in administrating an agency is to prepare a realistic budget, seek approval from funding sources, and then monitor expenditures to ascertain that spending limits will not be exceeded.

Working with the Media

The news media include television, radio, and newspapers. Good communication with the media is an effective way to bring attention to one's cause and to influence decision makers of funding sources. For example, a homeless shelter in a community may contact a television station and ask that the station do a brief news program on the desperate plight of the homeless being turned away from the shelter in the winter because all existing beds are full—the aim being to initiate a fund-raising campaign to expand the square footage of the shelter so as to increase the number of beds available.

Conducting a Needs Assessment

Needs assessment (NA) is a term that has acquired wide usage and a variety of meanings. It has been used to refer to a statewide comprehensive appraisal of problems and needs. It has also been used on a smaller scale to refer to assessment of a community's needs or an agency's assessment of its clients' needs. For example, a homeless shelter in a community may conduct a needs assessment of its clientele. On a large or small scale, needs assessment refers to efforts of acquiring and making sense out of information so it can be used as an aid in making decisions.

An NA is conducted for various reasons. A sponsoring group may know that a need exists, but without documentation it will be difficult to convince decision makers and others of the necessity for action. In the same vein, an NA can increase the visibility of an issue or condition.

An agency or organization may conduct an NA to determine whether its efforts are addressing the most critical needs. Especially when new money is involved, NAs can be used to gain information about various problem areas to determine which area most needs attention.

NAs are frequently required by funding agencies. Various government and private funding organizations have policies that include a needs assessment as part of the proposal development process.

Two broad categories of data are used in NAs. One is already existing information, and the other is information that needs to be generated.

Sources of existing information for every community include census records, state labor department and health department statistics, and agency records and reports. These data can serve as statistical indicators of

Exhibit 10.6   The Mercado Central, an Example of Asset-Based Community Development

Many American (and foreign) cities have pockets of deeply troubled communities. These pockets have high rates of: crime, violence, unemployment, welfare dependency, gangs, drug involvement, homelessness, and vacant and abandoned land and buildings.

There are two paths for seeking to find solutions for deteriorated communities: the deficiency-oriented model, and the asset-based approach. Both of these approaches will be briefly discussed.

The deficiency model focuses attention on what is "wrong" with a community. A key instrument used in the deficiency model is a "needs" survey, which focuses on the deficits in a community. The deficiency model often leads to the creation of "client neighborhoods." The creation of a client neighborhood is often accelerated by the mass media with its focus on emphasizing the spectacularly problematic components of a client neighborhood. It is apt to lead residents in these neighborhoods to view themselves as deficient victims who are incapable of taking charge of their lives and of their community's future. Targeting resources based on a "needs map" directs funding to service providers rather than directly to the residents. The service providers, with the deficiency approach, then relate to the residents as "clients." This approach furthers the perception that only outside experts can provide "real help." Such an approach hinders the development of the leadership capacities of the residents. Furthermore, service providers are under funding pressure to provide annual evidence that problems continue to intensify—in order for funding to be renewed. All of these factors tend to lead to the deepening of the cycle of dependence.

The asset-based model focuses on the development of policies and activities based on the assets, skills, and capacities of lower income people and their neighborhoods (Kretzmann & McKnight, 1993). The asset-based approach believes that significant community development occurs only when local community people are committed to investing themselves and their resources in improving the community. This approach believes sustainable development of a community must start from within the community—rather than waiting for significant help to arrive from outside the community. Instead of viewing the residents of a deteriorated neighborhood as being "clients," this model views residents as being "citizens"—who have untapped resources, assets, capabilities, and potential. The focus is on the community's assets, capacities, and abilities. In addition, every community has a number of citizens' associations—where the citizens assemble to share common interests and activities, and to solve problems. (Every community has associations with religious, athletic, cultural, and recreational purposes.) These associations are key instruments in having the potential for community development.

Additional assets in a community are: private businesses; public institutions such as police and fire stations, parks, schools and libraries; social service agencies; hospitals; and medical clinics.

The key to asset-based community development is mobilizing the assets of individuals, associations, businesses, and public institutions to build a community from inside out.

How can this mobilization be accomplished? Mathie and Cunningham (2008) edited a text that summarizes a number of successful efforts in many countries—in Egypt, Brazil, the United State, Ecuador, Vietnam, Canada, Morocco, India, South Africa, Kenya, and the Philippines. The mobilization of one of these efforts, Building the Mercado Central in Minneapolis, will be summarized (Sheehan, 2008).

The Mercado Central is located on Minneapolis's Lake Street. Historically this area was a commerce center. However, in the 1960s the area experienced serious deterioration. Established businesses began to close their doors. Homeowners fled this area. City services no longer were sufficient to upgrade the aging infrastructure. By 1970, this area was a "seedy" district with pawn shops, liquor stores, bars, and adult sex businesses.

Today, the Mercado Central is a thriving retail business cooperative that was developed by the Latino immigrant community in Minneapolis. More than 40 established businesses are located in this area. It is the hub of this community. It is a place of pride and culture for Latinos, and for non-Latinos.

The Mercado Central is a central market place where people gather to socialize, shop, celebrate, share news, and share concerns. Traditional *mercados* in Latin American cities are in the center of a city and are designed to be an informal place for families to shop, socialize, and dine.

What led to the transformation of this "seedy area" in the 1970s to a thriving central market area that Latinos and non-Latinos now cherish?

According to Sheehan (2008), it began in 1990 when five Salvadoran immigrants asked Juan Linares, a social worker from Catholic Charities, to make St. Stephen's (the local Catholic church) available to community access during the week. The immigrants wanted a place to pray, and gather, during the week. (The church had been locked during the week.) Juan Linares had moved to the USA from Mexico City. Juan Linares' request that this church be opened during the week was granted. The Salvadoran immigrants then requested some church masses be held in Spanish. With the assistance of *Isaiah* (a multidenominational, congregation-based community organizing coalition in Minneapolis) the first Spanish mass was conducted at St. Stephen's in 1991. The deacon, Carl Valdez, in this area (at the request of Juan Linares) then arranged for 12 bilingual priests to commit to a weekly rotation at St. Stephens.

(From the 1970s to the 1990s this area of the city increasingly saw Latino immigrants settle in this neighborhood. These Latino immigrants were from Mexico, Central and South America, Cuba and Puerto Rico.)

The deacon, Carl Valdez, then visited over 200 families in the neighborhood to discuss their desire to build a spiritual community in this area. He also asked them whether they were willing to help build such a spiritual community. In 1995 a church was established in St. Stephen's Parish called Sagrado Corazon, which resulted in over 750 Latino families regularly attending this new Spanish-focused church. This church eventually became the center from which Latino residents would mobilize to build their local economy and to address community concerns.

Exhibit 10.6 (*continued*)

From these church families, a "sponsoring team" of community members was formed to develop an action plan that addressed the community's concerns about what the community believed were unfair immigration practices of the Immigration and Naturalization Service (INS). This team wanted the INS to transform its interactions with Latino residents in ways that respected language barriers and other concerns.

Juan Linares and Salvador Miranda (one of *Isaiah's* community organizers) then began working with congregation members to develop a "Community Talent Inventory" (CTI) that was focused on developing entrepreneurial skills within the community and building relationships among community members. This CTI identified a desire for targeted entrepreneurial training.

Since an entrepreneurial training program in Spanish was already offered in the neighboring city of St. Paul, the provider of this training, Neighborhood Development Center, agreed to offer this training to this geographic area in Minneapolis.

During this 16-week entrepreneurial training, the participants began to discuss how they could develop individual businesses that would be profitable, without competing with one another. The participants agreed to develop a "cooperative" that would allow each business owner to make a profit, while working together and supporting each other's efforts.

Reflecting on their assets and cultures, this cooperative decided to build the Mercado Central, which is a central marketplace for people to gather, shop, and socialize.

The plan that emerged from the coordinating committee was fairly complex. A plan was developed for the Mercado Central. Land was purchased. A business development plan was formulated for the business start-ups. In addition, financing for the Mercado Central was obtained from about 25 sources—including banks, the city of Minneapolis, foundations, local corporations, non-profit development organizations, and the Catholic Campaign for Human Development.

Many residents of this geographic area contributed their time, talents, capabilities, and assets to transform this geographic area from a "seedy district" into a thriving community that is a source of pride and a cultural treasure.

An asset-based community development has the potential to turn other deteriorated neighborhoods into communities that will prosper and flourish.

---

the extent of problems or conditions. Another potential source of existing information is studies conducted at some previous time for a different purpose.

One good source of information is the regional planning commission that serves the given geographical area. In addition to possessing certain statistical information, individuals on planning commissions can be helpful in directing you to other sources. City and county planning units can also be valuable sources of information.

Sometimes information that is not presently available will need to be generated. This can be done in many ways—for example, community forums, or·interviews with selected individuals, community leaders, frontline workers, or clients.

One common way to generate data is the survey. Three survey techniques used to gather information are (1) the telephone interview, (2) the mailed questionnaire, and (3) the person-to-person interview.

Exercise 10.5: Participating in a Needs Assessment

Goal: This exercise is designed to give you experience in participating in a needs assessment.

Step 1: Needs assessments usually seek to survey consumers of services about their views regarding gaps in services. Because you are a consumer of services at this campus, two questions will be asked. Specify what you see as the main areas that the social work program needs to improve on in providing educational services to students.

First, specify the major unmet needs of the social work program at this campus. (Unmet needs may include shortage in number of needed faculty members, lack of an MSW program, insufficient number of field placement sites, more support staff needed, etc.)

Step 2: Specify the major unmet needs of this college or university.

Step 3: (Optional) The instructor may choose to collect the information from each student and then compile it. This information should then be made available to the students in the class. The class may then brainstorm about how to meet the identified needs in these areas.

Influencing Decision Makers

Influencing others is a common role for social workers. Workers want to influence their clients to become motivated to take actions to improve their life circumstances. In community practice there is often a need to influence people with decision-making power—such as elected and appointed officials, supervisors, administrators, and board members of agencies. People with decision-making power are apt to control financial resources. Community practitioners need to become skilled in influencing decision-makers to make favorable decisions for funding needed new social programs and services.

One way to influence decision-makers is by emails. The internet now facilitates the ease in which social workers can influence decision-makers.

Exercise 10.6: Getting Involved in Political Activity

Goal: This exercise is designed to show you that getting involved in political activity is remarkably easy to do.

Step 1:   Identify a current political issue at the state or federal level that you feel strongly about. Specify this issue.

Step 2:   Identify the e-mail address of one of your state or federal legislators (your instructor may be able to assist with this; state chapters of NASW are also a valuable resource in this area). Specify this e-mail address.

Step 3:   Compose an e-mail that summarizes your views on the issue identified in step 1. (Write what you compose here.)

Step 4:   Send the e-mail. Specify, here, the response that you receive from your legislator. (Remember: Do not be timid. Legislators want to hear from constituents.)

Sometimes social workers in community practice have an opportunity to communicate directly with decision-makers. In such direct interactions there are a number of suggestions to maximize the chances of a preferred decision. A worker probably will be anxious, but it is important to appear calm and competent (with practice, a worker can learn to "put on a mask" of being calm, even though anxious). Using a relaxation technique prior to the interaction (see Chapter 14) may help the worker to relax. Also, the worker needs to make direct eye contact with the decision-makers, and display appropriate nonverbal communication. The worker also needs to carefully prepare what he/she wants to say, contemplate possible questions, and rehearse his/her answers to such questions.

COMMUNITY ASSETS APPROACH

There are a number of theories about how best to inspire positive changes in a community. One of the most prominent theories is the community assets approach. It is a strengths-based approach and is described in Exhibit 10.6.

In practically all community development projects social workers use a problem-solving approach. The process can be described in a variety of ways but includes these steps:

1. Identify as precisely as possible the problem or problems.
2. Generate possible alternative solutions.
3. Evaluate the alternative solutions.
4. Select a solution or solutions to be used and set goals.
5. Implement the solution.
6. Follow up to evaluate how the solution worked.

Exercise 10.7: The Assets of My Home Community

Goal: This exercise is designed to assist you in using a strengths-based approach to community practice.

Knowledge of community assets is as important as knowledge of community needs. Knowledge of assets provides hope of improving community life and often helps identify resources that may be used to improve identified community needs. Specify the assets and resources that exist in your home community. (Examples of assets include positive community values, financial resources, low unemployment rate, low crime rate, diversity in population, high educational levels achieved, existence of such clubs as Rotary, good transportation systems, a good public library system, and people having pride in their community.)

SUMMARY

The following summarizes the chapter's content in terms of the learning objectives presented at the beginning of the chapter.

1. Define community and community practice.
   Barker (2003) defined a community as "a group of individuals or families [who] share certain values, services, institutions, or geographic proximity" (p. 83).
   Community practice is the process of stimulating and assisting the local community to evaluate, plan, and coordinate its efforts to provide for the community's health, welfare, and recreational needs.

2. Understand the history of community practice.
   Community practice in social work began in the 1800s with the charity organization movement and the settlement house movement. All social welfare agencies and organizations become involved at times in community practice efforts.

3. Understand three models of community practice.
   Three models of community practice are the locality-development (also called community-development), social planning, and social-action models.

4. Comprehend knowledge needed for community practice.
   Communities differ in many characteristics from one to another. Therefore it is essential for community practitioners to know, in depth, the community they are working in. A questionnaire is provided in Exhibit 10.5 to serve as a guide for what information social workers should seek to learn about the community they are serving.

5. Describe force field analysis.
   Force field analysis is a tool to help the planners of a proposed community change to analyze the forces impacting the change and weighing the pros and cons of the proposal.

6. Identify skills for community practice.
   Social workers in community practice need to be skilled at fulfilling the following roles: advocate, empowerer, activist, mediator, negotiator, educator, initiator, coordinator, public speaker, and staff supervisor. Additional skills inherent in community practice include the following: evaluating outcomes, fundraising, budgeting, working with the media, conducting a needs assessment, and influencing decision makers.

7. Describe the community assets approach.
   There are two paths for seeking to find solutions for deteriorated communities: the deficiency-oriented model, and the asset-based approach.
   The deficiency model focuses attention on what is "wrong" with a community. A key instrument used in the deficiency model is a "needs" survey, which focuses on the deficits in a community. The deficiency model often leads to the creation of "client neighborhoods."
   The asset-based model focuses on the development of policies and activities based on the assets, skills, and capacities of lower income people and their neighborhoods. The asset-based approach believes that significant community development occurs only when local community people are committed to investing themselves and their resources in improving the community.

EXERCISES

1. Community Needs Assessment

Goal: To conduct a community needs assessment.

Step 1: Form groups of five.

Step 2: Select a community and use the questions in Exhibit 10.5 to conduct a community needs assessment.

Note: Alternatively, the entire class can assess one community, with groups focusing on different topics.

2. Needs Assessment and Proposal Development

Goal: To conduct a needs assessment and develop proposals to meet the needs identified.

Step 1:   Form groups of five or six. Your task will be to conduct a needs assessment of an issue on campus or in the surrounding community and then develop a proposal to meet the needs identified.

Note: This assignment may be a major course assignment. Alternatively, make as much progress as you can in a class period to conduct a needs assessment and develop a program proposal. For example, if the latter approach is used, ask the following questions:

> a.   What are the most urgent, unmet needs of our social work program?
> b.   What evidence or documentation is there that these are urgent, unmet needs?
> c.   What additional information needs to be sought to determine fully whether these needs are urgent and unmet?
> d.   What specific, realistic proposals do we have for meeting the needs that have been identified?

Step 2:   The subgroups present their needs assessments and proposals in oral or written form. The instructor provides feedback to the subgroups.

3. Identifying Community Values

Goal: To examine the values of your home communities.

Note: Community values influence the types of services that are publicly available and supported by a community.

> Break into groups of three or four. Discuss your home communities' reactions to the following community activities:

> a.   High school students seek to establish in their school a clinic that dispenses contraceptive materials.
> b.   An avowedly lesbian woman launches a campaign to seek election to a local political office (such as to the city council).
> c.   A group of working parents requests the local school system to establish an all-day kindergarten, partially to meet the needs of working parents.
> d.   An AIDS support group seeks authorization to use the public meeting room of the library for its weekly meetings.
> e.   A local organization seeks the establishment of an additional (or the first) shelter for the homeless in your neighborhood.

4. Analyzing Community Practice Efforts

Goal: To analyze community practice efforts.

Step 1:   Form groups of three. Select a community change or community planning effort to report on to the class. An example of a planning effort is the efforts of a community group to establish a homeless shelter.

Step 2:   Research information on the questions that follow on your selected community change effort. Try to interview at least one planner.

QUESTIONS

a.   What are the goals of the planning effort? How many planners are involved? Who are the planners, and what are their planning credentials? Why is this planning effort being undertaken?

b.   Which of the three community practice models is this planning group primarily using? What characteristics of this model are being displayed by the planners? Does this planning effort have some characteristics of the other models? If "yes," which models, and what characteristics of these models does it have?

c.   What are the results of this planning effort—that is, to what extent are the goals being accomplished? What are the strengths and shortcomings of this planning effort?

PRACTICE EVALUATION AND PROGRAM EVALUATION

In the past few decades, accountability has become a major emphasis in social work. Funding sources demand research evidence that funds allocated are having a beneficial effect. As essential component of accountability is evaluation. In broad terms evaluation is designed to assess whether services provided, or programs provided, are effective and efficient. If the goals and objectives of services, or of programs, are unmet, then these services and programs are neither effective nor efficient. The importance of social workers conducting research is underscored by "practice-informed research" being recognized by the Council on Social Work Education as being one of the key competencies that social workers need to attain; 2008 EPAS states "Social workers . . . evaluate their own practice, and use research findings to improve practice, policy, and social service delivery." In addition, the NASW Code of Ethics states, "Social workers should promote and facilitate evaluation and research to contribute to the development of knowledge." Thus, social workers have an ethical obligation to engage in research and evaluation.

There are two types of evaluation—practice evaluation and program evaluation.

Practice evaluation involves assessing the effectiveness of providing services to clients (such as counseling, group treatment, and family therapy). Program evaluation involves assessing the effectiveness of social service programs (such as the Affordable Health Care Act, child protective services program, and AA).

This chapter will help prepare students to:

Describe process evaluation and outcome evaluation
Describe four approaches to outcome evaluation
Understand evidence-based practice
Understand the ethics of evaluation

PROCESS EVALUATION

Process evaluation is an assessment, generally by clients, as to the aspects of the services received that were useful or detrimental. Feedback about techniques and incidents that blocked or enhanced process is of immense value to the provider of services. With this information, the social worker can hone certain skills and approaches. Positive feedback can build confidence. If the feedback is highly critical, it can be humbling and even devastating. It is far better to make changes suggested by the evaluation than to reject and "deny" the feedback and repeat the same mistakes in providing future services. Social workers need to welcome criticism and be prepared to respond to it constructively, which is the way that social workers expect clients to take constructive criticism.

Process evaluation can be conducted orally by asking clients to discuss the aspects, techniques, materials, and discussions that were constructive and those that were counterproductive. An advantage of such an oral evaluation is that most clients enjoy a verbal discussion. A disadvantage is that some may be inhibited from giving negative feedback verbally as there is a social norm in such situations to focus on the positives.

Process evaluation can also be accomplished by a brief questionnaire that is given to clients. Three key questions follow:

1. Summarize the strengths of the contact. (Cite specific discussions, skills and techniques used by the social worker, and perhaps materials received.)

2. Summarize the shortcomings of the contact. (Cite specific discussions, skills and techniques used by the social worker, and perhaps other information that was desired.)
3. Briefly outline specific suggestions for changes.

In process evaluations, clients typically cite positive factors more than negative ones. Such positive feedback not only has a "stroking value," but also enables providers of services to be more aware of their strengths so that they are apt to increase the use of these strengths in the future.

Negative feedback is as valuable, and often more valuable, than positive feedback. It informs the social worker of aspects that need improvement, which the worker can then attend to.

Another way of evaluating process is by "peer review," a form of quality control. Peer review is conducted by having a peer (usually another social worker) attend a worker's meeting with a client. (Some agencies have one-way mirrors so that the observer can unobtrusively observe the worker with a client.) Prior to a peer review, the agency or organization should agree upon a set of standards or criteria that reflect quality service provision. A peer review is a review of a small portion of the total package of services that are provided. That small portion may be typical or atypical of the total package. When a peer review is being conducted, the client's permission for another worker to be present should be obtained, and the purpose of another worker being present should be explained. (Many colleges and universities use a peer-review process in which tenured faculty in a department sit in on some of the classes of recently hired faculty.)

A variation of the peer-review process is taping (either audio or video) a worker's meeting with a client. That tape is played back and reviewed by the social worker and the "evaluator." Prior to taping a meeting, the worker should explain the reasons for wanting to tape the meeting, indicate who will view the tape, and then ask the client's permission to tape the meeting.

Exercise 11.1: Your Process Evaluation of a Group

Goal: This exercise is designed to familiarize you with process evaluation.

Step 1:   Describe a group that you participated in, which has now ended.

Step 2:   Summarize the following:

a) Strengths of this group:
b) Shortcomings of this group:
c) Suggestions for how this group could have been improved:

Outcome Evaluation

Outcome evaluation approaches can be used to assess the effectiveness of social work practice (i.e., services to clients) and social work programs. Outcome evaluation involves assessing the extent to which the goals have been accomplished in practice with clients or with social work programs. Four approaches to measure goal attainment are single-subject design, goal achievement scaling, task achievement scaling, and satisfaction questionnaire.

Single-Subject Design

Single-subject design has become increasingly popular in the helping professions in the past two decades. There are more than a dozen variations of single-subject design, some of which are very complex and rigorous (Bloom, Fischer, & Orme, 2009). Fortunately, the simpler designs can be used by entry-level social workers in many direct practice situations. The basic elements of the design are described here.

Single-subject design has been identified by several other terms—single-system design, single N or N = 1 research, intensive or ideographic research, single case-study design, single-organism research, time-series research or design, and single-case experimental design (Sheafor & Horejsi, 2007). The phrase *single-subject* indicates a focus of research attention on a single client—which is usually an individual but can be a small group or a family.

In a single-subject design, the client becomes the control group. For this reason, the approach is relatively easy to incorporate into a practitioner's usual services.

The steps in the research process involve:

1. Specifying the outcome
2. Selecting a suitable measure
3. Recording baseline data
4. Implementing intervention and monitoring the outcome
5. Assessing change
6. Inferring effectiveness

The first step in single-subject design is to specify the outcome of interest. The selected outcome should reflect the needs of the client and what is realistic to achieve. It also must be an outcome that can be defined specifically and measured. For example, for a bulimic client who is binging and purging, an appropriate outcome may be cessation of purging. For a family in which there are frequent heated arguments, an appropriate outcome may be a sharp reduction in heated arguments.

The second step in the design process is to select a suitable measure. The target behavior that the practitioner and client hope to change (such as reduction in heated arguments) must be specified in such a way that it can be measured in some reliable way. There are a variety of ways for measuring client outcomes, including direct observation, self-reports from the client, and standardized measures. Standardized measures include tests, questionnaires, rating scales, inventories, and checklists. A variety of standardized measures have been developed to measure variables such as self-esteem, level of assertiveness, level of depression, anxiety level, degree of marital satisfaction, burn-out, amount of stress, potential for suicide, and generalized contentment (Hudson, 1992).

The third step is to record baseline data. Baselining involves collecting data for a period of time before implementing the intervention. The objective of baselining is to establish the base rate of the outcome measure before intervention occurs. This baselining rate can then be used to provide a basis of comparison for the occurrence of the target behavior (behavior to be changed) before, during, and after intervention.

The fourth step is to implement intervention and monitor outcomes. For example, for a client who is generally nonassertive, the intervention may be to have the client participate in an assertiveness training group.

The fifth step is to assess change. This step involves a comparison of the occurrence of the target behavior before, during, and after treatment. Often the occurrence of the target behavior during these three time periods can be displayed on a graph, as shown in Figure 11.1.

The sixth step in the process is to infer effectiveness. This step involves demonstrating logically and empirically that the intervention is the only reasonable explanation for the observed change in the client

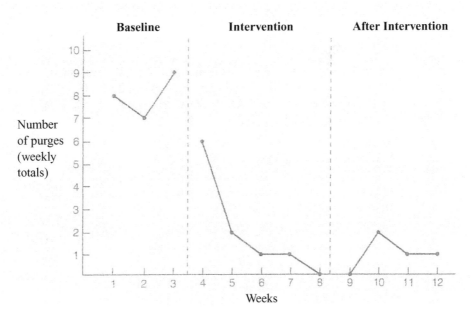

Figure 11.1

Intervention results for a client with bulimia

outcome. In essence, this stage involves ruling out other possible explanations for the observed change. The primary criterion for inferring causality is concomitant variation; that is, the observed change in the outcome must occur at (or soon after) the time the intervention was implemented. If positive changes begin during the baseline period, then logically we have to conclude that something other than the intervention may have contributed to the positive changes. Likewise, if change occurs too long after intervention, then other possible factors may be responsible for the change. If we examine the chart for the Intervention Results for a Bulimic Client (Figure 11.1), we can logically conclude that the intervention had a positive effect, as the number of purges per week declined sharply during and after intervention. However, the usual goal with bulimic clients is complete cessation of purging. Since the client is still purging periodically, additional interventions may be advisable.

In some situations in single-subject research, it is necessary to use a multiple baseline, which indicates the use of more than one baseline as a means of measuring change. Sheafor and Horejsi (2007, p. 394) summarize an example of where a multiple baseline might be used:

> In work with a child having trouble in school, one baseline might focus on frequency of school attendance, a second on grades received for weekly assignments, and a third on a teacher's weekly rating of the student's level of cooperation in the classroom. Unless the target behavior is highly specific, multiple baselines are usually necessary in order to capture the impact of an intervention.

Exercise 11.2: Applying Single-Subject Design to Alleviating One of Your Bad Habits

Goal: This exercise is designed to assist you in understanding and applying single-subject design.

Step 1: Identify a bad habit that you have and that you want to reduce in frequency or eliminate entirely. It might be, for example, drinking fewer alcoholic beverages or quitting smoking.

Step 2: For alleviating this habit, specify the following:

    a) Your outcome:
    b) A suitable measure to determine progress:
    c) Your baseline data:
    d) Implementing intervention and monitoring the outcome:
    e) Assessing change:
    f) Inferring effectiveness:

Step 3: Being realistic, after completing this evaluation, do you have a commitment to alleviating your undesired habit?

Goal Achievement Scaling

Another approach to evaluating social work practice is ask a client (or clients) to rate the degree in which the goals that were set in initial meetings with the client(s) have been attained. This rating is usually done at the termination of services—or a few weeks after termination of services.

An example of a rating scale is:

____ All my goals that were set have been attained.
____ Most of my goals that were set have been attained.
____ About half of my goals that were set have been attained.
____ Most of the goals that were set have not been attained.
____ None of the goals that were set have been attained.

(As stated in Chapter 3, it is highly desirable to specify each goal so that it can be "measured." A measurable goal is a goal that is stated in such a way that the extent of progress toward attaining the goal can be measured.)

Task Achievement Scaling

The objective of this approach is to gauge the degree to which clients and/or the social worker have completed agreed-upon tasks. With this approach, the work toward accomplishing clients' goals is broken down into many separate actions or tasks. The tasks are selected by mutual agreement of the clients and the worker. Usually a deadline is set for completion of each task. Task Achievement Scaling refers to a procedure for rating the degree to which each agreed-upon task has, in fact, been achieved.

Reid and Epstein (1972), in using this approach, utilize a four-point scale to record progress on each task:

4 = Completely achieved
3 = Substantially achieved, action is still necessary
2 = Partially achieved, considerable work needs to be done
1 = Minimally achieved or not achieved

Where appropriate, they have a fifth rating; "No" for "No opportunity to work on task." With this approach, only results are rated—not effort, motivation, or good intentions. The appealing features of this approach are its simplicity and the fact that it can be used when more rigorous procedures are not feasible because of insufficient time, insufficient data, or difficulties in finding a suitable way to measure changes in the target behavior. The approach also has limitations. For example, if the tasks are erroneously conceptualized to be constructive in resolving the client's problems, then completing the tasks may have little effect on resolving the client's problems.

Satisfaction Questionnaire

Still another way to assess the outcome is to have clients fill out a questionnaire that measures level of satisfaction. An example of such a questionnaire for a group is the Group Member Satisfaction Questionnaire shown in Figure 11.2.

Such a questionnaire is a relatively simple and inexpensive way to measure clients' satisfaction level with services received. The questionnaire can be filled out at the last contact with clients, or can be mailed some time later. Questions that evaluate process (described earlier in this chapter) can be added to the questionnaire. With this approach, it is assumed that the higher the level of satisfaction, the greater the extent to which goals have been attained.

Figure 11.2
Group Member Satisfaction Questionnaire

Thank you for taking a few minutes to evaluate your experiences in our group. Your answers to this brief questionnaire will help us to improve future groups. Feel free to offer your comments. To assure anonymity, please do not sign your name.

1. Did you accomplish what you expected when you joined the group?
   _____ Yes, completely
   _____ Mostly
   _____ No real progress
   _____ Worse off now than before
   Comments _____

2. Do you feel the group accomplished its goals?
   _____ Yes, completely
   _____ Mostly
   _____ No real progress
   _____ The group was an utter failure
   Comments _____

3. How do you feel about the group leader?
   _____ Very satisfied
   _____ Satisfied
   _____ No feelings one way or another
   _____ Dissatisfied
   _____ Very dissatisfied
   Comments _____

4. How do you feel about the other members of the group?
   _____ Satisfied with everyone
   _____ Satisfied with some, and dissatisfied with others
   _____ No feelings one way or another
   _____ Dissatisfied with most of the other members
   _____ Dissatisfied with all of the other members
   _____ Very dissatisfied with all of the other members
   Comments _____

Exercise 11.3: Applying a Satisfaction Questionnaire to a Group You Participated In

Goal: This exercise is designed to assist you in applying a satisfaction questionnaire.

Step 1:   Describe a group that you participated in that has now ended.

Step 2:   Answer the questions from the Satisfaction Questionnaire that appears in Figure 11.2 for the group you identified.

PROGRAM EVALUATION

Much of the discussion in this chapter thus far has focused on evaluating social work practice with individuals, families, and groups. All of the approaches described earlier (single-subject design, goal achievement scaling, task achievement scaling, and satisfaction questionnaire) can also be used to evaluate social work programs. Because social work programs often have complex components, an in-depth description of program evaluation is beyond the scope of this text. The Affordable Health Care Act, for example, has many complex components, and therefore more sophisticated evaluation approaches than those described in this chapter are needed to evaluate such questions as: a) Is the quality of care provided under the Affordable Health Care Act better than the care of our former health care system? b) Is the Affordable Health Care program more cost-effective and efficient than the former health care system? c) What are the strengths and shortcomings of the Affordable Health Care Act? d) What changes should be made in the provisions of the Affordable Health Care program? and e) Which population groups are better served under the Affordable Health Care program, and which population groups were better served under the former health care system?

EVIDENCE-BASED PRACTICE

Basing one's practice on the best available evidence is often referred to as *evidence-based practice* (EBP). The concept of EBP evolved in the field of medicine in response to the realization that many patients did not receive the most effective treatments available, sometimes with unfortunate outcomes. The assumption was that practitioners were not informed about the best treatments or perhaps were influenced more by authority and tradition than by empirical evidence (Gambrill, 2006). The evolving paradigm of EBP not only emphasized the importance of empirical evidence in one's practice but also included skills for finding the best evidence and applying it to one's work. EBP is now well established in medical schools and is rapidly being adopted in social work programs as well (Rubin, 2007).

EBP is actually a broader concept than just using evidence-informed interventions. It incorporates using one's clinical expertise and the client's values and preferences when deciding what intervention to use (Sackett et al., 2000). Evidence-based intervention should be used only when you are competent to do the intervention and it is compatible with the client's wishes and situation. Evidence-based intervention is not only good practice; it is ethically required. As stated in the NASW *Code of Ethics*, competent social work practice requires that we base our practice "on recognized knowledge, including empirically based knowledge, relevant to social work and social work ethics" (National Association of Social Workers, 1996. 4.01c).

Although the term *evidence-based interventions* implies that some interventions are "evidence-based" and others are not, it is an oversimplification to think of EBP that way. There are many types of empirical evidence, ranging from the findings of randomized clinical trials (highly controlled control group studies), to simple follow-up studies, to descriptive studies and evolving best practices. EBP considers all of the evidence that is available and uses it to inform one's choice of intervention, consistent with one's professional competence and the client's preferences. For this reason it seems more accurate to describe this approach as "evidence-informed practice" than simply EBP (E. Gambrill, personal communication, September 2006).

Some EBP advocates argue that to treat anyone using treatments without known effectiveness is unethical. Also, some advocates assert that if one treatment program works better than other available treatment approaches, professionals have an ethical obligation to use it in order to best serve clients/patients. Advocates also have asserted that only interventions with demonstrated effectiveness should be supported financially. This assertion links demonstrations of effectiveness with funding through managed care systems (Gambrill, 1999).

There are seven steps in EBP:

Step 1. The professional first of all needs to be motivated to use EBP. A professional may be motivated to use EBP because the approach fosters using effective treatment strategies. However, if a managed care system mandates the use of EBP, the professional may resent forced use.

Step 2. The professional needs to formulate a clear and answerable question that is based on the client's problems and needs. The question should cover such aspects as diagnosis, likely results of various treatment strategies, side effects, prognosis, likely benefits, and costs. An example of a question is, "What are the most effective strategies to treat a 44-year-old recently divorced male who has a bipolar disorder?"

Step 3. Search the literature for relevant research that could help answer the question. EBP places greatest credibility on randomized control trials (RCTs). An RCT is an experiment in which participants are randomly assigned to either a treatment group or a control group. Ideally, neither the participant nor the treating professional knows which group is which. After a course of treatment (or control), improvement is measured by comparing pretreatment status with post-treatment status. If the treated group improves significantly more than the control group, the conclusion is that the treatment works (that is, it is better than no treatment).

Step 4. Carefully and critically appraise the research information for its validity and applicability to the client's needs and circumstances. Also to be considered in this appraisal process are (a) the client's wishes and needs (both stated and implicit) and (b) the professional's competencies to apply the various treatment strategies.

Step 5. Formulate and apply an intervention based on the appraisal in step 4. The selected intervention is based on what has been called the "best available evidence."

Step 6. Monitor the intervention (to verify that it was applied appropriately), and evaluate the benefits and side effects.

Step 7. The professional shares the results with others in order to add to the "best available evidence."

There are a number of Evidence-Based Practice Registries and Databases that are "libraries" of the effectiveness of interventions. Two of these libraries are:

The Campbell Collaboration Library
http://www.campbellcollaboration.org/library.php
This library provides free online access to systematic reviews in the areas of social welfare, criminal justice, and education. The library is a peer-reviewed source of reliable evidence of the effects of interventions.

The Cochrane Library
http://www.interscience.wiley.com/cgi-bin/mrwhome/106568753/HOME
This library contains high-quality, independent evidence to inform healthcare decision-making. The reviews in this library provide the combined results of the world's best medical research studies and are recognized as the "gold standard" in evidence-based health care.

THE ETHICS OF EVALUATION

Process evaluation and outcome evaluation are integral to practice because evaluations tell us if we are making progress and when we can terminate the helping process. Such evaluations also further build a social work knowledge base of what works, and what does not work. Because evaluations are a part of normal practice, evaluations need to be treated ethically as any other aspect of practice. As such, the usual ethical requirements of practice discussed in earlier chapters apply—including informed consent, confidentiality, and client access to records.

In regard to evaluative research it is important to note that additional ethical guidelines are required to protect clients as research subjects. The distinction between evaluation as a practice activity and evaluative research as a knowledge-building activity is important to note—although that distinction is sometimes ambiguous. As a general rule, if the primary purpose of the evaluation is to further develop the knowledge base of social work, rather than to deliver a service to a client, then the researcher needs to adhere to additional ethical guidelines. For example, if the researcher is planning to present the results to a professional meeting or to publish the results in a journal, then the researcher needs to adhere to the following additional guidelines. These guidelines are stated in the NASW Code of Ethics, section 5.02, "Evaluation and Research", at www.naswdc.org. These guidelines state that the researcher must assure that clients/subjects will not be exposed to undue risks as a consequence of their participation in the research project. Furthermore, the subjects must be fully informed of the nature of the research, including the intervention itself and the measurements and design requirements of the research. In addition, clients/subjects must be informed that their participation is completely voluntary; and, if they choose not to participate, they must be informed there will not be any adverse consequences. And, if they choose to participate, and then decide to withdraw, they should be informed there will be no adverse consequences for withdrawing.

Universities and other research organizations are required to have an institutional review board (IRB). The IRB is a committee that has been formed to review, approve, and monitor biomedical and behavioral research involving humans. The number one priority of IRBs is to protect human subjects from physical or psychological harm. IRBs often conduct some form of risk-benefit analysis in an attempt to determine whether a proposed research project should be approved to be conducted. IRBs are regulated by the Office for Human Research Protections within the federal Department of Health and Human Services. IRBs were established in 1974, after the public became aware that some research projects had major ethical violations and severe adverse consequences to human subjects.

One example of severe unethical components in a research study was the Tuskagee syphilis experiment that was conducted between 1932 and 1972 by the U.S. Public Health Service to study the natural progression of untreated syphilis in rural African American men who were informed they were receiving free health care from the U.S. government. The Public Health Service partnered with the Tuskagee Institute in 1932, and enrolled a total of 600 impoverished sharecroppers from Macon County, Alabama. Of these men, 399 had previously contracted syphilis before the study began, and 201 did not have the disease. The men were given free medical care, meals, and burial insurance for participating in the study. Those infected by syphilis were never informed they had the disease, nor were they treated for it. They were instead told they were being treated for "bad blood," which was a local term for such illnesses as fatigue, anemia, and syphilis. The study was particularly unethical because in the 1940s penicillin became recognized as an effective treatment for syphilis; and the researchers of this research project continued the study without treating any participants and withholding penicillin and information about it from the infected subjects in the study! The victims of the study included numerous men who died of syphilis, their wives who contracted the disease, and their children—many of whom were born with congenital syphilis. Revelation of the unethical components in this research study by a whistleblower was a major reason why IRBs were created.

SUMMARY

The following summarizes this chapter's content in terms of the learning objectives presented at the beginning of the chapter.

1. Describe process evaluation and outcome evaluation.

   Process evaluation is an assessment; generally by clients, as to the aspects of services that were useful or detrimental. Outcome evaluation involves assessing the extent to which the goals have been accomplished in practice with clients or with social work programs. Four approaches to measure goal attainment are single-subject design, goal attainment scaling, task achievement scaling, and satisfaction questionnaire.

2. Describe four approaches to outcome evaluation.

   Single-subject design indicates a focus of research on a single client—which is usually an individual but can be a small group or a family. In a single-subject design, the client becomes the control group. The steps in the research process involve:

   a. Specifying the outcome
   b. Selecting a suitable measure
   c. Recording baseline data
   d. Implementing intervention and monitoring the outcome
   e. Assessing change
   f. Inferring effectiveness

   In goal attainment scaling, a client (or clients) rate the degree in which the goals that were set in initial meetings with the client(s) have been attained. With task achievement scaling the focus is on the clients and/or social worker rating the extent to which agreed upon intervention tasks have been successfully completed. A fourth approach to outcome evaluation is to have clients fill out a questionnaire that measures the level of satisfaction with services received. With this approach, it is assumed that the higher the level of satisfaction, the greater the extent to which goals have been attained.

In regard to program evaluation, all four of these outcome approaches can also be used. Because social work programs often have complex components, an in-depth description of program evaluation is beyond the scope of this text.

3. Understand evidence-based practice.

Evidence-based practice (EBP) involves basing one's practice on the best available evidence of what interventions are most effective. In addition to scientific evidence, it incorporates using one's clinical expertise and the client's values and preferences.

4. Understand the ethics of evaluation.

Process evaluation and outcome evaluation are integral to practice because evaluations tell us if we are making progress and when we can terminate the helping process. Such evaluations also further build a social work knowledge base of what works, and what does not work. Because evaluations are a part of normal practice, evaluations need to be treated ethically as any other aspect of practice. As such, the usual ethical requirements of practice discussed in earlier chapters apply—including informed consent, confidentiality, and client access to records.

The distinction between evaluation as a practice activity and evaluative research as a knowledge-building activity is important to note—although that distinction is sometimes ambiguous. As a general rule, if the primary purpose of the evaluation is to further develop the knowledge base of social work, rather than to deliver service to a client, then the researcher needs to adhere to additional ethical guidelines. These guidelines state that the researcher must assure that clients/subjects will not be exposed to undue risks as a consequence of their participation in the research project. Furthermore, the subjects must be fully informed of the nature of the research, including the intervention itself and the measurements and design requirements of the research. In addition, clients/subjects must be informed that their participation is completely voluntary.

EXERCISES

1. Evaluating and Ending the Class

Goal: To demonstrate how to effectively use evaluation.

Note: The instructor of the course should lead this exercise.

Step 1: The instructor begins by expressing a number of positive thoughts and feelings that she or he has about the class. The instructor may also mention a few memorable experiences.

Step 2: The group sits in a circle and the instructor asks: "Is there anything that anyone wants to express before the class ends? Is there any unfinished business that we should deal with?"

Step 3: The instructor leads a discussion through questions such as: "Do you believe this course has helped prepare you to be a social worker?" "What else might have been done to better prepare you to be a social worker?" "What do you see as the strengths of this course?" "What do you see as the shortcomings of this course?" "How might this course be improved?" (An alternative to a verbal discussion of the questions in this step is to have the students record their responses anonymously on a sheet of paper and then hand them in.)

Step 4: The members express what they will most remember about this course and/or what they feel they have learned. Each member should be given an opportunity to express this.

Step 5: Each member expresses nonverbally how she or he felt about being in this class at the first session and how she or he now feels about having been in the class. (This step is optional.)

Step 6: The leader asks each member to give an imaginary gift to the person on his or her right. Each person should take a turn so everyone can hear what the gifts are. When giving or receiving the gift the members extend their hands to symbolize the giving or receiving of the gift. Examples of such gifts are the time-management key to ending procrastination, a warm sun for a smiling personality, a heart for happier relationships, positive and rational thinking for handling unwanted emotions, and the gift of meditation for reducing stress. (This step is optional.)

Step 7:   The instructor may end the class by administering a student course evaluation, by saying some final words, or in some other appropriate way.

A positive, optional , way to end the class is for the instructor to distribute a small container (such as a small paper bag) to each student, with a magic marker. Each student then writes her or his first name on the container that was distributed to her or him. The instructor then distributes a packet of papers (each sheet about 2 inches by 3 inches) to each student. Each student then anonymously writes something positive to each of his/her classmates and then places the comments in the respective container for each classmate. After the distribution is completed, each student then reads (silently) the comments that were placed in his/her container.

2.. Assessing Social Work Competencies and Behaviors

Goal: This exercise is designed to help students self-assess the extent to which they have acquired the competencies and behaviors for social work practice.

Step 1:   The instructor states the purpose of this exercise. The instructor instructs the students to review the material, presented in Chapter 1, on the competencies and behaviors identified by the CSWE in 2015 (EPAS) for effective social work practice.

Step 2:   The instructor makes photocopies of the following list of competencies and behaviors. Each student is given one of these lists.

Step 3:   Each student anonymously rates him/herself on the extent to which he or she has attained each of these competencies and behaviors according to the following five-point scale.

1.	I have attained this behavior (in the range of 80 to 100%)
2.	I have largely attained this behavior (in the range of 60 to 80%)
3.	I have partially attained this behavior (in the range of 40 to 60%)
4.	I have made a little progress in attaining this behavior (in the range of 20 to 40%)
5.	I have made almost no progress in attaining this behavior (in the range of 0 to 20%)

EPAS 2015 Competencies & Behaviors   Student Self-Assessment

Student Assessment Scale	1	2	3	4	5

Competency 1: Demonstrate Ethical and Professional Behavior

	1	2	3	4	5
Makes ethical decisions by applying the standards of the NASW Code of Ethics, relevant laws and regulations, models for ethical decision-making, ethical conduct of research, and additional codes of ethics as appropriate to context	1	2	3	4	5
Uses reflection and self-regulation to manage personal values and maintain professionalism in practice situations	1	2	3	4	5
Demonstrates professional demeanor in behavior, appearance, and oral, written, and electronic communication	1	2	3	4	5
Uses technology ethically and appropriately to facilitate practice outcomes	1	2	3	4	5
Uses supervision and consultation to guide professional judgment and behavior	1	2	3	4	5

Competency 2: Engage Diversity and Difference in Practice

	1	2	3	4	5
Applies and communicates understanding of the importance of diversity and difference in shaping life experiences in practice at the micro, mezzo, and macro levels	1	2	3	4	5
Presents her/himself as a learner and engages clients and constituencies as experts of their own experiences	1	2	3	4	5
Applies self-awareness and self-regulation to manage the influence of personal biases and values in working with diverse clients and constituencies	1	2	3	4	5

Competency 3: Advance Human Rights and Social, Economic, and Environmental Justice

Applies her/his understanding of social, economic, and environmental justice to advocate for human rights at the individual and system levels   1   2   3   4   5

Engages in practices that advance social, economic, and environmental justice   1   2   3   4   5

Competency 4: Engage in Practice-informed Research and Research-informed Practice

Uses practice experience and theory to inform scientific inquiry and research   1   2   3   4   5

Applies critical thinking to engage in analysis of quantitative and qualitative research methods and research findings   1   2   3   4   5

Uses and translates research evidence to inform and improve practice, policy, and service delivery   1   2   3   4   5

Competency 5: Engage in Policy Practice

Identifies social policy at the local, state, and federal level that impacts well-being, service delivery, and access to social services   1   2   3   4   5

Assesses how social welfare and economic policies impact the delivery of and access to social services   1   2   3   4   5

Applies critical thinking to analyze, formulate, and advocate for policies that advance human rights and social, economic, and environmental justice   1   2   3   4   5

Competency 6: Engage with Individuals, Families, Groups, Organizations, and Communities

Applies knowledge of human behavior and the social environment, person-in-environment, and other multidisciplinary theoretical frameworks to engage with clients and constituencies   1   2   3   4   5

Uses empathy, reflection, and interpersonal skills to effectively engage diverse clients and constituencies   1   2   3   4   5

Competency 7: Assess Individuals, Families, Groups, Organizations, and Communities

Collects and organizes data, and applies critical thinking to interpret information from clients and constituencies   1   2   3   4   5

Applies knowledge of human behavior and the social environment, person-in-environment, and other multidisciplinary theoretical frameworks in the analysis of assessment data from clients and constituencies   1   2   3   4   5

Develops mutually agreed-on intervention goals and objectives based on the critical assessment of strengths, needs, and challenges within clients and constituencies   1   2   3   4   5

Selects appropriate intervention strategies based on the assessment, research knowledge, and values and preferences of clients and constituencies   1   2   3   4   5

Competency 8: Intervene with Individuals, Families, Groups, Organizations, and Communities

Critically chooses and implements interventions to achieve practice goals and enhance capacities of client and constituencies   1   2   3   4   5

Applies knowledge of human behavior and the social environment, person-in-environment, and other multidisciplinary theoretical frameworks in interventions with clients and constituencies   1   2   3   4   5

Uses inter-professional collaboration as appropriate to achieve beneficial practice outcomes   1   2   3   4   5

Negotiates, mediates, and advocates with and on behalf of diverse clients and constituencies   1   2   3   4   5

Facilitates effective transitions and endings that advance mutually agreed-on goals   1   2   3   4   5

Competency 9: Evaluate Practice with Individuals, Families, Groups, Organizations, and Communities

Selects and uses appropriate methods for evaluation of outcomes   1   2   3   4   5

Applies knowledge of human behavior and the social environment, person-in-environment, and other multidisciplinary theoretical frameworks in the evaluation of outcomes   1   2   3   4   5

Critically analyzes, monitors, and evaluates intervention and program processes and outcomes   1   2   3   4   5

Applies evaluation findings to improve practice effectiveness at the micro, mezzo, and macro levels   1   2   3   4   5

Step 4:   The instructor collects each of the lists and then calculates the mean scores on each item. At a future class period, the instructor shares this information with the students and holds a discussion with the students that is focused on the students providing information on changes in the program/curriculum that the students believe will improve the ratings on low-rated items.

3. Assessing Social Work Competencies and Behaviors in Field Placement

Goal: This exercise is designed to facilitate students and the social work program in assessing the extent to which students have acquired the competencies and behaviors for social work practice while the students are in field placement.

Step 1:   This field instrument may be used by agency field supervisors to evaluate the performance of the interns they are supervising. One way of using the instrument is to evaluate the intern at the end of field placement. The instrument is completed by the field instructor and reviewed with the student intern and faculty liaison for the dual purposes of providing a grade for the field placement as well as assessing the individual student's attainment of social work behaviors and competencies. Another approach is for field instructors to complete the evaluation mid-way through the length of the field placement (i.e., mid-semester for a one-semester field placement or mid-year for a two-term field placement), then again at termination of the field placement. With either approach, benchmarks (as specified in 2015 *EPAS*) need to be established.

Rating Scale for Evaluation of Field Placement Performance

Midterm   ☐   **Final**   ☐

Name of Intern _____   **Date** _____

Instructions for Rating Interns on the 9 Competencies in the First Part of the Evaluation:

The standard by which an intern is to be compared is that of a new beginning-level social worker. The 9 competencies that are specified in this evaluation form are those established in 2015 by our national accrediting organization (the Council on Social Work Education). Under each competency statement are several items that we ask that you rate according to the following criteria.

1   The intern has excelled in this area

2   The intern is functioning above expectation for interns in this area

3   The intern has met the expectations for interns in this area

4   The intern has not as yet met the expectations in this area, but there is hope that the intern will meet the expectations in the near future

5   The intern has not met the expectations in this area, and there is not much hope that the intern will meet the expectations in this area in the near future

n/a   Not applicable, as the intern has not had the opportunity to demonstrate competence in this area

Comments may be made under any competency statement, if desired. Please be sure to indicate those areas in which you think the intern is particularly strong and those areas that need improvement.

This evaluation is intended to give the intern feedback about her or his performance. The agency supervisor's rating of these items will not directly be used to calculate the grade that is given to the intern. The faculty supervisor has the responsibility of assigning the grade for the course. The grade that is assigned will be based on: **the faculty supervisor's overall evaluation of the student's performance in placement in conjunction with the agency supervisor's evaluation; intern logs; seminar participation; and assigned papers.**

If you prefer to use another evaluation system **in addition** to this form to evaluate a student's performance, please discuss this with the faculty supervisor.

Competency 1: Demonstrate Ethical and Professional Behavior

Makes ethical decisions by applying the standards of the NASW Code of Ethics, relevant laws and regulations, models for ethical decision-making, ethical conduct of research, and additional codes of ethics as appropriate to context	1	2	3	4	5	na
Uses reflection and self-regulation to manage personal values and maintain professionalism in practice situations	1	2	3	4	5	na
Demonstrates professional demeanor in behavior, appearance, and oral, written, and electronic communication	1	2	3	4	5	na
Uses technology ethically and appropriately to facilitate practice outcomes	1	2	3	4	5	na
Uses supervision and consultation to guide professional judgment and behavior	1	2	3	4	5	na

    <u>Comments:</u>

Competency 2: Engage Diversity and Difference in Practice

Applies and communicates understanding of the importance of diversity and difference in shaping life experiences in practice at the micro, mezzo, and macro levels	1	2	3	4	5	na
Presents her/himself as a learner and engages clients and constituencies as experts of their own experiences	1	2	3	4	5	na
Applies self-awareness and self-regulation to manage the influence of personal biases and values in working with diverse clients and constituencies	1	2	3	4	5	na

    <u>Comments:</u>

Competency 3: Advance Human Rights and Social, Economic, and Environmental Justice

Applies her/his understanding of social, economic, and environmental justice to advocate for human rights at the individual and system levels	1	2	3	4	5	na
Engages in practices that advance social, economic, and environmental justice	1	2	3	4	5	na

    <u>Comments:</u>

Competency 4: Engage in Practice-informed Research and Research-informed Practice

Uses practice experience and theory to inform scientific inquiry and research	1	2	3	4	5	na
Applies critical thinking to engage in analysis of quantitative and qualitative research methods and research findings	1	2	3	4	5	na
Uses and translates research evidence to inform and improve practice, policy, and service delivery	1	2	3	4	5	na

    <u>Comments:</u>

Competency 5: Engage in Policy Practice

Identifies social policy at the local, state, and federal level that impacts well-being, service delivery, and access to social services	1	2	3	4	5	na
Assess how social welfare and economic policies impact the delivery of and access to social services	1	2	3	4	5	na
Applies critical thinking to analyze, formulate, and advocate for policies that advance human rights and social, economic, and environmental justice	1	2	3	4	5	na

    <u>Comments:</u>

Competency 6: Engage with Individuals, Families, Groups, Organizations, and Communities

Applies knowledge of human behavior and the social environment, person-in-environment, and other multidisciplinary theoretical frameworks to engage with clients and constituencies	1 2 3 4 5 na
Uses empathy, reflection, and interpersonal skills to effectively engage diverse clients and constituencies	1 2 3 4 5 na

Comments:

Competency 7: Assess Individuals, Families, Groups, Organizations, and Communities

Collects and organizes data, and applies critical thinking to interpret information from clients and constituencies	1 2 3 4 5 na
Applies knowledge of human behavior and the social environment, person-in-environment, and other multidisciplinary theoretical frameworks in the analysis of assessment data from clients and constituencies	1 2 3 4 5 na
Develops mutually agreed-on intervention goals and objectives based on the critical assessment of strengths, needs, and challenges within clients and constituencies	1 2 3 4 5 na
Selects appropriate intervention strategies based on the assessment, research knowledge, and values and preferences of clients and constituencies	1 2 3 4 5 na

Comments:

Competency 8: Intervene with Individuals, Families, Groups, Organizations, and Communities

Critically chooses and implements interventions to achieve practice goals and enhance capacities of client and constituencies	1 2 3 4 5 na
Applies knowledge of human behavior and the social environment, person-in-environment, and other multidisciplinary theoretical frameworks in interventions with clients and constituencies	1 2 3 4 5 na
Uses inter-professional collaboration as appropriate to achieve beneficial practice outcomes	1 2 3 4 5 na
Negotiates, mediates, and advocates with and on behalf of diverse clients and constituencies	1 2 3 4 5 na
Facilitates effective transitions and endings that advance mutually agreed-on goals	1 2 3 4 5 na

Comments:

Competency 9: Evaluate Practice with Individuals, Families, Groups, Organizations, and Communities

Selects and uses appropriate methods for evaluation of outcomes	1 2 3 4 5 na
Applies knowledge of human behavior and the social environment, person-in-environment, and other multidisciplinary theoretical frameworks in the evaluation of outcomes	1 2 3 4 5 na
Critically analyzes, monitors, and evaluates intervention and program processes and outcomes	1 2 3 4 5 na
Applies evaluation findings to improve practice effectiveness at the micro, mezzo, and macro levels	1 2 3 4 5 na

Comments:

Overall Evaluation at MIDTERM:

Please check one of the following at the midterm evaluation. At the final evaluation do <u>NOT</u> complete this section.

☐ This intern is excelling in field placement by performing above expectations for interns.

☐ This intern is meeting the expectations of a field placement intern.

☐ This intern is functioning somewhat below the expectations of a field placement intern. There is a question whether this intern will be ready for beginning level social work practice by the end of placement.

☐ This intern is functioning below the expectations of a field placement intern. There is considerable concern that this intern will not be ready for beginning level social work practice by the end of placement. This intern should perhaps be encouraged to pursue another major.

<u>Comments/elaboration:</u>

FINAL OVERALL EVALUATION:

Please check one of the following at the final evaluation. At the midterm evaluation do <u>NOT</u> complete this section.

☐ This intern has excelled in field placement by performing above expectations for interns. If an appropriate position were open at this agency, for a beginning level social worker, this intern would be considered among the top candidates for this position.

☐ This intern has met the expectations of the field placement. This intern is ready for beginning level social work practice.

☐ This intern is not yet ready for beginning level social work practice.

☐ This intern is not yet ready for beginning level social work practice, and has demonstrated serious problems in performance, and perhaps should be encouraged to pursue another major.

<u>Comments/elaboration:</u>

Signature of Agency Field Instructor _____

Agency _____ Date _____

The following section should be completed by the intern:

My agency supervisor and faculty supervisor have discussed this evaluation with me, and I have received a copy. My agreement or disagreement follows:

    I agree with the evaluation   ☐

    I do not agree with the evaluation   ☐

Intern's Signature _____ Date _____

☐ If the intern disagrees with the evaluation she/he should state that disagreement in writing and submit a copy to both the agency supervisor and the faculty supervisor. The disagreement should be specific and should also relate to the items in the evaluation.

NOTE TO FACULTY

This exercise may be very valuable in obtaining information for reaffirmation of accreditation by the Commission on Accreditation of the CSWE.

CHAPTER

12 SOCIAL WORK PRACTICE WITH DIVERSE GROUPS

LEARNING OBJECTIVES

The profession of social work has had a long tradition of seeking to protect the rights of vulnerable populations and advocating equal opportunities for members of vulnerable populations. For example, the *Code of Ethics* of the National Association of Social Workers (2008) states:

> Social workers should act to prevent and eliminate domination, exploitation, and discrimination against any person, group, or class on the basis of race, ethnicity, national origin, color, age, religion, sex, sexual orientation, marital status, political belief, mental or physical disability, or any other preference, personal characteristic, or status.

The *Code* also states:

> Social workers should act to expand choice and opportunity for all persons, with special regard for vulnerable, disadvantaged, oppressed, and exploited persons and groups.
> Social workers should promote conditions that encourage respect for the diversity of cultures and social diversity within the United States and globally. (National Association of Social Workers, 2008).

Social workers have an obligation to promote social and economic justice for those who are oppressed or victimized by discrimination. The Council on Social Work Education (2015) states social work educational programs need to "provide a learning environment in which respect for all persons and understanding of diversity and difference are practiced." In *Educational Policy and Accreditation Standards*, the Council on Social Work Education (2015) states that social work educational programs are mandated to have a commitment to diversity, "including but not limited to age, class, color, culture, disability and ability, ethnicity, gender, gender identity and expression, immigration status, marital status, political ideology, race, religion/spirituality, sex, sexual orientation, and tribal sovereign status." (Tribal sovereignty refers to the right of Native American tribes to govern themselves, define their own membership, manage tribal property, and regulate tribal business and domestic relations. It further recognizes the existence of a government-to-government relationship between such tribes and the federal government. There are over 500 federally recognized Native American tribes in the United States.) This chapter will help prepare students to:

Define key terms involving diversity
Identify stereotypes
Comprehend three general principles of social work practice with diverse groups
Understand the cultures of diverse groups and understand effective intervention approaches
Describe macro strategies to promote social and economic justice

DEFINITION OF KEY TERMS

Unfortunately, there has been a long history of prejudice, discrimination, and oppression against vulnerable populations in our culture. Some definitions may be useful.

Stereotypes are fixed mental images of a group that are applied to all its members. Stereotyping is the attribution of a fixed and usually inaccurate and unfavorable conception to a category of people.

Prejudice means prejudging, making a judgment in advance of due examination. Prejudice is a combination of stereotyped beliefs and negative attitudes, so that prejudiced individuals think about members of a minority group in a predetermined, usually negative, categorical way.

Discrimination involves taking action against people because they belong to a category. Discriminatory behavior often derives from prejudiced attitudes.

Oppression is the unjust or cruel exercise of authority or power. Members of vulnerable populations in our society are frequently victimized by oppression from segments of the white power structure. Oppression and discrimination are closely related, as all acts of oppression are also acts of discrimination.

A *minority group* is a group that has a subordinate status and is subjected to discrimination. It is not size that is critical in defining a group as a minority but rather lack of power. Women comprise the majority in our society but are a minority according to this definition.

Diverse groups are groups with characteristics that are distinct from the dominant group in a society. Many diverse groups in our society are also vulnerable populations. In regard to diversity, it should be noted that everyone has "multicultural diversity." We differ from one another in terms of such variables as age, economic status, education, family type, gender, personality type, ethnicity, religion, geographic origin, sexual orientation, communication patterns, attire, language, political views, physical abilities, lifestyle, and so forth. Therefore, when we meet someone who, for example, is Native American, it is essential to recognize that there are many other facets of that individual in addition to just his or her ethnicity.

Social justice is an ideal condition in which all members of a society have the same basic rights, protection, opportunities, obligations, and social benefits. Economic justice is also an ideal condition in which all members of a society have the same opportunities for attaining material goods, income, and wealth.

In working with diverse groups, a social worker needs (1) to be aware of personal stereotypes and preconceptions about diverse groups, (2) to have knowledge about the diverse groups that he or she is working with and the special needs of those groups, and (3) to be aware of which intervention techniques are apt to be effective with those groups and which are not.

STEREOTYPES

Stereotypes are closely related to the way we think, as we seek to perceive and understand things in categories. We need categories to group things that are similar in order to study them and to communicate about them. We have stereotypes about many categories, a few of which will be mentioned: football players, priests, mothers, delinquent children, fathers, Democrats, accountants, lawyers, school teachers, Mormons, Muslims, Italians, Germans, and politicians. Stereotypes often contain some useful and accurate information about a member in any category. Yet, each member of any category has many characteristics that are not suggested by the stereotypes, and is apt to have some characteristics that run counter to some of the stereotypes.

A major danger of stereotypes is that if we believe a negative stereotype of a diverse group, we are apt to stereotype individual members of that diverse group as being "such and such," while overlooking the abilities and capacities of the members (such as their intelligence, morals, work ethic, and other unique and positive attributes).

There have been many groups in the history of the United States that have been negatively stereotyped, and then discriminated against. A few of these groups are: Native Americans, persons with a disability, women, Italians, Irish people, Chinese Americans, Japanese Americans, Arab Americans, older persons, gays, bisexuals, lesbians, transgender persons, overweight persons, persons of short stature, African Americans, persons receiving public assistance, persons receiving a mental illness label, persons who are disfigured, people who are poor, Hispanic-Americans, Mormons, and Muslims. Given this short list of those who have been victimized by discrimination, it is clear that a vast majority of people living in the United States have been negatively stereotyped and victimized by discrimination.

Exercise 12.1: Have You Been Victimized by Negative Stereotyping and Discrimination?

Goal: This exercise is designed to further your knowledge of negative stereotyping and discrimination.

Step 1:   Review your past. Consider a variety of characteristics you have, including: sex, ethnicity, race, height, appearance, social status, economic status, mental or physical disabilities, religion, athletic ability, sexual orientation, marital status, political beliefs, age, etc. Write down any incident where you believe you were negatively stereotyped and victimized by discrimination.

Step 2:   If you were negatively stereotyped and discriminated against, write down your thoughts, feelings, and any actions that you may have taken about this stereotyping and discrimination.

It should be noted that negative stereotyping and discrimination can occur independently of each other:

A) Someone who does not have negative stereotypes (a rare phenomenon) and does not discriminate generally upholds American values of equality and freedom. Such a person is not prejudiced against other groups and does not discriminate against them;

B) Someone who does not have negative stereotypes, but does discriminate may discriminate against certain groups because it seems financially or socially convenient to do so;

C) Someone may hold negative stereotypes about a group, but yet recognize that social pressures or laws are opposed to discrimination, and therefore may not discriminate; and

D) Someone may hold negative stereotypes and discriminate against other groups. Such a person does not believe in the values of equality and freedom.

What are the causes of negative stereotyping and discrimination? There are a variety of causes, many of which will be summarized here:

A) The Belief in White Supremacy: White supremacy is the belief that white people are superior to people of other racial backgrounds. This belief has led whites to discriminate against people of color. White supremacy was a dominant belief in the United States before the Civil War and for decades after Reconstruction. The Ku Klux Klan still advocates and asserts white supremacy.

B) The Belief in "The One True Religion": Some people are raised to believe that their religion is the one true religion. They believe they will go to heaven, whereas those who believe in some other religion will go to eternal damnation. Such a belief system often leads such people to feel superior to people who believe in some other religion. They tend to view people who do not hold their religious beliefs as being "heathens" and as being inferior. With this belief, they tend to believe they have a right to treat the "heathens" in an inferior manner. The influence of the "one true religion" has led to an extensive number of wars between societies. Societies in which the leaders believe they have the "one true religion" tend to believe they are justified in spreading their chosen religion with any possible means, including going to war.

C) Socialization Patterns: Negative stereotyping is often a learned phenomenon, transmitted from generation to generation through socialization patterns. From childhood on, all of us hear negative stereotypes about certain groups, which are apt to gradually become incorporated into our thought processes. (You may want to reflect, here, on the negative stereotypes you have heard about certain diverse groups.)

D) Frustration-Aggression: All of us, at times, become frustrated when we are unable to achieve or obtain something we desire. Sometimes we are able to strike back at the source of our frustration, but many times we realize it is not in our best interest to directly retaliate. Some of us then displace our anger and aggression onto a scapegoat; and the scapegoat may include a group of people, such as a minority group.

E) Competition and Exploitation: Our society is highly materialistic and competitive. Competitiveness may lead some people to exploit (discriminate against) subordinate groups. Historically, many white people in positions of power in our society have exploited people of color.

F) Insecurity and Inferiority: Some insecure people feel better about themselves when they are putting down other groups; they then can tell themselves that they are "better than those people."

G) Projection: Projection is a psychological defense mechanism by which we attribute to others characteristics that we are unwilling to recognize in ourselves. For example, a minority group may serve as a projection of a prejudiced person's lusts and fears. People who view African Americans as lazy and preoccupied with sex may be projecting their own internal concerns about their industriousness and their sexual fantasies onto this group. Or, some people who are homophobic may be attempting to hide from themselves some same-sex desires that they have.

What are your negative, and positive, stereotypes about a wide variety of groups? It is essential that social workers are aware of their negative stereotypes (i.e., "tapes" in their heads) so that they are able to confront and counteract those negative stereotypes when providing services to members of these groups. (Social workers have a moral obligation to treat each client with respect, fairness, and dignity.) How do you identify your negative stereotypes? Exercise 12.2 may assist you in becoming more aware of your stereotypes.

Exercise 12.2: Whom Would I Be Hesitant to Marry?

Goal: This exercise is designed to identify some of your personal stereotypes that you need to be aware of in order to develop an objective approach to social work practice with diverse groups.

Step 1:   Assume you are single. Place an X by anyone you would be hesitant to marry.

____ Person who is blind
____ Person who is deaf
____ A cross dresser
____ An older person (over age 65)
____ Person who has genital herpes
____ Someone who has previously been married
____ Person who has had cancer in the past
____ Person who has been labeled mentally ill
____ Person who has young children from a prior relationship
____ Person who is bisexual
____ Transgender person
____ Person who has cerebral palsy
____ Person who has recently declared bankruptcy
____ A Muslim
____ An atheist
____ A Jew
____ An undocumented immigrant
____ A Pakistani
____ A Hungarian
____ An Eskimo
____ A Mexican
____ A white Protestant
____ A Roman Catholic
____ A German
____ A Yugoslav
____ A Norwegian
____ A Samoan
____ An Arab
____ A Russian
____ A Chinese-American
____ A Japanese-American
____ A Native American
____ A white American
____ A Korean
____ A Puerto Rican
____ Person who has a mild cognitive disability
____ Person who was incarcerated in the past
____ A Vietnamese

Step 2:   As specifically as possible, state (next to each group that you checked) the reasons why you would be hesitant to marry a member of that group.

Step 3:   Do you believe you hold negative stereotypes about the individuals you checked? Explain your answer to this question.

EMPOWERMENT

For many of the last ten decades, social work and other helping professions have largely focused on diagnosing the shortcomings, pathology, and dysfunctions of clients. One reason may be that Freudian psychology was the primary theory used in analyzing human behavior from the early 1900s to the 1960s. Freudian theory is based on a medical model which has concepts that are geared to identify illness and pathology. It has very few concepts to identify strengths. Since the 1960s social work has largely shifted to focusing on a systems model, which emphasizes the importance of identifying both strengths and weaknesses. Identifying the strengths of clients is perhaps more important than identifying the shortcomings. Empowerment counters hopelessness and powerlessness with an emphasis on the ability of each person to address problems competently, beginning with a positive view of self.

A key goal of social work practice is empowerment, which is the process of helping individuals, groups, families, organizations, and communities to increase their personal, interpersonal, socioeconomic, and political strength and influence through improving their circumstances. Social workers who are involved in empowerment-focused practice seek to facilitate clients to understand their environment, make good choices, take responsibility for their choices, improve their life situations through becoming involved in forming alliances with persons facing similar challenges, and then engaging in advocacy. Empowerment-focused practice seeks to gain a more equitable distribution of resources and power among different groups in society.

STRENGTHS PERSPECTIVE

The strengths perspective is closely related to empowerment. Social workers using the strengths perspective seek to identify, use, build on, and reinforce the abilities and strengths that people have, in contrast to the pathological perspective, which focuses on their deficiencies. One example of the strengths perspective is the Asset-Based Model of Community Development, which is described later in this chapter.

Another example is the life of Temple Grandin (2011). Temple was born on August 29, 1947. She did not begin to speak until she was nearly 4 years old. She instead communicated her frustrations by screaming. At age 3 she was diagnosed by physicians as being autistic, who urged her parents to place her in an institution. (If she had been placed, she probably would have received institutional care for the remainder of her life.) Temple's mother thought there was more that could be done to help Temple. Temple received speech therapy and began to talk at age 4 and also began to make developmental progress. Temple's mother also hired a nanny who spent hours playing games with Temple and her sister. Temple had a supportive mother, supportive teachers, and supportive mentors who focused on helping Temple develop her capabilities to the fullest. Although she had many challenges, including being taunted and teased by her classmates in school, Temple graduated from high school; earned her bachelor's degree in psychology from Franklin Pierce College in 1970; received her master's degree in animal science from Arizona State University in 1975; and her doctoral degree in 1989 from the University of Illinois at Urbana-Champaign. She is now a professor at Colorado State University. She is a philosophical leader of both animal welfare and autism advocacy movements. She is a best-selling author on animal welfare and autism. She advocates early interventions to address autism, and urges that autistic children have supportive teachers who can direct the fixations of autistic children in fruitful directions. Temple urges that no one should be stereotyped as having "no hope for the future" because of receiving a mental/physical disability diagnosis (such as autism). Her life story dramatically demonstrates that having supportive people in one's early years that emphasize the strengths of a person, rather than the limitations, can have amazing outcomes.

The strengths perspective is more fully described in Chapter 3.

Exercise 12.3: The Strengths Perspective Applied to a Homeless Family

Goal: This exercise is designed to have you apply the strengths perspective to a case scenario.

Step 1:   Read the following scenario:

Ms. Kerr was recently evicted from her two-bedroom apartment. She had been working at a small business that did not offer health insurance coverage to her. She is a single mother with three children, ages 7, 9, and 10. She developed pneumonia, which hung on because she could not pay to see a physician. The small business experienced financial problems, and her employment was terminated. She has been seeking another job but has not found one. She wants a job that has health benefits. Being unable to pay rent, she was evicted from her apartment. She cares a lot for her children, and they display respect for her. The children are all doing well in school. Ms. Kerr and her children lived on the street for 3 days and nights but then located a homeless shelter at the Salvation Army. They have been at the homeless shelter for the past 2½ weeks. The children are fairly healthy and are respectful of the services they are receiving from the shelter. Ms. Kerr has largely recovered from her pneumonia, partly because of the physician's visit she asked the Salvation Army to arrange for her.

Step 2:   List the strengths that you identify in this family.

CULTURAL COMPETENCE

It is a mistake for a social worker to conclude that working effectively with a different cultural group represents insurmountable obstacles and barriers. In actuality, the similarities between worker and client almost always outweigh the dissimilarities.

There are a number of guidelines/principles that compose cultural competence in social work practice (National Association of Social Workers, 2001; Dhopper and Moore, 2001). These guidelines/principles are "ideal" standards. It should be noted most social workers are working towards meeting these standards; many social workers have some limitations in meeting some of these standards.

Social workers need to:

A) Be aware of culture and its pervasive influence.
B) Learn about their own culture.
C) Learn about other cultures, particularly of the major client groups they serve.
D) Need to adapt social work skills and intervention approaches to best serve clients of diverse groups.
E) Function in accordance with the ethics, values, and standards of the profession.
F) Be knowledgeable about community resources and services, and make appropriate referrals for their diverse clients.
G) Be aware of the impacts of social policies and programs on diverse client populations, and advocate for improvements in these programs.
H) Advocate for personnel practices (in hiring, admissions, and retention) in social work agencies and educational programs that facilitate diversity within the social work profession.
I) Participate in training and educational programs that advance cultural competence in social work practice.
J) Provide or advocate for the conveying of information and services (including using interpreters) in language that clients comprehend.

Exercise 12.4: Cultural Competence in Social Work Practice

Goal: This exercise is designed to assist you in assessing standards of cultural competence that you need to work on.

Step 1: Review the standards for cultural competence that are listed in this chapter.

Step 2: List the standards (using the letters A, B, C, etc.) that you believe you have significant competence in.

Step 3: List the standards that you believe you need to improve on in order to be competent.

Step 4: Describe your strategies/plans for improving on becoming more competent for the standards you identified in Step 3.

CULTURAL HUMILITY

In recent years the social work profession has been advocating the adoption of the construct of "cultural humility" into social work practice. Cultural humility is somewhat related to cultural competence. The two will be contrasted. The goal of cultural competence is to build an understanding of diverse cultures in order to better and more appropriately provide services. The goal of cultural humility is to encourage personal reflection and growth around culture in order to increase the cultural awareness of service providers.

Three factors are involved in a worker progressing toward cultural humility. The first factor is a lifelong commitment to self-evaluation and self-critique. This factor encourages lifelong learning with no end goal, but with an appreciation of the journey of growth and understanding. We never arrive at a point where we are done learning!

The second factor of cultural humility is a commitment to fixing power imbalances where no power imbalance ought to exist. This factor encourages social workers to realize their own power, prejudices, and privilege; and to be willing to accept that acquired credentials and educational degrees alone are insufficient to address social inequality. This factor encourages workers to embrace the idea of learning with and from clients.

CULTURES OF DIVERSE GROUPS AND EFFECTIVE INTERVENTION APPROACHES

Social workers sometimes make the mistake of using their own cultural, social, or economic values as the norm. See, for example, Exhibit 12.1.

The third factor of cultural humility is a commitment to develop partnerships with people and groups who advocate for advancing the human rights of members of diverse groups. Advocacy groups can often have more of an impact on changing oppressive policies, practices, and systems than individuals acting alone. This factor of cultural humility offers clients a mechanism by which they can be seen and heard.

Cultural humility is a tool (a mindset) that should be used by social workers to gain more insight into their personal biases, and to better connect with members of diverse groups. Social workers need to be aware that they can never be truly "competent" about any culture that differs from their own culture.

If a social worker has been subjected to the prejudices and discrimination that a client is experiencing and was raised in a similar environment to the client, that worker may be more perceptive about and empathetic to that client. For example, a worker who is a lesbian may be more perceptive and understanding (than heterosexual workers) of the "coming out" challenges that a client faces who recently recognized that she is more intimately interested in women than in men. Similarly, a Hmong social worker whose parents immigrated to the United States from Laos may be more perceptive (than non-Hmong workers) of the challenges experienced by Hmong children whose parents also immigrated to the USA from Laos.

It should be noted, however, that a helping professional does not need to be a member of the client's minority group in order to provide high quality services to a client. A perceptive and empathetic helping professional who has had few life experiences that a client has had may well be able to provide higher quality services than a helping professional who has shortcomings in being empathetic and perceptive—even though that helping professional has had many life experiences similar to the client's. The following example quoted in Sager, Brayboy, and Waxenberg (1970) illustrates this point:

> In answering the question of whether a white middle-class psychiatrist can treat a black family, I cannot help but think back over my own experiences. When I first came to New York and decided to go into psychotherapy I had two main thoughts: (1) that my problems were culturally determined, and (2) that they were related to my Catholic upbringing. I had grown up in an environment in which the Catholic Church had tremendous influence. With these

---

Exhibit 12.1   Case Example of a Social Worker Mistakenly Viewing a Case from the Worker's Values

Mary and Robert Robins are seeking to adopt a young child. They contacted Catholic Social Services and were being interviewed by Jessica Warner (a social worker), who was gathering information about whether the agency and the Robinses should move ahead with the adoption. The Robinses were financially and emotionally stable. He was 31, and she was 29. They had been trying to conceive for the past four years, to no avail. They had sought fertility counseling, and the tests showed Mr. Robins had a very low sperm count. So they decided to apply for an adoption. During the interview, when asked, Mr. Robins acknowledged that his parents' marriage had considerable strife.

Mr. Robins indicated his mother was now retired, after having been a well-respected school teacher for 36 years. She had primarily raised Mr. Robins and his three siblings. All the siblings were now adults and no longer living at home. Mr. Robins' father, Earl, had been, and still was, an alcoholic for most of the 43 years that he was married. When intoxicated, he had often been verbally abusive to his wife and his children. This information became the focus of Ms. Warner's attention. She inquired what Earl's source of income had been and currently was. It was indicated that Earl had been a part time carpenter but had not worked for the past 13 years, due to a stroke that he had suffered, which left his right side partially paralyzed. (Against his physician's

advice, Earl continued to drink.) At this point, Ms. Warner was dumbfounded. She asked Mr. and Mrs. Robins why Mr. Robins' mother did not seek a divorce. Mr. Robins said his mother was a long-time church-goer who believed that marriage was for a lifetime; (until death do we part). Ms. Warner did not let the subject rest at this point. She urged Mr. Robins to have a private lunch with his mother, where he was instructed to urge his mother to seek a divorce.

Wanting to be compliant with Ms. Warner's instructions (as he did not want this issue to be an adverse factor in the adoption application), he had lunch with his mother to suggest she consider pursuing a divorce. His mother stated the social worker was crossing a boundary that she had no right to cross. She strongly indicated it was her decision to stay married, and certainly not the social worker's. At the next interview with Ms. Warner, Mr. Robins relayed what had transpired. Ms. Warner later discussed with her supervisor whether she had gone too far in recommending Mr. Robins' mother seek a divorce. The supervisor stated she had probably "gone too far"; her focus should be on the adoption application of the Robins, and not on trying to resolve the marital strife between Earl and his wife. The supervisor added that divorce is sometimes warranted, but that decision is up to the two spouses in a marriage.

factors in mind, I began to think in terms of the kind of therapist I could best relate to. In addition to being warm and sensitive, he had to be black and Catholic. Needless to say, that was like looking for a needle in a haystack. But after inquiring around, I was finally referred to a black, Catholic psychiatrist.

Without going into too much detail, let me say that he turned out to be not so sensitive and not so warm. I terminated my treatment with him and began to see another therapist who was warm, friendly, sensitive, understanding and very much involved with me. Interestingly enough, he was neither black nor Catholic. As a result of that personal experience, I have come to believe that it is not so much a question of whether the therapist is black or white but whether he is competent, warm and understanding. Feelings, after all, are neither black nor white. (pp. 210–211)

For any client (including a member of a vulnerable population) that a worker has, the worker needs a variety of skills to bring about positive changes. Such skills include: relationship building, empathy, problem solving skills, ability to apply knowledge of intervention strategies, and listening skills. A worker's effectiveness is also enhanced by having a working knowledge of a client's minority group and its unique characteristics.

There are an immense number of vulnerable populations (i.e., minority groups) in our society. A partial list include: racial groups, ethnic groups, women, children, older persons, people with a mental or physical disability, the homeless, those living in poverty, the LGBT population, and some religious groups. It is beyond the scope of this chapter to describe the unique characteristics of all the vulnerable populations in our society. Instead, a few characteristics will be summarized to illustrate the importance of learning about the cultural and social background of the client. When a social worker has a new client of a vulnerable population that the worker is unfamiliar with, the worker has an obligation to learn as much as possible about the unique challenges and characteristics of that population.

If a female client begins talking about her partner, it is a mistake to assume the partner is a man and refer to the person as "he" or "him." The client may be a lesbian. Such an erroneous assumption may lead the client to terminate the interview, and to end further contact. Obviously this caution applies to male clients as well. The helping professionals now realize that attempts to change a client's sexual orientation are usually unsuccessful. Conversion therapy (also known as "reparative therapy" or "sexual reorientation therapy") is a dangerous practice that purports to change a person's sexual orientation from gay to straight. This type of therapy has been discredited by virtually all major American medical, psychological, psychiatric, and professional counseling organizations. Persons who have undergone conversion therapy have reported depression, increased anxiety, and in some cases, suicidal ideation, with no change in their sexual orientation. Sexual orientation appears to be firmly established early in life (Bell, Weinberg, & Hammersmith, 1981).

Most persons who are uncertain of their sexual identity orientation will benefit from talking to an LGB-affirming counselor. Such a counselor has expertise in helping people who are experiencing feelings of same-sex attraction to explore such feelings. If a person then determines he or she has same-sex attractions, that person needs to examine if he or she wants to "come out," and with whom to share this information. (Most larger cities have local LGBT community centers that willingly provide the names of LGB-affirming counselors to inquiring persons—including to inquiring helping professionals.)

In the United States and many European countries (such as France, Germany, and Spain) using direct eye contact is accepted and considered to be a sign of attentiveness, honesty, confidence, and respect for what the other is saying. In Native American cultures and in some Latin-American cultures, the opposite is true. Direct eye contact in these cultures is considered to be aggressive, rude, and confrontational. Social workers and other professionals need to respect this cultural pattern by seeking to substantially reduce direct eye contact.

Some clients do not speak or understand English. In such situations, if the worker is not fluent in the language spoken by the client, it is necessary for the worker to use an interpreter. There are some guidelines for using an interpreter. Bilingual children should not be used as interpreters. To use a child of the client adversely changes the role of the child in family relationships. Serving as conveyors of sensitive family information is not an acceptable role for a child in a family to play. Often, it places the child in an unpleasant and awkward situation. Also, a child lacks an adult's knowledge base, which reduces the child's value as an interpreter. For example, if a husband and wife are having intimacy issues (or financial issues), it is clearly inappropriate and counterproductive to use one of their children as an interpreter.

Another guideline when using an interpreter is that a worker needs to relate and talk to the client, not to the interpreter. If the worker talks primarily to the translator, it places the client in the role of a bystander, rather than being the central figure in the dialogue between the worker and the client.

Our culture places a high value on physical beauty. Americans spend billions of dollars each year on cosmetics, exercise programs, clothes, food supplements, and special diets to look more attractive. Beauty in our culture is identified with goodness, and lack of being attractive with evil. For example, Snow White was beautiful, and the evil witch was ugly. Sadly, this emphasis on the body beautiful has led those with a disability to be the brunt of cruel jokes, sometimes being bullied, and occasionally being shunned or treated as inferior. Wright (1960) has noted that the emphasis on the body beautiful has also led many people in our society to believe that those with a disability ought to feel inferior. Wright has coined the term "requirement of mourning" for this expectation of society. Many able-bodied people who spend a great deal of time and money on seeking to be physically attractive want a person with a disability to mourn the absence of physical perfection. Another consequenc of the body beautiful cult is that people with a disability are sometimes pitied.

There have been a huge number of persons with a disability who have been very "successful." A short list follows:

Stevie Wonder	Songwriter, producer, singer and musician has been blind most of his life
Julius Caeser	Roman emperor had epilepsy
George Washington	President had a learning disability
George Patton	Noted World War II general had dyslexia
Ludwig van Beethoven	Famous musician and composer had a serious hearing disorder
Franklin D. Roosevelt	President had polio as a child which resulted in a serious mobility disability
Winston Churchill	Prime minister of Great Britain had a learning disability
Thomas Edison	Inventor had a learning disability
Albert Einstein	Mathematician/physicist had a learning disability
Ray Charles	Singer and musician was blind
Helen Keller	Advocate for people with a disability was blind, deaf, and mute
Temple Grandin	Prominent PhD, author, and inventor is autistic

Persons with a physical or mental disability can live productive, happy and fruitful lives when they receive the support and encouragement they need. In working with a person who has a disability, it is important for social workers to assess not only the severity and extent of the disability but also the strengths and special talents of that person. In seeking to participate fully in our society, persons with a disability must face the challenges created by their disability and also the additional challenges created by society's reaction to disability. When working with persons with a disability, social workers need to provide assistance in both areas. In addition, social workers have an obligation to advocate for eradicating prejudices and discrimination against persons with a disability to ensure equal opportunities and rights for them.

In working with persons with a disability (and with other vulnerable populations) it is important for a social worker to have a focus on empowering people to maximize self-determination and independence. The following principle is relevant here: "If you give them fish, you feed them for a day; if you teach them to fish, you feed them for a lifetime." Empowering people was discussed at greater length in an earlier section of this chapter.

Historically and at the present time religious institutions have assisted African-Americans both materially and psychologically. African-American churches have been responsive to the needs of their community members, while governmental units (federal, state, and local jurisdictions) have often not put a high priority on meeting the needs of African-Americans. Second, African-American churches provide material, emotional, and spiritual assistance to members as well as advice. Examples of church programs include food and clothing programs, and visiting programs to the sick and shut-in. Finally, African-American churches play a prominent role in uplifting their members which increases their self-esteem and self-worth. In working with African-Americans, it is important for social workers to recognize the important role that African-American churches play, and to seek to form alliances with these churches in order to maximize the provision of services to this population. African-American churches are natural support systems that workers need to utilize in working with African-Americans who face challenges.

Zuniga (2003) has noted that Mexican American families tend to encounter such obstacles as fear of formal social and legal systems and therefore a hesitance to deal with these systems; prejudice from non-Mexican Americans; and lack of understanding by non-Mexican Americans of their culture and values.

Zuniga (2003) indicates Latino families tend to become involved with natural support systems such as extended families; religious institutions; godparents; and merchants and social clubs. These natural support systems are often resource systems for Latino families. In working with Latino families who face challenges, it is important for social workers to form quality relationships with these natural support systems so as to utilize these resources.

Women and girls throughout the world continue to experience: inequality (e.g., males being primarily in decision-making positions in government, in corporations, and businesses); discrimination (including gender pay inequalities and sexual harassment); violence (including sexual assaults and domestic violence); and the role of expectations of having the majority of child-rearing responsibilities. (See Exercise 12.5: Roles of Men and Women in Your Family)

Exercise 12.5: Roles of Men and Women in Your Family

Goal: This exercise is designed to assist you in examining gender-role patterns in your family.

Step 1:   Who are the primary caregivers in your family?

____ Men

____ Women

____ Shared equally between the sexes

Why do you think this has occurred?

Step 2:   Who primarily has performed the domestic tasks in your family?

____ Men

____ Women

____ Shared equally between the sexes

Why do you think this has occurred?

Step 3:   Who have been the primary financial providers in your family?

____ Men

____ Women

____ Shared equally between the sexes

Why do you think this has occurred?

Step 4:   For yourself, do you want these gender roles to continue in your future in your family?

____ Yes

____ No

If your answer is "'no," specify what you intend to do to change the gender roles you will fulfill in the future.

Feminism is a social movement that seeks to improve the status and well being of women. It is described in Exhibit 12.2, along with "Principles of Feminist Intervention."

Exercise 12.6: Feminist Intervention

Goal: This exercise is designed to further your understanding of feminist issues and feminist intervention.

Step 1:   Describe the plight of a female who you know could benefit from feminist intervention. Do not give identifying information (such as last name) of this person in your description.

Step 2:   Speculate about how a social worker could use principles of feminist therapy to counsel this person.

Exhibit 12.2   Principles of Feminist Intervention

Barker (2003, p. 161) defines *feminism* as "the social movement and doctrine advocating legal and socioeconomic equality for women. The movement originated in Great Britain in the eighteenth century." Barker (2003, p. 161) then defines *feminist social work* as "the integration of the *values*, skills, and knowledge of social work with a feminist orientation to help individuals and society overcome the emotional and social problems that result from *sex discrimination*."

Barker (2003, p. 161) defines *feminist therapy* as follows:

A psychosocial treatment orientation in which the professional (usually a woman) helps the client (usually a woman) in individual or group settings to overcome the psychological and social problems largely encountered as a result of *sex discrimination* and sex-role stereotyping. Feminist therapists help clients maximize potential, especially through *consciousness-raising*, eliminating sex stereotyping, and helping them become aware of the commonalities shared by all women.

Nine principles of feminist intervention have been identified (Kirst-Ashman & Hull, 2012; Van Den Berg, 1992, pp. 95–110; Van Den Berg & Cooper, 1987):

1. *A client's problems should be viewed "within a sociopolitical framework"* (Van Den Berg & Cooper, 1987, p. 613). Feminist intervention is concerned with the inequitable power relationship between women and men and is opposed to all "power-over" relationships, regardless of gender, race, class, age, and so on. Such relationships lead to oppression and domination. Feminism is concerned with changing all social, economic, and political structures based on the relationships between the haves and the have-nots. The problems of the have-nots are often rooted in a sexist social and political structure. Another way of stating this principle is that the "personal is political." According to Van Den Bergh (1992, p. 103):

   This principle maintains that what a woman experiences in her personal life is directly related to societal dynamics that affect other women. In other words, an individual woman's experiences of pejorative comments based on sex are directly related to societal sexism. For ethnic minority women, racism and classism also are factors that affect well-being.

   A primary distinguishing characteristic of feminist treatment is to help the client analyze how her problems are related to systematic difficulties experienced by women in a sexist, classist, and racist society.

2. *Traditional sex roles are pathological, and clients need encouragement to free themselves from traditional gender-role bonds.* Women are put in a double bind because of *femininity achievement incompatibility*. There is a traditional view in our society that a woman cannot be both feminine and an achiever. Achievement, erroneously, is thought to reduce a woman's femininity, and the truly feminine woman is thought to be someone who does not

seek to be an achiever. Traditionally, women have been socialized to fill a "learned helplessness" role. Van Den Bergh (1992, p. 101) describes the effects of such sex-role stereotyping:

Sex-role stereotypes suggest that women should be submissive, docile, receptive, and dependent. The message is one of helplessness; that women cannot take care of themselves and are dependent upon others for their well-being. This sets up a dynamic in which a woman's locus of control is external to her self, preventing her from believing that she can acquire what she needs on her own in order to develop and self-actualize. In other words, oversubscription to sex-role stereotypes engenders a state of powerlessness in which a woman is likely to become involved in situations where she becomes victimized. . . . For example, because young girls are socialized to be helpless, when they become women they tend to have a limited repertoire of responses when under stress; e.g., they respond passively.

In feminist treatment, clients are helped to see how their difficulties may be related to oversubscription to traditional sex-role stereotypes. They are shown that by internalizing traditional sex roles, women are inevitably set up to play passive, submissive roles and experience low self-esteem and self-hatred. The feminist approach asserts that clients need encouragement to make their own choices and pursue the tasks and achievements they desire, rather than be constrained by traditional sex roles.

3. *Intervention should focus on client empowerment.* Van Den Bergh (1992, p. 104) describes the empowerment process:

Helping women to acquire a sense of power, or the ability to affect outcome in their lives, is a crucial component of feminist practice. Empowerment means acquiring knowledge, skills, and resources that enhance an individual's ability to control her own life and to influence others. Traditionally women have used indirect, coven techniques to get what they want, such as helplessness, dependency, coyness, and demureness.

Empowerment is fostered in a variety of ways: (1) by helping the client define her own needs and clarify her personal goals so she can derive a sense of purposefulness; (2) by providing the client with education and access to resources; (3) by helping the client see that the direction and ability to change lie within herself (that is, alterations in her life will result only from her own undertakings); and (4) by focusing on the identification and enhancement of the client's strengths rather than on her pathologies. Women need to be empowered so they can increase their ability to control their environments to get what they need.

Exhibit 12.2   (*continued*)

4. *Clients' self-esteem should be enhanced.* Self-esteem and self-confidence are essential for empowerment. Self-esteem can be enhanced in a variety of ways. The worker should try to be an encouraging person. The worker should help clients identify and recognize their unique qualities and strengths. Many clients with low self-esteem tend to blame themselves for everything that is wrong. For example, a battered woman typically tends to blame herself for being battered. These clients need to look more realistically at those areas in which they are blaming themselves and feeling guilt. They need to distinguish where their responsibility for dysfunctional interactions ends and other individuals' responsibility begins.

5. *Clients should be encouraged to develop their identity (sense of self) on the basis of their own strengths, attributes, qualities, and achievements.* It is a serious mistake for a woman to develop her identity in terms of her spouse or dating partner. Women need to develop an independent identity that is not based on their relationships with others.

6. *Clients need to value and develop social support systems with other women.* In a society that devalues women, it is all too easy for some women to view other women as insignificant. With social support systems, women can ventilate their concerns and share their experiences and the solutions they've found to similar problems. They can serve as brokers in identifying resources and can provide emotional support and nurturance to one another.

7. *Clients need to find an effective balance between work and personal relationships.* Feminist intervention encourages both women and men to share in the nurturant aspects of their lives and in providing economic resources.

8. *The nature of the relationship between practitioner and client should approach equality as much as possible.*

Feminist practitioners do not view themselves as experts in resolving clients' problems but, rather, as catalysts whose role is helping clients empower themselves. Feminist practitioners try to eliminate dominant-submissive relationships. Regarding an egalitarian relationship, Van Den Bergh (1992, p. 104) notes,

> Obviously, there is an innate power differential between practitioner and client because the former has expertise and training as an "authority" However, the feminist admonition is to avoid abusing that status; "abuse" in this sense might be, for example, taking all credit for client change, or using terminology and nomenclature that are difficult for the client to understand.

9. *Many clients can benefit from learning to express themselves assertively.* The steps in assertiveness training are described in Module 2. As indicated earlier, many women are socialized to be passive and nonassertive, and as a result, they have difficulty expressing themselves assertively. Clients can be helped through individual and group counseling.

Clients who learn to express themselves assertively will experience increased self-confidence and self-esteem. They will be better able to communicate their thoughts, feelings, and opinions. Also, learning to express oneself assertively is an important component of empowerment.

Many women feel considerable anger over being victimized by sex discrimination and gender stereotyping. Some of these women turn these feelings inward, resulting in depression. Assertiveness training can help women recognize their right to be angry and also help them identify and practice constructive ways to express their anger assertively, rather than aggressively.

MACRO STRATEGIES TO PROMOTE SOCIAL AND ECONOMIC JUSTICE

Social Programs

Thousands of social programs have been enacted at national, state, and local levels to promote social and economic justice for a variety of vulnerable populations. A few examples are presented here.

The 1935 Social Security Act initiated a variety of programs for several vulnerable populations. Aid to the Blind provided financial assistance to low-income people of any age whose vision is 20/200 or less with correction. Aid to the Disabled provided financial assistance to low-income people, ages 18 to 65, who have a permanent disability Old Age Assistance provided financial assistance to low-income older persons (ages 65 and older). Aid to Dependent Children provided financial assistance to low-income mothers with children under age 18 and no father in the home.

In the 1960s President Lyndon Johnson declared a War on Poverty. Various anti-poverty programs were created, including Head Start, Medicare, and Medicaid. (Medicare helps older persons pay the high cost of health care; Medicaid primarily provides medical care for recipients of public assistance.)

In 1975, the U.S. Congress passed the Education for All Handicapped Children Act. This legislation mandates that all school districts identify students with physical, developmental, learning, and social-emotional problems that hamper their education. Once the children are identified, school districts are then required to develop specialized programs to meet their needs. In 2004, this law was renewed under the Individuals with Disabilities Act (IDEA).

In 1990, the U.S. Congress passed the Americans with Disabilities Act. This act prohibits discrimination against persons with a disability, in employment or by limiting access to public accommodations (such as restaurants, stores, museums, and theaters). The law requires that new public buildings be accessible to persons with a disability and requires that barriers in existing public buildings be removed if the changes can be accomplished without much difficulty or expense.

In 1996, the Personal Responsibility and Work Opportunity Reconciliation Act established the Temporary Assistance for Needy Families (TANF) program. TANF replaced the Aid to Families with Dependent Children (AFDC) program originally created in 1935. Each state receives a block grant from the federal government and is allowed substantial flexibility in setting up and operating the TANF program. Program purposes include providing assistance to needy families so that children can remain in their own homes; reducing dependency by helping recipients acquire job skills, encouraging work and marriage; eliminating out-of-wedlock pregnancies; and encouraging two-parent families. Unlike AFDC, TANF sets time limits and work requirements for recipients.

In 2010, the Affordable Health Care Act established a national health insurance plan in the United States.

Social workers have an obligation to be involved in enacting and implementing social programs to meet the needs of individuals and groups subjected to discrimination and oppression. Ways that social workers can participate in the enactment of needed social programs include running for political office, calling and writing to political officials to express their views about needed programs, campaigning for persons running for office who support the enactment of needed social programs, lobbying for needed programs, and joining and becoming active in groups that support the enactment of needed social programs. A more detailed list and discussion of macro-level strategies appears in Kirst-Ashman and Hull (2015).

Mass-Media Appeals

Newspapers, radio, and television at times present programs designed to explain the nature and harmful effects of prejudice and to promote social and economic justice for populations at risk. Mass media reaches large numbers of people simultaneously. By expanding public awareness of the existence of discrimination and its consequences, the media can strengthen control over highly prejudiced people. But it has limitations in changing prejudiced attitudes and behaviors; it primarily provides information and seldom has a lasting effect in changing deep-seated prejudices through propaganda. Broadcasting platitudes like "all people are brothers and sisters" and "prejudice is un-American" is not very effective. Highly prejudiced people are often unaware of their own prejudices. Even if they are aware, however, they generally dismiss mass-media appeals as irrelevant to them or as propaganda. Mass media has probably had a significant impact in reducing racial discrimination by showing nonwhites and whites working harmoniously in commercials, on news teams, and on TV shows.

Civil Rights Laws

In recent decades, equal rights laws have been enacted in areas such as employment, voting, housing, public accommodation, and education for a variety of vulnerable populations.

Populations benefiting from federal civil rights laws include people of color, women, persons with disabilities, and older persons.

Civil rights laws prohibit overt discrimination in specified areas. For example, in 1986 the U.S. Congress outlawed most mandatory age-related retirement policies, which had discriminated against older persons. The passage of a civil rights law protects the vulnerable population only in the area or areas specified in the law. The legislation does not provide protection in areas that are not specified. As a result, subtle discrimination often persists because it is hidden and therefore difficult to document.

How effective are laws in curbing discrimination and reducing prejudice? Proponents of civil rights legislation make certain assumptions. The first is that new laws will lessen discriminatory behavior. The laws redefine what was once "normal" behavior (discrimination) as now being "deviant." It is expected that attitudes over time will change and become more consistent with the mandated nondiscriminatory behavior. The second assumption is that the laws will be enforced.

Civil rights laws enacted after the Civil War, however, prohibited discriminatory behavior against African Americans but were seldom enforced and gradually eroded. It is also unfortunately true that some officials find ways to evade the intent of the law by eliminating only extreme, overt symbols of discrimination without changing other practices. Thus, the enactment of a law is only the first step in the process of changing prejudiced attitudes and practices. However, as Martin Luther King, Jr., noted, "The law may not make a man love me, but it can restrain him from lynching me, and I think that's pretty important" (www.quotationspage.com, 2004).

Activism

The strategy of activism attempts to promote social and economic justice through direct confrontation of policies involving discrimination and oppression. Activism has three types of politics: the politics of creative disorder, the politics of disorder, and the politics of escape (Johnson, 1973, pp. 374–379).

The *politics of creative disorder* operates on the edge of the dominant social system and includes school boycotts, rent strikes, job blockades, sit-ins (for example, at segregated restaurants), public marches, and product boycotts. This type of activism is based on the concept of nonviolent resistance. A classic illustration of nonviolent resistance began on December 1, 1955, when Rosa Parks, an African American in Montgomery, Alabama, refused to give up her seat on a bus to a white person. (Exhibit 12.3 describes Rosa Parks's act of courage.)

The *politics of disorder* reflects alienation from the dominant culture and disillusionment with the political system. In this type of activism, those being discriminated against resort to mob uprisings, riots, and other forms of violence.

In 1969, the National Commission on Causes and Prevention of Violence reported that 200 riots had occurred in the previous 5 years, when inner cities in the United States erupted (Johnson, 1973, p. 376). In the early 1980s, there were again some riots in Miami and in other U.S. inner cities. In 1992, race riots devastated parts of Los Angeles after the acquittal of four white police officers charged with using excessive force to arrest Rodney King, an African American; the brutal arrest had been videotaped. The focus of most of these riots has been aggression by people of color against white-owned property.

Riots and similar forms of activism have a long history in the United States, including draft riots in New York in 1863 and race riots in Chicago in 1919. The 1969 Stonewall riots involving gays against the police in New York is sometimes considered the beginning of the gay rights movement in this country. Riots are

---

Exhibit 12.3 Rosa Parks's Act of Courage Sparked the Civil Rights Movement

On December 1, 1955, Rosa Parks was in a hurry. She had a lot of things to do. When the bus came to the boarding area where she was standing in Montgomery, Alabama, she got on without paying attention to the driver. She rode the bus often and was aware of Montgomery's segregated seating laws, which required blacks to sit at the back of the bus.

In those days in the South, black people were expected to board the front of the bus, pay their fare, then get off and walk outside the bus to reboard on the back. But Rosa Parks noted the back was already crowded, standing-room only, with black passengers even standing on the back steps of the bus. It was apparent to Rosa that it would be all but impossible to reboard at the back. Besides, bus drivers sometimes drove off and left black passengers behind, even after accepting their fares. Rosa Parks spontaneously decided to take her chances. She paid her fare in the front of the bus, then walked down the aisle, and took a seat toward the back of the bus that was still in the area reserved for whites. At the second stop after boarding, a white man got on and had to stand.

The bus driver saw the white man standing and ordered Rosa Parks to move to the back. She refused, thinking," I want to be treated like a human being."

Two police officers were called and they arrested Rosa. She was taken to city hall, booked, fingerprinted, jailed, and fined. Her arrest and subsequent appeal all the way to the U.S. Supreme Court were the catalyst for a year-long boycott of the city buses by blacks, who composed 70% of the bus riders. The boycott inspired Martin Luther King, Jr., to become involved. The boycott ended when the Supreme Court declared Montgomery's segregated seating laws unconstitutional.

Rosa Parks's unplanned defiance of the segregated seating law sparked the civil rights movement. This movement not only has promoted social and economic justice for African Americans but also has served to inspire other groups to organize to advocate for their civil rights. These groups include other racial and ethnic groups, women, older persons, persons with a disability, and LGBT individuals.

common across the globe as a tool to bring about change. The sparks that set off riots can be as diverse as citizens lacking basic goods and services (for example, gas riots in Jamaica, 1999) to responding to oppression and ethnic/religious differences, as happened in India in 2004. Typically, riots are used as a tool when other efforts to end long-standing grievances and oppression have not been successful. Recent riots and demonstrations include the Occupy Wall Street effort in the USA in 2011, and in Greece in 2014 and 2015 in opposition to government austerity measures.

The *politics of escape* engages in passionate rhetoric about the oppression of populations. Because the focus is not on arriving at solutions, the rhetoric is not productive, except perhaps for providing an emotional release.

The principal value of activism or social protest seems to be that it informs the public of the existence of certain problems. The civil rights protests in the 1960s made practically all Americans aware of the discrimination to which nonwhite groups were being subjected. Since then, at least some of the discrimination has ceased, and race relations have improved. Continued protest beyond a certain (although indeterminate) point, however, appears to have had little additional value.

Affirmative Action Programs

Affirmative action programs provide for preferential hiring and admission requirements (for example, admission to medical schools) for minority applicants. Affirmative action programs cover minority groups, including women, many groups of color, and persons with a disability. (Women—though in the majority in the United States—are considered a minority group because for generations they have been subjected to discrimination and have been denied equal opportunities.) Affirmative action programs also require that employers must (1) make active efforts to locate and recruit qualified minority applicants, and (2) in certain circumstances, have hard quotas under which specific numbers of minority members must be accepted to fill vacant positions (for example, a university with a high proportion of white, male faculty may be required to fill half of its faculty vacancies with women and members of other minority groups). Affirmative action programs require that employers must demonstrate, according to a checklist of positive measures, that they are not guilty of discrimination.

A major dilemma with affirmative action programs is that preferential hiring and quota programs involve reverse discrimination, which sometimes arbitrarily excludes qualified majority group members. Several successful lawsuits have claimed reverse discrimination. The best-known case has been that of Alan Bakke, who was initially denied admission to the medical school at the University of California, Davis, in 1973. He alleged reverse discrimination because he had higher grades and higher scores on the Medical College Admissions Test than several minority applicants who were admitted under the university's minorities quota policy. In 1978, his claim was upheld by the U.S. Supreme Court in a precedent-setting decision (Sindler, 1978). The Court ruled that strict racial quotas were unconstitutional, but the Court did not rule that race could not be used as one among many criteria in making admissions decisions.

Supporters of affirmative action programs note that the majority group expressed little concern about discrimination when its members were the beneficiaries instead of the victims of discrimination. They also assert there is no other way to rapidly make up for past discrimination against minorities—many of whom may presently score slightly lower on qualification tests because they have not had the opportunities and the quality of training that the majority group members have had.

With affirmative action programs, some minority group members are given preferential treatment, which results in some whites being discriminated against. But minority group members still face more employment discrimination than whites do. Affirmative action programs raise delicate and complex questions about achieving equality through giving preferences in hiring and admissions to minorities. Yet no other means has been found to end subtle discrimination in hiring and admissions.

Admission to educational programs and well-paying jobs are crucial elements in working toward integration. The history of immigrant groups who have "made it" (such as the Irish, Japanese, and Italians) suggests equality will be achieved only when minority group members gain middle- and upper-class status. Once such status is achieved, the minority group members become an economic and political force to be reckoned with. Dominant groups are then pressured into modifying their norms, values, and stereotypes. For this reason, numerous authorities have noted that the elimination of economic discrimination is a prerequisite for achieving equality and harmonious race relations (Kornblum & Julian, 2009). Achieving educational equality between races is also crucial because lower educational attainments lead to less prestigious jobs, lower incomes, lower living standards, and the perpetuation of racial inequalities from one generation to the next.

Critics of affirmative action assert that it is a highly politicized and painful remedy that stigmatizes many of those it was meant to help. Affirmative action is now perceived by many in our society as a system of preferences for the unqualified. Critics further assert that although affirmative action may have been necessary 40 years ago to make sure that minority candidates received fair treatment to counter the social barriers to hiring and admission that stemmed from centuries of unequal treatment, such programs are no longer needed. They assert that it is wrong to discriminate against white males for the sole purpose of making up for an injustice that somebody's great-grandfather may have done to somebody else's great-grandfather. They assert that it is wrong for the daughter of a wealthy African American couple, for example, to be given preference in employment over the son of a homeless alcoholic who happens to be white.

In 1996, voters in the state of California passed Proposition 209, which explicitly rejects the idea that women and other minority group members should get special consideration when applying for jobs, government contracts, or university admission. This affirmative action ban became law in California in August 1997. In addition, numerous lawsuits have been filed objecting to reverse discrimination. If the courts rule in favor of those filing the lawsuits, the power of affirmative action programs will be sharply reduced. In November 1997, the U.S. Supreme Court rejected a challenge to the California law that ended racial and gender preferences in that state. This Supreme Court action clears the way for other states and cities to ban affirmative action. The states of Washington and Michigan have since voted to abolish the use of affirmative action in public university admissions.

Supporters of affirmative action believe that if we abandon affirmative action, we return to the old-boy network. They assert that affirmative action has helped a number of women and people of color to attain a good education and higher-paying positions and thereby to remove themselves from the ranks of the poor. They assert that in a society in which racist and sexist attitudes remain, affirmative action is necessary to give women and people of color a fair opportunity at attaining a quality education and well-paying jobs.

Is there a middle ground for the future of affirmative action? Zuckerman (1995) recommends:

> The vast majority of Americans would probably accept a return to the original notion of affirmative action—an aggressive outreach to minorities to make sure they have a fair shot. They would probably see a social benefit in accepting that racial justice might be relevant in a tiebreaker case, or might even confer a slight advantage. The goal must be a return to policies based on evenhandedness for individuals rather than for groups. Then employers can concentrate on whether a minority applicant is the right person for the job rather than being moved by whether the applicant looks litigious. All employees could take it for granted that they had a fair shot. (p. 112)

Exercise 12.7: Your Thoughts on Affirmative Action Programs

Goal: This exercise is designed to assist you in analyzing the merits and shortcomings of affirmative action programs.

Step 1: Specify the merits and benefits of affirmative action programs. (With affirmative action programs, some minority group members are given preferential treatment, which results in some whites being discriminated against.)

Step 2: Specify the shortcomings of affirmative action programs.

Step 3: Specify your recommendation about whether affirmative action programs should be (a) continued, (b) discontinued, or (c) changed in a direction you suggest. Explain your rationale.

Confrontation of Jokes and Discriminatory Actions

Jokes and sarcastic remarks about people of color, women, persons with a disability, and other populations at risk perpetuate stereotypes and prejudices. It is important that we all seek to tactfully but assertively indicate that we do not view such remarks as humorous or appropriate. We must also tactfully and assertively point out the inappropriateness of discriminatory actions by others against vulnerable populations. Such confrontations make explicit that jokes and discriminatory actions involving vulnerable populations are harmful; this has a consciousness-raising effect. Gradually, such confrontations will help reduce prejudices and discriminatory actions.

Asset-Based Community Development

Asset-based community development is described in exhibit 10.6, "The Mercado Central" (pp. 224–225). A case example of the approach is also presented in this exhibit.

SUMMARY

The following summarizes the chapter's content in terms of the learning objectives presented at the beginning of the chapter.

1. Define key terms involving diversity.
   The following terms were defined: Stereotypes, prejudice, discrimination, oppression, minority group, diverse groups, and social justice.
2. Identify stereotypes.
   Material is presented to help students identify their stereotypes about diverse groups. Negative stereotyping and discrimination can occur independently of each other; for example, someone may hold negative stereotypes about a group, but yet not discriminate against that group. There are a variety of causes of negative stereotyping and discrimination—including the belief in white supremacy.
3. Comprehend four general principles of social work practice with diverse groups.
   Four principles were described: empowerment, strengths perspective, cultural competence, and cultural humility.
4. Understand the cultures of diverse groups and understand effective intervention approaches.
   There are an immense number of vulnerable diverse groups in our society. A partial list includes: racial groups, ethnic groups, women, children, older persons, people with a mental or physical disability, the homeless, those living in poverty, the LGBT population, and some religious groups. It is beyond the scope of this chapter to describe the unique characteristics of all the vulnerable groups in our society. Instead, a few characteristics were summarized to illustrate the importance of learning about the cultural and social background of the client. Also, examples of effective intervention approaches with selected vulnerable groups were presented.
5. Describe macro strategies to promote social and economic justice.
   The following strategies were described: social programs, mass-media appeals, civil rights laws, activism, affirmative action programs, and confrontation of jokes and discriminatory actions.

EXERCISES

1. Understanding Stereotypes

Goal: To increase understanding of the origins and effects of stereotypes, and to explore ways to change negative stereotypes.

Step 1: In subgroups of three or four students, make a list on flip chart paper of common stereotypes of people who are:

Muslim	Bankrupt
Native American	Divorced
HIV positive	Mexican American
On public assistance	Autistic

Step 2: Each group tapes its lists on a wall that displays the stereotypes to the whole class.

Step 3: A class discussion is then held on the following questions:

1. Which stereotypes are accurate, and which are erroneous?
2. Are the stereotypes largely positive or negative?
3. What are the impacts of the stereotypes on those who belong to the category?
4. Where did these stereotypes come from?
5. What can be done to change inaccurate negative stereotypes in a positive direction?

2. Understanding Feminist Therapy

Goal: Assist students in understanding and applying feminist intervention.

Step 1:   The instructor either explains the principles of feminist intervention, or asks the students to read the content on feminist intervention in this chapter.

Step 2:   The instructor asks for a female volunteer to play the role of a client. The volunteer needs to select a challenge that a woman might face, such as being sexually harassed by her male employer, while needing to keep her job as she is a single "mom" with two young children. After a student volunteers to play this role in counseling, the instructor asks for a second volunteer to play the role of the therapist. Once a second person volunteers, the instructor asks the "therapist" to realistically apply as many principles of feminist intervention as possible.

Step 3:   The "therapist" counsels the "client."

Step 4:   A class discussion is then held on what the "therapist" did well in applying the principles of feminist intervention, and what else the "therapist" might have done to apply the principles of feminist intervention.

3. Jedi Starwing to Aquarii

Goal: Assist students in identifying some of their positive and negative stereotypes about various ethnic and racial groups.

Step 1:   Form subgroups of four or five persons. The instructor reads the following to the subgroups:

The United States has recently discovered a planet in a distant galaxy that appears to have a climate and atmosphere remarkably similar to the Earth. Scientists are virtually assured that this planet, named Aquarii, can support human life. In addition, the United States has recently completed building a new spaceship, named Jedi Starwing, that can travel at the speed of light. It can transport 20 people. At the same time that space travel to another planet appears to be a reality, a new comet called The Obliterator is discovered and is found to be on a collision course for Earth. Scientists predict it will strike the Earth in approximately two and one-half months. A huge explosion, much worse than a nuclear war, is predicted. Some scientists are even predicting the comet will cause the Earth to disintegrate. The President of the United States has commissioned your subgroup to choose the racial and ethnic backgrounds of the twenty people who will be selected to board Jedi Starwing, and to then fly to Aquarii to continue the human race. The twenty people may come from one ethnic/racial background, or from a variety (up to 20) backgrounds. After your subgroup provides its selections, the President will select, consistent with your choices, people in their twenties, including ten men and ten women. All the persons selected will be fluent in the English language.

Step 2:   After the subgroups make their selections, a representative from each subgroup states its choices. (These may be written on the board.) Each representative states the reasons for the subgroup's selections.

Step 3:   A class discussion is held on whether the selections were based on stereotypes of racial and ethnic groups.

4. What If I Woke Up Tomorrow and My Sexual Orientation Had Changed???

Goal: This exercise is designed to help students better understand some of the issues confronting the LGB population today, and to examine their ideas and stereotypes about heterosexuality and same-sex attractions.

Step 1:   Form subgroups of four to five people. Discuss the following questions: "How would the life of a heterosexual person change if she/he woke up tomorrow being sexually attracted to same-sex relationships?" "How would the life of a person who is gay change if she/he woke up tomorrow having heterosexual attractions?" Subsidiary questions might include: "How would this change her/his relationships to family members and friends?" "Would this affect his/her work life?" "How might her/his social life be affected?"

Step 2:   After the subgroup discussions, each subgroup chooses someone to summarize the discussion. The representative from each subgroup then shares a summary of the discussion with the class.

Step 3:   The instructor may choose to end the exercise by making some summary statements regarding what was learned from this exercise.

SPIRITUALITY AND RELIGION IN SOCIAL WORK PRACTICE

LEARNING OBJECTIVES

You are a social worker for the following clients. An older male client who displays manic-depressive symptoms informs you that he recently had an intense spiritual experience. As a result, he wants to quit his job, separate from his wife and grown children, and make pilgrimages to holy sites. How do you respond to his stated intentions?

A married mother of seven children who is a devout Roman Catholic is pregnant. Her husband and she both work full-time, but their combined earnings are well below the poverty level for their family size. She and her husband come to see you about their options for this pregnancy. They ask whether you believe abortion is a morally acceptable option. How do you respond?

A 75-year-old male with a terminal degenerative illness is in intense pain that painkillers are unable to relieve. He asks you for a referral for physician-assisted suicide. How do you respond?

A married couple contacts you for advice about a plan to physically kidnap their son from a religious cult. The son dropped out of college after joining this cult and now lives in a distant state in a cult commune. How do you respond to their request for advice?

Such questions pose various moral, ethical, and value dilemmas. Bullis (1996) notes,

> The spiritual issues clients raise are as diverse as the clients themselves. For some, grief over the loss of a loved one, a job or career, a marriage, or a child is spiritual. For some, decisions over pregnancy, marriage, separation and divorce, disease, terminal illness, or debilitating illness are spiritual. For others, the experience of depression, alienation, isolation or ennui evokes spiritual issues. For sull others, crises of war, immigration, child custody disputes, child abuse, or domestic violence trigger spiritual concerns. Spiritual questions deserve thoughtful, deliberate, and authentic responses. (p. 9)

This chapter will help prepare students to:

Understand a rationale for the use of spirituality and religion in social work practice
Describe four prominent religions
Describe spiritual and religious assessments of clients
Describe spiritual and religious interventions with clients
Describe social work and religion in limited partnership

SPIRITUALITY AND RELIGION

A major thrust of social work education is to prepare students for culturally sensitive practice. Because religion and spirituality play important roles in all cultures, it is essential that social workers comprehend the influence of religion and spirituality in human lives. The Council on Social Work Education's *Educational Policy and Accreditation Standards* (2015) requires that accredited baccalaureate and master's programs provide practice content in this area so that students will develop approaches and skills for working with clients with differing religious and spirituality backgrounds.

Spirituality and religion are separate though often related dimensions. *Spirituality* is a broad concept with room for many dimensions. In general, it includes a sense of connection to something larger than ourselves, and it typically involves a search for meaning in life. Spirituality is a universal human experience—something that touches all of us. Some may seek meaning through their connections to art or nature. Some may find their spirituality is intricately linked to their association with a synagogue, church, mosque, or temple. Others may define their spirituality as being a relationship with a higher power; they may even pray to this higher power, but view the higher power as being unrelated to a specific religious organization. A person's definition of spirituality may change as the years go by.

Religion is an organized system of beliefs, rules, and ceremonies used to worship a god or a group of gods. For some people the religious organization they belong to largely determines their spiritual beliefs. For others, their spiritual beliefs are distantly related to any organized religion.

Social work has historical roots in religious organizations. The philanthropic founders of social work were inspired by Judeo-Christian religious traditions. Jewish scriptures and religious law requiring the emulation of God's creativity and caring have spurred social welfare activities for many centuries. Similarly, the Christian biblical command to love one's neighbor as oneself is interpreted as establishing a moral responsibility for social service. This idea drove the development of charity organizations and philanthropy in the United States during the nineteenth century. Social workers need to be trained for effective practice with religiously oriented clients. Many social issues today—abortion, use of contraceptives, acceptance of gay, lesbian, bisexual, and transgendered (LGBT) individuals, reproductive technology, roles of women, prayer in public schools, physician-assisted suicide—have religious dimensions.

Social workers need to have an appreciation and respect for religious beliefs that differ from their own chosen beliefs. There is a danger that those who believe that their religion is the "one true religion" will tend to view people with divergent religious beliefs as ill-guided, evil, mistaken or in need of being "saved." More wars have been fought over religious differences than for any other reason. A major source of intolerance, discrimination, and oppression is this notion: "My religion is the one true religion. Anyone who believes as I do will go to heaven. Those who follow in some other religion are heathens condemned to eternal damnation."

Furman (1994, p. 10) notes, "The goal of incorporating religious and spiritual beliefs in social work curricula should include a broad array of knowledge of many different religious and spiritual beliefs, primarily to expand students' understanding and sensitivity." As a beginning effort to move in this direction, Exhibit 13.1 summarizes information on four prominent religions: Judaism, Christianity, Islam, and Buddhism. These religions were selected because of their prominence, but there are hundreds of other religions in the world. Practicing social workers should have a knowledge and appreciation of the religious beliefs and value systems of their clients.

RATIONALE FOR THE USE OF SPIRITUALITY AND RELIGION IN SOCIAL WORK PRACTICE

Traditionally, social work literature has tended to ignore the impact of religion or spirituality on social work practice. Loewenberg (1988) identified several reasons for this neglect: The psychoanalytic movement (which social work was involved with for many years) rejected religious approaches to furthering the personal and social well-being of people. Economic, political, and professional competition has at times existed between members of the clergy and secular social workers. In the United States, the separation of church and state led many social workers to avoid spiritual assessments and interventions with clients. Some social workers avoid spiritual aspects of human behavior because of their perception that spirituality and social work are totally distinct from one another. Spirituality has been viewed (erroneously) as having only heavenly concerns, and social work has been viewed (erroneously) as having only earthly concerns.

As noted in Chapter 1, the pioneers of the social work profession (such as Jane Addams, who founded Hull House) often used interventions that had religious or spiritual components (such as initiating and leading Bible classes) in providing services to their communities. In addition, many religious organizations are heavily involved in providing social services. Examples of such organizations include Jewish Social Services, Catholic Charities, Lutheran Social Services, YMCA (Young Men's Christian Association), and YWCA (Young Women's Christian Association). Twelve-step self-help groups also have a spiritual component, emphasizing recognition of a "higher power." Examples of 12-step self-help groups include Alcoholics Anonymous, Emphysema Anonymous, Smokers Anonymous, Gamblers Anonymous, Narcotics Anonymous, Overeaters Anonymous, and Families Anonymous.

Social work, historically and philosophically, has links to spirituality. Philosophically, social work and spirituality are natural allies in working for personal and social well-being. Social workers and the clergy have numerous similar goals. Both promote personal and community welfare, both urge the ending of interpersonal violence, and both are advocates for family values.

The spiritual aspects of a person's life should be an important area of assessment by both social workers and the clergy. To ignore this aspect is a serious error. As indicated earlier, spiritual beliefs often are major determinants in clients' decisions in such areas as terminating a pregnancy, seeking a divorce, seeking physician-assisted suicide, entering the military (which may lead to deadly combat with an enemy), and using reproductive technology.

Exercise 13.1:   Understanding Your Religious Beliefs, and Your Spiritual Beliefs

Goal: This exercise is designed to assist you in understanding and becoming comfortable with your religious beliefs.

Step 1:   Summarize your religious and spiritual beliefs.

Step 2:   If you have questions about religion that you experience discomfort about (and many people have questions), specify these questions.

Step 3:   If you wrote questions in the previous step, specify what you hope to do to obtain answers—such as talking to a member of the clergy or taking a course in the philosophy of religion.

Step 4:   Do you believe there is "one true religion"?

___ Yes   ___ No

If your answer is "yes," what is this religion, and what evidence do you have?

Step 5:   If a social worker firmly believes that his or her religion is the one true religion, can that worker fully accept clients who adhere to other religious faiths?

___ Yes   ___ No

Explain your view.

> In a study from a national probability sample of clinical social workers ($N = 283$) in the United States, Kuarfordt and Sheridan (2009) found that these social workers received limited content on religion and spirituality in their social work educational program. The authors highly recommend:
>
> > attention to religious and spiritual diversity should be addressed in the curriculum to the same degree as other aspects of human diversity, such as race, gender, age, class, or sexual orientation. (p. 401)
>
> In another study, Sheridan and Amatovon Hemert (1999) found that while social work students want more content on religion and spirituality in their social work education, they are receiving relatively little exposure to content on religion and spirituality in their educational program.

SPIRITUAL AND RELIGIOUS ASSESSMENTS OF CLIENTS

> In the twentieth century many social workers (and psychologists and psychiatrists) ignored religious and spiritual aspects of clients' lives in their assessments. Today, helping professions increasingly recognize the importance of attending to religious and spiritual matters in assessments. The CSWE *Educational Policy and Accreditation Standards* (2015) identifies religion and spiritual development as important areas for social workers to attend to in their work with individuals, groups, families, organizations, and communities. The American Psychiatric Association's *Diagnostic and Statistical Manual–5* (2013) recognizes spiritual and religious issues as an important area of assessment. For example, section V62.89, titled "Religious or Spiritual Problem," (p. 725) states,
>
> > This category can be used when the focus of clinical attention is a religious or spiritual problem. Examples include distressing experiences that involve loss or questioning of faith, problems associated with conversion to a new faith, or questioning of spiritual values that may not necessarily be related to an organized church or religious institution.
>
> What kinds of questions are useful in a spiritual or religious assessment with a client? Here are a few suggestions:
>
> 1. What are your main religious and spiritual beliefs?
> 2. What is your current religious or spiritual affiliation?

Exhibit 13.1   Four Prominent Religions

Judaism Judaism is the religion of the Jews. Jews believe in one God, the creator of the world who delivered the Israelites out of their bondage in Egypt. The Hebrew Bible is the primary source of Judaism. (The Hebrew Bible was adopted by Christians as part of their sacred writings, and they now call it the "Old Testament.") God is believed to have revealed his law (Torah) to the Israelites; part of this law was the Ten Commandments, which were given to Moses by God. The Israelites believed God chose them to be a light to all humankind.

Next in importance to the Hebrew Bible is the Talmud. The Talmud is an influential compilation of rabbinic traditions and discussions about Jewish life and law. The Talmud consists of the Mishnah (the codification of the oral Torah) and a collection of extensive early rabbinical commentary. Various later commentaries and the standard code of Jewish law and ritual (Halakhah) produced in the later Middle Ages have been important in shaping Jewish practice and thought.

Abraham (who lived roughly 2,000 years before Christ) is viewed as an ancestor or father of the Hebrew people. According to Genesis, he came from the Sumerian town of Ur (now part of modern Iraq) and migrated with his family and flocks via Haran (the ancient city of Nari on the Euphrates) to the "Promised Land" of Canaan, where he settled at Shechem (modern Nablus). After a sojourn in Egypt, he lived to be 175 years old and was buried with Sarah, his first wife. By Sarah, he was the father of Isaac (whom he was prepared to sacrifice at the behest of the Lord) and grandfather of Jacob ("Israel"). By his second wife, Hagar (Sarah's Egyptian handmaiden), he was the father of Ismael, the ancestor of 12 clans. By his third wife, Keturah, he had six sons who became the ancestors of the Arab tribes. He was also the uncle of Lot. (Interestingly, Abraham is regarded as being an important ancestor or father in Judaism, Christianity, and Islam.)

All Jews see themselves as members of a community with origins around the time in which Abraham lived. This past lives on in its rituals. The family is the basic unit of Jewish ritual, although the synagogue plays an important role. Observation of the Sabbath, which begins at sunset on Friday and ends at sunset on Saturday, is the central religious ritual. The synagogue is the center for community worship and study. Its main feature is the "ark," a cupboard containing the handwritten scrolls of the Pentateuch (the five books of Moses in the Hebrew Bible, comprising Genesis, Exodus, Leviticus, Numbers, and Deuteronomy). Rabbis are primarily teachers and spiritual guides.

There is an annual cycle of religious festivals and days of fasting. Rosh Hashanah, the Jewish New Year, falls in September or October. During the New Year's Day service, a ram's horn is blown as a call to repentance and spiritual renewal. The holiest day in the Jewish year is Yom Kippur, the Day of Atonement, which comes at the end of 10 days of penitence following Rosh Hashanah; Yom Kippur is a day devoted to fasting, prayer, and repentance for past sins. Another important festival is Hanukkah, in December, commemorating the rededication of Jerusalem after the victory of Judas Maccabees over the Syrians. Pesach, the Passover festival, occurs in March or April, commemorating the exodus of the Israelites from Egypt; the festival gets its name from God's passing over the houses of the Israelites when he killed the firstborn children of Egyptian families.

Christianity Developed out of Judaism, Christianity is practiced in numerous countries and is centered on the life and work of Jesus of Nazareth in Israel. The earliest followers were Jews who, after the death and resurrection of Jesus, believed Jesus to be the Messiah, or Christ, promised by the prophets in the Old Testament. He was declared to be the Son of God. During his life he chose 12 men as disciples who formed the nucleus of the church. This communion of believers believed that Jesus would come again to inaugurate the "Kingdom of God." God is believed to be one in essence but threefold in person, comprising the Father, Son, and Holy Spirit, or Holy Ghost (known as the Trinity). Jesus Christ is also wholly human because of his birth to Mary. The Holy Spirit is the touch or "breath" of God, which inspires people to follow the Christian faith. The Bible is thought to have been written under the Holy Spirit's influence.

Jesus Christ was the son of Mary and Joseph yet also the Son of God, created by a miraculous conception by the Spirit of God. He was born in Bethlehem (near Jerusalem) but began his ministry in Nazareth. The main records of his ministry are the New Testament Gospels, which show him proclaiming the coming of the Kingdom of God and, in particular, the acceptance of the oppressed and the poor into the Kingdom. The duration of his public ministry is uncertain, but from John's Gospel we get the impression of a 3-year period of teaching. Jesus was executed by crucifixion under the order of Pontius Pilate, a Roman ruler. The date of death is uncertain, but it is considered to be when Jesus was in his early 30s.

At the heart of the Christian faith is the conviction that through Jesus' death and resurrection, God has allowed humans to find salvation. Belief in Jesus as the Son of God, along with praying for forgiveness of sin, brings forgiveness of all sin. Many Christians believe that those who ask for forgiveness of their sins will join God in heaven, while unbelievers who do not ask for forgiveness of their sins will be consigned to hell. The Gospel of Jesus was proclaimed at first by word of mouth, but by the end of the first century A.D. it was written and became accepted as the authoritative scripture of the New Testament. Through the witness of the 12 earliest leaders (Apostles) and their successors, the Christian faith, despite sporadic persecution, spread through the Greek and Roman world, and in A.D. 315 it was declared by Emperor Constantine to be the official religion of the Roman Empire. Christianity survived the break-up of the Empire and the "Dark Ages," largely through the life and witness of groups of monks in monasteries. The religion helped form the basis of civilization in the Middle Ages in Europe. Since the Middle Ages, major divisions of Christianity have separated as a result of differences in doctrine and practice.

Islam Islam is the Arabic word for "submission" to the will of God (Allah). Islam is also the name of the religion originating in Arabia during the seventh century through the prophet Muhammad. Followers of Islam are known as Muslims, or Moslems.

Exhibit 13.1   (*continued*)

Muhammad was born in Mecca. He was the son of Abdal-lah, a poor merchant of the powerful tribe of Quaraysh, hereditary guardians of the shrine in Mecca. Muhammad was orphaned at age 6 and raised by his grandfather and uncle. His uncle Abu Talib trained him to be a merchant. At the age of 24, Muhammad entered the service of a rich widow, Khadijah, whom he eventually married. They had six children. While continuing as a trader, Muhammad became increasingly drawn to religious contemplation. Soon afterward he began to receive revelations of the word of Allah, the one and only God. These revelations given to Muhammad by the angel Gabriel over a period of 20 years were eventually codified into the Quran (Koran). The Quran commanded that the numerous idols of the shrine should be destroyed and that the rich should give to the poor. This simple message attracted some support but provoked a great deal of hostility from those who felt that their interests were threatened. When his wife and uncle died, Muhammad was reduced to poverty, but he began making a few converts among pilgrims to Mecca. Muhammad eventually migrated to Hegira. The name of this town was changed to Medina, "city of the prophet." This migration marks the beginning of the Muslim era. After a series of battles with warring enemies of Islam, Muhammad was able to take control of Mecca, which recognized him as chief and prophet. By A.D. 630, he had control over all Arabia. Two years later he fell ill and died in the home of one of his nine wives. His tomb in the mosque at Medina is venerated throughout Islam.

The religion of Islam embraces every aspect of life. Muslims believe that individuals, societies, and governments should all be obedient to the will of God as set forth in the Quran. The Quran teaches that there is one God, who has no partners. He is the Creator of all things and has absolute power over them. All persons should commit themselves to lives of praise-giving and grateful obedience to God, for everyone will be judged on the Day of Resurrection. Those who have obeyed God's commandments will dwell forever in paradise; those who have sinned against God and have not repented will be condemned eternally to the fires of hell. Since the beginning of time, God has sent prophets (including Abraham, Moses, and Jesus) to provide the guidance necessary for the attainment of eternal reward.

Devout Muslims have five essential religious duties, known as "the pillars of Islam." (1) The Shahadah (profession of faith) is sincere recitation of the twofold creed: "There is no god but God" and "Muhammad is the Messenger of God." (2) The Salat (formal prayer) must be performed at fixed hours five times a day while facing toward the holy city of Mecca. (3) Alms giving through the payment of Zakat ("purification") is regarded primarily as an act of worship and is the duty of sharing one's wealth out of gratitude for God's favor, according to the uses stated in the Quran. (4) There is a duty to fast (Saum) during the month of Ramadan (the ninth month of the Muslim year, during which Muslims abstain from eating and drinking between sunrise and sunset). (5) The pilgrimage to Mecca is to be performed if at all possible at least once during one's lifetime.

Shariah, the sacred law of Islam, applies to all aspects of life, not just religious practices. This sacred law is found in the Quran and in the sunnah (the sayings and acts of Muhammad).

Buddhism Buddhism originated in India about 2,500 years ago and is derived from the teachings of Buddha (Siddharta Gautama). Buddha is regarded as one of a continuing series of enlightened beings.

Buddha was born the son of the rajah of the Sakya tribe in Kapilavastu, north of Benares. His personal name was Siddharta, but he was also known by his family name of Gautama. At about age 30 he left the luxuries of the court, his beautiful wife, and all earthly ambitions. He became an ascetic, practicing strict self-denial as a measure of personal and spiritual discipline. After several years of severe austerities, he saw in meditation and contemplation the way to enlightenment. For the next four decades he taught, gaining many followers and disciples. He died at Kusinagara in Oudh.

The teaching of Buddha is summarized in the Four Noble Truths, the last of which asserts the existence of a path leading to deliverance from the universal human experience of suffering. A central tenet of Buddhism is the law of Karma, by which good and evil deeds result in appropriate rewards or punishments in this life or in a succession of rebirths. It is believed that the sum of a person's actions is carried forward from one life to the next, leading to an improvement or deterioration in that person's fate. Through a proper understanding of the law of Karma and by obedience to the right path, humans can break the chain of Karma.

The Buddha's path to deliverance is through morality (Sila), meditation (samadhi), and wisdom (panna). The goal is nirvana, which is the "blowing out" of the fires of all desires and absorption of the self into the infinite. All Buddhas are greatly revered, with a place of special accordance being given to Gautama.

There are two main branches of Buddhism, dating from its earliest history. Theravada Buddhism adheres to the strict and narrow teachings of the early Buddhist writings; in this branch, salvation is possible for only the few who accept the severe discipline and effort to achieve it. Mahayana Buddhism is more liberal and makes concessions to popular piety; it teaches that salvation is possible for everyone. It introduced the doctrine of the bodhisattva (or personal saviour). A bodhisattva is one who has attained the enlightenment of a Buddha but chooses not to pass into nirvana. Rather, this person voluntarily remains in the world to help lesser beings attain enlightenment. This view emphasizes charity toward others. Mahayana Buddhism asserts that all living beings have the inner potential of Buddha nature. Buddha nature is a kind of spiritual embryo that holds out the promise to all people that they can eventually become Buddhas because they all have the potential for Buddhahood.

3. Would you describe yourself as strict or lenient (casual) in following the values and principles of your religious or spiritual affiliation?
4. What changes have occurred in your religious and spiritual orientation since your childhood years? What events or experiences were associated with these changes?
5. What was the religious or spiritual faith of your parents? Were they strict or casual in their beliefs?
6. How have your parents' beliefs influenced you in the past? Do their beliefs still influence you? If "yes," how?
7. What do you think are the most important spiritual beliefs held by your parents? Do you currently hold these same beliefs?
8. What are the main religious beliefs of the people closest to you (such as a spouse or partner)?
9. In what religious or spiritual orientation were they raised? Have they remained with this orientation? Why, or why not?
10. What, if any, religious or spiritual issues have caused problems with those you are closest to? Are there some current unresolved spiritual issues with your partner?
11. How comfortable are you with your current religious and spiritual beliefs?
12. Are you currently struggling with religious or spiritual issues? If "yes," what are those issues?

Exercise 13.2: A Religious and Spiritual Assessment

Goal: This exercise is designed to give you practice in conducting a religious and spiritual assessment.

Step 1:   Ask a friend or acquaintance the 12 questions for conducting a religious and spiritual assessment. Summarize the answers here.

Step 2:   If the person has current religious or spiritual issues, specify your recommendations for resolving these issues.

> When you are conducting a spiritual assessment, your clients may ask you what your religious affiliation is. How should you respond? If your spiritual or religious affiliation differs from that of your clients, they may erroneously believe that the difference will interfere with rapport, with your comprehension of their spiritual dilemmas, and with solutions you may suggest. Therefore, a useful response is, "Our agency has a policy that instructs us not to share our religious affiliation." (To ensure honesty, you may well want to request that your agency adopt such a policy.) The underlying reason for a client asking this question may be that the client is trying to determine if the worker has the necessary knowledge, skills, and qualifications to help him or her. Therefore, it may be useful for the worker to add something like the following: "I think it is highly desirable for clients to assess whether a professional person they are beginning to work with has the necessary expertise to assist them in problem-solving the challenges they are facing. Let me briefly summarize my background and training related to your personal challenges." (The worker then summarizes his or her background and training.) The worker then adds: "If you have further questions, now or in the future, about my background and training, I'd be happy to answer such questions."
>
> Nelson and Wilson (1984) identify an exception to the guideline that social workers generally should not share their religious beliefs with clients. In their view it is ethical for social workers to share their religious beliefs with a client if three conditions are met: (1) There is a high probability that such sharing will assist in problem-solving the client's issues. (2) The discussions related to sharing are held within the clients own belief systems. (3) Such sharing is defined within the intervention contract. (At the present time, few intervention contracts discuss such sharing.)

SPIRITUAL AND RELIGIOUS INTERVENTIONS WITH CLIENTS

> Which spiritually related interventions should social workers use, and which should not be used? This is an important question! Spiritually related interventions vary widely, from referring clients to 12-step self-help groups, using or recommending religious literature in counseling, teaching spiritual meditation to clients, meditating spiritually with clients, praying privately for clients, praying with clients in counseling, using religious language or metaphors in counseling, touching clients for "healing" purposes, reading scripture

with clients in counseling, helping clients clarify religious or spiritual values in counseling, referring clients to religious counselors or to members of the clergy, exploring religious elements in dreams, recommending religious penance or some other religious ritual in counseling, to performing exorcism. Which of these interventions are appropriate, and which are inappropriate? The social work profession and the judicial system have not established clear-cut guidelines, but a review of social work literature provides some ideas. However, many questions remain unanswered.

Sherwood (1981) and Keith-Lucas (1985) provide some guidelines for social workers with strong religious beliefs:

1. At times you may encounter major conflicts between the values of the social work profession and your religion. Possible areas of conflict include abortion, rights to be accorded to LGBT individuals, military combat service, use of contraceptives, use of reproductive technology, and physician-assisted suicide. Integrating faith and practice involves difficult judgments and compromise because every choice will advance certain values at the expense of other values.

2. It is possible to work with clients whose values are at variance with yours. It is acceptable for you to express your own values, when appropriate, as long as they are clearly labeled as yours and as long as you emphasize that clients have the right and responsibility to make their own choices (and to then be accountable for the consequences).

3. A social agency, particularly a secular one, is not an appropriate setting for a social worker espousing his or her religious beliefs.

4. When working in a social agency, you have an obligation to carry out the policy of the agency. For example, in a public health clinic, you must adhere to the agency's policies on issues such as discussing the use of condoms with gays and with unmarried clients as a means of AIDS prevention, providing birth control information to teenagers, discussing abortion as an option to a problem pregnancy, and discussing strategies for obtaining clean needles with IV drug addicts. Keith-Lucas (1985, p. 32) notes, "One has no right to ignore policies or give them subtly some other meaning than that which the agency intends. Clients have a right to rely on an agency's consistency and Government or a Board of Trustees that its money be spent as it directs."

5. Should you be asked at the employing agency to do something that you cannot in good conscience do, you have three choices. One is to resign. The second is to refuse to carry out the policy (in which case you may be fired). The third is to advocate for a change in agency policy.

Many religiously affiliated agencies employ social workers who are not very religious. What should you do when a religiously affiliated agency asks you to do something that runs counter to the values of your profession? For example, what should pro-choice social workers do when employed by a Catholic agency that has a strict policy against discussing abortion as an option for clients? Workers in such a setting certainly have an obligation to follow agency policy and to not discuss abortion—but they also have an obligation to follow the pro-choice position of the social work profession. Workers in such a selling can resign, request that the agency change its policy (which a Catholic-affiliated agency in this situation will not do), adhere to the policy of the agency, or ask to be reassigned to another unit of the agency where they will not be serving pregnant clients. (It is perfectly ethical for a Catholic-affiliated agency to have a pro-life policy as long as clients know about it ahead of time. It is not ethical for an agency to call itself a "Pregnancy Counseling Center"—implying it offers all options—if it does not offer abortion as an option.)

The following guidelines may be useful in helping you decide which spiritual or religious interventions are appropriate (and inappropriate) to use:

1. Social workers should not use interventions that have the potential of resulting in harm to the client or to others whom a client interacts with. If you were to use such an intervention, you would be at risk of being sued for malpractice. For example, an intervention that is inappropriate for social workers to engage in with clients is a religious ritual involving the sacrifice of an animal.

2. Social workers should never engage in actions that can be construed as seeking to convert a client to the social worker's religious beliefs. Thus, encouraging a devout Buddhist to read the Bible is inappropriate.

3. Some interventions (such as leading a Bible class with clients that emphasizes adherence to Christian principles and values) may be appropriate in some sectarian (religiously affiliated) settings but will be inappropriate in most secular (not religiously affiliated) settings.

4. When you have questions about which spiritually related interventions are appropriate (or inappropriate), consult with your supervisor.
5. Social workers should use interventions with proven therapeutic value and generally avoid using techniques with no proven value.
6. Interventions that are clearly beyond the purview of social work should not be used. For example, administering sacraments (such as Communion) is the purview of designated members of the clergy and certainly beyond the purview of social workers.
7. Spiritually related interventions should generally be limited to those specifically identified in the intervention contract with the client. Such an intervention contract should be approved by the worker's supervisor or agency director.
8. It is crucial that social workers gain an understanding of their clients' religious and spiritual beliefs, traditions, and rituals—and of the laws related to these religious and spiritual practices. Three examples will be presented. Members of the Native American Church, a religious organization, use peyote (a hallucinogenic drug derived from a cactus plant) for ceremonial purposes; a number of states have now passed statutes allowing this church to use this illegal drug for sacramental purposes. In a major 1993 U.S. Supreme Court decision, *Church of the Lukumi Babalu Aye v. City of Hialeah* (Bullis, 1996, pp. 89–92), the Court ruled that the City of Hialeah, Florida, could not prohibit members of the Santeria faith from sacrificing live animals (including chickens, pigeons, pigs, doves, ducks, goats, sheep, and turtles); this decision follows the precedent of other Supreme Court decisions that unusual or popularly distasteful spiritual practices are sometimes afforded First Amendment protection when the religious practice is a central ritual component of spiritual importance for a religious organization. In another area, Bullis (1996) notes several court decisions that have generally sided with cult members when their parents have sought to rescue or kidnap them from seemingly unusual and even bizarre spiritual groups. The courts have generally asserted that cult members' First Amendment rights and their ethical rights of self-determination outweigh the wishes of parents and other family members. Social workers who assist or even encourage parents in rescuing and deprogramming an adult son or daughter from an unpopular cult should be prepared to defend themselves against a suit for false imprisonment, intentional infliction of emotional distress, and other torts.

Bullis (1996) conducted a study to determine whether clinical social workers believe it is professionally ethical to use a variety of religious and spiritual interventions. Survey questions were sent to 294 clinical social workers in Virginia; 116 (44%) responded. Most clinical social workers in this survey believe that it is professionally ethical to use a variety of religious and spiritual interventions. The study also found that these clinical social workers use a wide variety of such interventions in their practice. Most social workers in the survey reported that they use the following religious and spiritual interventions in their practice:

■ Explore client's religious background
■ Explore client's spiritual background
■ Use or recommend spiritual books
■ Pray privately for client
■ Use religious language or metaphors
■ Use spiritual language or metaphors
■ Recommend participation in religious program (Sunday school, religious education)
■ Recommend participation in spiritual programs (meditation groups, 12-step programs, men's/women's groups)
■ Help clients clarify religious values
■ Help clients clarify spiritual values
■ Refer clients to religious counselors
■ Refer clients to spiritual counselors
■ Help clients develop ritual as a clinical intervention (house blessings, visiting graves of relatives, and so on)
■ Explore religious elements in dreams
■ Explore spiritual elements in dreams
■ Recommend religious/spiritual, forgiveness, penance, or amends
■ Share their (the workers') own religious/spiritual beliefs or views

With the recent attention to spirituality by a variety of helping professionals (including social workers, psychologists, and psychiatrists), it is anticipated that ethical guidelines increasingly will be developed related to the use of spiritual and religious interventions.

In a review of court decisions involving which spiritual and religious interventions are appropriate (and inappropriate) to use in social work practice, Schoener (2000) concludes that spiritual and religious interventions are appropriate if *all* of the following conditions exist: (1) There is no evidence the interventions physically or emotionally harm clients. (2) The helping professionals inform clients of the spiritual and religious interventions that they use before contracting with clients for services. (3) The helping professionals are *in no way* using the spiritual and religious interventions to persuade clients to join a particular religious faith.

SOCIAL WORK AND RELIGION IN LIMITED PARTNERSHIP

Ram Cnaan in *The Newer Deal* (1999) indicates that in the United States the "devolution revolution" (the federal government's surrender of its responsibility for the welfare of its citizens) has been gaining momentum since the 1980s. Devolution of social welfare is a broad national process that originated with the Reagan administration to shift responsibility for the administration of funding of social and health services to state and local governments and to nonprofit organizations. Devolution includes two complementary trends: privatization of service delivery and the end of some entitlements (such as the replacement of the program Aid to Families with Dependent Children with the program Temporary Assistance to Needy Families). Cnaan (1999) notes,

> Devolution is the antithesis of the welfare state in which the central government assumes full responsibility for the social and health needs of individuals with low income. In the United States, the process of devolution has resulted in the replacement of federal allocations for social services by smaller block grants to states. The states, in turn, asked counties and cities to do more with less and to engage nonprofit organizations in the provision of services. This process culminated in 1996 welfare reform legislation. This legislation not only substantially reduced the responsibility of the federal government for social welfare but also heightened both the visibility and the role of the religious-based services providers as a viable replacement. (pp. x and xi)

An important outcome of the devolution revolution is that the religious community (as it was in the 1800s) is again becoming a major provider of social services. The role of religious-based services provision in maintaining the local social services infrastructure is stronger than ever. Most religious groups now provide social and community services as a means to witness their faith, to fulfill religious teachings and beliefs, and to simply "do good" in providing for those in need in the community.

From 2008 to 2014 the United States, and many other countries, were in a very serious economic recession. Because of the shortage of funds, states and the federal government made serious cutbacks in federal funding for social welfare and social work programs. As a result, church-affiliated social service organizations were asked to expand their services to people in need and as a result are becoming even more prominent in the provision of social services.

In regard to the principle of church and state separation in the United States, Cnaan (1999) notes,

> Despite all the attempts to separate church and state in the United States, the two are quite interwoven.
>
> We would like to believe that church and state can be fully separated. However, this is not the case. In a country that calls upon the religious community to do more for the welfare of strangers and that willingly pays religious-based groups to do so, church-state separation is merely an ideal. Politicians recognize that the separation does not exist. Managers of religious-based social services also know it. After all, more than 50 percent of the budgets of Catholic Charities, Jewish Family and Children's Services, and Lutheran Social Ministries, to name just a few agencies, comes from the public coffers. It is now time for the profession of social work, its leaders, its scholars, and its practitioners to acknowledge the same: the church-social work separation is unwarranted.
>
> If the religious community is to be even more deeply involved in social services provision, then we must learn how to cooperate with organized religion to improve the lot of those whom we serve and whose interests we represent. We must apply a more pluralistic model, one that enables both sides to maintain their ideological and value stances while collaborating where possible and when beneficial for both. (pp. 300–301)

Congregations and church-affiliated organizations provide a wide range of social services, many of them partly financed by the purchase of care arrangements with federal, state, and local governmental units. Examples of social services provided by congregations and church-affiliated organizations include: counseling; telephone reassurance; free use of church buildings for meetings by self-help groups, such as Alcoholics Anonymous, Narcotics Anonymous, AL-Anon, Alateen, and Overeaters Anonymous; emergency food assistance; congregate meals; soup kitchens; emergency shelter; mobile meals; cash assistance; housework for older persons and those with a disability; food preparations; legal help; brokering services; child care; after-school care; adult day care; tutoring; employment help; pregnancy counseling; foster care; housing for health clinics; food banks; housing rehabilitation; adoption services; and refugee resettlement.

Religious congregations and organizations are not solely "member-serving" organizations but also are "other-serving" organizations that are committed to improving the quality of life in their communities. Clearly, a limited partnership is emerging between social work and the religious community. Cnaan (1999) recommends the following:

1. That baccalaureate and master's programs in social work teach students about the increasing role of the religious community in the provision of local social services, which would include field placements that prepare graduates to work more effectively within religious-based social service organizations.

2. That social work professionals form coalitions with religious-based social services and other religious groups when planning and implementing community projects as a means of increasing both the legitimacy and the resource base of the projects, because religious organizations have the trust and support of many local residents.

3. That social work professionals offer consultative services to religious congregations to assist them in expanding or reorganizing the programs they provide to the community.

4. That baccalaureate and master's programs in social work educate students on the boundary issues between social work and religious organizations. At times the values and principles of the profession of social work and those of religious organizations will conflict. When conflicts occur (for example, between the pro-choice position of social work and the pro-life position of some religious organizations), social work professionals need strategies for resolving such conflicts.

Exercise 13.3: Benefits and Dangers of the Religious Community Being a Major Provider of Social Services

Goal: This exercise is designed to assist you in analyzing the merits of social services being provided by the religious community.

Step 1: Specify the merits and benefits of the religious community being a major provider of social services.

Step 2: Specify the dangers and questions raised by the religious community being a major provider of social services.

Step 3: If you were a client needing counseling who faced a dilemma (such as whether to terminate a pregnancy, whether to "come out" as being gay or lesbian, whether to seek physician-assisted suicide, or whether to use reproductive technology), would you prefer to go to a church-affiliated agency or to an agency that is not affiliated with a church?

____ Church-affiliated agency

____ Agency that is not affiliated with a church

Explain your rationale.

SUMMARY

The following summarizes the chapter's content in terms of the learning objectives presented at the beginning of the chapter.

1. Understand a rationale for the use of spirituality and religion in social work practice.
   A major thrust of social work education is to prepare students for culturally sensitive practice, including helping social workers comprehend the influence of religion and spirituality in human lives. The philanthropic founders of social work were inspired by Judeo-Christian traditions to pursue social work. Social workers need to have an appreciation and respect for religious beliefs that differ from their own chosen beliefs. Although social work literature has largely ignored religion's or spirituality's impact on social work practice, there has been a resurgence in recent years to attend to the spiritual aspects of clients' lives. Philosophically, social work and spirituality are natural allies in working for personal and social well-being. Spiritual beliefs are major determinants in a wide variety of clients' decisions.

2. Describe four prominent religions.

Judaism, Christianity, Islam, and Buddhism are described in this chapter. It should be noted there are hundreds of other religions.

3. Describe spiritual and religious assessments of clients.

EPAS (2015) of the Council on Social Work Education identifies religious and spiritual beliefs of clients as being important areas for social workers to attend to. This chapter summarizes the kinds of questions that are useful in a spiritual and religious assessment of clients.

4. Describe spiritual and religious interventions with clients.

Some guidelines regarding appropriate and inappropriate interventions are provided. However, many questions remain unanswered in this area. It is crucial that social workers gain an understanding of their clients' religious and spiritual beliefs, traditions, and rituals—and of the laws and court decisions related to these religious and spiritual practices.

5. Describe social work and religion in limited partnership.

A limited partnership between social work and religion is emerging in the provision of social services in communities. Both social work and religion attend to the social and personal well-being of people.

EXERCISES

1. Respecting Clients' Spiritual and Religious Beliefs and Practices

Goals: To gain background information about diverse religions, learn to respect religious beliefs that differ from your own, and become more comfortable with your own religious beliefs.

Step 1:   Read Exhibit 13.1.

Step 2:   Form groups of three and discuss the following questions:

a. Some religions assert that God is all-good, all-knowing, and all-powerful. If God has these three characteristics, why would God allow diseases like AIDS or send people to eternal damnation?

b. What evidence is there that God ever existed or currently exists?

c. Most prominent religions have a "bible"—that is, a book of sacred scriptures. Is one of these bibles more accurate in being the word of God than the others? If your answer is "yes," which book is it, and what evidence do you have?

d. Is there "one true religion"? If your answer is "yes," what is it, and what evidence do you have?

e. Can a social worker who believes strongly that his or her religion is the one true religion fully accept clients who adhere to other religious faiths?

Step 3:   Class discussion of group thoughts.

Step 4:   How does intolerance of others' religious beliefs contribute to other forms of prejudice, such as racism, sexism, and homophobia?

2. Timeline of Your Religious and Spiritual Journey

Goal: To describe the chronology of your religious and spiritual journey.

Step 1:   Draw a timeline of your religious and spiritual experiences. Begin by drawing a straight line at the bottom of a sheet of paper and numbering the line with numbers corresponding to your current age; a 22-year-old student would have 22 numbers. Note significant religious and spiritual events that occurred at various ages—significant experiences with people, places, ideas, books, movies, churches, and so on. End with a summary of your current religious and spiritual beliefs and values.

Step 2:   Form groups of three or four and share your timelines. (You may choose not to share.)

3. Using Religious and Spiritual Interventions

Goal: To explore the ethics of using religious and spiritual interventions in practice.

Step 1:   You are a social worker at a *secular* (not religiously affiliated) agency. For each intervention in the following table, mark on a separate sheet of paper whether you believe the intervention is professionally ethical for you to use and whether you personally would be comfortable using this intervention at your agency.

Step 2: List the 26 numbers and the possible responses on the chalkboard. Ask each student to mark his or her responses on the chalkboard.

Step 3: Lead a discussion of the items and student responses.

Interventions	Professionally Ethical to Use		Personally Comfortable Using	
	Yes	No	Yes	No
1. Lead a Bible class				
2. Explore client's spiritual background				
3. Help clients clarify spiritual values				
4. Recommend participation in spiritual programs (meditation groups, 12-step programs, men's/women's groups)				
5. Explore client's religious background				
6. Explore spiritual elements in dreams				
7. Help clients develop ritual as a clinical intervention (house blessings, visiting graves of relatives, and so forth)				
8. Refer clients to religious counselors				
9. Use or recommend spiritual books				
10. Use spiritual language or metaphors				
11. Refer clients to spiritual counselors				
12. Pray privately for client				
13. Explore religious elements in dreams				
14. Help clients clarify religious values				
15. Recommend participation in religious programs (Sunday school, religious education)				
16. Teach spiritual meditation to clients				
17. Use religious language or metaphors				
18. Recommend religious/spiritual forgiveness, penance, or amends				
19. Share your own religious/spiritual beliefs or views				
20. Participate in client's rituals as a clinical intervention				
21. Use or recommend religious books				
22. Meditate spiritually with clients				
23. Pray with client in session				
24. Read scripture with client				
25. Touch client for "healing" purposes				
26. Perform exorcism				

4. Providing Services in Cases with Religious or Spiritual Issues

Goal: This exercise is designed to assist students in setting goals and objectives in working with cases involving religious or spiritual issues.

Step 1: State the goal of the exercise. Ask students to form subgroups of about five students each. Ask the subgroups to arrive at a consensus as to the goals and objectives they would set for each of the following situations. Have each subgroup select a representative to summarize the goals and objectives they arrived at for each case scenario.

a. You are a social worker at a secular agency A married couple asks your help in rescuing (kidnapping) their 19-year-old daughter from a religious cult. The daughter dropped out of college and joined this cult. She is living in a distant state in a commune sponsored by this cult. Her parents ask for a referral to an organization that rescues adult children from such cults and also asks your help in deprogramming her once she is rescued (kidnapped). How do you respond?

b. You are a social worker at a secular agency in a community where a religious group that practices voodoo wants to relocate (voodooism includes the practice of witchcraft). An organization forms in your community with the objective of stopping this religious group from relocating to your community. The organization contacts your agency requesting any help you can provide. How do you respond?

c. You are a hospital social worker, and a nurse approaches you for help. A Haitian patient has requested that his spiritual adviser conduct a healing ceremony in his hospital room. The patient and his spiritual adviser practice voodooism. The nurse is concerned that the ceremony may be inappropriate in a hospital that is loosely affiliated with the Catholic church and that the ceremony may upset other patients. How do you respond to this nurse's concerns?

d. You are a protective services worker. A child abuse report comes in from a teacher at an elementary school that an 8-year-old boy is being emotionally abused. His parents practice the Santeria religion and require that their son attend ritual slaughters of lambs, pigs, and turtles. The schoolteacher asserts that forcing the child to attend such sacrifices is upsetting to him and therefore constitutes emotional abuse. You investigate and find that the child does become upset after attending such ceremonies but does not appear to be unduly traumatized. How would you proceed with this case? What would be your goals?

Step 2: After the subgroups conclude their discussions, ask the representatives for the subgroups to share their responses to the first case scenario with the class. After the representatives give their summaries, briefly discuss how you would proceed. The second, third, and fourth case scenarios are processed in the same manner. (Point out that some statutes and court decisions discussed in this chapter may provide guidance in setting goals and objectives for these case scenarios.)

14 | SURVIVING AND ENJOYING SOCIAL WORK

LEARNING OBJECTIVES To be of help to others, helping professionals must first take care of themselves. Good emotional and physical health are internal resources that helping professionals need to be able to help others. In this chapter, we focus on how to survive and enjoy a career in social work. This chapter will help prepare students to:

Understand common concerns of students related to majoring in social work
Describe safety guidelines for social workers
Describe burnout, stress, and stress management techniques
Comprehend strategies for enjoying social work and your life

STUDENTS' COMMON CONCERNS

One of the surprises I found in teaching social work students is that although they have a number of common concerns, they believe their concerns are so unique and "secret" that they are reluctant to share and discuss them with others. In this section, I examine a number of these concerns and offer some suggestions for resolving them.

Will I Be Able to Make It in Field Placement?

Associated with this concern are numerous specific concerns: Will I be accepted and liked by the agency staff? Will I be accepted and liked by the clients who are assigned to me? Will I be able to help clients? Will the clothes I wear be acceptable? Will my shortcomings do me in? (*Every* student perceives a number of personal shortcomings—such as unusual tone of voice, inability to speak clearly, a low level of interviewing skills, questionable personal appearance, or inability to start and maintain a conversation. Students by far are their own harshest critics.) Am I emotionally stable enough to handle field placement? Will I be able to speak on the telephone? Will I be able to learn to do all the paperwork? Will I be attacked by clients? Will my car hold up, or will I be able to get where I'm supposed to be? Will I become too anxious and get stage fright when I'm assigned certain tasks?

In 35 years of supervising students in field placement, I have heard these and many similar concerns from practically every student. The students I worry about when arranging field placements are those who deny having such concerns; I have found that they generally are not perceptive about themselves. If people are not perceptive about personal concerns and emotions, it generally means they won't be perceptive about the thoughts and emotions of clients and therefore won't make skillful counselors.

Practically every student is anxious before field placement and during at least the first few weeks at placement. This anxiety is to be expected. You will find in field placement that your moderate level of anxiety will drain your energy. When you leave in the evening, you may be exhausted.

Although such anxiety and concerns are normal, there are ways to reduce some of these concerns.

1. In many social work programs, students have considerable input in choosing their field placement setting. If you have such input, use this opportunity to visit the agency you are considering for a placement. Meet with agency staff, ask them to describe the agency's programs and also discuss the expected tasks for student interns. Certain other concerns, such as expected dress code, can also be discussed. If after the visit you have serious reservations about taking a placement at that agency, discuss your reservations with the faculty who coordinate field placements. If your concerns are not

allayed after this discussion, many programs allow you to visit another agency to explore doing a field placement there.

2. Ask other students who are currently in field placement or who have completed field placement to share and discuss their experiences and concerns. This will give you a better idea of what placement is like and may provide answers to some of your concerns. It is particularly useful to talk with students who have worked at the agency you are considering.

3. Discuss your concerns with faculty who coordinate field placements at your school. They will be able to answer some of your concerns and provide additional information about the agency.

4. Volunteer in your classes to role-play simulated counseling situations. Videotaping these sessions is particularly useful. Reviewing the tapes will enable you to assess and further develop your interviewing skills. Zastrow and Navarre (1979) found that videotaped role-playing of counseling situations also develops students' confidence in their counseling capacities.

5. Express any concerns you have to your agency supervisor. Make sure you understand agency procedures and policies and expectations for student interns. Open communication between you and your agency supervisor is an important key to making it in field placement.

These suggestions will reduce some, but certainly not all, of your concerns about whether you will make it in field placement. It is normal to be anxious at the beginning. As the weeks pass and you receive feedback that you are doing well, you will become more relaxed.

Will I Conduct a Satisfactory Interview with My First Client?

Concerns that relate to this question include the following: How will I know what to say? How will I keep the conversation going? If I say the wrong thing, won't it be a calamity for the client? How will I introduce myself? Will clients discover that I am only a student and therefore feel they are being used as guinea pigs to train me? What if I become tongue-tied and am unable to say anything? Am I really ready to assume the awesome responsibility of counseling others? I've got personal problems that are unresolved—how can I possibly help others?

Before seeing their first client, some students become so concerned that they can't sleep the night before; others develop tension headaches. A few students have told me they couldn't eat or developed diarrhea or were nauseated. It happens. If you have severe reactions, you are not alone. Just remember, it is highly unlikely that you will "bomb" during your first interview. Most anxious students report that once the interview began they relaxed and the interview went fairly well.

Here are suggestions for reducing your concerns:

1. Role-play simulated counseling situations, ideally playing the roles of both counselor and client. Videotaping and reviewing the tape is particularly helpful. Such role-playing will give you practice in counseling.

2. To prepare for the interview, identify your objectives, and think about the kinds of questions you will need to ask to accomplish them. Review the material in Chapters 4 and 5 on how to begin and end interviews, how to build a relationship, and how to begin to explore the client's problems.

3. Clients are much less fragile than beginning counselors believe they are. If you fail to cover something, you can probably do so at some future interview. If you fail to phrase a question properly, you won't cause a calamity in the client's life. It is irrational to expect that if you make some mistakes in the first interview you will cause a disaster for the client. No one has that kind of power. Clients have been exposed to situations much more traumatic and chaotic than talking to you; they survived those experiences; they will survive talking to you.

4. Review the interview with your agency supervisor or your faculty supervisor to identify which aspects you did well and which ones you need to improve. Don't expect perfection—in your first interview or in *any* interview. You *will* make mistakes; everyone does. Remember, the main purpose of field placement is *training*—helping you test and further develop your social work skills and techniques. Therefore, agency staff expect you to make mistakes. The students who generally do best in placement are those who readily seek to apply the theoretical material they have learned about social work practice, because this facilitates the development of their social work skills. It is a serious mistake to "hang back" in field placement for fear of making mistakes. Focusing on making few errors in order to get a high grade usually leads student interns to "hang back," and this usually *lowers* their grade.

5. If you have specific questions before the first interview, ask your agency supervisor. Perhaps you are wondering whether you should inform the client that you are a student. Different agencies handle

this question differently. Your agency supervisor wants to hear your questions and concerns. Only by hearing your questions can your agency supervisor determine "where you are" and how to be most helpful to you. Agency supervisors were once in training themselves. They are fully aware of the pressures and anxieties of being in field placement and are committed to helping you. Many have told me that the questions students ask frequently bring a fresh, new perspective to their practice, which leads them to make improvements in their counseling and interviewing approaches.

Will I Ever Be Able to Interview as Well as My Supervisor?

When student interns observe the interviewing and counseling skills of their agency or faculty supervisor, many become disheartened because they realize their skills are not as highly developed. They tend to "awfulize" and erroneously conclude they never will do well at interviewing and counseling. *Of course* your skills are not as good as your supervisor's; you haven't had 30 years in the field! Rome was not built in a day, and neither are interviewing skills. You *will* get better. Be patient, observe carefully, and *don't* think negatively!

How Do I Separate the Roles of Counselor and Friend?

Students generally have a small caseload in field placement, which allows them to spend considerable time with clients. It is not uncommon for clients to begin to become attracted to their worker because sharing personal concerns fosters an attachment. Students are also generally young and physically attractive, which also fosters attachments. Questions that students in field placement frequently have include, "Is this client beginning to see me as someone he wants to get socially involved with—how do I handle this?" "This client has invited me to her home—should I go?" "This client has suggested we have a cup of coffee (or dinner) together—should I go?" "This client has suggested we go to a park (or play golf, or go to a bar, or play cards)—should I go?"

There are no *yes* or *no* answers to these questions. Most agencies frown on and some prohibit fraternizing with clients. For example, if you as a probation officer socialize extensively with a probationee, problems may arise. The probationee might violate some conditions of probation and then try to use the friendship with you to avoid the consequences. Also, other probationees and parolees who become aware of the friendship may conclude they no longer have to rigidly adhere to the conditions of probation or of parole because you are "a nice guy" and "a soft touch." In addition, administrative officials will view the friendship as a conflict-of-interest situation and will disapprove highly of such a relationship.

Furthermore, if you become socially involved with a client, it is difficult to counsel that person effectively. The client, for example, may no longer be willing to accept suggestions from you—he may misinterpret the suggestions as being put-downs. Counseling someone you are socially involved with elicits clashes, not unlike when you tried to teach your sister how to drive a car.

Nevertheless, the attraction of client to counselor *can* be a component of a helping relationship and one that occasionally can be used positively. I've seen elderly, apathetic, depressed male clients in nursing homes become attracted to female student interns. These interns then used this attraction to motivate these elderly men to become involved in programs at the nursing home (such as hobbies and craft activities). Once involved in the programs, they started to enjoy them and as a result became more energetic, happier, and more active.

How, then, should counselors decide whether to accept social invitations from clients? The guideline is simple. *If* you believe doing something with your client will help you develop a working relationship and would be constructive for the client, then do it. Going to a park and talking helps some clients relax and develops the kind of atmosphere in which they will feel free to share and discuss their secret personal concerns. However, *if* you believe that accepting an invitation has the potential for being destructive to the helping process, then don't do it. If you believe going to a park will lead the client to conclude that you want to become romantically involved, then tactfully decline the invitation. (Establishing professional boundaries with clients is discussed at greater length in Chapter 2.)

It is useful for beginning workers to understand the essential difference between friendship with a client and a professional relationship. Friendship is for *both* of you to *give* and *receive*; a professional relationship involves the helping person *giving* and the client *receiving*.

Beginning counselors often wonder how, in practice, to separate the roles of counselor and friend. With experience, this problem usually disappears. Experienced counselors become more perceptive in determining the intents behind invitations from clients and more skillful in conveying the boundaries of the professional relationship. Experienced counselors also have more cases; this reduces the amount of time spent per client, which reduces socializing opportunities.

How Do I Avoid Becoming Too Emotionally Involved?

At one time or another, every counselor becomes overly emotionally involved in a case. I recently supervised a student in a child welfare unit at a public welfare department. One case assigned to this student involved a 14-year-old girl who had been in a series of foster homes since she was 3. The student, Linda H., became fairly attached to the girl. This client wanted to date, which her conservative foster parents could not accept. Considerable friction developed, and the foster parents suggested to the agency that it would be best for the girl to be placed in a different foster home. Because the girl felt rejected, Linda H. arranged a meeting between the foster parents and the girl to try to work out a compromise, but the meeting resolved nothing. After considerable effort, Linda H. found another foster home, and a trial visit was attempted. Linda H. indicated that she "felt like a nervous mother" about this visit. (Right away this statement led me to believe she was becoming overly involved.) The trial visit went fairly well, but after a day of reflecting, these foster parents decided they did not want to take a foster child at this time. Not only did the girl feel rejected, unloved, and depressed, but Linda H. became so depressed that she had to take 2 days off from her placement. She sympathized, rather than empathized, with the girl. Fortunately, she realized she was too emotionally involved at this point to search for another foster family. (She did ask the foster parents to keep the girl for a few more days until a new placement could be found, which they consented to do.)

As Linda H.'s example indicates, counselors who are too emotionally involved have a reduced capacity to help clients discuss their problems and to explore alternative solutions objectively with clients. Several types of irrational thinking lead to overinvolvement. Exhibit 14.1 lists these types of irrational thinking and presents rational self-challenges to counter them.

Exhibit 14.1   Irrational Thinking Leads to Emotional Overinvolvement, Which Can Be Changed by Rational Self-Challenges

Irrational Thinking

1. "This client has shared his problems, and therefore I must help this client resolve these problems." (Such thinking leads to taking ownership of the client's problems.)

2. "If things (events) don't work out for clients, I have failed. I am at fault for their problems. I am a failure."

3. "If things don't work out for clients, it is *awful, terrible, overwhelming, unbearable.*"

4. "If I don't solve the client's problems, the consequences for the client, the client's family, and others close to the client will be tragic, unbearable." (Overly involved counselors often view the consequences as being more tragic than the clients themselves view the consequences.)

5. "I've tried the only approach there is, and it failed. There is no hope. Things are certainly bleak for this client. I feel overwhelmed—I give up!"

Rational Self-Challenges

1. "Clients own their problems and have the responsibility for resolving them. I do not have the power to resolve them. All I can do is help clients explore their problems, explore alternative solutions, and encourage clients to select a resolution approach."

2. "Everyone has ups and downs. We are all fallible, and we all have problems. If one resolution approach does not work out for a client, it only means that approach failed. It in no way means I am a failure. What the client and I need to do is to examine why that approach did not work out, explore other alternatives, select one, and try that."

3. "As Ellis and Harper (1977) pointed out, it is irrational to conclude that a problem is awful, overwhelming, or unbearable. Adverse events are often inconvenient and problematic, but assigning labels such as 'awful' only leads to unwanted emotions. Instead of viewing problems as being overwhelming, I need to take each problem one at a time and in a step-by-step fashion develop strategies to deal with each."

4. "Clients own their problems and have the responsibility to resolve them. I am not God; I have no miracle power to resolve problems. All I can ever do is 'give it my best shot' in counseling. It is irrational and counterproductive to overexaggerate consequences. If the selected approach doesn't work, the client needs to select and try another."

5. "There is always hope. Even though I am unaware of other alternatives, there may well be others. I need to talk to an authority in this area to learn about other alternatives."

Beginning counselors are much more likely than experienced counselors to become overly involved. With experience, counselors increasingly learn that clients own their problems, that clients are the primary problem-solvers, and that to be of optimal assistance, counselors need to remain objective rather than exaggerating the consequences of resolution approaches that don't work out. (The main reason counselors are less successful in counseling close friends and relatives is because they are too involved to be objective.)

Yet even experienced counselors at times become involved. I speak from experience. A few years ago I was asked to provide professional help to a client for a number of personal problems—including burnout, grief over her husband's death, drinking problems, insomnia, depression, and lack of meaning in work or in living. She was highly respected in her profession. I realized I was giving myself the following irrational thinking that was leading to overinvolvement: "I must solve her problems. If she resigns her position this will be tragic, as several thousand people will be adversely affected. If this person resigns, it will be awful." By countering my thinking with rational self-challenges, I was able to help her explore her problems, one at a time, and we developed strategies to handle each.

What should you do when you feel emotionally involved in a case (for example, taking it home with you by thinking about it for several hours)? Here are three possible strategies:

1. Discuss the case with others, particularly your supervisor. Other people are often able to offer suggestions on alternatives and may be able to suggest ways to become more objective and less emotionally involved.
2. Do a rational self-analysis (described in Module 1) of your unwanted emotions about a case. This will help you identify your irrational thinking so that you can counter it with rational self-challenges.
3. Seriously consider transferring the case to another worker if your involvement is simply too intense. It is irrational to expect to be able to handle all cases optimally. You will handle some cases better than your fellow workers, and they will handle other cases better than you. Intense emotional involvement with a case for an extended period lessens your objectivity and indicates a transfer is necessary.

Do I Really Want a Career in Social Work?

Related concerns include the following: Do I have capacities to be a competent social worker? What area of social work (for example, mental health, corrections) should I pursue? Will a career in social work pay me enough money to live the way I want to live? (See Exhibit 14.2.) What do I really want to do with my life? What will my parents, friends, and relatives think of me if I become a social worker? Is there a profession or vocation that I would find more enjoyable and gratifying?

Most of these questions can be answered only by you. As far as the money question goes, faculty members in your social work department will be able to tell you about average starting salaries in your area for graduates of baccalaureate and master's programs in social work. Starting salaries vary considerably in different regions and in different positions. Pay increases are largely deter mined by you—your skills, your efforts to obtain advanced degrees, and your efforts to seek administrative and supervisory positions that generally pay more than direct services positions. Psychotherapists in private practice (who have an MSW degree and 2 or more years of counseling experience) can earn more than $100,000 per year. Skills at grant writing, consultation, public speaking, and developing new programs also are often financially rewarded.

But how do you determine whether social work is the right career for you and, if so, which area of social work to pursue? Only you can decide. Here are some suggestions that may help you:

1. Relax. Don't be in a hurry to make a final career decision. Some social work students think they have to make such decisions within a few weeks. Thinking about the pros and cons makes them so anxious they can't make any decision. In one sense you've got the rest of your life to make career decisions. Today people routinely start new careers in their 40s, 50s, 60s, and even 70s.
2. Try a trial-and-error approach. If you find one area of social work unsatisfying, try another. Skills learned in one area won't be wasted. You may find one area fulfilling for a while, but then find you need new challenges. If you really don't think you want a career in social work, fine; try something else—you may like it. Perhaps someday you'll change your mind and want to try social work again. No problem. You can take refresher or continuing education courses or attend workshops to polish your skills and learn new techniques and revised procedures. We have students in our undergraduate courses in their 40s, 50s, and 60s who are just now pursuing a career in social work. Do not think that this is your *final* career decision. Times change, agencies change, our interests and values change, and—yes, our careers change too.

Exhibit 14.2   What Do Social Workers Make?

Social work, as most everyone knows, is not one of the highest-paying professions. What do social workers really make?

They make a teenager in a dysfunctional family find a focus in school and in his life. They locate two children to adopt for an infertile couple who yearn to be parents, and they rescue these two children from the alternative of being raised in a series of foster homes. They facilitate, through counselling, a marital couple problem-solving their marital issues, and thereby prevent a divorce.

They place a battered wife and her three children in a domestic violence sheller and then work with this family to find new directions in their lives. They empower a recently arrived Hmong refugee family living in poverty to learn English, to receive job training services, to be connected with necessary medical and dental care, and to find housing, and they place the parents in jobs that allow the family members to escape from poverty. They instruct and facilitate a young adult with anger management issues to learn to express her anger in an assertive manner and thereby empower her to get what she wants, rather than allowing her anger to get her involved in physical confrontations with others.

They empower a postpartum depressed mother with a young baby to challenge her negative and irrational thinking patterns and thereby alleviate the depression—and thereby also provide a better life for herself, her child, and her husband. They provide sexual assault services to a rape victim and thereby help her put her life back together. They assist a suicidal gay teenager to become aware and accepting of his sexual orientation and to begin to develop a lifestyle that provides direction and meaning to his life.

They provide a diversion program for first-time offenders for shoplifting (and similar offenses) that provides restitution to the victims and also deters these offenders from committing future crimes. They help organizations to recognize institutional patterns of racism and then make changes to reach out to better serve people of color.

They assist an older employee to make a solid financial plan for retiring and to also connect him with volunteer opportunities that will be gratifying for him and also benefit the community. They serve as a catalyst in a deteriorating community to form a grassroots organization to improve the neighborhood.

They provide family group conferencing to a family in which abuse is occurring, which empowers the family to end the abuse and keeps the family intact. They connect (broker) an alcoholic female in her 20s with AA and start her one-day-at-a-time recovery. They empower a secretary to become assertive to confront her employer about the sexual innuendoes that he makes, which thereby ends the sexual harassment.

They provide hospice services to a terminally ill male cancer patient, thereby relieving the pain associated with the disease and helping him make the most of his remaining days; they also provide services to the family members to help them through this difficult time—and then provide bereavement services to the family members after the patient dies. They find a quality group home for an autistic young adult and also place him in a job at a fast-food restaurant and job-coach him until he learns how to do the tasks that are assigned. They inform a 16-year-old pregnant teenager of her options and help her make plans for the adoption option she selects.

What do social workers make? They get paid to help other people—that's something most people would be inclined to do anyway. They make more than most people will ever make. They make a difference.

Do not idly sit back and wait for some unknown force to decide your career path for you. You are in the driver's seat, and it's up to you to decide on the *first* destination of your journey and then to drive yourself there.

Exercise 14.1: My Concerns about Majoring in Social Work

Goal: This exercise is designed to have you identify your concerns about majoring in social work and to problem-solve these concerns.

Step 1: Specify your concerns about majoring in social work.

Step 2: Are your concerns consistent or inconsistent with the "common concerns" of other students?

      ___ Consistent   ___ Inconsistent   ___ Uncertain

      Explain your view.

Step 3: If you have concerns that are not mentioned in this chapter, specify your plans for problem-solving those concerns.

SAFETY GUIDELINES FOR SOCIAL WORKERS

Several years ago, I was teaching a class in a weekend MSW program. The students had attained their BSW and now were working on attaining an MSW. Most of the students had full-time jobs in social work during the week. I was summarizing these safety guidelines for social workers. When I finished summarizing these safety guidelines, one of the students raised her hand and stated the following: "I was working as a child protective services worker two year ago, and out agency received a call to investigate a case involving a husband and wife who had a two-year-old child—the parents were suspected of neglecting the child, as a neighbor called in and said the child was crying nearly day and night. I went to the home, rang the doorbell, and the husband opened the door. I stated my name and indicated the name of the agency that I worked for. I saw the wife on a couch moaning 'help me-help me'. I rushed to the couch, which was obviously a mistake on my part. The husband slammed the door and pulled out a pistol. (We had been trained by our agency to remain calm in such a situation.) I noticed the wife had several bruises on her face—and later found out she also had a fractured hip from being battered by her husband. I also noted the husband was slurring his words, and appeared intoxicated. I knew I was in a potentially life-threatening position. Fortunately, I remembered I had programmed my cell phone to speed dial 911 by pressing a button. I reached in my coat pocket, put my hand on the phone, and pressed the 911 button—with my hand in my coat pocket. I began calmly talking to the husband, who was quite agitated. After a minute or two I asked if the address I was at was 201 Jefferson St. The husband indicated it was, without knowing that I was communicating this information to the police dispatcher. Four minutes later three police officers knocked on the door, and the husband opened the door and surrendered." I stated how impressed I was by this social worker being so prepared, and by being skilled in following through on her plan to obtain police help by unobtrusively dialing 911 on her cell phone. I indicated that "in a nutshell" this student had demonstrated the key components of a social worker being prepared to handle a very dangerous situation.

The social work perspective views violence as erupting in context rather than residing within the "violent individual." Rather than viewing some people as inherently violent, social workers understand that most violent behavior occurs because of interactions between the environmental context, the worker's interaction with the potentially violent client, and the client's internal dynamics. People differ in their tendency toward violent behavior and in the speed with which they convert emotions into violent behavior. The immediate context tempers whether a person with a shorter fuse (that is, more prone to violence) gets further agitated. Violent behavior is often a defensive reaction—the person expects harm or perceives a threat. Because the immediate environmental context is important, social workers are often able to use their skills to deter potentially violent behavior.

Environmental Signals of Danger

Context—the environment—may signal a violent situation. Certain situations have more potential for violence than others. Consider these scenarios. A protective services worker decides to remove a child from a home in which one, or both, of his parents are abusing him. A social worker at a battered women's shelter takes a resident to her home (where the batterer may be present) to pick up her belongings. A social worker at a police department goes with a police officer to a home where domestic violence is reportedly occurring. A social worker at a neighborhood center works with juvenile gang members to curb criminal activity. In assessing risk in these and other potentially violent situations, social workers need to determine the following:

■ Are there people present who are inciting the situation?
■ Are colleagues present who can assist me?
■ Are there obvious weapons present or objects that can be used as weapons?

Client Signals of Danger

Weinger (2001), in a review of the literature on social worker safety, has identified client signals that indicate an increased risk of violence. These are listed in Exhibit 14.3.

The best predictor of violent outbursts is a history of violent expressions. Clients who have a history of violent reactions stand a greater chance of becoming violent again. Therefore, if at all possible, workers should read clients' records before meeting with them. Diagnoses of antisocial personality disorder, borderline personality, and schizophrenia are also associated with proneness to violence.

Another indicator is a history of substance abuse. Alcohol intoxication lowers inhibitions and interferes with a client's judgment. Use of such drugs as cocaine, PCP, and amphetamines increases the risk of violence because these drugs increase the potential for agitation, suspicion, grandiosity, and delusional beliefs.

Exhibit 14.3   Client Signals of Danger

Signal Type	Behavior
Angry verbalizations	Swearing, threatening statements, complaining, sarcasm
Emotional distress	Suspicious, hostile, irritable, unhappy, angry
Thinking difficulties	Confused, disoriented, hallucinations, paranoid ideas
Bodily changes	Trembling, heavy breathing, shakes, sweating
Speech	Sharp, loud, pressured speech
Signs of intoxication	Slurred speech, flushed face, unsteady gait, dilated pupils, lack of coordination
Body movements	Exaggerated movements, pacing, shifting positions, flailing arms, threatening gestures, clenched fists, pounding of fists on objects, wringing of hands, tense muscles
Facial cues	Muscle tension in face and neck, paleness, gritting teeth, dilated pupils, glaring, scowling
Agitation	Hyperactive, tenseness, ill at ease, overly anxious

Yet another indicator is a history of child abuse or of witnessing repeated abuse at home when growing up. Sadly, children who have been abused are more prone to violence as adults. Other indicators of an increased risk of violence include fitting these categories: male, military combat experience, and having been incarcerated.

Regarding all these warning signals, Weinger (2001) astutely notes three caveats:

> First, although knowing the predictive factors may increase awareness, there are many false positives. Persons who do not resort to violence may also have these risk factors. . . . Second, in fueling the flames of racism we have often linked violence and crime to race. Although research has demonstrated that when different groups live in the same social, economic, and political environment their rate of violence is comparable, we have not always absorbed these findings into our mind-sets. Because of these distortions, for example, a social worker may too readily suspect an African American client and may overlook the warning signs exhibited in contact with a White client. . . .

Finally, there is a potential to use predictors of violence in a way that will create more risk to the clinician. If clinicians forsake their level of alertness because a client doesn't meet the criteria for potential risk factors, they may overlook important signals. It is important to realize that a client who presents or does not present risk factors can exhibit assaultive behaviors. (p. 37)

Worker Signals of Danger

Pay attention to your gut feelings. This is crucial. You are already in social work because of your inherent ability to empathize and understand people. You pick up on signals probably a lot better than the proverbial "man on the street." *Use this ability here as well.* This doesn't always mean you will be correct in your assessment. You can be misled by personal biases, by cultural biases, and by misinformation. Also, always remember that gestures, body language, and verbal expressions have different meanings in different cultures.

The Assault Cycle

Kaplan and Wheeler (1983) note that most assaults follow a predictable pattern of five phases:

1. *Triggering phase:* Everyone has a baseline of normative behaviors. In the triggering phase, an event occurs that ignites the first deviation from the baseline demeanor. The event can be infinitely varied—such as receiving criticism or receiving a speeding ticket.
2. *Escalation phase:* Clients become increasingly emotionally aroused. Their speech, behavior, and emotions move away from their normative expressions. The best time to intervene is early in this

cycle. Interventions can involve active listening, nonjudgmental listening, and problem solving, to prevent the agitation from escalating further.

3. *Crisis phase:* Clients are so aroused physiologically and psychologically that they are unable (or at least not inclined) to control angry and hostile feelings. They become verbally or physically aggressive. At this point, interventions such as active listening and problem solving are no longer effective. It is time to attend to your own safety, the safety of others, and the safety of the aggressive client.

4. *Recovery phase:* Clients begin to return to baseline behaviors but are still in a precarious state. If further events upset them, they can rapidly return to the crisis phase. To support the recovery, pace your interventions in response to clients' cues, and perhaps reassure them that they will be safe. Avoid disapproving comments, and do not explore the reasons for, and consequences of, the behavior.

5. *Postcrisis depression phase:* At this point, clients have calmed down and returned to baseline behaviors. They may even be more subdued than their normal baseline behaviors. They may be mentally and physically exhausted. They are likely to feel remorse and shame, which then make them more receptive to social work interventions. In this phase, Weinger (2001) notes,

> It may be appropriate to reflect on the assaultive episode with the client . . . to help the client discuss the consequences of the behavior and deal with feelings of fear or guilt that someone got hurt . . . to understand the dynamics or events that preceded her or his losing control, and to consider appropriate choices and behavioral options for the future when she or he becomes anxious or angry. (p. 35)

This progression of reactions provides clues about when and how interventions can deescalate the situation. Thus, during the crisis and recovery phases, active listening and problem solving probably won't be helpful, yet these same techniques may be more than usually effective during the postcrisis phase.

Preventing Violence

The best way to deal with violence, of course, is to prevent it from happening in the first place. Usually the most constructive way to do this is to lessen perceived threats and feelings of helplessness. Fortunately, a variety of options help do just this.

Deescalate Verbal Communication. Help clients express their feelings and thoughts—that is, let them vent. To do this, use your skills of active listening and reflecting feelings. This helps clients feel worthy. Use disarming (see Chapter 7)—that is, find some truth in what the client is saying, and then express this "agreement." Disarming also helps the client feel understood and validated and perhaps more open to examining another point of view. Use empathy (see Chapter 7)—that is, paraphrase what clients say. Restating their thoughts and feelings helps them reflect and move to problem solving.

Encourage clients to problem-solve. This can also help deescalate verbal communication. Weinger (2001, p. 38) notes that violence-prone clients have difficulty generating nonviolent solutions. They may need help thinking of nonviolent options.

It may be time for small talk. Sometimes redirecting clients' attention to less emotionally charged subjects deescalates verbal communication. For example, say, "It's really getting warm in here. Let's take a walk. We'll come back to this later."

Avoid aggressive, confrontational, or macho responses when a potentially violent client is emotionally upset. Such responses increase the likelihood of violence.

Deescalate Nonverbal Communication. Weinger (2001, p. 39) recommends approaching the client from an angle (rather than head-on or from the back) in order to convey a nonconfrontational approach. Approach the client casually and gradually, so as not to appear aggressive. Maintain some distance, so that the client doesn't feel his or her personal space is being violated. Individuals with a history of violence often require a wider personal space than do less violent individuals (Weinger, 2001, p. 39). Avoid touching the client (other than shaking hands). Touching can be perceived as a challenge, or it may arouse emotionally charged memories of past physical abuse.

Some eye contact with potentially violent clients may be useful. It conveys interest, and it enables you to be watchful. However, sustained eye contact (and definitely glaring) should be avoided.

If your client's body language is agitated, mirror his or her body language, but do so at a somewhat slower and softer pace. This conveys that you are "in sync" with the client, that you are an ally. Once the client feels in sync with you, gradually reduce the intensity of your movements; often unconsciously the client will model this reduced level of activity. With this approach, you are literally leading the client to a more relaxed state.

Set Limits. Many angry clients fear losing control. For such clients, Weinger (2001, p. 40) recommends that you say something like, "It's okay to be angry, but it's not okay to strike out. What can I do to help you feel more in control right now?" This statement clarifies that physical aggression is not acceptable. The tone and wording should support the client's worth and should not increase feelings of powerlessness. Don't come across as a parent. Don't be nonassertive. Both can trigger additional arousal. Set limits in a confident, assertive, but neutral tone.

Stay Calm and Generate Options. As much as possible, remain calm. Communicate calmness, both verbally and nonverbally, even if you are agitated and frightened. An even, slow, soft-toned voice and a confident nonjudgmental, nonauthoritarian approach will reassure an agitated person but won't pressure him or her. Conveying your agitation can provoke aggression.

Remaining calm also helps you figure out constructive options (including escape strategies). Fear and anxiety interfere with generating and assessing appropriate options. Use relaxation techniques (described later in this chapter) and self-talk (Module 1) to calm yourself.

Safeguards in the Workplace

The nature of your work setting can increase or decrease the risk of violence. Disorganization, cold-appearing surroundings, staff conflict, isolated offices, overcrowding, and lack of an alarm system can contribute to the likelihood of client violence.

Safety accommodations in the workplace vary according to the field of social work practice and the type of clients. Different settings need different safeguards. Typical workplace safeguards include the following:

1. Metal detectors. Some settings (such as some schools and courthouses) now use metal detectors that screen for weapons. There should also be a dependable planned-response system when a weapon is detected.
2. Alarm systems and other security devices include cellular phones, intercoms, panic buttons, and handheld or mounted buzzers. Again, when using these systems, have a dependable, planned, and *rehearsed* response system in place.
3. Possible weapons. Be aware of items in the workplace that can be used as weapons. Limit the presence of potential weapons such as soda bottles, pens, ashtrays, vases, pictures, and radios. When interviewing potentially violent clients, remove your clothing accessories that can be used in harmful ways, such as neckties, dangling earrings, and necklaces.
4. Interview rooms should be in view and have two exits (for escape purposes). The agency may also choose to have a special interview room with a large window that other staff can view into or have a one-way mirror for viewing from the outside.
5. Furniture should be arranged so that staff (and clients) can make quick exits. Chairs that are light in weight can be picked up by workers and used as shields.
6. Pleasant surroundings. Waiting rooms and interview rooms should be designed for comfort and for stress reduction. Try to have soft lighting, comfortable chairs, current magazines, and calming color schemes (such as pastel colors).

Response Planning

Planning for "what if" scenarios needs to be an ongoing part of staff training and meetings. The following guidelines are useful:

1. Report and record all violent incidents. Agency administration should keep records.
2. Have a policy that informs clients and workers that violence will not be tolerated.
3. Schedule initial interviews with clients at times when other staff are present. Workers should never be alone in the office or building with clients who are identified as potentially violent.
4. Have strategies in place for summoning immediate help from other staff—such as cell phones or panic buttons.
5. Plan how the agency will respond to agitated clients—including when and how police should be called and how other staff are expected to respond.
6. Role-play and rehearse what staff will say and do when clients are verbally combative or physically combative.

7. Keep your colleagues informed of potentially violent clients.
8. Keep waiting time to a minimum. Clients waiting for service should be treated in a respectful, courteous manner and given an approximate estimate of the length of time they will have to wait.

Home Visits

Specific safety precautions need to be tailored to the individual situation. However, the following are some safety guidelines for home visits.

If possible, have clients come to the office, where safety is more easily achieved. If the meeting cannot be held in the office, try to hold it in some other public place, such as a library or restaurant.

If the visit must be held in the home, arrange for two workers (or a worker and a supervisor) to attend. If the potential for violence is especially high (as in helping a woman at a battered women's shelter retrieve belongings from home when the batterer is present), arrange for a police officer to accompany you.

Before you leave the office for a home visit, make sure your supervisor or another staff member knows where you are going, what time you expect to return, your cell phone number, and the name of your client and his/her address.

Before home visits, obtain as much information as possible about your clients. Review the file for evidence of a history of violence and for risk factors (such as alcohol or other drug abuse). Determine whether others in the household present a risk. Also, find out whether there is an aggressive dog in the home or yard.

At the beginning of the visit, note exit routes. Wear shoes that facilitate a rapid exit. Don't wear expensive jewelry and clothes in deteriorating neighborhoods. Such items underscore that you are from a different socioeconomic class and thus unlikely to relate to the client's circumstances. They also tempt muggers and others in the neighborhood. Wear professional attire that presents you as a nonthreatening person.

Carry a cell phone and have it on. (Workers should call the agency if they anticipate being late.) Cellular phones should be programmed with agency and emergency numbers for quick dialing.

Present yourself as a confident, assertive person. Timid or aggressive behavior can elicit aggressive responses. If other people are present and appear threatening near your destination, you may choose to return at another time or day—and perhaps take another staff member along.

Park your vehicle in a place that allows for a quick escape. If a noisy argument is occurring at your destination, consider returning at another time. Before your visit, make sure the vehicle is in good working order and that you have plenty of gas. Lock all valuables in the trunk, leaving nothing valuable in view inside the car. Park in a well-lighted location.

Schedule visits early in the day if at all possible. Most crimes occur from mid-afternoon to early evening.

Become knowledgeable of the neighborhood where your client lives. If the client lives in a high-crime area, you should consider using the "buddy system."

Once at the location, make a visual assessment of the situation before leaving the car. If concerned about safety you may want to call your client and ask him/her to accompany you to the building.

As you enter a house, do a quick visual scan looking for signs of danger, such as weapons or drugs. Be watchful of *all* persons in the home. Ask who else besides your client is at home. If there are signs of danger, promptly and politely postpone the visit, saying something like, "I'm sorry, you're going to have to excuse me. I just remembered I'm supposed to be at another meeting. I'll call you this afternoon to arrange another time when we can meet." It's best, at least at first, to stay near the entrance door, in case a quick exit is needed. The bottom line when conducting a home visit is to *remain calm*. Being calm helps you generate and assess your options. And always trust your gut feelings. If it feels dangerous, it probably is.

BURNOUT, STRESS, AND STRESS MANAGEMENT

Ron Pakenham is 10 days behind in his paperwork. He has been a juvenile probation and parole officer for the past 3½ years. Both his agency director and the juvenile judge are pressuring him to do his paperwork. Mr. Pakenham also has problems at home. His mother has emphysema, and he and his wife are going through a divorce. While working on his paperwork, he receives a call from a houseparent at a group home for adolescent youths, inquiring when high school is starting in fall. (Mr. Pakenham supervises two teenage boys at this home.) Mr. Pakenham replies, "Hey, I don't know. You'll have to call the school system. I'm not your errand boy. Don't you know I have more important things to do than to hunt information for you?" Moments later, Mr. Pakenham regrets his response. Pondering his family problems and his mountain of paperwork, Mr. Pakenham realizes he is nearing burnout.

Definitions and Symptoms of Burnout

Burnout is a serious problem for helping professionals. Pines and Aronson (1981) defined *burnout* as

> a state of mind . . . accompanied by an array of symptoms that indicate a general malaise: emotional, physical, and psychological fatigue; feelings of helplessness, hopelessness, and a lack of enthusiasm about work and even about life in general. (p. 3)

Maslach and Pines (1977) studied burnout extensively among social workers, psychiatrists, psychologists, prison personnel, psychiatric nurses, legal aid attorneys, physicians, child-care workers, teachers, ministers, and counselors. They summarized a number of symptoms:

> Burnout involves the loss of concern for the people with whom one is working. In addition to physical exhaustion (and sometimes even illness), burnout is characterized by an emotional exhaustion in which the professional no longer has any positive feelings, sympathy, or respect for clients or patients. A very cynical and dehumanized perception of these people often develops, in which they are labeled in derogatory ways and treated accordingly. As a result of this dehumanizing process, these people are viewed as somehow deserving of their problems and are blamed for their own victimization, and thus there is a deterioration of the quality of care or service that they receive. The professional who burns out is unable to deal successfully with the overwhelming emotional stresses of the job, and this failure to cope can be manifested in a number of ways, ranging from impaired performance and absenteeism to various types of personal problems (such as alcohol and drug abuse, marital conflict, and mental illness). People who burn out often quit their jobs or even change professions, while some seek psychiatric treatment for what they believe to be their personal failings. (pp. 100–101)

Freudenberger (1977) described burnout as follows:

> Briefly described, burnout includes such symptoms as cynicism and negativism and a tendency to be inflexible and almost rigid in thinking, which often leads to a closed mind about change or innovation. The worker may begin to discuss the client in intellectual and jargon terms and thereby distance himself from any emotional involvement. Along with this, a form of paranoia may set in whereby the worker feels that his peers and administration are out to make life more difficult. (pp. 90–91)

Burnout as a Reaction to High Levels of Stress

We don't always differentiate being "burned out" from feeling alienated, indifferent, apathetic, cynical, discouraged, mentally or physically exhausted, and overwhelmed by stress. To better understand burnout, it is useful to conceptualize it as one reaction to high levels of stress. This suggests that stress management strategies can be used to prevent and treat burnout.

Stress is a contributing factor in most illnesses, including heart attacks, migraine headaches, diabetes, allergies, colds, cancer, arthritis, insomnia, emphysema, hypertension, and alcoholism (Sapolsky, 1998). It is also a contributing factor in numerous emotional and behavioral difficulties, including depression, anxiety, suicide attempts, spouse abuse, child abuse, physical assaults, irritability, and stuttering (Sapolsky, 1998). Becoming skillful in reducing stress is an effective way to prevent emotional and physical disorders, and it is also an effective adjunct to treatment for emotional and physical disorders (Sapolsky, 1998).

Stress can be defined as an emotional and physiological reaction to stressors. A stressor is a demand, situation, or circumstance that disrupts our equilibrium and initiates the stress response. Possible stressors include crowding, noise, death of a friend, excessive cold, loss of a job, toxic substances, arguments—the list is infinite.

Hans Selye (1956), one of the first authorities on stress, found that we have a three-stage reaction to stress—alarm, resistance, and exhaustion—and he called this three-stage response the "General Adaptation Syndrome."

In the *alarm* stage, the body recognizes the stressor, such as an argument, then reacts to it by preparing to fight or flee. Our physiological reactions are complex and numerous and are summarized only briefly here (for an extended discussion, see Sapolsky, 1998). The body sends messages from the brain (hypothalamus) to the pituitary gland to release its hormones. These hormones trigger the ad renal glands to release adrenaline. Adrenaline increases the rate of breathing and heartbeat, increases perspiration, raises blood sugar

Exhibit 14.4 Conceptualizing Stressors, Stress, and Stress-Related Illnesses

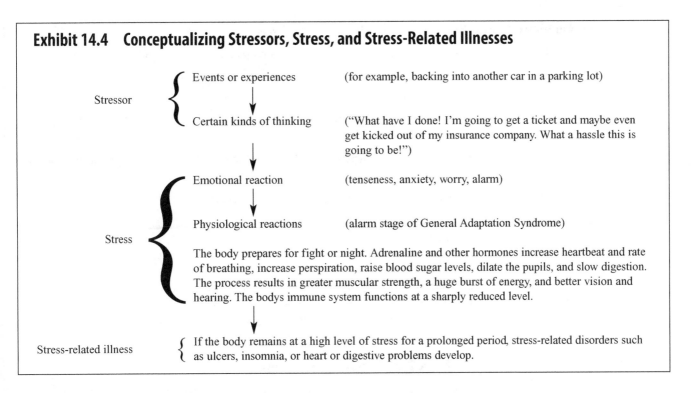

level, dilates the pupils, and slows digestion. This results in a huge burst of energy, better hearing and vision, and greater muscular strength—all reactions that increase our capacity to cope with the situation. During the alarm stage, the body's immune system functions at a sharply reduced level. (The immune system fights germs, bacteria, and viruses and facilitates healing within the body.)

In the *resistance* stage, the body becomes relaxed. When the body is relaxed, the immune system functions at its optimal capacities. During this stage, the body (and the immune system) repair any damage caused during the alarm stage. Most stressors cause the body to go through only the alarm and resistance stages. During our lifetimes we experience these two stages innumerable times.

Are you aware that stress can be beneficial? It increases concentration and enhances our capacities to accomplish physical tasks. A life without stress would be boring and might even be impossible. Even dreaming produces some stress.

Stress that causes long-term damage results when the body remains in a stage of high stress for an extended period. When this happens, the body is unable to repair the damage and eventually reaches the *exhaustion* stage. This stage is characterized by the development of one or more stress-related illnesses, such as ulcers, hypertension, or arthritis.

Numerous authorities on stress note two components of stressors: the events or experiences encountered and our thoughts and perceptions about these events. This conceptualization of stressors, stress, and stress-related illnesses (Exhibit 14.4) suggests two general approaches for reducing stress: Change the distressing events, or change your thoughts and perceptions about the events.

Exhibit 14.6 provides material on traumas and stress disorders.

Exercise 14.2: Events and Self-Talk as Stressors

Goal: This exercise is designed for you to recognize your current stressors and to assist you in realizing that stressors consist of distressing events and self-talk associated with those events.

Step 1: Specify the events that are currently stressors in your life.

Step 2: For each stressful event, specify your self-talk associated with the event. (Self-talk may intensify or decrease your overall feeling of being under stress.)

Step 3: Which form of a stressor (the event or the associated self-talk) do you believe is the major contributor to the level of stress that you experience? Explain your views on this issue.

Exercise 14.3: My Physiological Reactions to High Levels of Stress

Goal: This exercise is designed to assist you in recognizing how you physiologically react to high levels of stress.

Step 1: Specify two events in the past week that were very stressful to you—where you physiologically were in the alarm phase.

Step 2: What physiological reactions do you remember having? Review the material on reactions to stress. Specify the physiological reactions that you remember having.

Step 3: Specify the stress-related illnesses that you have experienced. Also indicate (as well as you can) the starting and ending times for these illnesses.

Step 4: Rate the importance to you of learning and using stress management strategies:

Not important	Somewhat important	Fairly important	Very important	Absolutely essential

As noted earlier, burnout is one reaction to high levels of stress (Exhibit 14.5). Burnout is caused primarily by what we tell ourselves about events or experiences: "I've had it." "What's the use, whatever I try won't work." "I'm going to give up—I am no longer going to make an effort." Avoiding self-defeating thoughts reduces burnout.

Structural Causes of Stress That May Lead to Burnout

Because burnout is one possible reaction to, or consequence of, high stress levels, it therefore follows that events (structural factors) that contribute to high stress levels also contribute to burnout. Edelwich (1980) identified structural factors associated with work that contribute to high stress levels and lead to burnout:

- Too many work hours
- Career dead end
- Too much paperwork
- Insufficient training
- Not appreciated by clients
- Not appreciated by supervisor
- Not paid enough money

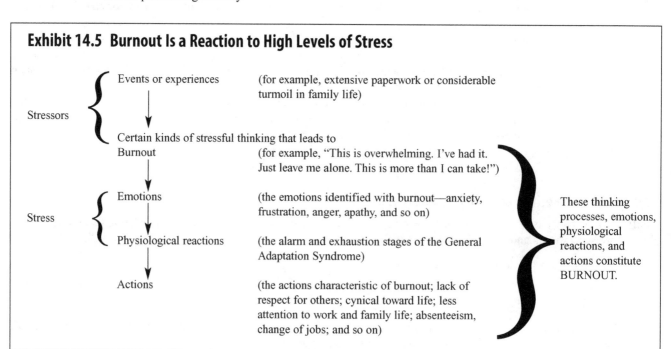

Exhibit 14.5 Burnout Is a Reaction to High Levels of Stress

Stressors
- Events or experiences   (for example, extensive paperwork or considerable turmoil in family life)
- Certain kinds of stressful thinking that leads to
  Burnout   (for example, "This is overwhelming. I've had it. Just leave me alone. This is more than I can take!")

Stress
- Emotions   (the emotions identified with burnout—anxiety, frustration, anger, apathy, and so on)
- Physiological reactions   (the alarm and exhaustion stages of the General Adaptation Syndrome)
- Actions   (the actions characteristic of burnout; lack of respect for others; cynical toward life; less attention to work and family life; absenteeism, change of jobs; and so on)

These thinking processes, emotions, physiological reactions, and actions constitute BURNOUT.

- No support for important decisions
- Powerlessness
- System not responsive to clients' needs
- Bad office politics
- Sexism
- Too much travel
- Isolation from peers
- No social life

Edelwich added that people who seek careers in the helping professions are particularly vulnerable to burnout because many enter this field with unrealistic expectations. They expect (1) that the services they provide will decisively improve the lives of practically all their clients, (2) that they will be highly appreciated by the employing agency and practically all clients, (3) that they will be able to substantially change bureaucracies to be more responsive to clients' needs, and (4) that there will be many opportunities for rapid advancement and high status. The frustrations experienced at work and the gradual recognition that many of these expectations are unrealistic are contributing factors to stress and to burnout.

Maslach (1976) found that large caseloads in the helping professions are a major cause of stress and burnout:

> Burnout often becomes inevitable when the professional is forced to provide care for too many people. As the ratio increases, the result is higher and higher emotional overload until, like a wire that has too much electricity flowing through it, the worker just burns out and emotionally disconnects. (p. 19)

A lack of approved *timeouts* at work is another source of stress and may be a factor in burnout. Timeouts are not merely short coffee breaks; they are opportunities for professionals having a stressful day to switch to less stressful tasks. Timeouts are possible in large agencies that have shared work responsibilities.

Additional causes of burnout include poor time management, inability to work effectively with other people, lack of purpose or undefined goals in life, and inability to handle effectively emergencies that arise (Pines & Aronson, 1981).

Clients can add to staff burnout (Maslach, 1978). *Some* clients cause high levels of stress, particularly those with depressing or emotionally draining problems (such as terminally ill clients, belligerent clients, suicidal clients, obnoxious clients, incest cases, and severe abuse cases). Chronic clients who show no improvement (such as an alcoholic family in which the problem drinker denies a drinking problem) can lead to frustration and high stress levels for workers. So can clients who remind workers of personal difficulties they presently face, such as providing marriage counseling services when workers are having marital difficulties at home. Extensive home responsibilities, such as taking care of a terminally ill parent, can also drain energy needed at home and at work.

Taking "ownership" of clients' problems contributes to burnout. When a client tells you his or her innermost secrets and problems, you may want to rescue that person. Helping professionals, especially in their early years of practice, often fall victim to the "white knight" fantasy. You cannot slay your client's dragons. Clients must slay their own dragons. Remember, we are called helping professionals, *not* rescuing professionals!

Exercise 14.4: A Time When I Burned Out

Goal: This exercise is designed to help you recognize what you can do when you experience burnout.

Step 1: Describe a time in your life when you experienced burnout. When you were experiencing burnout, did you conclude (for a while), "I can't take this anymore"?

Step 2: If you have recovered from feeling burned out, describe what helped you to recover. If you are still feeling burned out, speculate about what you need to do to make progress in recovering.

Approaches to Manage Stress and Prevent Burnout

Okay, you ask, so what can I do to avoid burnout? Lots of things, it turns out. What follows is a small sampling of strategies. The key is to select strategies you will be most motivated to use. These strategies parallel healthy diet plans—they work for those who put forth effort to make them work. (The references provide expanded reading on these strategies.)

Exhibit 14.6   Traumas and Stress Disorders

Physical trauma is an injury to the body caused by violence or accident, such as a fracture, bruise, and so forth. Psychological trauma is an emotional wound or shock, often having long-lasting effects. Physical traumas often lead to psychological traumas.

Traumatic experiences often involve a threat to life or safety, but any situation that leaves one feeling overwhelmed and alone can be traumatic even if it does not involve physical harm. It's not the objective facts that determine whether an event is traumatic, but one's subjective emotional experience of the event.

A stressful event is most likely to be traumatic if:

- It happened unexpectedly.
- One is unprepared for it.
- It happened repeatedly.
- One felt powerless to prevent it.
- Someone was intentionally cruel.

Traumas can come in a huge variety of ways. The following is a short list: serving in combat in the military, being physically or sexually abused as a child, a sexual assault, an auto accident, the breakup of a significant relationship, a humiliating or deeply disappointing experience, and the discovery of a life-threatening illness or disabling condition.

People are more likely to be traumatized by a stressful experience if they are already under a heavy stress load or have recently suffered a series of losses. Not all potentially traumatic events lead to lasting psychological and emotional damage; some people rebound quickly from even the most shocking and tragic experiences, while others are devastated by experiences that appear on the surface to be "mildly upsetting."

Traumatic experiences in childhood can have a severe and long-lasting impact. Children who have been traumatized see the world as a dangerous and frightening place. When childhood trauma is unresolved, this sense of fear and helplessness carries over into adulthood, setting the stage for further trauma.

Emotional symptoms of trauma include:

- Denial, shock, or disbelief
- Anxiety and fear
- Withdrawing from others
- Feeling numb or disconnected
- Anger, irritability, mood swings
- Confusion, difficulty concentrating
- Guilt, self-blame, shame
- Feeling hopeless or sad

Physical symptoms of trauma include:

- Aches and pains
- Fatigue
- Muscle tension

- Being startled easily
- Racing heart beat
- Agitation and edginess
- Difficulty concentrating

These emotional and physical symptoms gradually fade *if* the impacted person makes progress in coming to terms with the trauma. But even if the person is progressing in resolving the trauma, the person may be troubled from time to time by painful memories and emotions. Triggers for reliving the painful event include the anniversary of the event, or sounds and images of the situation that remind the traumatized individual of the traumatic experience.

There are two stress disorders associated with severe traumas: acute stress disorder and posttraumatic stress disorder (PTSD). Acute stress disorder is an anxiety disorder in which fear and related symptoms are experienced soon after a traumatic event and last less than a month (American Psychiatric Association, 2000).

Posttraumatic stress disorder is an anxiety disorder in which fear and related symptoms continue to be experienced long after a traumatic event (American Psychiatric Association, 2000). Primary symptoms of PTSD include flashbacks or intrusive memories, living in a constant state of "red alert," and avoiding things that remind the impacted person of the traumatic event.

Working through trauma can be painful, scary, and potentially retraumatizing. The "healing" work is best done with a competent trauma expert. Trauma treatment involves:

- Processing the trauma memories and feelings
- Discharging the pent-up emotions/energy associated with the trauma
- Learning how to control strong emotions
- Rebuilding the capacity to trust other people

Treatment approaches for PTSD include the following:

- Cognitive-behavioral therapy, such as rational therapy (described in Module 1), in which the person learns to reframe the disturbing traumatic thoughts.
- Antianxiety drugs, which help control the anxieties and tensions associated with PTSD. Such medication provides some relief but needs to be combined with a "talk" therapy approach.
- Eye movement desensitization and reprocessing (EMDR), which incorporates elements of cognitive-behavioral therapy, in which the impacted persons move their eyes in a rhythmic manner from side to side while flooding their minds with images of the objects and situations they try to avoid. These back-and-forth eye movements are thought to work by "unfreezing" traumatic memories, which then can be processed and resolved.

Goal Setting and Time Management. Not knowing what you want out of life is distressing and even depressing. Many people muddle through life without ever setting goals. The result? Frustration and boredom. (Boredom, by the way, is highly stressful.) The solution? Realistic goal setting. What do you get? Increased self-confidence, improved decision making, a greater sense of purpose, and an improved sense of security. Do you set goals, or do you muddle?

Time is life, and to waste time is to waste life. Managing your time well is empowering. Time management approaches help you set goals and use your time effectively to reach short-term and lifetime goals (Lakein, 1973). First, set lifetime and short-term goals. (Admittedly this can be a lengthy process, but failure to set goals almost guarantees feeling unfulfilled and dissatisfied.) Next, write down tasks that will help you accomplish your high-priority goals—both short-term and lifetime. Then prioritize tasks according to what is most important to do to accomplish each goal. Do the high-priority tasks first and—generally—ignore doing the low-priority (low-payoff) tasks. Low-priority tasks consume time and interfere with your high-priority tasks.

Exercise 14.5: My High-Value Goals and Tasks

Goal: This exercise is designed to assist you in specifying your short-range and long-range goals, and to identify tasks that will help you achieve these goals.

Step 1:   List your goals for the next 6 months on one sheet of paper, and list your long-range goals on another.

Step 2:   Prioritize your goals by assigning "A" to high-value goals, "B" to medium-value goals, and "C" to low-value goals. Next, rank the A, or high-value, goals in order: A-1, A-2, A-3, and so on.

Step 3:   List the tasks needed to achieve the specified A goals.

Step 4:   Prioritize each task's value in achieving each of your A goals using the A, B, C, and so forth approach.

Note: If this process is conscientiously followed, you will have a clear vision of your goals in life and what you need to do to achieve these goals.

Positive Thinking. Is your cup half full or half empty? You and you alone choose how you view your "cup of life." Negative self-talk ("I've had it. I'm no longer going to try. I'm just going to go through the motions. I'm giving in.") becomes self-fulfilling.

Choose positive thinking. Taking a positive view and positive action not only leads to others' liking you, but you will also feel worthwhile, you will like yourself, you will be productive and creative, and good things will happen. (Positive thinking is discussed more fully later in this chapter.)

Travel through life at a "relaxed cruising speed." Look at the scenery with enjoyment, remain calm during crises and emergencies, approach work thoughtfully and strive to be creative, and enjoy your leisure.

Changing "Burnout Thoughts." Rational therapy (Module 1) demonstrates that what we tell ourselves about our experiences causes our emotions and shapes future actions. Burnout is thus primarily determined by our thinking processes.

Although we cannot change events that happen to us, we can think rationally and positively about events. Challenge your "burnout thoughts": "I am *not* going to give up. I've handled challenges in the past, and I can handle this one. One step at a time, that's what I have to do. When the going gets tough, I get going."

Keys to changing "burnout thoughts": (1) Recognize when you are thinking them. (2) Select positive thoughts that challenge burnout ones. And (3) every time you start thinking burnout thoughts, replace them with positive thoughts.

Relaxation Techniques. Burnout doesn't happen in a day, but it does happen one day at a time. The days accumulate, and bingo, you're in burnout. So challenge burnout one day at a time. How? By taking the time to relax. The relaxation response is a powerful challenge to burnout. Use it. Three relaxation techniques are described in Exhibit 14.7.

Research has demonstrated that using a relaxation technique is physiologically and psychologically more refreshing and energy restoring than deep sleep (Seaward, 2005). Many users, in fact, have reported that they needed less sleep after they began relaxing, which suggests that a regenerative process occurs during relaxation (Seaward, 2005). Relaxation techniques have been used successfully in the treatment of many stress-related disorders including hypertension and asthma (Seaward, 2005). They also have been effective in decreasing the use of drugs, alcohol, and cigarette smoking (Seaward, 2005); alleviating sleep disorders; and accelerating the bodily healing process.

Relaxation techniques have been found to have a number of other positive effects. They are useful in treating phobias and in treating people with emotional problems (Seaward, 2005). Regular practice of a technique improves learning ability, perceptual motor performance, ability to recover from stress, perceptual

Exhibit 14.7   Three Relaxation Techniques

This exhibit presents a set of instructions that a worker can use in teaching an individual, or a group, to relax. (The instructions in this exhibit will assume a group is being instructed; the instructions can easily be revised for use with one individual.) Three relaxation techniques are taught: deep breathing relaxation, meditation by repeating the work "relax," and favorite relaxation place.

The worker explains that using a relaxation technique is one way to reduce stress and then leads the group in the following meditative exercise. (The worker should feel free to modify, and add to, the following material.)

"I will now lead you in three relaxation exercises. The purpose is to show you that through meditating you can reduce stress and anxiety. You can do this exercise by yourself whenever you are anxious or want to relax. You can do it, for example, before giving a speech in class, taking a crucial exam, or going to bed at night.

Herbert Benson (1975), who wrote the book, *The Relaxation Response*, has identified four key elements common to relaxation approaches that help people to relax. These four elements are (1) being in a quiet place; (2) getting in a comfortable position; (3) having an object to dwell on, such as your breathing or a phrase that you continually repeat silently to yourself; and (4) having a passive attitude in which you let go of your day-to-day concerns by no longer thinking about them. Having a passive attitude is the key element in helping you to relax.

Now, I want you to form a circle. (Wait until a circle is formed.) I will lead you in three types of relaxation exercises. First, we will do a deep-breathing exercise. Then, we will move into repeating the word *relax* silently to ourselves. Third, I'll have you focus on visualizing your most relaxing place. We will move directly from the first to the second, and then from the second to the third without stopping. When we do this exercise, don't worry about anything unusual happening. There will be no tricks. Concentrate on what I'm telling you to focus on, while taking a passive attitude where you let go of your everyday thoughts and concerns. Everyday thoughts and concerns may occasionally enter your mind, but seek to let go of them when they do.

Before we start, I want each of you to identify one of your most relaxing scenes. It may be lying in the sun on the beach or by a lake. It may be sitting in warm water in a bathtub reading a book. It may be sitting by a warm fireplace. Is there anyone who hasn't identified a relaxing scene? (Wait until everyone has identified one.)

OK, we're ready to start. (If possible, dim the lights, or turn out some of them.) First, I want you to close your eyes and keep them closed for the entire exercise. Next, get in a comfortable position. If you want, you can sit or lie on the floor. (Take 5 or 6 minutes for each of the three relaxation exercises. Speak softly and slowly. Pause frequently, sometimes for 20 seconds or more without saying anything. Feel free to add material to the following instructions.)

First, I want you to focus on your breathing. Breathe in and out slowly and deeply. . . . Breathe in and out slowly. . . . as you breathe out feel how relaxing it feels. . . . While exhaling, imagine your concerns are leaving you. . . . as you're breathing in and out, feel how you're becoming more calm, more relaxed, more refreshed. . . . Just keep focusing on breathing slowly in and out. . . . Don't try to be in sync when I'm talking about breathing in and out. . . . Find a breathing rhythm that's comfortable for you. . . . Breathe in slowly and deeply, and then slowly breathe out. . . . You've got the power within you to get more and more relaxed. . . . All you have to do is focus on your breathing. . . . Breathe in slowly and deeply, and then slowly breathe out. . . . If other thoughts happen to enter you mind, just let them drift away as effortlessly as possible. . . . The key to becoming more relaxed is to let go of your day-to-day concerns. . . . To do this, all you need to do is simply focus on your breathing. . . . Breathe in slowly and deeply, and then breathe out.

Now, we will switch to repeating silently to yourself the word *relax*. Keep your eyes closed. . . . just keep repeating to yourself the word *relax*. . . . Keep repeating *relax* to yourself silently and slowly. . . . All of us encounter daily stressors. . . . It is impossible to avoid daily stressors. . . . The important thing to remember about stress management is not to seek to avoid daily stressors but to find ways to relax when we are under high levels of stress. . . . An excellent and very simple way to learn to relax is to sit in a quiet place, in a comfortable position, and silently repeat to yourself the word *relax*. . . . *relax*. . . . *relax*. . . . By simply repeating the word *relax* to yourself, you have the power within you to become more and more relaxed. . . . Find a nice comfortable pace for repeating the word *relax* to yourself. . . . The pace should be slow enough so that you can relax. . . . But not be so slow that thoughts about your day-to-day concerns enter your mind. . . . Remember, the key to relaxing is letting go of your day-to-day concerns. . . . If such concerns begin to enter your mind, focus more of your attention on repeating *relax* silently and slowly to yourself. . . . By repeating *relax* to yourself, you will find it will appear to have magical powers for you, as you will find yourself becoming more and more relaxed and refreshed. . . . [Have the members repeat *relax* for 5 or 6 minutes.]

Now, we will switch to focusing on your most relaxing scene. Don't open your eyes. . . . Focus on being in your most relaxing place. . . . Feel how good and relaxing it feels. . . . Just dwell on how relaxing it feels. . . . Enjoy everything about how calm and relaxing this place is. . . . Feel yourself becoming calmer, more relaxed. . . . Enjoy the peacefulness of this place. . . . Feel yourself becoming more relaxed, more renewed and refreshed. . . . Enjoy all the sights and sounds of this special place for you. . . . Notice and cherish the pleasant smells and aromas. . . . Feel the warmth, peacefulness, and serenity of this very special place for you. . . . Whenever you want to become more relaxed, all you have to do is close your eyes, sit quietly, and visualize yourself being in this very relaxing place. . . . The more you practice visualizing being in your relaxing place, the quicker you will find yourself becoming relaxed. . . . It will appear to you that

Exhibit 14.7 *(continued)*

your relaxing place has magical, relaxing powers for you, but in reality you are simply relaxing yourself by letting go of your day-to-day concerns and instead focusing on enjoying the peacefulness of your most relaxing place. . . . If you have to give a speech or are facing some other stressful situation, you can learn to reduce your level of anxiety by simply closing your eyes for a short period of time and focusing your thoughts on being in your most relaxing place. . . . You always have the power within you to reduce your level of anxiety. . . . All you have to do is close your eyes and visualize being in your very special relaxing place. . . . Continue to visualize, now, being in this very relaxing place. . . . Feel yourself becoming more relaxed, refreshed, and calm. . . . If you're feeling drowsy, that's fine. . . . Feeling drowsy is an indication that you're becoming more and more relaxed. . . . You're doing fine. . . . Just keep on visualizing being in your very relaxing place. . . . You will become more and more relaxed by simply letting go of your day-to-day concerns and by enjoying this very special relaxing place. . . . (Pause for a minute or two, then continue this exercise.)

Unfortunately, in a minute or so it will be time to open your eyes. But there is no hurry. I will slowly count backwards from five to one, and then ask you to open your eyes shortly after we reach one. . . . (5) Enjoy how relaxed you feel. You may now feel warmer, drowsy, and so relaxed that you feel you don't even want to move a muscle. . . . Enjoy this very special feeling. . . . It is

healthy to become this relaxed, as your immune system functions best when you are relaxed. . . . (4) Slowly begin to become more alert. . . . There is no rush. . . . There is no hurry. . . . Take your time to become more alert. Anytime you want to relax, all you need to do is use one of these three relaxation approaches. With practice you will gradually get better at relaxing by using these approaches. . . . (3) You should now focus on becoming more alert. . . . Take your time. . . . we still have a half-minute or so. . . . Examine whether you want to make a commitment to use relaxation exercises to reduce the daily stress you encounter. . . . (2) We are nearly at the time to be alert. . . . You should now work toward becoming more and more alert. . . . (1) Slowly open your eyes. . . . There is no hurry. . . . Take your time to get oriented. A word of caution: if you have to drive someplace soon, please walk around for several minutes before trying to drive a car, as you may be so relaxed now that you may not be alert enough to drive safely."

Step 3. The worker then asks questions such as "What do you think of these three approaches?" "How relaxed did you get?" "Did any of you have trouble getting relaxed?" "If yes, why?" "Which of the three approaches did you like better and why?" (If the members are very relaxed and drowsy, they may feel they do not have the energy to respond to these questions. The worker should respect such a "mood" and not pressure members to respond.)

acuity, work productivity and job satisfaction, and creativity (Seaward, 2005). Using a technique improves psychological health; heightens self-awareness; increases self-actualization; reduces anxiety, depression, and aggression; reduces reaction time; increases recall ability; and improves academic performance (Seaward, 2005).

The potential medical value in eliciting the relaxation response is dramatically described by Benson (1975):

> The prevention of stress-related diseases carries with it enormous significance, certainly for the individual and his family in terms of their own physical and mental well-being, and for society as a whole through huge dollar savings in health expenditures. It is possible that the regular elicitation of the Relaxation Response will prevent the huge personal suffering and social costs now being inflicted on us by high blood pressure and its related ailments. (pp. 156–157)

Exercise. Regular exercise reduces stress (period). Choose an exercise program that you enjoy (be it softball or belly dancing). You will get fit (which of course you will feel good about), and you will have increased energy to meet crises and emergencies. Negative aspects of your job and home life won't seem so bad. Exercising uses up fuel, reduces heart rate and blood pressure, and sets off numerous physiological changes that reduce stress and induce the relaxation response (Seaward, 1994).

And don't forget to eat properly, get sufficient sleep, and get appropriate medical care.

Outside Activities. Have a life. Family and friends, church and meditation, hobbies and travel, fun—find the mixture that makes you healthy. These are your antidotes to stress and burnout and the sources of your inner strengths.

Reward yourself for tasks done well. We don't hesitate to compliment others for jobs done well; don't forget to take pride in your own work well done and in a life well lived. Take a mental health day. In periods of extended stress, take a day off and do only the things you want to do. (Some agencies now allow a certain number of mental health days with pay.) You will return to work more effective and ready to face challenges.

Social Support Systems. Develop trusting and mutually caring relationships at work. We all need a "lifeline." Maslach (1976) noted,

> Our findings show that burnout rates are lower for those professionals who actively express, analyze and share their personal feelings with their colleagues. Not only do they consciously get things off their chest, but they have an opportunity to receive constructive feedback from other people and to develop new perspectives of their relationship with patients/clients. This process is greatly enhanced if the institution sets up some social outlets such as support groups, special staff meetings or workshops. (p. 19)

Social support groups (at work or outside work) let us let our hair down, help us "kid around," share our lives, keep in touch, and give us a source of security that helps when crises arise. Support groups have several essential features (Greenberg, 1980): (1) The group meets regularly. (2) The same people at tend. (3) A feeling of closeness has developed. (4) There is an opportunity for spontaneity and informality. Possible support groups come in many "shapes and sizes": coworkers, friends, sport or hobby groups, family, church groups, and community organizations such as Parents Without Partners.

Variety at Work. No doubt about it—doing the same thing day in and day out becomes exhausting. The simple fact is, emotionally draining work (such as suicide counseling or hospice work) can be done only for limited periods, or burnout will rear its ugly head. Therefore, it is important to structure your practice so that you have a variety of job tasks during the week. Also, participating in workshops, conferences, continuing education courses, and in-service training programs adds variety and helps you grow professionally.

Humor. It is impossible to say enough about laughter as a coping mechanism. Humor relaxes us, makes work more enjoyable, and takes the edge off. Humor at work and at home relieves stress and helps prevent burnout.

Distressing Events. Bad things happen—to us, to friends and family we care about, and to clients we care about. Competent people lose their jobs, friends die, romantic relationships end, we question our faith—the list is endless.

When distressing events arise, what can you do? Actually, many things. It is important to confront events head-on to attempt to improve the situation. Power is always better than helplessness. For example, if you feel beginning burnout, identify what is frustrating and exhausting you at work and then develop new approaches for handling these responsibilities. One worker finds incest cases particularly exhausting, whereas another finds working with the terminally ill more draining—consider exchanging these cases. If you are frustrated because program objectives and job expectations are unclear, get clarification from your supervisor.

Many distressing events get less distressing when we confront them head-on and take positive action. Not all events or situations can be changed. For example, you may not be able to change certain distasteful aspects of your job. In such situations, the only constructive remaining alternative is to bite the bullet and accept them. It is counterproductive to spend time complaining about a situation you cannot change.

Exercise 14.6: Stress Management Techniques for Me

Goal: This exercise is designed to familiarize you with available stress management techniques.

Step 1: Review the material in this chapter on stress management techniques. List those techniques that you have used. Briefly describe whether the technique was beneficial to you in helping reduce the level of stress you were experiencing.

Step 2: Specify stress management techniques that you are planning to use in the future.

ENJOYING SOCIAL WORK AND YOUR LIFE

To gather material to write this section, I asked friends who have practiced social work for several years to summarize their satisfactions and frustrations about pursuing a career in social work. Here is one reply.

> It is difficult to find the right words to describe my satisfaction with having made a decision to be a social worker. I have worked in a protective services unit of a public welfare department for two years, as a probation and parole officer for three years, and now am a director of a group home for teenage males who have conflicts with their parents.

Exhibit 14.8   Mindfulness

A key principle of social work practice is: "In order for a social worker to help others, he or she must first take care of himself/herself!" An analogy may help to emphasize this principle. One of the first things an airline flight attendant says when the plane is preparing to take off is: "If there is an emergency and the cabin loses pressure, your oxygen mask will drop down, and the first thing you need to do is take care of yourself by putting on your oxygen mask—then you can begin to plan your exit from the pane and assist others." Like many professionals, social workers may experience a fair amount of stress. Social workers need to have quality self-care plans and practices, so that they can maintain their physical, mental, and emotional well-being. There are numerous ways that social workers, and other persons, can reduce and relieve stress and burnout. These self-care practices include: healthy eating, quality sleep, regular exercise, and learning to "let go" of disturbing thoughts about past traumatic events. In a very real sense, social workers have an ethical obligation to take care of themselves—so that they can then assist others (National Association of Social Workers Code of Ethics, 1999).

Mindfulness practice is another tool that social workers (and other persons) can readily use to reduce stress. Mindfulness meditations have increasingly been utilized in a variety of settings, including: mental health agencies, schools, and medical settings (Follette, Palm, & Pearson, 2006). Mindfulness is a state of consciousness with enhanced attention to moment-to-moment experience (Kabat-Zinn, 2012). Mindfulness teaches us to be unconditionally present. Mindfulness is paying attention on purpose, with a focus on the present—in a non-judgmental manner. An emphasis is placed on seeing and accepting things as they are, without trying to change them.

There are a number of benefits to mindfulness meditation. It has been found to: reduce rumination (that is, reduce thinking negatively about past, present, or future events), reduce stress, boost working memory, improve affect, decrease depression, increase focus and suppress distracting information, increase cognitive flexibility, increase the ability to communicate one's emotions to a partner, enhance self-insight, increase intuition, decrease anxieties, increase physical well-being, increase information processing speed, promote empathy, increase compassion for others, improve self-concept, and increase quality of life (Kabat-Zinn, 2012).

There are a large number of different mindfulness exercises. The following is an example of an exercise you can try. Find a quiet, comfortable place to sit down. This might be on a chair, or on a cushion on the floor. If it is a cushion on the floor, you may choose to cross your legs. Take a posture that is upright, but not rigid. Your back should be straight, with the curve in the lower back that is naturally there. For the next several minutes, just focus on your breathing. Your eyes may be closed, or open. Do not try to control the flow of your breathing—just focus on the air going in and out of your body. Notice how the air feels as it enters and exits. Notice how your stomach and rib cage rises and falls as you breathe in, and then out. Also, acknowledge your feelings, images, memories, and thoughts—and allow them to float along, like a gently moving white cloud on a very pleasant day. Allow your thoughts to come and go without judging them. Then focus again on your breathing. Expect your mind to wander—acknowledge the thoughts, images, and memories—without placing judgment on them. Return to focus your attention on your breathing, and feel your body gradually relaxing as you breathe in and out. Remember that mindfulness meditation is about practicing being mindful of whatever happens. It is NOT about getting ourselves to stop thinking. With mindfulness, we are trying to be with ourselves as we already are, not trying to change ourselves into some preconceived notion of how we ought to be instead. Seek to practice this meditation technique a few times a day. Gradually, as the days pass, increase the time that you meditate to around 20 minutes at a time.

One of the satisfying aspects of social work is that there is a wide variety of areas where a person can work. When I found myself becoming stale as a probation officer, it was inspiring to look forward to moving on to something else. If this job becomes routine and no longer something I would look forward to doing, I would again move on to some other social work position.

I truly find it gratifying to work with people. If you don't like working with people, then certainly this is the wrong job to have. I know this sounds "naive," but when I feel I've been of some help in assisting someone to better handle a personal or social problem, it really makes me feel good. It should be noted I'm no longer as idealistic as I was when I was going to college and thought I would be able to help the vast majority of my clients. I've learned that most clients simply aren't sufficiently motivated to put forth the time and effort needed to improve their lives—it's like exercising; we all know exercising will improve our health and keep us trim, but only a few people are willing to put forth the time and effort.

Social work is a challenging profession. Every client's problem is unique. For that matter, every client's personality is unique. Interacting with new people, and developing somewhat different treatment strategies with each client is a challenge. Through helping clients I also grow as a person and learn more about myself. Also challenging, and often learning experiences, are speaking to groups in the community, and seeking to develop new services when a need arises. Also educational (and a way of seeing old friends) are in-service training sessions that are held at the agencies I've worked at.

I don't want to give an ever-glowing picture of social work. There are also frustrations. At every agency there seem to be occasional personality conflicts between staff. (Such conflicts are furthered by staff members being pitted against each other for merit increases, for desired task assignments, and for who will get to go to conferences.)

Another frustration is the amount of paperwork. At the three agencies I've worked at, 10 to 15 hours per week are spent on paperwork.

Some social workers complain this profession doesn't pay enough. I've found that in social work there are some jobs that pay a lot more than others. When I first started out, my annual salary was pretty low, but now that I'm a director of this group home I have no complaints.

Another thing that is frustrating is being aware that there are a few workers who are cynical, who always look at the negative side of things, and who really appear to be only interested in drawing their paycheck, rather than helping people. With their negative attitude, I frankly don't see how they can ever help anyone. If I was a client of theirs, I would become even more discouraged and apathetic. To me, these social workers are "deadwood" and are on "welfare" themselves as they are drawing a check without doing anything productive. These people either burned out years ago or were never "encouraging" persons who were motivated to help others.

All in all I really am delighted I chose a career in social work. I enjoy working with most clients (certainly not all of my clients as some I do find obnoxious) and with most of the other staff. I hope this information will be useful to you, and if you ever want someone to speak in your classes, give me a "jingle."

One factor identified by this social worker is the importance of being an "encouraging" person. Chapter 5 noted this as a crucial characteristic of effective counselors. Closely related to this is positive thinking, which is important not only in working with clients but also in enjoying life.

Become a Positive Thinker

In *A Treasury of Success Unlimited*, W. Clement Stone (1966) presented some of the basic principles of positive thinking:

Your most precious, valued possessions and your greatest powers are invisible and intangible. No one can take them. You, and you alone, can give them. You will receive abundance for your giving. The more you give—the more you will have!

Give a smile to everyone you meet (smile with your eyes)—and you'll smile and receive smiles. . . .
Give a kind word (with a kindly thought behind the word)—you will be kind and receive kind words. . . .
Give appreciation (warmth from the heart)—you will appreciate and be appreciated. . . .
Give honor, credit and applause (the victor's wreath)—you will be honorable and receive credit and applause. . . .
Give time for a worthy cause (with eagerness)—you will be worthy and richly rewarded. . . .
Give hope (the magic ingredient for success)—you will have hope and be made hopeful. . . .
Give happiness (a most treasured state of mind)—you will be happy and be made happy. . . .
Give encouragement (the incentive to action)—you will have courage and be encouraged. . . .
Give cheer (the verbal sunshine)—you'll be cheerful and cheered. . . .
Give a pleasant response (the neutralizer of irritants)—you will be pleasant and receive pleasant responses. . . .
Give good thoughts (nature's character builder)—you will be good and the world will have good thoughts for you. . . . (pp. 9–10)

Few living Americans can write or speak on the power of positive thinking with more authority than W. Clement Stone. Beginning as a newsboy on the streets of Chicago, Stone applied the principles of positive thinking to amass and share with others a fortune in excess of $160 million (Mandino, 1966).

Harold Sherman (1966), in "The Surest Way in the World to Attract Success—or Failure," further elaborated on positive thinking:

"You might know this would happen to me!" Is this a comment you have made, not once, but many times, when things have gone wrong? . . . Certainly—you *knew* it was going to happen—and it did. Your *faith* in "things going wrong" caused the "power of TNT' [thinking negative thoughts] within you to work *against* you instead of for you. There is a great law of mind by which your thinking and your conduct should always be guided: "Like attracts like."

Think good thoughts; you will eventually attract good things. Think bad thoughts, you will ultimately attract bad things.

Simple—easy to remember—but also easy to forget. . . .

Get this point clearly in mind: *you* supply the material (by the nature of your thoughts) out of which your creative power builds your future. If the material is inferior, comprised of mental pictures of failure, despair, defeat and the like, you can readily see that only unhappy results can be materialized from them. . . .

Whatever conditions you are facing at the moment are the result of your past thinking—good and bad. These conditions cannot change until you have first changed your thinking. . . .

Things first happen in your mind before they can happen in this outer world. What are you picturing? Do you want it to happen? If not, you are the only one who can prevent it. Your future success or failure is in your hands— where it should be. (pp. 111–113)

Numerous books have been written about positive thinking philosophy (*Looking Out for No. 1,* by Robert Ringer, 1977; *Move Ahead with Possibility Thinking,* by Robert Schuller, 1973; *Positive Thinking Everyday,* by Norman Vincent Peale, 1993; and *Positive Thinking,* by Vera Pfeiffer, 1993—to name but a few). Positive thinking certainly has considerable merit. However, there is a potential danger. Every accomplishment requires certain abilities. For those who set goals above their capacities, positive thinking creates a false sense of hope. When people (particularly those suffering from emotional problems like anxiety or depression) fail to achieve unrealistic goals, they are headed for a downturn. Authorities now suggest replacing *positive thinking* with *optimal thinking* to avoid the pitfall noted above. In optimal thinking, we look for all *realistic* options for a situation. Then we assess the merits and shortcomings of those options, and finally we select the option that appears to be most constructive. (The optimal thinking approach uses the principles of the problem-solving process described in Chapter 1.)

Positive thinking usually gets people started on a project. Many people don't realize their own potential, and a bright outlook and positive action help them achieve their goals. It is your choice. You can think and act negatively about events that happen to you, or you can think and act positively about those same events. Positive thinking helps you enjoy your career and your life.

Develop an Identity

What kind of person are you? What do you want out of life? What kind of person do you want to be? These questions are among the most important ones you will ever face. Without answers, you are not prepared to make major life decisions. Unfortunately, many people muddle through life and never contemplate these questions. Those who don't have a clue about these questions may find themselves depressed, indecisive, anxious, and unfulfilled. All too often, their lives are carbon copies of Stan Sinclair's.

At age 18, Stan graduated from high school. Unable to find a job, he enlisted in the army for a 3-year hitch. At 20, he started dating Julia Johnson while he was stationed in Illinois. He liked Julia. She became pregnant, and they decided to get married. Money was tight, and Julia wanted to live near her relatives. Two months after his discharge, Stan became a father. Needing a job in the area, he became a gas station attendant because it was the only employment he could find. Two and one-half years later, an opening occurred in an auto assembly plant. The pay was better, so Stan applied and was hired. The job was relatively easy but monotonous. Stan faithfully attached mufflers to new cars, over and over, for 40 hours a week. During the next 8 years, Stan and Julia had three more children. The pay and fringe benefits, combined with his family and financial responsibilities, locked Stan into this assembly-line job until he retired at age 65. The morning after he retired, he looked into the mirror and began asking, finally, the key questions. Was it all worth it? Why did he feel empty and unfulfilled? What did he want out of the future? Never having in the past figured out what he wanted out of life, his only answer was a frown.

Identity Development. Identity is our sense of who we are—knowledge and a feeling of the ways in which we are separate, distinct persons. Identity development is a life-long process, and our identity changes throughout our lifetime. During the early years, our sense of who we are is largely determined by the reactions of others. A long time ago, Cooley (1902) suggested that this labeling process results in the *looking glass self*—that is, people experience their self-concept through their perceptions of how others relate to them. For example, if a neighborhood identifies a male youth as a "trouble-maker" (a delinquent), the neighbors will not trust him, may accuse him of delinquent acts, and will label his semi-delinquent and aggressive behaviors as "delinquent." The youth begins to realize that this label gives him prestige and status, at least among his peers. In the absence of objective ways to gauge whether he is, in fact, a delinquent, the youth will rely on the subjective evaluations of others. Thus, gradually, as people relate to him as a delinquent, he begins to perceive himself in that way and begins to become a delinquent in earnest.

Fortunately, identity development is a lifetime process, and positive changes are possible even for those with negative self-concepts. There are two key principles to remember: (1) We cannot change the past. (2) What we want out of the future and our motivation to achieve what we want are more important than any past experiences in determining our future.

How to Determine Who You Are. Forming an identity involves thinking about, and arriving at, answers to these questions: (1) What do I want out of life? (2) What kind of person am I? (3) What kind of person do I want to be? The most important decisions you make in your life may well depend on your answers to these questions.

This is not to say that these questions are easy to answer. They require considerable contemplation and trial and error. But if you are to lead a gratifying, fulfilling life, it is imperative to find a direction so you can live the kind of life you find meaningful. Here are some questions to consider:

1. What is satisfying/meaningful/enjoyable to me? (Only after you know this will you be able to consciously seek activities that make your life fulfilling and avoid those activities that are meaningless or stifling.)
2. What is my moral code? (One possible code is to seek to fulfill your needs and to do what you find enjoyable, doing so in a way that does not deprive others of the ability to fulfill their needs.)
3. What are my religious beliefs?
4. What kind of career do I want? (Ideally, you should choose work that you find stimulating and satisfying, that you are skilled at, and that earns you enough money to support the lifestyle you want.)
5. What are my sexual mores? (Find a code that you are comfortable with and that helps you meet your needs without exploiting others. There is no one right code. What works for one may not work for another because of differences in lifestyles, life goals, and personal values.)
6. Do I want to marry? (If yes, to what type of person and when? How consistent are your answers here with your other life goals?)
7. Do I want to have children? (If yes, how many, when, and how consistent are your answers here with your other life goals?)
8. What area of the country/world do I want to live in? (Climate, geography, type of dwelling, rural or urban setting, closeness to relatives or friends, and characteristics of the neighborhood.)
9. What do I enjoy doing with my leisure time?
10. What kind of image do I want to project to others? (Your image will be composed of your dressing style and grooming habits, your emotions, personality, degree of assertiveness, capacity to communicate, material possessions, moral code, physical features, and voice patterns. You need to assess your strengths and shortcomings honestly in this area and seek to make improvements.)
11. What type of people do I enjoy being with and why?
12. Do I desire to improve the quality of my life and that of others? (If yes, in what ways, and how do you hope to achieve these goals?)
13. What types of relationships do I want to have with relatives, friends, neighbors, and people I meet for the first time?
14. What are my thoughts about death and dying?
15. What do I hope to be doing 5 years from now? 10 years? 20 years?
16. How can I achieve the goals that I identified here?

To have a well-developed sense of identity, you will at some time need answers to most, but not all, of those questions. Very few of us arrive at rational, consistent answers to all the questions. But having at least contemplated them will provide a reference for you as you embark on life after college.

Note that the questions are simple to state, but arriving at answers is a complicated, ongoing process. In addition, expect some changes in your life goals as time goes on. Your circumstances will change in unexpected ways. Activities and friends you enjoy in the future may not be what you enjoy now. Be flexible as life throws you curves. Rigid adherence to a certain path is a sure prescription for failure.

Exercise 14.7: Arriving at a Better Sense of Who You Are

Goal: This exercise is designed to assist you in identifying who you are and what you want out of life.

Step 1:   Answer the 16 questions listed above.

Step 2:   Has this exercise been useful in focusing you on who you are and what you want out of life?

____ Yes   ____ No

Explain your view.

Use Rational Challenges to Develop a Success Identity

Some people muddle through without a clear sense of what they want or who they are; others wallow in self-pity, seeing themselves as failures. I once compared people who have a success identity with those who have a failure identity:

> Success identities are characterized by the following kinds of self-talk. "I have accomplished many of the things I have tried in the past." "I am a competent, worthwhile person." "I, similar to other people, have certain special talents." "Trying something new is challenging and stimulating." "I look forward to trying something more complicated that has the opportunity for substantial payoffs, and which will test and further develop my special talents." "Trying new things helps me grow as a person and helps provide meaning to living." "I look forward to each new day with its opportunities for involvement in activities that will be gratifying and fulfilling."
>
> Do you give yourself these types of positive self-talk, or do you give yourself the following negative kinds of self-talk, . . . characteristic of those with a "failure identity"? "I can't accomplish anything I try." "I'm inferior to other people." "Why can't I be as competent, capable, or attractive as others?" "I'm a failure." "I can't afford to risk trying anything new as it will reveal my weaknesses to others." "I wish people would stop picking on me, and making cutting comments about my shortcomings." "I've got a number of personal problems that are overwhelming me and draining my energy." "There just is no hope for a brighter tomorrow." "My problems are certainly more confusing and unresolvable than those that other people have." "Life is certainly the 'pits' and really not worth living." "I wish I was someone else." "I wonder why such and such hurt me so badly—I just can't stop thinking about it." "What did I do wrong to deserve all this misery?"
>
> Such self-talk by people with failure orientations generates a variety of negative emotions, including excessive worry, fatigue, anxiety, boredom, depression, loneliness, and general feelings of misery. (Zastrow, 1979, pp. 92–93)

Manley (1977) also noted:

> A sense of failure becomes a further problem since it limits the amount of risk-taking behavior in which we are willing to engage. If we feel that we are failures, we will feel threatened by any new behavior patterns that we perceive as risky. Accordingly, we will be very reluctant to try any such behaviors. This means that we will continue to operate as we have in the past, thereby creating somewhat of a "rut." To the degree that we follow this practice, we are precluded from growing psychologically or expanding our behavioral responses. We are stultifying ourselves from greater use of our potential and becoming a more complete individual. We learn and grow by our experiences. If we limit ourselves to only the "tried and true" modes of behavior, we are putting disabling constraints on ourselves and seriously limiting our growth potential. (p. 38)

To be an "encouraging" person as you work with clients and to feel good about yourself, it is essential that you have a positive, success self-concept. A very simple formula helps people who view themselves as failures improve their lives; they shift their thinking from focusing on negative items to focusing on positive items.

One way to change a failure identity into a success identity is to identify the failure self-talk and then challenge this with rational self-talk (see Module 1 for how to write a rational self-analysis). A feeling of failure is an emotion similar to any other emotion. This feeling results mainly from negative self-talk, and this emotion can be changed by rational self-challenges.

Exercise 14.8: Changing a Failure Identity into a Success Identity

Goal: This exercise is designed to demonstrate that by changing your failure self-talk to success self-talk, you will move in the direction of having a success identity.

Step 1: Review the material on writing a rational self-analysis in Module 1, and also review the case example in this chapter, "Developing a Positive Self-Concept."

Step 2: Write a rational self-analysis in which you identify your failure self-talk, and then challenge this with rational self-talk.

Step 3: Do you believe that if you practice using rational self-talk to challenge your failure self-talk, you will move in the direction of having a success identity?

____ Yes   ____ No   ____ Uncertain

Explain your views.

SUMMARY

The following summarizes the chapter's content in terms of the learning objectives presented at the beginning of the chapter.

1. Understand common concerns of students related to majoring in social work.

    To be of help to others, social workers must first take care of themselves. Good emotional and physical health are internal resources that social workers need to have to be of help to others. This chapter presents material on how to survive and enjoy social work and, in a broader sense, how to enjoy living.

    Although social work students have a number of common concerns, often they are reluctant to share them with others. The following concerns are discussed, and suggestions for resolving them are given: Will I be able to make it in field placement? Will I be able to handle my first interview with my first client? I'm really depressed because my supervisor is able to handle an interview much better than I—will I ever be able to do that well? How should I separate the role of counselor from that of friend? How can I avoid becoming too emotionally involved with clients' problems? Do I really want to pursue a career in social work?

2.. Describe safety guidelines for social workers.

    Safety guidelines for social workers are presented. In the social work perspective, violence erupts in context, rather than residing within the "violent individual." The immediate environmental context is important, so social workers are often able to use their skills to deter potentially violent behavior. Social workers need to be aware of the following signals of danger: environmental cues, client cues, and worker cues. Most assaults follow a predictable pattern of five phases: triggering, escalation, crisis, recovery, and post-crisis depression.

    Numerous strategies for preventing violence are summarized. Techniques to deescalate verbal communication and nonverbal communication are discussed. In some situations, it is important for social workers to state acceptable limits for clients to express their discontent. Agencies need environmental safeguards (such as workers having cellular phones) and response systems to deter potential violence. Guidelines were presented to increase worker safety during home visits.

3. Describe burnout, stress, and stress management techniques.

    Burnout is a major problem encountered by helping professionals. The symptoms and causes of burnout are discussed and suggestions given for reducing stress and preventing burnout. Because burnout is one reaction to high levels of stress, it follows that stress management techniques are also useful in preventing burnout.

4.. Comprehend strategies for enjoying social work and your life.

    The chapter ends by providing tips on how to enjoy social work and life. The value of positive thinking is described. Also, the importance of developing a sense of who you are and what you want out of life is discussed, and suggestions are given for developing such an identity. Having a failure identity is contrasted with having a success identity, and a rational self-analysis is presented as one approach that is useful in challenging and changing a failure identity.

EXERCISES

1. Reducing Stress and Preventing Burnout

Goal: This exercise is designed to help students reduce stress and prevent burnout.

Step 1: Describe the purpose of this exercise. Using the material in this chapter, define stress and burnout. Indicate that burnout is one reaction to high stress levels. Also summarize a variety of strategies to reduce stress and prevent burnout. (These strategies are outlined in this chapter. It may be helpful to prepare and distribute a handout that identifies these strategies.)

Step 2: Ask students to write answers to the following questions on a sheet of paper:

   a. A few problematic situations that are presently causing high levels of stress in my life are ___.
   b. My current ways of handling these high levels of stress are ___.
   c. Ways in which I could better handle these situations and become more relaxed are ___.

Step 3: Ask students to form subgroups of three and have them share what they wrote. Indicate that the subgroups may be able to offer additional suggestions on how to handle the stress-producing situations and on how to relax. Also indicate that each student has a right to privacy and is not expected to self-disclose what he or she wants to keep private.

Step 4: After the subgroups have concluded their discussions, ask whether there are questions or comments about what was discussed.

2. Positive and Negative Thinking Become Self-Fulfilling Prophecies

Goal: This exercise is designed to help students become aware that positive and negative thinking often become self-fulfilling prophecies.

Step 1: Indicate the purpose of the exercise. Indicate that we always have a choice of thinking either positively or negatively about events that happen to us. Also indicate that both positive and negative thinking frequently become self-fulfilling prophecies. For example, if we go for a job interview and think we have a good chance to get the job, we will be more relaxed and probably better able to sell ourselves. If we think negatively, we will be more anxious and probably less able to present ourselves with confidence. Give additional examples if desired.

Step 2: Ask students to write on a sheet of paper a situation in which positive thinking led to a self-fulfilling prophecy for themselves or for someone close to them. Also ask students to write a situation in which negative thinking led to a self-fulfilling prophecy for themselves or for someone close to them.

Step 3: Ask for volunteers to share what they wrote. Also ask the class if they are aware of any situations in which positive thinking led to undesirable results or negative thinking resulted in desirable consequences.

3. Law of Attraction

Goal: This exercise presents a unique strategy to help students improve their lives.

Step 1: Ask students to brainstorm about the qualities that they admire in others. The instructor lists all these qualities on the board. (The instructor should seek to elicit a long list.)

Step 2: The instructor then indicates that the Law of Attraction asserts that a person's thoughts (both conscious and unconscious) dictate the reality of that person's life, whether or not he or she is aware of it. The Law further asserts that if you really want something and truly believe it's possible, you'll get it. Furthermore, if you place a lot of attention and thought onto something you don't want, you'll probably get that too. For example, if you continue to worry and dwell on your belief that your romantic life "is in the pits," that belief system (along with the way you present yourself in accordance with this belief system) will lead you to have unhappy romantic relationships.

The instructor adds that the Law of Attraction asserts that we are always sending out vibes/vibrations of what we are thinking/feeling. If we are thinking bad thoughts, we will have bad feelings and will be sending out negative vibes. If we are thinking good/positive thoughts, we will have good feelings and will be sending out good vibes.

We like to be with people who send out good vibes, and who have the qualities you listed in this exercise. We generally do not like to associate with people who are sending out bad vibes.

In order for a salesperson to be successful, he or she needs to be sending out good vibes, so that customers will want to converse with him or her. In order for a social worker to be effective with clients, he or she also needs to be sending our good vibes, so that clients will want to converse with him or her. This rule applies to most professionals—physicians, attorneys, psychologists, psychiatrists, guidance counselors, teachers, and so on.

The Law of Attraction asserts that if you present yourself as exhibiting the qualities that were listed in this exercise, many doors will be opened up for you; and you will be successful, happy, contented, relaxed, and so on.

Are you willing to make a commitment to presenting yourself to others as having the characteristics you listed in this exercise?

Counseling Theories Resource Manual

Prominent theories of counseling are summarized and critiqued in this manual. Use it as a reference guide in your future practice and as a primer in your current coursework.

An effective social worker needs knowledge of comprehensive counseling theories and specialized intervention techniques to determine precisely what problems exist and how to intervene effectively. In a comprehensive counseling theory, the theorist proposes a counseling approach that can be used to treat practically all personal problems. There are a number of contemporary comprehensive counseling theories, including rational therapy, behavior modification, and reality therapy. These theories typically present material on (1) personality theory, or how normal psychosocial development occurs; (2) behavior pathology, or how emotional and behavioral problems arise; and (3) intervention, or how to change emotional and behavioral problems.

An effective counselor generally knows several intervention approaches and, depending on the problems being presented by the client, is able to select a strategy with a high probability of success. In addition to comprehensive counseling theories, social workers also use specialized intervention techniques for specific problems—for example, assertiveness training for people who are shy or overly aggressive and parent effectiveness training for parent-child relationship difficulties. Conscientious workers strive to gain working knowledge of a wide variety of intervention techniques, but it is nearly impossible to acquire working knowledge of all the comprehensive and specialized intervention approaches that are available. The material in this manual summarizes approaches that social workers commonly use. Case examples illustrate how each approach is used.

MODULE

RATIONAL THERAPY

LEARNING OBJECTIVES

Rational therapy asserts that unwanted emotions and dysfunctional behaviors are primarily determined by our thought process rather than by external events. This module will help prepare students to:

Comprehend rational therapy

ALBERT ELLIS

The founder of rational therapy, Albert Ellis (1913–2007) practiced psychoanalytic approaches to therapy during the late 1940s and early 1950s. He became disenchanted with both the results and the approach when he observed that even patients who achieved incredible insight into their childhood and unconscious processes continued to experience emotional difficulties.

Ellis developed a new approach, *rational therapy* (also called *rational-emotive therapy*), in which he treated clients by challenging and changing their irrational beliefs. Ellis (1957) was able to demonstrate significant effectiveness using this new approach.

In 1959, Ellis established the Institute for Rational Living in New York City, which provides adult education courses in rational living and a moderate-cost psychotherapy clinic for clients. In 1968, Ellis founded the Institute for Advanced Study in Rational Psychotherapy, which provides helping professionals with extensive training in rational therapy and also provides seminars and workshops throughout the country.

The Albert Ellis Foundation was established in 2006 to promote rational-emotive behavior therapy and the works of Albert Ellis. The foundation was created to ensure that Ellis's lifework would be protected and promoted and to advocate for the legal and human rights of Ellis himself.

Ellis was also recognized nationally as an authority on sexuality. In addition to running workshops and seminars and being a practicing psychotherapist, he wrote 54 books and more than 600 articles.

Rational therapy has had an enormous impact on both professionals and the public. The principles of rational therapy have been applied to assertiveness training, sexuality, adolescence, law and criminality, religion, executive leadership, children's literature, music, feminism, philosophy, personal problems, alcoholism, marriage and the family, and sex adjustment and therapy.

SELF-TALK DETERMINES OUR FEELINGS AND ACTIONS

Most people believe that our emotions and our actions are determined primarily by the events that happen to us. According to rational therapists, however (Ellis, 2000), the primary cause of all our emotions and actions is *self-talk—what* we tell ourselves about the events that happen to us:

Event
↓
Self-talk
↓
Emotion
↓
Actions

305

This is not a new idea. The Stoic philosopher Epictetus wrote in the first century A.D., "Men are disturbed not by things, but by the view which they take of them" (Ellis, 2000). Exhibit M1.1 illustrates this process.

Self-talk determines how we feel and act. By changing our self-talk, we can change how we feel and act. We cannot always control events that happen to us, but we do have the power to think rationally about them and thereby change our unwanted emotions and ineffective actions.

Maultsby (1977) indicated that thinking is irrational if it does one or more of the following:

1. Does not fit the facts (is not based on objective reality)
2. Hampers you in protecting your life
3. Hampers you in achieving your short- and long-term goals
4. Causes significant trouble with other people
5. Leads you to feel emotions that you do not want to feel

We cannot always control events, but we can think rational thoughts about each experience. Lembo (1974) notes,

> We can think rationally or irrationally about *the things that will happen to us* and insist that we will not be a failure if our boss fires us or that we will be a worthless no-account if we are dismissed from our job; that nothing catastrophic will happen if our parents die or that it will be horrible and unbearable if they do die. (p. 9)

Because we determine our feelings and our behaviors by means of self-talk, we truly are in control of our lives. If we are unhappy, unfulfilled, unsatisfied, frustrated, depressed, grief-stricken, or whatever, it is primarily our own doing. Lembo (1974, p. 10) notes, "We have the ability to create a satisfying life for ourselves, and we will succeed in doing so if we rationally manage the thoughts we tell ourselves."

Exercise M1.1: Self-Talk Causes Our Emotions

Goal: This exercise is designed to illustrate that it is primarily self-talk (rather than the event) that causes our emotions.

Step 1: Specify a negative emotion that you recently experienced.

Step 2: Describe the event associated with this emotion.

Step 3: Specify your self-talk associated with this event.

Step 4: Review the discussion of self-talk being the primary source of our emotions. Is it not true that if you had given yourself a different set of self-talk about this event, you would have felt differently?

    ____ Yes   ____ No   ____ Uncertain

Step 5: Do you now believe that self-talk is the primary source of our emotions? Explain your views.

ADDITIONAL ASPECTS OF SELF-TALK

Our emotional reactions to repeated occurrences of an event become nearly automatic because we rapidly give ourselves a set of self-talk responses to them. For example, a few years ago I counseled a woman who became intensely emotionally upset every time her husband (who had a drinking problem) came home intoxicated. As we examined this situation, it became clear that because of repeated occurrences, she routinely gave herself the following self-talk on seeing him inebriated:

Self-talk: "He's foolishly spending the money we desperately need in this family."
                "He's making a fool of himself and me in that condition."
                "He's setting a terrible example for our children."
                "One of these days he's going to have a serious accident, get hurt, and then what will we do?"

Emotion: Anger, frustration, some depression, general unhappiness.

We are often unaware of how self-talk affects us, and it behooves counselors to discover this self-talk. Several years ago I counseled a married woman who expressed a strong desire to continue having extramarital affairs but was afraid her husband would find out about them and end the marriage. Although she was fully aware of her emotional desire for having affairs, she was unaware of the self-talk that generated this feeling. I got her to look at the self-talk that was driving her desire to have extramarital sex, and she gradually discovered the underlying self-talk "I enjoy the feeling of being able to seduce someone to whom I am attracted." 'The people I seduce feel somewhat obligated to me." "The conquest of someone who is very attractive is three-quarters of the thrill."

Another aspect of self-talk is *layering*, in which what Ellis termed the "emotional Consequence" (C) becomes a new "Activating Event" (A) by "Tom" giving himself additional self-talk (B) about his initial reaction. Ellis (1973) described layering as follows:

> Once the individual [Tom] becomes emotionally upset—or, rather, upsets himself—another startling human thing frequently occurs. Most of the time, he *knows* that he is anxious, depressed, enraged, or otherwise agitated; and he also generally knows that his symptoms are undesirable and (in our culture) socially disapproved. For who approves or respects highly agitated or "crazy" people? He therefore makes his emotional Consequence (C) or symptom into another Activating Event (A).
>
> Thus, he originally starts with something like "(A) I did poorly on my job today; (B) Isn't that horrible! What a worm I am for failing!" and he winds up with (C) feelings of anxiety, worthlessness, and depression. He now starts all over: "(A) I feel anxious and depressed, and worthless. (B) Isn't *that* horrible! What a worm I am for feeling anxious, depressed, and worthless!" Now he winds up with (C) even greater feelings of anxiety, worthlessness, and depression. Or, in other words, once he becomes anxious, he frequently makes himself anxious about being anxious. Once he becomes depressed, he makes himself depressed about *being* depressed. Et cetera! He now has two consequences or symptoms for the price of one; and he often goes around and around in a vicious cycle of (1) condemning himself for doing poorly at some task; (2) feeling guilty or depressed because of his self-condemnation; (3) condemning himself for his feelings of guilt and depression; (4) condemning himself for condemning himself; (5) condemning himself for seeing that he condemns himself and for still not stopping condemning himself; (6) condemning himself for going for psychotherapeutic help and still not getting better; (7) condemning himself for being more disturbed than other individuals; (8) concluding that he is indubitably hopelessly disturbed and that nothing can be done about it; and so on, and so forth. (p. 178)

Although self-talk is often based on our attitudes, beliefs, and values, it is a distinct entity. It has a here-and-now quality; it represents those thoughts we tell ourselves in the present. Although we hold thousands of beliefs, attitudes, and values, our self-talk at a given time is based on only a fraction of them. Self-talk is also driven by our needs, wants, and motives.

Exercise M1.2: Understanding Layering

Goal: This exercise is designed to help you understand the concept of "layering."

Reflect on a time when your awfulizing about an event led you to feel "bad." Then, because you were feeling "bad," you proceeded to awfulize about other "bad" things happening in your life—which led you to feel even worse. Specify (a) the original bad event, (b) your original set of negative self-talk, (c) how you then felt, (d) your second set of negative self-talk because you were feeling "bad," and (e) how you then felt.

CHANGING UNWANTED EMOTIONS

Rational therapy is increasingly used to change unwanted emotions. Rational therapy asserts that all emotions are primarily determined by self-talk, even the emotion of love. Individuals often believe that love is a feeling beyond their control. The language of love reinforces this erroneous belief: "I just *couldn't help it*, he swept me off my feet," "I *fell* in love," and "*It was* love at first sight." But in reality, the emotion of love is based primarily on self-talk:

Event: A woman's ideal date is a man who is tall and athletic, has dark hair, is a good conversationalist, and likes pop music. She meets a man in one of her classes who is 6 feet tall, a football player, has dark hair, is personable, and likes pop music.

Her self-talk: *I can hardly believe I've finally met someone I'm really attracted to. This person is really handsome, charming, the kind of person I'd really like to get to know better and to go out to dinner with.*

Her emotion: Feelings of infatuation.

There are five ways to change an unwanted emotion. Three are constructive: getting involved in a meaningful activity, changing the negative and irrational thinking underlying the unwanted emotion, and changing the distressing event. Two are destructive: abuse of alcohol, drugs, and food; and suicide. We will discuss each of the five in turn.

Getting Involved in Meaningful Activity

Practically everyone encounters day-to-day frustrations and irritations—having a class or two that aren't going well, working at a job that's unpleasant, coping with a dull social life. Dwelling on such irritations will spawn such unwanted emotions as depression, anger, frustration, despair, or feelings of failure. Which of these emotions a person has will directly depend on the person's self-talk.

Meaningful enjoyable activity, however, produces satisfaction and a healthful distraction from unwanted emotion. Individuals can learn the value of meaningful activity by writing an "escape" list of activities they find motivating, energizing, and enjoyable—taking a walk, playing golf or tennis, going to a movie, shopping, knitting, visiting friends, and so on. By having an "escape" list of things they enjoy doing, individuals can nip unwanted emotions in the bud. They can use enjoyable activities to take their minds off their day-to-day concerns and irritations. The positive emotions they experience will stem directly from the things they tell themselves about the enjoyable things they are doing.

In urging individuals to compile and use an escape list, rational therapy is not suggesting that people should avoid doing something about unpleasant events. If something can be done to change a distressing event, all constructive efforts should be tried. However, we often do not have control over unpleasant events and cannot change them. But we always have the capacity to control and change what we tell ourselves about the unpleasant events.

Exercise M1.3: Using Meaningful Activities to Change Unwanted Emotions

Goal: This exercise demonstrates that when we are awfulizing about something and therefore feeling bad, we can alleviate the unwanted emotions by getting involved in meaningful activities.

Step 1:   Describe a time when you were awfulizing about something and therefore feeling bad and then alleviated the unwanted emotions by getting involved in something you enjoyed doing.

Step 2:   Reflect on this experience. Is it not true that getting involved in enjoyable activities stopped you from awfulizing (that is, you stopped thinking about the unpleasant event and instead switched to thinking about an activity you were enjoying)? Also, when you stopped awfulizing, did you find your unwanted emotions alleviated?

Changing Self-Talk[1]

A second approach to changing unwanted emotions is to identify and then alter the negative and irrational thinking that leads to them. Maultsby (1977) developed *rational self-analysis* (RSA), which is very useful for alleviating undesirable emotions. The goal in RSA is to change unwanted emotions (such as anger, guilt, depression, or shyness). An RSA is done by recording the event and self-talk on paper. An RSA has six parts (see Exhibit M1.1).

1. *Part A (facts and events):* Simply state the facts or events that occurred.
2. *Part B (self-talk):* Write all of your thoughts about A. Number each statement (1, 2, 3, 4, and so on). Write "good," "bad," or "neutral" after each self-talk statement to show how you believe each B-section statement reflects on you as a person. (The RSA case example on page 310 illustrates the mechanics of an RSA.)
3. *Part C (emotional consequences):* Write simple statements describing your gut reactions and emotions stemming from your self-talk in part B.
4. *Part D(a)* is written *only* after you have written sections A, B, and C and *only* after you have reviewed all five guidelines for rational thinking. Part D(a) is a "camera check" of part A. Reread part A and ask your-

---

[1]This description of rational self-analysis is adapted from Charles Zastrow, *Talk to Yourself Using the Power of Self-Talk,* © 1979, pp. 32–36, Prentice-Hall, Inc., Englewood Cliffs, New Jersey. Reprinted by permission of the author.

Exhibit M1.1   Format for RSA

A	**D(a)**
Facts and Events	Camera Check of A
B	**D(b)**
Self-Talk	Rational Debate of B

1. _____   1. _____
2. _____   2. _____
and so on   and so on

C	**E**
Emotional Consequences of B	Emotional Goals and Behavioral Goals for Similar Future Events

---

self, "If I had a video of what happened, would it verify what I wrote as 'fact'?" Videos record facts, not personal beliefs or opinions.

An example in part B of a personal opinion that is mistaken as a fact is "Karen made me look like a fool when she laughed while I was trying to make a point." In D(a) (the video check of A), you correct the opinion part of this statement by writing only the factual part: "I was attempting to make a serious point when Karen laughed." Then add the personal opinion part of the statement to B ("Karen made me look like a fool").

5. *Part D(b)* challenges and thus may change negative and irrational thinking. Take each B statement separately. Read B–1 first and ask yourself whether it is inconsistent with any of the five criteria for rational thinking. According to Maultsby (1977), thinking is irrational if it does one or more of the following:

1. Does not fit the facts (is not based on objective reality)
2. Hampers you in protecting your life
3. Hampers you in achieving your short- and long-term goals
4. Causes significant trouble with other people
5. Leads you to feel emotions that you do not want to feel

If the self-talk statement is consistent with the five criteria for rational thinking, merely write "that's rational." If, however, the self-talk statement meets one or more of the criteria for irrational thinking, then think of an alternative self-talk to that B statement. This new self-talk statement is crucially important in changing your undesirable emotion and needs to be rational and to be a self-talk statement you are willing to accept as a new opinion for yourself. After writing down this D(b–1) self-talk in the D(b) section, then consider B–2, B–3, and so on, in the same way.

6. Under *part E*, write down the new emotions you want to have in similar future A situations. In writing these new emotions that you desire, keep in mind that they will follow from your self-talk statements in your D(b) section. Section E may also contain a description of certain actions you intend to take to help you achieve your emotional goals when you encounter future A's.

Rational self-challenges will work only if clients actively practice using the rational self-challenges they develop. Self-challenges work best when used by clients every time they start the original negative, irrational self-talk.

Exercise M1.4: Changing Unwanted Emotions with a Rational Self-Analysis

Goal: This exercise demonstrates that writing and then using the rational debates will change unwanted emotions.

Step 1:   Review the material on a rational self-analysis. Write a rational self-analysis on an unwanted emotion you recently experienced.

Step 2:   Do you believe that if you apply the rational debates to your negative and irrational self-talk, you will be able to change unwanted emotions? Explain your views.

CASE EXAMPLE   RATIONAL SELF-ANALYSIS: COPING WITH A SEXUAL AFFAIR

Cindy sought counseling after her boyfriend Jim told her that a few months earlier he had become sexually involved with Linda. Jim and Cindy had dated for 2 years. But they began to argue frequently and so decided not to see each other during the summer. In the fall, they again felt strongly about each other and resumed their relationship. A few weeks later, Jim (after Cindy questioned him) informed her about Linda.

Cindy told the counselor that she wanted to better handle her unwanted feelings about this affair. After discussing them in some depth, the counselor informed her that she could counter her undesirable emotions with a rational self-analysis, and Cindy wrote the following RSA.

A (FACTS AND EVENTS)	D(a) VIDEO CHECK OF A
My boyfriend, Jim, informed me that he had sex with Linda, after a party where they had both been drinking.	This is all factual. I know this because Jim told me himself. Jim and I are very close, and I know he wouldn't lie to me.

B (SELF-TALK)	D(b) CINDY'S RATIONAL DEBATE OF B
B–1 It's not fair! How could Jim do such a thing to me? (bad)	D(b–1) Jim had sex with Linda. I'll just have to accept that. People are human and fallible, I can't expect to always be treated with fairness. Besides, Jim and I had broken up, so I'm sure they didn't have me in mind when they did it. At the time they were sexually involved, neither Jim nor I had any commitment to each other. Truth be told, I also considered having a fling this summer and would have had I met the right guy.
B–2 That creep just had sex with Linda because he wanted a piece of _____. (bad)	D(b–2) Jim probably had sex with Linda for other reasons. I know he's not the type who uses a woman merely for relief of his sexual tensions. It is also a mistake to label him a creep. No one is a creep. People are humans. If I mislabel him a creep, it may lead me to view him in terms of an inaccurate label.
B–3 Jim and Linda had no good reasons for doing what they did. They only did it because they were both drunk. What a couple of jerks! (bad)	D(b–3) Alcohol obviously had something to do with their having sex. I know that Jim is much less inhibited when he has had a few drinks. I don't know about Linda, though. The drinking can't be the only reason they had sex. Maybe they felt attracted to each other and wanted to have sex. I've got to remember that this summer Jim and I had no commitments to each other, and therefore I do not have the right to expect that he would be celibate to please me. Also, it is a mistake for me to refer to Jim or Linda as being a "jerk." People are people.
B–4 Linda must be some kind of cheap tramp. Only a tramp would have sex with a guy she didn't love. (bad)	D(b–4) I don't even know Linda, so I shouldn't judge her like this. Furthermore, I have no way of knowing how Linda felt about Jim. Maybe she felt she loved him at the time. A woman isn't necessarily loose if she has sex with a guy.
B–5 Jim must think he's some kind of stud now. (bad)	D(b–5) Jim has told me that he has had sex with only two women. My idea of a "stud" is a guy who thinks he can have sex with any woman who comes along. I know Jim better than that. He doesn't think he could, nor would he try to, conquer just any woman.

CASE EXAMPLE   *(continued)*

B–6   Jim and I will never again be able to have a good sexual relationship of our own now that he has someone else to compare me to. I just know that he'll be thinking of Linda from now on. (bad)

D(b–6)   Jim and I love each other. Jim told me that he does not love Linda. Just because Jim had sex with Linda does not mean our relationship will always be adversely affected. We can communicate easily during sex, and it has always been satisfying so far. It would be silly for Jim to compare our entire relationship to the one night he spent with Linda.

B–7   This is the worst thing that Jim could have done. (bad)

D(b–7)   This is not the worst thing that Jim could have done. What he did was not a crime, like murder or rape, which would have been worse. The situation would be worse if Jim had slept with Linda while he was still seeing me. I'm glad to know that he would never do that.

B–8   Now that I know Jim had sex with Linda, our whole relationship will be ruined. (bad)

D(b–8)   The fact that Jim had sex with Linda does not have to ruin our relationship. The event occurred in the past. It's over. Past sexual experiences should have no bearing on the future of our relationship. I want the relationship to continue, and I don't want to see it ruined.

B–9   I should never have broken up with Jim. Then he would never have slept with Linda. It's all my fault. (bad)

D(b–9)   It's not my fault at all. I broke up with Jim because I felt it was the best thing to do at the time. I know Jim would not have been unfaithful to me had we still been dating, but we weren't dating at the ume this happened. I had no way of knowing he would some day go to bed with Linda, and knowing would not have changed my decision to break up with him. It's not my fault because I wasn't even involved.

B–10   From now on, whenever I hear Linda's name mentioned I'm going to have a fit! I won't be able to handle it! (bad)

D(b–10)   When I hear Linda's name mentioned, I don't have to respond by having a fit. I can handle my feelings by being calm and not letting the mention of her name bother me.

C MY EMOTIONS	E MY EMOTIONAL AND BEHAVIORAL GOALS
I feel guilty, hurt, angry, upset, and jealous. (very bad)	I want to get over my unwanted emotions that I have had about this affair. I want to put this affair in our past. At the time it happened, Jim and I had no commitments to each other. What is important to Jim and me is our present and future relationship and not what happened one evening when Jim and I had broken up.

Changing the Distressing Event

A third way to change unwanted emotions is to change the distressing event. There is an infinite number of distressing events: losing a job, the break-up of a romantic relationship, receiving failing grades, being in an automobile accident, and so on. In some cases, constructive action can be taken to change the distressing event. For example, if a man is terminated from a job, he can seek another; when he finds one, he will feel better. If a student is getting failing grades, a conference with the instructor may give the student some ideas about how to improve the grades. If the suggestions appear practical and have merit, the student will feel better.

Not all distressing events can be changed. For example, a woman may have a job that she needs and be forced to interact with other employees who display behaviors she dislikes. If that individual cannot change the behaviors of the others, the only other constructive option is to "bite the bullet" and adapt to the circumstances. However, when it is practical to change distressing events, they should be changed. When constructive changes in events are made, a person probably will feel better because he or she will then (in all likelihood) be having more positive self-talk related to the constructive changes that have been made.

Exercise M1.5: Changing Unwanted Emotions by Changing Events

Goal: This exercise demonstrates that unwanted emotions can be changed by changing the event that is associated with the unwanted emotion.

Step 1:   Describe a time in your life when you were awfulizing about something and therefore feeling bad and you then changed the event—which resulted in your stopping awfulizing. For example, you may have had an unpleasant job, which you then changed. Or you may have been in an abusive relationship, which you then ended.

Step 2:   Is it not true that you stopped feeling bad after changing the unpleasant event because you stopped awfulizing and then had more positive self-talk related to the constructive changes that you made? Explain your views on this.

Two Destructive Ways of Dealing with Unwanted Emotions

I strongly discourage using either of the following two ways of dealing with unwanted emotions. I present them here only to complete the list of ways to deal with unwanted emotions.

One method is to relieve intense unwanted emotions temporarily through the use of alcohol, other drugs, or food. When the effects of the drug wear off, the person's problems and unwanted emotions remain, and there is a danger that through repeated use the person will become dependent on the drug. Some people overeat for the same reasons—loneliness, insecurity, boredom, and frustration. The process of eating and the feeling of having a full stomach provide temporary relief from intense unwanted emotions. Such people are likely to become overweight or bulimic—or both.

The other destructive way to relieve unwanted emotions is suicide. This is the ultimate destructive approach to dealing with unwanted emotions. If you know of someone who is contemplating suicide, you have a legal right and an ethical obligation to seek to connect that person with professional help—even when the suicidal person requests that you do not inform anyone else of his or her intentions.

Exercise M1.6: Changing Unwanted Emotions by Abusing the Use of Alcohol, Other Drugs, or Food

Goal: This exercise demonstrates that unwanted emotions can be changed temporarily through the abusive use of alcohol, other drugs, or food.

Step 1:   Describe someone you know who emotionally was feeling bad and turned to abusive use of alcohol, other drugs, or food. If you do not know anyone who did this, describe a time in your life when you were feeling bad and resorted to the abusive use of alcohol, other drugs, or food.

Step 2:   Is it not accurate that the abusive use of alcohol, other drugs, or food only provides temporary relief? Give a short explanation of your views on this question.

ASSESSING AND CHANGING DYSFUNCTIONAL BEHAVIOR

Self-talk is the primary determinant not only of our emotions but also of our actions:

Event
↓
Self-talk
↓
Emotion
↓
Actions

In a nutshell, our actions are primarily determined by self-talk (our cognitions). Our thoughts determine our actions. To demonstrate this principle, reflect on the last time you did something bizarre or unusual. What self-talk statements were you giving yourself (that is, what were you thinking) before and during the time when you did what you did?

Rational therapy maintains that the reasons for any dysfunctional act (including crime) can be determined by examining what the offender was telling himself or herself before and during the time when the act was being committed. Two examples of cognitions that lead to dysfunctional behavior are the following:

Cognition: A 16-year-old sees an unlocked Audi with the keys in it and thinks, "Hey, this is the ultimate car to drive. Let me take it for a ride."

Behavior: Car theft.

Cognition: A 23-year-old male is on his third date with the same woman. He brings her to his apartment and thinks, "She is really sexy. Since I've wined and dined her three times, now it's time for her to show her appreciation.

"I'll bet she wants it as much as I do. I'll show her what a great lover I am. If she says, 'Don't,' I know she really means 'Don't stop.' I'll use a little force if I have to. When it's over, she'll really love me."

Behavior: Date rape.

It should be noted that the cognitions underlying each dysfunctional behavior may vary considerably among perpetrators. For example, possible cognitions for shoplifting a shirt might be the following. "This shirt would look really nice for the wedding I'm going to on Saturday. Since I'm buying a number of other items from this store, they still will make a profit from me even if I take this without paying for it." Another may be: "This will be a challenge to see if I can get away with taking this shirt. I'll put it on in the fitting room and put my own shirt and coat on over it, and no one will even see me walk out of the store with it. Since I've taken a number of things in the past, I'll act real casual as I walk out of the store." Or: "My son really needs a decent shirt. He doesn't have any nice ones to wear. I don't get enough money from public assistance to buy my children what they need. I know my son is embarrassed to wear the rags that he has. I'll just stick this shirt under my coat and walk out with it."

Assessing human behavior is largely a process of identifying the cognitions that underlie unwanted emotions or dysfunctional behavior. The stages of this process are as follows:

1. Identify as precisely as possible the unwanted emotions or dysfunctional behavior that a client has.
2. Identify the cognitions, or thinking patterns, that the client has during the time when the client is having unwanted emotions or is displaying dysfunctional behavior. There are two primary ways of identifying these cognitions. One way is to ask the client what he was thinking before and during the time when the client was having unwanted emotions or displaying dysfunctional behavior. If this approach does not work (perhaps because the client refuses to divulge what he was thinking), a second approach is to obtain information about the client's life circumstances at that time. Once these life circumstances are identified, the professional conducting the assessment needs to place herself mentally into the life circumstances of the perpetrator and then reflect on the kinds of cognitions that would lead this client to have his specific unwanted emotions or dysfunctional behavior. For example, if the client is a 16-year-old female who has run away from home and is unemployed, it is fairly easy to identify (to some extent) the kinds of cognitions that would lead such a person to turn to prostitution.

One deduction that can be made from the principle that thinking processes determine dysfunctional behaviors and unwanted emotions is that *to change dysfunctional behaviors or unwanted emotions it is necessary for the affected person to change his or her thinking patterns.* This concept is illustrated in Exhibit M1.4. Also see the Case Example "Using Rational Therapy to Change Irresponsible Behavior" on page 315.

Exercise M1.7: Our Actions Are Determined by Our Thoughts

Goal: This exercise demonstrates that most of our actions are determined by what we think.

Step 1:   Describe something embarrassing that you did.

Step 2:   Describe what you were thinking that led you to do the embarrassing thing that you described.

Step 3:   Can you identify any actions that you engaged in that were not partially influenced by what you were thinking? If "yes," specify such actions.

Step 4:   In criminal court proceedings, prosecuting attorneys are expected to identify the "motive" for why the defendant committed the alleged crime. Is not the search for the motive a search to identify the thinking patterns that led the defendant to commit the alleged crime? Explain your views.

Step 5:   Is it not true that to stop engaging in dysfunctional or deviant behaviors, a person needs to change the thought patterns underlying the dysfunctional behaviors? Explain your views.

Step 6   As an example, what interventions might be used to change the abusive behavior of a husband who abuses his wife?

RATIONAL THERAPY IS AN EDUCATIONAL PROCESS

Learning how to think rationally and to counter irrational and negative self-talk is a process. Clients can learn to analyze and change irrational self-talk in a variety of ways: instruction by their counselor, viewing videotapes and films, reading books and pamphlets, and attending workshops or seminars on rational therapy. Ellis demonstrated that the basic principles of analyzing irrational self-talk and thinking rationally can be successfully taught both to adults and to elementary and secondary school students.

Rational therapists teach clients how to analyze irrational self-talk using probes, confrontation, explanations, interpretations, humor, and suggestions that help clients discover their irrational thinking. Once clients become aware of their irrational self-talk, rational therapists use a variety of techniques to help them change.

AN ECLECTIC APPROACH

Rational therapists use whatever approaches show promise in changing irrational self-talk. Ellis (1979, p. 186) noted, "The rational therapist uses role playing, assertion training, desensitization, humor, operant conditioning, suggestion, support, and a whole bag of other 'tricks.'"

Rational self-challenges (including RSAs) are often used to change unwanted emotions. For certain unwanted emotions, such as depression, rational therapists may attempt to get clients involved in meaningful or enjoyable activities (for example, playing golf, joining a social club). Reality therapists (see Module

---

Exhibit M1.2   Our Thinking Determines Our Behaviors and Our Emotions

A few years ago I was describing to a class the concept that our thinking primarily causes our emotions and our actions. A male student voluntarily self-disclosed the following:

> What you're saying makes a lot of sense. It really applies to something that happened to me. I was living with a female student whom I really cared about. I thought, though, that she was going out on me. When I confronted her about it, she always said I was paranoid and denied it.
>
> Then one night I walked into a bar in this town and I saw her in a corner in a "clutch" position with this guy. I told myself things like "She really is cheating on me. Both of them are playing me for a fool." Such thinking led me to be angry.

> I also told myself "I'm going to set this straight. I'm going to get even with them. I'll break the bottoms off these two empty beer bottles and then jab each of them with the jagged edges." I proceeded to knock off the bottoms on the bar, and then started walking toward them. I got to within eight feet of them and they were still arm in arm and didn't see me. I began, though, to change my thinking. I thought that if I jabbed them, the end result would be that I would get 8 to 10 years in prison, and I concluded she isn't worth that. Based on this thinking I decided to drop the beer bottles, walk out, and end my relationship with her—which is what I did.

3) use this approach to change unwanted emotions. Rational therapists theorize that getting clients involved in enjoyable activities works because it switches their negative focus to a positive one, which then changes their emotions.

For people who are shy or prone to temper outbursts, rational therapists may use assertiveness training techniques (see Module 2). For clients with drinking problems, rational therapists may supplement therapy by getting clients involved in Alcoholics Anonymous.

Homework assignments are frequently given. Shy clients try out assertive approaches that they role-played in counseling. They may write an RSA in which they identify and challenge the negative and irrational self-talk that makes them feel shy. A male client who states he can't stand to be rejected by the opposite sex might ask three different females out on dates to test the hypothesis that he can indeed survive rejection. Clients also read books to help them learn and apply the basic concepts.

CASE EXAMPLE   USING RATIONAL THERAPY TO CHANGE IRRESPONSIBLE BEHAVIOR

Dan Barber, age 4½, was taken to the emergency room of St. Mary's Hospital in a midwestern city. He was unconscious and severely bruised, and he had a broken arm. Dan was brought in by neighbors after Mr. Barber telephoned them. Dan had a concussion, sustained from what appeared to be several blows. Seven weeks earlier Dan had been rushed to the hospital for a broken leg. That time Mr. Barber stated Dan fell down a stairway. Protective Services was contacted by the hospital, and in the initial interview Mr. Barber acknowledged that he beat Dan on both of these occasions. Why? The following is Mr. Barber's account of the thinking processes (self-talk) that led him to abuse his son.

Dan is my only son. His mother and I got a divorce 8 months ago. I'm an accountant and up until about a year ago I really thought I had it made. Mary is very attractive, and we got along well. We had a nice house, and I had a good income—many days I worked 11 or 12 hours, getting overtime pay. Mary primarily took care of our son.

One day I arrived home and there was a note from my wife saying she was leaving me. I was shocked and couldn't believe it. A few weeks later I received papers indicating she had gotten a divorce in Mexico. Shortly afterward I heard she married a person from the same church I used to go to. I really don't understand how she could leave both Dan and me, without even talking about it. I guess I've been so involved with my work that I didn't realize how she felt.

As time went by after she left I discussed my problems with some of our neighbors. A few indicated that several men over the years visited with my wife during the day when I was at work. Apparently she had been having affairs for a long time.

My mother moved in after Mary left, to help take care of Dan.

In the past few months, I have been wondering if Dan is really my own son.

At this point Mr. Barber was asked to indicate what he was thinking during the last time he abused Dan. The events and self-talk are put into the format presented earlier.

Event: That evening I came home from work feeling exhausted. I wanted just to relax and have a peaceful evening. My mother went grocery shopping, and I guess I was feeling sorry for myself. Dan was quite noisy, and I told him to stop making so much noise. But he continued.

Self-talk: "I can't take any more of this."
"Here I have to take care of a kid who may not even be my own."
"This kid reminds me of the hurt that Mary has caused me. I have a right to even the score."
"I can't stand this! I've got to shut this brat up!"
"My father beat me when I did wrong—that's the best way to show kids who's the boss."

Emotion: Anger, revenge, hostility, frustration.

Actions: Hitting Dan, knocking him down several times. (Mr. Barber added, "Once I started hitting Dan, I thought I was evening the score with Mary, and didn't want to stop.")

At first, Mr. Barber indicated he couldn't understand how he could lose control and abuse his son. He appeared remorseful and desirous of changing his actions. Through therapy, he gradually came to understand that he controlled his emotions and actions and that he could change his unwanted emotions and actions by changing his self-talk. He knew he had severely hurt his son and that he could lose him if the abuse was not curbed.

Mr. Barber's concerns about being Dan's biological father were relieved by the results of DNA testing, and he learned through rational therapy how to challenge and change the self-talk that led him to abuse his son. Mr. Barber was also instructed to leave Dan in the care of his mother whenever he felt an urge to abuse Dan. If the grandmother wasn't available, Mr. Barber agreed to call the Protective Services worker to ventilate his feelings over the phone rather than at Dan. Mr. Barber also received counseling about his feelings toward his wife and about the importance of focusing his thoughts and energies on the present and future rather than wallowing in self-pity and dwelling on the past.

COMMON IRRATIONAL BELIEFS

Rational therapy seeks to refute clients' irrational beliefs. Clients are confronted with their irrational beliefs. Therapists ask, "Where is it written that you must succeed at everything you try in order to feel good about yourself?" or "What evidence do you have that your girl friend *must* treat you fairly?"

Several writers (Criddle, 1974; Ellis, 1958; Ellis & Harper, 1977; Hauck, 1972; Raimy, 1977; Zastrow, 1979, 1993) have identified common beliefs that generate negative or irrational self-talk. For a list, see Exhibit M1.5. Thinking of "needs," "shoulds," "musts," "awful," and "unbearable" distorts reality and frequently leads us to overact. A more rational philosophy is "I would like to be treated reasonably well by people and life."

Exercise M1.8: Changing My Irrational Beliefs

Goal: This exercise is designed to assist you in identifying and eliminating your irrational beliefs.

Step 1:   Review the irrational beliefs in listed in Exhibit M1.4. Write down any irrational beliefs that you have (which may or may not be listed in the exhibit). For each irrational belief that you have, write down the rational belief that you should instead focus on developing for yourself.

Step 2:   Do you think you can make progress in changing your irrational beliefs by seeking to refute your irrational beliefs by challenging them with your rational beliefs? Explain your views.

WHAT REALLY CAUSES CHANGE?

Client-centered therapy, psychoanalysis, rational therapy, feminist intervention, behavior therapy, transactional analysis, reality therapy, hypnosis, meditation, and crisis intervention are all used to treat a wide range of emotional and behavioral problems: people who are depressed, who are lonely, who have marital or other interpersonal relationship problems, who have disabling fears and phobias, who are overly aggressive, who have drinking problems, or who suffer from grief, shame, or guilt. These therapies differ substantially in explaining why therapeutic change occurs. How can all these distinct and diverse therapies produce positive change in clients? What produces changes in therapy? Is there a single explanation?

Practically every theory postulates a different view of why change occurs. In reviewing this dilemma, Raimy (1977) stated,

> Psychotherapists today are faced with an insistent, nagging problem: since widely diverse methods of treatment for similar problems have their successes as well as their failures, how can one defend a given set of treatment procedures as superior to others? Clearly, since quite different, even contradictory, methods of treatment produce similar results, explanations for the success of treatment must be sought outside the realm of method or technique. (p. 1)

Exhibit M1.3   Common Beliefs That Generate Negative Self-Talk

1. The belief that it is a dire necessity to be loved or approved of by everyone for everything you do. A more rational idea is to do the things you want to do as long as you do not hinder others. No matter how hard you try, you will never get everyone to like you, as what will please one may displease another. Your opinion of yourself is much more important than others' views of you.

2. The belief that you should be thoroughly competent, skilled, and achieving in all possible respects if you are to consider yourself worthwhile. This idea represents a demand for perfection that is simply impossible to achieve. All humans are fallible. We all make mistakes. Achieving something does not make you a "better person." We all have intrinsic worth because we exist. If you fail at something, it does not make you a failure but only a person who has failed at something.

3. The belief that it is awful and catastrophic when things are not the way you would like them to be. In actuality, nothing is awful. Awful connotes that certain circum-

stances are more than "100 percent" negative. Events or circumstances are at times inconvenient, but they never are "awful." By telling ourselves that certain inconvenient events (such as a broken engagement) are awful, we are causing ourselves to overreact emotionally. In actuality we have limited control over events that happen to us. You can try to change reality, but you better stop *demanding* that it be as you say—there is a great deal of evidence that neither you nor I runs the world. Rational therapy seeks to "deawfulize" thinking.

4. The belief that there will be justice in the world and in interpersonal relationships. Humans are fallible, and injustices can be expected to occur. To expect justice in all interactions is unrealistic and will lead you to react with anger or frustration when an injustice occurs. "Complete justice" does not exist, and it never did. A more rational philosophy is to seek to change conditions so they become more fair. But if you come to realize that it is impossible to change an "unfair" situation, you

Exhibit M1.3 *(continued)*

had better become resigned to its existence and stop telling yourself how awful it is.

5. The belief that human unhappiness (and happiness) is externally caused and that you have little or no ability to control your unwanted emotions. The external environment can only cause you physical pain, never emotional pain. You cause all your emotions by your self-talk, and thereby you can control and relieve any uncomfortable emotion by changing your negative or irrational self-talk.

6. The belief that if something is or may be dangerous or fearsome you should be terribly concerned about it and should keep dwelling on the possibility of its occurring. Worriers frequently believe the act of worrying has a "magical" value of preventing the worst from occurring. Of course, worrying has no magical power. Chronic worrying seldom achieves the results that calm deliberation and careful study do. Excessive worry often incapacitates a person to the point that the feared event is not avoided but often brought about. If you are a chronic worrier, analyze your self-talk to discover what is rational fear and what is irrational fear. Worriers will find that most of their fears are irrational and can be countered with rational self-challenges.

7. The belief that you should depend on others and that you need someone stronger than yourself on whom to rely. Any time you enter into a dependent relationship, you become vulnerable to the whims of the person you are dependent on. It is usually far better to stand on your own feet and gain faith in yourself by doing what you can for yourself and for others. There is no guarantee that someone else's judgment is right—in fact, all humans are fallible. The only way you become efficient at acting on your own judgment is to practice doing it.

8. The belief that your past is an all-important determinant of your present behavior and that because something once strongly affected your life it will indefinitely have a similar effect. In actuality, what you want out of life, now and in the future (along with your motivation to achieve what you want), is a much stronger determinant of what your life will be.

9. The belief that what other people do is vitally important to your existence and that you should make great efforts to change them in the direction you would like them to be. Forcing others to behave in a certain way frequently makes them rebel. In actuality, you have a right to live the way you want to as long as you do not hinder others in living the way they want to. You own your life and others own theirs, and you should respect their right to live the way they want to.

10. The belief that other people's problems are also yours and that you should become quite emotionally involved in other people's problems. You can do very little in controlling the emotions and behaviors of others, although you can do a great deal about controlling your own. When other people have problems, they *own* them; you don't. Becoming emotionally involved by psychologically taking on joint ownership usually is more destructive than helpful. The best way to help others is to recognize their problems are theirs and be an emotionally calm person who is available to help arrive at a sensible attack on the problems.

11. The belief that people with a stereotyped label (for example, ex-convict, mentally ill, mentally retarded, whore, juvenile delinquent, welfare mother) are somehow categorically different from "normal" people and should be viewed with suspicion and avoided. In actuality, such a label (at best) refers only to a small proportion of their past or present behavior. Every person is unique. Stereotypes that are based on labels are frequently myths without a factual base. We will get to know other people much more realistically if we interact with them as "unique persons" rather than in terms of expectations based on labels. The same approach is applicable to interacting with people having labels with more positive stereotypes;—for example, priests, professors, executive directors, police officers, counselors, school principals, judges.

12. The belief that human happiness can be achieved by inaction. There is no magical way in which happiness is suddenly going to happen to you. We get out of life what we put into it. If you are bored or unhappy, there are two ways of counteracting these problems: challenging the irrational self-talk or getting involved in meaningful activities. People are the happiest when they are fully absorbed in satisfying activities.

13. The belief that what you *want* are needs that *must* be fulfilled. In actuality, you have very few *needs*—you need food, water, and shelter to exist. The consequences of thinking in terms of needs are often self-defeating. Thinking in terms of needs implies life-and-death consequences. Faced with such consequences, you will tend to panic and think and behave irrationally, and thus self-defeatingly. Ellis (1973) coined the term *musterbation* for people who behave irrationally because they erroneously perceive their wants to be needs that *must* be fulfilled.

14. The belief that people and life *should* always be pleasing, and if they are not, they are awful and unbearable. This erroneous belief is operating when you give yourself the following self-talk about an unpleasant experience: "I *should* be treated in a totally satisfying way; it is *awful* when I'm not." But where is the evidence that people and life *should* treat anyone in a perfectly gratifying way? Everything in life is imperfect. Nothing completely lasts or fully satisfies. All people are fallible. Demanding "I should be treated in a certain way" requires that others act and that events unfold according to your private wishes. You have neither the control over others nor are you (or for that matter, anyone) such a superspecial person that the world *should* revolve around you.

Thinking psychologically in terms of "needs," "shoulds," "musts," "awful," and "unbearable" is a distortion of reality and frequently leads us to overact. Instead of using "shoulds" and "musts" in our interactions with others, a more rational philosophy is "I would like to be treated reasonably well by people and life."

What Causes Disturbing Emotions and Ineffective Actions?

Before we attempt to provide an explanation of what produces positive changes in therapy, it is important to identify the primary determinants of emotional and behavior problems. The most important point about the rational therapy formula (Event → Self-talk → Emotion → Actions) is that self-talk determines how we act.

By changing our self-talk, we can change how we act. Generally we cannot control events that happen to us, but we have the power to think rationally and thereby change *all* of our unwanted emotions and dysfunctional behaviors. Self-talk is hypothesized as the primary determinant of all actions and all emotions, including love, fear, anger, grief, depression, anxiety, shame, happiness, hate, and frustration. Zastrow (1979, 1993) has also shown that self-talk is the primary determinant of our self-concept, our sense of success or failure, our personality, and stress-related illnesses.

Restructuring Thinking: Is This the Key Therapeutic Agent?

Rational therapy asserts that discomforting emotions and dysfunctional actions arise primarily from negative or irrational self-talk. If this conceptualization is accurate, an important corollary is that any therapy technique that succeeds in changing emotions or actions is effective primarily because it changes self-talk. In other words, self-talk appears to be the key therapeutic agent in all approaches that produce positive changes.

Exercise M1.9: Is Restructuring Thinking the Key Therapeutic Agent?

Goal: This exercise is designed to have you reflect on what causes therapeutic change.

Step 1:   Describe an unwanted emotion that you recently had that you no longer have.

Step 2:   Did restructuring your thinking lead to the unwanted emotion ceasing to exist? Describe what you believe led to your unwanted emotion ceasing to exist.

Step 3:   Describe a dysfunctional behavior (such as procrastinating about something) that you recently engaged in but no longer engage in.

Step 4:   Did restructuring your thinking lead you to stop engaging in this dysfunctional behavior? Describe what you believe led you to no longer engage in this dysfunctional behavior.

Step 5:   Provide your thoughts on the assertion that changing self-talk in a more positive and rational direction is the key therapeutic agent in changing unwanted emotions and dysfunctional behaviors.

EVALUATION OF RATIONAL THERAPY

Rational therapy is one of the most widely used therapy approaches. DiGiuseppe, Miller, and Trexler (1977) summarized a large number of outcome studies conducted on rational therapy and found that more than 90% of these studies supported its claims. Ellis (2008) noted that more than 200 outcome studies have been published showing that rational therapy is effective in changing the thoughts, feelings, and behaviors of individuals with various kinds of disturbances. DiGiuseppe, Terjesen, Rose, Doyle, and Vadalakis (1998) stated that studies conducted on rational therapy show that the approach usually works better than no therapy and that rational therapy is often more effective than other methods of psychotherapy.

Rational therapy has been used successfully to treat clients with a wide range of problems, including unwanted emotions (depression, anxiety, fears and phobias, guilt, shame), sexual problems and sexual dysfunctions, worrying, marital problems, interaction problems, alcoholism, shyness, and such irresponsible actions as committing crimes, procrastination, and jealous actions. Its major hypotheses are also useful in child rearing, education, and executive management.

By asserting that we primarily cause our unwanted emotions and irresponsible behaviors by what we think, the approach squarely puts responsibility on us for improving our lives. We are in charge of our lives and have the power to alleviate unwanted emotions and change ineffective actions. Zastrow (1979, 1993) theorized that our self-talk has immense effects on our lives that we only now are beginning to understand. Self-talk, for example, plays a major part in chronic stress, and chronic stress causes a wide range of stress-related illnesses, including ulcers, migraine headaches, insomnia, diarrhea, heart problems, digestive problems, cancer, hypertension, and obesity. It is also hypothesized that success at any competitive game is substantially determined by the kind of self-talk we give ourselves.

Rational therapy has made a substantial contribution to psychotherapy. Yet there are some important unanswered questions:

1. *Physiology of self-talk and emotions.* As yet we do not precisely know the physiological components of thinking or of emotions. The brain, of course, is important in enabling us to think. But what precisely takes place in the brain that leads us to conceptualize our thoughts? Are other pans of the body involved in thinking? Thinking is related to memory. But what precisely is memory, and how do we "store" and "recall" experiences that we have? And how are memory and thinking physiologically related?

   If self-talk primarily causes our emotions, what are the physiological processes involved? What different physiological processes occur for such varied emotions as love, depression, happiness, anger, sorrow, and so on? And how, physiologically, do certain types of self-talk and certain kinds of emotional states influence our health?

2. *Separating* the *effects of self-talk from the effects of physiological factors.* For people with injuries or abnormal conditions in the brain, it is at times extremely difficult to separate the effects of their medical conditions from those of self-talk. Injuries in different areas of the brain cause changes in a person's emotions and behaviors (Rosenhan & Seligman, 1995). Abnormal conditions of the brain result from a wide range of factors, including brain tumors, disorders such as cerebral palsy, chronic alcoholic intoxication, Alzheimer's disease, general paresis, AIDS, and cerebral arteriosclerosis. Such medical conditions are a factor in causing confusion, incoherence, clouding of consciousness, loss of recent or past memory, reduction in reasoning capacities, listlessness, apathy, reduction in intellectual capacities, and sometimes perceptual changes. Although these conditions can have permanent or long-lasting effects on thinking patterns and emotional reactions, other factors also change mental activity—such as high fever, toxins or poisons, and the intake of drugs and alcohol.

   Even with the presence of these factors, one's self-talk about these conditions also affects one's emotions and behaviors. Separating which effects result from other factors and which from self-talk often is difficult.

3. *Nature versus nurture. Nurture* can be defined as the sum of the influences modifying the expression of the genetic potentialities of a person. The theory of human behavior presented in this module focuses on nurture determinants, as it states human behavior is determined by events and self-talk. This theory fails to include genetic factors, which obviously influence human behavior.

4. *The importance of experiences or events themselves.* According to critics of rational therapy, the events that happen to a person are as important in determining behavior as the self-talk about such experiences (and perhaps even more important). These critics point out that events such as poverty, discrimination, child abuse, overprotective parents, inadequate education, and being victimized by crime are major determinants of human behavior.

5. *Boundaries of self-talk.* Rational therapy theorizes that self-talk has immense effects on our lives, and many of these effects are summarized in this module. But what are the limits of the effects of self-talk? In reference to this question, Zastrow (1979) presented the following example:

   A college student recently asked if her mother's long-time concern about giving birth to a child with a "dwarf" arm might have led to her youngest being born with a malformed arm.

   The student mentioned that her mother had been mildly concerned for a number of years that she would give birth to a child with a malformed arm. This young woman and her older brother were born without having such a malformation. However, shortly after the mother became pregnant the third time, a neighbor woman gave birth to a child with a malformed arm. This led the mother to have intense concerns that the child she was carrying would be born with a "dwarf" arm. When the child was born, it in fact was born with a "dwarf" arm.

   After I had given several lectures on the effects of self-talk in one of my classes, the student asked whether I thought this malformation was partly caused by self-talk or was just a matter of coincidence.

   In truth, I answered I didn't know—and I still don't know. We know certain drugs (such as thalidomide and excessive drinking) can cause malformations. So can having certain illnesses, such as German measles, during the time when the mother is pregnant. There is also speculation that the mother's emotional state while pregnant can influence the emotional and physiological development of the unborn child (Ainsworth et al., 1966; Dunn, 1977). Is it possible that this mother's thoughts and fears about having a malformed child might have been a factor in the child's being born with a malformed arm? . . .

Daily I become aware of new ways in which my life, and that of others, is being influenced by self-talk. And, as I discuss the concept with others, the discussion usually ignites their relating to me specific incidents in which their self-talk has had a powerful effect on them.

At this point I frankly do not know what the boundaries are for the effects of self-talk. It may well be that we are only at the "tip of the iceberg" in understanding all its effects. (pp. 327–328)

SUMMARY

The following summarizes the module's content in terms of the learning objectives presented at the beginning of the module.

1. Comprehend rational therapy.

   Rational therapy asserts that the primary cause of all our emotions and actions is not our experiences but rather what we tell ourselves about events that happen to us. Generally we cannot control events, but we can think rationally and thereby change unwanted emotions and dysfunctional actions. Self-talk has a here-and-now quality because it represents our present thoughts. Self-talk is frequently based on our attitudes, beliefs, values, wants, needs, drives, and motives.

   The theory asserts there are three constructive ways to change unwanted emotions:

   a) getting involved in meaningful, enjoyable activities,
   b) challenging and changing negative self-talk to more positive and rational self-talk, and
   c) changing the distressing event.

   Rational therapy asserts that assessing human behavior is largely a process of identifying the cognitions that underlie unwanted emotions or dysfunctional behavior. Rational therapy asserts that the key therapuetic change agent in any therapy techniques is changing a person's thinking from self-talk that is negative or irrational to self-talk that is more rational and positive. Rational therapy is a cognitive-behavioral approach to therapy.

   Unanswered questions remain about rational therapy, including how self-talk physiologically leads to emotions and what the limits of the effects of self-talk are.

EXERCISES

1. Changing Unwanted Emotions

Goal: This exercise is designed to illustrate many of the principles of rational therapy and to demonstrate to students how to change unwanted emotions.

Step 1:   Begin by asking students to think about the last time they were "sad" or "angry." Ask what made them sad or angry. List three or four responses on the chalkboard under each heading. The students in all probability will give you "events" as being the source of these emotions.

Step 2:   Indicate to the students that what they told you was *not* the primary source of their emotions. Indicate instead that emotions are determined primarily by self-talk rather than events. For each "event" response given by a student, have the student tell you about personal self-talk that led to the emotion or guess what the self-talk is. For example, if a student says, "I became sad because I received a speeding ticket," you might suggest the self-talk that led to being sad was something like "This is awful. I sure am stupid for driving so fast. Now my insurance rates will go up. Woe is me. I don't have enough money to pay for tickets and increased insurance payments. I'm a bad person for getting a ticket."

Step 3:   Further demonstrate the principles of rational therapy by asking the students, "What would be your self-talk if the person you were elating for the past 4 years informed you that he or she no longer wanted to date you?" Write this event on the chalkboard. Ask students what would be their self-talk, and what would be the resulting emotions from each self-talk statement. Write these self-talk statements and the resulting emotions on the board. Using the five criteria for determining rational thinking, ask the students to identify which of the self-talk statements are irrational and to give the reasons they are irrational. For each irrational self-talk statement, ask the class to come up with rational self-challenges to challenge and change the irrational self-talk statement.

Step 4: Explain to students how to write a rational self-analysis. (Show them examples from this module or distribute a handout of a completed RSA.)

Step 5: Indicate that there are only three constructive ways to change an unwanted emotion:

  a. Challenge negative and irrational thinking with rational self-challenges.
  b. Get involved in meaningful and enjoyable activities, which stops a person from thinking negatively and irrationally.
  c. Change the distressing event(s). If you are successful in doing this, you are likely to feel better because you will then give yourself more positive self-talk.

Step 6: As a homework assignment, ask students to write a rational self-analysis on an unwanted emotion they have. Ask students their thoughts on the merits and shortcomings of rational therapy.

2. Positive Affirmations

Goal: This exercise is designed to provide students with another approach to change negative and irrational thinking.

Step 1: Indicate that some people find writing a rational self-analysis too time-consuming and cumbersome. An alternative is to use positive affirmations. A positive affirmation is a positive assertion that helps in achieving emotional and behavioral goals. The process of writing a positive affirmation also enables a person to identify negative and irrational thinking that he or she may be unaware of.

Step 2: Instruct the students in the following process of writing a positive affirmation. Have each student select a realistic emotional or behavioral personal goal that he or she is currently struggling with. The following are examples:

"I believe I am a person of worth."
"I will no longer be depressed about _____."
"I will no longer get angry and aggressive when _____ occurs."
"I will lose 5 pounds in 2 months."
"I will stop smoking today."
"I will limit my drinking of alcoholic beverages to two drinks when I go out."
"I will no longer feel guilty about _____."
"I believe I am an attractive person."
"I will assertively express myself when _____ occurs."

Step 3: Have each student start writing on a sheet of paper the selected positive affirmation. When negative thoughts enter students' minds, have them record those thoughts and then continue writing the positive affirmation, using the following format:

Positive Affirmation	Negative Thoughts
"I will lose 5 pounds in 2 months."	
"I will lose 5 pounds in 2 months."	
"I will lose 5 pounds in 2 months."	"I overeat when I'm bored, depressed, or lonely."
"I will lose 5 pounds in 2 months."	
"I will lose 5 pounds in 2 months."	"I will need to develop an exercise program, which I hate to do."
"I will lose 5 pounds in 2 months."	"One reason I'm fat is because I snack between meals."
"I will lose 5 pounds in 2 months."	"I will have to limit the number of beers that I have when I go out—beer is putting a lot of weight on me."
"I will lose 5 pounds in 2 months."	"I wonder if I really want to make all the changes that I will have to make to lose 5 pounds."
"I will lose 5 pounds in 2 months."	
"I will lose 5 pounds in 2 months."	
"I will lose 5 pounds in 2 months."	

Step 4:   Ask students to write for 10 to 15 minutes. Ask for volunteers to share what they wrote. Have the class discuss the merits and shortcomings of writing positive affirmations. One advantage of repeated writing of the affirmation is that it trains the mind to accept the positive affirmation more readily.

3. Assessing and Changing Dysfunctional Behaviors

Goal: This exercise is designed to have students evaluate the merits and shortcomings of focusing on cognitions in assessing and changing dysfunctional behaviors.

Step 1:   Explain the theory, described in this module, that thinking processes primarily determine behavior. The theory asserts that the reasons for unusual or dysfunctional behavior can always be identified by determining what the perpetrator was thinking before and during the time the act was being committed.

Step 2:   Divide the class into several subgroups (ranging in size from three to six). Give each subgroup a different problematic or dysfunctional behavior. Examples include (a) alcoholism, (b) child abuse, (c) bulimia, (d) date rape, (e) suicide attempt, and (f) compulsive gambling.

Step 3:   Instruct each subgroup to (a) identify the *thinking processes* that would lead a person to engage in the dysfunctional behavior and (b) identify the interventions that would be most effective in changing the thinking patterns of the perpetrator to "curb" the dysfunctional behavior. Instruct each subgroup to identify several intervention strategies or options, because (in one sense) social work practice involves "options planning." Give the subgroups 10 or more minutes to arrive at their answers.

Step 4:   Ask each subgroup to select a representative to share with the class what the subgroup arrived at for both thinking processes and interventions. Ask a representative to share what his or her subgroup arrived at. Then ask the class to discuss whether the representative identified thinking processes (as the exercise instructed) or focused on describing events and personality characteristics that the subgroup thought were related to the dysfunctional behavior. Also ask the class whether the subgroup may have overlooked some important intervention strategies and options. Continue this process for each subgroup: A representative of the group presents the groups findings, and then the class discusses them.

Step 5:   After the presentations and discussions end, ask the class for their thoughts on the merits, difficulties, and shortcomings of focusing on cognitions to assess and change dysfunctional behaviors.

4.. Improving Your Self-Concept

Goal: To improve your self-concept.

Step 1:   The leader asks each student to list on a sheet of paper her or his good qualities—what she or he likes about herself or himself.

Step 2:   The leader asks each student to then list what he or she dislikes about himself or herself.

Step 3:   The leader then asks each student to write down, for each negative quality listed in step 2, what positive things he or she will tell himself or herself whenever this student starts "awfulizing" about a negative quality. (The refuting positive quality may be a quality listed in step 1.)

Step 4:   The leader explains that a negative self-concept stems from negative and irrational self-talk that people give themselves. One way to improve a negative self-concept is to identify the underlying negative self-talk and then challenge this self-talk with positive thoughts about oneself.

MODULE

BEHAVIOR THERAPY

LEARNING OBJECTIVES

No one person is credited with developing behavioral approaches to psychotherapy. Behavior therapists vary considerably in both theory and technique. The main assumption in this counseling approach is that maladaptive behaviors are acquired primarily through learning and can be modified through additional learning. This module will help prepare students to:

Comprehend three learning processes
Understand behavior intervention techniques used by social workers

FOUNDERS

Learning theory has been the philosophical foundation for behavior therapy even though there has never been agreement about which learning theory is the core of behavior therapy. Numerous authorities have advanced somewhat different theories of how people learn. Pavlov, a Russian who lived between 1849 and 1936, was one of the earliest. Other prominent learning theorists include E. L. Thorndike (1913), E. R. Guthrie (1935), C. L. Hull (1943), E. C. Tolman (1932), and B. F. Skinner (1938). Behavior therapists who have achieved international recognition for developing therapies based on learning principles include R. E. Alberti and M. L. Emmons (1970), A. Bandura (1969), B. F. Skinner (1948), J. B. Watson and R. Rayner (1920), and J. Wolpe (1958).

Despite the wide variation in behavior therapy approaches and techniques, there are some common emphases. One is that the maladaptive behavior (such as bedwetting) is the problem and needs to be changed. This approach is in sharp contrast to the psychoanalytic approach that views the problematic behavior as a *symptom* of some underlying, unconscious causes. Psychoanalysts assert that the underlying causes must be treated to prevent the substitution of new symptoms or the return of old symptoms, but behavior therapists assert that treating the problematic behavior will not result in symptom substitution.

Behavior therapists assert that counseling approaches must be tested and validated by rigorous experimental procedures. This focus requires that the goals of therapy be articulated in behavioral terms that can be measured. Baseline levels of problematic behaviors are established before counseling to measure whether the approach is producing the desired change in the rate or intensity of responding.

The use of behavior modification therapy in counseling has increased dramatically during the past 40 years. Behavior therapy intervention techniques are now among the most widely used techniques in counseling and psychotherapy (Wilson, 2008).

Behavior therapists have devoted little attention to developing a behavioral model of personality. Behaviorists generally believe that environmental conditions or experiences are of much greater influence in controlling behavior than are internal personality traits.

TYPES OF LEARNING PROCESSES

Before we examine the prominent behavior therapy techniques, it behooves us to discuss three types of learning processes: operant conditioning, respondent conditioning, and modeling. These three learning processes form the theoretical basis of behavior therapy techniques.

Operant Conditioning

According to learning theory, much of human behavior is determined by positive and negative reinforcers. A *positive reinforcer* is any stimulus that, when applied following a behavior, increases or strengthens that behavior. Common examples include food, water, sex, attention, affection, and approval. The list of positive reinforcers is inexhaustible and highly individualized. Praise, for example, is a positive reinforcer when and only when it maintains or increases the behavior with which it is associated (for example, efforts to improve one's writing skills). A *negative reinforcer* (or *aversive stimulus*) is any stimulus that a person will terminate or avoid if given the opportunity. Common examples include frowns, electric shock, and criticism. The same stimulus—for example, the smell of Limburger cheese—can be a negative reinforcer for one person and a positive reinforcer for another.

There are four basic learning principles involving positive reinforcers and aversive stimuli:

1. If a positive reinforcer (for example, food) is presented to a person following a response, the result is positive reinforcement. With positive reinforcement, the occurrence of a given behavior is strengthened or increased.
2. If a positive reinforcer is withdrawn following a person's response, the result is punishment.
3. If an aversive stimulus (for example, an electric shock) is presented to a person following a response, the result is punishment. (As can be seen, there are two types of punishment.)
4. If an aversive stimulus is withdrawn following a person's response, the result is negative reinforcement. In negative reinforcement, a response (behavior) is increased by removing an aversive stimulus (for example, fastening ones seat belt to turn off the obnoxiously loud and annoying buzzer).

In sum, positive and negative reinforcements increase behavior, and punishment decreases behavior. Principles of operant conditioning are used in several behavioral techniques described in this module, including assertiveness training, token economies, contingency contracting, and aversive techniques.

Exercise M2.1: Operant Conditioning

Goal: This exercise is designed to assist you in understanding and applying operant conditioning.

Step 1: Describe an experience in which a behavior of yours was increased by a positive reinforcer.

Step 2: Describe an experience in which a behavior of yours was decreased by a negative reinforcer.

Respondent Conditioning

Respondent learning has also been called "classical" or "Pavlovian" conditioning. Many diverse everyday behaviors are considered respondent behaviors—perspiring, salivating, and, more important, many anxieties, fears, and phobias. A key concept in respondent learning is *pairing*: the idea that behaviors are learned by being consistently paired over time with other behaviors or events.

To explain respondent conditioning, let's first define the following key terms:

- *Neutral stimulus (NS):* a stimulus that elicits little or no response
- *Unconditioned stimulus (UCS):* a stimulus that elicits an innate, or unlearned, response
- *Unlearned response (UR):* a response that is innate—for example, salivating because of food in the mouth
- *Conditioned response (CR):* a new response that has been learned
- *Conditioned stimulus (CS):* an original neutral stimulus that, through pairing with an unconditioned stimulus, now begins to elicit a conditioned response

Respondent learning asserts that when a neutral stimulus (NS) is paired with an unconditioned stimulus (UCS), the neutral stimulus will elicit a response similar to the response elicited by the UCS. That new response is called a conditioned response (CR) because it has been learned. The originally neutral stimulus, once it begins to elicit the response, becomes the conditioned stimulus (CS). Thus, it is possible for an event that originally elicited no fear whatsoever (for example, being in the dark) to elicit fear when it is paired with a stimulus that does elicit fear (for example, horrifying stories about being in the dark). This learning process is indicated in the following paradigm:

1. *UCS* (horrifying stories about being in the dark) → elicits *UR* (fear)
2. *NS* (being in the clark) paired with *UCS* → elicits *CR* (fear)
3. *NS* becomes *CS* → elicits *CR* (fear)

The *CS-CR* bond can be broken by respondent extinction or by counterconditioning. *Respondent extinction* involves continuing presentation of the conditioned stimulus without any further pairing with the unconditioned stimulus. Respondent extinction gradually weakens and eventually eliminates the CS-CR bond. Implosive therapy, discussed later in this module, is based on this principle.

Counterconditioning is based on the principle that the CS-CR bond can be broken by using new responses that are stronger than, and incompatible with, old responses that are elicited by the same stimulus. For example, it is possible to teach a person to relax (new response) instead of becoming anxious (old response) when confronted with a particular stimulus (for example, the prospect of flying in a small plane). In vivo desensitization (also discussed later in this module) is based on counterconditioning.

Exercise M2.2: Respondent Conditioning

Goal: This exercise is designed to assist you in understanding and applying respondent conditioning.
Describe an experience in which a behavior of yours was shaped by respondent conditioning.

Modeling

Modeling is a technique in which the client changes his or her behavior as a result of observing another person's behavior—that is, learning by vicarious experience or imitation. Much of everyday learning is thought to take place through modeling—using both live models and symbolic models (such as films). Modeling has been used in behavior modification to develop new behaviors that are not in a person's repertoire—for example, showing a youngster how to swing a bat. Modeling has also been used to eliminate anxieties and fears—for example, using a model in assertiveness training. Anxieties and fears are reduced or eliminated through modeling by exposing fearful observers to modeled events in which the model performs the feared activity without experiencing any adverse effects and even enjoys the experience.

Exercise M2.3: Modeling

Goal: This exercise is designed to assist you in understanding and applying the principles of modeling.
Describe an experience in which you learned a new behavior by modeling.

THEORY OF COUNSELING

Behavior therapy rests on the assumption that all behavior occurs in response to stimulation, internal or external. The first task of the behavior therapist is to identify the probable stimulus-response (S-R) connections that are occurring for the client. This part of the counseling process is called a *behavioral*, or *functional*, *analysis*. The following illustrates an S-R connection: For a person who fears heights, the stimulus (S) of flying in a small plane elicits the response (R) of intense anxiety and avoidance of the stimulus.

Before and during the time the behavior therapist performs a behavioral analysis, he or she also attempts to establish a working relationship with the client. (The characteristics of a working relationship are described in Chapter 5.) In regard to this emphasis on establishing a working relationship, Chambless and Goldstein (1979) stated,

> Although behaviorists are often portrayed as cold and mechanical, a study of recordings of therapy sessions yields a different picture. When measured on variables used in the study of client-centered therapy, behavior therapists showed high warmth and positive regard for their clients (equal to other psychotherapists in the study) and higher empathy and self-congruence than the other therapists. (p. 243)

Chambless and Goldstein (1979) also described sources of information for making a behavioral analysis:

> The behavior therapist may base the [behavioral] analysis on interviews with the client and important people in the client's life or on information gained by having the client keep a journal. Questionnaire data are often useful. Interpersonal problems may be more clearly defined if the therapist and client role play interactions with which the client reports difficulty. When the therapist has a difficult time making the analysis, observing the client in the situation where the problem occurs may lead to a wealth of information. Obviously, there are times when this would be impossible or in poor taste, but direct observation is used much less frequently than it should be. (pp. 244–245)

During the analysis, the behavior therapist attempts to determine the stimuli associated with the maladaptive responses. Through this analysis, both client and counselor arrive at an understanding of the problem and generally how it developed. This insight does not treat the problem but is useful because it reduces client anxiety; clients no longer feel possessed or overwhelmed by unknown, mysterious forces. Errors about hypothesized S-R connections at this diagnostic stage usually lead to ineffective interventions because the interventions will be focused on treating S-R connections that are *not* involved in perpetuating the maladaptive behavior.

A behavioral analysis begins with the behavior therapist taking a detailed history of the presenting problem, its course, and particularly its association with current experiences. In making such an analysis, it is crucial to obtain specific, concrete details about the circumstances in which the presenting problem arises. If, for example, clients are shy in some situations, it is important to identify the specific interactions in which they are shy. Furthermore, it is important to determine why they are shy: Is it because they do not know how to express themselves, or is it because they have certain fears? The choice of an intervention depends on such information. If clients do not know how to express themselves, a *modeling* approach through role-playing might be used. However, if they have the response potential but are inhibited by certain fears, a desensitization procedure (described later in this module) to reduce these fears might be used.

The objective in the behavioral analysis is to identify the antecedent stimuli that are generating the maladaptive responses. Once the behavior therapist identifies these connections, he or she discusses them with the client, to help the client gain insight and to obtain from the client feedback on possible erroneous connections. Client and counselor then agree on the goals for the treatment. How counseling will proceed and the techniques to be used are described to the client. This information gives the client some idea of her or his role in the intervention. Orne and Wender (1968) found that this knowledge fosters positive outcomes and reduces the dropout rate.

ASSERTIVENESS TRAINING

Assertiveness training has become the most frequently used method in modifying unadaptive interpersonal behavior. It is particularly effective in changing both timid behavior and aggressive behavior. Wolpe (1958) originally developed this approach, and it has been further developed by a variety of authors, including Alberti and Emmons (1970) and Fensterheim and Baer (1975). Interest in assertiveness training has grown enormously in the past four decades, sparked by the recognition that sex-role stereotyping has led to a general lack of assertiveness in women. Assertiveness training groups are now widely offered. During the past few decades, increasing numbers of men are also getting involved, either individually or through groups, in assertiveness training. Outcome research on assertiveness training has found the approach to be effective in assisting participants to become more assertive (Cormier & Cormier, 1991).

Overview of Assertiveness Training

Do you handle put-downs well? Are you reluctant to express your feelings and opinions openly and honestly in a group? Are you frequently timid in interacting with people in authority? Do you react well to criticism? Do you sometimes explode in anger when things go wrong, or are you able to remain calm? Do you find it difficult to maintain eye contact when talking? If you are uncomfortable with someone smoking near you, do you express your feelings? Are you timid in arranging a date or social event? If you have trouble in any of these situations, there is, fortunately, a useful technique—assertiveness training—that helps people become more effective in such interpersonal interactions.

Assertiveness problems range from extreme shyness, introversion, and withdrawal to inappropriately flying into a rage that results in alienating others. A nonassertive person is often acquiescent, fearful, and afraid of expressing his or her real, spontaneous feelings. Frequently, resentment and anxiety build up, which may result in general discomfort, feelings of low self-esteem, tension headaches, fatigue, and perhaps a destructive explosion of temper, anger, and aggression. Some people are overly shy and timid in nearly all interactions. Most of us, however, encounter occasional problems in isolated areas in which it would be to our benefit to be more assertive. For example, a bachelor may be quite effective and assertive in his job as store manager but still awkward and timid when attempting to arrange a date.

There are three basic styles of interacting with others: *nonassertive*, *aggressive*, and *assertive*. Alberti and Emmons (1975) summarized characteristics of these styles:

> In the *nonassertive* style, you are likely to hesitate, speak softly, look away, avoid the issue, agree regardless of your own feelings, not express opinions, value yourself "below" others, and hurt yourself to avoid any chance of hurting others.

In the *aggressive* style, you typically answer before the other person is through talking, speak loudly and abusively, glare at the other person, speak "past" the issue (accusing, blaming, demeaning), vehemently expound your feelings and opinions, value yourself "above" others, and hurt others to avoid hurting yourself.

In the *assertive* style, you will answer spontaneously, speak with a conversational tone and volume, and look at the other person, speak to the issue, openly express your personal feelings and opinions (anger, love, disagreement, sorrow), value yourself equal to others, and hurt neither yourself nor others. (p. 24)

Simply stated, *assertive behavior* is being able to express yourself without hurting or violating the rights of others.

Assertiveness training is designed to lead people to realize, feel, and act on the assumption that they have the right to be themselves and to express their feelings freely. Assertive responses generally are not aggressive responses. The distinction between these two types of interactions is important. Let's look at two examples of nonassertive, aggressive, and assertive behavior.

You are a social worker driving in a car with an associate to a conference in another city. The associate lights up a pipe; you soon find the smoke irritating and the odor somewhat stifling. What are your choices?

1. *Nonassertive response:* You attempt to carry on a "cheery" conversation for the 3-hour trip without commenting about the smoke.
2. *Aggressive response:* You increasingly become irritated until exploding, "Either you put out that pipe or I'll put it out for you—the odor is sickening."
3. *Assertive response:* In a firm, conversational tone, you look directly at the associate and state, "The smoke from your pipe is irritating me. I'd appreciate it if you put it away."

At a party with friends, during small-talk conversation, your husband gives you a subtle put-down by stating, "Wives always talk too much." What do you do?

1. *Nonassertive response:* You don't say anything but feel hurt and become quiet.
2. *Aggressive response:* You glare at him and angrily ask, "John, why are you always criticizing me?"
3. *Assertive response:* You carry on as usual. On the drive home, you calmly look at him and say, "When we were at the party tonight, you said that wives always talk too much. I felt you were putting me down when you said that. What did you mean by that comment?"

Steps in Assertiveness Training

You can train yourself to be more assertive. Here are 12 steps.

Step 1: Examine your interactions. Are there situations that you need to handle more assertively? Do you at times hold back your opinions and feelings for fear of what would happen if you expressed them? Do you occasionally lose control and lash out angrily at others? To study your interactions, keep a diary for a week or longer, recording the situations in which you acted timidly, aggressively, and assertively.

Step 2: Select those interactions in which it would be to your benefit to be more assertive. They may include situations in which you were overly polite, overly apologetic, timid, or allowed others to take advantage of you while you were harboring feelings of resentment, anger, embarrassment, fear of others, or self-criticism for not having the courage to express yourself. Overly aggressive interactions in which you exploded in anger or walked over others also need to be dealt with. For each set of nonassertive or aggressive interactions, you can become more assertive, as shown in the next steps.

Step 3: Concentrate on a specific incident in the past in which you were either nonassertive or aggressive when you wanted to be assertive. Close your eyes for a few minutes and vividly imagine the details, including what you and the other person said, and how you felt at the time and afterward.

Step 4: Write down and review your responses. Ask yourself the following questions to determine how you presented yourself:

a. *Eye contact.* Did you look directly at the other person in a relaxed, steady gaze? Looking down or away suggests a lack of self-confidence. Glaring is an aggressive response.
b. *Gestures.* Were your gestures appropriate, free flowing, and relaxed and used effectively to emphasize your messages? Awkward stiffness suggests nervousness; other gestures (such as a clenched fist) signal an aggressive reaction.

c. *Body posture.* Did you show the importance of your message by directly facing the other person, by leaning toward that person, by holding your head erect, and by sitting or standing appropriately close?

d. *Facial expression.* Did your facial expression show a stern, firm pose consistent with an assertive response?

e. *Voice tone and volume.* Was your response stated in a firm, conversational tone? Shouting may suggest anger. Speaking softly suggests shyness, and a cracking voice suggests nervousness. Tape recording and listening to one's voice is a way to practice increasing or decreasing the volume.

f. *Speech fluency.* Did your speech flow smoothly, clearly, and slowly? Rapid speech or hesitation in speaking suggests nervousness. Tape recording assertive responses that you try out in problem situations is a way to improve fluency.

g. *Timing.* Were your verbal reactions to a problem situation stated at a time close to the incident that would appropriately permit you and the other person time to review the incident? Generally, spontaneous expressions are the best, but certain situations should be handled at a later time. For example, a challenge to some of your boss's erroneous statements should be made in private rather than in front of a group in which he or she is making a presentation.

h. *Message content.* For a problem situation, which of your responses were nonassertive or aggressive and which were assertive? Study the content and consider why you responded in a nonassertive or aggressive style. (At this point, it is very helpful to identify the self-talk that led you to act nonassertively or aggressively, and to challenge this self-talk with rational, assertive self-challenges—see Module 1.)

Step 5: Observe one or more effective models. Watch the verbal and nonverbal approaches that are assertively used to handle the types of interactions with which you are having problems. Compare the consequences between their approach and yours. If possible, discuss their approach and their feelings about using it.

Step 6: Make a list of alternative approaches for being more assertive.

Step 7: Close your eyes and visualize yourself using each approach. For each one, think through what the full set of interactions would be, along with the consequences. Select one, or a combination of approaches, that you believe will be most effective for you to use. Through imagery, practice using this approach until you feel comfortable with it.

Step 8: Role-play the approach with a friend or counselor. If certain segments of your approach appear clumsy, awkward, timid, or aggressive, practice modifications until you become comfortable with the approach. Obtain feedback from the other person on the strengths and shortcomings of your approach. Compare your interactions to the verbal and nonverbal guidelines for assertive behavior in step 4. It may be useful for the other person to role-play one or more assertive strategies that you could then practice using.

Step 9: Repeat steps 7 and 8 until you develop an assertive approach that you believe will work best for you and that you are comfortable with.

Step 10: Use your approach in a real-life situation. The previous steps are designed to prepare you for the real event. Expect to be somewhat anxious when first trying to be assertive. If you are still too fearful of attempting to be assertive, repeat steps 5–8. For those few individuals who fail to develop the needed confidence to try being assertive, professional counseling is advised—expressing yourself and effective interactions with others are essential for personal happiness.

Step 11: Reflect on the effectiveness of your effort. Did you remain calm?[1] Considering the nonverbal guidelines for assertive behavior discussed in step 4, what components of your responses were assertive, aggressive, and nonassertive? What were the consequences of your effort? How did you feel after trying out this new set of interactions? If possible, discuss how you did in regard to these questions with a friend who observed the interactions.

---

[1]Getting angry at times is a normal human emotion, and it needs to be expressed. However, the anger should be expressed in a constructive, assertive fashion.

Step 12: Expect some success, but not complete personal satisfaction, with your initial efforts. Personal growth and interacting more effectively with others is a continual learning process. Quite appropriately, "pat yourself on the back" for what you did well—you earned it. But also note the areas in which you need to improve.

Use these steps for improving your assertive efforts. These steps are not to be followed rigidly. You need to develop a process that works best for you.

Helping Others Become More Assertive

Either as a friend or as a social worker, you can be very helpful in assisting another person—your "client"—to become more assertive. The following guidelines are suggested:

1. Together identify situations or interactions in which your client needs to be more assertive. Get information about such interactions from your observations and knowledge of the person and from discussing in depth the interactions in which the person feels a need to be more assertive. You may also ask the person to keep a diary of interactions in which she or he feels resentment over being nonassertive and interactions in which she or he was overly aggressive.
2. Develop together some strategies for the person to be more assertive. Small assignments with a high probability of successful outcomes should be given first. A great deal of discussion and preparation should take place between the two of you in preparing for the "real event." For a person who is generally shy, introverted, and nonassertive in all interpersonal relationships, it may be necessary to explore in great detail the connection between nonassertive behavior and feelings of resentment or low self-esteem. In addition, for very shy people, certain attitudes, such as "don't make waves" or the "meek will inherit the earth," may need to be dealt with before developing strategies for the person to be more assertive.
3. Role-playing is a very useful technique in preparing for being assertive. The helper first models an assertive strategy by taking the shy person's role. Shy clients concurrently role-play the role of the person with whom they want to be more assertive. Then the roles are reversed; clients role-play themselves, and the helper plays the other role. Besides the previously mentioned benefits of modeling and practice experience, role-playing has the added advantage of reducing the shy person's anxiety about attempting to be assertive. For feedback purposes, if possible, record the role-playing on audio or videotape.
4. Explain the 12 steps described earlier that your client can use on his or her own to handle future problem situations involving assertiveness. If possible, provide reading material on these steps.

Although individuals must be able to express themselves in their own unique styles, an additional guideline is often useful. A good rule is to start sentences with "I feel" rather than making threatening or aggressive statements. (I-messages are further described in Module 4.) Frequently, we don't take the time to express our real feelings to others. As a result, we end up creating serious misunderstandings, hurt feelings, and verbal fights that take 10 times as long to work through.

Consider the following example of two busy people, a working mother and her 15-year-old son:

Mother: John, please do the dishes for me tonight.
John: I can't, I'll do them tomorrow.
Mother: (*Getting angry*) You never do anything for me.
John: I said I'll do the dishes tomorrow.
Mother: And you always forget. I asked you to clean your room 2 weeks ago, and you still haven't done that. (*Now angry*) I just don't know what I'm going to do with you. Just for that you can't go camping this weekend.

And the argument has ignited. Contrast this to the following approach:

Mother: John, I feel very tired this evening. I had a bad day at work, and I still have to do all the washing and ironing tonight. Could you please help me out by doing the dishes?
John: I'm sorry you had a bad day. I'm supposed to be at basketball practice in 5 minutes. I'll be back at 8:30, would it be all right if I did them then?
Mother: Yes, if you don't forget.
John: I won't.

Assertiveness training is relatively simple to comprehend. Skill, common sense, and ingenuity, however, are needed to create an effective strategy for a real-life situation. The joy and pride resulting from being able to express oneself assertively are nearly unequaled.

Exercise M2.4: Becoming Assertive

Goal: This exercise is designed to assist you in understanding and applying the principles of assertiveness training.

Step 1: Describe a behavior in which you are routinely nonassertive and want to become more assertive.

Step 2: Review the material on assertiveness training. Visualize yourself being assertive in this situation. Describe what you will say, and describe what you want to communicate with your nonverbal behavior.

Step 3: Describe a behavior in which you are routinely aggressive and want to become more assertive.

Step 4: Visualize yourself being assertive in this situation. Describe what you will say, and describe what you want to communicate with your nonverbal behavior.

Step 5: Are you now committed to trying to be assertive when these problematic situations in which you have been nonassertive or aggressive arise again?

BEHAVIOR REHEARSAL

This technique enlarges the client's repertoire of coping behaviors. Behavior rehearsal has four stages.

First, the counselor prepares the client by explaining the importance of acquiring new behaviors (for example, to express anger assertively rather than aggressively), getting the client to accept behavioral rehearsal as a useful device, and reducing any initial anxiety over the prospect of role-playing. The second stage involves selecting target situations. Together, counselor and client select one or more rehearsal situations that relate directly to the situations in which the client is having difficulty (for example, learning to respond assertively rather than aggressively when the client is criticized by his coworkers). The third stage is the actual behavior rehearsal. Counselors sometimes model an appropriate response pattern first. For example, the client may take on the role of a critical coworker while the counselor role-plays an assertive response to receiving criticism from a coworker. Frequently, then, the roles are reversed and the client role-plays responding assertively to being criticized by a coworker (with the counselor as coworker). The fourth stage is the client's actual use of the newly acquired skills in real-life situations.

After the final stage, client and counselor review the client's performance and feelings about the experiences. Sometimes clients are asked to keep diaries describing the real-life situations they encounter, their behavior, its consequences, and so on.

TOKEN ECONOMIES

Tokens are symbolic reinforcers, not unlike poker chips or lines on a tally sheet, that can be exchanged for reinforcement rewards such as candy or increased privileges. An exchange system—an "economy"—is set up that specifies exactly what the tokens can be exchanged for and how many tokens are needed to get particular items or privileges. Target behaviors (such as going to school or making a bed) are specified. These earn tokens; a certain response rate earns a particular number of tokens. For example, attending school every day for 2 weeks earns 10 tokens at an adolescent group home, and 10 tokens can be exchanged for attending a sports event.

Token economies have been successfully used in a wide variety of institutional settings, including mental hospitals, training schools for delinquents, classrooms for students with emotional problems, schools for individuals with cognitive disabilities, sheltered workshops, and group homes for adolescents. Considerable evidence supports the effectiveness of token economies (Kazdin, 1977b), which have been used to effect positive changes in a wide variety of behaviors, including personal hygiene, social interactions, job attendance and performance, academic performance, domestic tasks such as cleaning, and personal appearance. At times, token economies are arranged so that clients not only earn tokens for desired behaviors but also lose tokens for undesired behaviors (for example, instigating a fight).

Effective token economies are, however, more difficult to establish than it appears at first glance. Prochaska (1979) summarized important factors that need to be given attention in establishing a successful token economy:

> Some of the more important considerations include staff cooperation and coordination, since the staff must be more observant and more systematic in their responses to clients than in a noncontingent system. A variety of attempts at establishing token economies have failed because the staff did not cooperate adequately in monitoring the behavior of residents. Effective token economies must also have adequate control over reinforcements, since an economy becomes ineffective if residents have access to reinforcements by having money from home or being able to bum a cigarette from a less cooperative staff member. Problems must be clearly defined in terms of specific behaviors to be changed in order to avoid conflicts among staff or patients. Improving personal hygiene, for example, is too open to interpretation by individuals, and patients may insist that they are improving their hygiene even though staff members may disagree. There is much less room for misunderstandings if personal hygiene is defined as clean fingernails, no evidence of body odor, clean underwear, and other clear-cut rules. (p. 3a)

It is interesting to note that the system of employers hiring employees to work has many components of a token economy. Employers pay cash to employees to do tasks that are specified by the employer. Employees then decide what products and services they will then purchase with the cash they received.

Exercise M2.5: Token Economy

Goal: This exercise is designed to assist you in understanding a token economy.

Describe a token economy that you participated in. Perhaps it was a token economy that a former teacher used with the class. Perhaps it was a system that your parents used to pay you for you doing work that they wanted completed.

CONTINGENCY CONTRACTING

Closely related to token economies is contingency contracting. Contingency contracts provide clients with a set of rules that govern the change process. Contracts may be *unilateral*—that is, clients may make contracts with themselves. For example, a person with a weight problem may limit himself to a certain calorie intake, using a system of rewards for staying within the calorie limit and negative consequences for going over the limit. Contracts may be *bilateral* and specify the obligations and the mutual reinforcements for each party. Kanfer (1975, p. 321) noted that a good contingency contract has the following seven elements:

1. A clear and detailed description of the required instrumental behavior.
2. Criterion for the time or frequency limitations that constitute the goal of the contract.
3. Specified positive reinforcements, contingent on fulfillment of the criterion.
4. Aversive consequence(s), contingent on nonfulfillment of the contract within the specified time or with the specified frequency.
5. Bonus clause with additional positive reinforcements obtainable if the person exceeds the minimal demands of the contract.
6. Specified means by which the contracted response is observed, measured, and recorded and a procedure for informing clients of their achievements during the contract's duration.
7. Delivery of reinforcement contingencies to follow the response as quickly as possible.

Helping professionals increasingly find contingency contracts useful. Such contracts specify desired goals, tasks to be performed to meet these goals, tasks for the client and for the therapist, and the deadline for completing tasks. Kanfer (1975) indicated that marriage counseling is one area in which contingency contracts are especially effective. Each spouse agrees to change behaviors that irritate the other. There is a specified system of reinforcements and consequences depending on the extent to which the contract provisions are met.

Formulating contracts with clients in both one-to-one settings and in group settings has a number of advantages. Contracts guide clients for specific actions they need to take to improve their situations. Contracts have a motivational effect because when people commit to the terms of a contract, they usually feel a moral obligation to follow through. In addition, reviewing whether commitments made in contracts are being met provides counselors and clients with a method for measuring progress.

Exercise M2.6: Contingency Contracting

Goal: This exercise is designed to assist you in understanding and applying contingency contracting.

Step 1: Identify a behavior that you want to change (such as stopping smoking, stopping procrastinating on a project, or having only two alcoholic beverages when you go out).

Step 2: State your behavioral goal.

Step 3: Specify what tasks you need to accomplish to reach your goal.

Step 4: State your time frame for accomplishing the tasks.

Step 5: Specify the means of monitoring your progress toward accomplishing the tasks.

Step 6: Specify how you will reward yourself if you achieve your goal.

Step 7: Specify what you will do whenever you engage in behavior inconsistent with your goal (for example, donating $10.00 to a charity).

IN VIVO DESENSITIZATION[2]

In vivo (from the Latin "in life") *desensitization* is a real-life desensitization process in which a person gradually approaches an actual feared event or stimulus while being in a relaxed state. To carry out in vivo desensitization, the following three steps should be taken:

1. Make a ranked list of fear-producing situations, arranging items from least to most anxiety-producing. (This step is identical to the construction of anxiety hierarchies in systematic desensitization.)
2. Learn to produce or achieve relaxation, perhaps by meditation, deep-breathing relaxation, or imagery relaxation.[3]
3. Gradually approach an actual feared event while remaining relaxed.

A 22-year-old male college student used in vivo desensitization to overcome several situations (themes) connected with a fear of heights. He first became skilled at producing the relaxation response by imagery of his ideal relaxation place. (His ideal relaxation place was lying on the beach in Cabo, Mexico. With practice he became skilled at relaxing himself by fully focusing his thinking on relaxing in Cabo.) He then gradually approached feared situations while remaining in a relaxed state with his imagery of Cabo. For example, he countered his fear of tall buildings by looking out the window in the lower floors and gradually moving upward while thinking about being relaxed in Cabo. He also used this approach to overcome his fears of taking amusement park rides and of flying in small planes.

Watson and Tharp (1972) indicated that in vivo desensitization is an effective method for eliminating fear and anxiety reactions associated with specific stimuli (events).

EXPOSURE THERAPY

Exposure therapy is based on the principle of *extinction*. In exposure therapy, clients expose themselves to stimuli or situations that they previously feared and avoided. The "exposure" can be in real life (*in vivo*) or in fantasy (*in imagino*). In the latter case, clients are asked to imagine themselves in the presence of the feared stimulus (for example, a snake) or in the anxiety-producing situation (for example, giving a presentation in class). The theory behind exposure therapy is that the occurrence of an anxiety response will gradually lessen when the fear-producing stimulus situation is continuously presented in the absence of the reinforcement that perpetuates the fear.

Exposure therapy has been found by researchers to be effective in treating panic disorders, specified phobias, agoraphobia (abnormal fear of crossing or being in open spaces), social phobia, posttraumatic stress disorder, and obsessive-compulsive disorder (Emmelkamp, 1994). Several researchers suggest that

---

[2]Excerpted from Charles Zastrow, "In Vivo Desensitization," in *Talk to Yourself: Using the Power of Self-Talk*, © 1979, pp. 190–193. Reprinted by permission of author.
[3]These three relaxation techniques are described in Chapter 14.

the following features must be present in exposure treatments for the client to achieve maximum benefits (Barlow & Cerny, 1988):

1. Exposure should be of long duration.
2. Exposure should be repeated until all fear and anxiety is eliminated.
3. Exposure should be graduated, starting with low-anxiety stimuli or situations and progressing to high-anxiety stimuli or situations.
4. Clients must attend to the feared stimulus and interact with it as much as possible.
5. Exposure must produce anxiety.

According to exposure therapy, panic attacks or phobias are essentially "false alarms" issued by the body in response to a cue or signal that the client has learned to associate with danger or threat. Through the process of extinction, it is theorized, the anxiety or fear elicited in reaction to the false alarm will gradually subside as the client learns that there is no basis for the fear associated with the false alarm.

A recent innovation with exposure therapy is the use of virtual reality computer-simulated environments. For example, at the University of Washington in Seattle, people with serious fears of spiders are treated by using virtual reality in which they simulate entering a kitchen, chasing a tarantula around a countertop, and flushing it down a sink (Ritter, 2000). At U.S. Department of Veterans Affairs medical centers in Atlanta and Boston, some Vietnam veterans with posttraumatic stress disorder are visiting "Virtual Vietnam," a re-creation of the wartime environment that still haunts them (Ritter, 2000). Virtual reality is also being used to treat a wide variety of other phobias—including fear of flying, fear of public speaking, and fear of heights (Ritter, 2000). The idea is to teach people how to manage fears and then (through virtual reality) take them to whatever situations terrify them. There they learn that they can control their emotions and that these situations are not so scary after all. The advantage of virtual reality is that it can provide the feared environment in the counselor's office, which saves time and money. No more driving to the airport for fear-of-flying treatment!

AVERSIVE TECHNIQUES

An *aversive stimulus* is any stimulus that an organism (person) will avoid or terminate if given the opportunity. Examples include electric shock, unpleasant imagery, holding ones breath, stale cigarette smoke, vile-smelling substances, white noise, and shame.

In a review of aversive methods, Sandler (1986) found aversive therapy has been used to treat self-injurious behavior (such as head banging and self-biting), enuresis, sneezing, stuttering, alcoholism, cigarette smoking, overeating, gambling, sexual deviations (for example, fetishes and transvestism), and aggressive behavior. The following are some illustrations of aversive techniques.

Vogler, Lunde, Johnson, and Martin (1970) served cocktails to alcoholic clients in a simulated lounge arrangement. Each time clients took a drink, they were given an electric shock, and the shock was maintained until they spat out the drink. The investigators did a follow-up and concluded the treatment led to abstinence. Alcoholic clients have also been treated using aversive therapy by giving them an emetic drug (for example, Antabuse) that produces nausea or vomiting when they take a drink. Sometimes the emetic drug is mixed with the drink. This combination of alcohol and emetic is usually given for a week to 10 days. Eventually, just the sight of a drink is sufficient to induce nausea and discomfort in many clients (Phares & Trull, 1997, p. 390).

Positive reinforcement approaches are generally more effective than approaches based on punishment. Punishment is often counterproductive because it can lead to the client's becoming hostile about the treatment procedures. Also, punishment may have only temporary effects. When clients realize they are no longer under surveillance, they may engage in the dysfunctional behavior again. Aversive techniques probably should be used only when all other intervention approaches have failed. In general, aversive procedures should be applied only to people with seriously debilitating problems (such as alcoholism or sexual deviations) and who are in despair because nothing else has worked.

COGNITIVE BEHAVIORAL-MODIFICATION TECHNIQUES

A major trend in behavior therapy in the past four decades has been toward recognizing the role of cognition (thinking processes) in human behavior. Following the observations of cognitive therapists such as

Alben Ellis (1962) and A. T. Beck (1976), cognitive-behavioral therapists have accepted the notion that changing one's thoughts often changes one's feelings and behavior.

The traditional paradigm of behavior therapy has been S (stimulus) $\rightarrow$ R (response). Cognitive-behavioral therapists insert an additional element into this paradigm:[4]

$$S \qquad \rightarrow \qquad O \qquad \rightarrow \qquad R$$

(stimulus)   (cognitions of organism)   (response)

The following techniques developed to change cognitions—thought stopping and covert assertion, diversion, and reframing—are examined in this section.

Thought Stopping and Covert Assertion

Thought stopping helps clients whose major problems involve obsessive thinking and ruminations about events that are very unlikely to occur (such as worrying that a plane they will be taking in 2 weeks will crash or that they are becoming mentally ill). The client is first asked to concentrate on and express aloud her obsessive, anxiety-inducing thoughts. As she begins to express those thoughts, the counselor suddenly and emphatically shouts "Stop." This procedure is repeated several times until the client reports that her thoughts are being successfully interrupted. Then responsibility for the intervention is shifted to the client, so that the client now tells herself "Stop" out loud when she begins to think about the troubling thoughts. Once the overt shouting is effective in stopping the troubling thoughts, the client begins to practice saying "Stop" silently to herself whenever the troubling thoughts begin.

Rimm and Masters (1974) supplemented the thought-stopping technique with covert assertion. In addition to interrupting obsessive thoughts by saying "Stop," the client is encouraged to produce a positive, assertive statement that is incompatible with the content of the obsession. For example, a client who worries about becoming mentally ill (when there is no basis for such thinking) may be encouraged to add the covert assertion "Screw it! I'm perfectly normal" whenever he interrupts the obsessive thinking with "Stop."

Mahoney (1973) successfully used thought stopping and covert assertion as part of a comprehensive program for overweight clients. Mahoney first instructed clients to become aware of such self-statements as "I just don't have the willpower" and "I sure can taste a strawberry sundae." Clients then were trained to use thought stopping and covert assertion to combat these thoughts.

Exercise M2.7: Applying Thought Stopping and Covert Assertion

Goal: This exercise is designed to demonstrate how to use thought stopping and covert assertion.

Step 1:   This may sound strange, but start awfulizing about a current problem in your life. Awfulize for about 5 minutes about this problem. After 5 minutes, yell "Stop" to yourself (either out loud or silently).

Step 2:   Think of a positive, assertive statement that is incompatible with the content of the obsession. From now on, whenever you start awfulizing about your problem, yell "Stop" and use your covert assertion.

Step 3:   Specify what you were awfulizing about.

Step 4:   Specify the covert assertion you came up with.

Step 5:   Indicate whether the thought stopping and covert assertion approach worked for you.

Step 6:   If the technique did not work very well, indicate why you believe it did not.

Diversion

Diversion is used with clients who have strong unwanted emotions such as loneliness, bitterness, depression, frustration, and anger. As indicated in Module 1, unwanted emotions stem primarily from negative and irrational thinking. When clients with unwanted emotions engage in physical activity, work, social interaction, or play, they will usually switch their negative cognitions to more positive cognitions related to the new

---

[4]This paradigm is similar to the paradigm of rational therapists: Events $\rightarrow$ Self-talk $\rightarrow$ Emotion $\rightarrow$ Actions. See Module 1 on rational therapy.

activity. Once they focus their thinking on the diversion activity that they are finding meaningful and enjoyable, they experience more pleasing emotions.

Diversion is used in both rational therapy (see Module 1) and cognitive-behavioral therapy, which are closely related. In fact, rational therapy is often classified as a cognitive-behavioral approach.

Exercise M2.8: Applying the Diversion Technique

Goal: This exercise is designed to demonstrate that most people can change an unwanted emotion by means of diversion.

Step 1:   Think about a situation in your past that you tended to awfulize extensively about, until you used diversion to stop the awfulizing and thereby diverted your thoughts away from the unwanted emotion. (For example, you may have awfulized about someone breaking up with you.)

Step 2:   Specify what you were awfulizing about. Also describe your resulting unwanted emotion(s).

Step 3:   Describe the diversion technique that you used.

Step 4:   Describe the effects of your diversion technique.

Step 5:   Are you willing to try diversion the next time you start awfulizing?

——— Yes   ____ No

Explain your view.

Reframing

Reframing is assisting a client to change cognitions that are causing unwanted emotions or dysfunctional behaviors. There are an infinite number of problematic cognitions that need reframing. Examples of problematic cognitions are the following.

Negative Thinking. When unpleasant events occur (such as receiving a lower grade on an exam than anticipated), we always have the choice of thinking positively or negatively. If we take a positive view and focus on problem solving, we are likely to identify and initiate actions to improve the circumstances. However, if we think negatively, we often develop unwanted emotions (such as depression and frustration) and fail to focus on how to solve the problem. With negative thinking, we may not do anything constructive and may even engage in destructive behavior.

When a client is thinking negatively, a counselor can use reframing to help the client realize he is thinking negatively. At times it is helpful to remind clients that both negative and positive thinking become self-fulfilling prophecies (see Module 1). Then, by asking clients to identify some positive aspects of the situation, counselors assist clients in thinking more positively. (If clients are unable to identify any positives, counselors suggest some.) Clients may then be encouraged to tell themselves "Stop" whenever they begin to think negatively and instead to focus on telling themselves positive aspects of the situation. Some people take a negative view of most events; for such people, reframing through using positive cognitions is difficult and time-consuming. However, if they succeed in learning to think positively, they often make substantial gains.

Awfulizing. When distressing events occur, most of us tend to awfulize—we exaggerate the negatives. When we awfulize, we focus only on the negatives and do not identify constructive actions to improve the situation. When clients are awfulizing, counselors can usually help them identify such thought processes by simply inquiring, "I wonder if you're awfulizing?" Counselors can then assist their clients to give themselves positive cognitions oriented toward problem solving.

When clients awfulize about distressing events that occurred, it is also helpful for the counselor to reframe the awfulizing by relating stories such as "Good luck? Bad luck? Who knows?" (De Mello, 1978):

> There is a Chinese story of an old farmer who had an old horse for tilling his fields. One day the horse escaped into the hills and when all the farmer's neighbors sympathized with the old man over his bad luck, the farmer replied, "Bad luck? Good luck? Who knows?" A week later the horse returned with a herd of wild horses from the hills and this time the neighbors congratulated the farmer on his good luck. His reply was, "Good luck? Bad luck? Who knows?" Then, when the farmer's son was attempting to tame one of the wild horses, he fell off its back and broke his leg. Everyone thought this very bad luck. Not the farmer, whose only reaction was, "Bad luck? Good luck? Who knows?" Some weeks later the army marched into the village and conscripted every able-bodied youth they found there. When they saw the farmer's son with his broken leg, they let him off. Now was that good luck? Bad luck? Who knows? (p. 140)

The point here is that distressing events often are crises but they also frequently lead those involved to make positive changes in their lives.

Catastrophizing. This technique (Beck & Weishaar, 1989) is used when clients are "catastrophizing" over anticipated feared events. Decatastrophizing involves continually asking clients "what if" an anticipated, undesired consequence occurs. The following is a dialogue with a 21-year-old college student who fears expressing his thoughts and feelings in class:

Counselor: What do you think will happen if you begin expressing your views in your classes?

Client: My voice may crack, and the others may laugh at me.

Counselor: It is unlikely that your voice will crack. But even if it does and the students happen to laugh a little, is that really worse than your anger and frustration over not sharing your thoughts?

Client: I don't know.

Counselor: Which is worse when you're asked a question in class? Shrugging your shoulders and appearing tongue-tied, or responding as well as you can even though your voice may crack?

Client: I hear what you're saying.

Counselor: What other negative consequences might occur if you begin expressing yourself in class?

Client: *(pause)* None that I can think of.

Counselor: What positives may come from your speaking up in class?

Client: I'd probably get more out of the class and feel better about myself. Enough of this. I get the message loud and clear. I will commit myself to speaking up at least once a week in each of my classes.

People who catastrophize usually exaggerate the feared consequences. Decatastrophizing demonstrates that even if such consequences occur (which they seldom do), they aren't as severe as feared.

Personal Problem Is Unresolvable. Redefining is used for clients who believe a problem is beyond their personal control (Beck & Weishaar, 1989). A person who believes "Life is boring" may be encouraged to think, "The only reason I'm bored is because I don't have special interests and because I'm not initiating activities. It's not life that is boring; it's my thinking processes that make me feel bored. I need to get involved in activities I enjoy and initiate interactions with people I like." Redefining is accomplished by counselors first demonstrating that emotions, such as boredom, stem primarily from thoughts (see Module 1). Next, counselors demonstrate that if clients think more positively and realistically, they will feel better. Together, client and counselor then identify the negative thinking patterns that are causing clients to believe the problem is beyond their personal control. Finally, they identify cognitions that the client commits to using to counter cognitions that are causing unwanted emotions and ineffective behaviors.

For a listing of additional problematic cognitions that should be reframed, see Exhibit M1.5 Common Beliefs that Generate Negative Self-Talk in Module 1 on rational therapy.

It is somewhat difficult to specify what is and is not a cognitive-behavioral technique. In addition to techniques described here, Cormier and Cormier (1991) identified the following as cognitive-behavioral techniques: role-playing, problem-solving efforts, meditation, muscle relaxation, and paradoxical suggestions (see Module 4). Module 1 notes that changing irrational and negative cognitions may be the key psychotherapeutic change agent. Because practically all effective psychotherapeutic techniques change cognitions, then, in a broad sense, practically all psychotherapeutic techniques can be considered cognitive-behavioral techniques.

Exercise M2.9: Applying Reframing

Goal: This exercise is designed to assist you in understanding and applying reframing.

Step 1:   Specify an unwanted emotion you are currently (occasionally) experiencing or a dysfunctional behavior you sometimes engage in.

Step 2:   Specify the cognitions that underlie your unwanted emotion or dysfunctional behavior.

Step 3:   Specify a "reframe" for each of those cognitions.

Step 4:   When you have this unwanted emotion in the future or when you are tempted to engage in your dysfunctional behavior, do you think it will be useful to focus your thinking by using your specified "reframes"? Explain your views.

EVALUATION OF BEHAVIOR THERAPY

Behavior therapy comprises a range of intervention techniques, some of them more effective than others. Also, behavior therapy rests on a variety of different learning theories, and behaviorists have never agreed on which learning theory should be the main focus of behavior therapy. Particularly controversial among behavior therapists is the learning approach advocated by cognitive-behavioral therapists, that states that emotions and actions are largely determined by our thoughts. Cognitive techniques are incompatible with the traditional principles of behaviorism, which has ignored cognitive processes because they cannot be measured and tested. Traditional behaviorism has endeavored to explain all behavior in terms of stimuli-response connections.

During the past 60 years behavior therapy has experienced a dramatic growth in new treatment techniques and in their adoption by members of the helping professions. Two pivotal books that inspired this development were *Science and Human Behavior* (Skinner, 1953) and *Psychotherapy by Reciprocal Inhibition* (Wolpe, 1958). Behavior therapists have developed, and are continuing to develop, more intervention techniques than therapists in any other psychotherapeutic area are developing.

Behavior therapy is to be highly commended for its emphasis on testing the effectiveness of its intervention techniques. This is consistent with the demand by the public that human services be accountable. Approaches shown to be effective that are widely being used include assertiveness training, behavior rehearsal, contingency contracting, token economies, and systematic desensitization and exposure therapy. The future for behavior therapy is indeed bright. Helping professionals (psychologists, psychiatrists, social workers, guidance counselors, psychiatric nurses) are increasingly being trained in behavior techniques.

Some criticisms can be made of behavior therapy:

1. Research has focused on applying the techniques to problems that are readily tested in laboratory situations, with successful results, but these problems are not the kinds of problems that clients commonly face. As Prochaska (1979) noted,

    > So what if desensitization can reduce a college coed's fear of white rats? Does that have anything to do with the devastating problems that therapists are confronted with daily in their clinical practices? Who ever sees a snake phobic in a clinic? Most behaviorists would do themselves justice when planning a study if they asked the key clinical question for any outcome research—the so-what question. So what if having college students imagine vomiting in their lunches leads to a loss of a pound a week? So what if some of the loss lasts for four months? There is plenty of evidence that eighty-five percent of the people who lose weight through any means regain it within two years. How come only a tiny fraction of their studies use a two-year follow-up? Are the authors more concerned with completing a thesis quickly or rushing to publish than with establishing a really useful therapy? (p. 354)

2. Problems that clients face in the real world often involve arriving at some decision. Should a pregnant 17-year-old teenager have an abortion or carry the pregnancy to full term? How do you get a person with a drinking problem to admit he has a problem and make a decision to seek help? Should sons and daughters of an older parent seek to place him or her in a nursing home? How do you help a teenager who has run away from home make future plans about where to live? Behavior therapy does not help clients arrive at such decisions. The focus of behavior therapy is on changing maladaptive behavior, not on arriving at decisions.

3. Behavior therapy is an amalgam of techniques, which leads to the potential for theoretical chaos. Some techniques are based on operant conditioning, others on classical conditioning and modeling principles, still others on cognitive theories. Phares and Trull (1997) note,

    > Without an integrating theoretical framework, individual clinicians may find themselves flailing about in a morass of competing techniques, each claiming to be forms of behavior therapy. What is needed is a systematic theoretical position that will incorporate the techniques, classify them, and help the clinician decide when and under what conditions to employ one technique over another. Such a theoretical framework would be infinitely more efficient than multiple rules of thumb. (p. 404)

SUMMARY

The following summarizes the module's content in terms of the learning objectives presented at the beginning of the module.

1. Comprehend three learning processes.

   Behavior therapy is based on learning theory. Behavior therapists assume that maladaptive behaviors are acquired primarily through learning and can be modified through additional learning. Numerous learning theories have been developed, and no consensus exists about which learning theory should be the basis of behavior therapy. Intervention techniques are tested with rigorous experimental procedures.

   Behaviorists postulate there are three types of learning processes: operant conditioning, respondent conditioning, and modeling.

2. Understand behavior intervention techniques used by social workers.

   Behavior therapy assumes that all behavior occurs in response to stimulation, internal or external. Behavior therapists do a behavioral analysis, which involves identifying the probable stimulus-response connections of the maladaptive behavior. Behavior therapists attempt to establish working relationships with their clients. Once the behavioral analysis is completed, the findings are discussed with the client, and client and counselor agree on treatment goals.

   This module summarizes the following intervention techniques: assertiveness training; behavior rehearsal; token economies; contingency contracting; in vivo desensitization; exposure therapy; aversive techniques; and cognitive behavioral-modification techniques (including thought stopping and covert assertion; diversion; and reframing).

   The main trend in behavior therapy is growing recognition of the role of cognition in human behavior. Some behavior therapists now identify themselves as cognitive-behavioral therapists and accept the notion that changing thoughts often changes feelings and behaviors. These theorists use techniques such as thought stopping and covert assertion, diversion, and reframing.

EXERCISES

1. Learning to Be Assertive

Goal: This exercise is designed to help students learn how to be assertive in problematic interactions where in the past they were either nonassertive or aggressive.

Step 1:   Describe the purpose of this exercise. Explain the differences between nonassertive, aggressive, and assertive behavior. Indicate that everyone is nonassertive or aggressive in some situations in which it would be more constructive to be assertive. Ask students to silently identify a situation in the past in which they wished they had been assertive rather than aggressive or nonassertive. Give some examples such as the following: The situation may involve being told to do something you did not want to do. Or perhaps someone was smoking a cigarette near you, which bothered you. Or perhaps someone made a put-down comment about you. Or perhaps you're unable to express what you feel about certain situations to your parents or to someone you're dating. Before proceeding further, ask whether the students have identified such a situation in which they wished they had been assertive. Do not proceed to the next step until everyone has identified a situation.

Step 2:   State the following: "We will now do a visualization exercise that is designed to help you learn to be more assertive in the situation you identified. There will be no tricks in this exercise. Close your eyes and keep them closed during this exercise. Get as comfortable as possible in your chair, and slowly take a couple of deep breaths to become relaxed.

   "Focus on a specific incident in your past when you wanted to be assertive but instead were either nonassertive or aggressive. Visualize all the details of what happened. (*Pauses a few seconds after asking each of the following questions.*) What was said to you? What did you fail to say that you wanted to say? What did you say that you didn't want to say? How did you feel about what was said? How do you now feel about this incident? Your nonverbal communication is as important in being assertive as is verbal communication. Think about your nonverbal communication. What did you communicate with your facial expressions? What did you communicate with your body posture? Did you look down or away from the other person? Did you glare at the other person? What did your gestures communicate? What were your voice tone and volume like? Did your voice crack? Did you yell or speak softly? Did you speak rapidly or with hesitation? During this incident, which of your verbal and nonverbal communications were nonassertive? Which were aggressive? Which were assertive?

"Now, let's turn to focus on how to handle this situation more assertively when it arises again. Continue to keep your eyes closed. What might you say that would assertively handle this situation? (*Pause.*) What changes do you need to make in your nonverbal communication to present yourself more assertively? (*Pause.*) Is there someone you know who would be good at handling this situation assertively? (*Pause.*) If there is someone, what would this person say or do? (*Pause.*) Does this assertive model give you some ideas on how you might assertively handle this situation? (*Pause.*)

"Continue to visualize various approaches that might work for you. Also, visualize yourself using each of these approaches. For each approach, imagine the full set of interactions that would occur if you were to use the approach. (*Pause.*)

"Now select an assertive approach that you believe would best work for you when the nonassertive or aggressive situation arises again in the future. Are you now sufficiently prepared and confident to use this approach in a real-life situation? If not, you may want to visualize further what you might say or do to increase your confidence. Or you may want to select another approach that you would be more comfortable in using. Or you may want to role-play your approach with a friend so that you become more comfortable using the approach. (*Pause.*)

"The real test will come when you try out your assertive approach in a real-life situation. The next time your problematic situation arises, use your assertive approach. After trying it out, analyze how it turned out. Pat yourself on the back for what you did well. Identify aspects of your nonverbal and verbal communication that you need to improve to express yourself more assertively. Visualize ways in which you might more assertively express yourself in the areas you need to work on.

"Above all, congratulate yourself on your efforts to become more assertive. You've earned feeling good about yourself. Learning to express yourself in situations that you're comfortable in is one of the greatest thrills you'll ever experience. Okay, gradually open your eyes, and take a little while to relax."

Step 3: Ask whether there are any questions or comments about the exercise. Then ask whether there are any situations students would like to see others in the class role-play. If students suggest some situations, have other students role-play these. If no situations are suggested, ask for volunteers to role-play situations you suggest, such as these:

    a. Ask someone to put out a cigarette that is bothering you.

    b. Refuse to accept an alcoholic drink that a friend wants to buy for you when you prefer not to drink any more alcoholic beverages that day.

    c. Say "no" when someone asks to borrow something you don't want to lend, such as a sweater.

2. Anger Management

Goal: The purpose of this exercise is to help students learn assertive and constructive ways to express their anger.

Step 1: Describe the goal of this exercise. Indicate that many people have not learned to express their anger assertively for a variety of reasons. Some of us have been brought up to believe it is wrong to get angry, so we deny our anger. Some of us, through modeling, have learned to express our anger aggressively, thereby lashing out and hurting others. Indicate that we have a right to all our emotions. It is normal to become angry at times. Others do not have a right to try to convince us that we should not be angry when we are angry.

    When anger is not expressed assertively, it is often expressed destructively. We may aggressively hurt others. Or we may try to deny we are angry and instead turn the anger inward and become depressed. Or we may recognize the anger but fail to express it, which can result in anxiety. Or anger may lead to guilt if we punish ourselves for getting angry when we erroneously believe we should not get angry. Or we may seek to relieve our angry feelings through excessive drinking or eating.

Step 2: Explain that there are assertive and constructive ways to express anger. These ways include the following:

    a. Express angry feelings assertively so no one is hurt. When expressing anger assertively, it is advisable to use non-blaming I-messages rather than you-messages. (See Module 4 for a description of I-messages.)

    b. Express angry feelings at the time we become angry so we do not stew about it. If we delay expressing anger, the hostility may build, and we may explode and lash out at others.

    c. Admit to ourselves when we are angry, so that we do not try to hide our anger from ourselves. Through acknowledging our anger, we are better able to focus on finding constructive ways to express our anger.

    d. Blow off steam nondestructively through physical activities such as jogging, hitting a pillow or a punching bag, taking a walk, or lifting weights whenever it is counterproductive to express our anger or when we feel we seem about to explode.

    e. Seek to counter negative and irrational self-talk by writing out a rational self-analysis (see Module 1).

Step 3: Ask each student to complete the following three statements on a sheet of paper:

       a. Three or four things that make me angry are
       b I usually express my anger by
       c. Things that I can do to better handle and express my anger are

Step 4: Have students form subgroups of three people each to share what they wrote and to receive additional suggestions on how to express their anger more effectively. (Indicate that students have a right to privacy and therefore do not have to self-disclose anything they want to keep private.)

Step 5: Form a circle and ask students whether they have any questions or comments about the exercise or about what was discussed in the subgroups.

3. Reframing

Goal: This exercise is designed to demonstrate to students how to reframe cognitions resulting from awfulizing.

Step 1: Describe the technique of reframing, and illustrate the process of awfulizing by giving a few examples of occasions in which you awfulized.

Step 2: Instruct each student to record his or her responses to the following questions and instructions on a sheet of paper. Indicate that students will not be required to reveal their responses.

       a. Briefly describe a distressing event over which you awfulized.
       b. Specify your awfulizing cognitions about this distressing event.
       c. For each awfulizing cognition, specify a more positive and realistic cognition that you could give yourself about this event. (Ideally, many of these countering cognitions will facilitate problem solving.)
       d. Indicate the approximate length of time that you awfulized over this event.
       e. Are you still awfulizing about this event?
       f. Do you believe that countering the awfulizing cognitions with more positive and realistic cognitions would have shortened the time you spent awfulizing?

Step 3: Ask for volunteers to share their responses to those questions. End by asking students to indicate their thoughts on the merits and shortcomings of the use of reframing in therapy.

REALITY THERAPY

Reality therapy is based on choice theory. The approach emphasizes the importance of relationships and also asserts that there are dynamic interactions between our thoughts, emotions, actions, and physiology. This module will help prepare students to:

Comprehend reality therapy

WILLIAM GLASSER

The founder of reality therapy is William Glasser (1925–2013). Glasser developed two versions of reality therapy. The first, developed in the 1960s, is based on identity theory (Glasser, 1965). The second, developed during the past two decades, is based on choice theory (Glasser, 1998). This second version is described in this module.

Glasser is an internationally recognized psychiatrist. He graduated from Case Western Reserve Medical School in Cleveland, Ohio, in 1953. In 1956, he became a consulting psychiatrist to the Ventura School for Girls, a California state institution for the treatment of delinquent girls. Glasser grew skeptical of the value of orthodox psychoanalysis. At the Ventura School, he set up a new treatment program based on the principles of his reality therapy. The program showed promise, and participants expressed enthusiasm. In 1966, Glasser began consulting in the California school system and applied the concepts of reality therapy to education. His emphasis on the need for schools to highlight involvement, relevance, and thinking continues to have a profound impact on the educational system.

Glasser does not believe in the concept of mental illness. His point of view on mental illness is presented later in this chapter. He has written more than 20 books. In 1967, he founded the Institute for Reality Therapy, which has trained over 60,000 people worldwide in reality therapy. In recent years, Glasser's major focus has been to teach the world his views on choice theory, the new psychology described in this module.

OVERVIEW OF CHOICE THEORY

Choice theory is an *internal* control psychology: It explains why and how we make the choices that determine the course of our lives. According to Glasser (1998), we choose everything we do. A major assumption of choice theory is that we carry around in our heads pictures of what reality is like and of how we would like it to be. Glasser (1984, p. 32) asserts, "All our behavior is our constant attempt to reduce the difference between what we want (the pictures in our heads) and what we have (the way we see situations in the world.)" By *pictures*, Glasser means *perceptions* from our senses of sight, hearing, touch, smell, and taste. Some examples will clarify this idea. Each of us has a detailed idea of the type of person we would like to date or form a relationship with; when we find someone who closely matches these characteristics, we seek to form a relationship. Each of us carries around a mental picture album of our favorite foods; when we're hungry, we select an item and go about obtaining that food.

How do we develop these pictures/albums/ideas that we believe will satisfy our needs? According to Glasser, we begin to create our albums at an early age (perhaps even before birth), and we spend our whole life enlarging them. Essentially, whenever what we do gets us something that satisfies a need, we store the picture of it in our personal albums. Glasser (1984) gives the following example of this process by describing how a hungry child added chocolate-chip cookies to his picture album:

> Suppose you had a grandson and your daughter left you in charge while he was taking a nap. She said she would be right back, because be would be ravenous when he awoke and she knew you had no idea what to feed an eleven-month-old child. She was right. As soon as she left, he awoke screaming his head off, obviously starved. You tried a bottle, but he rejected it—he had something more substantial in mind. But what? Being unused to a howling baby, and desperate, you tried a chocolate-chip cookie and it worked wonders. At first, he did not seem to know what it was, but he was a quick learner. He quickly polished off three cookies. She returned and almost polished you off for being so stupid as to give a baby chocolate. "Now," she said, "he will be yelling all day for those cookies." She was right. If he is like most of us, he will probably have chocolate on his mind for the rest of his life. (p. 19)

When this child learned how satisfying chocolate-chip cookies are, he placed the picture of these cookies in his personal picture album.

The pictures in our albums do not have to be rational. Anorexics picture themselves as fat and starve themselves to come closer to their irrational picture of unhealthy thinness. Rapists have pictures of satisfying their power needs and perhaps sexual needs through sexual assault. To change a picture, we must replace it with one that will reasonably satisfy the need in question. People who are unable to replace a picture may endure a lifetime of misery. Some battered women, for example, endure brutal beatings and humiliations in marriage because they cannot picture themselves as worthy of a loving relationship.

Glasser notes that whenever the picture we see and the one we want to see differ, a *signal* generated by this difference leads us to behave in a way that will obtain the picture we want. We examine our behaviors and choose one or more that we believe will help us reduce this difference. These behaviors include straightforward problem-solving efforts as well as manipulative strategies such as anger, pouting, and guilt. People who act irresponsibly or ineffectually either have failed to choose responsible behaviors from their repertoires or have not yet learned responsible courses of action.

Glasser believes we are driven by five innate needs and that as soon as one need is satisfied another need or perhaps two or more needs acting together push for satisfaction. Our first need is *survival.* This includes such vital functions as breathing, digesting food, sweating, regulating blood pressure, and meeting the demands of hunger, thirst, and sex. Our second need is *love and belonging.* We generally meet this need through family, friends, pets, plans, and material possessions.

Our third need is *power.* Glasser says this need involves getting others to obey us and to then receive the esteem and recognition that accompanies power. Our drive for power sometimes conflicts with our need to belong. Two people in a relationship may struggle to control it rather than create an equalitarian relationship.

Our fourth need is *freedom.* People want the freedom to choose how they live their lives, to express themselves, to read and write what they choose, to associate with whom they select, and to worship or not worship as they believe.

Our fifth need is *fun.* Glasser believes learning is often fun; it gives us a great incentive to assimilate what we need to satisfy our needs. Classes that are grim and boring are major failings of our educational system. Laughing and humor help fulfill our needs for fun. Fun is such a vital part of living that most of us have trouble conceiving of life without it.

AXIOMS OF CHOICE THEORY

Glasser has a list of principles of choice theory. He calls these principles "axioms." A summary of these axioms follows:

1. The only person whose behavior we can control is our own. No one can make us do anything we do not want to do—as long as we are willing to endure the consequences: punishment for not doing what others want us to do. If we choose to do what others want us to do under the threat of severe punishment, we tend to become passive-aggressive and not perform very well. When we try to force others to do what they do not want to do, they may choose not to do it—or resort to passive aggression and not perform well.

Exercise M3.1: Seeking to Change Someone and Being Controlled by Someone

Goal: This exercise is designed to illustrate that we are inclined to attempt to change others and that others sometimes attempt to control us. The consequences of attempting to control others are also examined.

Step 1:   Describe a situation in which you attempted to change someone's behavior—perhaps the irritating actions of someone you were dating.

Step 2:   Were you successful in changing the behavior of this person? What were the emotional reactions of this person to your attempts at change?

Step 3:   If the person changed the behavior that you found irritating, do you think the change occurred because you forced this person to change or because he or she "chose" to change?

Step 4:   Describe a situation in which someone (perhaps a parent or someone you were dating) sought to change some behavior of yours that he or she found irritating.

Step 5:   Did you change your behavior? How did you feel about someone trying to change (or control) you?

Step 6:   If you changed the behavior, did you do so because someone forced you to change or because you "chose" to change?

Note: Isn't it interesting that we think we have a right to attempt to change irritating behavior of people we are dating, but we don't like others to attempt to change us!

2.   All we can give to or get from other people is information. How each person deals with that information is his or her own choice. For example, a teacher can assign readings but is not responsible if some students choose to ignore the assignment. The teacher should not feel personally responsible for students who choose not to do the reading. The teacher, of course, can choose the consequences that students who fail to do the assignment will face—such as lower grades.

3.   According to Glasser, all we can do from birth to death is "behave," and behavior consists of four inseparable components: acting, thinking, feeling, and physiology. Each of these components of what Glasser terms "total behavior" interacts with and affects the other three. (Axioms 4 and 5 elaborate on this interaction.)

4.   All long-lasting psychological problems are relationship problems. Our usual way of dealing with an important relationship that is not working out the way we want it to is to choose misery—emotional misery and physical misery. Relationship problems are a partial cause of many other problems, such as fatigue, pain, weakness, and autoimmune diseases (such as fibromyalgia and rheumatoid arthritis). Glasser (1998) states,

> Most doctors believe that adult rheumatoid arthritis is caused by the victims' immune systems attacking their own joints as if these joints were foreign bodies. Another way of putting it is that their own creative systems are trying to protect these people from a perceived harm. If we could figure out a way to stop this misguided creativity, millions of people who suffer from this disease and a host of other relentless diseases, called autoimmune diseases, could be helped. (pp. 137–138)

5.   The human brain is very creative. A woman who was sexually abused as a child may develop a dissociative identity disorder to psychologically shield herself from the emotional pain of the abuse. Glasser believes that almost all medical problems for which physicians are unable to identify a cause are partially created by the ill person's brain to deal with the unhappiness that the person is experiencing. Unhappiness is the force that inspires the creativity inherent in the brain to be a partial cause of symptoms described in the *DSM-IV* (American Psychiatric Association, 2000): aches and pains (such as migraine headaches), physical illnesses (such as heart disease, cancer, adult asthma, and eczema).

Regarding the brain creating the symptoms in the *DSM-IV*, Glasser (2003) describes how unhappiness may lead the brain to create hallucinations:

> Suppose, instead of your creativity presenting an idea to you as a thought, it created a voice uttering a threat or any other message directly into the auditory cortex of your brain. You would hear an actual voice or voices; it could be a stranger or you might recognize whose voice it was. It would be impossible, just by hearing it, for you to tell it from an actual voice or voices. (p. 114)

Because we can hear voices, our brain can create voices that we hear when no one else is around. Because we can see, our brain can create visual hallucinations. Because we can feel pain, our brain can create pain—perhaps in greater severity and duration than what we experience from an injury or illness. Because we are able to fear, our brain can and does create disabling phobias. (See Exhibit M3.1.)

Exercise M3.2: The Creativity in Our Brains

Goal: This exercise is designed to assist you in understanding that our thoughts are sometimes a cause of somatic problems, emotional difficulties, and behavioral dysfunctions.

Step 1: Identify a somatic problem (such as migraine headaches) of unknown physical cause that you or someone close to you has. Speculate how thoughts may be a factor in causing the somatic problem.

Step 2: Identify an emotional or behavioral problem that you or someone close to you has. Speculate on how thoughts contributed to this emotional or behavioral problem.

Exhibit M3.1   Our Thoughts Impact Our Physiological Functioning: Healing Thoughts versus Disease-Facilitating Thoughts

Diseases and medical conditions are caused by a variety of factors: what we eat; exposure to germs, viruses, and bacteria; genetics; too much or too little exposure to sun; lack of exercise; lack of sleep; and thoughts. The following are examples of how our thoughts impact our physiological functioning.

1. Under hypnosis, "I will feel no pain" → painless surgery without anesthesia
2. Under hypnosis, "Something hot is burning my arm" → blister
3. Deep-breathing relaxation, "I am relaxing" → painless dental drilling without anesthesia
4. "I no longer want to live" → death within a few years
5. "I don't want to die yet" → a person ravaged by cancer continues to live
6. When I have a cold, the thought "I must get all these things done" → cold lasts for weeks
   When I have a cold, the thought "I will take time off to rest and relax" → cold lasts for only a few days
7. Hangover, "My head is killing me" → intense headache
   Hangover, "I will relax and ignore the pain in my head" → headache soon subsides (the same is true for most other headaches)
8. "I am worried about such and such," or "I have *so* much to do tomorrow" → unable to fall asleep
9. "I will have serious complications if I have this surgery" → complications likely
10. "The plane I'm going to fly on is going to crash" → anxiety, panic attacks (panic attacks, if frequent, will lead to a variety of illnesses, including hypertension and heart problems)
11. A woman thinks she is pregnant but isn't → morning sickness and enlarged belly
12. Relaxing thoughts → immune system functions well, fights off illnesses, and facilitates healing

13. Alarming thoughts (such as "I miss ____ *so much!*" → high stress level → various illnesses, such as heart problems, colitis, stomach problems, skin rashes, ulcers, aches and pains, headaches, cancer, colds, and flu. (Immune system is suppressed when a person experiences high levels of stress.)
14. "I will do well today in this sport, by focusing on ____" → success at tennis, golf, bowling, baseball, etc.
15. "I am too fat; but by controlling my eating, I can control part of my life" anorexia and various health problems
16. "By throwing up after eating, I can maintain my weight and figure and also enjoy the taste of food" → bulimia and various health problems
17. "I need several drinks each day to get through the day and numb my pain" → alcoholism
18. "I love food *so much that I don't care what happens to me*" → compulsive overeating, obesity, diabetes, and various other health problems
19. "I need to get more work done, in a shorter time, for the next 10 years" → Type A personality, hypertension, heart problems, and strokes
20. "I'll never forgive ____ for what s/he did," or "I'll get even with her/him if it's the last thing I do" → hostility and heart problems and strokes
21. "Sex is disgusting," or "My partner stinks," or "My partner is inept at lovemaking" → lack of sexual arousal and other sexual dysfunctions

Note: Module 1 demonstrates that all our emotions and all our actions/behaviors are largely determined by our thoughts. Module 3 suggests our thoughts have a major impact on our physiological functioning. It appears our thoughts have a major impact on our lives!

6. Barring untreatable physical illnesses or severe poverty, unsatisfying relationships are the primary source of crimes, addictions, and emotional and behavioral disorders.
7. It is a serious mistake (and irrational to expect positive results) to seek to control others by nagging, preaching, punishing, or threatening to punish them. As indicated earlier, the only person we can effectively control is ourself. To progress in improving human relationships, we need to give up seeking to control others through nagging, preaching, putting down, or threatening punishment.

Exercise M3.3: The Effects of Nagging and Preaching

Goal: This exercise is designed to increase your awareness of the effects of nagging, preaching, put-downs, or threats of punishment.

Step 1: Describe a situation in which someone tried to control you by nagging, preaching, putting you down, or threatening punishment.

Step 2: How did you feel about someone attempting to control you with those external control strategies?

Step 3: Did you change your behavior? If you did, was it because you were forced to change or because you "chose" to change?

Step 4: Describe a situation in which you attempted to change someone by nagging, preaching, put-downs, or threats of punishment.

Step 5: How did that person emotionally react to your external control attempts?

Step 6: Did that person change his or her behavior? If the person did change, was it because you forced him or her to change or because he or she "chose" to change?

8. The unsatisfying (problematic) relationship is always a current one. We cannot live happily without at least one satisfying relationship. In a quality relationship between two people, each person seeks to meet his or her own needs and wants and those of the other person too.
9. The *solving circle* is a good strategy for two people who know choice theory to use to redefine their freedom and improve their relationship. Glasser advocates its use in marital and dating relationships. Each person pictures his or her relationship inside a large circle—the solving circle. An imaginary circle is drawn on the floor. Each person sits on a chair within the circle. The two persons are told there are three entities in the solving circle: the two persons and the relationship itself. The two persons are asked to agree that maintaining the relationship takes precedence over what each person wants. In the circle, each person tells the other what he or she will agree to do to help the relationship. Within those limits, the two persons must reach a compromise on their conflicts.
10. Painful events that happened in the past have a great deal to do with what we are today, but dwelling on the painful past contributes little or nothing to what we need to do now—which is to improve an important, present relationship.

Exercise M3.4: Improving an Unhappy Relationship

Goal: This exercise is designed to assist you in improving, through problem solving, a significant relationship in your life.

Step 1: Identify and briefly describe a significant relationship in your life that you would like to improve.

Step 2: Do you believe the unhappy components in this relationship may be having an adverse impact on your physical or mental well-being? Please explain. (If you cannot identify a problematic current relationship, describe a past unhappy relationship and indicate how it negatively affected your physical and mental well-being.)

Step 3: Speculate about what you might do to improve a current problematic relationship.

11. It is not necessary to know our past before we can deal with the present. It is good to revisit the pans of our past that were satisfying, but it is even better to let go of what was unhappy.

Exercise M3.5: Letting Go of Grudges

Goal: This exercise is designed to assist you in letting go of strong feelings of being wronged by others.

Step 1: Describe a situation that you still awfulize about in which you feel that someone severely wronged you.

Step 2: Does it do you any good to continue to awfulize about this? Research shows hostility toward others is a major factor leading to heart disease and other stress-related illnesses (Leyden-Rubenstein, 1998). By holding a grudge, are you not adversely impacting your physical and mental well-being? Speculate about how holding a grudge may currently be affecting you.

Step 3: Speculate about what you can do to let go of this grudge.

12. We can satisfy our basic needs only by satisfying one or more pictures in our "quality world." Our quality world consists of three kinds of need-satisfying pictures: people (such as parents), things (such as a car and clothes), and beliefs (such as our religious and political beliefs). We experience the most freedom when we are able to satisfy one or more pictures in our quality world. We give up part of our freedom when we put pictures into our quality world that we cannot satisfy.

13. When we have difficulty in getting along with other people, we usually make the mistake of choosing to employ *external control psychology.* We attempt to coerce or control others by nagging, preaching, moralizing, criticizing, or using put-down messages.

14. Because relationships are central to human happiness, improving our emotional and physical well-being involves exploring how we relate to others and looking for ways to improve how we relate to others (particularly those people to whom we feel closest).

15. It is therapeutic to discuss our "total behavior" by means of verbs. For example, it is much more accurate to say "I am choosing to depress" or "I am depressing" than to think "I am suffering from depression" or "I am depressed." When we say "I am depressing," we are immediately aware that we are choosing to depress and have the option to do and feel something else (such as "I will go golfing and enjoy the day.") People who say "I am depressed" mistakenly tend to believe the depressing is beyond their control. In addition, they are likely to mistakenly believe the depressing has been caused by what someone else has done to them. To recognize that we have the power to choose to stop depressing (or to stop angering or frustrating, and so on) is a wonderful freedom that people who adhere to the view that they are largely controlled by others will never have.

Exercise M3.6: Expressing Negative Emotions by Means of Verbs

Goal: This exercise is designed to demonstrate that expressing our negative emotions by means of verbs assists us in recognizing that we are *choosing* to feel a certain way and could *choose* to feel positive emotions instead.

Step 1: List all the negative emotions you have felt in the past week.

Step 2: Rephrase all these negative emotions by means of verbs—for example, "I am angering" instead of "I am angry"

Step 3: Does this exercise help you to understand that we *choose* to feel negative emotions and could choose to feel positive ones instead? Explain your thoughts on this.

16. All four components of behavior (thinking, feeling, acting, and physiology) are subject to choice, but we have direct control over only the acting and thinking components. We do, however, control our physiology and our feelings through how we choose to act and think. It is not easy to change our actions and thoughts, but when we succeed in coming up with more satisfying actions and thoughts, we gain a great deal of personal freedom.

Exercise M3.7: Changing Our Feelings and Improving Somatic Problems

Goal: This exercise is designed to demonstrate that negative emotions can be changed and some somatic problems can be improved by changing our thoughts and actions.

Step 1: Describe how you changed a negative emotion by changing your thoughts or actions.

Step 2: Describe how you improved a somatic problem (perhaps a headache) by changing your thoughts or actions.

17. Whenever you feel as if you lack the freedom you want in a relationship, it is because you, your partner, or both of you are unwilling to accept a key axiom of choice theory: *Only you can control your own life.* The more both you and your partner learn choice theory, the better you will get along with one another. Choice theory supports the golden rule.

18. People choose (although some are unaware of their choice) to play the mentally ill roles that are described in the *DSM-5* (American Psychiatric Association, 2013). These people have the symptoms described in the *DSM-5*, but they are not mentally ill (if mental illness is defined as a disease of the mind). These people do not have an untreatable or incurable mental illness. The symptoms are only an indication that these people are not as healthy as they could learn to be. See Exhibit M3.2 and Case Example "Reality Therapy."

Exhibit M3.2   Two Approaches to Mental Illness

Much of the language relating to emotional disturbances is a familiar part of our lexicon. We use *crazy, psychotic, neurotic, nervous breakdown, insane, sick, uptight,* and *mad* to express judgments (often unfavorable) about unusual behavior or unusual emotions. Whatever term we use, we often have only a vague idea of its technical meaning. Amazingly, though, we act as if the label is completely accurate and then relate to the person as if the label is absolutely correct. However, we all know it is impossible to define these terms precisely.

Helping professionals use two approaches to diagnose people who display emotional disturbances and abnormal behaviors: the medical model and the interactional model.

Medical Model

This model presents emotional and behavioral problems as illnesses comparable to physical illness. Mental illness labels use medical terminology (for example, *schizophrenia, paranoia, psychosis,* or *insanity*) to describe emotional problems. Adherents of this approach believe the disturbed person's mind is affected by an internal condition. This condition, they assert, results from genetic endowment, metabolic disorders, infectious diseases, internal conflicts, chemical imbalances, unconscious use of defense mechanisms, or traumatic early experiences.

The medical model has a lengthy classification of mental disorders defined by the American Psychiatric Association. (See Chapter 1 for a summary of the numerous specific mental disorders that are classified in *DSM-IV* [American Psychiatric Association, 2000].)

The medical model arose in reaction to the historical notion that the emotionally disturbed were possessed by demons and could therefore be blamed for their disturbances. The medical model treats the disturbed as in need of help and has stimulated enormous amounts of research into the nature of emotional problems. Therapeutic approaches owe their development to the medical model.

Interactional Model

Critics of the medical model assert that medical labels have no diagnostic or treatment value and may actually have an adverse effect. Thomas Szasz (1961) was one of the first authorities to assert that mental illness is a myth—that it does not exist. Szasz's theory is interactional; it focuses on the processes of everyday social interaction and the effects of labeling.

Beginning with the assumption that the term *mental illness* implies a "disease of the mind," Szasz categorized all so-called mental illnesses into three types of emotional and behavioral disorders and discussed the inappropriateness of calling them "mental illnesses":

1. *Personal disabilities,* such as excessive anxiety, depression, fears, and feelings of inadequacy. Szasz said such so-called mental illnesses may be appropriately considered "mental" (in the sense that thinking and feeling are "mental" activities), but he asserts that they are not diseases.

2. *Antisocial acts,* such as bizarre homicides and social deviations. (Homosexuality used to be listed in this category but was removed from the American Psychiatric Associations list of mental illnesses in 1974.) Szasz said such antisocial acts are actually social deviations and not "mental" or "diseases."

3. *Deterioration of the brain with associated personality changes.* This category includes the "mental illnesses" in which personality changes result from brain deterioration caused by arteriosclerosis, chronic alcoholism, AIDS. general paresis, or serious brain injury. Common symptoms are loss of memory, listlessness, apathy, and deterioration of personal grooming habits. Szasz says these disorders can appropriately be considered "diseases" but are diseases of the brain rather than of the *mind.*

Szasz (1961) asserted that calling people with emotional problems "mentally ill" is as absurd as calling the emotionally disturbed "possessed":

> The belief in mental illness as something other than man's trouble in getting along with his fellow man is the proper heir to the belief in demonology and witchcraft. Mental illness exists or is "real" in exactly the same sense in which witches existed or were "real." (p. 84)

In reality, being labeled "mentally ill" occurs in three steps: the person displays some deviant behavior; the behavior is not tolerated by the family or community; and the professional labeler, usually a psychiatrist, believes in the medical model and assigns a mental illness label. Scheff (1966) and Mechanic (1962) offered evidence that family and community intolerance of deviant behavior and the professional labelers' belief in the

Exhibit M3.2   *(continued)*

medical model are more crucial than the behavior itself in determining whether someone will be labeled "mentally ill."

The point here is that people have emotional problems, not mystic "mental illnesses." Thus, reality therapists use the following terms to describe behavior: *depression, anxiety, obsession, compulsive, excessive fear, feelings of failure.* These are personal problems, not illnesses. Medical terms (for example, *schizophrenia* or *psychosis*) are not useful because no distinguishing symptom indicates whether a person has or does not have the "illness." In addition, Rosenhan and Seligman (1995) pointed out that considerable variation exists among cultures regarding what is mental illness. Indeed, psychiatrists themselves frequently disagree in their "medical" diagnoses.

In a dramatic study, psychologist David Rosenhan (1973) demonstrated that professional staff in mental hospitals could not distinguish between "sane" and "insane" people. Rosenhan and seven "normal" associates went to 12 mental hospitals in five different states and claimed to hear voices. After they were admitted, these pseudopatients said they had stopped hearing the voices. Although they then began to behave completely normally, the hospital personnel were unable to recognize the difference between their sanity and the "insanity" of the other patients. The pseudopatients were confined to the hospitals for an average of 19 days and then discharged with a diagnosis of "schizophrenia in remission."

Medical labels have several adverse labeling effects. People who are labeled *mentally ill* (and frequently their therapists) believe that they have a disease for which unfortunately there is no known "cure." The label gives them an excuse for not taking responsibility for their actions (for example, innocent by reason of insanity). Because there is no known "cure," the disturbed frequently idle away their time waiting for someone to discover a cure rather than assuming responsibility for their behavior, examining the reasons for their problems, and making efforts to improve. Other undesirable consequences of the label *mentally ill* are that those so labeled lose legal rights; can be stigmatized as dangerous, unpredictable, untrustworthy, or of "weak" character; and find it more difficult to secure employment or receive a promotion (Rosenhan & Seligman, 1995).

An even more harmful effect is that "mentally ill" people view themselves as different and therefore play the role of the "sick" person. Everyone needs to evaluate feelings, opinions, and abilities. In the absence of objective, nonsocial criteria, people rely on other people to gauge the validity of their beliefs and feelings. If others define us as mentally ill and react to us accordingly, we may begin to say, "I must be crazy, because other people treat me as if I were insane."

Authorities who adhere to the interactional model raise a key question, because expectations generally guide behavior: "If we relate to people with emotional problems as mentally ill, how can we expect them to act in emotionally healthy and responsible ways?" Also, a diagnosis of mental illness carries a greater stigma than does one of physical illness.

Szasz (1967) also argued that the mental model is used (perhaps unintentionally) to control people who do not conform to social expectations. The former Soviet Union had a long history of labeling dissenters (including poets, writers, and intellectuals who would be respected in this country) as mentally ill and sending them to concentration camps or to insane asylums. In the past, psychiatrists in Russia often concluded that people who did not accept Marxist-Leninist philosophy were psychologically impaired. Are some psychiatrists using the mental illness label to control the behavior of nonconformists in our country? Szasz (1967) asserted that they are. As an example, he cited listing homosexuality as a mental disorder by the American Psychiatric Association. As another example, Szasz (1963) quoted Dana L. Farnsworth, a Harvard psychiatrist and an authority on college psychiatric services:

> Library vandalism, cheating and plagiarism, stealing in the college or community stores or in the dormitories, unacceptable or antisocial sexual practices (overt homosexuality, exhibitionism, promiscuity), and the unwise and unregulated use of harmful drugs are examples of behavior that suggest the presence of emotionally unstable persons. (p. 76)

Mental illness labels have a "boundary" effect, defining what behaviors a society considers "sick" and pressuring citizens to avoid such behaviors. Szasz's point is that nonconformists can be adversely affected by the use of the medical model.

Labeling as the Primary Cause of Chronic "Mental Illness"

We must, of course, ask "If mental illness does not exist, why do some people go through life as if they were mentally ill?" Scheff's theory (1966) provides an answer. Scheff hypothesizes that labeling is the most important determinant of chronic functional "mental illness."

Scheff began by first arriving at a definition of *mental illness:*

> One source of immediate embarrassment to any social theory of "mental illness" is that the terms used in referring to these phenomena in our society prejudge the issue. The medical metaphor "mental illness" suggests a determinant process which occurs within the individual: the unfolding and development of disease. In order to avoid this assumption, we will utilize sociological, rather than medical concepts to formulate the problem. (p. 31)

The symptoms of mental illness can thus be viewed as violations of social norms. For Scheff's purposes the term *mental illness* refers to persons assigned this label by professionals.

Literally thousands of studies have been conducted to identify the origins of long-term mental disorders. Practically all of these studies identified the causes as somewhere inside a person (for example, metabolic disorders, unconscious conflicts, heredity factors). These research efforts are based on medical and psychological models of human behavior. Yet, amazingly, despite this extensive research, the determinants of chronic mental disorders (such as schizophrenia) are largely unknown. Scheff suggested that the major determinants are not medical but are our social processes (that is, our interactions with others).

Exhibit M3.2 (*continued*)

Scheff's theory is summarized here. Everyone, at times, violates social norms and commits acts that could be labeled symptoms of mental illness. For example, a person may on occasion angrily engage in fights with others, or experience intense depression or grief, or be highly anxious, or use drugs or alcohol to excess, or have a fetish, or be an exhibitionist, or commit a highly unusual and bizarre act.

Usually the person who has unwanted emotions or who commits deviant acts is not identified (labeled) as being mentally ill. In such cases, the unwanted emotions and deviant actions are usually not classified as symptoms of a mental illness but instead are ignored, unrecognized, or rationalized in some other manner.

Occasionally, however, such norm violations are perceived by others as being "abnormal." The offenders are then labeled *mentally ill* and consequently related to as if they are mentally ill. When people arc publicly labeled, they are highly suggestible to cues from others. They realize they have done something unusual and turn to others to obtain an assessment of who they really are. In the absence of objective measures of their sanity, they rely on others for this assessment. If others relate to them as if they are mentally ill, they begin to define and perceive themselves as being mentally ill.

Traditional stereotypes of mental illness define the mentally ill role, both for those who are labeled mentally ill and for people they interact with. Frequently people they interact with reward them for enacting the social role of being mentally ill. The rewards may be sympathy and attention, such as not having to hold a job or not being held responsible for wrongdoing, or they fulfill the requirements of other roles.

In addition, the "mentally ill" are punished for attempting to return to conventional roles. They are viewed with suspicion and have considerable difficulty obtaining employment.

The effect of all this is a gradual change in one's self-concept. People thus labeled begin to view themselves as different, as insane, and a vicious circle is created. The more one enacts the role of being mentally ill, the more one is defined and treated as mentally ill, and so on. Unless interrupted, the cycle leads to a "career" of long-term mental illness. Scheff concluded that with this process, labeling is the single most important determinant of chronic mental illness.

If labeling is an important determinant of chronic functional mental illness, significant changes are suggested in certain diagnostic and treatment practices. Mental health personnel are frequently faced with uncertainty in deciding whether a person has a mental disorder. An informal norm has been developed to handle this uncertainty: When in doubt, it is better to judge a well person ill than to judge an ill person well. This norm is based on two assumptions taken from treating physical illness: (1) A diagnosis of illness results in only minimal damage to the status and reputation of a person. (2) Unless the illness is treated, the illness will become progressively worse. However, both of these assumptions are questionable. Unlike medical treatment, psychiatric treatment can drastically change a person's status in the community; for example, it can remove rights that are difficult to regain. Furthermore, if Scheff is right that labeling is the key determinant in leading to long-term mental illness, the exact opposite norm should be established ro handle uncertainty— namely, when in doubt, do not label a person mentally ill. This would be in accord with the legal approach that follows the norm "When in doubt, acquit" or "A person is innocent until proven guilty."

If labeling is indeed a major determinant of mental illness, certain changes are also suggested in treating violators of social norms. One is to attempt to maintain people with problems in their local community without labeling them *mentally ill* or sending them to a mental hospital, where their playing the role of the mentally ill is likely to be reinforced. In the past few decades, the field of mental hygiene has been moving in this direction. Another outgrowth of Scheff's theory would be increasing public education efforts to inform the general public of the nature of emotional and behavioral problems and the adverse effects that result from inappropriate labeling.

The adverse effects of labeling ultimately raise the issue of the value of labeling anyone mentally ill.

Source: This material is adapted from the following articles: (1) Charles Zastrow, "When Labeled Mentally Ill," in *The Personal Problem Solver,* edited by Charles Zastrow and Dae H. Chang, © 1977, pp. 163–169. Adapted by permission of Prentice-Hall, Inc., Englewood Cliffs, New Jersey; (2) Charles Zastrow, "Understanding Deviant Behavior," in *Talk to Yourself: Using the Power of Self-Talk,* © 1979, pp. 117–124. Reprinted by permission of the author.

CASE EXAMPLE   REALITY THERAPY

A number of years ago when I [the author] was employed as a social worker at a maximum security hospital for the criminally insane, my supervisor asked me to develop and lead a therapy group. When I wondered aloud who should be in the group and what its objectives should be, my supervisor indicated those decisions would be mine. He added that no one else was doing group therapy at the hospital and that the hospital administration thought it would be desirable to develop such a program.

Being newly employed at the hospital and wary because I had never been a group leader before, I asked myself, "Who is in the greatest need of group therapy?" and "If the group members do not improve, or even deteriorate, how will I be able to explain this—that is, cover my tracks?" I concluded that I should select those identified as being most ill (those labeled *chronic schizophrenics*). Because such patients are generally expected to show little improvement, I felt I would not be blamed if group members

CASE EXAMPLE   *(continued)*

did not improve. However, if they did improve, I thought it would be viewed as a substantial accomplishment.

First I read the case records of the 11 residents who were diagnosed as chronic schizophrenics. I then met individually with each of these residents to invite them to join the group. (To my surprise, each of the residents appeared to be very different from the impressions I received from reading the case records.) I explained the purpose of the group and the probable topics to be covered. Eight of the 11 who were contacted decided to join; some frankly stated they would join primarily because it would look good on their records and increase their chances for an early release.

The approach I used in counseling these group members was based on reality therapy. I began the first group meeting by stating I knew what the "key" was to their being discharged from the hospital and asked if they knew what that might be. This statement got their attention. I indicated that the key was very simple—they had to learn to "act sane" so that the medical staff would think they had recovered. At the first meeting the purpose and the focus of the group were presented and described. Our purpose was not to review the past but to make life in the present more enjoyable and meaningful and to plan for the future. Various topics would be covered: how group members could convince the hospital staff they no longer needed hospitalization; how they could prepare for returning to their home community (for example, learning an employable skill while at the institution); and what to do when they felt depression or some other unwanted emotion or had an urge to do something that would get them into trouble again after their release. Also to be covered were discussions on how to improve relationships with people who were important to them. Occasionally films covering some of these topics would be shown and discussed. The group would meet for about 1 hour each week for 12 weeks.

This focus on improving the current circumstances of the group members stimulated their interest, but soon they found it uncomfortable and anxiety-producing to examine what the future might hold for them. They also became uncomfortable after being told they had considerable control over their future. They reacted to this discomfort by stating that they were "mentally ill" and therefore had some internal condition that was causing their strange behavior. Further, since no cure for their schizophrenia had yet been found, they believed they could do little to improve.

I told them that their excuses were "garbage" (stronger terms were used) and spent a few sessions convincing them that the term *chronic schizophrenic* was a meaningless label. I spent considerable time in explaining the myth of mental illness—that people do not have a "disease of the mind," though they may have emotional problems. I went on to explain that what had gotten them locked up was their deviant behavior. The only way for them to get out was to stop such behavior and convince the staff that they would not exhibit it if released.

The next excuse they tried was that broken homes or inferior schools or broken romances or other misfortune had "messed up" their lives for good, and they could do little about their situation. "Garbage," I told them. True, their past experiences were important. But, I emphasized, what they *wanted* out of their future and the motivation they had to achieve their goals were more important in determining the future.

Finally, after working through a number of excuses, we focused on how they could better handle specific problems: how to handle being depressed, how to stop exhibiting behavior considered "strange," how to present themselves as being "sane" to increase their chances of an early release, and how to adjust to returning to their home communities. We also focused on what kind of work or career they desired upon their release and how they could prepare themselves for their selected careers by learning a skill or trade while at the institution. Another focus was to help them examine what they wanted out of the future and the specific steps they would have to take to achieve their goals. Also discussed was how they could improve relationships that were important to them.

The results of this approach were encouraging. Instead of idly spending much of the time brooding about their situation, group members became motivated to take action. At the end of the 12 weeks, the eight members spontaneously stated that the meetings were making a positive change in their lives and requested that another social worker from the hospital be assigned to continue the group after I left to return to school. This was arranged. Three years later on a return visit to the hospital, I was informed that five of the eight group members had been released to their home communities and two of the others had shown improvement. One group member's condition was described as "unchanged."

19. A mentally healthy person enjoys being with most of the people he or she knows—especially important people such as family and friends. A mentally healthy person likes people and is more than willing to help an unhappy friend, colleague, or family member to feel better. A mentally healthy person laughs a lot and leads a mostly tension-free life. He or she enjoys life and has no trouble accepting others who are different. He or she does not focus on criticizing others or trying to change others. He or she is creative. A mentally healthy person, when unhappy (no one can be happy all the time), knows why she or he is unhappy and will attempt to do something about it.

Exercise M3.8: A Mentally Healthy Person

Goal: This exercise is designed to help you identify what you need to work on to improve your mental well-being.

Step 1: Review Glasser's definition of a mentally healthy person. Describe components of your current life that are consistent with mental well-being.

Step 2: Identify components of your life that you need to work on to improve your mental well-being.

Step 3: For the components that you need to work on, speculate about courses of action to take to improve your mental well-being.

PRINCIPLES OF REALITY THERAPY

1. It is what you choose to do in a relationship, not what others choose to do, that is the focus of reality therapy.
2. People choose the behaviors that have led them into counseling because it is a way perceived by them as being their best effort to deal with an unsatisfying relationship or with no relationship at all. For example, an alcoholic chooses to drink because she or he sees such behavior as the best way to cope with the challenges in living that she or he is facing.
3. The task of the counselor is to help unhappy clients choose new relationship-improving behaviors. These new behaviors will also help clients satisfy one or more of their five basic needs: survival, love and belonging, power, freedom, and fun.
4. Satisfying the need for love and belonging is the key to satisfying the other four needs because the five basic needs can be satisfied only when we have good relationships with other people.
5. Because love and belonging (like all the other basic needs) can be satisfied only in the present, reality therapy focuses almost entirely on the here-and-now.
6. Although most of us have been traumatized in the past, we are victims of our past only if we currently choose to be. The solution to our problems is rarely found in explorations of the past; one exception may be a focus on past successes.
7. The symptoms or the pain that clients choose (because of their unhappiness) is not important to the counseling process. The focus in counseling needs to be on improving present relationships. (It is usually a fruitless endeavor to seek to determine why one discontented person may choose to depress, another to drink, a third to obsess, and a fourth to be crazy).
8. A continuing goal of reality therapy is to create a choice-theory relationship between the counselor and the client. By experiencing a satisfying relationship, the client can learn a lot about a model relationship and how to improve the troubled relationship that brought him or her into counseling.
9. As long as clients continue to use the choice-theory concepts they've learned in counseling, the therapy never ends.
10. During marriage or couple counseling, Glasser (2000) urges the use of *structured reality therapy*. This approach emphasizes that marriage is a partnership and the only way to help a troubled couple is to focus on what's best for their marriage, rather than on what may be best for one or the other spouse. Any marital counseling that allows one partner to blame the other will harm the marriage. Couples are urged to never say or do anything in a relationship that experience indicates will drive the two further apart. They are urged to say and do only what will bring them closer or keep them close. Couples are also instructed to use the solving circle (described earlier) extensively.

Exercise M3.9: The Solving Circle

Goal: This exercise is designed to have you speculate about the merits and shortcomings of the solving circle.

Step 1: Specify difficulties you are currently having in a relationship that is significant to you.

Step 2: Review the material on solving circles. Do you believe that using a solving circle with the person you are currently having difficulties with would be useful? (If possible, try to become involved in an actual solving circle with this person.) Speculate about the merits and shortcomings of the solving circle.

11. Reality therapy is a "doing" approach: Clients are guided in the direction of actually doing something about their problems.

12. Glasser notes that all of us are *responsible* for the behaviors we engage in because we can't be anything but *responsible* for everything we choose to do.

13. The reality therapist looks for every opportunity to teach choice therapy to clients and their families so that everyone involved can begin the process of replacing external control psychology with choice theory.

14. A symptom is a cry for help. People use symptoms to avoid situations that they fear will increase their frustration.

15. Good or bad, happy or sad, people choose everything they do all day long.

Exercise M3.10: Symptoms as a Cry for Help

Goal: This exercise is designed to assist you in recognizing that emotional difficulties, dysfunctional behaviors, somatic problems, and relationship problems are cries for help.

Describe how someone you know is demonstrating that his or her emotional difficulties, relationship problems, dysfunctional behaviors, or somatic problems are cries for help.

CAN OUR THOUGHTS ALTER OUR GENETIC CODE?

Dr. Bruce Lipton (2008) is a former medical school professor (University of Wisconsin) and research scientist (Stanford University School of Medicine). He has conducted a number of experiments on the molecular mechanisms by which cells process information. He has found genes do not, in fact, control our behavior; instead, genes are turned on and off by influences outside the cell. These influences include our thoughts, perceptions, and beliefs. Dr. Lipton asserts that our thoughts and beliefs, true or false, positive or negative, affect genetic activity and actually alter our genetic code. He further asserts that we can retrain our consciousness to create healthy thoughts and beliefs, and that doing so will result in a profoundly positive impact on our bodies and on our lives.

EVALUATION OF REALITY THERAPY

Reality therapy is a commonsense approach to counseling. The first version (Glasser, 1965) has been found to be quite effective in producing positive changes (Eysenck, 1965; Glasser & Wubbolding, 1995; Stuart, 1970). It has been successfully applied in a variety of settings, including corrections, mental health, education, unemployment, public welfare, and treating delinquency. Relatively little research has been conducted on the newer version (Glasser, 2000). It does have potential to become a leading approach to counseling.

Critics of choice theory and reality therapy point out that the theory does not explain why some people commit robbery but others commit murder or white-collar crimes, or neglect their children, and so on.

SUMMARY

The following summarizes the module's content in terms of the learning objectives presented at the beginning of the module.

1. Comprehend reality therapy.
   Choice theory is an internal control psychology. According to choice theory, all behavior is an attempt to reduce the difference between what we want and what we have. Glasser believes that we are driven by five innate needs: survival, love and belonging, power, freedom, and fun.

   The only behavior we can control is our own. All behavior is "total behavior" and is made up of four inseparable components: acting, thinking, feeling, and physiology.

   All long-lasting psychological problems are relationship problems, human brains are very creative, and almost all medical problems for which physicians are unable to identify the cause are partially created by the ill person's brain to deal with unhappiness. Unsatisfying relationships are the primary source of crimes, addictions, and emotional and behavioral disorders.

It is a serious mistake to seek to control others by nagging, preaching, punishing, or threatening to punish them. The solving circle is a good strategy for two people who know choice theory to use in redefining their freedom and improving their relationship. It is not necessary to know our past before we can deal with the present. It is therapeutic to view our "total behavior" in terms of verbs.

All total behavior (thinking, feeling, acting, and physiology) is chosen, but we have direct control over only the acting and thinking components. People choose (although some are unaware of their choice) to play mentally ill roles. Mental illness is a myth.

Reality therapy focuses on improving unhappy relationships and on the here-and-now. Reality therapy focuses on having clients understand and apply the concepts of choice theory. During marriage or couple counseling, the solving circle is often used. Reality therapy is a "doing" approach. Clients are guided in the direction of doing something about their problems. A symptom is a cry for help.

EXERCISE

1. The Mental Illness Debate

Goal: To identify the arguments about whether mental illness exists.

Step 1. At a class session some students form two panels. One will argue that mental illness exists; the other, that mental illness is a myth. Panel members are given a few days to gather information and prepare their arguments. Panel members may interview counselors and therapists in the community and read reference materials.

Step 2. At the selected class date, a debate is held. At the end of the debate, students who did not participate on either panel summarize the strong points made by the debaters.

PROMINENT SPECIFIC INTERVENTION TECHNIQUES

LEARNING OBJECTIVES

Modules 1, 2, and 3 presented intervention techniques that are components of comprehensive theories of psychotherapy. Module 4 summarizes some intervention techniques that were developed independently of any comprehensive theory of psychotherapy. We'll call them *specific intervention approaches*. This module will help prepare students to:

Describe Play Therapy, Parental Education, Crisis Intervention, Solution-Focused Therapy, Mediation, and Narrative Therapy

PLAY THERAPY

Play therapy is used with young children. Play is seen as a young child's most natural vehicle for self-expression and is therefore viewed by play therapists as a means for relating to, and communicating with, young children. Play therapy serves many purposes: making a diagnosis, forming a relationship, ventilating feelings, working through unwanted emotions, teaching desired new behaviors, and modeling alternative behavior. Play therapists' approaches range from almost totally nondirective to highly directive. Play therapy is used by counselors with widely diverging orientations, including reality therapy, rational therapy, and behavior therapy.

CASE EXAMPLE   PLAY THERAPY

Dawn, age 7, was a second grader who was referred by her teacher to a school social worker. Academically and socially she was functioning far behind her peers, even though tests showed she was of normal intelligence. The social worker observed her in her play interactions with peers. She was withdrawn and tried to avoid competitive game situations. Forced to participate, she would quit whenever she fell behind. When the social worker discussed Dawn's behavior with her teacher, the teacher indicated that Dawn shied away from doing her assignments and seldom completed any. Dawn was observed for a few sessions in a playroom at school. At one point, Dawn held the mother doll and called the baby girl "stupid" and stated, "You'll never be able to do what your brother does." The social worker felt that Dawns academic and social problems were resulting from Dawn's having such a low self-concept that she had virtually given up trying. Dawn's interactions with the dolls suggested her mother might be contributing to her low self-concept by disparaging her. Several

meetings were then held with Dawn's parents, with Dawn present for two of these. The social worker observed that the mother was highly critical of Dawn without ever praising her. Dawn was placed in a special educational program for the next 18 months; here she received close attention and considerable praise for her academic and social efforts. The worker also counseled the parents on how they were contributing to her low self-concept and how they needed to praise Dawn for her efforts and to get her more involved in interests she had. On three separate occasions Dawn, her parents, Dawn's brother, and the social worker met in a playroom. The family members were encouraged to play together in various games, and the parents were instructed to praise Dawn whenever she made efforts to participate positively. Also, Dawn's mother was encouraged to refrain from disparaging Dawn. After this intensive program, Dawn was able to rejoin her class at the start of the fourth grade and had become much more outgoing and self-confident.

Source: In the classic *Play Therapy,* Axline (1947) provided a number of other case examples in which play therapy has been used for diagnostic purposes, for helping children to understand themselves and their problems better and to resolve their problems.

Whittaker (1974) described play therapy as follows:

The therapist may use initial play sessions for diagnostic purposes to observe such things as relationship, attention span, areas of preoccupation, areas of inhibition, direction of aggression, wishes and fantasies, and self-perception. Depending upon orientation, the therapist typically encourages free play with a variety of available materials (paints, dolls, punching bags, puzzles, clay), interprets the child's affect to him ("You seem to be angry at the doll"), and finally offers insights into the child's behavior. The child may experience some regression to earlier levels of functioning while in the play situation and also may practice newly acquired skills and try on new behaviors. A central notion of play therapy is that the child is expressing symbolically through play the conflicts he is experiencing in the outside world. In the relative safety of the play situation, these conflicts can be worked through and—so the theory goes—transferred to the child's real-life situation. (pp. 225–226)

Play therapy generally takes place in a playroom, with only the child and the therapist present. At times other children are present, which helps the child learn to interact more effectively with others. Occasionally parents attend the play therapy sessions, which helps them better understand their child and learn more effective interaction approaches with their child. Play materials include dolls (usually a doll family), puppets, clay and finger paints, crayons, a sandbox, toy animals, soldiers and weapons, and cutting-out materials. In play therapy, children are generally allowed to express themselves as freely as they desire. Usually minimal limits are set: establishing the duration of the play sessions, forbidding the willful destruction of play materials, and forbidding the child from physically attacking others in the playroom. (See Case Example "Play Therapy.")

Some protective services programs use anatomically correct dolls to gather information from young children who are suspected victims of sexual abuse. A worker first forms a relationship with a child and then asks the child to show, with the dolls, what the alleged perpetrator did. In some jurisdictions, this process is videotaped and is available for court use if formal charges are brought against the alleged perpetrator.

Exercise M4.1: The Beneficial Effects of Playing for Me

Goal: This exercise is designed to assist you in understanding the beneficial effects of "play" for you in childhood and in adulthood.

Step 1:   Specify your favorite play activities in your childhood.

Step 2:   Summarize what you learned from play activities in your childhood.

Step 3:   Specify your current "play" and "fun" activities.

Step 4:   Specify the benefits of your current "play" and "fun" activities.

PARENTAL EDUCATION: PARENT EFFECTIVENESS TRAINING

The main goal of parental education programs is to help parents understand child behavior and develop child-rearing skills. Most programs rest on the assumption that rearing children is a difficult and complex task for which society ill prepares young people. Numerous theoreticians have developed somewhat different educational programs: Dreikurs (1964), Ginott (1965), Gordon (1970), Patterson (1971), and Spock (1957). These programs use a variety of educational formats: short courses, small discussion groups, and programmed self-instruction.

Probably the most popular program is Parent Effectiveness Training (PET), developed by Thomas Gordon (1970). PET courses are offered in hundreds of communities and have been endorsed by numerous public and private agencies serving parents and youth. The PET system has been found to work effectively with children of all ages. It fosters warmer and more harmonious relationships between parents and their children, and children learn to become more responsible. The basic concepts of this approach are presented here, partly because some of the techniques, such as active listening, I-messages, and no-lose problem solving, can be used by not only parents and parent surrogates (such as teachers, principals, counselors, and youth leaders) but also anyone who wants to interact more effectively with others.

Parents Are People, Not Gods

Gordon urges parents to be "real" in their relationships with children. "Realness" is much more important and more easily achievable than always being consistent in displaying feelings, putting up a "united front," and being unconditionally tolerant and accepting. In a close relationship, it is impossible to hide our true feelings, so it is normal and real for parents to be accepting of some behaviors of their children and nonaccepting of other behaviors. Parents should recognize their true feelings and not attempt to convey false acceptance when they dislike what their children are doing. It is normal and real for one parent to be more accepting than the other, and one parent may feel accepting and the other nonaccepting of the same behavior. Being honest and human in interacting with children will improve a relationship substantially more than will conveying false acceptance or trying to always be consistent.

Who Owns the Problem?

PET asserts that appropriate parental responses depend on the answer to the question "Who owns the problem?" We own a problem only when the situation affects our ability to get our needs met in a concrete and tangible way. If the *child* owns a problem, then *active listening* is an appropriate technique for a parent to use. If the *parent* owns the problem, then *I-messages* are appropriate for the parent to use. If the situation involves a conflict between the parent and the child in meeting the needs of both, then *no-lose problem solving* is an appropriate technique. If the situation involves a conflict in values between the parent and the child, Gordon provides guidelines for *resolving collisions of values*.

PET Techniques

Active Listening. When a 16-year-old boy announces "I hate school, and I'm going to drop out," his parents can respond in a variety of ways: ordering him to stay in school, warning him that he'll be sorry if he drops out, moralizing by saying dropping out would not be proper or right, giving advice by saying he should discuss his intention with the high school counselor, and so forth. Such approaches are generally not effective or productive in helping children express their feelings, explore their problems, and arrive at a comfortable solution.

Active listening is a much more effective way of interacting: (1) The receiver of a message tries to understand what the sender's message means or what the sender is feeling. (2) The receiver then expresses this understanding in her or his own words and returns this understanding for the sender's verification. The receiver does *not* send any message of her or his own—such as a question, advice, feelings, or an opinion. The aim is to feed back only what the receiver feels the sender's message means. Active listening is a difficult skill to learn and takes practice to master.

In the following exchange, the parent consistently uses the active listening technique:

Youth: I hate school, and I'm going to drop out.
Parent: You're fed up with school and thinking about leaving.
Youth: Yes I am! My teachers are real bummers this year.
Parent: You're disappointed with your current teachers.
Youth: Especially my Spanish teacher. He asks us questions in Spanish and expects us to understand what he's saying. All I hear is words that I can't understand.
Parent: You're having trouble understanding your Spanish teacher when he speaks in Spanish.
Youth: I've been getting A's and B's on tests, but the other students appear to understand Spanish better when it is spoken.
Parent: Your grades show that you are doing well in Spanish, but you have trouble understanding Spanish when it is spoken.
Youth: Yeah, I wonder what I could do to learn to understand people better when they speak Spanish.
Parent: You're wondering how you can better learn to hear and speak in Spanish.
Youth: Maybe I could talk to my teacher. He'd know. He might have some ideas.

Gordon listed some advantages of using the active listening technique. It facilitates problem solving by the child, which fosters the development of responsibility. By talking a problem through, a person is more likely to identify the root of the problem and arrive at a solution than by merely thinking about a problem. A child who feels that his or her parents are listening is more likely to listen to their point of view. In addition, the relationship between parent and child is likely to improve because a child who feels he or she is being heard and understood by another person is likely to feel warmth toward the listener. Finally, the approach helps the child explore, recognize, and express personal feelings.

Gordon noted that parents need to have certain attitudes to use the technique effectively. Parents must view the child as a separate person with his or her own feelings. Parents must be able to accept the child's feelings, whatever they may be. Parents should genuinely want to be helpful and must want to hear what the child has to say. And parents must trust the child's capacities to handle personal problems and feelings.

Parents initially make three common mistakes as they use the technique: (1) They guide the child's behavior or thinking toward what the parents think the child should do. If parents have this intention, children are likely to feel they are being manipulated, and the approach may be counterproductive. (2) Parents parrot back the words rather than the intended meaning or feeling. For instance, if a daughter yells at her father "You stupid jerk," an appropriate response geared to the message would be "You're angry with me," rather than parroting the words "You think I'm a jerk." (3) Parents use active listening at the wrong time. If a child does not want to talk about her or his feelings or is simply too tired, the parent should respect the child's right to and need for privacy.

I-Messages. Active listening is used when the child has the problem. However, many occasions arise when the child causes a problem for the parent. For example, a child talks loudly in church, or gets too close to a precious glass vase, or is about to walk on a new carpet with muddy shoes, or is driving recklessly. In such cases, entirely different communication skills are required. Confronted with such situations, many parents send either a *solution message* (they order, direct, command, warn, threaten, preach, moralize, or advise) or a *put-down message* (they blame, judge, criticize, ridicule, or name-call). Solution and put-down messages can have devastating effects on a child's self-concept and are generally counterproductive in helping a child become responsible.

Solution and put-clown messages are primarily you-messages: "You do what I say," "Don't you do that," "Why don't you be good," "You're lazy," "You should know better." PET advocates that parents instead send *I-messages* on those occasions when a child is causing a problem for them. Suppose a child is walking on a clean carpet with dirty shoes. Instead of saying, "John, get off that carpet, you're a pig!," PET urges parents to use an I-message: "I shampooed the living room rug today and want to keep it clean as long as possible."

I-messages are nonblaming messages that communicate only how the sender of the message believes the receiver is adversely affecting the sender. I-messages do not provide a solution, and they are not put-down messages. It is possible to send an I-message without using the word *I,* for the essence of I-messages is a nonblaming statement of how the parent feels the child's behavior is affecting the parent. For example, a parent riding in a car driven by a 17-year-old son who is exceeding the speed limit may say, "Driving fast really terrifies me."

You-messages are generally put-down messages that convey to children either that they should do something or that they are bad. In contrast, I-messages communicate to children much more honestly the effect of the behavior on the parent. I-messages are also more effective because they help children learn to assume responsibility for their own behavior. An I-message tells children that the parent trusts them to respect the parent's needs, that the parent is leaving the responsibility with them, and that the parent is trusting them to handle the situation constructively.

You-messages frequently end up in a struggle between parent and child, whereas I-messages are much less likely to produce an argument. I-messages lead to honesty and openness in a relationship and generally foster intimacy. Children, as well as adults, often do not know how their behavior affects others. I-messages produce startling results. Parents frequently report that their children express surprise on learning how their parents really feel.

The following are examples of you-messages and I-messages:

YOU-MESSAGES	I-MESSAGES
1. Don't you ever kick me again; you're a real pain.	Ouch! That kick really hurt me.
2. John, you stop pestering me now!	John, I am very tired today, and I just do not have the energy to play with you this evening.
3. You're a reckless driver, and someday you'll kill someone.	I'm afraid to ride with you when you drive so fast.

I-messages work only if the child does not want his or her actions to adversely affect his parent. A child who does not want to cause discomfort in his or her parent will seek to change the adversive behavior when an I-message is used. However, if a child enjoys causing discomfort in his or her parent, then I-messages may result in an *increase* in the adversive behavior, because the child is now more fully aware of how to cause parental discomfort.

Exercise M4.2: I-Messages and You-Messages

Goal: This exercise is designed to assist you in understanding I-messages and you-messages and to understand the consequences of each type of message.

Step 1: Reflect on your childhood. Did your parents primarily use I-messages or you-messages? Describe the kind of messages your parents sent to you.

Step 2: Summarize the affects of these messages on you.

Step 3: Reflect on your current life. Identify someone significant to you (perhaps a boss or someone you are dating or married to) who is currently interacting with you by using either I-messages or you-messages. Specify what this person tends to say to you with either I-messages or you-messages.

Step 4: Summarize the affect of these I-messages or you-messages on you.

No-Lose Problem Solving. In every parent-child relationship, situations inevitably arise in which the child continues to behave in a way that interferes with the needs of the parent. Conflict is part of life and is not necessarily bad. Conflict occurs because people are different and have different needs and wants, which at times do not match. What is important is not how frequently conflicts arise but how they get resolved. Generally conflicts create a power struggle. In many families the power struggle is resolved by one of two win-lose approaches.

Most parents try to resolve the conflict by having the parent win and the child lose. Parents generally have the greater authority. When the parent wins, the child resents the parent, the child is less motivated to carry out the solution, and the child has no opportunity to develop self-discipline and self-responsibility. Such children may rebel or become dependent and withdrawn.

Alternatively, the win-lose conflict is resolved when parents give in to their children out of fear of frustrating their children or fear of conflict. These children come to believe their needs are more important than anyone else's, and they generally become self-centered, selfish, demanding, impulsive, and uncontrollable. They a reviewed by others as being spoiled, they have difficulty interacting with peers, and they do not respect the property or feelings of others.

Of course, few parents use either approach exclusively. Oscillating between the two approaches is common. Evidence indicates that both approaches lead to the development of emotional problems in children (Gordon, 1970, p. 161). The two win-lose approaches are illustrated in the following situation:

Parent Wins—Child Loses

Mother: Since I'm now working, we need to divide the work tasks around the house. I'll continue to do most of the work, but from now on I'd like you to wash the dishes in the evening.

John: But I don't like washing dishes.

Mother: Well, I don't like cooking and washing and ironing clothes, but I have to do them. We all have to do things we don't like to do.

John: Washing dishes is for girls.

Mother: Look, I'm not going to argue with you about this. You're now old enough to help out. In this family we all have to contribute. If you don't do the dishes, you won't receive your allowance. In fact, from now on, every evening you do not wash dishes, 50 cents will be deducted from your weekly allowance.

Child Wins—Parent Loses

Mother: Since I'm now working, we need to divide the work tasks around the house. I'll continue to do most of the work, but from now on I'd like you to wash the dishes in the evening.

John: But I don't like washing dishes.

Mother: Why?

John: Washing dishes is for girls.

Mother: But many boys help their mothers with the dishes.

John: Tom and Gary don't help their mothers. What would they say about me washing dishes?

Mother: You may be right. Could you instead help me with washing clothes, or dusting, or cleaning your room?

John: Aw—Mom, those things are for girls, too.

Mother: (*Dejectedly*) Well, okay. I'll try to do these things while also working.

Exercise M4.3: My Win-Lose Struggles with My Parents

Goal: This exercise is designed to assist you in understanding the adverse consequences of win-lose struggles.

Step 1:   Reflect on your childhood. Specify whether you were frequently, occasionally, or seldom involved in win-lose situations with your parents.

Step 2:   Describe some of the win-lose situations that you had with your parents.

Step 3:   Specify who tended to win and who tended to lose.

Step 4:   Specify the affects of these win-lose situations on you and on your parents.

Step 5:   Are you currently in a win-lose situation with someone important to you? If "yes," describe the situation and describe your current feelings about this situation.

Gordon seriously questioned whether power is necessary or justified in a parent-child relationship. As children grow older, they become less dependent, and parents gradually lose their power. Rewards and punishments that worked in younger years are less effective. Children resent those with power over them, and parents frequently feel guilty after using power. Gordon believed that parents continue to use power because they have little experience in using nonpower methods of influence.

Gordon describes a new approach, the *no-lose approach*, to resolve conflicts. In this approach, parent and child resolve their conflicts by finding their own unique solutions acceptable to both. Gordon (1970, p. 237) listed six steps of no-lose problem solving:

1. Identify and define the needs of each person.
2. Generate possible alternative solutions.
3. Evaluate the alternative solutions.
4. Decide on the best acceptable solution.
5. Work out ways of implementing the solution.
6. Follow up to evaluate how it worked.

The following example illustrates this approach:

Mother: Since I'm now working, I will have less time to do the work that needs to be done around the house. I would appreciate it if you would help me out with some of the things that need to be done.

John: I suppose I could help—what needs to be done?

Mother: The meals need to be cooked, dishes washed, the house cleaned, grocery shopping done, and the garbage taken out.

John: Let's see. I'd be willing to vacuum the floor and dust. Will my allowance be increased? I'd like to get a new bike.

Mother: Yes, since we'll have some more money now that I'm working, we could increase your allowance, with the increase dependent on how much additional work you do.

John: In addition to helping to clean the house, I'd be willing to wash the clothes if you show me what to do. I also could carry out the garbage.

The no-lose approach is simple to state: Each person in the conflict treats the other with respect, neither person tries to win by using power, and a creative solution acceptable to both parties is sought. There are two basic premises to no-lose problem solving: (1) All people have the right to have their needs met. (2) What is in conflict is not needs but solutions to those needs. This approach offers several advantages. It motivates children to carry out the solution because they participated in the decision. It develops children's thinking skills and responsibility. It requires less enforcement, eliminates the need for power, and improves relationships with parents.

Exercise M4.4: No-Lose Problem Solving

Goal: This exercise is designed to assist you in understanding and applying the no-lose approach to problem solving.

Step 1:   Describe a situation in the past in which you had an interpersonal conflict with someone and you used no-lose problem solving, or describe a current situation in which you have an interpersonal conflict with someone and you now seek to apply no-lose problem solving.

Step 2:   Specify the following for this situation:

     a. Identify and define the needs of each person.
     b. Generate possible alternative solutions.
     c. Evaluate the alternative solutions.
     d. Decide on the best acceptable solution.
     e. Work out ways of implementing the solution.
     f. Follow up to evaluate how the solution worked.

Step 3:   Summarize the merits and shortcomings of no-lose problem-solving.

> ***Resolving Collisions of Values.*** Collisions of values are common between parents and children, particularly as the children become adolescents and young adults. Likely areas of conflict include sexual behavior, clothing and hairstyles, religion, choice of friends, education, plans for the future, use of drugs, and eating habits. On these topics, emotions run strong, and parents generally seek to influence their offspring to follow the values the parents consider important. Teenagers, however, often think their parents' values are old-fashioned and stupid and declare that they want to make their own decisions about these matters.
>
> Gordon described three constructive ways in which parents and teenagers can seek to resolve such conflicts. (For the sake of simplicity, I use the term *mother* here, although a father or a teenager also can use these techniques.)
>
> 1. The mother models the values she holds important. If she values honesty, she should be honest. If she values responsible use of drugs, she should not get drunk or drink and drive, for example. If she values openness, she should be open. She asks herself if she is living according to the values she professes. If her values and behaviors are incongruent in certain areas, she needs to change either her values or her behavior in the direction of congruency. Congruence between behavior and values is important if she wants to be an effective model.
> 2. The mother acts as a consultant to her teen. A good consultant finds out whether the teen would like to consult with her. If the answer is "yes," she makes sure she has all the available pertinent facts. She then shares these facts—once—so the teen understands them. She leaves the teen the responsibility of deciding whether to follow the advice. A good consultant is well informed and does not nag; otherwise, she may not be used as a consultant again.
> 3. The mother reduces tensions by modifying her own values. After she examines her teen's values, she may realize they have merit, and she can then move toward those values or at least toward understanding why the teen holds them.
>
> In summary, PET is intended to improve relationships between parents and children and to develop responsibility in children. Many parents who participate in PET courses or read Gordon's *Parent Effectiveness Training* find them to be effective. In recent years, PET concepts have been found useful not only for improving relationships between parents and children but also for improving interactions and communication between people in all manner of transactions.
>
> PET techniques work if influencees respect influencers and want a positive relationship with them. If the influencee neither respects nor wants a positive relationship with the influencer, these techniques don't work.

CRISIS INTERVENTION

Ell (1995) notes that crisis intervention is appropriate in an infinite number of situations, including serious illness or trauma, death of a loved one, disasters, violent crimes, moving away from home, and unplanned pregnancy. Crisis intervention (CI) is grounded in the belief that in a crisis situation current levels of functioning are disrupted and previously manageable internal psychological difficulties are stirred up. CI views the emotional disturbances presented by people facing crisis as the result of (1) the stressful situation they face and (2) underlying emotional dispositions that come to the surface only in crisis situations. CI postulates that underlying emotional difficulties are ingredients of all personalities. People are viewed as being fairly normal in their general adjustment, with the crisis being a major cause of a person's emotional difficulties. See Exhibit M4.1.

CI services often have two tasks. One is to resolve the current crisis. The other is to resolve problems the person has been denying or ignoring. For example, if a woman is fired from a job because of drinking problems, services might focus not only on helping her find another job but also on breaking down her denial of her drinking problem. Golan (1979, p. 500) noted that at the point of crisis "a minimal effort . . . can produce a maximal effect; a small amount of help, appropriately focused, can prove more effective than extensive help at a period of less emotional accessibility." (See Case Example "Crisis Intervention.")

Crisis intervention services are generally brief and provided when the client is in desperate need emotionally. The specific treatment techniques are borrowed from other approaches. Here are a few examples: Role-playing helps a pregnant single woman gather her nerve to inform her parents and her sexual partner. Confrontation helps a person arrested three times for drunken driving acknowledge that he has a drinking problem. A person whose engagement has been broken learns to counter unwanted emotions with a rational self-analysis. A young woman who has been raped is given immediate medical attention and counseling on both legal implications and on her thoughts and feelings about the assault. A counselor uses the active listening technique in counseling someone who is suicidal.

Whittaker (1974) provided a summary of crisis counseling services:

> Requisite worker skills include the ability to function effectively and efficiently in an emotionally tense atmosphere and to give support and direction while at the same time helping the client to develop autonomous coping skills.
>
> Crisis intervention generally progresses in the following manner: (1) An attempt is made to alleviate the disabling tension through ventilation and the creation of a climate of trust and hope. (2) Next the worker attempts to understand the dynamics of the event that precipitated the crisis. (3) The worker gives his impressions and understanding of the crisis and checks out these perceptions with the client. (4) Client and worker attempt to determine specific remedial measures that can be taken to restore equilibrium. (5) New methods of coping may be introduced. (6) Finally, termination occurs—often after a predetermined number of interviews—when the agreed-upon goals have been realized. (p. 212)

Exhibit M4.1   The Effects of a Crisis

A. Before a crisis a person is functioning in a groove, that is, a relatively routine, stable kind of living with only minor changes.

B. A crisis arises (for example, being fired from a job) that places a person in an unfreezing position. This unfreezing position is emotionally charged, and the person's lifestyle is highly vulnerable to change. In such a crisis, a person may either take the constructive (C) path or the destructive (D) path.

C. This constructive path has the person (perhaps with the assistance of others) gaining an awareness of why the crisis arose. The person develops adaptive ways of handling the crisis, and thereby grows through acquiring problem-solving skills that will better enable him or her to solve future crisis situations.

D. If the destructive path is followed, the person does not satisfactorily resolve the crisis. Unsolved aspects of the crisis remain, and the person is apt to develop maladaptive coping patterns. The person remains in an emotionally charged situation, and is less able to face future crises that arise. Problems may well begin to snowball (for example, when a single, pregnant woman denies the pregnancy and makes no effort to begin making decisions that she will have to face).

CASE EXAMPLE   CRISIS INTERVENTION

John Franzene (age 28) went to work intoxicated one day and was promptly fired. John became incensed and yelled obscenities at his supervisor. He then went to a local tavern and drank until he passed out. A friend took him home. When his wife found out that John had been fired from his job as a janitor, she packed her bags that evening and took the two children to live with her mother. She indicated that this was the "last straw."

John is an alcoholic and drinks an average of eight bottles of beer and a pint of whiskey every day. He has been drinking excessively for the past decade. Three years ago, his wife separated from him because he was abusive to her and the children, both physically and verbally, when intoxicated. At that time John promised to stop drinking if his wife would only return; she did, and 3 weeks later he again began drinking. Five years ago he lost his position as an elementary school teacher because of his drinking and his frequent absenteeism. Two years ago, he lost his driver's license for driving while intoxicated. In the past 5 years, he has lost three other jobs.

The next day John went to his mother-in-law's home to try to talk his wife into returning. She refused to speak to him. John, feeling sorry for himself, went to a local tavern and again got drunk. He blamed his supervisor for his current difficulties. While intoxicated he decided to "straighten this matter out." He went to the office where he had been fired and got into a fight with his supervisor. He was arrested. While in jail, he got the "DTs" (delirium tremens), which really scared him. He was transferred to a hospital. The doctor at the hospital explored his interest in receiving help for his drinking problem. John indicated he was willing to talk about it to someone, and he was referred to Tom Halaska, the hospital social worker.

For the first time in his life, John acknowledged that he had a drinking problem and needed help. Mr. Halaska met with John on several occasions during the next 4 days. The ways that alcohol was affecting his life (including his job and his family life) were traced, and John gained an awareness that he got into trouble only when he was drinking. Mr. Halaska explored the reasons John drank, and it became clear that he drank excessively either when he was with male friends in a tavern or when he sought to relieve unwanted emotions of feeling tense, moody, or depressed. John appeared at this time to be sincerely committed to giving up drinking. Mr. Halaska suggested that one thing he would have to do to give up drinking was to stop meeting his friends at a tavern. John indicated that saving his marriage meant more to him than hanging out with his friends. Mr. Halaska arranged a meeting between John and his wife. His wife agreed to return if John would first go 1 month without drinking, promise never to drink again, and actively participate in AA meetings. John agreed. Mr. Halaska referred him to an AA group and also referred him to the outpatient treatment unit of the mental health center. Among other services, this outpatient treatment service provided marriage counseling services to John and his wife and helped him explore job opportunities.

John occasionally stops by the hospital to visit Mr. Halaska briefly. It has now been 14 months since he had a drink. He is a sales clerk at a clothing store and is seeking a teaching position. He reports that he and his wife are getting along better than they ever have.

Note: Additional case examples using crisis intervention are presented in Greenstone and Leviton (2011).

Crisis intervention services are provided in traditional and nontraditional settings, including runaway centers, rape crisis centers, "hot lines," hospital emergency rooms, mental health clinics, suicide prevention services, neighborhood centers, crisis hostels, halfway houses, detention facilities, and self-help groups such as Parents Anonymous. Crisis intervention services are provided by both professionals and paraprofessionals and volunteers.

Exercise M4.5: Crisis Intervention in My Past

Goal: This exercise is designed to assist you in understanding crisis intervention services.

Step 1: Describe a crisis you had in the past.

Step 2: Specify how you resolved this crisis (crisis intervention services include both assistance from others and your own problem-solving resources).

SOLUTION-FOCUSED THERAPY

Solution-focused therapy is also called "solution-oriented therapy" and "strategic therapy." Solution-focused therapists ask clients *what* is happening now and *how* it should be changed. They do not ask *why.* This approach focuses not on pathology (the approach of fixing what is wrong) but on identifying clients' requests. This focus has a profound effect on what interventions are used. For clients, learning to be the persons they want to be is quite different (and often less time-consuming) than learning why they are the way they are. Solution-focused therapy has been developed by a variety of researchers, including Berg and Miller (1992), DeJong and Miller (1995), and de Shazer (1988).

Solution-focused therapy emphasizes two intervention techniques. One is developing well-formed goals with clients that are within their frame of reference. The other is developing solutions with the client based on "exceptions."

What are well-formed goals? Berg and Miller (1992) identify seven characteristics of well-formed goals in solution-focused therapy:

1. The goals are important to clients. Clients should want to achieve these goals, and the goals should be expressed in the clients' language. The only time the worker should object to the desired goals of a client is when a stated goal will result in danger to the client (such as the goal of terminating the client's life) or to others (such as the goal of physical retaliation for a perceived wrong).
2. The goals are modest. Small goals are easier to achieve than large goals.
3. The goals are concrete, specific, and behavioral, so that both client and worker can observe when progress is being made. For example, "going out to lunch with a friend three times a week" is a concrete, specific, and behavioral goal.
4. The goals describe the presence of something (for example, "taking walks") rather than the absence of something (for example, "no longer feeling discouraged").
5. The goals express beginnings ("arranging a pleasant vacation with my spouse for this summer") rather than endings ("having a happy marriage"). Stating goals as a beginning process helps clients conceptualize the first steps they need to take to achieve their desired ends.
6. The goals are realistic. Clients can achieve them within the context of their lives.
7. The goals are perceived by clients as involving "hard work." Goals call for changes in what clients do, and change is difficult. Clients are generally motivated to work hard to achieve highly desired goals.

Setting well-formed goals assumes that goals are negotiated between the worker and client. Expressing goals in such a way that they are consistent with these guidelines often requires considerable effort.

DeJong and Miller (1995) assert that a "miracle" question is often a superb way to assist clients in formulating goals:

Suppose while you are sleeping tonight a miracle happens. The miracle is that the problem that has you here talking to me is somehow solved. Only you don't know that because you are asleep. What will you notice different tomorrow morning that will tell you that a miracle has happened? (p. 731)

Additional questions asked in this vein include

What is the very first thing you notice after the miracle happens?
What will your husband (child, friend) notice about you that gives him the idea that things are better for you?
When he notices that, what might he do differently?
When he does that, what will you do?
And when you do that, what will be different around your house? (p. 731)

These questions shift clients' attention from their difficulties and pathologies to imagining a future in which their problems are resolved. The questions provide an opportunity for workers to help clients formulate goals consistent with the guidelines.

What are "exceptions"? In solution-focused therapy, exceptions are those occasions in clients' lives when their problems could have occurred but did not. For example, a married couple characterize their recent years as "continual fighting"; the worker asks the couple to describe times when they weren't fighting. Workers focus on the *who, what, when,* and *where* of exception times (rather than on the problem times), and an in-depth exploration of client problems is avoided. The result is growing awareness in both worker and client of the client's strengths relative to his or her goals rather than the client's deficiencies relative to his or her problems. Once these strengths are brought to clients' awareness, they can mobilize them to move in the direction of achieving their miracle.

In another example of the exceptions strategy, a worker asks a depressed client to do this homework assignment: "Pay attention to the times when you are not depressed or when the depression is less of a problem. What is different about those times?" During the next session, the worker asks the client what she did differently during those times when she noticed the depression was not a problem or was less of a problem. Such a question implies that the client already has the skills to function in a more satisfying manner.

The essence of solution-focused therapy is as follows. The counselor helps the client to define what he wants (his goals), and then helps the client identify courses of action to attain these goals.

In a study of 275 clients, Berg and DeJong (1996) found a 77% success rate using solution-focused therapy. Forty-five percent of the clients indicated that their treatment goal was met, and another 32% indicated some progress in attaining their treatment goal.

Solution-focused therapy is highly consistent with the strengths perspective in social work, which is described in Chapter 3. Solution-focused therapy, task-centered therapy, and some forms of cognitive behavior therapy (see Module 2) are examples of brief therapies. Brief therapies are becoming increasingly popular with clients and with funding sources as society and individuals clamor for approaches that result in significant change in a short time and at a reasonable cost.

A shortcoming of solution-focused therapy is that the approach cannot be used with clients who deny a problem exists—for example, alcoholics who are in denial about their drinking problem. The approach cannot be used with people who are in denial because they do not want to change their problematic behavior. Solution-focused therapy can be used only with clients who want to change their problematic behavior(s).

MEDIATION

Moore (1986) defined *mediation* as follows:

> Mediation involves the intervention of an acceptable impartial and neutral third party who has no authoritative decision-making power to assist contending parties in voluntarily reaching their own mutually acceptable settlement of issues in dispute. . . . Mediation leaves the decision-making power in the hands of the people in conflict. Mediation is a voluntary process in that the participants must be willing to accept the assistance of the intervenor if the dispute is to be resolved. Mediation is usually initiated when the partners no longer believe that they can handle the conflict on their own and when the only means of resolution appears to involve impartial third-party assistance. (p. 6)

During the past four decades, mediation has been used increasingly to resolve conflicts between disputing groups. As far back as 1913, the federal government established the use of federal mediators to help resolve issues between employers and employees (Moore, 1986, p. 21). Mediated settlements were expected to prevent costly strikes or lockouts and to protect the welfare and safety of Americans. Federal use of mediation in labor disputes set a precedent, encouraging many states to pass laws and to train a cadre of mediators to handle intrastate labor conflicts.

Mediation is currently used in a variety of ways. The Civil Rights Act of 1964 created the Community Relations Service of the U.S. Department of Justice to use mediation to resolve disputes relating to discriminatory practices based on race, color, or national origin (Moore, 1986, pp. 21–22). Diverse private agencies, civil rights commissions, and state agencies now use mediation to handle charges of sex, race, and ethnic discrimination. The federal government funds Neighborhood Justice Centers that provide free or low-cost mediation services to the public to resolve disputes informally, inexpensively, and efficiently (Mayer, 1995, pp. 618–620). Disputes settled through mediation are resolved much more efficiently and creatively than those resolved in court. Mediation is also used in schools to resolve issues between students, between students and faculty, between faculty members, and between faculty and administration. The criminal justice system uses mediation to resolve disputes in correctional facilities—for example, for prison riots, hostage negotiations, and institutionalized grievance procedures. Mediation is used extensively in family disputes involving child custody and divorce proceedings, disputes between parents and children, conflicts involving adoption and the termination of parental rights, and domestic violence situations. Moore (1986, p. 23) stated, "In family disputes, mediated and consensual settlements are often more appropriate and satisfying than litigated or imposed court outcomes." Mediation also is used to settle disputes between business partners, private individuals, government agencies and individuals, landlords and tenants, businesses and customers, and disputants in personal injury cases.

Many professionals now occasionally act as mediators to help people or groups in conflict resolve their concerns. Such professionals include attorneys, social workers, psychologists, and guidance counselors. A few social workers, attorneys, and other professionals work full-time as mediators—often in public or private mediation agencies.

Various models describe the mediation process (Moore, 1986). The one developed by Blades (1985) is summarized here. Blades viewed the mediation process as involving five stages:

1. *Introduction/commitment:* This stage usually is accomplished in a 1- to 2-hour session. The mediator sets ground rules, describes mediation, answers questions, discusses fees, and seeks to gain a commitment to the process from the two parties. The mediator also seeks to develop an understanding of the more pressing issues, gains a sense of the personal dynamics of the two parties, and tries to ascertain whether they are ready and willing to mediate. If one or both parties are unwilling to mediate, then the mediation probably should not proceed. If one or both parties are hesitant to proceed, the mediator usually describes the alternatives to mediation—such as a lengthy and expensive court battle.

2. *Definition:* The two parties, with the mediator's assistance, define the areas in which they already agree and disagree. At this stage certain disputes, such as divorce mediation, require a considerable amount of information.

3. *Negotiation:* Once the two parties agree on the issues in conflict and relevant factual information on these issues is obtained, the two parties are ready to begin negotiating. At this stage, the mediator seeks to have the parties focus on one issue at a time. A problem-solving approach is used in which the needs of each party are first identified and alternatives are generated. The mediator recedes into the background when discussions are proceeding well and steps in when emotions intensify or when the two parties are overlooking creative solutions that will meet their needs.

4. *Agreement:* Once alternatives are generated and related facts are evaluated, the two parties are ready to begin making agreements on the issues. The role of the mediator is to maintain a cooperative atmosphere and to keep the two parties focused on a manageable number of issues. The mediator summarizes areas of agreement and provides legal or other information necessary to a discussion. The mediator helps the two parties examine the merits and shortcomings of the options. During this stage, the mediator praises the parties for the progress they are making and gets them to praise themselves for progress made. The mediator seeks to create a positive atmosphere.

5. *Contracting:* In this final stage of mediation, the two parties review the agreements and clarify any ambiguities. The agreements are almost always written in the form of a contract, which is available for future reference. Either party, the mediator, or everyone together may write the contract. The contract expresses what each party agrees to do, may set deadlines for the diverse tasks to be completed, and may specify consequences if either party fails to meet the terms of the contract. Mediators seek to have specific agreements stated in concrete form to prevent future controversies. The ultimate goal of mediation is a contract in which no one is a loser and by which both parties willingly abide.

One of the major techniques mediators use is a caucus (Moore, 1986). At times a mediator, or either party, may stop the mediation and request a caucus. During a caucus, the two parties are physically separated from each other, and there is no direct communication between them. The mediator meets with one of the parties or with each party individually. Caucuses are called for many reasons: to vent intense emotions privately, to clarify misperceptions, to reduce unproductive or repetitive negative behavior, to clarify a party's interests, to provide a pause for each party to consider an alternative, to convince an uncompromising party that the mediation process is better than going to court, to uncover confidential information, to educate an inexperienced disputant about the processes of mediation, or to design alternatives that will later be brought to a joint session.

Caucuses allow parties to express in private the concessions they are willing to make. Usually such concessions are contingent on the other party's making certain concessions. During caucuses, mediators go back and forth, relaying information from one party to the other to develop a consensus.

NARRATIVE THERAPY

Narrative therapy, originally developed by therapists in Australia and New Zealand, is a recent approach. Michael White (1995) and other narrative therapists assert that our sense of reality is organized and maintained by the stories through which we circulate knowledge about the outside world and about ourselves. People who present negative, dead-end stories about themselves feel inadequate, defeated, overwhelmed, and without future choices. Narrative therapists insist that "the person is never the problem; the person has a problem." In other words, a problem is something one has, not something one is. A person with a problem does not have to change his or her nature but does have to fight the influence of the problem in his or her life.

All of us need to select from the huge amount of information the world throws at us all the time. We need to organize what we see, hear, feel, and remember into a meaningful "story." This always introduces biases: We notice and remember things we find interesting, important, and in line with our beliefs, expectations, and prejudices. We ignore, forget, or play down things that are contrary to the way we see the world. Things we notice and remember tend to confirm and strengthen our story about ourselves and our world. This works fine for most people—because they live reasonably happily within their world. Problems arise when a person is stuck in a story that makes him, her, or others unhappy. Examples are stories involving beliefs like these:

- "I am a violent person; I have a short fuse (and can't help it)."
- "I am no good, useless, have no worth; no one could possibly love me."
- "The world is a terribly dangerous place, and I am helpless in the face of its threats."

Such beliefs lead the person to erroneously believe "there is something wrong with me." Narrative therapy is a search for events that prove these beliefs to be false.

There are always exceptions: events that occurred but didn't fit the story and so were ignored, played down, or forgotten. They can be used to "write a new story," one that separates the problem from the way the person sees himself or herself. Once the problem is found and named, it can be fought. In the process, the person does not have to change. He or she discovers a past, an identity, that was always there but hidden by the biases of the previous story. The new story liberates the person from the shackles of the problem. Therapeutic help comes in the form of learning to reduce the power of problem-saturated stories and reclaiming one's life by substituting previously subjugated stories in which the person was successful.

Techniques used by narrative therapists include the following:

- *Externalizing the problem:* The problem becomes the opponent and is not viewed as a characteristic of the client. If a client is "depressed" or has a "gambling addiction," the problem becomes the *oppressor* that the client and the therapist will work against. Externalizing places the problem outside the client. This technique facilitates the client's seeing that he or she can overcome this *oppressor*, which paves the way for finding different solutions rather than blaming the client for the problem. The therapist can then proceed to deconstruct a preferred story.
- *Exceptions:* Narrative therapists seek to find exceptions—that is, occasions in clients' lives when their problems could have occurred but did not. Such exceptions can facilitate the beginning of a new (more preferred) story.
- *Positive narratives:* Narrative therapists help clients search for positive stories (things that they are doing well or things that are going well) in their lives. Such positive stories can give clients a sense of empowerment.
- *Support for positive narratives:* Narrative therapists use letters and certificates and seek to involve significant others to help clients reauthor their stories in a positive direction. Sharf (2008) notes:

    Letters written by the therapist summarize the session and externalize the problem. Such letters are positive and highlight the client's strengths. They focus on the unique outcomes of exceptions to the problem. Direct quotes from the session may be used. Also, questions or comments that the therapist thought about after the session can be included. Letters are mailed between sessions and at the end of therapy. Clients often report rereading the letters to help them to continue to make progress on the problem. Certificates, usually used with children, help to mark change and foster pride in having made changes. (p.425)

    Sharf (2008) also notes:

    Support for client stories can also come from parents, siblings, friends, or others. In family therapy, a therapist may ask questions such as "Mother, how do you see Jennie overcoming Anger?" or "Dad, how do teachers see Jennie fighting Anger at school?" These questions support the client's stories and provide ways to have several people supporting client change. From a narrative point of view, the client has a receptive audience to applaud or appreciate her progress.

    Although narrative therapists may use a variety of other approaches related to understanding the client's story, all focus on how the client can look differently at her story to bring about a new sense of hope or accomplishment. Family and others work with the client to bring about a new narrative that fights the externalized "problem."

It is interesting to note that narrative therapy is a cognitive therapy approach as it seeks to change self-defeating stories (cognitions) into preferred (more positive) stories.

SUMMARY

The following summarizes the module's content in terms of the learning objectives presented at the beginning of the module.

1. Describe play therapy, parental education, crisis intervention, solution-focused therapy, mediation, and narrative therapy.

   Play therapy is primarily used with young children. It serves many purposes: making a diagnosis, forming a relationship, ventilating feelings, working through unwanted emotions, teaching desired new behaviors, and modeling alternative behavior.

   The main goal of parental education programs is to help parents understand child behavior and develop child-rearing skills. Parent effectiveness training has four techniques that anyone can use to improve interactions with others: active listening, I-messages, no-lose problem solving, and resolving collisions of values.

   Crisis intervention emphasizes the importance of providing services to clients when they are experiencing crises. Crisis intervention seeks to promote effective coping that can lead to positive growth by acknowledging the problem, recognizing its impact, and learning more effective behaviors for coping with similar experiences.

   Solution-focused therapy spends little time dealing with underlying psychic issue that clients may have; instead the focus is on attaining the positive outcomes that clients seek.

   Mediation is used by a variety of professions to resolve conflicts between two or more people.

   Narrative therapists insist that a problem is something a person has, not something a person is. The goal of narrative therapy is to help the client reclaim his or her life by "writing a new story" in which the person is successful and happy.

EXERCISES

1. Using I-Messages

Goal: This exercise is designed to demonstrate how to phrase I-messages.

Step 1: Explain the goal of this exercise. Indicate that I-messages are a nonblaming description of the effects a person is having on the sender of the message. I-messages do not involve giving a solution message or a put-down message.

Step 2: Ask the class how to formulate I-messages in a variety of situations. The following are examples:

   a. Someone is smoking a cigarette near you, and the smoke is bothering you.
   b. You're riding in a car that a friend is driving dangerously fast.
   c. Someone is playing a stereo loudly in a building, which is interfering with your studying.
   d. A friend has just made another comment about your being overweight.
   e. A person you're dating continues to write to someone he or she dated in the past.

Step 3: Some of the responses given by students may well be you-messages. If that occurs, ask the class to indicate why the message is a you-message and not an I-message. If the class is having trouble formulating I-messages, ask students to discuss whether we are socialized in our society to use primarily you-messages.

2. Active Listening

Goal: This exercise is designed to have students practice and further develop their active listening skills.

Step 1: Explain the purpose of the exercise and describe what active listening is and what it is designed to accomplish. Indicate that active listening involves using two types of statements: reflecting feelings and restating content.

Step 2: Have students pair off. (Participate if there is someone without a partner.) Have one member of each pair select a topic to discuss for about 10 minutes. The topic may involve (a) a philosophical or moral issue such as abortion, (b) a problem with a friend or a relative, or (c) a problem at school.

Step 3: Ask the member who selected the topic to discuss it for about 10 minutes. The listener should try to respond solely with active listening statements.

Step 4: After the discussion, ask the presenter to discuss with the listener the quality of the active listening statements. Did the listener make the mistake of making suggestions, asking questions, or beginning to talk about personal experiences? Did active listening motivate the presenter to continue talking? Did the presenter perceive the active listening statements as primarily "natural" or "artificial"?

Have the listener discuss with the presenter his or her thoughts and feelings about using active listening statements. Did the listener want to make other types of statements? If so, what?

Step 5: Reverse the roles and repeat the process.

Step 6: Ask students to form a circle and discuss the merits and shortcomings of active listening. Did any unique or unusual events occur?

3. Narrative Therapy

Goal: This exercise is designed to assist students in comprehending narrative therapy.

Step 1: Students read the section on narrative therapy in the text.

Step 2: Each student writes down a problem that a friend or relative is having (students are told to withhold identifying information about this person). The problem might be excessive drinking, smoking too much, being depressed, excessive gambling, an eating disorder, and so on.

Step 3: Each student writes down his or her speculation about the self-defeating story that is leading to the problem.

Step 4: Volunteers are asked to share what they wrote. The class discusses what narrative therapy techniques may be useful in deconstructing the self-defeating story and reconstructing a preferred story.

SUGGESTED COUNSELOR'S RESPONSES TO CLIENT'S STATEMENTS

The following are suggested responses to the client's statements in Exercise 3, Chapter 5 (pp. 113–114):

1. "I sense that you feel strongly about this and that you've given this a lot of thought. I'd like to explore this further with you, as I care very much about you as a person. It makes me uncomfortable if you think that the only reason I meet with you is because I'm getting paid. Working with you and with the other clients I have is personally very gratifying. Perhaps I have miscommunicated with you, verbally or nonverbally. I'd like to hear more about why you've reached the conclusion that I don't care about you as a person."

2. "You're really feeling as if you're caught in a dilemma. Obviously in this situation, as in many situations, you can't please everyone. But are you aware that the most important person to please is yourself? You're the one who has to live with your decisions. I'm wondering what your feelings are toward Kent and what your feelings are about getting married at this time in your life. I'm also wondering why your parents dislike Kent. Let's examine these one at a time. What are your feelings toward Kent?"

3. "Yes, I did, I took them two summers ago when I was vacationing in the Colorado Rockies. But we're here to talk about you and how your life is going. Let's begin by discussing how you're doing in school. Could you please tell me your midterm grades for each of your classes?"

4. "I sense this is extremely difficult for you to reveal. You are probably feeling very vulnerable at this point. I'm pleased that you shared this with me, and I want you to know that I have an open mind about sexual orientation. It took real courage for you to talk about this, and I now believe we are in a much better position to help you make some decisions about your future. Can you tell me more about this person you're involved with?"

5. "It's true that I am neither black nor have I lived in an inner city. But I'm interested in you and in working with you. Just because I'm white doesn't mean we can't work together. Everyone, including me, has personal problems. You, too, have some personal problems. By taking each one, one at a time, and examining them and then coming up with some realistic ways of resolving them, I firmly believe we can make progress. Just as a teacher doesn't have to be blind to teach students with a visual disability, a counselor doesn't need to have the same color of skin to work with people who have personal problems. Have I said or done anything to lead you to believe that I am prejudiced against people of color?"

6. "I'm sorry you're still involved with drugs, especially since you were using drugs when you committed the offenses that resulted in your being sent here. I don't like to see you get into trouble, but I have no choice. I have to report this. I made it crystal clear to you at our first meeting that the consequences of drug involvement would probably be an extension of the time you spend here. As you know, we do have a drug treatment program. I suggest you seriously consider participating in this program. Participation in this program, now, may not only lead to an earlier release but may also help you become drug free. Are you interested in participating in this program?"

References

Addams, J. 1959. *Twenty Years of Hull House.* New York: Macmillan (original publication, 1910).

Adler, R. B., & N. Towne. 1981. *Looking Out/Looking In*, 3rd ed. New York: Holt, Rinehart and Winston.

Aguilar, I. 1972. "Initial Contacts with Mexican-American Families." *Social Work 17* (May), pp. 186–189.

Aguilar, M. A. 2001. "Catholicism." In *Spirituality within Religious Traditions* in *Social Work Practice*, eds. M. Van Hook, B. Hugen, & M. Aguilar, pp. 120–145. Pacific Grove, CA: Brooks/Cole.

Ahn, H. N., & N. Gilbert. 1992. "Cultural Diversity and Sexual Abuse Prevention." *Social Science Review 66,* no. 3, pp. 410–427.

Ainsworth, M. D., et al. 1966. *Deprivation of Maternal Care.* New York: Schocken Books.

Alberti, R. E., & M. L. Emmons. 1970. *Your Perfect Right: A Guide to Assertive Behavior.* San Luis Obispo, CA: Impact Publishers.

———. 1975. *Stand Up, Speak Out, Talk Back!* New York: Pocket Books.

Alexander, C. A. 1982. "Professional Social Work and Political Responsibility." In *Practical Politics: Social Work and Political Responsibility,* eds. M. Mahaffey & J. W. Hanks. Silver Spring, MD: National Association of Social Workers.

Alexander, K. 1993. "Changes in Delivery of Services for Students with Limited English." *The Advocate 1,* no. 2, p. 1.

Alinsky, S. D. 1969. *Reveille for Radicals.* New York: Basic Books.

———. 1972. *Rules for Radicals.* New York: Random House.

Alter, C., & W. Evens. 1990. *Evaluating Your Practice: A Guide to Self-Assessment.* New York: Springer.

American Association of Community Gardens. 2008. *Benefits of Community Gardening.* Retrieved March 2, 2008, from http://www.co.ramsey.mn.us/NR/rdonlyres/DA2B45C9-B882-4012-A1617A826D4E40E4/857/Benefits_of_Community_Gardening.pdf.

American Professional Credentialing Services. 1996. *Administration and Scaling Manual for the OQ® 45.2.* Wharton, NJ: Author (September).

American Psychiatric Association. 2000. *Diagnostic and Statistical Manual of Mental Disorders, Fourth Edition Text Revision.* Washington, DC: Author.

———. 2013. *Diagnostic and Statistical Manual of Mental Disorders, Fifth Edition.* Washington, DC: Author.

Appleby, G. A. 2001. "Dynamics of Oppression and Discrimination." In *Diversity, Oppression, and Social Functioning: Person-in-Environment Assessment and Intervention,* eds. G. A. Appleby, E. Colon, & J. Hamilton, pp. 36–52. Boston: Allyn & Bacon.

Asch, S. E. 1955. "Opinions and Social Pressure." *Scientific American 193,* no. 5, pp. 31–35.

Bach, G., & P. Wyden. 1981. *The Intimate Enemy.* New York: Avon.

Baer, R. A. 2003. Mindfulness training as a clinical intervention: A conceptual and empirical review. *Clinical Psychology: Science And Practice 10*(2), 125–143. Doi:10.1093/slipsy/bpg015.

Baer, D. M., R. Harrison, L. Fradenburg, D. Peterson, & S. Milia. 2005. "Some Pragmatics in the Valid and Reliable Recording of Directly Observed Behavior." *Research on Social Work Practice 15,* pp. 440–451.

Bandura, A. 1969. *Principles of Behavior Modification.* New York: Holt, Rinehart & Winston.

Banfield, F. K., J. Terris, & N. Vorsanger. 2001. *Solving Sprawl Models of Smart Growth in Communities across America.* Washington, DC: Natural Resources Defense Council.

Barker, R. L. 2003. *The Social Work Dictionary,* 5th ed. Washington, DC: National Association of Social Workers.

Barlow, D. H., & J. A. Cerny. 1988. *Psychological Treatment of Panic.* New York: Guilford.

Barlow, D. H., S. C. Hayes, & R. O. Nelson. 1984. *The Scientist Practitioner.* Elmsford, NY: Pergamon Press.

Barlow, D. H., & M. Hersen. 1984. *Single Case Experimental Designs,* 2nd ed. Elmsford. NY: Pergamon Press.

Barocas, H. A. 1972. "Psychodrama Techniques in Training Police in Family Crisis Intervention." *Group Psychotherapy* and *Psychodrama 25,* pp. 30–31.

Beck, A. T. 1976. *Cognitive Theory and the Emotional Disorders.* New York: International Universities Press.

Beck, A. T., A. J. Rush, B. F. Shaw, & G. Emery. 1979. *Cognitive Therapy of Depression.* New York: Guilford.

Beck, A. T., & M. E. Weishaar. 1989. "Cognitive Therapy." In *Current Psychotherapies,* 4th ed., eds. R. J. Corsini & D. Wedding, pp. 284–320. Itasca, IL: Peacock.

Becker, D. G. 1968. "Social Welfare Leaders as Spokesmen for the Poor." *Social Casework 49,* no. 2 (Feb.), p. 85.

Belgrave, F. Z., & K. W. Allison. 2006. *African American Psychology: From Africa to America.* Thousand Oaks, CA: Sage.

Bell, A. P., M. S. Weinberg, & S. K. Hammersmith. 1981. *Sexual Preference.* Bloomington, IN: Indiana University Press.

Bellack, A. S., & M. Hersen, eds. 1998. *Behavioral Assessment: A Practical Handbook,* 4th ed. Boston: Allyn & Bacon.

Bemner, R. M. 1962. "The Rediscovery of Pauperism." In *Current Issues in Social Work Seen in Historical Perspective.* New York: Council on Social Work Education.

Benjamin, A. 1974. *The Helping Interview*, 2nd ed. Boston: Houghton Mifflin.

Benson, H. 1975. *The Relaxation Response.* New York: Morrow.

Berg, I. K, & P. DeJong. 1996. "Solution-Building Conversations: Co-Constructing a Sense of Competence with Clients." *Families* in *Society* (June), pp. 376–391.

Berg, I. K, & S. D. Miller. 1992. *Working with the Problem Drinker: A Solution-Focused Approach.* New York: Norton.

Bergman, A. 1989. "Informal Support Systems for Pregnant Teenagers." *Social Casework 70,* no. 9, pp. 526–533.

Bernanos, G. 1970. As quoted in J. C. DeBoer, *Let's Plan: A Guide to the Planning Process for Voluntary Organizations.* New York: United Church Press.

Bernstein, B. E. 1975. "The Social Worker as a Courtroom Witness." *Social Casework 56,* no. 9 (Nov.), pp. 521–525.

Berwick, D. 1980. "Nonorganic Failure to Thrive." *Pediatrics in Review 1,* pp. 265–270.

Billingsley, A. 1993. *Climbing Jacob's Ladder: The Enduring Legacy of African-American Families.* New York: Simon & Schuster.

Black, B. J. 1977. "Milieu Therapy." In *Encyclopedia of Social Work,* 17th ed., pp. 919–927. New York: National Association of Social Workers.

Blades, J. 1985. *Mediate Your Divorce.* Englewood Cliffs, NY: Prentice-Hall.

Blatner, A. 1995. "Psychodrama." In *Current Psychotherapies*, 5th ed., eds. R. J. Corsini & D. Wedding. Itasca, IL: Peacock.

Bloom, M. 1975. *The Paradox of Helping: Introduction to the Philosophy of Scientific Practice*. New York: Wiley.

———. 1983. "Empirically Based Clinical Research." In *Handbook of Clinical Social Work,* eds. A. Rosenblatt & D. Waldfogel, pp. 560–582. San Francisco: Jossey-Bass.

Bloom, M., J. Fischer, & J. G. Orme. 2006. *Evaluating Practice: Guidelines for the Accountable Professional,* 5th ed. Boston: Allyn & Bacon.

———. 2009. *Evaluating Practice: Guidelines for the Accountable Professional,* 6th ed. Boston: Pearson/Allyn & Bacon.

Blythe, B. J., & T. Tripodi. 1989. *Measurement in Direct Practice.* Newbury Park, CA: Sage.

Booth, A., K. Carver, & D. A. Granger. 2005. "Biosocial Perspectives on the Family." In *Exploring Family Theories*, eds. B. B. Ingoldsby, S. R. Smith, & J. E. Miller, pp. 227–246. Los Angeles: Roxbury.

Boyte, H. C. 1989. "People Power Transforms a St. Louis Housing Project." *Occasional Papers* (Jan.) Chicago: Community Renewable Society, pp. 1–5.

BPD. 2006. "Definition of Generalist Practice." Discussed and advanced by the BPD Social Work Continuum Committee and approved by the BPD Board of Directors.

Brammer, R. 2004. *Diversity in Counseling.* Belmont, CA: Brooks/Cole.

Branston, G., & R. Stafford. 2006. *The Media Student's Book*, 4th ed. London: Taylor & Francis.

Brave Heart, M. Y. H. 2001. "Culturally and Historically Congruent Clinical Social Work Interventions with Native Clients." In *Culturally Competent Practice*, eds. R. Fong & S. Furuto, pp. 285–298. Boston: Allyn & Bacon.

Brawley, E. A. 1983. *Mass Media and Human Services: Getting the Message Across.* Beverly Hills, CA: Sage.

———. 1995. *Human Services and the Media: Developing Partnerships for Change.* Newark, NJ: Harwood Academic Publisher.

Brieland, D., L. B. Costin, & C. R. Atherton. 1985. *Contemporary Social Work: An Introduction to Social Work and Social Welfare*, 3rd ed. New York: McGraw-Hill.

Briggs, H. E., W. Feyerherm, & W. Gingerich. 2004. "Evaluating Science-Based Practice with Single-Subject Designs." In *Using Evidence in Social Work Practice: Behavioral Perspectives*, eds. H. E. Briggs & T. L. Rzepnicki. Chicago: Lyceum Books.

Brown, B. B. 1977. *Stress and the Art of Biofeedback.* New York: Bantam Books.

Bullis, R. K. 1996. *Spirituality in Social Work Practice.* Washington, DC: Taylor & Francis.

Bureau of Labor Statistics. 2010. *Persons with a Disability: Labor Force Characteristics Summary.* Washington, DC: Author.

———. 2013. *Persons with a Disability: Labor Force Characteristics Summary.* Retrieved from: http://www.bls.gov/news .release/disabl.nr0.htm.

Campbell, J. A. 1988. "Client Acceptance of Single-System Evaluation Procedures." *Social Work Research & Abstracts 24,* pp. 21–22.

———. 1990. "Ability of Practitioners to Estimate Client Acceptance of Single-Subject Evaluation Procedures." *Social Work 35,* pp. 9–14.

Canadian Association of Social Workers. 2005. *Code of Ethics and Guideliners for Ethical Practice.* Retrieved from www.caswacts.ca.

Cartwright, T. J. 1973. "Problems, Solutions and Strategies: A Contribution to the Theory and Practice of Planning." *AIP Examination Readings.* Washington, DC: American Institute of Planners.

Center for Social Research and Development. 1974. *Analysis and Synthesis of Needs Assessment Research in the Field of Human Services.* Denver: University of Denver.

Chambless, D. L., & A. J. Goldstein. 1979. "Behavioral Psychotherapy." In *Current Psychotherapies*, 2nd ed., ed. R. Corsini. Itasca, IL: Peacock.

Chicago Tribune. 1998. "Model Minority Doesn't Tell?" (Jan. 3), p. 18.

Christie, R., & F. Geis. 1970. *Studies in Machiavellianism.* New York: Academic Press.

Ciminero, A. R., K. S. Calhoun, & H. E. Adams, eds. 1986. *Handbook of Behavioral Assessment*, 2nd ed. New York: Wiley.

Clements-Nolle, K., R. Marx, & M. Katz. 2006. "Attempted Suicide among Transgender Persons: The Influence of Gender-Based Discrimination and Victimization." *Journal of Homosexuality 51*, no. 3, pp. 53–69.

Clifton, R. L., & A. M. Dahms. 1980. *Grassroots Administration: A Handbook for Staff and Directors of Small Community-Based Social-Service Agencies.* Belmont, CA: Wadsworth.

Cnaan, R. A. 1999. *The Newer Deal: Social Work and Religion in Partnership.* New York: Columbia University Press.

Cohen, N. E. 1958. *Social Work in the American Tradition.* Hinsdale, IL: Dryden Press.

Coleman, J. W., & D. R. Cressey. 1995. *Social Problems*, 8th ed. Englewood Cliffs, NJ: Prentice-Hall.

Compton, B., & B. Galaway. 1975. *Social Work Processes.* Homewood: IL: Dorsey Press.

———. 1999. *Social Work Processes*, 6th ed. Pacific Grove, CA: Brooks/Cole.

Congress, E. P. 2000. "What Social Workers Should Know About Ethics: Understanding and Resolving Practice Dilemmas." *Advances in Social Work 1*, no. 1 (Spring), pp. 1–25.

———. 2004. "Cultural and Ethical Issues in Working with Culturally Diverse Patients and Their Families: The Use of the Culturagram to Promote Cultural Competent Practice in Health Care Settings." In *Social Work Visions from Around the Globe: Citizens, Methods, and Approaches.* Binghamton, NY: Haworth Press, pp. 249–262.

Cooley, C. H. 1902. *Human Nature and the Social Order.* New York: Scribner.

Cooper, M. 1990. "Treatment of a Client with Obsessive Compulsive Disorder." *Social Work Research & Abstracts 26,* pp. 26–32.

Corcoran, K., & J. Fischer. 2007. *Measures for Clinical Practice*, 4th ed. New York: Free Press.

Corcoran, K., & W. J. Gingerich. 1994. "Practice Evaluation in the Context of Managed Care: Case-Recording Methods for Quality Assurance Reviews." *Research on Social Work Practice 4*, pp. 326–337.

Corey, G. 2004. *Theory and Practice of Group Counseling.* Belmont, CA: Brooks/Cole.

Cormier, W. H., & L. S. Cormier. 1991. *Interviewing Strategies for Helpers.* Pacific Grove, CA: Brooks/Cole.

Council on Social Work Education. 1982. *Curriculum Policy for the Master's Degree & Baccalaureate Degree Programs in Social Work Education.* New York: Author, adopted May 24.

———. 1992a. *Curriculum Policy Statement for Baccalaureate Degree Programs in Social Work Education.* Alexandria, VA: Author.

———. 1992b. *Curriculum Policy Statement for Master's Degree Programs in Social Work Education.* Alexandria, VA: Author.

———. 2008. *Educational Policy and Accreditation Standards.* Alexandria, VA: Author.

———. 2015. *Educational Policy and Accreditation Standards,* Alexandria, VA: Author.

Cournoyer, B. R. 2004. *The Evidence-Based Social Work Skills Book*. Boston: Allyn & Bacon.

Criddle, W. D. 1974. "Guidelines for Challenging Irrational Beliefs." *Rational Living* (Spring), pp. 8–13.

Crosbie, J. 1993. "Interrupted Time-Series Analysis with Brief Single-Subject Data." *Journal of Consulting and Clinical Psychology 61*, pp. 966–974.

Davenport, J., & J. Davenport. 1982. "Utilizing the Social Network in Rural Communities." *Social Casework 63* (Feb.), pp. 106–112.

Davidson, D. 2000. "Issues Facing Elderly Gay Men and Lesbians." Retrieved from www.keln.org/bibs/Davidson.html.

Davie, J. S., & A. P. Hare. 1956. "Button-Down Collar Culture: A Study of Undergraduate Life at a Men's College." *Human Organization 14*, pp. 13–20.

Davis, K., & W. Newstrom. 1989. *Human Behavior at Work*, 8th ed. New York: McGraw-Hill.

Davis, L. V. 1994. *Building on Women's Strengths*. New York: Haworth.

De Mello, A. 1978. *Sadhana: A Way to God*. Garden City, NY: Image Books.

de Shazer, S. 1988. "The Death of Resistance." *Family Process 23*, pp. 79–93.

Dean, R. 2001. "The Myth of Cross-Cultural Competence." *Families in Society 82*, no. 6, pp. 623–630.

DeBoer, J. C. 1970. *Let's Plan: A Guide to the Planning Process for Voluntary Organizations*. New York: United Church Press.

DeJong, P., & I. K. Berg. 1998. *Interviewing for Solutions*. Pacific Grove, CA: Brooks/Cole.

DeJong, P., & S. D. Miller. 1995. "How to Interview for Client Strengths." *Social Work 40*, no. 6 (Nov.), pp. 729–736.

Delbecq, A. L., & A. Van de Ven. 1971. "A Group Process Model for Problem Identification and Program Planning." *Journal of Applied Behavioral Science* (July–Aug.).

Deming, W. E. 1986. *Out of the Crisis*. Cambridge, MA: Massachusetts Institute of Technology, Center for Advanced Engineering Study.

Deparle, J. 2007. "Cultivating Their Own Gardens." *New York Times*, September 30.

Devore, W., & E. G. Schlesinger. 1996. *Ethnic-Sensitive Social Work Practice*, 4th ed. Boston: Allyn & Bacon.

———. 1998. *Ethnic-Sensitive Social Work Practice*. 5th ed. Boston: Pearson.

Dhopper, S. S., & S. E. Moore. 2001. *Social Work Practice with Culturally Diverse People*. Thousand Oaks: CA: Sage.

Dickson, D. T. 1998. *Confidentiality and Privacy in Social Work*. New York: Free Press.

DiGiussepe, R., N. Miller, & L. Trexler. 1977. "A Review of Rational Emotive Psychotherapy Outcome Studies." *Counseling Psychologist 7*, no. l.

DiGiuseppe, R. A., M. Terjesen, R. Rose, K. Doyle, & N. Vadalakis. 1998. "*Selective Abstractions Errors in Reviewing REBT Outcome Studies: A Review of Reviews*." Poster presented at the 106th Annual Convention of the American Psychological Association, San Francisco (Aug.).

Dolgoff, R., & D. Feldstein. 1980. *Understanding Social Welfare*. New York: Harper & Row.

Dolgoff, R., F. M. Loewenberg, & D. Harrington. 2009. *Ethical Decisions for Social Work Practice*. Belmont, CA: Brooks/ Cole.

Dorfman, D. 1998. *Mapping Community Assets Workbook*. Portland, OR: Northwest Regional Educational Laboratory.

Downs, S. W., E. Moore, E. J. McFadden, & L. B. Costin. 2000. *Child Welfare and Family Services*, 6th ed. Boston: Allyn & Bacon.

Dreikurs, R. 1964. *Children: The Challenge*. New York: Hawthorn Books.

Drucker, P. F. 1954. *The Practice of Management*. New York: Harper.

Dumont, M. 1968. *The Absurd Healer*. New York: Viking Press.

Dunn, J. 1977. *Distress and Comfort*. Cambridge, MA: Harvard University Press.

Earl, J. 2006. "Pursuing Social Change Online: The Use of Four Protest Tactics on the Internet." *Social Science Computer Review 24*, no. 3, pp. 362–377.

Edelwich, J. 1980. *Burn-Out*. New York: Human Sciences Press.

Egan, G. 1985. *Change Agent Skills in Helping and Human Service Settings*. Pacific Grove, CA: Brooks/Cole.

Ell, K. 1995. "Crisis Intervention: Research Needs." In *Encyclopedia of Social Work*, 19th ed. Washington, DC: National Association of Social Workers.

Ellis, A. 1957. "Outcome of Employing Three Techniques of Psychotherapy." *Journal of Clinical Psychology 13*, pp. 344–350.

———. 1958. "Rational Psychotherapy." *Journal of General Psychology 58* (Jan.), pp. 35–49.

———. 1962. *Reason and Emotion in Psychotherapy*. New York: Lyle Stuart.

———. 1973. "Rational-Emotive Therapy." In *Current Psychotherapies*, ed. R. Corsini, pp. 167–206. Itasca, IL: Peacock.

———. 1979. "Rational-Emotive Therapy." In *Current Psychotherapies*, 2nd ed., ed. Raymond Corsini, pp. 185–229. Itasca, IL: Peacock.

———. 2000. "Rational Emotive Behavior Therapy." In *Current Psychotherapies*, 6th ed., eds. R. J. Corsini & D. Wedding, pp. 168–204. Itasca, IL: Peacock.

———. 2008. "Rational Emotive Behavior Therapy." In *Current Psychotherapies*, 8th ed., eds. R. J. Corsini & D. Wedding, pp. 187–222. Belmont, CA: Brooks/ Cole.

Ellis, A., & R. Harper. 1977. *A New Guide to Rational Living*. North Hollywood, CA: Wilshire Books.

Emmelkamp, P. M. G. 1994. "Behavior Therapy with Adults." In *Handbook of Psychotherapy and Behavior Change*, 4th ed., eds. A. E. Bergin & S. L. Garfield, pp. 379–427. New York: Wiley.

Eriksen, K. 1979. *Communication Skills for the Human Services*. Reston, VA: Reston Publishing.

Etzioni, A. 1964. *Modern Organizations*. Englewood Cliffs, NJ: Prentice-Hall.

Eysenck, H. J. 1961. "The Effects of Psychotherapy." In *Handbook of Abnormal Psychology*, pp. 697–725. New York: Basic Books.

———. 1965. "The Effects of Psychotherapy." *International Journal of Psychiatry 1*, pp. 97–144.

Falck, H. E. 1966. "Integrating the Rural Welfare Department into the Community." In *Can Welfare Keep Pace?*, ed. M. Morton. New York: Columbia University Press.

Family Village Disability Culture. 2010. "Famous People and Disabilities." Retrieved September 13, 2010, from www.familyvillage_wisc.edu/general/famous.html.

Faul, A. C., S. L. McMurtry, & W. W. Hudson. 2001. "Can Empirical Clinical Practice Techniques Improve Social Work Outcomes?" *Research on Social Work Practice 11*, 277–299.

Fellin, P. 1987. *The Social Worker and the Community*. Itasca, IL: Peacock.

Fensterheim, H., & J. Baer. 1975. *Don't Say Yes When You Want to Say No*. New York: Dell.

Ferguson, T. 1996. *Health Online*. Reading, MA: Addison-Wesley.

Fine, L. J. 1979. "Psychodrama." In *Current Psychotherapies*, 2nd ed., ed. R. J. Corsini. Itasca, IL: Peacock.

Fischer, J., & K. Corcoran. 2006. *Measures for Clinical Practice*, 4th ed. New York: Oxford University Press.

Flanagan, J. 1977. *The Grass Roots Fundraising Book: How to Raise Money in Your Community*. Chicago: Swallow Press.

———. **1995.** *The Grass Roots Fundraising Book: How to Raise Money in Your Community*. Raleigh, NC: Contemporary Press.

Follette, V., K. Palm, & A. N. Pearson. 2006. Mindfulness and trauma: Implications for treatment. *Journal of Rational-Emotive & Cognitive-Behavior Therapy 24*(1), 45-62. Doi:10.1007/s10942-006-0025-2.

Fong, R. 2003. "Cultural Competence with Asian Americans." In *Culturally Competent Practice*, pp. 261–281. Pacific Grove, CA: Brooks/Cole.

Ford, J., D. Young, B. Perez, R. Obermeyer, & D. Rohmer. 1992. "Needs Assessment for Persons with Severe Mental Illness: What Services Are Needed for Successful Community Living?" *Community Mental Health Journal 28*, no. 6, pp. 491–503.

Frank, J. D. 1973. *Persuasion and Healing*, 2nd ed. Baltimore: Johns Hopkins University Press.

Franklin, A. J. 1999. "Therapeutic Support Groups for African American Men." In *Working with African American Males*, ed. L. E. Davis, pp. 5–14. Thousand Oaks, CA: Sage.

Freedman, N., & R. Sherman. 1987. *Handbook of Measurements for Marriage and Family Therapy*. New York: Brunner/Mazel.

Freeman, E. M. 1994. "Women Who Work outside the Home: Multicultural and Multigenerational Influences on the Family Adjustment Process." In *Building on Women's Strengths*, ed. L. V. Davis. New York: Haworth.

French, J. R. P., & B. Raven. 1968. "The Bases of Social Power." In *Group Dynamics: Research and Theory*, 3rd ed., eds. D. Cartwright & A. Zander. New York: Harper & Row.

Freudenberger, H. J. 1977. "Burn-Out: Occupational Hazard of the Child Care Worker." *Child Care Quarterly 6*, pp. 90–99.

Frey, G. A. 1990. "A Framework for Promoting Organizational Change." *Families in Society 71*, no. 3, pp. 142–147.

Furman, L. E. 1994. "Religion and Spirituality in Social Work Education: Preparing the Culturally-Sensitive Practitioner for the Future." Paper presented at Midwest Biennial Conference on Social Work, April 28–29, St. Paul, MN.

Galan, F. 2001. "Interventions with Mexican American Families." In *Culturally Competent Practice*, eds. R. Fong & S. Furuto, pp. 255–268. Boston: Allyn & Bacon

Galper, J. H. 1975. *The Politics of Social Services*. Englewood Cliffs, NJ: Prentice-Hall.

———. **1980.** *Social Work Practice: A Radical Perspective*. Englewood Cliffs, NJ: Prentice-Hall.

Gambrill, E. 1999. "Evidence-Based Practice: An Alternative to Authority-Based Practice." *Families in Society: Journal of Contemporary Human Services 80*, no. 4, pp. 341–350.

———. **2006.** "Evidence-Based Practice and Policy: Choices Ahead." *Research on Social Work Practice 16*, pp. 338–357.

Ganz, M., 2009. *Why David Sometimes Wins: Leadership, Organization, and Strategy in the California Farm Worker Movement*. New York: Oxford University Press.

Garland, J. A., H. Jones, & R. Kolodny. 1965. "A Model for Stages of Development in Social Work Groups." In *Explorations in Group Work*, ed. S. Bernstein. Boston: Milford House.

Garvin, C. D., & F. M. Cox. 2001. "A History of Community Organizing since the Civil War with Special Reference to Oppressed Communities." In *Strategies of Community Intervention*, 6th ed., eds. J. Rothman, J. L. Erlich, & J. E. Tropman, pp. 64–99. Itasca, IL: Peacock.

Gates. G. J. (2001). *Gay and Lesbian Families in the United States: Same-Sex Unmarried Partner Households*. Washington, DC: Urban Institute.

Ghali, S. B. 1992. "Understanding Puerto Rican Traditions." *Social Work 27*, no. 1 (Jan.), pp. 98–102.

Gibb, J. R. 1961. "Defensive Communication" *Journal of Communication 11*, pp. 1741–148.

Gibson, G., & K. Ottenbacher. 1988. "Characteristics Influencing the Visual Analysis of Single-Subject Data: An Empirical Investigation." *Journal of Applied Behavioral Science 24*, pp. 298–314.

Gingerich, W. J. 1979. "Procedure for Evaluating Clinical Practice." *Health and Social Work 4*, pp. 105–130.

———. **1983.** "Significance Testing in Single-Case Research." In *Handbook of Clinical Social Work*, eds. A. Rosenblatt & D. Waldfogel, pp. 694–720. San Francisco: Jossey-Bass.

———. **1990.** "Expert Systems and Their Potential Uses in Social Work." *Families in Society 71*, pp. 220–228.

———. **1995a.** "Expert Systems." In *Encyclopedia of Social Work*, 19th ed., ed. R. L. Edwards, pp. 917–925. Washington, DC: NASW Press.

———. **1995b.** "MY ASSISTANT: Computer-Assisted Record-Keeping for the Case Manager." Poster session at the Nineteenth Annual Symposium on Computer Applications in Medical Care, New Orleans, LA.

———. **2002a.** "Computer Applications for Social Work Practice." In *Social Worker's Desk Reference*, eds. A. R. Roberts & G. J. Greene, pp. 23–28. New York: Oxford University Press.

———. **2002b.** "Online Social Work: Ethical and Practical Considerations." In *Social Worker's Desk Reference*, eds. A. R. Roberts & G. J. Greene, pp. 81–85. New York: Oxford University Press.

Gingerich, W. J., & A. Broskowski. 1996. "Clinical Decision Support Systems." In *The Computerization of Behavioral Healthcare*, ed. T. Trabin, pp. 11–38. San Francisco: Jossey-Bass.

Ginott, H. G. 1965. *Between Parent and Child*. New York: Macmillan.

Ginsburg, L. 1998. *Social Work in Rural Communities*, 3rd ed. Alexandria, VA: Council on Social Work Education.

Glasser, W. 1965. *Reality Therapy*. New York: Harper & Row.

———. **1972.** *The Identity Society*. New York: Harper & Row.

———. **1984.** *Control Theory*. New York: Harper & Row.

———. **1998.** *Choice Theory: A New Psychology of Personal Freedom*. New York: HarperPerennial.

———. **2000.** *Reality Therapy in Action*. New York: HarperCollins.

———. **2003.** *Warning: Psychiatry Can Be Hazardous to Your Health*. New York: HarperCollins.

Glasser, W., & R. Wubbolding. 1995. "Reality Therapy." In *Current Psychotherapies*, 5th ed., eds. R. J. Corsini & D. Wedding, pp. 293–321. Itasca, IL: Peacock.

Golan, N. 1979. "Crisis Theory." In *Social Work Treatment*, 2nd ed., ed. F. J. Turner, pp. 499–531. London: Free Press.

Goldenberg, I., & H. Goldenberg. 1991. *Family Therapy, An Overview*, 3rd ed. Pacific Grove, CA: Brooks/Cole.

———. **2004.** *Family Therapy: An Overview*, 6th ed. Pacific Grove, CA: Brooks/Cole.

Googins, B., V. A. Capoccia, & N. Kaufman. 1983. "The Interactional Dimension of Planning: A Framework for Practice." *Social Work 18* (July–Aug.), pp. 273-278.

Google Maps User Guide. 2008. Retrieved March 8, 2008, from http://local.google.com/support/bin/answer.py?hl-en&answer-68480.

Gordon, T. 1970. *Parent Effectiveness Training*. New York: Wyden.

Grandin, T. 2011. *The Way I See It*, 2nd ed. Arlington, TX: Future Horizons.

Green, J. W. 1999. *Cultural Awareness in the Human Services*. Boston: Allyn & Bacon.

Green, R. G., M. Kiernan-Stern, & F. R. Baskind. 2005. "White Social Workers' Attitudes about People of Color." *Journal of Ethnic & Cultural Diversity in Social Work 14*, nos. 1–2, pp. 47–68.

Greenberg, H. M. 1980. *Coping with Job Stress*. Englewood Cliffs, NJ: Spectrum.

Greenleaf, R. K., L. C. Spears, & S. R. Covey. 2002. *Servant Leadership: A Journey into the Nature of Legitimate Power and Greatness*. Mahwah, NJ: Paulist Press.

Greenstone, J. L. & S. C. Levinton. 2011. *Elements of Crisis Intervention: Crises and How to Respond to Them*, 3rd ed., Belmont, CA: Brooks/Cole.

Grier, W. H., & P. M. Cobbs. 1968. *Black Rage*. New York: Basic Books.

Grohol, J. M. 2000. *The Insider's Guide to Mental Health Resources Online, 2000/2001 Edition*. New York: Guilford Press.

———. 2003. *The Insider's Guide to Mental Health Resources Online, 2002/2003 Edition*. New York: Guilford Press.

Gross, E. R. 1996. "Deconstructing Politically Correct Practice Literature: The American Indian Case." In *Multicultural Issues in Social Work*, eds. P. L. Ewalt et al., pp. 241–254. Washington, DC: NASW Press.

Grossman, J. M., & B. Liang. 2008. "Discrimination Distress among Chinese American Adolescents." *Journal of Youth Adolescence 37*, pp. 1–11.

Grotevant, H. D., & C. I. Carlson. 1987. "Family Interaction Coding Systems: A Descriptive Review." *Family Process 26*, p. 49.

Guthrie, E. R. 1935. *The Psychology of Learning*. New York: Harper & Row.

Hall, C. J. 2007. "Perceptions of Need and the Ethicality of the Male Social Work Practice." *Families in Society 88*, no. 2, pp. 214–222.

Hare, A. 1962. *Handbook of Small Group Research*. New York: Free Press.

Harper, K. V., & J. Lantz. 1996. *Cross-Cultural Practice: Social Work with Diverse Populations*. Chicago: Lyceum Books.

Harper-Dorton, K., & J. Lantz. 2007. *Cross-Cultural Practice: Social Work with Diverse Populations*. Chicago: Lyceum.

Hartman, A. 1978. "Diagrammatic Assessment of Family Relationships." *Social Casework 59* (Oct.), pp. 465–476.

Hauck, P. A. 1972. *The Rational Management of Children*. New York: Libra Publishers.

Hayes, S. C., & L. A. Greco. 2008. Acceptance & Mindfulness Treatments for Children & Adolescents: A Practitioner's Guide. Oakland, CA: New Harbinger Publications.

Hayes, S. C., J. B. Luoma, F. W. Bond, A. Masuda, & J. Lillis. 2006. Acceptance and Commitment Therapy: Model, Processes and Outcomes. *Behavior Research & Therapy 44*(1), 1–25.

Hepworth, D. H., & J. Larsen. 1986. *Direct Social Work Practice: Theory and Skills*, 2nd ed. Pacific Grove, CA: Brooks/Cole.

———. 1993. *Direct Social Work Practice*, 4th ed. Pacific Grove, CA: Brooks/Cole.

Hepworth, D. H., R. H. Rooney, & J. A. Larson. 1997. *Direct Social Work Practice*, 5th ed. Pacific Grove, CA: Brooks/Cole.

Herrnstein, R. J., & C. Murray. 1994. *The Bell Curve: The Reshaping of American Life by Differences in Intelligence*. New York: Free Press.

Hersen, M., & A. S. Bellack, eds. 1988. *Dictionary of Behavioral Assessment Techniques*. Elmsford, NY: Pergamon Press.

Hersey, P., & K. Blanchard. 1977. *Management of Organizational Behavior: Utilizing Human Resources*, 3rd ed. Englewood Cliffs, NJ: Prentice-Hall.

Hick, S. F., & J. G. McNutt. 2002. *Advocacy, Activism, and the Internet*. Chicago: Lyceum Books.

Hollis, F. 1972. *Casework: A Psychosocial Theory*. New York: Random House.

Hower, D. 1994. "David Hower's Definition of Total Quality." *Reporter* (Aug. 29), p. 10. Whitewater: University of Wisconsin–Whitewater.

Hudson, W. W. 1982. *The Clinical Measurement Package: A Field Manual*. Pacific Grove, CA: Brooks/Cole.

———. 1992. *Walmyr Assessment Scales*. Tempe, AZ: Walmyr.

Hull, C. L. 1943. *Principles of Behavior*. New York: Appleton-Century-Crofts.

Hull, G. H. 1978. "The Parents' Anonymous Sponsor: A Professional Helping Role." Paper presented at the Child Welfare League of America Regional Conference, Omaha, NE.

———. 1990. *Social Work Internship Manual*. Eau Claire: University of Wisconsin–Eau Claire, Department of Social Work.

Hyde, J. S., & J. DeLamater. 2006. *Understanding Human Sexuality*, 9th ed. New York: McGraw-Hill.

———. 2011. *Understanding Human Sexuality*, 10th ed. New York: McGraw-Hill.

International Federation of Social Workers and International Association of Social Workers. 2004. *Ethics in Social Work, Statement of Principles*. Retrieved from www.ifsw.org.

Ivey, A. E., & M. B. Ivey. 1999. *Intentional Interviewing and Counseling*. Pacific Grove, CA: Brooks/Cole.

Jackson, D. D. 1965. "The Study of the Family." *Family Process 4*, pp. 1–20.

Jaffee, S., & J. S. Hyde. 2000. "Gender Differences in Moral Orientation: A Meta-Analysis." *Psychological Bulletin 126*, pp. 703–726.

Janis, I. 1971. "Group Think." *Psychology Today 15*, no. 6. (November), pp. 43–46, 74–76.

Jayaratne, S., & R. L. Levy. 1979. *Empirical Clinical Practice*. New York: Columbia University Press.

Johnson, D. W., & F. P. Johnson. 1975. *Joining Together*. Englewood Cliffs, NJ: Prentice-Hall.

———. 1987. *Joining Together*, 3rd ed. Englewood Cliffs, NJ: Prentice-Hall.

———. 2000. *Joining Together*, 7th ed. Boston: Allyn & Bacon.

———. 2009. *Joining Together*, 9th ed. Columbus, OH: Metrill.

Johnson, E. H. 1973. *Social Problems of Urban Man*. Pacific Grove, CA: Brooks/Cole.

Johnson, L. C. 1986. *Social Work Practice: A Generalist Approach*, 2nd ed. Boston: Allyn & Bacon.

Jones, R. R., R. S. Vaught, & M. R. A. Weinrott. 1977. "Time-Series Analysis in Operant Research." *Journal of Applied Behavior Analysis 10*, pp. 151–166.

Julia, M. 2000. *Constructing Gender*. Pacific Grove, CA: Brooks/Cole.

Juran, J. M. 1989. *Juran on Leadership for Quality: An Executive Handbook*. New York: Free Press.

Kabat-Zinn, J. 2012. *Mindfulness for Beginners: Reclaiming the Present Moment—and Your Life*. Boulder, CO: Sounds True.

Kabat-Zinn, J., A. O. Massion, J. Kristeller, L. G. Peterson, K. E. Fletcher, L. Pbert, et al. 1992. Effectiveness of a meditation-based stress reduction program in the treatment of anxiety disorders. *American Journal of Psychiatry 149*, 936–94.

Kadushin, A. 1972. *The Social Work Interview*. New York: Columbia University Press.

Kanfer, F. 1975. "Self-Management Methods." In *Helping People Change*, eds. F. H. Kanfer & A. P. Goldstein, pp. 309–355. Elmsford, NY: Pergamon Press.

Kaplan, S. G., & E. G. Wheeler. 1983. "Survival Skills for Working with Potentially Violent Clients." *Social Casework 64*, no. 6 (June), pp. 339–346.

Katz, A. H., & E. I. Bender. 1976. *The Strength in Us: Self-Help Groups in the Modern World.* New York: Franklin-Watts.

Kaufman, R., & S. Thomas. 1980. *Evaluation without Fear.* New York: New Viewpoints.

Kazdin, A. E. 1977a. "Assessing the Clinical or Applied Importance of Behavior Change through Social Validation." *Behavior Modification 1*, pp. 427–452.

——. **1977b.** *The Token Economy.* New York: Plenum.

Keegan, P. B. 1994. *Fundraising for Nonprofits: How to Build a Community Partnership.* New York: Harper Resource.

Keith-Lucas, A. 1972. *The Giving and Taking of Help.* Chapel Hill: University of North Carolina Press.

——. **1985.** *So You Want to Be a Social Worker: A Primer for the Christian Student.* St. Davids, PA: North American Association of Christians in Social Work.

Kelly, H. H., & A. J. Stahelski. 1970. "Social Interaction Basis of Cooperators' and Competitors' Beliefs about Others." *Journal of Personality and Social Psychology 16*, pp. 66–91.

Kelman, H. C. 1965. "Manipulation of Human Behavior: An Ethical Dilemma for the Social Scientist." *Journal of Social Issues 21*, no. 2, pp. 31–46.

Kertzner, R. M. 2007. "Developmental Issues in Lesbian and Gay Adulthood." In *The Health of Sexual Minorities: Public Health Perspectives on Lesbian, Gay, Bisexual, and Transgender Populations*, eds. I. H. Meyer & M. E. Northridge. New York: Springer.

Kilpatrick, A. C., & T. P. Holland. 2003. *Working with Families, an Integrative Model by Level of Need*, 3rd ed. Boston: Allyn & Bacon.

King, S. W., & R. S. Meyers. 1981. "Developing Self-Help Groups: Integrating Group Work and Community Organization Strategies." *Social Development Issues 5*, pp. 33–46.

Kiresuk, T. J., & S. H. Lund. 1978. "Goal Attainment Scaling." In *Evaluation of Human Service Programs*, eds. C. C. Attkisson, W. A. Hargreaves, M. J. Horowitz, & J. E. Sorensen, pp. 341–370. New York: Academic Press.

——. **2008.** *Understanding Generalist Practice*, 5th ed. Pacific Grove, CA: Brooks/Cole.

——. **2009a.** Understanding Generalist Practice, 5th ed. Belmont, CA: Brooks/Cole.

——. **2009b.** *Generalist Practice with Organizations and Communities*, 4th ed. Belmont, CA: Cengage.

Kirst-Ashman, K., & G. H. Hull. 2012. *Understanding Generalist Practice.* Pacific Grove, CA: Brooks/Cole.

——. **2015.** *Generalist Practice with Organizations and Communities.* Pacific Grove, CA: Brooks/Cole.

Klingensmith, M. 2014. Can those aged 45 to 64 be saved from misery in retirement? How? Downloaded from http://www.remappingdebate.org/article/can-those-aged-45-64-be-saved-misery-retirement-how-() May 29.

Knopf, R. 1979. *Surviving the BS (Bureaucratic System).* Wilmington, NC: Mandala Press.

Koop, J. 1988. "Self-Monitoring: A Literature Review of Research and Practice." *Social Work Research & Abstracts 24*, pp. 8–20.

Kornblum, W., & J. Julian. 2004. *Social Problems*, 11th ed. Upper Saddle River, NJ: Pearson Education.

——. **2009.** *Social Problems*, 13th ed. Boston: Allyn & Bacon.

Kratochwill, T. R., ed. 1978. *Single Subject Research: Strategies for Evaluating Change.* New York: Academic Press.

Krech, D., R. S. Crutchfield, & E. L. Ballachey. 1962. *Individual in Society.* New York: McGraw-Hill.

Kretzmann, J. P., & J. L. McKnight. 1993. *Building Communities from the Inside Out.* Chicago: ACTA Publications.

Krueger, A. 2014. Rising income inequality causing "unhealthy division in opportunities." Downloaded from http://huffington post.com/2012/01/12/alan-krueger-income-inequality_n_1202861.html May 12.

Kuarfordt, C. L. & M. J. Sheridan. 2009. "Understanding the Pathways of Factors Influencing the Use of Spiritually Based Interventions." *Journal of Social Work Education 45*, no. 3, (Fall), pp. 385–405.

Kübler-Ross, E. 1969. *On Death and Dying.* New York: Macmillan.

Laird, J. 1998. "Theorizing Culture: Narrative Ideas and Practice Principles." In *Re-visioning Family Therapy*, ed. M. McGoldrick, pp. 20–30. New York: Guilford.

Lakein, A. 1973. *How to Get Control of Your Time and Your Life.* New York: Signet.

Landers, S. 1993. "AIDS Deepens Duty-to-Warn Dilemma." *NASW News* (Jan.), p. 3.

Lee, C. C. 1999. "Counseling African American Men." In *Working with African American Males*, ed. L. E. Davis, pp. 39–44. Thousand Oaks, CA: Sage.

Lefrancois, G. R. 1996. *The Lifespan*, 5th ed. Belmont, CA: Wadsworth.

Lembo, J. 1974. *Help Yourself.* Niles, IL: Argus Communications.

Lewin, K. 1969. "Quasi-Stationary Social Equilibria and the Problem of Permanent Changes." In W. G. Bennis, K. D. Benne, & R. Chin (Eds.), *The Planning of Change*, 2nd ed. New York: Rinehart & Winston.

Lewis, M. L., D. L. Scott, & C. Calfee. 2013. "Rural Social Service Disparities and Creative Social Work Solutions for Rural Families Across the Life Span." *Journal of Family Social Work 16*, pp. 101–115.

Lewis, R. G., & M. Keung Ho. 1975. "Social Work with Native Americans." *Social Work 20* (Sept.), pp. 378–382.

Leyden-Rubenstein, L. 1998. *The Stress Management Handbook.* New Canaan, CT: Keats Publishing.

Liberman, R. 1971. "Behavioral Approaches to Family and Couple Therapy." *American Journal of Orthopsychiatry 40*, pp. 106–118.

Lie, G., & C. T. Lowery. 2007. "Cultural Competence with Women of Color." In *Culturally Competent Practice*, ed. D. Lum, pp. 351–388. Belmont, CA: Brooks/Cole.

Lieberman, M. A., E. D. Yalom, & M. B. Miles. 1973. "Encounter: The Leader Makes the Difference." *Psychology Today 6*, pp. 69–76.

Lipton, B. H. 2008. *The Biology of Belief.* Carlsbad, CA: Hay House.

Loewenberg, F. 1988. *Religion and Social Work Practice in Contemporary American Society.* New York: Columbia University Press.

Loewenberg, F., & R. Dolgoff. 2004. *Ethical Decisions for Social Work Practice*, 7th ed. Pacific Grove, CA: Brooks/Cole.

Loewenberg, F., & R. Dolgoff. 1971. *Teaching of Practice Skills in Undergraduate Programs in Social Welfare and Other Helping Services.* New York: Council on Social Work Education.

Losoncy, L. 1977. *Turning People On.* Englewood Cliffs, NJ: Prentice-Hall.

Lum, D. 2007. *Culturally Competent Practice*, 2nd ed. Belmont, CA: Brooks/Cole.

Maguire, L. 2002. *Clinical Social Work.* Belmont, CA: Brooks/Cole.

Mahoney, M. J. 1973. "Clinical Issues in Self-Control Training." Paper presented at the meeting of the American Psychological Association, Montreal.

Maier, N. R. F. 1970. *Problem Solving and Creativity in Individuals and Groups.* Pacific Grove, CA: Brooks/Cole.

Maluccio, A. 1979. "Perspectives of Social Workers and Clients on Treatment Outcome." *Social Casework 60*, pp. 394–401.

Mandino, O., ed. 1966. *A Treasury of Success Unlimited.* New York: Hawthorn Books.

Manley, M. J. 1977. "How to Cope with a Sense of Failure." In *The Personal Problem Solver*, eds. C. Zastrow & D. Chang. Englewood Cliffs, NJ: Prentice-Hall.

March, J. G. 1956. "Influence Measurement in Experimental and Semi-Experimental Groups." *Sociometry 19*, no. 4 (Dec.), pp. 260–271.

Marti-Costa, S., & I. Serrano-Garcia. 1987. "Needs Assessment and Community Development: An Ideological Perspective" In *Strategies of Community Organization: Macro Practice*, eds. F. M. Cox et al. Itasca, IL: Peacock.

Martinez-Brawley, E., & J. Blundall. 1989. "Farm Families' Preference toward the Personal Social Services." *Social Work 34*, no. 6, pp. 513–522.

Maslach, C. 1976. "Burned-Out." *Human Behavior 5* (Sept.), pp. 16–22.

———. **1978.** "The Client Role in Staff Burn-Out." *Journal of Social Issues 34*, pp. 11–24.

Maslach, C., & A. Pines. 1977. "The Burn-Out Syndrome in the Day Care Setting." *Child Care Quarterly 6*, pp. 100–113.

Masters, W. H., & V. E. Johnson. 1970. *Human Sexual Inadequacy.* Boston: Little, Brown.

Mathie, A., & G. Cunningham (Eds.). 2008. *From Clients to Citizens.* Warwichshire, United Kingdom: Practical Action Publishing.

Mauksch, H. O. 1975. "The Organizational Context of Dying." In *Death: The Final Stage of Growth*, ed. E. Kübler-Ross, pp. 7–26. Englewood Cliffs, NJ: Prentice-Hall.

Maultsby, M. C., Jr. 1977. "The ABC's of Better Emotional Self-Control." In *The Personal Problem Solver*, eds. C. Zastrow & D. Chang, pp. 3–18. Englewood Cliffs, NJ: Prentice-Hall.

Mayer, B. S. 1995. "Conflict Resolution." In *Encyclopedia of Social Work*, 19th ed., pp. 613–621. Washington, DC: National Association of Social Workers.

McGregor, D. 1960. *The Human Side of Enterprise.* New York: McGraw-Hill.

McLellan, A. T., L. Luborsky, G. E. Woody, & G. P. O'Brien. 1992. "An Improved Diagnostic Evaluation Instrument for Substance Abuse Patients: The Addiction Severity Index." *Journal of Nervous and Mental Diseases 168*, pp. 26–33.

Mead, M. 1935. *Sex and Temperament in Three Primitive Societies.* New York: Morrow.

Mechanic, D. 1962. "Some Factors in Identifying and Defining Mental Illness." *Mental Hygiene 46*, pp. 66–74.

Miley, K. 1992. "Religion and Spirituality as Central Social Work Concerns." Paper presented at the Midwest Biennial Conference on Social Work, April 9–10, LaCrosse, WI.

Milgram, S. 1963. "Behavioral Study of Obedience." *Journal of Abnormal and Social Psychology*, pp. 371–378.

Miller, W. R. & S. Rollnick. 1981. *Motivational Interviewing: Preparing People to Change Addictive Behavior.* New York: Guilford Press.

Minuchin, S., & H. C. Fishman. 1981. *Family Therapy Techniques.* Cambridge, MA: Harvard University Press.

Montague, A. 1964. *Man's Most Dangerous Myth: The Fallacy of Race*, 4th ed. Cleveland: World.

Mooney, L. A., D. Knox, & C. Schacht. 2011. *Understanding Social Problems*, 7th ed. Belmont, CA: Wadsworth.

Moore, C. W. 1986. *The Mediation Process.* San Francisco: Jossey-Bass.

Mor Barak, M. E. 2005. *Managing Diversity: Toward a Globally Inclusive Workplace.* Thousand Oaks, CA: Sage.

Moreno, J. L. 1946. *Psychodrama*, vol. 1. Boston: Beacon House.

Mullen, E. J., & H. L. Magnabosco, eds. 1997. *Outcomes Measurement in the Human Services.* Washington, DC: NASW Press.

National Association of Social Workers. 1982. *Standards for the Classification of Social Work Practice.* Washington, DC: Author.

———. **1996.** *Code of Ethics.* Revised and adopted by the 1996 Delegate Assembly of NASW.

———. **2001.** *Cultural Competence in Social Work Practice.* Washington, DC: NASW.

———. **2008.** *Code of Ethics.* Revised and adopted by the 2008 NASW Delegate Assembly.

National Highway Traffic Safety Administration. 2001. *Community How-to Guide: Needs Assessment and Strategic Planning.* Washington, DC: Author.

Nelson, A., & W. Wilson. 1984. "The Ethics of Sharing Religious Faith in Psychotherapy." *Journal of Psychology and Theology 12*, no. 1, pp. 15–23.

Netting, F. E., P. M. Kettner, & S. L. McMurtry. 1998. *Social Work Macro Practice*, 2nd ed. New York: Longman.

———. **2003.** *Social Work Macro Practice*, 3rd ed. Boston: Allyn & Bacon.

———. **2007.** *Social Work Macro Practice*, 4th ed. Boston: Allyn & Bacon.

Netting, F. E., P. M. Kettner, S. L. McMurtry, & M. L. Thomas. 2011. *Social Work Macro Practice*, 5th ed. Boston: Allyn & Bacon.

Nichols, M. P., with R. C. Schwartz. 2005. *The Essentials of Family Therapy*, 2nd ed. Boston: Pearson.

North, C. S., & E. M. Smith. 1994. "Comparison of White and Nonwhite Homeless Men and Women." *Social Work 39*, no. 6, pp. 639–647.

Norton, D. G. 1978. "Incorporating Content on Minority Groups into Social Work Practice Courses." In *The Dual Perspective.* New York: Council on Social Work Education.

Nurius, P. S., & W. W. Hudson. 1993. *Human Services Practice, Evaluation, and Computers.* Pacific Grove, CA: Brooks/Cole.

O'Connor, G. 1972. "Toward a New Policy in Adult Corrections." *Social Service Review 46* (Dec.), pp. 482–493.

Ogles, B. J., M. J. Lambert, & S. A. Fields. 2002. *Essentials of Outcome Assessment.* New York: Wiley.

Omachonu, V. K., & J. E. Ross. 1994. *Principles of Total Quality.* Delray Beach, FL: St. Lucie Press.

Orne, M. T., & P. H. Wender. 1968. "Anticipatory Socialization for Psychotherapy: Method and Rationale." *American Journal of Psychiatry 124*, pp. 1202–1212.

Osborn, A. F. 1963. *Applied Imagination: Principles and Procedures of Creative Problem Solving*, 3rd ed. New York: Scribner.

Parsonson, B. S., & D. M. Baer. 1978. "The Analysis and Presentation of Graphic Data." In *Single Subject Research: Strategies for Evaluation Change*, ed. T. R. Kratochwill, pp. 101–165. New York: Academic Press.

Patterson, D. A. 2000. *Personal Computer Applications in the Social Services.* Boston: Allyn & Bacon.

Patterson, G. R. 1971. *Families.* Champaign, IL: Research Press.

Peale, N. V. 1993. *Positive Thinking Everyday.* New York: Fireside.

Pfeiffer, J. W., & J. E. Jones. 1976. "Role Functions in a Group." In *1976 Annual Handbook for Group Facilitators*, eds. J. W. Pfeiffer & J. E. Jones, pp. 136–138. La Jolla, CA: University Associates.

Pfeiffer, V. 1993. *Positive Thinking.* Rockport, MA: Element Books.

Phares, E. J., & T. J. Trull. 1997. *Clinical Psychology*, 5th ed. Pacific Grove, CA: Brooks/Cole.

Pierce, D. 1993. "Developing a Framework for Social Work Practice with Lesbian Women and Gay Men." Paper presented at CSWE Annual Program Meeting, New York, Feb.

Pincus, A., & A. Minahan. 1973. *Social Work Practice: Model and Method.* Itasca, IL: Peacock.

Pines, A., & E. Aronson. 1981. *Burnout: From Tedium to Personal Growth.* New York: Free Press.

Posavac, E. J., & R. G. Carey. 1980. *Program Evaluation: Methods and Case Studies.* Englewood Cliffs, NJ: Prentice-Hall.

Powell, T. J. 1987. *Self-Help Organizations and Professional Practice.* Silver Spring, MD: National Association of Social Workers.

Prochaska, J. O. 1979. *Systems of Psychotherapy.* Pacific Grove, CA: Brooks/Cole.

Prochaska, J. O. & C. C. DiClemente. 1982. "Trans-Theoretical Therapy—Toward a More Integrative Model of Change." *Psychotherapy: Theory, Research and Practice 19*, no. 3, pp. 276–288.

Pruger, R. 1978. "Bureaucratic Functioning as a Social Work Skill." In *Educating the Baccalaureate Social Worker: Report of the Undergraduate Social Work Curriculum Development Project*, eds. B. L. Baer & R. Federico. Cambridge, MA: Ballinger.

Pruitt, M. W. 2002. "Size Matters:" A Comparison of Anti- and Pro-Gay Organizations' Estimates of the Size of the Gay Population." *Journal of Homosexuality 42*, no. 3, pp. 21–30.

Putnam, R. D. 2000. *Bowling Alone: The Collapse and Revival of American Community.* New York: Simon Schuster.

Raimy, V. 1977. *Misunderstandings of the Self.* San Francisco: Jossey-Bass.

Raiz, L., & S. Saltzburg. 2007. "Developing Awareness of the Subtleties of Heterosexism and Homophobia among Under-graduate, Heterosexual Social Work Majors." *Journal of Baccalaureate Social Work 12*, no. 2, pp. 53–69.

Ramirez, M. 2013. An Examination of Homophobia and Social Work Practice Among a Sample of School Social Workers. Dissertation Abstracts International Section A: Humanities and Social Sciences, 75(5A)(E).

Reamer, F. G. 2013. "Social Work in a Digital Age: Ethical and Risk Management Challenges." *Social Work*, pp. 163–172.

Reichert, E. 2007. *Challenges in Human Rights: A Social Work Perspective.* New York: Columbia University Press.

Reid, W., & L. Epstein. 1972. *Task-Centered Casework.* New York: Columbia University Press.

———. **1977.** *Task-Centered Practice.* New York: Columbia University Press.

Reid, W., & A. Shyne. 1969. *Brief and Extended Casework.* New York: Columbia University Press.

Richie, B. E. 2003. "Gender Entrapment and African American Women: An Analysis of Race, Ethnicity, Gender and Intimate Violence." In *Violent Crime: Assessing Race and Ethnic Differences*, ed. D. F. Hawkins, pp. 198–201. Cambridge, UK: Cambridge University Press.

Riessman, F. 1965. "The 'Helper Therapy' Principle." *Journal of Social Work 10*, no. 2 (April), pp. 27–34.

———. **1987.** "Foreword." In *Self-Help Organizations and Professional Practice*, ed. T. J. Powell. Silver Spring, MD: National Association of Social Workers.

Rimm, D., & J. Masters. 1974. *Behavior Therapy.* New York: Academic Press.

Ringer, R. J. 1977. *Looking Out for No.1.* New York: Fawcett Books.

Ritter, M. 2000. "Virtual Reality Coming into Vogue as Therapy." *Wisconsin State Journal* (July 2), pp. 1A, 10A.

Rivera, F. G., & J. L. Erlich. 1992. *Community Organizing in a Diverse Society.* Boston: Allyn & Bacon.

Roethlisberger, F. J., & W. J. Dickson. 1939. *Management and the Worker.* Cambridge, MA: Harvard University Press.

Rogers, C. R. 1970. *Carl Rogers on Encounter Groups.* New York: Harper & Row.

Rome, S. H., & S. Hoehstetter. 2010. "Social Work and Civic Engagement: The Political Participation of Professional Social Workers." *Journal of Sociology and Social Work 37*, no. 3, pp. 107–129.

Rommell, R. 2014. Drinking deeply ingrained in Wisconsin's culture. Downloaded from http://www.jsonline.com/news/wisconsin/31237904.html May 30.

Rosenhan, D. 1973. "On Being Sane in Insane Places." *Science 179*, pp. 250–257.

Rosenhan, D. L., & M. E. Seligman. 1995. *Abnormal Psychology*, 3rd ed. New York: Norton.

Rossi, P. H., H. E. Freeman, & S. R. Wright. 1979. *Evaluation: A Systematic Approach.* Newbury Park, CA: Sage.

Rothenberg, P. S. 2007. *Race, Class, and Gender in the United States*, 7th ed. New York: Worth.

Rothman, J., & J. E. Tropman. 1995. *Strategies of Community Intervention*, 5th ed., Itasca, IL: Peacock.

Rubin, A. 2007. "Proceedings of the Conference on Improving the Teaching of Evidence-Based Practice in Social Work" [Special issue]. *Research on Social Work Practice 17*, no. 5.

Rubin, A., & K. S. Knox. 1996. "Data Analysis Problems in Single-Case Evaluation: Issues for Research on Social Work Practice." In *Research on Social Work Practice 6*, pp. 40–65.

Rubin, H. J., & I. S. Rubin. 1992. *Community Organizing and Development.* New York: Macmillan.

Ruoss, M. 1970. As quoted in J. C. DeBoer. *Let's Plan: A Guide to the Planning Process for Voluntary Organizations.* Princeton, NJ: Pilgrim Press.

Saleeby, D. 1997. *The Strengths Perspective in Social Work Practice*, 2nd ed. Upper Saddle River, NJ: Pearson Education, Inc.

———. **2002.** *The Strengths Perspective in Social Work Practice*, 3rd ed. Boston: Allyn & Bacon.

———. **2012.** *The Strengths Perspective in Social Work Practice*, 6th ed. Upper Saddle River, NJ: Pearson.

Sandler, J. 1986. "Aversion Methods." In *Helping People Change*, 3rd ed., eds. F. H. Kanfer & A. P. Goldstein, pp. 191–235. Elmsford, NY: Pergamon Press.

Sandoval, J. 1985. "Crisis Counseling: Conceptualizations and General Principles." *School Psychology Review 14*, pp. 257–265.

Sapolsky, R. 1998. *Why Zebras Don't Get Ulcers.* New York: W. H. Freeman.

Sardar, Z. 2001. "More Hackney Than Bollywood," *New Statesman 14* (July 30), pp. 14–16.

Satir, V. 1967. *Conjoint Family Therapy*, rev. ed. Palo Alto, CA: Science & Behavior Books.

———. **1972.** *Peoplemaking.* Palo Alto, CA: Science & Behavior Books.

Schachter, S. 1959. *The Psychology of Affiliation.* Stanford, CA: Stanford University Press.

Schaefer, R. T. 1993. *Racial & Ethnic Groups*, 5th ed. New York: HarperCollins.

———. **2004.** *Racial & Ethnic Groups*, 9th ed. Upper Saddle River, NJ: Pearson Education.

———. **2008.** *Racial & Ethnic Groups*, 10th ed. Upper Saddle River, NJ: Pearson Education.

———. **2010.** *Racial & Ethnic Groups*, 12th ed. Upper Saddle River, NJ: Prentice Hall.

———. **2012.** *Racial & Ethnic Groups*, 13th ed. Upper Saddle River, NJ: Prentice Hall.

Scheff, I. 1966. *Being Mentally Ill.* Hawthorne, NY: Aldine.

Schiele, J. H. 1996. "Afrocentricity: An Emerging Paradigm in Social Work Practice." *Social Work 41* (May), pp. 284–294.

Schoener, G. R. 2000. "Duty to Warn or Protect." Paper presented at Professional At Risk: Ethical Dilemmas Workshop at the University of Wisconsin–Madison, Nov. 13.

Schuller, R., II. 1973. *Move Ahead with Possibility Thinking.* Moonachie, NJ: Pyramid Publications.

Schwartz, G. 1989. "Confidentiality Revisited." *Social Work* (May), pp. 223–226.

Seaward, B. L. 1994. *Managing Stress.* Boston: Jones & Bartlett.

———. 2005. *Managing Stress,* 5th ed. Boston: Jones & Bartlett.

Segal, Z. V., J. M. G. Williams, & J. D. Teasdale. 2002. *Mindfulness-based cognitive therapy for depression.* New York: Guilford Press.

Selye, H. 1956. *The Stress of Life.* New York: McGraw-Hill.

Shadish, W. R., T. D. Cook, & D. T. Campbell. 2002. *Experimental and Quasi-Experimental Designs for Generalized Causal Inference.* Boston: Houghton Mifflin.

Sharf, R. S. 2008. *Theories of Psychotherapy and Counseling,* 4th ed. Belmont, CA: Brooks/Cole.

Sheafor, B., & C. R. Horejsi. 2007. *Techniques and Guidelines for Social Work Practice,* 8th ed. Boston: Allyn & Bacon.

Sheafor, B. W, C. R. Horejsi, & C. A. Horejsi. 1988. *Techniques and Guidelines for Social Work Practice.* Boston: Allyn & Bacon.

Sheehan, G. 2008. "Building the Mercado Central," In A. Mathie & G. Cunningham, *From Clients to Citizens.* Warwickshire, United Kingdom: Practical Action Publishing, pp. 63–84.

Sheridan, M. J. & K. Amato-von Hemert. 1999. "The Role of Religion and Spirituality in Social Work Education and Practice: A Study of Student Views and Experiences." *Journal of Social Work Education 35,* no. 1, (Winter), pp. 125–141.

Sherif, M. 1936. *The Psychology of Social Norms.* New York: Harper & Row.

Sherman, H. 1966. "The Surest Way in the World to Attract Success—or Failure." In *A Treasury of Success Unlimited,* ed. O. Mandino, pp. 111–113. New York: Hawthorn Books.

Sherwood, D. A. 1981. "Add to Your Faith Virtue: The Integration of Christian Values and Social Work Practice." *Social Work and Christianity 8* (Spring–Fall), pp. 41–54.

Shorkey, C., E. Garcia, & L. Windsor. 2010. "Spirituality as a Strength in the Latino Community." In R. Furman & N. Negi (Eds.), *Social Work Practice with Latinos.* Chicago: Lyceum, pp. 161–183.

Shostrom, E. L. 1969. "Group Therapy: Let the Buyer Beware." *Psychology Today 2,* no. 12 (May), pp. 36–40.

Sims, C. M. 2010. "Ethnic Notions and Healthy Paranoias: Understanding of the Context of Experience and Interpretations of Healthcare Encounters Among Older Black Women." *Ethnicity & Health 15*(5), pp. 495–514.

Sindler, A. P. 1978. *Bakke, DeFunis and Minority Admissions: The Quest for Equal Opportunity.* New York: Longmans, Green.

Skinner, B. F. 1938. *The Behavior of Organisms.* New York: Appleton-Century-Crofts.

———. 1948. *Walden Two.* New York: Macmillan.

———. 1953. *Science and Human Behavior.* New York: Free Press.

Skoe, E. E. A., A. Cumberland, N. Eisenberg, K. Hansen, & J. Perry. 2002. "The Influence of Sex and Gender-Role Identity on Moral Cognition and Prosocial Personality Traits." *Sex Roles 46,* pp. 295–309.

Slater, P. E. 1958. "Contrasting Correlates of Group Size." *Sociometry 21,* no. 2 (June), pp. 129–139.

Slonim-Nevo, V., & Y. Anson. 1998. "Evaluating Practice: Does It Improve Treatment Outcome?" *Social Work Research 22,* pp. 66–74.

Spies, R. A., J. F. Carlson, & K. F. Geisinger. 2010. *The Eighteenth Mental Measurements Yearbook.* Lincoln: University of Nebraska Press.

Spock, B. 1957. *The Common-Sense Book of Baby and Child Care.* New York: Duell, Sloan & Pierce.

Spranger, E. 1928. *Types of Men.* New York: Hafner.

Starkweather, C. L., & S. M. Turner. 1975. "Parents Anonymous: Reflections on the Development of a Self-Help Group." In *Child Abuse Interventions and Treatment,* eds. N. C. Ebeling & D. A. Hill. Littleton, MA: PSG.

Stephenson, M. M. 1983. "The Talking Circle: A Resource for Personal and Community Development." Paper presented at the Eighth Annual Institute on Social Work in Rural Areas, July, Cheney, WA.

Stone, W. C. 1966. "Be Generous." In *A Treasury of Success Unlimited,* ed. O. Mandino, pp. 9–10. New York: Hawthorn Books.

Stuart, G. 2012. "What is the Strengths Perspective?" http://sustainingcommunity.wordpress.com/2012/05/30/what-is-the-strengths-perspective/.

Stuart, R. B. 1970. *Trick or Treatment.* Champaign, IL: Research Press.

———. 1976. "An Operant-Interpersonal Program for Couples." In *Treating Relationships,* ed. D. H. L. Olson. Lake Mills, IA: Graphic.

Suppes, M. A., & C. Wells. 2003. *The Social Work Experience, An Introduction to Social Work and Social Welfare,* 4th ed. New York: McGraw-Hill.

Szasz, T. 1961. "The Myth of Mental Illness" In *Clinical Psychology in Transition,* comp. J. R. Braun. Cleveland: Howard Allen.

———. 1963. *Law, Liberty and Psychiatry.* New York: Macmillan.

———. 1967. "The Psychiatrist as Double Agent." *Trans-Action 4,* pp. 3–25.

Taylor, F. W. 1947. *Scientific Management.* New York: Harper & Row.

Taylor, W. L., D. M. Piché, C. Rosario, & J. D. Rich. 2007. *The Erosion of Rights: Declining Civil Rights Enforcement under the Bush Administration.* Washington, DC: Citizens' Commission on Civil Rights.

Teasdale, J. et al. 2000. Prevention and relapse/recurrent in major depression by mindfulness-based cognitive therapy. *Journal of Counseling and Clinical Psychology 68*(4), 615–623.

Tessler, R., R. Rosenheck, & G. Gamache. 2001. "Gender Differences in Self-Reported Reasons for Homelessness." *Journal of Social Distress and the Homeless 10,* no. 3, pp. 243–254.

Thomas, E. J. 1978. "Research and Service in Single-Case Experimentation: Conflicts and Choices." *Social Work Research and Abstracts 14,* pp. 20–31.

———. 1984. *Designing Interventions for the Helping Professions.* New York: Sage.

Thorman, G. 1982. *Helping Troubled Families: A Social Work Perspective.* New York: Aldine.

Thorndike, E. L. 1913. *The Psychology of Learning.* New York: Teachers College Press.

Thyer, B., & J. Wodarski. 2004. *Handbook of Empirical Social Work Practice.* New York: Wiley.

Thyer, B. A., & L. L. Myers. 2007. *A Social Worker's Guide to Evaluating Practice Outcomes.* Alexandria, VA: Council on Social Work Education Press.

Toch, H. 1970. "The Care and Feeding of Typologies and Labels." *Federal Probation 34* (Sept.), pp. 46–57.

Tolman, E. C. 1932. *Purposive Behavior in Animals and Men.* New York: Appleton-Century-Crofts.

Toseland, R. W., & R. F. Rivas. 2007. *An Introduction to Group Work Practice,* 6th ed. Boston: Allyn & Bacon.

———. 2012. *An Introduction to Group Work Practice,* 7th ed. Boston: Allyn & Bacon.

Touliatos, J., B. F. Perlmutter, & M. A. Straus, eds. 1990. *Handbook of Family Measurement Techniques.* Newbury Park, CA: Sage.

Tripodi, T. 1994. *A Primer on Single-Subject Design for Clinical Social Workers.* Washington, DC: NASW Press.

Tubbs, S. I., & J. W. Baird. 1976. *The Open Person.* Columbus, OH: Merrill.

Turner, K. 2009. Mindfulness: The present moment in clinical social work. *Clinical Social Work Journal 37*(2), 95–103. Doi:10.1007/s10615-008-0182-0.

United Nations. 1948. *Universal Declaration of Human Rights.* Adopted December 10, 1948. General Assembly Resolution, 2200 AXXI. New York: United Nations.

University of Pittsburgh Law Review. **1975.** *"Tarasoff v. Regents of University of California: The Psychotherapists Peril"* 37, pp. 159–164.

Urban Institute. 2013. *LGBT Youth Face Higher Rate of Dating Abuse.* Retrieved from: http://www.urban.org_url.cfm?id= 904600&RSSFeed=Urban.xml.

U.S. Census Bureau. 2005. *Americans with Disabilities: 2005.* Washington, DC: Author.

Van de Ven, A., & A. L. Delbecq. 1971. "Nominal versus Interacting Group Processes for Committee Decision-Making Effectiveness." *Academy of Management Journal 14*, no. 2 (June), pp. 203–212.

Van Den Bergh, N. 1992. "Feminist Treatment for People with Depression." In *Structuring Change*, ed. K. Corcoran, pp. 95–110. Chicago: Lyceum Books.

Van Den Bergh, N., & L. B. Cooper. 1987. "Feminist Social Work." In *The Encyclopedia of Social Work*, pp. 610–618. Washington, DC: National Association of Social Workers.

Vogler, R. E., S. E. Lunde, G. R. Johnson, & P. L. Martin. 1970. "Electrical Aversion Conditioning with Chronic Alcoholics." *Journal of Consulting and Clinical Psychology 34*, pp. 302–307.

Watson, D. L., & R. G. Tharp. 1972. *Self-Directed Behavior: Self-Modification for Personal Adjustment.* Pacific Grove, CA: Brooks/Cole.

Watson, J. B., & R. Rayner. 1920. "Conditioned Emotional Reaction." *Journal of Experimental Psychology 3*, no. 1, pp. 1–14.

Wegscheider, S. 1981. *Another Chance: Hope and Health for the Alcoholic Family.* Palo Alto, CA: Science & Behavior Books.

Weick, A., C. Rapp, W. P. Sullivan, & W. Kisthardt. 1989. "A Strengths Perspective for Social Work Practice." *Social Work 34*, pp. 350–354.

Weil, M., & D. N. Gamble. 1995. "Community Practice Models." In *Encyclopedia of Social Work*, 19th ed., vol. 1, pp. 577–594. Washington, DC: NASW Press.

Weinger, S. 2001. *Security Risk: Preventing Violence against Social Workers*, Washington, DC: NASW Press.

Weiss, C. H. 1972. *Evaluation Research.* Englewood Cliffs, NJ: Prentice-Hall.

White, M. 1995. Reauthoring Lives: Interviews and Essays. Adelaide, South Australia: Dulwich Centre Publications.

Whittaker, J. K. 1974. *Social Treatment.* Hawthorne, NY: Aldine.

Wiger, D. E., & K. B. Solberg. 2001. *Tracking Mental Health Outcomes: A Therapist's Guide to Measuring Client Progress, Analyzing Data, and Improving Your Practice.* New York: Wiley.

Wigmore, J. H. 1961. *Evidence in Trials at Common Law*, vol. 8 (rev.), ed. J. T. McNaughton. Boston: Little, Brown.

Wilensky, H., & C. Lebeaux. 1965. *Industrial Society & Social Welfare.* New York: Free Press.

Williams, E. E., & F. Ellison. 1996. "Culturally Informed Social Work Practice with American Indian Clients: Guidelines for Non-Indian Social Workers." *Social Work 41*, no. 2, pp. 147–151.

Wilson, S. J. 1978. *Confidentiality in Social Work: Issues and Principles.* New York: Free Press.

Wilson, T. G. 2008. "Behavior Therapy." In *Current Psychotherapies*, 8th ed., eds. R. J. Corsini & D. Wedding, pp. 223–262. Belmont, CA: Brooks/Cole.

Winship, J., & A. Hall. 2004. "Social Exclusion: Understanding Barriers Facing Homeless and Immigrant Latino Students." A presentation at the Oxford Round Table: Addressing the Education Needs of At Risk Children, Oxford, England, March 22, 2004.

Wolpe, J. 1958. *Psychotherapy by Reciprocal Inhibition.* Stanford, CA: Stanford University Press.

Wright, B. A. 1960. *Physical Disability: A Psychological Approach.* New York: Harper & Row.

www.quotationspage.com. (2004). Martin Luther King. Retrieved from www.quotationspage.com/quotes/ Martin Luther King Jr.

Yahoo News. 2004. "Report: CIA Gave False Info on Iraq," July 9.

Young, J. 1989. *Fundraising for Nonprofit Groups.* Bellingham, WA: Self Counsel Press.

Zastrow, C. 1973. "The Nominal Group: A New Approach to Designing Programs for Curbing Delinquency." *Canadian Journal of Criminology and Corrections* (Jan.), pp. 109–117.

———. **1979.** *Talk to Yourself: Using the Power of Self-Talk.* Englewood Cliffs, NJ: Prentice-Hall.

———. **1993.** *You Are What You Think: A Guide to Self-Realization.* Chicago: Nelson-Hall.

Zastrow, C., & R. Navarre. 1977. "The Nominal Group: A New Tool for Making Social Work Education Relevant." *Journal of Education for Social Work 13* (Winter), pp. 112–118.

Index

Note: Page numbers followed by "f" refer to figures.

About the Author

Charles H. Zastrow, MSW and PhD, is Professor Emeritus in Social Work at the University of Wisconsin–Whitewater. He chaired the Social Work Department for 6 years at this campus. He has also been the Assistant Director and Professor in the Social Work Program at George Williams College of Aurora University at Williams Bay, Wisconsin. He has worked as a practitioner in a variety of public and private social welfare agencies and has chaired 28 social work accreditation site visit teams for the Council on Social Work Education (CSWE). He has served two terms as a Commissioner on the Commission on Accreditation of CSWE. He has been a Board Member of the Association of Baccalaureate Social Work Program Directors, Inc. (BPD). He has chaired the Commission on Educational Policy of CSWE. Dr. Zastrow is a Licensed Clinical Social Worker in the state of Wisconsin. In addition to *Generalist Practice in Social Work*, he has written four other textbooks: *Introduction to Social Work and Social Welfare* (11th ed.), *Social Work with Groups* (9th ed.), *Social Problems: Issues and Solutions* (5th ed.), and *Understanding Human Behavior and the Social Environment* (10th ed.) (with Dr. Karen Kirst-Ashman).